To Wendy
Merry Christmas, 1983
Love
Bill

JAPANESE

introduction by

M. F. K. Fisher

COOKING
A SIMPLE ART

Shizuo Tsuji
with the assistance of Mary Sutherland

KODANSHA INTERNATIONAL
Tokyo, New York and San Francisco

distributed in the United States by Kodansha International/USA, Ltd., through Harper & Row, Publishers, Inc., 10 East 53rd Street, New York, New York 10022.

published by Kodansha International Ltd., 12–21 Otowa 2-chome, Bunkyo-ku, Tokyo 112 and Kodansha International/USA, Ltd., 10 East 53rd Street, New York, New York 10022 and 44 Montgomery Street, San Francisco, California 94104

first edition, 1980
second printing, January 1981
third printing, March 1981

LCC 79–66244
ISBN 0–87011–399–2
JBC 2077–787583–2361

Library of Congress Cataloging in Publication Data

Tsuji, Shizuo, 1933–
  Japanese cooking.

  Includes index.
  1. Cookery, Japanese. I. Title.
TX724.5.J3T836   641.5952   79-66244
ISBN 0-87011-399-2

Contents

Introduction

It is strange, and perhaps inexplicable, that a person like me was asked by a person like Shizuo Tsuji to write a preface to his book.

Shizuo was a *Wunderkind* when I met him more than twenty years ago, and by now he is something of an *éminence grise* in the art of teaching young Japanese cooks to understand what their own food is based on, and where it comes from, and why it can be bountiful or scarce. His school in Osaka is called the Ecole Technique Hôtelière Tsuji, or in another Western language, the Tsuji Professional Culinary Institute. It is impressive, with more than 2,500 students. Their basic education is in their own national cooking, both past and present as well as regional. Once they have passed rigorous tests, about forty percent of them go on in their native field, hoping to make their mark in Japan's great restaurants, or to inherit their families' country inns, or even to enter the enormous wholesale food industry as buyers or purveyors. Another ten percent of the post-graduates stay on at the Institute to learn Chinese techniques. The rest, perhaps the most ambitious, study French *haute cuisine*, taught by the famous chefs Shizuo Tsuji entices to Osaka from Roanne, Collonges, Paris.

And that is the school I went to, for two peculiar and dreamlike weeks in October of 1978, with my sister Norah Barr. I wanted to see for myself what was happening in a chancy modern field of East-West eating.

Aside from our watching some forty-five private demonstrations at the two Tsuji buildings in Osaka (there will soon be another one in Tokyo), and coping with about thirty gastronomical onslaughts, no matter how gently subtle, in restaurants and inns and street-shops, we tasted seed pods and ginkgo nuts, and native fruits like "twentieth century" pears, as juicy as a ripe melon and as crisp as a frosty apple . . . seaweeds, dried or fresh, poached or swished through broths . . . plum jam, sour as Hell's wrath, in a tiny bowl with two quarter-inch cubes of fried liver from a sea bass . . . the ovaries of a sea slug, buried in froth skimmed from boiling crushed soybean . . . slender cucumbers, faintly sour from their vat of fermenting rice bran . . . ices made from fruit pulps, beaten without sugar and pressed back into their hollowed skins. . . .

I was *curious*, and I still am.

Until a few weeks before Norah and I flew to Japan, I had accepted Tsuji's compliments about my way of writing as part of his Oriental respect for older people, mixed with his natural pattern of flattery as a part of good manners. But when he asked me to come to Osaka as a professional, I suddenly realized that he was in earnest about my writing something for him, instead of merely being friendly and courteous.

Norah, who had met Shizuo and who knew of our long pleasant relationship, suggests that it is based on a strong mother-son feeling he has for me, somewhat as he does even more strongly for Madame Fernand Point, of La Pyramide, and as he does most strongly of all for Samuel Chamberlain, who was his "spiritual father," and who is now the constant image of his devotion. My sister's theory is thus a great compliment to me, if true!

Whatever the reasons, Shizuo did ask me to write some kind of introduction to the 220 recipes he has chosen, to prove to readers of the Western world that traditional Japanese cookery can and should be a useful part of our own way of eating. At times I am not completely sure that he is right. The preparation and serving of fine as well as routine Japanese food is more obviously mixed, than is ours, with other things than hunger.

At its best, it is inextricably meshed with aesthetics, with religion, with tradition and history. It is evocative of seasonal changes, or of one's childhood, or of a storm at sea: one thin slice of molded fish purée shaped like a maple leaf and delicately colored orange and scarlet, to celebrate Autumn; a tiny hut made of carved ice, with a little fish inside made of chestnut paste and a chestnut made of fish paste, to remind an honored guest that he was born on a far-north island; an artfully stuffed lobster riding an angry sea of curled waves of white radish cut paper-thin, with occasional small shells of carved shrimp meat tossing helplessly in the troughs. . . .

All this delicate pageantry is based on things that we Westerners are either unaware of or that we accept for vaguely sentimental reasons. Some of us still eat fish on cue, or matzo, because both priests and parents have taught us to, without much thought about anything but how good they will taste. The past is not as important as the present, nor is religious symbolism open in our thoughts. As children raised in lands of plenty, we do not learn to count on a curl of carrot and one fried ginkgo nut to divert us from the fact that the rest of the food on the plate consists of an austere mound of rice and two pinches of herb paste. We have never been taught to make little look like much, make much out of little, in a mystical combination of ascetic and aesthetic as well as animal satisfaction.

Not only are our ideas of what is delicate and rare different from those of the Japanese, but so is our conditioning. We North Americans, for instance, must combine many ethnical influences in our methods of cooking and eating, because we are all the offspring of other cultures. Our physical habits are different, so that we chew and swallow and sip and raise food to our mouths differently, with different tools.

There are many things about eating in Japan that we either accept instinctively or never learn or care to imitate. It is socially correct there, for instance, to make a loud sucking sound when one eats noodles (or drinks tea, on some social levels). This is basically sensible, since the cool air that goes into one's mouth with the food makes it possible to eat it steaming hot. But such noisy slurping is foreign to our own etiquette.

In much the same way, many Westerners, especially those of us with Anglo-Saxon backgrounds, have been taught not to pick our teeth, at table or indeed anywhere in public. In Japan, though, toothpicks are used almost ceremoniously by gentlemen at fine banquets or in public eating places, with one hand held like a curved fan before the mouth, while the other digs about. Small flat boxes, often very beautiful, hold the picks, which are wrapped in silky paper in fine restaurants.

Another difference, and one that Westerners accept more easily, is the Japanese way of eating, with chopsticks, the solid bits of food from a soup bowl, and then drinking the liquid from it. Like the other habits, this one is practical and simple—as is the custom of holding the bowl near one's chin, or using it as a catchall when transferring food to one's mouth after dipping it in the little bowls of sauces that are part of many meals.

Few people are completely austere by nature, and the Japanese enjoy the way food feels in their mouths and bellies as much as we do. They are basically more aware, possibly, of the functional beauty of a bowl or plate than we are. This does not mean, of course, that when a porter or streetcar conductor stops for a ten-minute lunch at a noodle-shop, he contemplates the pattern of the container, the significant tangle of the *udon* in their clear broth, the cloud-form of steam that rises, the symbolism of all this as a message both from Heaven and to it! He sucks the hot soup in as fast as he can, and pushes the thick noodles into his mouth with his chopsticks, from the bowl held close to it, and then he dashes back to work, untroubled by either aesthetics or an empty stomach.

Celebrations and festivals, though, are times for thoughtful attention, and fortunately there are many of them in Japan. It is then that tradition takes over, as far as modern life will let it, and perhaps an extravagantly lively sea bream will be bought instead of a can of mackerel, and the housewife will shave a cupful of the best dried bonito and use a slice of special seaweed to make a real *dashi*, instead of using a few spoonfuls of synthetic soup powder dissolved in boiling water.

Mostly, however, festive families will join millions of other people on the city streets and in the parks, and will treat themselves to an extra bottle of sticky soft drink and perhaps, in honor of Grandmother Itako or the first plum blossoms or the waning August moon, they will buy picnic boxes elegant with chicken, to lay out on a bench, instead of slurping their usual bowl of soup at a street-stand. It is doubtful that many will give a thought to the classical cookery of their country, formalized and artful, which few but the super-rich now taste.

And this is why some scientists and artists and intellectuals are worrying about the present and future of their national food, the Japanese *ryōri*. They hold seminars and debates about the fast-changing tastes in their country. They write books, like the six-volume *Nippon no Ryōri*, edited by Dr. Tadao Umesao, in hopes of showing housewives and even restaurant cooks that convenience-foods and microwave ovens and deep-freeze boxes can produce nourishment that need not be robbed of all its traditional taste and interest. Unless such a last-ditch effort works, most of the experts say, Japanese *ryōri*, as it has been known for the past two hundred years, is done for.

This concern for cultural standards is the reason for a book like Shizuo Tsuji's of course. Indirectly, it is probably my own reason for writing a preface to it: I want all of us, East or West, to fight against mediocrity and its gradually lower standards of eating, just as passionately as do my friend Tsuji and his learned peers in both Academe and the kitchen.

Shizuo does not expect a hundred million Japanese to crave fourteen courses of airy-fairy fantasy every night for dinner, any more than I expect every compatriot here at home to eat a daily sirloin steak with all the fixin's. We both wish, though, that the staples of our diets could stay honest. In Japan, *udon* noodles in broth can be delicious. In Italy and France and here, *pasta* can be fine—and so can hamburgers! The problem is to keep them *good*. The great international companies that will have increasing influence on our eating habits do not seem to care much, if at all, about helping our taste buds stay keen and alive, since if no really excellent food is procurable, they know that we will perforce buy an inferior substitute . . . and second-rate stuff is cheaper and apparently easier to market, anyway.

In Japan, there are not-bad dehydrated foods like soup powders and one-dish meals of wonton-in-broth, which even farm children eat instead of what their parents were raised on. But few manufacturers will bother to produce a commendable packaged staple like plain noodle soup. In somewhat the same way, here in North America anyway, decent bread is very hard to find, unless it is home-baked, because cheaper bread, almost zero in nutrition, is easier to produce and distribute. Everywhere, shoddy stuff is gradually the only procurable substitute for honest goods.

One formal definition of "shoddy" is "transparently imitative." Across the United States, so-called Japanese restaurants serve smelly copies of grease-soaked *tempura*, and from the Ginza in Tokyo, Big Macs and Kentucky fried chicken, fumy with additives and exhausted fats, spread out over a country where for hundreds of years small neighborhood food-shops have provided their own hot bowls and cold snacks, or their local versions of pickles and sweets. Often they have grown famous, as one generation after another has carried on the family recipes, so that canny travellers will stop in a certain village long enough to eat two bowls of a special shrimp soup, or take home some rolls of a fruit paste that has been exactly the same, past remembering.

Yet the Japanese have long been accustomed to "on the run" eating, and franchised soup-bars and pasta-parlors are now a thriving phenomenon. An American critic who has dismissed quick-food hamburger chains as "the quintessence of shoddiness in our times" warns us, just as Tsuji-san and his peers repeat on television and in university halls, that "by the time shoddiness becomes sufficiently visible . . . its roots have penetrated deeply" (Alan Rich, *New York Magazine*, December, 1978). And when does "shoddy" become "junk"?

We all ask this. Not enough of us are frightened. But books like this one are written—stubbornly, proudly—by people like Shizuo Tsuji who cannot tolerate letting their national taste falter and die.

Students of the influence of gastronomy on this national taste, and therefore on politics and such seemingly distant subjects, from Brillat-Savarin in France of the early nineteenth century to Umesao in present-day Japan, believe that what and how a man eats in his first few years will shape his natural appetite for the rest of his life. It will not matter if he begins as a potter's son and ends as an affluent banker. If he ate pure fresh food when he was a child, he will seek it out when he is old and weary, it is said. Dr. Umesao cites his own case: raised in Kyoto, where the flavors of every dish are believed, at least by the natives, to be subtler than anywhere else in Japan, he now stays near enough to his home town to return there every weekend, to buy fish that is fresh enough to satisfy his childhood recollections. In any other city, he says scornfully, the fish in markets is inedible. His palate, he adds, was shaped irrevocably when he was a child.

This theory, which I mostly agree with, has taken a double blow for me because of Shizuo's invitation to come to Osaka. Not only does my palate refresh itself daily with foods almost as simple as the first ones I knew, but

I feel that it has stayed young because of my natural curiosity about the best dishes that other countries have offered me. And now, after two weeks in Japan, I must admit with real astonishment that if I could eat as I did there under my friend's subtle guidance, I would gladly turn my back on Western food and live on Japanese *ryōri* for the rest of my life.

Such a pattern would be difficult for me to follow. There, few people without princely revenues and highly evolved palates are served the dishes Norah and I ate. I could never afford to buy them, even as an occasional luxury. For the same reason, neither could I go to the rare restaurants in Japan where such intrinsically *pure* food is still prepared, even if for political or professional or social reasons my reservation might be accepted.

Wealth is so much a part of protocol in Japan that one must know this Personage in Tokyo, that Eminence in Osaka, in order to make a reservation at a certain restaurant in Kobe for precisely 8:10 P.M. six months hence. This is out of my sphere of survival, except for the one such adventure in my life. I know, though, that the food I ate during those amazing days in 1978 has changed my whole palate, or, perhaps the gastronomers would say, it has simply strengthened the taste I acquired as a child. . .?

This is not to say that I could not and would not live well in Japan, just as I manage to do here in the States. I would eat seasonal fruits and vegetables in either place, and honest fresh-caught fish when available, and would surely find a source there for noodle dough now and then. . . .

For the first twenty years of my life I ate healthily of simple good American food. I grew up in Southern California, but our kitchen was generally ruled by Midwestern habits, overlaid by Ireland, Pennsylvania, and upper New York State through my grandparents and their forebears. That is to say, we had fresh bread and milk, "produce" from our own or neighboring gardens, and local meat and poultry with their accompanying butter and eggs and suchlike. Everything was taken as a matter of course, with small fuss except on holidays, when for dessert we ate Lady Baltimore cake and ice cream instead of rice pudding.

The next several decades of my life were spent partly in France and French Switzerland, with occasional stays in Cornwall and even Sweden, to accentuate the positive influence of my beginnings. I grew to know, sometimes actively, the ardors and ordeals of cooking in several European and American kitchens, and I went to as many high-style restaurants and hotels as opportunity offered, and read and talked and thought about the art of eating.

The result was that I agreed with my teachers that classical French and Chinese cuisines were the basic arbiters of an educated palate. I knew without any false modesty that my own would never be as well trained as I would like, but I felt no qualms about remaining a willing novice. And always I felt grateful for the simplicity and honesty of my first education in eating. Oddly enough, now that I have found what Japanese *ryōri* can be at its best—that is to say, the perfect food for me—I am not frustrated or sad. Perhaps that is because it is, to be blunt and brutal, almost unattainable. I know that never again can I eat as subtly and exquisitely, in effect as honestly, as I did for two weeks in my life. That is a *fait accompli*, an historical fact never to be repeated.

One immediate result of this intense experience is that when I cook for myself now, I am increasingly simple in both the sources of food and its preparation, and that when I must eat in other houses or restaurants, I find the dishes heavy and overflavored, and the supplies not fresh enough. When I first came home from Osaka, it was difficult to use butter, impossible for several weeks to drink milk, unnecessary to pick up a salt shaker or a peppermill.

Norah and I did not eat only as the industrial princes eat, in Japan. Shizuo sent us for lunches to the *best* noodle-shop in Osaka, the *best* tempura place in Kobe. But his humblest-seeming restaurants, which often seated only five or seven people at a time, were of such high quality that they sold all their scraps, all their used frying oils and suchlike, to lesser places. Their cooks, who worked across a snow-white cedar counter from us, were the most skilled in the country. Fish leaped from glass tanks to the cleavers and the pans and then into our mouths, in a ballet of accumulated motions and flavors.

After I returned to San Francisco, I went to a stylish new "Yaki Tori Bar," as it was called. Deft young chefs worked in traditional style behind the long dark counter we sat at, and the walls looked mysterious with dim shapes of pottery jugs and bottles, and there was a subtle smell of overused hot oil. The cooks laid little sticks of whatever we had asked for, two at a time, in front of us . . . bits of chicken, bits of fish, even ginkgo nuts, dipped into the suspicious fat and then grilled. Tea was served, or beer. The cups and dishes were very thick and brown, like the place and its pervasive smell, and its ultimate phoniness.

Westerners looked a little shy there, perhaps to watch everything being done so baldly in front of them. There were one or two Oriental couples, possibly Korean. The diners most at ease were an elderly Caucasian and his wife, plainly Old Hands, who used their chopsticks with skill, and seemed to be happy together in a vaguely familiar setting.

It was depressing. I wondered miserably why refrigeration had spoiled so much while it kept things from spoiling . . . why the bits of fish (albacore, it was called on the brown thick menu card) were flabby and sweetish, pulled on their little sticks from a series of iceboxes under the counter . . . why the cubes of chicken (really turkey) were half-frozen even after their oil bath and the ritual of sizzling over the grill. . . .

I knew, like a gong sounding far back in my head, what Japanese friends who worked with Norah and me in Osaka had meant when they half-cursed Tsuji-san for making it difficult for them ever to enjoy wholeheartedly the business meals they must return to in Tokyo. Average-to-good would never really satisfy them again.

I felt lost, full of misgivings about how to explain why I think the Japanese *ryōri*, the basic food that is now in such a state of flux, can be not only acceptable but welcome to our way of life, of eating. Then I thought, as we left the stylish and dubiously "honest" *ryōri-ya* in San Francisco, of how closely the best of Japanese cooking works with and influences the new styles in French and therefore Western food. High priests of *nouvelle cuisine* and *cuisine minceur* are good friends of Tsuji-san, and have worked with him both in Osaka and in their own country. All of them worship at the feet of Escoffier, the first great cook in our Western time to say to his apprentices, "Stay simple! Cook simply!"

The long-time association between the refinements of French and Chinese cooking seems to have shifted to one that is more applicable to our current life style, so that we now think easily in terms of French and Japanese similarities. We want to make less seem like more. We eat "lightly," compared with classical cooking rules, and in a Japanese rather than a Chinese way we shun many starches, fats, sugar.

We find high style in low calorie counts exactly right for our repudiation of the Edwardian silhouette (low paunches and high breasts and dangling jowls, and their final reward of apoplexy . . .), and try eagerly to imitate an artful curl of radish and one broiled mushroom elegantly placed on a thin bed of minced spinach as our password to the future. (*Où sont les sauces d'antan?*) Perhaps it started for us with Whistler and the "Japanese" simplicity of his mother's portrait? The fact remains that Zen austerity now intrudes on our old dreams of pastry shaped laboriously into towers of caramel and whipped cream and candied violets. . . .

Eastern countries have had more time than we Westerners to accustom their people to less rich food than we are used to. Here we load the tables, at Christmas and other celebrations and even for Sunday Noon Dinner, to prove that all's well with the world. In Japan, though, as in many other places on this shrinking planet, there is not space to grow enough food to feed all the people. So one perfect fruit (pear from home, papaya from Hawaii, coconut from Algeria) will be carved and arranged into symbolic patterns that can be religious (intricately Buddhist, less intricately Shinto perhaps), or merely sentimental (falling rain, the first cherry blossoms, a honeymoon in Honolulu). It will answer many hungers, and its design will be savored slowly. And the same dessert, in Paris or Denver, may taste equally delicious because it is low in calories, dietetically safe, a fashionable fantasy, straight from *Bocuse-Guérard et Cie* by way of Kyoto.

Obviously Europeans and Americans are deeply interested in changing their gastronomical patterns. They are sincere, whether for faddish reasons, newly discovered religious or economic convictions, or plain instinct, in wanting to stop eating as much as in the past, and in cutting down their conditioned dependence on fats, dairy products, starches, sugar. Some of them may have flocked like well-heeled lemmings to a fashionable spa in France, and then continued their newfound *bien-être* in the most stylish restaurants of London and New York. Others may have discovered dietary freedom in a hillside commune in California, or a quasi-Buddhist retreat near Barcelona. But all of them practice what they have been preached, at least for a while, and feel as restored spiritually by their brown rice and herb teas as by more worldly gods and goals.

This free acceptance, no matter how unwitting, of the intrinsic asceticism of Oriental cooking, is suspected by some observers to be a kind of intuitive preparation for the much leaner days to come to all of us who live on a polluted planet. What is now a stylish fad, or an "awakening," depending on both pocketbook and chronology, may become in the future an exotic recollection of the Good Old Days, when carrot curls and cashew nuts were eaten by caprice and not necessity. A latter-day MacLuhan might argue that our current preoccupation with culinary simplicity is really an instinctive recognition of our diminishing supplies of food ... of our need to accept austerity as the rule, after a long time of heedless Western glut.

All this sounds like some sort of celestial plot, a kindly trick of Nature, and perhaps it is. My friend Shizuo Tsuji wants to explain to us (as part of the plot?) his own theory of how and why the Japanese cuisine can be attractive to us. He believes that its combination of subtlety and simplicity has done much to keep Japan a strong nation, especially during the last hundred years of social changes and of revolutions and wars and cultural invasions. Even the Big Mac and "Kentucky" fried chicken cannot displace *udon*, he believes, as long as the noodles stay as honest as the broth they float in.

Tsuji-san is the first to admit to a love of ice cream, and is probably the first authority on traditional Japanese *ryōri* to invest in an expensive Western machine for it, and certainly the first reputable teacher of gastronomy to set his prize pupils to work at devising practical ways to make pure ice cream for their countrymen, without loading it with unhealthy sugar and unaccustomed milk products. He is, like his peers, aware that Japan can adjust to almost any change, and he is determined to keep that change beneficent rather than let it become one more compromise with mediocrity and shoddiness.

In Japan, red meat has been a status food since perhaps the late nineteenth century. Today it comes from cattle that were originally imported to please foreign palates, or from mammals caught and fast-frozen in far northern waters. It can be superb or routine, like broth made with special seaweed and dried bonito or with a synthetic *dashi* powder. In other words, one eats according to one's pocketbook—Kobe beef or fish, both prestigious in their own brackets.

This acceptance of imported gastronomical props shows in the three types of popular dishes in Japan, which are not native at all. At least half the population of more than a hundred million people like, eat, thrive on bowl-meals from China (*ramen* in soup), and India (curry-rice), and Italy (spaghetti with tomato sauce). In the same way sugar, which became available to the masses less than two hundred years ago, is now absorbed almost frantically, often as a chemical sweetener and mostly in soft drinks, laced according to their secret formulae with other potentially pernicious additives. Soybeans, which can be called a protein staple of the Japanese, whether eaten as packaged bean curd (*tōfu*) from the supermarket or as a salty fermented paste (*miso*), or as the ubiquitous soy sauce (*shōyu*), used to be bought from China, and now come largely from the Americas.

In other words, cooking is forever a compromise with historical fact and fancy, and Tsuji-san believes that there must be passionate leaders who know how to keep that compromise honest. As a Japanese, he wants his people to remember what has been best, gastronomically, in their history, and try to keep it intrinsic to the inevitable changes of the future.

As an American, a "Westerner," I agree. I want us to keep everything we know of honesty and quality, in eating habits formed during our short history, and shaped by our diverse ethnic heritage, so that we can bow in a basically healthy way to whatever the future may dictate. Inspired French cooks have simplified their art according to Japanese teachings, not too coincidentally, so that now we can eat either "nouvelle" or "minceur" in Pasadena as well as Paris. We can keep our inborn sense of *taste* as a cultural necessity to survival, thanks to the simplicity of flavors and satisfactions we learn daily from teachers who in turn have learned.

Escoffier said, "Cook simply!" The Japanese *ryōri* says, "Let little seem like much, as long as it is fresh and beautiful." The French and their Western cousins look at their medical records as well as their silhouettes, and agree to a new austerity that at its best returns them to a simpler and more honest way of living, and at its worst proves only that shoddiness can never be anything but a transparent imitation of the truth.

An authority on transferring the best of one national cuisine to another (in this case Diana Kennedy, who has studied and written wisely of Mexican foods for American readers and cooks) has said often and firmly that we must never try to *adapt* one cuisine to another, but instead *adjust* the two. As we come to know and use many of the finer things about traditional Japanese *ryōri*, therefore, Westerners can, with few changes in their hereditary conditionings, adjust themselves to some shifts in pattern and even in behavior without losing their own identity at the table.

Perhaps we can never sit with fascination through fourteen courses of nostalgic nibbles, each with its own place setting and each highly significant in one way or several. Quite probably we can never learn to slurp noodles with correct speed and enjoyment, especially if we were raised in the neo-Victorian tradition. We may never really like chopsticks, which I myself think are fine utensils for picking up small strange objects in the depths of bowls. But just as the Japanese adjusted their palates to sugar as an additive in the nineteenth century, and more lately to "Indian curry rice" and pasta with tomato sauce and even Kentucky fried chicken, and hamburgers in buns, and cokes, so we have adjusted to the imported versions of "tempura" and "sukiyaki" and daring displays of knifework with meats prepared before our dazzled eyes and broiled under our noses.

All these tricks have been adjusted, and skillfully. So why not an occasional long celebration of a birthday in the Japanese manner of a multitude of tiny courses? Why not a full lunch of fresh hot *udon* in good broth, perhaps with some slices of raw mushroom or even a few helpless bay-shrimp turning color at the bottom?

Yes, we can adjust to all this, and we must simplify our cooking just as the Japanese have done, by learning a few more of its complexities, while we still have time.

M. F. K. Fisher

Glen Ellen, 1979

Preface

My lifelong admiration for the incomparable M.F.K. Fisher is exceeded only by my gratitude for her friendship and her kindness in agreeing to write an introduction to this book. It really did my heart good to see the way Mrs. Fisher comprehended so well the spirit and soul of Japanese cooking, although it was her very first visit to this country and her first real encounter with Japanese cuisine.

I fear, however, that most people in the West think of Japanese cooking as something so utterly foreign to their way of life that it does not concern them at all—something they need never know anything about. The purpose of this book is to try and dispel that notion. Especially now, with the general world revulsion against additives and preservatives, there is a message for everyone in the Japanese food ethos with its insistence on natural goodness. And even though they may not admit it, those arbiters of *haute cuisine*, the great French chefs, have come to Japan and seen with their own eyes what we do here, and I think I can detect something of what they have seen emerging in their *nouvelle cuisine* and *cuisine minceur*.

This book has been a long time in the making. Of all the books yet published on the cuisine of this country, none has had so much time and effort spent on it as this volume. Here, for the first time, the secrets of the simple yet complex art of Japanese cooking have been laid bare for all to see.

Cooks the world over are notoriously secretive about their special recipes, but nowhere more so than in Japan. The way of teaching every Japanese art has traditionally been an imperfect passing down from master to disciple of jealously guarded personal interpretations. The master never explained; he merely demonstrated. And it was left to the more perceptive students to glean what they could of the master's art—filling in the gaps with their own ingenuity. Japanese cooking masters made it especially difficult. The part of his technique that a celebrated chef would demonstrate before his underlings was the virtuoso knifework and the finger dexterity that could only be achieved after years of experience and practice.

But that was mainly the decorative part of Japanese cooking. Its flavoring was far less complicated and too easily copied for a chef to take the chance of letting his juniors see how he blended his aromas. He would visit the kitchens in the dead of night, when the staff was asleep, to blend his subtle flavors. They could only guess how he had achieved his combinations. When all is said and done, Japanese cuisine is deceptively simple. Its key ingredients are but two: a rather delicate stock (*dashi*) made from *konbu* (giant kelp) and flakes of dried bonito, and *shōyu*, Japanese soy sauce. Its key requirements are also two: the pristine freshness and prime condition of materials used, and beauty of presentation.

Japanese cooking is the outcome of a long history and has a solid cultural background. But it is not an alien culture. Our culture is not difficult to understand. It is not really exotic at all, because the essence of Japan's culture is its closeness to nature. Like Japanese painting and poetry, our cooking, too, is simply the result of an acute awareness of the seasons.

Japanese culture was born of austerity, an austerity that even obtained in the very seat of culture—the imperial court of ancient Kyoto. The impoverished but cultivated court nobles learned to delight in the offerings of each changing season as it came, making the most of nature's provender when each article of food—fish, fowl, or vegetable—was at its prime. With meat made taboo from the introduction of Buddhism in the sixth century, the rich animal fats so familiar to Europeans were denied the Japanese, while the islands' temperate climate at the same time denied them nature's tropical largesse enjoyed in the countries where Buddhism began.

Making the most of nature's seasonal offerings with the utmost culinary artistry probably gave rise to the traditional formal Japanese meal as we know it today, with its many small courses—each a work of art on which much time and thought are spent, the receptacles, too, constituting an important part of the experience. While each dish in a Japanese meal could quite easily be expanded in quantity to make a sizeable entrée in the Western sense, it is a tradition of formal Japanese cuisine never to serve a large amount of any one thing. (In your own home, of course, such "rules" need not apply.) Perhaps this is its biggest difference in relation to other cuisines. A Japanese banquet consists of a great many small portions. The greater the variety, the more extravagant the hospitality.

If a formal Japanese meal seems to you like a mere succession of hors d'oeuvres, you can quite easily adjust the recipes in this book to suit a Western menu. There are soups to choose from, both thick and thin. One of the fish, fowl, or meat dishes need only be enlarged in quantity and served with one of the many tasty vegetable recipes, together with rice. And Japanese salads need no adjustment at all.

Few Westerners visiting Japan—and even few Japanese, for that matter—

are afforded the luxury of visiting an elegant and exclusive *ryōri-ya*, where the real Japanese cuisine in all its formal exquisiteness may be experienced. But fairly reasonable facsimiles can be had at Japanese inns; and specialty shops that serve only broiled eel or *sushi* or *tempura* are readily accessible. In fact, the specialty shops' expertise in their own dishes exceeds that of the exclusive *ryōri-ya*. There are plenty of other accessible restaurants that serve many popular dishes, including the convivial one-pot meals of traditional home hospitality such as *sukiyaki* and *shabu-shabu*. These are the dishes that the Western visitor to Japan probably enjoys the most and finds the most hunger satisfying.

Some Japanese dishes may at first seem flat and insipid to many Westerners. To those accustomed to rich, filling sauces and stocks using butter, flour, and meat juices, many of our foods may seem thin and lacking in substance. But you must learn to look for the subtle, natural aroma and flavor of ingredients, purposely not masked with anything stronger than a touch of bonito stock (*dashi*) or soy sauce. The broth used, for instance, to cook bean curd in *yudōfu* (page 436) is merely hot water containing a square of kelp. Anything else would mask the delicate but distinct aroma of the soybean from which the curd is made. Good *tōfu* has an intriguing taste all its own, highly appreciated by the Japanese gourmet.

Recipes for the many different forms of Japanese cooking are given here, with easy-to-follow directions, copious sketches of techniques, and color photographs of representative finished dishes, ingredients, and table settings. Apart from the intricate knifework of the experts, Japanese recipes are not hard to make. Their steps are not as difficult for the amateur as the complicated processes of French cuisine. The aesthetic principles underlying Japanese food may seen unfamiliar at first, but it is my aim in this book to make it clear to the reader just what those principles are. They are of the utmost importance. To grasp them is to stand on the threshold of a whole new culinary wonderland.

If an American, for instance, wants to try a bit of French cuisine, he or she might go out and buy a copy of Child and Beck's *Mastering the Art of French Cooking*. He or she would start with a very good idea of what the end result should be. To use a baseball simile, he would know where the "strike zone" was. With a Japanese recipe, however, unless you have been to this country and eaten the food, you will probably have little idea of what you will be aiming at. That is what this book is all about: to teach you the rules of the game, and where the "strike zone" is, so you will know what you are trying to achieve.

The very first rule is to avoid frozen foods. Dried foods are all right, but freezing destroys texture. Freshness and naturalness are the *sine qua non* of Japanese cuisine. Eschew the unnatural and artificial. If you live inland or in the mountains, do not cook seafood. Eat river fish and those caught in local lakes and streams. And eat them straight away, while they are fresh.

The soup and the raw fish are considered the test pieces of Japanese cuisine. They are the criteria by which a meal stands or falls. If the soup is good, it proves that the chef knows how to blend his bonito stock—the flavor base of all the dishes to come. And as for the raw fish, it speaks volumes. With no elaborate cooking processes and no French sauces to hide its nakedness, the *sashimi* dish can tell you at once whether or not your host—or the cook—sets high standards for the freshness and seasonal prime of his materials. When I enter a *sushi* restaurant, I can tell at a glance by the texture of their skins —like the bloom of youth on a young girl—whether the fish is really fresh. Frozen fish just has not the same intrinsic brilliance, even though it is sprinkled with water to make it shine. A dish of really fresh raw fish at the height of its prime, in dexterously sliced pieces beautifully arranged on an exquisite plate, is the high point of any Japanese meal. And you know that if the *sashimi* (raw fish) dish is good, your host—or the chef—will have chosen his vegetables and other ingredients with the same meticulous care.

I once wanted to serve a Japanese dinner in my flat in London and sent Mr. Hata, the head of the Japanese cooking division of my school in Osaka, who was traveling with me, to Billingsgate fish market to buy something for the raw fish course. He came back horrified, saying the fish looked listless and wan—as if they had all just come out of the hospital! The only thing he could find that was at all lively was the crayfish. He made us an excellent *sashimi* dish of that. Good fish restaurants in London like Wheelers send all the way to Dover to buy the fish directly from the boats as they come in. I know, because the proprietor is a good friend of mine. People run down English food, but there are many real connoisseurs of freshness there. They know, for instance, how good tomatoes are when just picked from the garden vine. The English love to grow their own runner beans and lift their own potatoes. Simply boiled, these homegrown vegetables have a natural flavor that is superb.

If you find it difficult where you live to get fish fresh enough for serving raw as *sashimi*, surely you know some enthusiastic angler. Get him to bring you a trout he has just caught. First, cut fillets, slice them, then apply the *arai* treatment. Briefly wash the slices in water, plunge them immediately into ice water until chilled, and drain. We do that with all freshwater fish to take away its muddy taste. Then arrange the fish slices artistically on a plain pottery plate, or if you do not have anything suitably artistic, use an attractive slab of wood (new wood has a marvelous fragrance), or even a flat stone, with a few leaves at one side. And there's your dish of *sashimi* in perfectly authentic Japanese style! You can even make your own chopsticks. It won't matter if they are knobbly. After all, that is what chopsticks are—a pair of sticks.

If you decide to grill the whole trout over charcoal, do it the Japanese way, over a very hot fire, only *just* cooked through to the bone and with the skin deliciously crisp. Lay a few thin slices of green onion at one side, and flavor the fish with a little soy sauce, lemon juice, and grated ginger.

Seafood is also washed thoroughly before it is served raw. Water is plentiful in Japan and we use a lot of it, especially when preparing raw fish. We have a sort of jingle, which liberally translates, "If it's fish, wash it twice, wash it thrice." Foreigners in Japan timidly trying their first piece of raw fish are usually very surprised when they find it does not taste at all fishy.

It is unlikely that many readers of this book will try to serve an authentic Japanese dinner in its entirety, but they might like to include a traditional Japanese dish in a menu of American, French, or Italian food. It would be just as artistically permissible, and interesting, as playing a modern cadenza in a Mozart concerto, or using a *biwa*—the ancient Japanese lute—in a modern symphonic work. It would please me to think that somewhere in San Francisco or New York someone who had read this book was serving, in the course of an otherwise completely American-style party, just one dish in the authentic Japanese manner—say a simple wooden slab with an aesthetic arrangement of leaves upon which was presented a Japanese salad or some fresh raw seafood.

As long as you know the rules, and know what authentic Japanese food is, there is almost no limit to the variations you can make with local ingredients. It is rather like playing the piano. After you have learned the rules, done your exercises, and practiced the correct fingering, you can put a little rubato into your Chopin, varying the tempo to suit your own artistic inclination.

Try serving cherrystone clams from New England with a dressing made of pureed kiwi fruit from New Zealand. Mix the puree with rice vinegar and add a few drops of Japanese soy sauce diluted with *dashi* stock, and you have a delicious salad authentically Japanese in concept. Be flexible and keep an open mind. If you cannot obtain some ingredient called for in the book, find something locally with the same kind of texture and aroma. Calves' brains are remarkably similar to bean curd! And sweetbreads make a fine substitute for the roe of bass and sea bream. Sweetbreads *teriyaki* would be delicious, too. And who knows, one day some of your innovations may be reimported into Japan.

Over the centuries the Japanese have adopted dishes from many countries. Today the Japanese eat a mixture of Western, Japanese, and Chinese food. Chinese noodles for lunch and curry-and-rice for dinner. But the *ramen* noodles are no longer really Chinese, and an Indian would not recognize the curry. The foreign dishes have been denatured to suit the Japanese palate, and, I am sorry to say, our own cuisine is no longer authentic. It has been polluted with frozen foods, which are freely used in heedless ignorance of tradition. Japan must be the only country in the world where the everyday fare is such a hodgepodge, and whose people know so little about their own traditional cuisine that they do not try to preserve its authenticity.

Tempura Soba—buckwheat noodles with deep-fried prawns—has been a popular favorite for years. But now these large shrimp are so scarce they are an exorbitant luxury. The dish would be perfectly authentic made with the still plentiful small shrimp, but no, the Japanese are such slaves to form —to the mere appearance of the dish, with the large decorative tails prominently displayed—that they would rather use large shrimp imported frozen all the way from Africa than be true to the traditional spirit of our cuisine. They have forgotten the very essence of *tempura*—the quick, light deep-frying of *very* fresh seafood.

One commendable adaptation on the modern food front here is the development of a really excellent instant *dashi*, far superior to the bouillon cubes of the West, all of which are terrible. While instant *dashi* cannot, of course, compare with the wonderful bouquet of stock made with freshly shaved dried bonito, it has simplified Japanese cooking enormously, and the wide availability abroad of instant *dashi* powders and Japanese soy sauce brings the basic makings of our traditional cuisine right to your door.

It is sad, however, to think that more and more young people in Japan will go through their lives never knowing the ineffable flavor of the real home-made *dashi* their grandmothers used to make. One cannot even buy those mahogany-colored dried bonito blocks any more at ordinary stores. It is only in the very expensive restaurants that one can now savor the true *dashi* that once was the pride of every home. The art of making *dashi* used to be handed down from mother to daughter and from mother-in-law to daughter-in-law. The boneless quarter of bonito, hard as wood, would be shaved with a special blade into a box fixed underneath to catch the thin flakes rich with the aroma of sea and sunshine. Then, before the fragrance had time to escape, the flakes would be quickly thrown into boiling water to release their goodness into the broth—strained and used forthwith to form the basis of many a dish for the whole family to enjoy.

Enjoyment. That is the aim of any good cuisine. The food is meant to be eaten and enjoyed. Food is only good if you enjoy eating it, however pleasing it may be to the eye. And to really enjoy the cuisine of Japan you must first develop a liking for the earthy bean taste of soy sauce and the ocean tang of kelp and bonito in our soup stock. Then, with this volume for your guide, it is my earnest hope that you will get to know some of these dishes and decide to introduce, from time to time, a little touch of Japan in your kitchen and at your table, wherever you may live.

The people of both Suntory and Kikkoman are rightfully proud of their products. My gratitude to both these companies for helping to make this ambitious book a reality.

Many people contributed their talents and energies to the making of this book. Some gave far more than any thanks of mine can adequately acknowledge. Mr. Kōichirō Hata, Chief of the Japanese Cuisine Division of the Ecole Technique Hôtelière Tsuji is a dedicated craftsman who expresses himself better with action than with words. His inestimable contribution, which forms the basis of this book, has been transformed into highly informative and easy-to-follow directions by Mary Sutherland, whose powers of organization are truly remarkable. After following a course of instruction with Mr. Hata in Osaka, she traveled to the United States to find out what Japanese foods—or their equivalents—were available abroad, and there she continued to be my "right hand" half a world away. Bilingual Hisako Harada of the Publications and Editorial Office of Ecole Technique spent invaluable hours checking and rechecking for accuracy of detail under the direction of Mr. Saburō Bando. I extend my gratitude to them and to all the staff members of the Ecole. My thanks are also due to longtime resident in Japan and writer Dorothy Britton (Lady Bouchier), whose sensitivity to things Japanese has enabled her to put my sentiments and thoughts into just the right words. And lastly, I am deeply indebted to the indefatigable editorial staff at Kodansha International, especially Katsuhiko Sakiyama, without whose competence and flair this work would never have reached completion, to Shigeo Katakura, who designed this book, and to Yoshito Suzuki, whose drawings bring words to life. Thank you.

Plate 1

Guest room of a formal Japanese restaurant. Japanese irises are arranged in green bamboo rafts on lacquer tables. A *sashimi* of the choicest sea bream is concealed in hollowed sections of bamboo stalk. The vermilion of the lacquer *saké* cups and the gold dust thinly applied on dried bamboo sheaths contrast with the green bamboo, the black tables, and the oxidized silver of the *saké* servers. Dinner has been set for five people—the number of *saké* cups indicates this.

Bold, beautiful calligraphy by the abbot of the famed Daitoku-ji temple is displayed on the wall. The ornamental scent ball of brocade hanging in the corner alcove is an essential accompaniment of the Boy's Day Festival, as are the irises. The colors and symbolism of each element —the green bamboo, irises, hanging scroll, ornamental ball, and oxidized silver—together form a tableau overflowing with the fresh ambience of early summer. (by courtesy of Kitchō, Osaka)

Fish

Plate 2

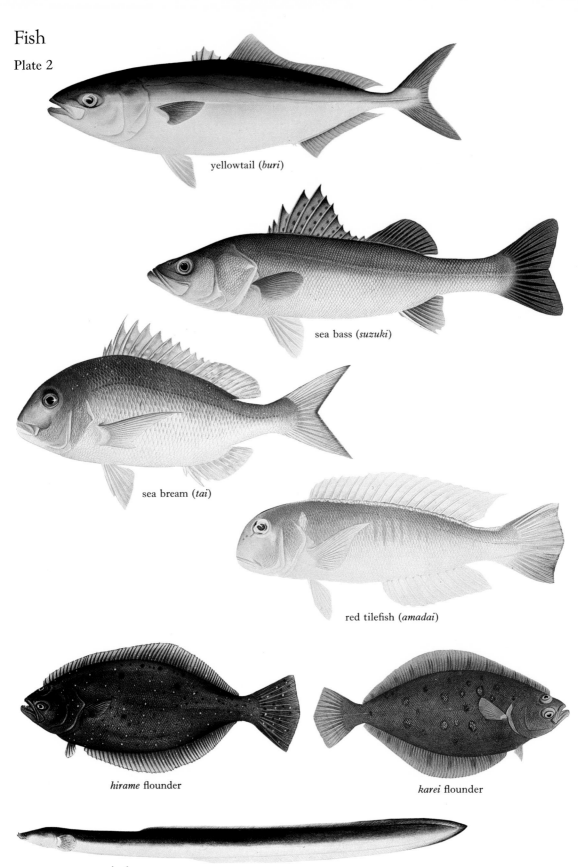

yellowtail (*buri*)

sea bass (*suzuki*)

sea bream (*tai*)

red tilefish (*amadai*)

hirame flounder

karei flounder

unagi eel

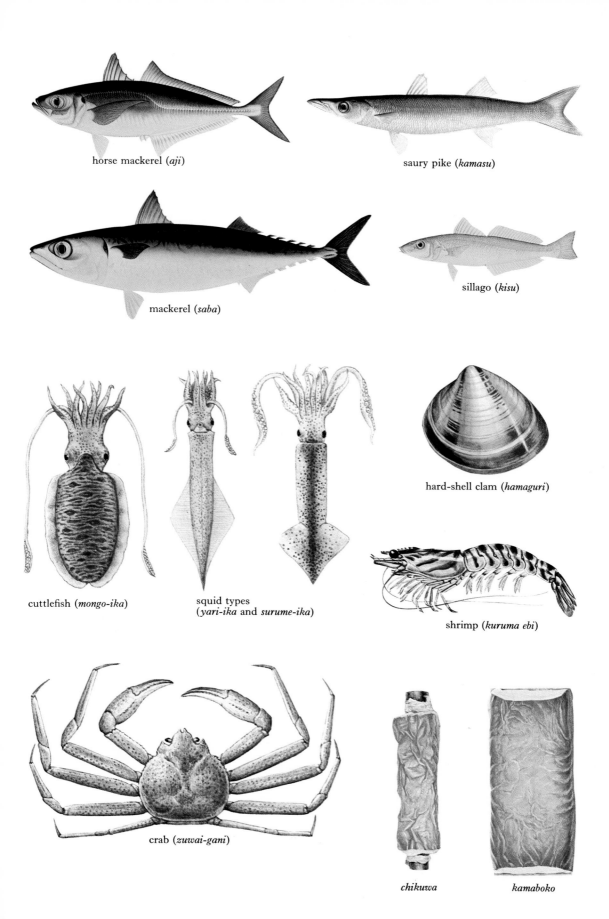

horse mackerel (*aji*)

saury pike (*kamasu*)

mackerel (*saba*)

sillago (*kisu*)

cuttlefish (*mongo-ika*)

squid types
(*yari-ika* and *surume-ika*)

hard-shell clam (*hamaguri*)

shrimp (*kuruma ebi*)

crab (*zuwai-gani*)

chikuwa

kamaboko

Vegetables

Plate 3

cucumbers (*kyūri*)

eggplant (*nasu*)

small green peppers (*ao-tōgarashi*)

Japanese squash
(pumpkins) (*kabocha*)

Chinese cabbage (*hakusai*)

kinome sprigs

spinach (*hōrensō*)

edible chrysanthemum
(*shungiku* or *kikuna*)

green and red *shiso* leaves

shiso seed pods (*hojiso*)

yuzu citron

trefoil (*mitsuba*)

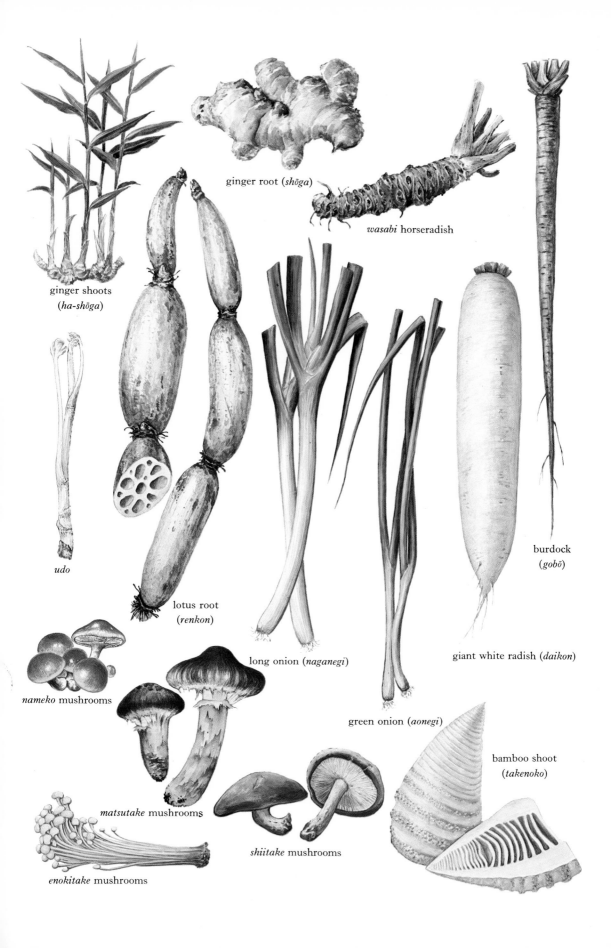

ginger root (*shōga*)

wasabi horseradish

ginger shoots
(*ha-shōga*)

udo

lotus root
(*renkon*)

long onion (*naganegi*)

green onion (*aonegi*)

giant white radish (*daikon*)

burdock
(*gobō*)

bamboo shoot
(*takenoko*)

nameko mushrooms

matsutake mushrooms

shiitake mushrooms

enokitake mushrooms

Plate 4

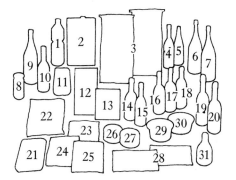

Some Japanese foods widely available in the United States.
1. light soy sauce.   2. dark soy sauce (1-gal can).   3. short-grain rice.   4. naturally brewed *mirin*.   5. artificially brewed *mirin*.   6. *saké*.   7. plum wine (*umeshu*).   8. sweet-&-sour sauce.   9. rice vinegar.   10. mild soy sauce.   11. *harusame* filaments (bean starch).   12. dried bonito flakes (*hana-katsuo*).   13. *tempura* batter mix.   14. *teriyaki* sauce.   15. dark (all-purpose) soy sauce.   16. noodle dipping sauce (cold).   17. *tempura* dipping sauce.   18. *sukiyaki* sauce.   19. *tonkatsu* sauce.   20. sesame oil.   21. *sōmen* noodles.   22. dried *shiitake* mushrooms.   23. instant *miso* soup (light).   24. instant *miso* soup (red).   25. instant clear soup.   26. water chestnuts.   27. bamboo shoots.   28. *udon* noodles.   29. red *miso*.   30. light miso.   31. *dashi* stock concentrate.

Plate 5

1. dry *wakame* seaweed. 2, 3. salted seaweed for garnishes or vinegared salads. 4. giant kelp (*dashi konbu*) for making *dashi* stock. 5. stick agar-agar (*kanten*). 6. thread agar-agar (*ito-kanten*). 7. *nori* seaweed (standard-size sheets open and folded). 8. *shiraita konbu* ("white-sheet" *konbu*). 9. *konbu* for rolled *sushi*. 10. *tororo konbu* (page 73). 11. *oboro konbu* (page 73). 12. *tsume konbu* (used for long simmering). 13. dried sardines (*niboshi*) for making stock. 14. dried bonito (*katsuo-bushi*) 15. dried bonito thread-shavings (*ito-kezuri-katsuo*). 16. dried bonito flakes (*hana-katsuo*)

Plate 6

1. dried giant white radish strips (*kiriboshi-daikon*). 2. dried gourd strips (*kampyō*). 3. thick dried *shiitake* mushrooms. 4. *iwatake* (*sashimi* garnish; see page 169). 5. dried *shiitake* mushrooms. 6. cloud ear mushrooms (*kikurage*). 7. *Suizenji nori* (*sashimi* garnish, for vinegared salads, or clear soups). 8. *bakudai* (*sashimi* garnish or for vinegared salads). 9. dried red peppers (*tōgarashi*). 10. red pepper flakes (*ichimi*). 11. seven-spice mixture (*shichimi*). 12. black sesame seeds. 13. white sesame seeds. 14. ground *sansho* pepper. 15. white poppy seeds.

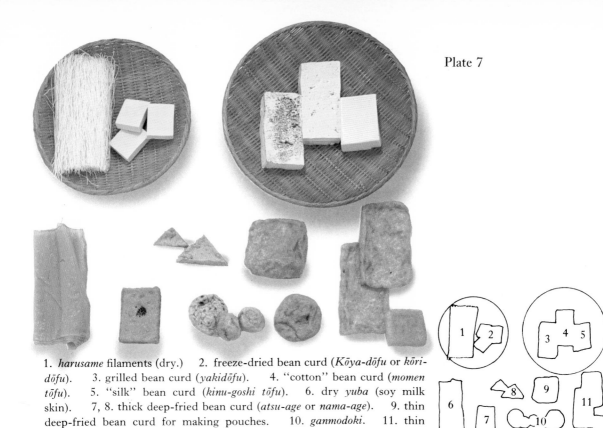

Plate 7

1. *harusame* filaments (dry.)   2. freeze-dried bean curd (*Kōya-dōfu* or *kōri-dōfu*).   3. grilled bean curd (*yakidōfu*).   4. "cotton" bean curd (*momen tōfu*).   5. "silk" bean curd (*kinu-goshi tōfu*).   6. dry *yuba* (soy milk skin).   7, 8. thick deep-fried bean curd (*atsu-age* or *nama-age*).   9. thin deep-fried bean curd for making pouches.   10. *ganmodoki*.   11. thin deep-fried bean curd (*aburage* or *usu-age*) (see pages 56–61).

Plate 8

1. wheat gluten (*fu*) sheets.   2. wheat gluten (*fu*) strips.   3. *mochi* (glutinous rice) cakes.   4. *Dōmyōji-ko* (glutinous rice meal).   5. *shiratamako* (glutinous rice starch).   6. *kuzu* starch.   7, 8. *konnyaku*, refined and unrefined.   9. *shirataki* (thread *konnyaku*) filaments.   10. *kishimen* noodles.   11. *udon* noodles.   12. green-tea buckwheat (*cha-soba*) noodles.   13. *sōmen* noodles.   14. egg *sōmen* noodles.   15. buckwheat (*soba*) noodles.   16. *hiya-mugi* noodles.

Plate 9

1. YELLOW FLOWER SHRIMP (page 226)—*garnishes:* squash; spinach (or chrysanthemum); *yuzu* citron rind
2. SOUSED SPINACH (page 429)
3. BAMBOO RICE (page 439)—*garnishes:* toasted and crumbled *nori* seaweed; *kinome* sprigs
4. CLAM CONSOMMÉ (page 155)—*garnishes:* thin *udo* slices; *kinome* sprigs
5. SEA BREAM SASHIMI (variation of recipe, page 160)—*garnishes:* shred-cut *daikon* and carrot; carrot curl; *shiso* buds; *bōfu; dip:* Tosa soy sauce

Summer

Plate 10

1. EGG "TŌFU" (page 216)—*garnish:* grated *yuzu* rind
2. POTATO-CHICKEN NUGGETS (page 411)—*garnish:* lemon wedge
3. STEAM-SIMMERED OCTOPUS (page 383)—*garnishes:* okra (sub. for *kinome*);
shred-cut ginger
4. SAKÉ-STEAMED ABALONE (page 378)—green sauce
5. GRILLED EGGPLANT (page 370)—*garnish:* dried bonito thread-shavings;
dip: soy sauce and ginger juice

Autumn

Plate 11

1. SEAFOOD PLATTER WITH PINE NEEDLES (page 197)
2. CHESTNUT RICE (page 279)
3. CLEAR CHICKEN SOUP (page 345)—*garnishes:* boiled chrysanthemum; *shiitake* mushrooms; carrot slices; lemon slice; chopped green onion
4. DEEP-FRIED FILLET OF TROUT (page 404)
5. STUFFED RED TILEFISH (page 361)—*garnish:* CHRYSANTHEMUM TURNIP (page 251)

Winter

Plate 12

1. FISH ONE-POT (page 259)
2. YELLOWTAIL TERIYAKI (page 200)—*garnish:* PICKLED GINGER SHOOTS (page 304)
3. VINEGARED CRAB (page 247)—*garnishes:* shred-cut cucumber and *yuzu* citron peel
4. DRENCHED RADISH (page 395)—*garnish:* kinome sprigs
5. SAVORY CUP CUSTARD (page 214)
6. SHELLFISH WITH MISO DRESSING (page 252)—*garnish:* benitade

Fish

Plate 13

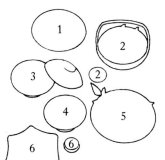

1. SAKÉ-SIMMERED FLOUNDER (page 224)—*garnish: kinome* sprigs
2. FLOUNDER TREASURE SHIPS (page 405)—*garnishes:* small green peppers; noodle "whisk"; lemon wedge; *dip:* salt
3. SEA BREAM STEAMED WITH BUCKWHEAT NOODLES (page 375)—*garnishes:* chopped green onion; *wasabi* horseradish; shreds of toasted *nori* seaweed
4. SEA BREAM SASHIMI (page 164)—*garnishes:* RED MAPLE RADISH (page 170); chopped green onion
5. GRILLED RED TILEFISH "WAKASA" (page 363)—*garnishes:* lemon wedge; pickled ginger shoot
6. YELLOWTAIL LEMON SASHIMI (page 352)—*garnishes: shiso* buds; *bōfu;* carrot curl; *wasabi* horseradish; *dip:* Tosa soy sauce

Plate 14

1. SIMMERING TŌFU (page 436)—*spicy condiments:* chopped green onion; dried bonito thread-shavings; grated ginger; dipping sauce in ewer
2. FOX NOODLES (page 312)
3. CHILLED FINE NOODLES WITH SHRIMP AND MUSHROOM (page 457) —*garnishes:* trefoil stalks; *kinome* sprigs; dipping sauce
4. NOODLES IN A BASKET (page 312)—*spicy condiments:* *wasabi* horseradish; chopped green onion; dipping sauce
5. TANGY WHITE SALAD (page 421)—*garnish: benitade*
6. FRIED AND SIMMERED FREEZE-FRIED TŌFU (page 399)—*garnish:* grated ginger

Rice Dishes

Plate 15

1. RICE BALLS (page 440)—triangles, ovals, and rounds
2. OHAGI (page 462)
3. SCATTERED SUSHI, OSAKA STYLE (page 449)
4. SUSHI PLATTER (pages 292–303)
   a. BATTERA SUSHI; b. NIGIRI-SUSHI; c. NORI-ROLL SUSHI; d. CUCUMBER SUSHI ROLL
5. RED RICE (page 280)
6. CHICKEN-'N-EGG ON RICE (page 283)

Fried and Skewered Dishes

Plate 16

TEMPURA (page 235)—shrimp; *anago* eel; sillago; lotus root; trefoil; *shiso*
leaves; *nori* seaweed; dipping sauce and grated *daikon*
YAKITORI (page 186)—(l to r) wing "stick"; chicken balls; gizzard; skin
and long onion; liver; thigh meat and long onion

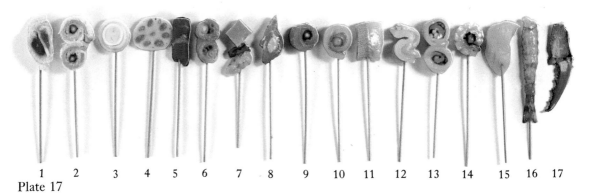

1 2 3 4 5 6 7 8 9 10 11 12 13 14 15 16 17
Plate 17

DEEP-FRIED MIXED KEBABS
The classical recipe is on page 418. The variations shown here before being coated and fried are
examples of the creative freedom possible with this dish. (l to r) 1. bread, beef, and marmalade roll;
2. bread, ham, and asparagus rolls; 3. pearl onion stuffed with boiled quail egg; 4. lotus root stuffed
with minced pork; 5. beef steak; 6. chicken breast fillet and green onion rolls; 7. ham, asparagus,
and shrimp; 8. salmon stuffed with *yuzu* citron *miso* (WHITE MISO DRESSING+grated *yuzu* rind);
9. salmon and asparagus roll; 10. sillago and ginkgo nut roll; 11. sillago fillet (*ryō-tsuma-ore* skewering, page 179); 12. ham between squid; 13. squid and asparagus rolls; 14. squid and *nori* seaweed
roll; 15. scallop; 16. shrimp; 17. crab claw.

Part One

Part One

❊ Part One Contents ❊

The Japanese Meal

This book goes beyond a presentation of authentic recipes for you to imitate. The real purpose is to teach you how to cook in the spirit of Japan, whose pure and restrained effects with food constitute an art. The book is designed to lay open the heart of Japanese cuisine so that you will understand and feel comfortable with fundamental techniques of Japanese cooking —apart from isolated recipes.

This is an ambitious goal, so the book has been divided into two parts. In Part One, the basic methods of food preparation are scrutinized, with some recipes included to illustrate the points of technique to be mastered. The second section is a collection of recipes without repetitive explanations of basic routines. Part One is for learning about Japanese food and for confidence in the kitchen. Part Two is for practice and fun. Once you feel secure with ingredients and methods, you can use Part Two as you would any Western cookbook.

Part One provides first of all a thorough introduction to general Japanese ingredients (you will be surprised at how many are easy to get at regular supermarkets), their properties, and whether any standard preparation, such as parboiling, is necessary beforehand. There is some discussion of alternate ingredients that will keep you in the "strike zone" of authentic Japanese cooking. Japanese kitchen utensils and table service are also examined. You will discover that, though a few Japanese utensils might be handy, you can cook Japanese with what you already have.

The Japanese meal is divided into consecutive courses according to method of preparation—a grilled dish comes before a steamed dish, and a steamed dish before simmered foods, and so on—and so the Part One chapters have been arranged in the proper sequence of a grand Japanese banquet. Each method chapter includes not only an explanation of the techniques involved but something about their cultural background and a few selected recipes characteristic of the category. For those who have never experienced firsthand the pleasure of Japanese hospitality in the form of a grand meal, this chapter arrangement will help to reinforce the idea of how a Japanese meal progresses.

While *miso* soup, rice, and pickles can make the bare minimum of a family repast, the ideal formal meal progresses in a more or less set order from clear soup and *sashimi* (fresh, uncooked fish) through entrées of grilled, steamed, simmered and fried foods to conclude with rice and pickles—and sometimes *miso* soup—followed by tea and fruit. The traditional basic formula, however, is much simpler—*ichijū sansai*, or "soup and three." That is, a soup and three main dishes as follows:

1. Fresh, uncooked fish (*sashimi*)
2. A grilled dish (*yakimono*)
3. A simmered dish (*nimono*)

This is the usual composition of a meal served to guests at home, always followed, of course, by rice, pickles, tea, and quite often fruit.

This basic formula of three is not unsimilar to that of a typical Western main course: fish or meat, fried potatoes, and boiled vegetables. The only difference is that in the West all three are served on the same large plate, instead of in small separate dishes or bowls as they are in Japan.

The Japanese custom of serving things in separate dishes emphasizes the importance placed on presentation. No Japanese, however humble, would think of serving food on just any old plate, relying on flavor alone to please. Each item is an artistic composition in which the receptacle, the food, and its arrangement are all carefully brought together to complement one another. The whole meal is a composition, too—a symphony of carefully orchestrated flavor, color, texture, and seasonal appropriateness. Japanese food is fresh and only lightly cooked. It is based on foodstuffs in season and prepared so that natural flavor is enhanced. Great care is taken not to over-cook. Cooked fish is just flaky, still moist; chicken is tinged with pink near the bone; vegetables are firm, not limp, still crisp. Basic seasonings—soy sauce and bonito-based *dashi* broth—are delicately fragrant, and, though added to most every dish, are used subtly, so as not to mask natural aromas.

Japanese foods are light, not greasy. Gentle simmering is one of the most popular methods of food preparation, especially good for maximum preservation of original flavor. In deep-frying, careful attention is paid to oil temperature so that little fat is absorbed by the food. Oil must be hot enough to "seal" the exterior of the food item the moment it is immersed. No grease penetrates, and natural juices are retained. This is why *tempura* done to perfection is so succulently light.

Fish appears on the Japanese menu with more frequency than beef or pork;

this is only logical because Japan is a land-poor country, a group of mountainous islands washed by fish-rich currents. But fish in Japan is served so delightfully fresh it is never "fishy." Fresh fish—bright-eyed and with firm, shiny scales—has a finer texture than red meat and a sophisticated, subtle, ocean-clean taste. Fresh fish that can be eaten raw as *sashimi* is not only delectable, but a low-calorie, low-carbohydrate, high-protein dish.

The *sashimi*—the fresh, uncooked fish—is, in fact, the highlight of any meal served to guests. The clear soup and the *sashimi* are the *chefs d'oeuvre* upon which the utmost artistry is lavished. Known in gastronomic parlance as *wan-sashi* (from *wan*, "soup bowl," and *sashi*, short for *sashimi*), these two dishes are the high point of the Japanese meal. In one's very best lacquer soup bowls a beautiful tiny "still life" of seafood and vegetables is composed within the crystal clear broth for the delectation of both eye and palate, followed by an equally beautiful arrangement, on one's very best plates, of skillfully sliced fillets of fresh, uncooked fish with some artistic garnish. In lieu of chinaware or pottery, the *sashimi* is sometimes presented on a plain, natural slab of fine-grained fragrant wood, beautiful in nature's simplicity, with only a leaf or two for garnish.

The Japanese meal has a definite beginning, an unmistakable middle, and a set end. In the basic "soup and three," the soup represents the beginning and the "three" comprise the middle. The end is always essentially rice, pickles, and tea. Within each of the three middle parts, if the meal is an elaborate one, several courses will be served and cleared in succession. If the meal is less formal, it may be served in three parts, with dishes being removed after each part is finished. If strictly informal or intimate (or if help is short), the entire meal can be laid out all at once—a method recommended for Western hosts.

Below is an outline of the complete Japanese banquet. Needless to say, courses may be embellished or subtracted, depending on the formality and importance of the occasion, and bearing in mind the basic "soup and three."

BEGINNING   Appetizer (*zensai*)
                    Clear soup (*suimono*)
                    Fresh, uncooked fish (*sashimi*)

MIDDLE   Grilled foods (*yakimono*) ⎤
                    Steamed foods (*mushimono*) ⎥ or One-pot dish
                    Simmered foods (*nimono*) ⎥ (*nabemono*)
                    Deep-fried foods (*agemono*) ⎦
                    Vinegared or "dressed" salad
                      (*sunomono* or *aemono*)

END   Boiled rice (*gohan*) ⎫
Miso soup (*miso-shiru*) ⎬ served together
Pickles (*tsukemono*) ⎭
Green tea (*ryokucha*)
Fresh fruit

Appetizers, or *zensai*, are typically an assortment of seasonal delicacies, attractively displayed and served in lilliputian portions. *Zensai* may be made from fish such as smoked salmon and other seafood like fresh shrimp, sea urchin, and squid. Vegetables such as cucumber and lotus root may be stuffed and cut crosswise into rounds. Ginkgo nuts and chestnuts may be eaten as *zensai* too. There is no disputing the fact that the ingredients and labor that go into a full complement of *zensai* are above what the average home cook can spend in terms of money and time. A vinegared food (*sunomono*) served in lieu of traditional *zensai* is more practical, especially if you have limited access to Japanese ingredients.

In a formal meal, *saké* is served from the very beginning; a toast is drunk even before the *zensai* course is touched. *Saké* is served throughout the meal until just before the rice course. However, *saké* is not drunk with soups, which should be imbibed as hot as possible. *Saké* is drunk lukewarm and is sipped between morsels of food—both hot and cold—to refresh the palate and increase the enjoyment of the temperature changes. *Saké* and rice do not go well together: *saké* is brewed from rice, and the two are too closely akin to enhance one another.

You will notice that the Japanese meal includes no sweet dessert as in the West, although sometimes—but not invariably—fruit appears at the end of the meal. The cup of plain green tea, however, is often accompanied by an *okashi*, or confection, as a sweet foil to the slight bitterness of the tea, rather like the chocolate mint wafer served with the demitasse of coffee in the West.

Although the authentic Japanese meal order has been given here, readers should feel free to use the recipes in this book in whatever way they please, as long as they bear in mind the spirit of Japanese cuisine, in which an artistic balance of textures, colors, flavors, seasonal freshness, and presentation is paramount.

In the West, of course, too, meals are put together with textural harmony and nutritional balance very much in mind, and people like to set an attractive table and use pretty dishes. Western dishes, however, tend to come in sets for the whole meal, so do not lend themselves to individual gastronomic compositions. A Japanese meal will use a great variety of dishes, not a homogeneous, patterned set.

To achieve balance in the Japanese manner there are two helpful guidelines. Make sure that the same ingredient is not used repeatedly. If shrimp *tempura* is going to be the highlight of the meal, for example, avoid shrimps in the hors d'oeuvres, clear soup, or vinegared salad. Secondly, let the dishes represent various cooking techniques. This is the intention of the "soup and three" formula, and if the meal has more than the three prescribed dishes, other techniques should be represented, rather than repeating any already used.

The recipes in this book are for servings that are slightly larger than those served in Japan. Thus, if you select one recipe for inclusion in an otherwise Western meal, portions will be adequate, though small in many cases. Integrating single Japanese dishes is highly recommended while learning Japanese cooking techniques, rather than being overly ambitious and attempting a complete meal in the Japanese manner straight away. The one-pot meals cooked at table, in particular, lend themselves to first efforts in Japanese cooking. The sample meals at the end of this chapter may be served all at once, as the Japanese often do, which is also helpful to the beginner.

You will not be cooking Japanese every day. (In fact, many readers will probably use this book as a takeoff point for ideas of their own.) There will be times, however, when you will want to review ingredients, precooking routines, and general methods, so cross-references are numerous. Page references embedded in recipes will direct you quickly to pertinent material for review, sparing you the task of thumbing through the general index.

The professional Japanese chef has countless helping hands to turn out many-course meals, each course unforgettably pure in taste, the cooking perfectly timed, the presentation a work of art. The home chef, who often cooks to entertain, could never hope to achieve the same results and at the same time join in the feast! Nonetheless, the basic principles that professionals follow to bring out the natural goodness of Japanese food underlie all the recipes in this book; the home chef can confidently base his work in his own kitchen on them. All the recipes here, whether standard fare or based on specialties of famed restaurants and inns, have been selected by a staff of professionals with the Western home kitchen in mind.

As you know, Japanese use chopsticks as their knife, fork, and spoon at table. Everyday ones are made of lacquer and may be beautifully decorated with intricate gilt or mother-of-pearl inlay patterns. For a formal meal, special plain cedar chopsticks are used.

There are also disposable chopsticks, which are in common use in restaurants, carry-out shops, and even inns. Each set is packaged in a long, narrow, open-ended envelope on which the name, address, and telephone number of the establishment are printed. They are used at home too, however, and may be purchased at oriental stores abroad. We suggest you use these for your Japanese meal because they are inexpensive and convenient. Simply set one pair in its envelope at each place. Such chopsticks come in a wide range of qualities, from disposable, soft pine sticks to quite elegant, finished cedar or bamboo sets.

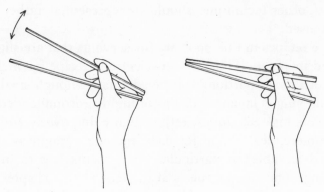

There are two main points to remember in using chopsticks. If you hold them too close to the point, leverage is lost, and it is harder to pick up foods. Secondly, do not hold chopsticks too tight. You will only get a cramp, and your ability to use them will be impaired.

Most Japanese food is cut into bite-sized pieces before serving so that it is easy to pick up with chopsticks. Knives are not necessary at the table for cutting, though occasionally chopsticks are used to "cut" through soft foods. Sometimes food is arranged in pieces that are a little larger than bite-sized— two or three bites, in fact. In this case, the etiquette is to pick up the morsel and carry it to your mouth and take one bite. While you are chewing and swallowing the first bite, continue to hold the remaining morsel in your chopsticks just off the plate. When you are ready for the next bite, lift the food to your mouth and continue eating. No matter how fascinating the conversation, it is considered bad form to gesture or point with chopsticks.

Chopsticks are set against low rests made of porcelain, pottery, bamboo, and the like. The same pair is used throughout the meal. During soup courses, when you are not using chopsticks, replace them on the rest. If there is no rest, you may lay the chopsticks across the lowest saucer, plate, or dish at your place. They are never left pointed down in soup or noodle bowls lest upsets ensue. In taking foods such as relishes or pickles from a common dish to your own individual plate, it is usual to turn the chopsticks round and use the handle end to serve yourself. There are two absolute taboos related to chopsticks: never stick chopsticks upright in a bowl of rice; never use your chopsticks to take something from someone else's chopsticks. These two things relate to Japanese funerary custom and must never be done at table.

For a very few dishes, SAVORY CUP CUSTARD (*chawan-mushi*) for example, chopsticks do not work well and spoons must be used. And when fruit is served as dessert, tiny forks or spears of bamboo are provided, and paring knives may sometimes be made available. In the main, however, chopsticks are the all-round eating utensil for the Japanese. It is nice to set your table with them when you cook Japanese, but do not feel compelled to use them if they are uncomfortable. You can use Western-style flatware and still eat in the Japanese spirit.

The menus that follow—a typical lunch and dinner for each of the four seasons of the year—will give you a good idea of that spirit: an acute awareness of nature that permeates not only its cuisine, but all the arts of Japan.

MENUS FOR THE FOUR SEASONS

Spring

lunch   MISO SOUP (WITH TŌFU AND WAKAME SEAWEED)
        ROLLED OMELETTE
        YŪAN-STYLE GRILLED CHICKEN
        SOUSED SPINACH or SPINACH WITH SESAME DRESSING
        RICE
        PICKLES
        TEA

dinner   CLAM CONSOMMÉ
        SEA BREAM SASHIMI
        BEAN CURD DENGAKU
        YELLOW FLOWER SHRIMP
        ASPARAGUS WITH MUSTARD DRESSING
        BAMBOO RICE
        PICKLES
        TEA

Summer

lunch   GRILLED EGGPLANT
        BEEF AND BURDOCK ROLLS
        CHILLED FINE NOODLES
        TEA
        WATERMELON

dinner EGG "TŌFU"

SAVORY OKRA

TROUT SASHIMI

DEEP-FRIED EGGPLANT

NAGASAKI-STYLE BRAISED PORK

VINEGARED OCTOPUS

RICE

TEA

FRESH PEACHES

Autumn

lunch BEATEN EGG SOUP

TEMPURA-ON-RICE

VINEGARED CRAB

PICKLES

TEA

dinner CLEAR CHICKEN SOUP

DEEP-FRIED MIXED KEBABS

SEA BREAM STEAMED WITH BUCKWHEAT NOODLES

CHINESE CABBAGE AND DEEP-FRIED TŌFU

CHESTNUT RICE

PICKLES

TEA

PERSIMMONS or PEARS

Winter

lunch ODEN

MIXED RICE

PICKLES

TEA

dinner SHELLFISH WITH MISO DRESSING

CHUNKY VEGETABLE SOUP

YELLOWTAIL TERIYAKI

SIMMERING TŌFU

STUFFED CRAB

SAVORY CUP CUSTARD

RICE

PICKLES

MANDARIN ORANGES

Ingredients

The adventurous cook who might be able to do acrobatics in the cuisines of France or Italy or Mexico inevitably is perplexed in a Japanese food store. Our shopper, the cook, brings to his nose cellophane packages, plastic tubs, and even bottles to sniff out information, and he pokes, handles, and wonders about everthing. Not many ingredients are familiar. Shopkeepers are as helpful as possible, but there is a difference between asking a salesperson for a specific item and requesting the equivalent of a basic Japanese cooking lesson from the clerk in the market.

The greatest barrier to learning Japanese cooking is not so much cooking techniques as ingredients. Simmering, steaming, grilling, and the like are the same or similar in other cuisines, but unfamiliar ingredients and their combinations are another matter.

The purpose of this section is to provide a simple and convenient guide to Japanese foods. Included are notes about storage and how long foods will keep. Where possible, information about the quantities in which foods are generally sold is given.

Unfortunately space does not permit an encyclopedic approach to the raw materials of Japanese cooking; but the ingredients of the recipes in this book plus a few others are discussed in this section or in the other chapters of Part One. These include the foods most often used in Japanese cooking, most of which may be obtained with relative ease in the United States.

In all cases the romanized Japanese name, an English equivalent, if any, and the name written in Japanese are given. The order of these names is dictated by convenience and usage, not consistency. Terminology in some cases is a problem, especially when an item appears on the market in a motley of different names provided by various packers (sometimes, charmingly, without recourse to an English dictionary).

Japanese foods are available in several kinds of stores in the United States —oriental food stores, healthfood and gourmet food stores, and a large number of supermarkets. An item like *kamaboko* (fish paste) might be found only at a Japanese store, but fermented bean paste (*miso*) is likely to be carried by most healthfood stores. Some Japanese staples like bean curd (*tōfu*) and soy sauce have become so popular that they are stocked by large national supermarket chains.

It is sometimes difficult to get good, fresh Japanese produce, so canned foods are indicated as well as Western vegetables that might substitute. Dried and salted foods are perfectly all right, but avoid frozen foods. Herbs and condiments, of course, are much better fresh. But do not get the notion that you must use only the ingredients given here, and remember to take advantage of local products. As you get better acquainted with Japanese cooking, you will gain a better understanding of which Western vegetables can be substituted; the more you experiment, the more you will become familiar—through successes as well as your friends' and family's occasional wry reactions—with what Japanese cooking is all about.

AGAR-AGAR (*kanten*; 寒天): Agar-agar is a sparkling, pure form of gelatin processed from a type of red seaweed called *tengusa*, or "heavenly grass," in Japanese. It has been used for a long time in the West as the standard culture medium in biological research, but only recently have its marvelous qualities as a gelatin begun to be recognized outside the Orient.

In Japanese cooking, agar-agar is used generally for sweets and confections in the same manner as conventional gelatin. Its qualities are different, however. As used in this book, agar-agar begins to set at 108° to 102°F/42° to 39°C, higher than room temperature. Its melting point in its pure state is 180°F/82°C. The temperature range shows how useful *kanten* was as a jelling agent in the days before refrigeration systems. For best results, however, refrigeration is recommended. Its texture is both firmer and more delicate than gelatin's, and it does not have gelatin's rubberiness. Further, it cannot be unmolded with a little heat, as gelatin can, but it does not adhere to vessel surfaces as gelatin does. It comes away easily, at least from flat (pan or mold) surfaces.

Originally, *kanten* was made by a complicated process of rinsing *tengusa* seaweed in fresh water, sun-bleaching, rerinsing, boiling, and molding. The feather-light *kanten* sticks that we buy today are made in modern factories in a different way—freeze-drying.

To use, tear the *kanten* stick into small pieces. Soak pieces in water to soften for at least 20 minutes. Wring out water and place pieces in cold water in a saucepan and bring to a simmer over medium heat *without stirring*. After simmering starts, stir occasionally until *kanten* dissolves. Do not boil on too high a heat or *kanten* will be deposited on sides of saucepan. The amount of water to be used with agar-agar varies greatly with the effect to be obtained and the ingredients it is combined with. There is no general rule. Follow recipes until agar-agar becomes familiar.

Agar-agar also comes in filament and powdered forms. The former is prepared just like the stick form and the latter like conventional gelatin powder. Some healthfood stores also carry a flake form. Read and follow directions on each package. Conventional (animal) gelatin can be used instead of agar-agar, but the result is different.

Since *agar-agar* sets so quickly, it also quickly seals in the freshness of fruits and other foods. Follow directions for each recipe here, but a general, helpful technique is to add hot *kanten* to room-temperature fresh ingredients.

Kanten is generally sold in both Chinese and Japanese stores in 2-stick packets. Each stick is about 10 inches (25 cm) long and 1 inch (2½ cm) square in cross-section and weighs only about ⅓ ounce (8–10 g).

AZUKI BEANS (*red beans*; 小豆): This small, red bean is the legume you will most frequently encounter in Japanese cooking besides soybeans (*daizu*). It is used in the cooking of many countries, so it is stocked in most supermarkets throughout the United States. For some historical reason this bean is commonly spelled *adzuki*. This spelling is a Victorian romanization; phonetically, *azuki* is correct.

These beans are steamed with glutinous rice on special occasions to make the festive RED RICE (*sekihan*; page 280). They are more commonly boiled with sugar to make SWEET RED-BEAN PASTE (*an*), which forms the base of a large percentage of Japanese sweet confections (see page 327). *An* is made in two textures: smooth puree (*koshi-an*) and "chunky," with beans partially crushed (*tsubushi-an*). If there is no time to make *an* from scratch, ready-made *an* is available canned and is stocked in most Japanese food stores.

BAMBOO SHOOTS (*takenoko*; 竹の子, 筍): Bamboo shoots are one of the most common ingredients in Asian cooking. The fibrous shoots are prized for their mild, unpretentious taste (they pick up the flavor of the soup, stew, or whatever they are simmered with) and their crunchy texture.

Canned shoots, packed in water, are available at all oriental food stores and some supermarkets. In a 15-ounce can (8 ounces dry weight) there are usually 2 to 3 small shoots, which make 2 cups of chopped shoot. Smaller and larger can sizes also exist.

Spring is the time when bamboo sends forth shoots. Fresh raw shoots in their brown husks appear on the market, and the flavor of bamboo shoot is associated with spring. Regardless of size, all shoots are thickly covered with many layers of husks. But by the time the husks are shucked and the base is trimmed off, the shoot is only about half its original size and weight. If a shoot is cooked *immediately* after being dug from the ground, it may be sweet. Usually, however, some time elapses before shoots get to market and in the kitchen, and they become acrid and bitter. This bitterness can be easily removed by boiling the shoot (preferably in the milky water from washing rice) for about 1½ hours, then cooling in a cold water bath. Husks should be peeled after boiling. This is a lot of work for an item that can be purchased canned, but many feel the flavor of the fresh shoot, and its ambience of spring, are worth the effort.

In Japan, bamboo shoots are also available year-round "fresh-cooked" and packed in water in plastic packs. Occasionally such water-packed bamboo is imported and available in the United States.

Before using either canned or water-packed bamboo, be sure to wash very thoroughly after slicing shoot in half lengthwise. There is a grainy white residue in the interior ridges of the shoots—a result of the commercial preparation process—which has a sour flavor and must be removed.

Once opened, water-packed and canned bamboo will keep about 10 days if stored in fresh water in a covered container in the refrigerator. Change the water every other day. But, as with any vegetable, bamboo is best used as soon as possible.

BEAN CURD (*tōfu*; 豆腐): Made from soybeans and extremely high in protein while low in cost.

Bean curd originated in China over two millennia ago, and its use spread throughout the Far East so completely that today from Indonesia to Korea and Mongolia no national cooking does without it. Bean curd was probably introduced to Japan around the eighth century. The "regular" Japanese type of bean curd (discussed first below) was made to meet Japanese tastes and is softer, whiter and more delicately flavored than the Chinese type. Both kinds are available in oriental food markets.

So-called regular bean curd is soft and easily digestible. It is an ideal food for slimming, having an extremely low ratio of calories to protein. A 6-ounce (180-g) portion of "regular" bean curd is merely 100 Calories, but 6 percent protein. (Other types of bean curd, such as freeze-dried bean curd, or *Kōya-dōfu*, may be as high as over 53 percent protein.) An extra attraction is that bean curd is low in carbohydrates and completely free of cholesterol.

Bean curd is made from dry soybeans, which are soaked in water till softened, then crushed and boiled. The crushed material is separated into pulp and milk. (The pulp becomes a bean curd by-product called *okara*, a food in its own right, described below.) To the soy milk is added a coagulant to make the milk separate into curds and whey. Fresh, warm curds are then poured into molds and left to settle for a few hours to take shape. The bean curd is then soaked in water to firm even more, to cool and to keep fresh. If you buy bean curd at one of the many thousands of family *tōfu* shops in Japan, you will see that standard-sized cakes are cut from blocks soaking in a large trough of water. In supermarkets in Japan and America, however, bean curd is sold packed in water in small plastic tubs.

In Japan, fresh bean curd is sold in cakes that fit nicely on the hand, a size convenient for cutting—about $3\frac{1}{2} \times 7 \times 1$ inch ($9 \times 18 \times 2\frac{1}{2}$ cm), weighing approximately $8\frac{3}{4}$ to $10\frac{1}{2}$ ounces (250 to 300 g). Recipes in this book calling for bean curd have been written with this standard Japanese cake in mind. Abroad, the dimensions (and thus weight) of cakes have not been standardized and vary depending on the kind of bean curd you buy and where you buy it. For example, Chinese bean curd is a little firmer in texture than the Japanese type, and cakes tend to be smaller. Excess moisture has often been pressed out beforehand, so Chinese cakes are sold "dry" in plastic bags in the refrigerator case. It is Japanese-style bean curd, however, that is generally stocked in American supermarkets.

Bean curd is used fresh, usually on the day it is made in Japan, where daily shopping at local stores is still a way of life. Shopping habits are different across the Pacific, however, and most bean curd in America, packaged in plastic tubs, is date-stamped like dairy products to give the consumer some idea of freshness. Use bean curd within 5 to 7 days of date manufactured. (Deep-fried bean curd keeps 1 week to 10 days.) Many American supermarkets sell regular bean curd in "jumbo" blocks, about 4 inches (10 cm) square and weighing 1 pound (450 g).

Bean curd must be kept under refrigeration. It will stay fresh longer in more water rather than less, so you may want to remove it from its plastic pack and let it rest in ample water. If you change the water daily, the bean curd will keep its freshness better. This food *cannot* be frozen successfully without a change in form. If you attempt to freeze bean curd at home, the result will be a sort of freeze-dried bean curd (described below), which is different from the regular item.

In Japan, the neighborhood *tōfu* maker has a number of bean curd products available, but there are 3 types of fresh *tōfu*. A scouting of oriental food stores, healthfood stores, and supermarkets should net you all three, if one store does not carry them all.

The type described here as "regular" is known in Japan as *momen* —"cotton" *tōfu*. In the process of making *tōfu*, a cloth is spread across the bottom of the settling tank and then soy milk is poured in. When coagulant is added and the soy milk forms curds, this cloth is used to drain the curds of water, and the resulting *tōfu* is comparatively coarser and more robust than *kinu-goshi*, or "silk," *tōfu*.

"Cotton" bean curd is the type most commonly used in Japan. Even if no specific type is mentioned on the label, you may safely assume that the *tōfu* you buy at the supermarket is the "cotton" type. This type may have to be drained or pressed before use, depending on the dish being made.

Kinu, "silk," is simply *tōfu* in which the curds are not drained. The result is much more delicate, thus the name. The package should be labeled "silk," "silk bean curd," or *kinu*. "Silk" bean curd gets the same parboiling and draining treatment as the regular kind, but it is far too delicate to be pressed. Its delicacy and fine texture are why it is enjoyed, and it is often used in elegant, clear soups. It is especially in demand in summer.

Yakidōfu is bean curd that has been lightly broiled. It is easy to recognize by the light mottling on its skin. Though it has been grilled, it is packed in water. Plastic tubs should be labeled "grilled bean curd" or "*yakidōfu*." This type of fresh bean curd has a firm texture and does not need the treatments of parboiling (except to freshen) or pressing (though it has a fuller flavor if pressed). It is most often used in one-pot communal dishes such as SUKIYAKI (page 267), or in some special dishes. If *yakidōfu* is not available, you can make your own by draining and pressing regular *tōfu* and lightly grilling each side on very high heat.

Tōfu is pressed when it is used for deep-fried foods or in dressed salads (*aemono*) in order to remove water.

There are several methods of pressing, but the simplest is to wrap briefly drained bean curd cakes in kitchen toweling. Place 2 dinner plates on the *tōfu* and let rest 30 minutes to 1 hour.

The most convenient way of cutting bean curd, especially when it is going into soups, is to hold it in the flat of your hand over the pot, as shown. Use a straight-bladed knife and gently press straight through— there is no need to saw.

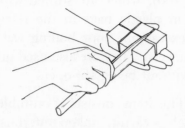 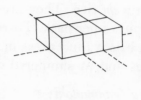

Even though freshly made bean curd is easy to find, there is one alternative if none is to be had. Powdered "instant" bean curd mix is sold in small boxes like flavored gelatin.

This form is handy to keep on the shelf, is not difficult to make, and its flavor is pleasant and close to the fresh. Its texture is midway between "cotton" and "silk" bean curd. In the package are included one envelope of powdered soy milk and one small packet of coagulant. These are dissolved in water over low heat, and the resulting milky liquid is poured into a pan to set. Refrigerate. Fresh bean curd is much cheaper, however.

When fresh bean curd is deep-fried in oil, another *tōfu* variety is created —*age*, which translates as "deep-fried bean curd." It is very simple to deep-fry fresh bean curd at home, but it is a bother if no other deep-frying is planned. Therefore, in Japan freshly deep-fried bean curd is sold by the neighborhood *tōfu* maker, and abroad it can be found in Japanese markets. It may be set out in glass cases like fresh pastries, or packed in plastic bags and displayed in the refrigerator case. This form of *tōfu* is never packed in water. Deep-fried bean curd keeps refrigerated a little over 1 week; it cannot be frozen. It is easily recognizable by its appealing, golden-brown color, but it is made in a variety of shapes for different cooking purposes (see color plate 7). All types fall into one of the following basic groups (the terminology differs somewhat in Osaka and Tokyo):

Thick cakes (*atsu-age* or *nama-age*; 厚揚げ or 生揚げ): Regular *tōfu* cakes deep-fried, or first cut into triangles or cubes. Because the cakes are left in their original thickness of about 1 inch (2½ cm), and because the deep-frying is relatively short, only the outside is crisped golden brown and the inside is as soft and white as fresh bean curd. This type of fried *tōfu* is often cut into small pieces and used in MISO SOUP or simmered dishes like ODEN. Pour boiling water over deep-fried bean curd cakes and lightly press them in paper towels to remove excess oil. This step is essential.

Thin deep-fried *tōfu* (*aburage* or *usu-age*; 油揚げ or 薄揚げ): Bean curd cakes cut into thin sheets then deep-fried. These can be slit open along one end to make "pouches" (see GOLD PURSES, page 400), which are stuffed with vegetable or with *sushi* rice. They are found in plastic bags in the refrigerator case, 3 to 5 pieces per pack. To remove excess oil, pour boiling water over sheets, drain briefly, and press in paper towels. They are also used in brothy noodle dishes and in simmered dishes without being slit open.

Mixed *tōfu* (*ganmodoki*; がんもどき): This item consists of crumbled bean curd, sesame seeds, slivered vegetables such as carrot, ginkgo nut, mushroom, and burdock, bound with grated mountain yam (*yama no imo*). This bean-curd-based mixture is formed into 3-inch (8-cm) patties or into 1½-inch (4-cm) balls, then deep-fried a golden brown. Used in the same manner as thick cakes.

Freeze-dried bean curd (*Kōya-dōfu* or *kōri-dōfu*; 高野豆腐 or 凍り豆腐): "Mt. Kōya bean curd" is named after the monastic site where, it is believed, Buddhist monks invented the food in their snowy, winter fastness long centuries ago. Its other name, *kōri-dōfu*, means "frozen bean curd."

Freezing turns all the water in bean curd cakes to ice; when thawed, all that is left is a spongy protein-packed square of *tōfu* "essence." Dehydrating by freezing changes the color and texture as well as size and weight. White, custardy bean curd becomes beige, featherlike in weight, with a fine, spongy texture.

Reconstitute before using by soaking in hot water for 5 minutes, then firmly press between your hands to squeeze out moisture and the milky fluid given off. Dampen, press again, and repeat this process until there is no more milky discharge, then press once more. Simmered in seasoned broth with vegetables, freeze-dried bean curd absorbs flavors nicely.

This item is sold in the form of small, flat cakes in cellophane packets of several ounces or sometimes in cartons with 5 to 10 cakes. Do not confuse them with some forms of wheat gluten cakes (*fu*), which they may resemble at first glance.

Soybean milk "skin" (*yuba*; 湯葉): In the process of making *tōfu*, before the coagulant is added, the soy milk may be allowed to separate so that a skin forms on top, while sediment drops to the bottom. The skin is carefully removed and treated as a delicacy. Only rarely is it sold fresh, but it is commonly available dried. Dried soybean milk skin, or *yuba*, is available in most Japanese food stores in a variety of forms—flat sheets, rolls, strips, and the like. It must be softened in an ample amount of tepid water for a few minutes before using.

Bean curd pulp or "lees" (*okara*; おから): The soybean pulp that is the by-product of *tōfu*-making looks like moist white sawdust. It can be used to great advantage in croquettes and the like. This crumbly white ingredient is fairly high in protein content and provides needed bulk and roughage. It is good simmered with diced vegetables, in light salads, and in soups. Sold fresh in ½- to 1-pound (225- to 450-g) plastic bags at Japanese food stores that sell homemade bean curd.

bean paste, fermented, see MISO

BONITO, DRIED (*katsuo-bushi*; かつお節): The bonito, a member of the mackerel family, has been an important part of the Japanese diet from very early times, perhaps as early as the eighth century. From about the fifteenth century, the fillets of this fish were dried and used as they are today.

Steam-processed bonito fillets, dried to woodlike hardness, are shaved into flakes and used as one of the two essential ingredients of basic soup stock —*dashi*. Making and using *dashi* stock in Japanese cooking is roughly analogous to making and using bouillon in classical French cooking. In the Japanese kitchen the cook cannot do much without *dashi*—and *dashi* means stock based on dried bonito and kelp (see the chapter on *dashi*, pages 146ff, for a fuller description of *katsuo-bushi*).

The "petrified" fillets can last indefinitely if they are kept dry. Shaving is done on a bladed utensil called a *katsuo-kezuri-ki* ("bonito shaver") made of wood, about half the width of a shoebox and made with a drawer to catch the flakes. A time-consuming process certainly, though nothing compares with the flavor of fresh stock made with just-shaved bonito. A variety of alternatives, which millions of Japanese employ, do exist. Instead of shaving dried bonito (difficult to obtain abroad) every time you make *dashi*, you can use one of the following for *dashi* stock, with from adequate to good results. The fresh shavings can be made for special occasions; at such times you will savor the bouquet of *dashi* as it should be made and vow to make fresh bonito flakes more often.

1. Packaged dried bonito flakes are called *hana-katsuo*, "flower bonito," or *kezuri-bushi*, "shaved [bonito] fillets." The fish shavings look like pale rose-colored wood shavings and are sold in cellophane packages of various sizes—from one-use packets to large bags. Store as you would potato chips or crackers, in an airtight container. Humidity is the greatest enemy.
2. Seasoned dried bonito flakes in disposable infusion bags, marketed as *dashi-no-moto*, or "stock essence," which category also includes the next type below. This product is like a large tea bag.
3. "Instant" *dashi* granules. This product is included in the ***dashi-no-moto***

category and is also sold under the name *hon-dashi* ("true *dashi*") in packets or small brown glass jars. The granules contain dried ground bonito and all other seasonings required for *dashi* stock. This preparation is rather strong—only 1 level tsp of instant *dashi* granules in 4 cups of simmering water produces a fully flavored stock. This instant preparation is excellent; the Japanese food industry has not only produced convenient, subtly flavored stock granules, but has also captured the aroma of the original quite successfully. After opening, keep in refrigerator tightly sealed for best flavor.

All these products for *dashi*-making are easily purchased in Japanese stores. In making Japanese food abroad, there will be instances when flexibility becomes necessary. As an alternative to *dashi* stock, you may decide to use (in order of preference) strained, *fat-free*, light chicken stock (bone or carcass stock is good) or diluted canned chicken broth.

Light chicken stock cannot be used as a substitute for *dashi* in all cases, but it works well enough in enough recipes to be mentioned here as an alternative. Your own experience will teach you when chicken stock is a felicitous substitute and when it is not.

ito-kezuri-katsuo (糸削りかつお). Dried bonito thread-shavings are a dried bonito product often called for as a garnish. Such "thread-shavings" look like rosy-beige excelsior, have a pleasant texture and taste of the sea. This product comes in boxes or cellophane packets and is sold in some Japanese stores in the U.S. If a dish calls for *ito-kezuri-katsuo* as a garnish, you may substitute regular *hana-gatsuo* or bonito shavings rubbed briskly between the palms.

buckwheat noodles, see SOBA NOODLES

BURDOCK (*gobō*; ごぼう): It is said that the long, slender root of this member of the aster family was used in ancient China as a medicine. In Japan, there is documentation that the vegetable was in the diet as early as the tenth century, when it was regarded as being a source of energy or as an aid to recovery from a serious illness.

The root is about ¾ inch (2 cm) at its widest point at the top and then tapers for about 18 to 24 inches (45–60 cm). The skin has the best flavor, so the root should be cleaned carefully, preferably scrubbed well with a stiff brush and any rootlets carefully trimmed off.

Once cut, *gobō* must be immediately submerged in a cold water bath to prevent discoloring and to eliminate bitterness. A drop or two of vinegar in the water helps whiten the root. If the cut burdock has turned brown, whiteness may be restored by simmering in lightly vinegared water, but this limits the root's use to dishes that are vinegary.

The flavor of burdock itself is rather neutral, but it becomes host to other flavors it absorbs during cooking—usually long simmering in seasoned liquids or sautéing in oil. The appealing, crunchy texture of burdock and the way that it combines well with oil is well demonstrated in the KINPIRA recipe on page 392.

Four major varieties of this biennial are cultivated in Japan in spring and fall, so there is a year-round harvest, and it is now grown to a limited extent in the United States. Most oriental provisions stores abroad carry this root fresh and sell it by the piece or in small bundles of 2 or 3. Burdock fresh from the garden tastes best, so look for roots that are firm and have no soft spots. *Gobō* is best stored buried in loamy earth, but it can be stored in the refrigerator wrapped in plastic for up to 2 weeks.

Cut, boiled burdock is available canned.

CABBAGE, CHINESE (*hakusai*; 白菜): This large, cylindrical head vegetable is pale green at the top of the crinkle-edged leaves and white at the stem, where stalks are thick and succulent.

Mild, almost sweet, with a more distinct flavor than lettuce, Chinese cabbage is much more delicate than Western round cabbage. It is used in many oriental cuisines: in Japan, it is simmered, used in one-pot dishes, and in soups, made into pickles, etc.

This vegetable is very widely available not only in oriental stores, but in supermarkets. It may also be called nappa, and is often labeled "celery cabbage."

Stores well refrigerated in vegetable crisper.

CHESTNUTS (*kuri*; 栗): Chestnuts are a favorite autumn flavor in Japan, and Japanese chestnuts are excellent. Tamba chestnuts are large and pleasantly mealy; Shiba chestnuts are small, firm, and sweet.

Chestnuts are cooked with rice to make CHESTNUT RICE (page 279), are included in steamed dishes (page 376), in grilled and "baked" dishes (page 197), and in almost every type of cooking. The nuts are used in a large number of Japanese sweets.

Shelling chestnuts involves work. The shell comes off rather easily, but the thin, bitter-tasting inner skin demands careful removal. There are a number of ways to accomplish this, depending on how much meat you are willing to waste. The easiest method involves the most waste. Let nuts soften in warm water for 2 hours, then cut off the hard, rough-textured "bottom," cut away the shells, and pare away inner skin, carving the nut into 6 or 8 facets.

Be sure not to confuse chestnuts with *water* chestnuts—a crisp bulb that is usually stocked in canned form by oriental food stores and many supermarkets because it is used in Chinese cooking and its American derivatives.

CHRYSANTHEMUM LEAVES, EDIBLE (*shungiku* or *kikuna*; 春菊 or 菊菜):   The perfume and blossoms of this Japanese vegetable are like chrysanthemums bred for garden display and cutting. But the edible foliage of the "spring" or "leaf" chrysanthemum (*shungiku* or *kikuna*; it goes by both names in Japan) are more deeply lobed and fuller than the decorative variety.

Fresh, young chrysanthemum leaves are so tender that they may be eaten raw. More commonly, however, they are parboiled briefly, shocked into retaining their bright green color with a cold water bath, and served in light salads. Chrysanthemum is also particularly well suited to one-pot dishes like SUKIYAKI (page 267); its fragrance and distinct, light, astringent flavor harmonizes with meat or fowl, onion, and other vegetables. Take care not to overcook in one-pot dishes—a minute or two in the seasoned broth is enough. If overdone, chrysanthemum leaves tend to develop a bitter aftertaste.

Chrysanthemum is used only fresh. It is in season in April and May, but it is grown year-round in Japan in greenhouses. It is seen more and more in Japanese stores abroad and is carried in a number of supermarkets, too. It is sold in bundles by weight, like spinach, but there does not seem to be a standard size in the U.S. yet. In Japan an average bundle is enough to serve 4 if used in a one-pot dish.

When buying this vegetable, look for bright green leaves and stalks that are strong and perky. If showing buds or flowers, the chrysanthemum leaves are already too old and tough.

The base of the central stem may be tough and may need to be trimmed away. Individual leaf sprigs should be separated from the central stem before cooking.

You may substitute fresh spinach, but the fragrance and flavor are, of course, different.

CLOUD EAR MUSHROOMS (*kikurage*; きくらげ): Known in English as "wood ear" and "cloud ear," or more simply packaged as "dried black fungus," *kikurage* is a fungus that looks more like chips of wrinkled bark than mushrooms when it is dried. *Kikurage* (which translates literally as "wood jellyfish") has been a staple in Chinese, Japanese, and Korean cooking since ancient times.

The dried form must be softened before use by soaking in tepid water for about 20 minutes. It becomes pliable, turns translucent, and has a surprising, almost crisp texture, though it is rather floppy. Used more for its pleasant texture than for its flavor, which is bland and neutral, *kikurage* typically appears in stir-fried dishes (Chinese), and in lightly vinegared salads. It only appears once in this book, in the KENCHIN STUFFING on page 361, which is also used in STUFFED CRAB (page 407).

COLTSFOOT (*fuki*; ふき): The plant has received this name because of the shape of its leaf. The edible part of this perennial is the long green stalk with a hollow center. *Fuki* is often served in simmered dishes, but it needs preparation before being used. Stalks are salted and allowed to rest briefly, then parboiled to draw out bitterness, and finally the fibrous outer veins (like strings on celery) are stripped away. The flavor is like celery, but lighter.

Occasionally available fresh in season in Japanese stores abroad. Look for stalks that are about the same overall diameter from root to top. Veins should be greeny white, not pink or red. Keeps fresh about a week under refrigeration. Some Japanese stores also carry canned *fuki* packed in water. This vegetable is expensive; celery can be used as a substitute.

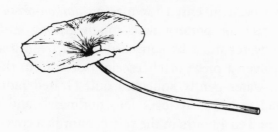

CUCUMBER (*kyūri*; 胡瓜): Japanese cucumbers are smaller, have a much clearer flavor, and are less watery than the type of cucumber generally found in markets in the U.S. The small, Japanese variety measures no more than 1 inch (2½ cm) in diameter and about 8 inches (20 cm) long. The skin is thinner than the U.S. cucumbers, and the seeds are vestigial—you do not have to remove seeds of Japanese cucumbers.

Japanese cucumbers are sometimes available in Japanese stores, but these have been air-freighted from Japan and might not always be crisp. You are better off shopping in a supermarket and selecting the youngest cucumbers available. Japanese cucumber seeds are listed in some seed catalogues, and the variety makes an occasional appearance in supermarkets.

Recipes in this book calling for cucumbers refer to the Japanese type unless otherwise stated. Generally, a Japanese cucumber equals ½ an American cucumber. The American type should be peeled and seeded when used in Japanese cooking.

DAIKON (giant white radish; 大根): The two characters that combine to make up the word *daikon* mean "great root." In cool weather, when growth is quick and steady, the typical *daikon* grows about 14 inches long, as thick as a girl's leg, and may weigh up to 4 or 5 pounds. Some varieties are thin and long, others fat and short, and there is one type like a huge turnip—one kind grown in the rich volcanic fields of Kyushu is as big and round as a soccer ball.

Daikon radish is thought to aid digestion, especially of oily foods, and it is one of the commonest ingredients in Japanese cooking. Simmered, it tastes good with many thick sauces.

Daikon flesh is dense and demands long cooking, so it may need rather long parboiling even when sliced very thin.

Perhaps its most frequent usage is in its finely grated form (*daikon-oroshi*); grated *daikon* is used as a condiment mixed into dipping sauces, in "salads," in steamed dishes, and in numberless other ways. Grated giant white radish always goes into TEMPURA DIPPING SAUCE, for example, in part because, as stated above, *daikon* is thought to be especially helpful in aiding the digestion of oils.

Special graters have been invented for making *daikon-oroshi*—of copper, aluminum, stainless steel, or pottery with rough grating surface, with or without holes. Excess water must be squeezed out of fresh gratings. To do this, *daikon* is grated over a piece of cheesecloth or cotton, the corners are gathered up, and the water gently squeezed out. Grated radish cannot be prepared too far ahead of time—it loses its "fluffiness" and gets soggy—but it will stand well for 3 to 4 hours in the refrigerator in a covered container.

This vegetable is so fundamental to Japanese cooking that it is easy to find in most Japanese stores abroad. Look for *daikon* that has tight skin and a fresh appearance. Avoid those that seem pithy, or smell too strong, or are limp, with soft, withered skin. *Daikon* is also appearing in supermarkets under the name "*daikon* radish," appropriately enough.

Happily, there are some Western radish varieties that will substitute adequately for *daikon*, and these may be purchased in supermarkets. Select the best of the largest *white* radishes. A few specific types to look for are the white icicle radish, about 5 inches (13 cm) long, about the size of a large carrot; celestial—also known as white Chinese—6 to 8 inches (15 to 20 cm) long and 3 inches (8 cm) in diameter; and all seasons radish. Sometimes they are simply marked as "oriental type." Radishes keep about 2 weeks in the refrigerator.

Daikon is good in other forms too. It is pickled in different ways, the most famous pickle being *takuan*, bright yellow, crunchy, and very pungent. *Takuan* may be purchased abroad in bottles, or sometimes in plastic half-pint tubs in the refrigerator case. Very occasionally it is seen in Japanese stores abroad in large wooden pickle barrels.

Dried radish shavings are also used in Japanese cooking. These are called *kiriboshi daikon*.

dashi, see BONITO, DRIED

EGGPLANT (*nasu*; なす): Eggplant is an important vegetable in Japan. A variety of eggplant types are used, all of which are smaller than the American.

With small Japanese eggplants, the flesh is tighter, less grainy, less watery, sweeter (though water soaking is still required to remove bitterness), and more fully flavored than the large American type. Four or 5 Japanese eggplants are roughly equivalent to one big American specimen.

There are of course, many kinds of eggplant in Japan—tiny globes; long and skinny ones; the plump, 4-inch (10-cm) ones, which are the most common; medium-sized spheres; the large, Western kind, and so forth.

Japanese eggplants are used in simmered dishes and are often deep-fried and grilled as well. They make a deeply colored, excellent pickle.

In America, especially in late July and early August, just before the height of the eggplant season, small eggplants—4 or 5 inches (10 or 13 cm) long—are on sale in supermarkets. *Recipes in this book are based on eggplants of this size, unless otherwise specified.*

You may occasionally find small eggplants imported from Japan at oriental food stores, but they will be expensive. Middle Eastern cooking also utilizes the same types of small eggplants, and they may be available in Greek or

Turkish markets. Some seed catalogs list small hybrid types that may be picked when they are only 3 to 5 inches (8 to 13 cm) long.

EGGS, QUAIL (*uzura no tamago*; 鶉の卵): Speckled brown eggs, 1 inch long, are to be found in the refrigerator case in large Japanese stores. Hard-boiled, shelled quail eggs are sold packed in water in small jars or cans. Buy the fresh eggs if possible. They will keep for about 2 weeks refrigerated.

These eggs are not much different in flavor from chicken eggs, but their size makes them an attractive ingredient—hardboiled and shelled—in soup or, 2 or 3 skewered, in one-pot dishes. On longer skewers they are good breaded and deep-fried in DEEP-FRIED MIXED KEBABS (page 418). Sometimes, quail eggs are cracked open and served raw, for example, with finely grated mountain yam (*yama no imo*), or in a nest of grated *daikon* (*daikon-oroshi*), served as a relish.

ENOKITAKE MUSHROOMS (えのき茸): With slender 5-inch (13-cm) whitish-yellow stems topped by tiny round caps, these mushrooms come fresh to market in clumps. They are mild-flavored, have a pleasant crispness and aroma, and are used in soups and one-pot dishes. Sometimes they are wrapped in foil with fish or fowl for grilling over charcoal. Most mushrooms are wiped clean because they absorb too much water if washed, but with *enokitake* the most practical course is just to cut off the spongy root (in Japan this is the shape and size of the mouth of the commercial cultivation bottles) about 1½ inches (4 cm) from the bottom and rinse the mushrooms in a colander, or hold under a tap, immediately before using.

The name of this mushroom derives from the *enoki* tree (Chinese hackberry), on whose stumps the mushroom grows. But *enokitake* mushrooms can be commercially cultivated so easily that this mushroom is the first Asian variety to become easily available abroad. Fresh *enokitake* may be purchased at oriental provisions stores and at some specialized greengrocers or gourmet shops, touted as a new salad ingredient (in which role it is indeed good). They are sold in plastic packages of 3 ounces (85 g), enough for one dish of 4 to 6 servings.

Fresh *enokitake* keeps in the sealed plastic packet in which it is sold for about a week under refrigeration. Some companies have made canned *enokitake* available, but fresh is preferred.

FISH PASTE (*kamaboko*; かまぼこ): *Kamaboko*, the generic name for a wide variety of pureed then steamed and (perhaps) grilled fish products, is derived from the medieval word for cattail. The first *kamaboko* of the fourteenth century (the *chikuwa* type described below) were obviously reminiscent of the dense cylindrical head of this very familiar marsh plant.

Standard ingredients of *kamaboko* are: pureed white fish such as cod or croaker or shark; a binding agent like *kuzu* or potato starch to help mold the pureed fish; and salt. Sometimes food colorings are used to tint the outer layer. After the pureed fish has been blended with a binding agent, molded into a desired shape, and, if necessary, colored, it is steamed. When cool, it is firm and has approximately the same texture as bologna.

The *kamaboko* that is sold in Japanese food stores in America is not imported from Japan; it is the product of small domestic packaging concerns. In English it is variously called fish cake, fish loaf, fish paste, and fish sausage. None of these terms is really accurate. As with many different foods, the foreign word is the best to use. Rather arbitrarily, because *kamaboko* starts as a thick puree and is often made into different forms, the term "fish paste" has been adopted here.

Kamaboko—usually made in cakes or rolls of 5 to 8 ounces (140 to 225 g), generally measuring no longer than about 8 inches (20 cm) and 1 to 2 inches wide—may be eaten without any more preparation than slicing. One may also heat it first in simmering water. It is good this way as an hors d'œuvre or a snack. Sliced *kamaboko* may be added to soups, to noodle dishes (pastel-tinted types are often used with noodles) and may be simmered in seasoned liquid, as in ODEN.

No matter what type of *kamaboko* you buy, keep it refrigerated. It will keep about 1 week. Two of the most popular types are:

Planked *kamaboko (ita-kamaboko*; 板かまぼこ): Before steaming, the white-fish puree is molded into a Quonset-hut shape on a rectangular piece of cypress wood. The cypress was essential to the old way of steaming, and it lent a woody aroma. Today, when production is carried out in modern factories, gleaming with sterilized stainless steel, the wood is retained for aesthetic reasons and, no doubt, because it acts as disposable cutting board. These cakes may be pure white; if grilled, they may be slightly browned on top; or they may have been tinted pink or green on the surface.

At Japanese stores in America, this kind of *kamaboko* is sold in 7-ounce (200 g) cakes on 6- × -2-inch (15- × -5-cm) cypress rectangles. It often comes in a thick plastic package that is simply put in hot water to heat. Check directions on any package you buy. Also available in 10- and 13-ounce (285- and 370-g) cans.

"Bamboo wheels" (*chikuwa*; 竹輪): This form of *kamaboko* predates all other kinds, but it came by its present name only after it became necessary to distinguish it from other shapes, such as the planked *kamaboko*.

The fish paste is molded around a thin segment of bamboo stalk (now, a stainless steel rod) before steaming. To brown the outer layer, the steamed paste is grilled.

In Japanese stores in America, *chikuwa* is sold in 8-ounce (225-g) plastic packs. Also available in 10-ounce (285-g) cans.

FLOURS: Wheat flour is not used much in traditional Japanese cooking. Noodles and deep-frying coatings and batters are the main uses for wheat flour in traditional cuisine. Of course, there are any number of modern dishes in the Japanese cooking genre that freely use wheat flour, and the Japanese fondness for European food means that wheat flour has a permanent place on most kitchen shelves. Types of flour in the Japanese pantry that are used for native-style cooking are rice and soybean.

Rice flour is available in 3 kinds: flour ground from ordinary short-grain rice, called *joshinko*, and 2 flours made from glutinous rice, called *mochiko* and *shiratamako*. Common rice flour (*joshinko*) is used for making sweet confections primarily. It is sold in 12-ounce (340-g) boxes or 8-ounce (225-g) paper tubes. *Mochiko* is ground from cooked glutinous rice (*mochi-gome*) and is mixed with water, then boiled to make a type of *mochi* cake (see MOCHI entry), or it may be used, if the need arises, as a thickener in (Western) sauces or foods that will be refrigerated or frozen because it inhibits the separation of liquids. *Shiratamako* is ground from raw glutinous rice and is used in a similar manner in making refined sweet confections.

Soy flour (*kinako*) is made by grinding roasted soybeans. It is nutty and fragrant. Sweetened with sugar, it is used in many traditional sweets. Soy flour is frequently sold in healthfood stores.

fuki, see COLTSFOOT

GINGER (*shōga*; 生姜): Fresh ginger root is carried in the produce section of many supermarkets. It is the fresh form, *never* the dried root or the powdered, that is used in Japanese cooking.

Choose ginger that is firm and tight. Avoid pieces that are flabby or have soft spots, as well as those having shriveled skin. Pare away skin of amount you will use just before using. Obtain juice by squeezing finely grated root.

The root may be stored in the refrigerator up to 2 weeks. Condensed moisture makes it go soft, so wrap the root in newspaper or paper toweling before storing in an airtight plastic bag. Fresh roots may be frozen—break off as many knobs as are needed and return unused portion to freezer.

Other varieties of ginger that you will come across in this book are:

hajikami shōga (recipe, page 304): Literally, "blushing ginger." These are pink, pickled shoots of a different variety of ginger and are eaten with grilled foods. You can make your own if you find the right shoots in early and late spring at an oriental market. Look for shoots that have tender, bright green, sprouting leaves and long, slender stalks with a pink blush at the bottom. You may also buy them already pickled and bottled.

beni-shōga and *gari:* These are two names for VINEGARED GINGER (recipe, page 304); the latter is *sushi*-shop jargon, the former is usually dyed bright red. Usually available at oriental provisions stores in small half-pint (¼ L) plastic tubs in the refrigerator case.

GINKGO NUTS (*ginnan*; ぎんなん): The fruit borne by the mature female ginkgo tree (*Ginkgo biloba*). Three layers must be removed from fresh nuts — a pulpy yellowish outer covering; a hard, smooth white nut case; and a thin, brownish inner skin. The spongy outer covering is extremely odiferous and liable to rot, so it is usually removed before nuts are brought to market. This still leaves two layers for the cook to take care of. The nut case is thin and can be cracked easily with a nutcracker, a knife, or whatever; for the inner skin, drop shelled nuts into hot water on the fire for a few minutes to loosen skins, then rub skins away (in the water) with a slotted spoon.

Raw nuts are a white color but turn pale green when cooked. They are used for their mild flavor and their attractive color, and are included in SAVORY CUP CUSTARD (page 214) and in other steamed dishes. They may be skewered in twos or threes and grilled, or deep-fried, or put into one-pot dishes.

Ginkgo nuts come onto the market in autumn and may be purchased fresh at some oriental food stores at that time of the year. Nuts may be stored in the refrigerator for several weeks. Ginkgo nuts are also available canned in water, but the canned nuts have little flavor, tend to crack and break apart, and are not a good substitute for the fresh nuts. Unless the fresh nuts are available, this ingredient may be eliminated.

GOURD SHAVINGS, DRIED (*kampyō*; 干瓢): Bottle calabash pith is shaved and dried to a long ribbonlike form. Buff-colored dried gourd strips have two primary uses—as something both edible and decorative to tie or fasten food and as a filling in such foods as ROLLED SUSHI (page 300).

Available in 1-ounce (30-g) cellophane packets, which will see you through several recipes. To soften, first wash then knead strips for one use in an ample amount of salt. This breaks down the fibers and increases absorbency. Wash in water, then boil until soft. Drain. Handle with some care: this vegetal "string," though very flexible, is not as strong as the cotton kitchen variety.

KINOME (young leaves of the prickly ash; 木の芽): The Japanese prickly ash, or *sansho* (*Zanthoxylum piperitum*), grows to be a 6- to 12-foot (2-4-meter) tree, with thorn-bearing branches. It is deciduous, and in early spring it sends out new leaves. These fragrant sprigs are plucked for use both as an aromatic and a colorful garnish and are associated with spring.

Kinome's refreshing bouquet—bright, with the mildest hint of mintiness—enlivens soups, simmered foods, grilled foods, and bean curd dishes such as DENGAKU (page 192)—in fact just about any Japanese dish. This is perhaps the most widely used garnish of professional Japanese chefs, which explains its appearance so often in this book. It is a pleasant addition, but not essential.

Kinome is available only in season even in Japan, because it is used fresh. It keeps, wrapped in plastic and refrigerated, for about 1 week.

If *kinome* is unavailable to you, or if spring has already slipped by (or is just approaching), use tiny sprigs of watercress or parsley merely to give a touch of bright green. There is no substitute for the springtime flavor of this herb.

The small pods that the prickly ash bears are dried and ground to yield fragrant *sansho* pepper (see entry).

KONBU (kelp or sea tangle; 昆布): One of the two basic ingredients of *dashi*, the stock on which so many Japanese dishes depend for their subtle flavor.

All Japanese *konbu* is of the *Laminaria* family and is mainly harvested off the northernmost island of Hokkaido. The deep olive brown kelp leaf is from 2½ to 12 inches (6 to 30 cm) wide and may reach lengths of many yards. Leaves are dried in the sun, cut, folded, and packaged. A ⅔-to-1-ounce (20-30-g) amount is the standard measure required to season stock or broth for 4 servings, so one package provides for many dishes. There are a number of grades—in this case, the more expensive are usually better quality.

Never wash or rinse *konbu*. Its speckled surface holds the flavor, and wiping the *konbu* clean with a lightly dampened towel is all it needs. Some Japanese cooks advocate lightly scoring *konbu* so that glutamic acid (a sort of natural flavor intensifier present in the leaf) is easily released during simmering.

Besides being used for *dashi*, in shred form *konbu* may also be deep-fried or sautéed as a vegetable.

Tororo and *oboro konbu* are yet other varieties. Fresh *konbu* leaves are soaked in vinegar, and from them these two types are shaved. The former is shaved along the length of the *konbu* leaf and is cut into thread form. The latter is shaved across the width and comes in sheet form. The core remaining after shaving is *shiraita konbu*. A piece of *shiraita konbu* looks like a very fine square of ecru-colored silk—it weighs about as much, too, and is similarly pliable and relatively strong. It is moistened with vinegar and used as an edible wrapper for a number of dishes. It has a unique, delicate, sweet ocean taste. The soft, thin sheets are folded many times over and wrapped individually in cellophane packs to keep each sheet at its freshest, and sold in packets of five.

KONNYAKU (devil's tongue jelly; こんにゃく) and SHIRATAKI (白滝): Most Japanese would fail if asked to describe the starchy root of *Amorphophalus konjac*, because it is never brought to market. Quite a bit of processing is necessary to bring it to palatable state—peeling, cooking, pounding, mixing it with milk of lime (like bean curd) to coagulate it, and then forming it into cakes.

It is the dense, gelatinous, dark brown to hazy gray cake—6×3×1½ inches (15×8×4 cm)—that is called *konnyaku*. *Konnyaku*'s flavor is neutral, and it is not porous enough to easily absorb flavors from foods it is cooked with. For this reason, *konnyaku* is always simmered for a long time.

This food has two filament forms. As *shirataki* ("white waterfall"), it is an ingredient in SUKIYAKI. Another filament form is *ito konnyaku*, "string *konnyaku*," which is thicker than *shirataki*.

In both cake and filament form, *konnyaku* should be parboiled in ample water before using. Let the jelly heat through well in circulating boiling water, then drain. You may cool it quickly in a cold water bath. Parboiling clarifies the flavor and makes the jelly firmer. After parboiling, the cakes may be sliced or torn into bite-sized pieces. Torn, rough edges increase the surface area for flavors to penetrate. Filaments may be chopped coarsely into 3- or 4-inch (8- or 10-cm) lengths for easier handling with chopsticks.

Konnyaku comes in unrefined ("black") and refined ("white") forms. One or both forms are available in all Japanese food stores. The fresh cake will be in a tub of water in the refrigerator case, probably alongside the bean curd. Canned *konnayku* is sometimes available.

Shirataki and *ito-konnyaku* are sold fresh, and loose knots of filaments will be found floating in water tubs in the refrigerator case (again, next to the bean curd). They also come in 2- to 4-cup quantities in sealed, sausage-shaped, clear plastic water packs. Packaged in this way, *shirataki* may be refrigerated or it may be found on the shelf. Both cake and filament *konnyaku* keep about 2 weeks in a bowl of water in the refrigerator if the water is changed daily.

LILY BULB (*yuri-ne*; ゆり根):   The bulb of several lily varieties ("mountain," "princess," and "devil"), quite different from those with white, trumpet-shaped flowers.

The smooth, white-skinned bulb looks rather like a peeled, large bulb of garlic with flattened cloves, but there is no other resemblance. Cooked lily bulb is mild tasting—slightly nutty and sweet—and it is appreciated for its soft, somewhat mealy texture. It is always parboiled beforehand to remove bitterness. Lily may be used, for example, in simmered *kinton*-type dishes (page 460), or in steamed dishes, typically SAVORY CUP CUSTARD (page 214). Despite this fairly wide range of uses, this is not a common food.

The fresh bulbs keep in damp sawdust in a dark, cool place for a few months. It is abundant in winter, and Japanese who grow lilies in their garden leave bulbs in the ground, protected from the cold with a thick layer of mulch or with plastic sheeting and dig them up as needed throughout the winter.

Choose bulbs that are well shaped with tightly clinging cloves. It is doubt-ful that this ingredient is available in the U.S.

LOTUS ROOT (*renkon*; 蓮根):   This rhizome has been a part of the Japanese diet for well over a millennium; mention of it is made in the eighth century *Man'yō-shū* poems. Raw, it has more texture than flavor; its flesh is fine and tight and it is decidedly crunchy. Lotus is very good in vinegared dishes; thinly sliced it may be used as a TEMPURA vegetable or put into simmered dishes. It is also widely used in Chinese cooking.

The thick, cream-colored rhizomes of this perennial grow in a form that resembles links of sausage. Size varies greatly, but the average size of link is from 5 to 8 inches (13 to 20 cm) long and about 2½ inches (6½ cm) wide. Tubular hollows run the length of each link and form an attractive pattern when the root is cut into rounds.

Lotus root is always scraped or pared. Because the cut root discolors quickly, much more quickly than pared apples, for instance, cut lotus must be immersed in lightly vinegared water till time to use. Use as quickly as possible—this is not an ingredient that can be prepared ahead of time.

Fresh lotus is becoming ever more available in oriental food stores in the U.S. In choosing fresh lotus, look for one without bruises or surface blemishes. If the skin is unblemished, the flesh is probably white (the major problem with lotus is discoloration). The root should be firm with no soft spots. Choose a large or small specimen; flavor does not change with size. Store in a dark, cool place as you would potatoes; keeps well but not as long as potatoes. Once a root link is cut, however, the remaining part of that link must be used within a few days.

Boiled and sliced lotus is sold in cans too, but try to find the fresh root, if possible. Dried sliced lotus is Chinese.

This vegetable also lends itself well to use in Western cooking. It combines well with other vegetables, and its crunchiness is pleasant. It also makes excellent pickles, chutneys, and relishes.

MATSUTAKE MUSHROOMS (松茸): The "pine mushroom" (*Armillaria edodes*) may possibly be the most delicious of all mushrooms. Scented with the fragrance of piney woods, these mushrooms that grow only in the wild in undisturbed stands of red pine are so highly prized that they tend to be used as the main ingredient or the primary focus of a dish. They are eaten lightly cooked.

The *matsutake* is a dark brown mushroom with a thick, meaty stem. It is usually eaten before the cap spreads open. Its season is limited to a few weeks in autumn, and it must be picked wild, giving a good excuse for a pleasant outing—the autumn *matsutake* hunt, a picnic where *matsutake* are grilled in the open air.

A few tips on *matsutake*: do not wash—wipe the cap with a damp cloth or rinse quickly, then trim off about ½ inch (1½ cm) of the stem bottom. Trim off as little as possible! If slicing lengthwise, cut slices not less than ¼ inch (¾ cm) thick. If slices are too thin, flavor is lost. Do not overcook; *matsutake*'s fresh, almost raw woodsiness should be retained.

Given its wonderful flavor, short season, and the fact that commercial cultivation is still impossible, *matsutake* are one of the most sought-after delicacies in Japan. Like truffles or any other such seasonal delicacy, *matsutake* have devotees as well as a body of esoteric lore. And, they are expensive! If you are able to treat yourself to the pleasure, they may be found fresh in season, sawdust packed and imported from Japan (or Korea), in a limited number of Japanese stores, chiefly those in California and New York, where many overseas Japanese reside. They are also savored in Korea, and one might search Korean stores as well. Spores have been successfully scattered in forests in America's Pacific Northwest, where the mushrooms are hunted and then sold by Japanese-food aficionados in the Seattle area.

Matsutake have been canned in water, but this is probably for Japanese living in remote places abroad without access to their native cuisine who cannot let an autumn pass without tasting *matsutake* just once. The canned item is nothing in comparison to the fresh. *Matsutake* are never dried.

MIRIN (味醂): Heavily sweetened wine, like a thin golden-colored syrup, used only in cooking to add a mild sweetness and to glaze grilled foods when used in a basting sauce. The alcohol content is 13–14 percent, and cooks often burn off the alcohol so only the sweet essence of *mirin* remains.

Since this wine is for cooking and not for drinking, and since its alcohol content is so low, *mirin* is not generally stocked in wine and liquor stores. But it is a standard stock item of Japanese food stores everywhere. Some brands have English-language labels reading "sweet cooking rice wine" or some such. *Mirin* comes in bottles in sizes from about 10 to 20 fluid ounces (300–600 mL). Only a few Tbsps are needed to prepare most dishes, so a bottle lasts for a while.

If you cannot find *mirin*, do not try to sweeten *saké* with sugar as is sometimes recommended. Rather, use sugar alone, substituting 1 tsp sugar for 1 Tbsp *mirin*.

MISO (fermented bean paste; 味噌): Packed with protein, and appealing because of its aroma and taste, *miso* is one of Japan's most important staples. Every Japanese—110 million—on the average consumes a few spoonfuls a day in one form or another. Since *miso* has been important in the Japanese diet for centuries, naturally it is used in a wide variety of dishes. It may be thinned and used as a dressing for vegetables; left in its thick state it is a pickling medium; it is also spread on grilled foods as in DENGAKU. It is consumed by nearly all Japanese in the form of *miso-shiru*—MISO SOUP—which is served for breakfast, and may also be served for lunch and dinner.

There are many different kinds of *miso*, each with its own aroma and flavor, color, and texture, but all are made by essentially the same method: crushing boiled soybeans and adding wheat, barley, or rice and injecting the mixture with a yeastlike mold. The mixture is allowed to mature for months, or even up to 3 years. Light, yellow *miso* are injected with rice mold (*kōji*) and are relatively sweet; very good for dressings. One company labels its product "rice *miso*," but "light *miso*" identifies the type. Red *miso*, made with barley *kōji*, is very savory; good for winter soups. Again, the same maker has "barley *miso*" on his package label, but "red *miso*" is sufficient identification.

A third, very dark and thick type is made with bean *kōji*. There is a great variety within and between these three basic types. Texture is somewhat independent of color. There are both smooth and chunky light and dark *miso*s, but dark *miso* tends to be denser than the light, physically as well as in flavor.

It might be helpful to begin learning about *miso* by buying small quantities of various kinds to see which flavor and texture you like best. Nearly a dozen kinds of *miso* are carried in Japanese food stores in the refrigerator cases, and healthfood stores carry, on the average, 3 or 4 kinds. You should have no problem finding *miso*, though labels vary according to maker (it may be called soybean paste, for example). You need not worry about using *miso* quickly. It will keep refrigerated up to a year. It is packaged in the United States in a variety of ways—in plastic tubs (cups, pints, and quarts); in squeeze-out tubes; jars of various sizes; and heavy-duty plastic bags ($\frac{1}{2}$ pound [225 g] and 1 pound [450 g]).

Brief descriptions of some of the most common types (from lightest and sweetest to darkest and saltiest) and how they are used should be helpful.

Shiro-miso, "white *miso*," is represented by *Saikyō miso*. Sweet and fine-textured. Good for soups and excellent for dressings.

Shinshū-miso. A deep yellow smooth *miso*, fairly salty, but tart. It is named for the region of central Honshu that includes present Nagano Prefecture. (Nagano still produces about 20 percent of all *miso* consumed.) Good for general cookery. The most commonly available *miso* in the United States is this type.

Inaka-miso. *Inaka* means "rural countryside," and this red *miso* comes in both sweet and salty types.

A typical red *miso* is *Sendai miso*, Sendai being the northern city where in former times high-quality red *miso* was made. This is a combination of rice, barley, and beans. Comes in both smooth and chunky textures. A good choice if you want *miso* for cooking rather than for dressings. Excellent for *miso* soups.

Hatchō-miso. Robust, strong, chunky, *hatchō-miso* is extremely rich and salty. Best for soups. This *miso* takes its name from the location of the two famous shops (still in operation) in Okazaki near Nagoya that claim to have originated this type of *miso* centuries ago. This is a typical *miso* made mainly of beans. Available in the U.S. Very dark colored, nearly fudge brown, and thick enough to cut with a knife. *Akadashi miso*, also often found in the U.S., is a subtype of this *miso*.

MOCHI (glutinous rice cake; 餅): The honorific form is *o-mochi*. Heavy, chewy *mochi* cakes are made by pounding hot steamed glutinous rice in barrel-sized wooden mortars with a large wooden mallet; then, handfuls of the sticky paste are scooped up and patted into rounds of various sizes. The sound of rice pounding was once common in the last days of December, when many households made fresh *mochi* for the New Year's festivities.

Today most *mochi* is machine processed and sold ready-made. The same kinds of ready-made *mochi* available in Japan are to be had at Japanese stores in America. Cakes may be freshly made by the proprietor, or they may be factory made and packed, vacuum sealed, in plastic. If fresh, the *mochi* will probably be in round cakes or in sheet form; if made commercially, *mochi* comes in packaged squares or in sheet form. *Mochi* cakes should be soft, but if the ones you buy seem hard, the cakes may be softened for use by soaking them overnight in cold water.

The usual way of eating *mochi* is simply to grill it and eat it with a flavor complement such as a soy sauce dip, a wrapper of toasted *nori* seaweed, or perhaps a generous amount of roasted and sweetened soy flour (*kinako*; see ABE RIVER MOCHI, page 469), and the like. (Recent influences have combined such things as butter and cheese and also applesauce with hot grilled *mochi*—with success.) When grilled, *mochi* will double in size, and a crisp skin will form. The same principles apply to grilling *mochi* as to marshmallows—do not let it blacken, but a crisp, well-browned skin is delicious.

If *mochi* gets very hard, dry, and full of cracks, it can be broken into small pieces and deep-fried. It will puff up in irregular shapes. Salted, these make a good snack or nibble.

Joshinko, *mochiko*, and *shiratamako* (see FLOURS entry) can be mixed with water to a paste and boiled to form *mochi*-like dumplings and confections.

MUSHROOMS (*kinoko*; 茸): The edible fungi that the Japanese enjoy are quite different from kinds popular in the West. Happily, with increased interest in oriental cooking, many Asian mushrooms are now becoming known, and some are readily available—fresh, dried, and canned—not only in oriental provisions stores but in supermarkets too.

Whereas, in occidental cuisines mushrooms are sautéed, creamed, stuffed, or used in stuffings, soups, and sauces, in traditional Japanese cooking, they rarely undergo such complicated preparation, and their woodsy fragrance and gentle flavor are emphasized by simple grilling or by being added to soups or one-pot dishes.

See CLOUD EAR MUSHROOMS, ENOKITAKE, MATSUTAKE, NAMEKO, and SHIITAKE entries.

MUSTARD (*karashi*; 芥子): The dry ground mustard used in Japan is very strong stuff, and a little goes a long way. It is prepared by mixing (Japanese) mustard powder with a bit of water to a very stiff paste and allowing it to ripen for about 10 minutes. A common practice is to mix the stiff paste in the bottom of a small bowl and invert it while the mustard flavor ripens. Mix only a small amount at a time, because the fullness of flavor fades quickly. Besides, you will not use very much at once.

Besides being sold in powdered form in oriental provisions stores in 1-, 2-, and 5-ounce (30-, 60-, and 140-g) round spice tins, Japanese mustard paste is also available in tubes.

Karashi is used very sparingly as a condiment with ODEN (page 402), and is a flavoring in some dressed salads (page 423). It may also be used to brighten soy-based dipping sauces—cautiously.

Japanese *karashi* is like some of the hotter European mustards, but without vinegar, and not as light or as mild as American mustard. Though purists may object, substitute any hot mustard you like, as long as it is not too vinegary or sweet.

NAMEKO MUSHROOMS (なめこ): This is one mushroom that even in Japan is more likely to be purchased bottled or canned than fresh. The fresh mushroom has a short shelf life, but it preserves well in heavy brine (20 percent).

Nameko are very much like button mushrooms, but they have a slippery, gelatinous coating, the texture of which contrasts pleasantly with the dark yellow or amber color of the mushroom and its woodsy flavor. *Nameko* are often used in clear and *miso* soups, in one-pot dishes, and in light salads.

Available at oriental stores in small- and medium-sized cans. Drain off water-packing before use.

noodles, buckwheat, see SOBA NOODLES

noodles, wheat, see UDON NOODLES and SŌMEN NOODLES

NORI SEAWEED (のり): Often rendered in English as "laver"—the Latin word for water plant—the word is used for some species of the *Porphyra* genus of marine algae. In some cooler parts of Europe, where this seaweed can be gathered, it may be used in stews or pickled. The dried sheet form is known as *Asakusa nori*, but is simply referred to as *nori* here.

Throughout Japan, porphyra is cultivated in sheltered shallows—from the 1600s until modern pollution, the offshore waters of Tokyo Bay were planted in bamboo stakes, against which it was discovered this dark brown alga would grow. It was gathered, washed in fresh water, and laid in thin sheets to dry like handmade paper on bamboo or wooden frames. *Nori* processing today is highly mechanized in order to produce the billions of sheets that the Japanese consume every year.

Dark brown or deep green *nori* sheets come in a standard size of $8 \times 6\frac{7}{8}$ inches ($20\frac{1}{2} \times 17\frac{1}{2}$ cm).

Toast *nori* by holding a sheet and passing only one side over a (gas) flame a few times till it becomes crisp. Toasting improves flavor and texture, and brings out fragrance. Untoasted *nori* is tough and tasteless.

Nori is normally used to wrap *sushi* (NORI-ROLL, page 300), to wrap RICE BALLS (page 440), or around rice crackers, etc. It is crumbled or cut into very thin strips and used as a garnish on many dishes.

Manufacturers package *nori* in several ways. When dried *nori* sheets are in the standard size, they are generally sold 10 sheets to a bundle or package. Sometimes the sheets are flat, sometimes folded in half—both cellophane packaged. Costly brands may come in tin boxes or canisters to keep the contents crisp and fresh.

Nori sheets may come toasted (*yaki-nori*) by the manufacturer or seasoned by being brushed with a soy-based sauce (*ajitsuke-nori*). Whatever kind of dried *nori* sheets you buy, for best flavor, once the package has been opened, keep out of the sunlight and in a tightly sealed jar.

Nori also comes packaged in sizes smaller than the standard; these have various uses. You may come across what might be called *nori* "miniatures," several 3-inch (8-cm) toasted strips in individual packs, with 50 or perhaps 100 small packs to a bundle. Each pack contains an individual serving used in the traditional Japanese breakfast. Strips are dipped in soy sauce and molded around mouthfuls of hot rice, or left dry and crumbled on top of rice in the bowl. It is convenient to use these small packs of toasted breakfast *nori* when you need a quick *nori* garnish.

A product that goes by the name of green *nori* (*ao-nori*) ought to be mentioned. It is sold in round shakers for use on a few dishes. It also appears as a flavoring on potato chips. It is a type of *nori*, but different from that used to make sheets.

OILS (*abura*; 油): For sautéing, deep-frying, and other cooking uses, pure vegetable oils are basic to Japan cooking. Animal fats are not used. There is, however, no reason to buy the very expensive, imported "authentic" oils that are on the shelves in Japanese stores. The bottles and cans displaying no English are simply labeled either *sarada* ("salad") or *tempura* oil or *goma abura* ("sesame oil"). At less than half the price, the American oils at your local supermarket will do perfectly.

Use a refined mixture of pure, cold-pressed vegetable oils—or choose a single pure vegetable oil. In Japan, for example, pure rapeseed oil is extremely popular, but across the Pacific, your choice might be soybean oil, peanut oil, corn oil, or cottonseed oil. Olive oil is *never* used because it is too heavy and has a dominating flavor.

The only other type of oil you will need for Japanese cooking—for seasoning rather than to cook with—is sesame seed oil. This oil is sold as 100 percent sesame oil or in various degrees of dilution with vegetable oil. It exudes an enchanting nutty fragrance that matches its nutty taste. This oil is now sold in many supermarkets, in Chinese stores (it is widely used in Chinese cooking), and in Japanese stores, where you can ask for it as *goma abura*. It is generally used in small amounts, so a medium-sized bottle of 14 ounces (400 mL) should last some time.

Deep-frying in oil is easily associated with Japanese cooking because of the wordwide popularity of *tempura*. Commercially made *tempura* oil is vegetable, but is not as highly refined as ordinary vegetable oil. You can add fragrance to *tempura* oil by adding sesame oil in up to a 50 percent mixture.

ONIONS: Aromatic vegetables of the genus *Allium* such as onions, leeks, shallots, and chives are used—raw or cooked—throughout the world in all cuisines.

Kinds vary widely from region to region, so what is common in one place is not in another. Some onion varieties are used for their bulbs, which may be small and tight, or large and grainy, globular or flattened, with colors of white, yellow, and red. Other types, of which scallions and leeks are two, produce edible, thick basal portions without a true bulb. The name "green onion" applies either to stalks of immature bulb onions or to fresh, young, non-bulb-bearing "scallions," which look and taste very much alike before they are fully grown.

In Japan, two types of onion are savored in traditional cooking; one or the other predominates, but both do not find equal favor in any area. In Tokyo, people are most familiar with and rely upon the *naganegi*, literally "long onion," which has received that name because, it should come as no surprise, it is quite long—generally 14 to 16 inches (35 to 40 cm) with diameter from 3/8 inch (1 cm) to 1 inch (2½ cm). The white part of the *naganegi* is also quite long in comparison to that of other onion types, and it is the white part of this onion that is used.

Osaka cooks use the *aonegi*, literally, "green onion," which is much slimmer and somewhat shorter than the long onion and has only a short white part: it is the green part that is mainly used. This onion is *not* the same as the green onion commonly found in U.S. markets.

Since this book centers on Osaka cooking, it is this *aonegi*, green onion, that is mostly used; recipes featuring the long onion are from Tokyo or other parts of the country that use this type. Both these onion types are available the year round in Japan, but the flavor of the *naganegi* is best in autumn. Both the long onion and green onion have a pleasant bitterness and a lightness of flavor not found in the conventional Western bulb onion. Of course, the flavors of these two Japanese onions also differ from each other, but they may be interchanged for practical purposes.

But, in fact, this advice is not practical. This section should be entitled "The Onion Problem." Where can one obtain these Japanese onion types in America, and, if not available, what are substitutes? Japanese onion types are *not* readily available. Some Japanese food stores may stock them. Substitutes? In the U.S., it seems that the same type of onion may be called different things in different places and that the preferences for onions in different places differ. The terms "green onion," "scallion" (and sometimes even "shallot") seem to be used for roughly the same thing. Size varies with season and local preference. As a general rule for supermarket shopping, obtain the largest onions that are called green onions or scallions. This is all very imprecise and embarrassing to a cookbook writer [and editor—ed.]. Not even seed catalogs that are supposed to supply the entire U.S. are of help.

Therefore, the quantities for onion(s) in the recipes are for Japanese varieties and sizes. You will have to play your local onion situation by ear. Perhaps you will find a kindly Japanese vegetable gardener or a Chinese produce market (some Chinese types are similar to *aonegi*). . . .

Leeks resemble long onions in shape, but are squatter and smaller, with coarser and tougher greens and a totally different flavor. Nonetheless, use them as substitutes for long onions in most cases, if available.

Other types of Japanese onions are *asatsuki*, *wakegi*, and *rakkyō*. The first two are like small green onions or baby scallions, with long grassy stems and firm white bottoms (though they, in fact, are botanically different) *Rakkyō* are a type of shallot and are pickled in light vinegar, not cooked. Pickled *rakkyō* are very pleasant and are available in oriental food shops.

What looks like flat chives or flat onion greens without a white part is actually a member of the lily family and is called *nira*. The flavor is delicate and garlicky.

Conventional bulb onions are used in Japanese cooking, but mostly in dishes introduced during the last century. If, after all this verbiage about onions, only bulb onions are available, of course use them and enjoy.

PEARS (*nashi*; 梨): The Japanese pear (*nashi*) has been part of the diet since the tenth century, but new strains of fruit have been developed recently. The "twentieth century" pear (*nijūseiki nashi*) is one of the most delicious and widely grown of the new varieties. Japanese pears are applelike in shape and

also in crispness, range in color from light yellow to brown, and have a tart juiciness entirely their own. In season from the end of August to the middle of October. Also available canned. Good as a dessert.

PEPPERS, BELL (*piman*; ピーマン): The bell pepper grown in Japan is small, thinner walled, and more delicate than the varieties marketed in the United States. The recipes in this book that include bell pepper are for the Japanese type. Roughly, Japanese bell peppers are about ⅓ the size of American, but the difference in thickness of flesh results in different cooking times.

Bell peppers were introduced to Japan only around the late nineteenth century. The name—*piman*—is a Japanization of the French *piment*. While Japanese use *piman* often and with great familiarity in the preparation of Western and Chinese dishes, this vegetable has integrated itself into the traditional cuisine in a mere two categories: grilled foods and deep-fried foods. *Piman* may be skewered and grilled as well as batter-fried. To the Japanese taste, bell peppers smell too strong when simmered and lose their shape and color when steamed, so they are not used in either of those food categories.

When shopping for bell peppers to use in Japanese recipes, buy the smallest and thinnest fresh peppers you can find.

PEPPERS, HOT RED CHILI (*tōgarashi*; 唐芥子): These small red chilies are used fresh (in season) or dried. *Tōgarashi* are sold in bunches dried on the stalk or in small quantities in plastic bags; the dried form also comes in rounds, in flakes, or in thread form. *Tōgarashi* plants are often used as decorative perennial borders because of their lovely white blossoms.

Tōgarashi seeds are dangerously hot, so always make sure that seeds are shaken out of the pod before using, as you would any hot chili pepper. Wash hands well after handling *tōgarashi* and do not touch your hands to your eyes to avoid unnecessary irritation.

Tōgarashi is also ground into a coarse sort of pepper. In recent years, this pepper has come to be called *ichimi*, or "one flavor," presumably because it is not mixed with other spices as is *shichimi*—seven-spice mixture (see entry this section). *Ichimi* is also one of the component ingredients of this seven-spice mixture.

To nonspeakers of Japanese, it might seem confusing, but the same word, *tōgarashi*, is often applied to small green peppers that are not hot and are used as a vegetable.

PEPPERS, SMALL GREEN (*ao-tōgarashi, shishi-tōgarashi*; 獅子唐芥子): Often abbreviated *shishi-tō* or "lion pepper" (which, in fact, is one type of *ao-tōgarashi*), this 3-inch (8-cm) Japanese species looks like a pungent green chili, but is mild and sweet. This popular pepper is a convenient size—a whole pepper is a single bite. As a substitute, however, seed and cut bell peppers into strips.

Ao-tōgarashi are an excellent side dish grilled or deep-fried. They also may be simmered with soy sauce and eaten with hot boiled rice. They are occasionally sold in Japanese food stores abroad. Keep refrigerated.

Hot red *tōgarashi* peppers, though similar in shape and size, should not be confused with these sweet green ones.

PERSIMMONS (*kaki*; 柿): Oriental persimmons are best when they are firm rather than soft. There are many varieties, some of which are seedless. The skin is astringent and must be peeled before the fruit is eaten. In season from September to November. A typical dessert.

Occasionally, in the countryside, one comes upon strings of persimmons hanging under farmhouse eaves drying in the autumn sun.

plums, unripe, see UME

POTATOES (*jaga-imo*; じゃが芋): White Irish potatoes were introduced to Japan by European traders in the sixteenth century via Jakarta, which name is echoed in the Japanese *jaga-imo*. Spuds did not really have much appeal for the Japanese till the late nineteenth century, when many foreign foods were experimented with. Today, mainly two kinds of white potatoes are found in Japanese markets, both thin-skinned and small by U.S. standards. Though Irish potatoes are used in most categories of traditional Japanese cooking, they have only a minor position.

Three other tubers—the sweet potato, "mountain yam" (*yama no imo*), and "field yam" (*sato imo*)—have more important places in Japanese cooking. Though the latter two are hardly touched upon in this book, they are sold fresh in Japanese stores abroad and are introduced in this section, under the YAMS entries.

radish, giant white, see DAIKON

red-bean paste, sweet, see AZUKI BEANS

RICE (*kome*; 米), see rice chapter, pages 270ff.

RICE BRAN (*nuka*; 糠):   Rice bran is one of the basic pickling media in Japan, where it can be purchased from neighborhood rice dealers—just ask for as many kilograms as it will take to fill your pickle barrel. At oriental food stores in America, *nuka* is sold in 1- to 5-pound (450-g to 2¼-kg) plastic bags, often shelved next to rice, flours, and other grains.

It might interest some readers to know that rice bran is an excellent detergent as well as wood polish. A cup or so of rice bran in a cotton drawstring bag can be used to wash dishes—with a softening effect on the hands. It may also be used in a dry cotton bag to wipe woodwork; over time, oil from bran has given stairs and floors of traditional houses a deep luster.

SAKÉ (rice wine; 酒):   *Dashi* stock, soy sauce, fermented bean paste (*miso*), and *saké* are the "big four," of Japanese cooking. One or more of these four substances is used in nearly every Japanese dish.

The same kind of *saké* used as beverage is used in the kitchen. Its role as a beverage is discussed in the tea and *saké* chapter, pages 330ff. Here the concern is with *saké* in cooking.

Rice wine was discovered by early Japanese to be a food tenderizer. Amino acids in *saké* account for this property. Moreover, *saké* acts to suppress saltiness, helps eliminate fishy tastes, and takes away strong odors. In some cases, when delicate flavors might expire, it acts to keep dishes alive.

In general, *saké* is used only in small quantities in cooking. But some rigorous cooks object to the smell of alcohol and burn off the alcohol in *saké* before using it in cooking. (Such *saké* is known as *nikiri-zaké*). Simply pour a few cups of *saké* into a saucepan and heat very gently. Ignite the *saké* and let the alcohol burn off. Set aside and use as needed. Make only as much as you will need for one cooking session. If you are in a hurry, just use *saké* from the bottle.

Saké is widely distributed in wine and liquor stores throughout the United States, and is inexpensive.

SANSHO (the pod of prickly ash; 山椒):   This greenish-brown ground spice made from the pod of the *sansho* tree is tangy but not hot. It is sometimes called "Japanese pepper," but it is not a form of pepper and does not resemble that spice. It is employed in Japanese cooking largely to mask the odor and to counter the taste of fat, particularly with fatty grilled foods such as chicken and eel.

The same tree that yields fragrant *kinome* leaves in the springtime also yields *sansho* spice. The tree's yellowish orange berries are harvested and dried in the autumn sun, and when the pods split open, the bitter black seeds are removed and discarded. The dried split pods are sometimes sold in whole form for home grinding, but most of the crop is commercially ground into a flaky powder and packed in small spice tins.

Sansho powder is available in these small tin spice boxes at most oriental provisions stores. Tinned ground *sansho* keeps its zesty fragrance for about a year on the shelf.

The berries are also pickled and used as a relish.

SESAME SEEDS (*goma*; 胡麻):   Both white and black sesame seeds are used in Japanese cooking in both whole and ground form.

To grind, first lightly roast or parch sesame seeds in a dry frypan. Be careful, it is easy to overroast the seeds. Keep seeds moving constantly over a medium flame by shaking pan and stirring. Toast *just until* golden and *immediately* pour out of pan into a *suribachi* grinding bowl (see page 105) or conventional mortar. The point when seeds become overroasted and aroma and flavor suffer is hard to tell by color.

Grind seeds until flaky and very aromatic. Grinding also releases some oil. You do not want a homogenous paste, but a rough, flaky mixture with some half-crushed seeds. Make only as much as you will need for one use; ground sesame is only good fresh. The ground form of sesame is used mainly in sauces and dressings.

Seeds to be used whole are also roasted to enhance flavor and aroma. Black seeds are somewhat stronger in flavor and aroma than the white. After roasting, they are sprinkled over rice or other dishes, such as omelette slices, as a color accent and when a strong sesame flavor is desired. You may substitute black poppy seeds for black sesame, though the flavor is different.

Toasting and grinding the white seeds may seem bothersome, but it is a very quick and simple process, and the results are rewarding. Sesame paste is not the same as freshly ground seeds and is not a good substitute, though a small amount may be used if there is no alternative.

Sesame oil (*goma abura*) is discussed under the OILS entry.

SEVEN-SPICE MIXTURE (*shichimi*; 七味): This snappy spice is a grainy, variegated collection of seven dried and ground flavors: red pepper (*tōgarashi*) flakes; roughly ground, brown *sanshō* pepper pods; minute flakes of dried mandarin orange peel; black hemp seeds (or sometimes white poppy seeds); dark green *nori* seaweed bits; and white sesame seeds.

Literally "seven flavors," *shichimi* may be blended to suit individual taste and is available in mild, medium, and hot strengths. In Japan, *shichimi* may be purchased from itinerant spice sellers who set up booths with small trays brimming with each spice at shrine festivals and neighborhood fairs. Passersby can ask this vendor to mix the spice to personal taste, requesting a bit more of this, or some of that. This mixed spice loses its aroma rather quickly, and so it is generally purchased in small quantities. A small, green-bottomed and orange-topped round spice can is the usual container, and this is how it is sold by vendors and in stores in Japan and in oriental provisions stores in the United States. The product has recently come to be packaged in small plastic zip-lock pouches too.

This ingredient is sold in the U.S. under several general names, one of which is misleading:

> seven-spice powder (*shichimi*)
> seven-spice red pepper (*shichimi tōgarashi*)
> *tōgarashi*

The last is a misnomer. The word *tōgarashi* refers only to hot red peppers or red-pepper flakes, which is also known as *ichimi* ("one-flavor") spice. See entry for PEPPERS, HOT RED CHILI.

Shichimi is lightly sprinkled over *udon* noodles, added to soups, and is used to season a wide variety of dishes.

SHIITAKE MUSHROOMS (椎茸): This mushroom is to Japanese, Chinese, and Korean cooking what the field mushroom or champignon is to Western cooking—abundant, versatile, easy to cultivate commercially and thus a popular ingredient.

Fresh *shiitake* have a distinctive, appealing "woodsy-fruity" flavor. They dry well, and the flavor of the dried mushroom is also excellent.

This mushroom is grown commercially in large quantities by inoculating cut logs of the *shii* tree (*Pasania cuspidata*) and other oak-related species with spores. *Shiitake* are double-cropped in Japan and are in season in spring and fall.

Fresh *shiitake* are dark brown, with smooth velvety caps (though the *shiitake* with white fissures in the cap are excellent). They are best when the caps are thick, the flesh is firm, and the cap edges are curled under. When the cap has flared out and become floppy, the mushroom is past its prime, though the flavor may still be all right. The inner meat is light pinky beige. When fresh caps are used whole, a simple or complex decorative cross is often notched into the caps. Extremely large caps may be cut in half. *Shiitake* stems are tough. Usually, for convenience, the entire stem is trimmed off because it takes longer to cook than the cap. If you like, use the stems, discarding only the hard root, in soups and stews or for soup stock.

Fresh *shiitake* in Japan seem to be darker with more velvety skin than those grown and sold in America as "black forest shiitake" in oriental stores and a number of specialized greengrocers. These American *shiitake* have yellowish, slick skins and appear a bit more spongy.

The mushroom is dried and packaged whole, sliced, in pieces, or crumbs, in a number of grades and package sizes. A 1-ounce (30-g) package holds 8 to 10 caps. This is how they are carried in nearly every oriental food store.

Dried mushrooms must be soaked in tepid water for 3 to 5 hours to soften. (The soaking water may be used for stock.) Cut away and discard hard parts of the stem after soaking. Often such softened *shiitake* are simmered in seasoned liquids and, sliced or coarsely chopped, used in any number of dishes—including mixed rice combinations and noodles. Dried *shiitake* keep almost indefinitely in an airtight container.

Fresh whole *shiitake* are used for their appearance, texture, and aroma. If the vegetable is to be chopped or sliced and then mixed with other foods, fresh and dried may be used interchangeably. If neither type of *shiitake* is available, substitute large fresh field mushrooms or whatever mushroom is available. There is a type of brown mushroom sometimes seen in American markets that resembles *shiitake* closely, though somewhat lighter in color.

shirataki, see KONNYAKU

SHISO (perilla, beefsteak plant; 紫蘇): The names "perilla" (after the plant's genus) and "beefsteak plant" (for the red species) are not more or less familiar or easy to remember than the plant's snappy Japanese name—*shiso*—and for that reason *shiso* is used in this book. *Shiso* is a member of the mint family.

Its natural habitat is China, Burma, and the Himalayas, and for centuries it has been cultivated in Japan. The plant is hardy, makes a good addition to an herb garden, and is cultivated in California. Fresh *shiso* leaves are available in many oriental provisions stores in the U.S.

Green (*ao-jiso*) and the red *shiso (aka-jiso)* have different uses.

The green appears mainly as a garnish, either whole or chopped, is a TEMPURA vegetable, and is incorporated (chopped) into ROLLED SUSHI (page 303). Fresh spearmint or basil may be substituted for the green species, though the flavors are not the same.

The red or magenta *shiso* is not as fragrant as the green. It is not a "ripe" stage of the green plant, but is a different species of the *Perilla* genus. It is available on the market only during June or early July and wilts very quickly after picking. Usually an entire plants with roots and stems are sold, but only the leaves are used.

Red *shiso* is used mainly in making PICKLED PLUMS (*umeboshi*; page 317), in making various kind of pickles, and in some local confections or sweets. Dark opal basil may be substituted in some cases.

In Japan, green *shiso*'s natural season is from spring to early autumn, but hothouse cultivation makes it available the year round. Make sure leaves are not wilted when purchased; they cannot be perked up in a cold water bath.

Stems of flowering seed pods (*hana hojiso*) are often used as a garnish for *sashimi*, as are the tiny sprouts (*mejiso*). The pods are scraped off the stem with chopsticks or fingers and mixed into the accompanying soy-based dipping sauce. Store sprouts in a cup of water and change water to keep them crisp, or wrap in damp paper and refrigerate.

You may come across salted or pickled varieties of *shiso*. These are to be eaten with rice.

shōyu, see SOY SAUCE

SOBA NOODLES (buckwheat noodles; そば): Discussed at length in the noodles chapter, page 305. A single serving is considered to be 100 grams (about 3½ ounces) of dried noodles, and standard packages are 500 grams, or 5 servings. For convenience, the amounts in the recipes are given in terms of pounds and fractions thereof—a single serving then becomes ¼ pound or 115 grams. Cooked noodles increase in weight 3 times over the dried form.

Dried *soba* is carried in Japanese food stores and sometimes in healthfood stores, where it may be labeled "Japanese pasta." Freshly made *soba* may be available in vacuum-sealed plastic packs.

SŌMEN NOODLES (fine wheat noodles; そうめん): Discussed at length in the noodles chapter, page 305. *Sōmen* comes in a few forms, one of which is of almost threadlike thinness.

SOYBEANS (*daizu*, 大豆, and *edamame*, 枝豆) : The type of soybean eaten as a fresh vegetable or selected for drying is exactly the same as is used to make soy sauce, *miso* paste, and *tōfu*. The beans grow in a bushy form, about 20 inches (50 cm) tall, with clusters of pods directly attached to stems. Beans are usually 2 to 3 to a pod; pods are around 2½ inches long, bright green, and fuzzy. In Japan, from mid-May to early autumn, every greengrocer and supermarket sells rooted and bound plants, stems full of green soybean pods. In season, they may be obtained at a few Japanese stores abroad. The recipe for SOYBEANS IN THE POD is given on page 471.

Mature soybeans, shelled and dried by the packer, look like almost oval yellow pearls. They are sold in packages as *daizu*, or "great beans." With dried beans you can make your own *tōfu* from scratch or simply soak or boil them to soften, then simmer them in seasoned stock until the beans are plump and serve as a side dish.

SOY SAUCE (*shōyu*; 醤油) : A pungent, brown salty sauce that is one of the primary seasonings of oriental cooking. It prevented foods from spoiling in the summer heat and it made it possible to preserve foods for winter months. The action of mold and brine on soybeans produced Japan's first, primitive soy sauce. New techniques were introduced from China in the eighth and ninth centuries, but it was not until the fifteenth century that production techniques were modified, and Japan began producing its own type of soy sauce. This accounts for the great difference between the sauces of the two countries. It was not until the sixteenth century, however, that soy sauce became widely used and commercially manufactured. Before that, it was made by farm families for their own or local use. It is also perhaps of mild interest to point out that, though Americans in the last decade have come to recognize soy sauce as an outstanding seasoning, they are by no means the first Western discoverers. Dutch traders in Nagasaki in the seventeenth century exported soy sauce to Europe, and it was the secret seasoning served at the court banquets of Louis XIV of France.

Soy sauce is made from soybeans, wheat, and salt. A mixture of carefully selected and roasted beans and wheat is inoculated with an *Aspergillus* mold. The resulting culture, which takes 3 days to grow, is called *kōji*. The *kōji* is then mixed with brine to make a liquidy mash. Mash is transferred to fermentation tanks for a leisurely brewing of one year. After brewing, raw soy sauce is separated from the "cake" (residual materials such as bean and grain hulls) and refined. Soy sauce today is pasteurized too.

There are three basic categories of soy sauce: natural Chinese, natural Japanese, and chemical synthetic.

Natural Chinese soy sauce in general is quite salty and has a dense flavor. There is a variety of types, from thick, dark reddish brown sauces to some that are as light and thin as Japanese-style soy sauce.

Natural Japanese soy sauces have relatively bright taste and aroma. Because far more wheat is used in Japanese soy sauces, they generally are "sweeter" and less salty than Chinese-style sauces. Japanese types are generally clearer in color and thinner than the dark, thick browns of Chinese soy sauce. Japanese themselves grade their soy sauce as "light" and "dark."

Synthetic soy sauce. The quality and good flavors of naturally brewed Japanese or Chinese soy sauces are reflected in the word "natural." Unhurried brewing to develop flavor and aroma takes a minimum of 4 to 6 months. Modern technology allows brewing to be shortened so that so-called fermentation takes 3 to 4 days. Natural ingredients are replaced by hydrolyzed vegetable protein and hydrochloric acid (to get the chemical reaction underway), and caramel and corn syrup provide coloring and flavor. Synthetic soy sauces in the American market are often sold under Chinese-sounding brand names. The sauce is thick and black. Before you put a bottle of soy sauce into your shopping basket, read all the labeling and make sure that you pick a brand that has been naturally brewed.

In only two places in this book are products recommended by name. When it comes to soy sauce, the answer is Kikkoman. This is because there are any number of mistakes to be made in shopping—choosing a Chinese type instead of Japanese soy sauce, or a chemical type rather than naturally brewed type. Without the right kind of soy sauce, your efforts at Japanese cooking simply will not result in Japanese dishes. Kikkoman is widely available in the U.S., is dependable, has the correct flavor and quality, and even has the Good Housekeeping seal of approval.

A quick scan of the recipes in this book will reveal that two types of soy sauce are called for—light and dark. The light type is favored in the Osaka area; dark has a wider popularity and might be called the "standard" type.

Light soy sauce (*usu-kuchi shōyu*) is amber in color, is clearer and thinner than the dark, but it is also *saltier*. It can be used on all foods. This soy sauce does not darken the color of the food, and it is salty enough so that foods may be seasoned without saturating them or coating them. Dark soy sauce (*koi-kuchi shōyu*) has a deeper color and more body. It is *less salty* and used in relatively greater quantities. It may be used, for example, as a basting sauce, or as a marinade base, in simmered dishes, and the like.

If you do your shopping at a Japanese store, you will have no problem obtaining both types. All Kikkoman light soy sauce is imported from Japan. It is generally used in smaller quantities than the dark type, so a small or medium-sized bottle will suffice. This is not only a suggestion for economy: once light soy sauce is opened, it darkens in time. In order not to defeat the aesthetic purpose of using light soy sauce, get in the habit of buying smaller bottles that will be used quickly.

You will almost certainly find Kikkoman soy sauce in supermarkets. This sauce is not imported. It is made in the Kikkoman factory in Walworth, Wisconsin, from soybeans, wheat, and salt produced in the U.S.A. The multicolored label on this product is in English, with highly visible lettering proclaiming the sauce to be "naturally brewed." But there is no clue whether this sauce is dark or light. *Kikkoman produces only dark soy sauce in America.* Purchase the dark Kikkoman sauce at a supermarket and a small bottle of imported light at a Japanese food store to keep down grocery bills. (Imported dark soy is stocked in Japanese food stores too, but at import prices.) Best stored in refrigerator to maintain freshness.

If you can obtain only dark soy sauce, how should you proceed if a recipe calls for light soy sauce? Sacrifice aesthetics and use only the dark.

If a recipe calls for a combination of light and dark, and you have only the dark on hand, total the amounts and use that quantity of dark sauce.

Kikkoman has a growing line of products now available in the American market. Among them, the two that are most related to Japanese cooking are *teriyaki* sauce and steak (*tonkatsu*) sauce. The former is advertised as a barbecuing sauce, and the latter as a Worcestershire-type sauce. Although "from-scratch" recipes for these sauces are included in this book, these commercial products are time-saving.

Tamari (たまり), used in oriental cooking and sold in healthfood stores and oriental food stores, is a thick, very dark liquid with a stronger flavor than soy sauce and a clear soy aroma. It is mainly made of soybeans and cultured and fermented like *miso*. It is sometimes described as raw soy sauce that has not been fully brewed, but this description is incorrect. Often *tamari* imported into the U.S. is just a brewed soy sauce. Even in Japan, it is hard to find the best *tamari*. In Japanese cooking, *tamari* is generally used as a dipping sauce or a base for basting sauce such as YAKITORI SAUCE, page 185.

SPINACH (*hōrensō*; ほうれん草): Japanese spinach is different from the spinach sold in the U.S. The leaf color is identical, but the leaves of Japanese spinach are smaller, more delicate, spear-shaped, and not deeply crinkled (easy to wash), in comparison to the large, roundish, waxy, heavily wrinkled and curled leaves of the type found in American markets. At the root, the stems of the Japanese spinach are pink. Spinach is sold with the rootlet in Japan, which may be eaten.

Cooked Japanese spinach is milder and sweeter than Western spinach. The leaf is prepared by parboiling. Wash leaves well; do not cut off roots. Bring a large pot of lightly salted water to a boil, add spinach, and cook briefly—only until just limp and color darkens. Remove and rinse until cool under cold running water. Drain well and gently wring out water from cooked leaves. Chop or use whole, as desired.

Spinach is available year round in Japan due to greenhouse cultivation, but it is best in its natural season—from fall to spring. It is sometimes carried in Japanese stores abroad.

Substitute fresh Western spinach, the younger the better.

SQUASH, JAPANESE (*kabocha*; かぼちゃ): This vegetable is also referred to as a pumpkin. The *kabocha* is no more than about 8 inches (20 cm) in diameter, turban-shaped, with a jade green, slightly waxy skin. Its flesh is bright yellow to medium orange, has a rich flavor, and is pleasantly smooth textured. There are a few varieties.

The *kabocha* is suitable for any number of cooking methods. It is cut into bite-sized pieces and simmered, with or without skin. It may also be deep-fried in slices as a TEMPURA vegetable.

This vegetable is grown rather widely on the West Coast and may be purchased in supermarkets there in the autumn. Otherwise, substitute acorn squash or small pumpkin. In Japan, it is a summer vegetable.

STARCHES AND THICKENERS: To thicken sauces and broths, Japanese cooks have traditionally turned to one of the three starches below. They are sold in Japanese food stores, and occasionally in healthfood stores. Using any one of the three will expand your knowledge of authentic Japanese ingredients, but you may substitute cornstarch.

Kuzu (くず): Sometimes incorrectly equated with arrowroot starch, *kuzu* is not only a good thickener, it is also known in the Orient for its medicinal properties. One of Japan's most pervasive wild plants, *kuzu* vine is listed in a ninth century literary work as an edible vegetable. It is no stranger to America. As a plant display at the Japanese pavilions at international expositions in Philadelphia (1876) and New Orleans (1883), *kuzu* was much admired for its prolific growth and ornamental shape. By the turn of the century, this riotous plant was spreading all over the South as a shade vine and as a fodder source. It is known in America as kudzu, the obsolete romanization (same as *adzuki/azuki*).

As a thickener, *kuzu* starch—extracted from the root of the vine—is excellent: it produces a sparkling, translucent sauce and adds shiny gloss to soups. It has a gentle, pleasant aroma, and does its work at fairly low temperatures. Because it is an alkali, it balances acidity, such as found in sweets. Dusted over foods to be deep-fried, it yields a light, crisp, almost crystalline snow-white coating.

Kuzu is available in Japanese food stores and healthfood stores, most often sold in small cellophane packets of 4 ounces (115 g). The starch looks like lumpy flour. The lumps easily crush into a fine powder and dissolve with a few stirs in a small amount of water. It is about the same strength as cornstarch, and is best stored in a tightly sealed jar. *Kuzu* is expensive.

Potato starch (*katakuriko*; 片栗粉):   In days long gone, a fine starch was extracted from the bulb of the *katakuri*, dog-tooth violet, but commercial manufacture of starch from this plant is expensive, which precludes its use commercially. The name *katakuriko*, or "dog-tooth violet starch," has come to glamorize starch processed from plain potatoes. This tasteless thickener is popular because of its moderate price. Like cornstarch, potato starch must be dissolved in a small amount of cold water before using.

Potato starch is sold in tubelike paper packages of about 8 inches (20 cm) long and 8 ounces (225 g) in weight. Once the paper tube is opened, it is convenient to store the starch in a small canister. *Katakuriko* is stronger than cornstarch, so use less.

Sweet rice flour (*mochiko*; 餅粉):   A fine flour ground from steamed glutinous rice. While *mochiko* is often used to make dumplings (*dango*) or confections, if necessary, it may be employed for thick, glossy (Western) sauces. It is widely sold in Japanese stores, healthfood stores, and gourmet food stores in 1-pound (450-g) boxes like cornstarch.

SWEET POTATO (*Satsuma-imo*; さつま芋):   In premodern times, southern Kyushu was the Satsuma fief, and because this potato was introduced to Japan from Okinawa by way of the old Satsuma domain, it is called the "Satsuma potato." There are a number of varieties. Botanically it is the same as the sweet potato familiar in the U.S.; the flavor of the Japanese varieties tends to be sweeter and the flesh firmer than the American. Hot baked sweet potatoes are sold by itinerant peddlers from autumn through spring, and the cry of the sweet potato man is familiar to everyone in Japan. Sweet potato slices are used in TEMPURA, and the potatoes are simmered to make a sweet dish associated with the New Year (*kinton*, page 460). There are also a number of sweet potato "candies."

Satsuma-imo are occasionally available in Japanese markets, but you may substitute American sweet potatoes or yams.

TREFOIL (*mitsuba*; 三つ葉): A member of the parsley family, this annual herb has thin greenish-white stalks approximately 6 to 7 inches (15 to 18 cm) long, topped with a compound leaf of three flat, deeply cut leaflets. Depending on the variety, the leaves range in color and size from pale to bright green and from small to rather full.

With a flavor somewhere between sorrel and celery and an attractive light green color, *mitsuba* is used in many Japanese dishes as a flavor and color accent. Used only fresh, it is often lightly parboiled beforehand to rid it of any "parsleyish" overtones. Also, professional cooks usually use only the stems because leaves and stems have different cooking times, but it is not necessary to be so fussy. Coarsely chopped, it is added to soups or to SAVORY CUP CUSTARD (page 214); whole trefoil is used in one-pot dishes and TEMPURA. It also goes well with vinegared vegetables and tastes good in light salads. No matter how it will be used, because the leaves become bitter and lose their fragrance when simmered too long or subjected to too much heat, *mitsuba* should be no more than lightly parboiled or very gently stir-fried in a scant amount of oil if preliminary treatment is required.

Various types of trefoil are available at different times of the year in Japan, as well as in the United States, where they are marketed by oriental provisions stores.

Whatever type of trefoil is available, always look for bunches that have strong, perky stems and leaves and are young and fresh looking. Wrapped in plastic or in the vegetable crisper, this vegetable keeps in the refrigerator about 1 week.

Similar to trefoil in appearance, but *not* a possible substitute are fresh coriander leaves, also known as cilantro and Chinese parsley. The flavor and odor of this herb are very strong, and it is not a part of Japanese cooking, though used to good advantage in other national cuisines.

UDO (うど): Though known to botanists as *Aralia cordata*, no English name has been given to *udo*. The Chinese characters used to write the word *udo* throw off a clue as to why this perennial is so highly regarded—the characters mean "to live alone."

The raw *udo* stalk has a delicate aroma, a flavor with a light fennelish overtone, and an appealing fresh crispness. *Udo* stalk is used in Japanese cooking almost raw. (If it is cooked, it is briefly parboiled, never steamed, grilled, or deep-fried.) Cut crosswise into thin slices or lengthwise into julienne strips, *udo* is used in vinegared and "dressed" salads (*sunomono* and *aemono*). It may also be added at the last minute to clear soups. Because there is a hint of bitterness in the skin and flesh, raw *udo* is generally peeled and the stalk is left in cold water for a few minutes. Then it is sliced or cut. Stalks grow several feet tall, but the stem is ready for eating before full maturity is reached. *Udo* is rarely seen in Japanese stores abroad—the difficulty is in keeping this vegetable fresh. *Udo* is in season from early spring to early autumn, but because thinner, more tender stalks are the best, from March to May is prime. Substitute celery, asparagus, or fennel.

UDON NOODLES (wheat noodles; うどん): Discussed at length in noodles chapter, page 305. The comments under the SOBA entry here also apply to *udon*. Comes in a fairly wide variety of sizes and lengths.

UME (梅): "Plum" has become such a common misnomer that correcting it seems no longer possible. Besides, it is not very important. This fruit is a species of apricot, *Prunus mume*. It is only used when unripe—the firm green fruit is used to make PLUM LIQUEUR (page 470), and after it has turned yellow but before it becomes sweet, it is used for PICKLED PLUMS (*umeboshi*, page 317).

UMEBOSHI (*pickled "plums"*; 梅干): The round red pickles are often made every June when green "plums" come onto the market. Unripe plums are soaked in brine, packed with red *shiso* leaves (which contribute not only flavor but dye the plums red), and left to mature in the salty bath (see page 317 for recipe for *umeboshi*).

Umeboshi have long been regarded as a tonic. Not only are they thought to aid digestion, they are also said to keep the intestinal tract clear. This may be one reason why *umeboshi* are part of the traditional Japanese breakfast,

—besides their strong acid-salty flavor, which is considered fresh and cleansing in the morning.

Particular dipping sauces sometimes require a jolt of tartness and utilize plum paste, or *bainiku*. This is pureed *umeboshi*. To make *bainiku*, pit several large *umeboshi* and rub the meat through a fine sieve. Bottled and canned *bainiku* in 1-ounce (30-g) quantities are available at many Japanese stores. Do not confuse Japanese *umeboshi* paste in small bottles or jars with sweet plum jam, often sold in cans in Chinese stores. The sweet plum puree is popularly used in Chinese-American cooking.

Home-made pickled plums are available in the refrigerator case in 1-pint (½-L) plastic tubs at many Japanese stores. You will also be able to find them bottled on the grocery shelf. Once a bottle has been opened, refrigerate. Keeps indefinitely.

VINEGAR (*su*; 酢): Japanese produce rice vinegar in a number of strengths, but no matter what the type of rice vinegar, it still will be milder than most Western vinegars.

Lightness and relative sweetness are characteristics of rice vinegar, and these seem to have caught on in the U.S. to such an extent that rice vinegar is stocked not only in oriental provisions stores but in many chain supermarkets as well.

If you must substitute another kind of vinegar, use cider vinegar, rather than anything synthetic. You might want to dilute it a bit with water or add a tiny amount of sugar, but the flavor will not emulate rice vinegar.

WAKAME SEAWEED (若布): Lobe-leafed *Undaria pinnatifida*, a member of the brown algae family. Prized for its flavor and texture, *wakame* is usually sold in Japan and Japanese stores abroad in dried form. In Japan, it is available fresh in early spring to summer.

Dried *wakame* must be softened by soaking in tepid water for about 20 minutes. The frond's spine is very tough, so if you find it has not been pared away by the processor, cut away any tough sections. *Wakame* is widely used in soups; it should not be simmered longer than a minute or so, however, to keep it from losing any of its important nutrients. Extremely high in nutrition, with no calories, *wakame* is a good salad ingredient. It goes well in light vinegary dressing—pleasant in texture with a fresh vegetable crispness. Its color and form are also appealing.

WASABI HORSERADISH (山葵): As indicated by its Latin name, *Wasabia japonica*, this plant that yields one of the strongest spices in Japanese cooking is unique to these islands. The name *wasabi* translates from the Japanese as "mountain hollyhock."

The plant's natural habitat is the marshy edge of cold and clear streams. In fact, *wasabi* cannot be cultivated well in other than cold, pure running water, and is grown in flooded mountain terraces.

Wasabi is sometimes compared to Western horseradish, but the two are not related. *Wasabi* is more fragrant and less sharp than white horseradish.

The edible part of the plant is the root. Shop for the root (green tops already disposed of) in water-filled pans at greengrocers in Japan. Before grating into a fine paste, cut out the "eyes" and pare away the tough brownish-green skin to reveal the delicately colored, pale green flesh. Rub on a fine grater, using a circular motion.

The biting yet fresh, cleansing taste of *wasabi* accompanies most raw fish dishes. Scant half-teaspoonful mounds of grated *wasabi* garnish *sashimi* plates and are mixed to taste with the soy-based dipping sauce that accompanies the dish. Likewise, smears of this grated spice are placed beneath the bite-sized pieces of raw fish that cover *sushi*.

Outside Japan, fresh *wasabi* roots are almost impossible to find, but two alternative products are available in most oriental provisions stores: powdered *wasabi* and paste *wasabi*.

Powdered *wasabi* comes in small round tins, just like powdered mustard. To prepare, add a small amount of tepid water to a small amount of powder, mix till smooth, and allow to stand, covered, for about 10 minutes to develop flavor.

Paste *wasabi* comes ready-to-use in small plastic tubes. It is on the shelf with dry things; once opened it must be refrigerated.

WHEAT GLUTEN (*fu*; 麩): Wheat gluten is typically used in soups, noodle broths, and one-pot dishes. Made not from all-purpose flour but rather from gluten flour, these "cakes" are in fact like frothy bread that is high in protein and low in starch. *Fu* is made in a great variety of shapes, many of them whimsical and decorative.

Even in Japan, *fresh fu* is available only in a few specialty shops: it is available in any grocery in its dried form.

Dried wheat gluten must be softened for 5 to 10 minutes in tepid water before using. The "cakes" will expand greatly. Press out excess water by gently squeezing between the palms of your hands.

YAMS, FIELD (*sato imo*; 里芋): The word yam in the United States is used for orange-fleshed sweet potatoes. Yam correctly designates a type of tuber very different from sweet potatoes and generally unfamiliar to the American public. There are a number of types of yam used in Japanese cooking.

One of the most important is the *sato imo*, rendered here as "field yam," but which has no common English name. This tuber is mentioned only in passing in this book, but it is a popular ingredient in Japanese cooking, mainly in simmered foods.

When cooked, it has a slightly gluey quality, which many Westerners feel needs getting used to, but its flavor is pleasant and mild. It is a common ingredient in ODEN (page 402).

There are two varieties of *sato imo*; the small one is known as *ko-imo* and the large one as *yatsugashira*. The season is from September to March. Thin- and soft-skinned yams are considered the best.

Because the skin is rather bitter, peel the tubers rather thickly and soak in water 30 minutes. Boil until soft in the water used to wash rice (add a little vinegar to bleach, if desired). Test for doneness by poking with a bamboo skewer. If the yam is soft throughout and there is no firm core, it is done. Rinse immediately in a water bath. Drain. Small yams are best peeled after boiling.

The small variety (*ko-imo*) is often available in Japanese food shops in the United States.

YAMS, MOUNTAIN (*yama no imo*; 山の芋):   Four popular types of the beige, hairy mountain yam are *naga-imo*, literally "long potato," *ichō-imo*, *Yamato-imo*, and *jinenjo*. Mountain yams are frequently in demand by Japanese abroad, so Japanese markets in large cities usually carry them, generally displayed in the sawdust-filled packing crate in which they arrived.

These yams have a gluey consistency when peeled and finely grated. The flavor of grated yam is mild and pleasant, but the texture is an acquired taste for most Westerners. This grated form is also used as an ingredient in many processed foods, often as a binder.

This raw grated yam is also considered to be an excellent digestive. It is served in combination with various other foods and is known as *tororo*.

YUZU CITRON (柚子): Japan has many types of citrus fruit, not all of which are sweet or good eating. One of these is the *yuzu* citron, which is used almost entirely for its marvelous aromatic rind. The sour flesh might be squeezed for its acid juice, but it is the small pieces and slivers of rind that add bright fragrance to soups, simmered dishes, pickles, relishes, and sweet confections. This yellow fruit, about the size of a tangerine, is in season from late November into January. The *yuzu* fragrance is entirely its own and resembles no citrus familiar to the West.

Yuzu is carried in some Japanese stores on the West Coast. Substitute lemon or lime.

Utensils

If your kitchen is well equipped for Western cooking, you can cook Japanese food. A few improvisations are necessary, but such things are fun and often encountered by the adventurous cook. You already have an intimate, friendly relationship with your basic equipment: good heavy pots; nests of stainless steel bowls and pans for mixing, soaking, marinating and performing the many steps of food preparation; wooden spoons, large slotted spoons, ladles, measuring cups and spoons, a chopping board, and knives.

Knives are so important that an entire chapter is devoted to them. It is not imperative that you buy Japanese knives, but you must have *good* knives with blades that can be used in the same way. A paring knife or a slicer, no matter how good, cannot cut and chop vegetables well. Probably the most versatile Japanese knife is the vegetable cutter (*nakiri-bōchō* or *usuba-bōchō*, page 111); it has no counterpart in the Western home kitchen and is a valuable tool.

For this discussion of Japanese utensils, a minimalist approach has been taken—only a few items are needed to supplement a Western kitchen and make Japanese cooking easier. Even most of these may be improvised.

For example, a place mat woven of plastic slats will roll seaweed *sushi* just as well as a traditional bamboo mat. Or, a baking paper circle with a center vent does almost the same job that a wooden drop-lid does.

Most or all of these utensils are to be found in oriental goods stores. They are also often carried in kitchen utensil stores that cater to international gourmet cooking. Though there are numerous beautiful Japanese cooking utensils, many are for special uses, and most are not available abroad.

BAMBOO DRAINING BASKETS (*zaru*; ざる): For draining off liquids and rinsing foods, for arranging, sorting and tossing, for salting, and for many other steps of food preparation, the Japanese cook has traditionally relied on bamboo baskets. Though utensils of metal and vinyl more like the Western colander have recently appeared on the market, bamboo is still preferred. The traditional tool, made out of a natural material, is the best and most convenient. Wash baskets in water and store in the open air, not in a cupboard.

BAMBOO MAT (*maki-su*; 巻す): This utensil is made by weaving strips of bamboo into a mat with strong cotton string. (The same weaving principle is used to make bamboo blinds.) It is used as an aid in forming and pressing various soft materials into cylindrical forms, as with ROLLED SUSHI and ROLLED OMELETTE, and to press out excess moisture. The mats are generally about 10 inches (25 cm) square, but vary somewhat in size, depending on the maker. The bamboo strips are either thick or thin. The thick-stripped mat is the more versatile; the thinner one is primarily for thin ROLLED SUSHI (*kappa-maki*, page 303).

After using the mat, wash it carefully under tepid running water and wipe dry. To avoid musty smells, let dry completely before storing. In lieu of a bamboo mat, you may use any small place mat that is woven in the same manner or has the same flexibility. Be careful to use one that is chemically neutral and color fast.

CHOPSTICKS (*hashi*; 箸): One or two pairs of long, kitchen chopsticks, a package of disposable cedar or pine chopsticks, and a few pairs of somewhat more elegant, finished chopsticks are good to keep on hand.

Kitchen chopsticks come in various lengths, starting at about 1 foot (30 cm). They are made of wood or bamboo and are usually joined at the top by a piece of string (remove this, if it hampers you) so they can be hung easily. Once you start using kitchen chopsticks, their ease of use and fitness for certain jobs will make you regret not "discovering" them earlier. They are unequaled for handling delicate foods, and you can stir, beat, turn foods, and perform many other cooking steps with *one hand*, which is also at a comfortable distance from spattering and heat. A short and a very long pair of kitchen chopsticks are convenient for various jobs, but a single pair will suffice. For arranging prepared foods on dishes, chopsticks are the ideal tool —they give you precise control and ability to arrange the most delicate foods. A pair of small, pointed chopsticks is best for this. If you do any amount of deep-frying, it is wise to get long metal chopsticks; if you use wooden or bamboo ones over and over in hot oil their tips become charred.

Disposable individual chopsticks are practical for everyday use. You can use them both in the kitchen and at table. But for guests and your own special occasions—or for everyday use—it is nice to have pairs of finished chopsticks in the house. There are so many kinds that no guides can be given other than to rely on your own taste. It is probably best to avoid plastic or slippery finishes, however (see page 50 for a discussion on how to hold chopsticks.)

DEEP-FRYING EQUIPMENT (*agemono no dōgu*; 揚げものの道具): Deep-frying is so common in Japan that special deep-frying utensils are likely to be found in most Japanese kitchens.

Deep-frying pot (*agemono-nabe*; 揚げ物鍋): Pots used for deep-frying have to be heavy enough to retain heat well and deep enough to hold sufficient amounts of oil. Naturally, Japanese have designed pots that meet these two criteria: thick cast iron or thick brass pots with ear-handles are made for hot oil. Avoid using a thin pot for deep-frying, because it simply cannot keep oil at a high, *even* temperature.

Net ladle (*ami-shakushi*; 網杓子): A scoop made of fine wire mesh is an excellent tool for skimming bits of batter from the oil and keeping oil clean.

Oil drainer (*abura-kiri*; 油きり用バット): A shallow pan fitted with a rack. Place sheets of absorbent paper towel on the rack and drain freshly fried foods for a few seconds before transferring them to individual serving dishes.

Long metal chopsticks with wooden grips (金属製の箸): The advantages of such metal chopsticks when working with hot oil are obvious.

EARTHENWARE CASSEROLES (*donabe*; 土鍋): The great advantage of these vessels is that they can be used directly on a flame, whereas conventional ovenproof ware (especially stoneware) can *never* be used on a direct flame. In fact, most are not earthenware, but made of a special refractory clay (like firebrick) and fired at a relatively high temperature. Japanese *donabe* can be used in an oven as well.

The special clay of *donabe* retains heat well and distributes it evenly, both of which are also great advantages with stove-top cooking (*donabe* are excellent for things like cheese fondue). Though *donabe* take a direct flame, the vessels must not be shocked with sudden high heat, but be heated gradually at first. Also, the unglazed outside must be *completely dry* before being put on a burner, or water in the porous clay will expand and crack the vessel. It should also not be kept empty on a flame. See also One-Pot Cooking chapter, pages 254ff, for a discussion of *donabe*.

GRATERS (*oroshigane*; おろし金): There are two kinds of Japanese graters, and both grate much finer than is usual in most Western cooking. The grater for giant white radish (*daikon*) gives a somewhat coarser result than the grater used for ginger or *wasabi* horseradish.

Japanese professional chefs use tin-coated copper graters; from the point of view of quality and durability, these are excellent but they are expensive and probably difficult to find abroad. The average home has graters made of stainless steel or aluminum or plastic; the older, traditional material is pottery. The traditional form of these utensils is a flat surface textured with raised spikes.

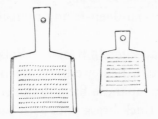

If you prefer the Japanese type, two graters are handy—one with spikes rather widely set on the grating surface for general all-purpose work; and one with tightly set, small spikes for fine grating of ginger and *wasabi* horseradish. Some manufacturers make "two-in-one" graters with surfaces of both types. Recently, a grater of stainless steel or plastic, with small spikes set around round holes, the whole grater often forming the top of a plastic box to catch the gratings, has become popular. This is an all-purpose grater for both *daikon* and ginger. If necessary, the finest hole, on a multipurpose Western grater can be used for *daikon* but not for ginger or *wasabi*.

Grate onto cheesecloth if liquid must be extracted from the grated material, or onto a dish for convenience in moving the gratings. (Actually the juice from grated ginger can be pressed out with your hands.) Hold the grater at a 45° angle, pressing it down so the base is firm and steady. For *wasabi*, grate gently, with a continuous *circular* motion, not in jerks or backward and forward.

Be sure to clean the grater so that nothing remains between the spikes. Wash in water, with a bit of salt and vinegar if you like.

GRINDING BOWL (MORTAR) (*suribachi*; すり鉢) AND PESTLE (*surikogi*; すりこぎ): These utensils are designed to crush and grind seedy materials with speed and little exertion.

The "mortar" is a sturdy high-fired pottery bowl textured with a combed pattern on the unglazed inside. The outside is usually glazed a rich, warm brown, though recently, for some reason, *suribachi* glazed hideous pink have appeared. The textured interior of the "mortar" acts like the surface of a grater, making the *suribachi* more efficient and easier to use than a conventional, smooth-surfaced mortar.

Bowls come in various sizes, from about 5½ inches (14 cm) in diameter to large ones more than a foot (30 cm) across. Recently, grinding bowls have been manufactured in molded plastic, but that plastic, while sturdy, does not have the necessary weight for the work. For the purposes of the home cook, a medium-sized pottery grinding bowl, about 9 inches (23 cm) across at the top, is the most versatile.

A wooden pestle may come with the *suribachi*. If you must buy your pestle separately, choose a long one to provide good leverage.

To use the mortar, set it on top of a damp cloth so that the bowl does not move while you work. Add the material to be ground gradually as you work. Hold the top of the pestle loosely in your cupped palm and keep this hand stationary. Place your other hand on the pestle about halfway up from the rounded tip. Rotate the pestle and press down so that the rounded tip crushes the contents of the mortar against the grooved ridges. Hold the pestle firmly yet loosely. Move with the whole of your arms from the shoulder.

To clean the mortar, you may need to use the tip of a bamboo skewer once in a while to loosen any hard bits that stick in the bowl's grooves. Wash with plain water and a stiff brush.

OMELETTE PANS (*makiyakinabe*; 巻き焼き鍋): The Japanese omelette is rolled as it is fried so that it forms a neat cylinder, equally as thick at the ends as at the middle. A rectangular pan was developed to allow the making of such omelettes or egg rolls. Some omelette pans are cast iron or heavyweight aluminum, but the best are heavy copper coated with tin.

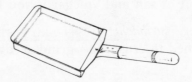

The melting point of tin is relatively low, so avoid putting a good tin-coated copper omelette pan over high heat while empty. After use, clean it by wiping it with oil and then a clean cloth. Do not scrub with abrasive pads or brushes; they wear away the tin. This pan is used for nothing but eggs, but it needs seasoning before its first use. Do this by sautéing a few sliced vegetables in a couple of Tbsps of oil.

SKEWERS (*kushi*; 串): You may already have long stainless steel barbecue skewers in your kitchen, but for Japanese cooking you need an assortment, including short, 8-inch (20-cm), bamboo skewers. Because skewers are used for so many grilled Japanese dishes, you can find many different kinds of skewers at Japanese provisions stores.

Long, 15-inch (35-cm) or longer, stainless steel skewers are good for large fish such as sea bream. Ten-inch (25-cm) lengths are convenient for smaller fish such as perch, but the long skewers can also be used (see pages 178ff for details on how to skewer fish).

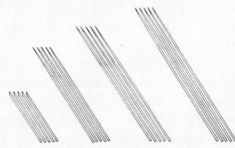

Points of metal skewers must be kept very sharp, a fact sometimes overlooked. Sharpen points on a whetstone, and you will eliminate skewering struggles. After use, sprinkle skewers with scouring powder and rub clean. If your skewers are steel, not stainless steel, wrap them in dry newspaper to prevent rust.

Bamboo skewers are used for such foods as YAKITORI chicken and DEEP-FRIED MIXED KEBABS (pages 186 and 418), which are eaten directly off the skewer. Points are liable to break or burn over the open fire, but there is something you can do to prevent this. Before skewering food, burn the skewer tip till just black and then plunge into water.

Bamboo skewers are also used to probe food to test for doneness, just as in Western cooking a fork pricks simmering vegetables to see if they are done. Bamboo skewers may be shortened and used for skewering shelled ginkgo nuts, parboiled quail eggs, and the like for one-pot dishes. You can also skewer raw shrimp lengthwise with bamboo skewers to keep them from curling during boiling.

You may wash and store bamboo skewers, or throw them away after one or several uses. They are inexpensive and disposable.

STEAMERS (*mushiki* 蒸し器 or *seiro* 蒸籠): Basically, two types of steamers are used in Japan—bamboo and metal. The first is a set of round wooden tiers placed over a boiling pot; each tier has a bamboo latticework bottom, so steam rises and circulates throughout. Such steamers are of Chinese design. The other, usually square in shape, has tiers with round holes in their bottoms; the set includes a big bottom pot that holds the boiling water.

In Japanese cooking, the food is often arranged first in individual serving vessels and then placed in the steamer. The square, modern steamers of metal are spacious and hold large amounts, but in fact the wooden type is more efficient because the material is an insulator and also absorbs moisture. See Steaming chapter for a discussion of steamers, pages 207ff.

WOODEN DROP-LID (*otoshi-buta*; 落し蓋): The drop-lid is a necessity in preparing simmered dishes (see pages 218ff). Made of wood, this lid is slightly smaller in diameter than the straight-sided pot, so that it fits down into the pot and floats directly on top of the foods being simmered. In this position, the drop-lid forces the even distribution of simmering liquid and heat penetration, makes flavors penetrate foods, and prevents the simmering liquid from breaking into a rolling boil. Because there is no boiling action, foods are not tumbled about, and the shapes of fragile ingredients are not harmed.

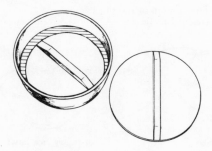

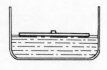

Wood is a natural material for drop-lids because it is not too heavy or too light and does not chemically interact with foods. To prepare a wooden drop-lid for its first use and eliminate woody odors, soak it first for a short time in a medium-strength solution of water and bicarbonate of soda (*or* in the cloudy water that runs off from rice when you wash it). Immediately before using, always soak the drop-lid in water for a few minutes; if a bone-dry lid is used, it is likely to absorb the juices of the pot and will carry that particular odor forever. After using, wash with water and mild soap, rinse, and let dry completely in the open air before storing.

If you see wooden drop-lids on sale at your Japanese goods stores, buy some because they are not regularly imported. They are not expensive. Drop-lids and alternatives are discussed in the Simmering chapter, pages 220ff.

DISHES

simmered or steamed foods   broiled or deep-fried foods

salad

rice   soup

place setting

soup bowl   SAVORY CUP CUSTARD cup   bowl for simmered or
(lacquer)   steamed foods

rice *donburi*   ordinary rice bowl

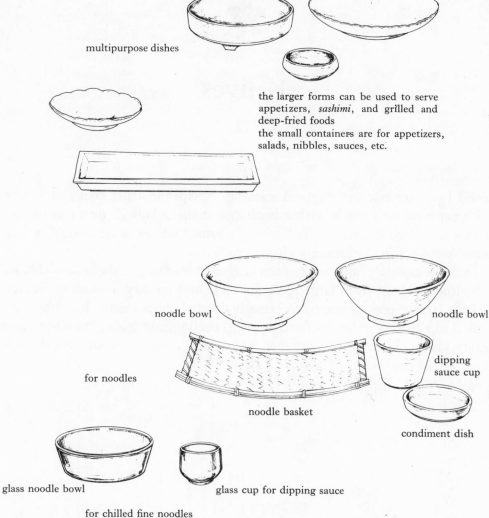

multipurpose dishes

the larger forms can be used to serve appetizers, *sashimi*, and grilled and deep-fried foods
the small containers are for appetizers, salads, nibbles, sauces, etc.

noodle bowl

noodle bowl

for noodles

noodle basket

dipping sauce cup

condiment dish

glass noodle bowl

glass cup for dipping sauce

for chilled fine noodles

donabe casserole

platter for food

dipping bowl

condiment dish

one-pot cooking set

Knives

Good tools are essential to good cooking. Recipes instruct cooks to accomplish some minor miracle with a *small* "good sharp knife," or a feat of skill with a *large* "good sharp knife." Sharply honed knives of good-quality steel are obviously foremost among kitchen tools.

In the completely outfitted French kitchen, for example, the array of bladed instruments range from large tools for meat and poultry, including cleavers to split large pieces of meat and straight-bladed choppers for breaking light bones, to a battery of knives for chopping, peeling, and paring, to all-purpose utility knives, to small instruments for scraping lemon zest or thin slices of other citrus rind.

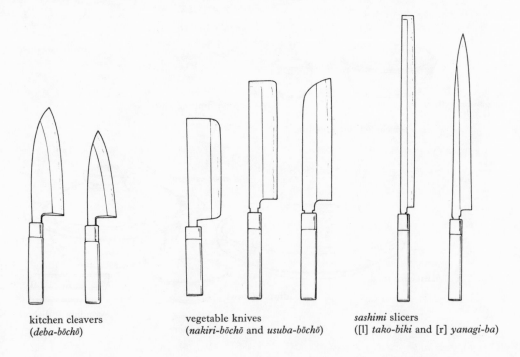

kitchen cleavers
(*deba-bōchō*)

vegetable knives
(*nakiri-bōchō* and *usuba-bōchō*)

sashimi slicers
([l] *tako-biki* and [r] *yanagi-ba*)

A similarly varied group of bladed instruments is to be found in the Japanese kitchen. Of course, the shapes of Japanese knives are different from those of the West because blade shapes evolve in conjunction with native techniques of food preparation and indigenous foods. There are three Japanese knives that do most of the work:

1. Kitchen carver (*deba-bōchō*): This is basically a fish knife, but it is used for basic cutting of fish, chicken (through light chicken bones too), and meat. It is made in many sizes; the medium and large sizes with blades from 7 to 12 inches (18 to 30 cm) long are for average or heavy work. This knife seems thick and heavy to most Westerners at first, but in fact it is very versatile and can do delicate work.

2. Vegetable knife (*nakiri-bōchō* and *usuba-bōchō*): In its round-ended version, this basic vegetable chopper is sometimes mistakenly described as a cleaver. It is much lighter than any cleaver. It is used for paring vegetables, for slicing, chopping, and mincing. All can be done with amazing efficiency and speed with this knife. For small quantities, it is quicker and easier to use than a food processor, and it can be cleaned with a few wipes of a towel.

The term *nakiri-bōchō* refers to the vegetable knife commonly used in the home kitchen; its blade is usually black. *Usuba* are vegetable knives for professional use, have a number of shapes, and the cutting edge is on *one side only*. In Osaka, the "sickle-style" vegetable knife, with a rounded top front end, is preferred to the standard rectangular Tokyo-style vegetable knife.

While you can make your Western chef's knife and meat slicer do the duty of the Japanese carver and fish slicer, there is nothing quite as efficient in the Western knife collection as this vegetable knife. If you are going to invest in any Japanese knife, this is the one to buy.

3. Fish slicer (*sashimi-bōchō*): Long, thin-bladed knife developed to cut boned fish fillets. Its second use is to cut prepared foods, for example, BEEF AND BURDOCK ROLLS.

There are two main shapes. In Osaka, the knife is pointed and is known as a "willow-leaf blade" (*yanagi-ba bōchō*). In Tokyo, it has a blunt end, not a point, and is called an "octopus cutter" (*tako-biki bōchō*). Both come in various sizes with blades ranging in length from 7 to 15 inches (18 to 39 cm).

A European meat slicer can do the same basic jobs.

In the United States, Japanese knives are sold in some oriental shops and may be carried by stores that sell kitchen equipment and, of course, by professional cooking supply houses. But, as the descriptions above have made very clear, you can make do with European-type knives.

These three basic Japanese knives are made in a number of sizes (and weights) with blades of different lengths. So when you think about which knives to buy, consider the shape and size that will be best for you. If you bone a lot of chicken or fish, you will find a medium-sized carver is handy. A fish slicer is what you need if, for example, you enjoy *sashimi*, or thin-sliced roast beef for that matter.

In buying knives in general, you should consider not only the knife best suited to the foods you prepare most often, but also the type of cutting edge and material from which the knife is made. With regard to these two features, Japanese knives distinguish themselves quite easily. They are forged so that usually one side of the blade only holds the cutting edge, and they are made—at least the edge—of high-quality, hard carbon steel. A Japanese knife's cutting edge is usually on the right because most users are right-handed, whereas ordinary Western knives are sharpened on both sides of the blade. A single-edged blade cuts much faster and more cleanly than a double-edged one. (Left-handed Japanese knives with the cutting edge on the left side of the blade are also manufactured, but are more expensive.)

In the world of knives, two materials are favored for blades: carbon steel and stainless steel. With the Japanese ancient tradition of sword-making, which utilizes sophisticated techniques of forging steel and is practiced even today, it is no wonder that the same advanced forging techniques and high-quality hard steel are used in Japan for knives. The blade of a carbon steel knife can be honed so fine that it literally can split a hair, but to maintain such sharpness a blade needs honing before every use. Carbon steel blades are precision instruments that demand respect and are the choice of the professional cook. In fact, many Japanese chefs have two sets of steel knives, using them on alternate days. After honing, they let one set of knives rest for a day so that "raw" metallic post-honing tastes have time to disappear from the blade's edge.

The highest-quality knives (called *hon-yaki*, or "true-forged") are made of hard steel and are extremely expensive. The ordinary kitchen blade (*kasumi*—"haze" or "mist") is made differently. If we look at a cross-section of the *kasumi* type, which is what you would most likely buy, we see that the blade is comprised of a thin layer of hard steel, covered by a thick layer of soft steel. Only a thin edge of hard steel is exposed to form the cutting edge of the knife.

This ordinary type of knife, still *far* superior to stainless steel in sharpness, is not as durable as a hard steel "true-forged" blade, and it rusts more easily. If left unwiped after use even for 5 or 10 minutes, the blade begins to discolor. But if it is cared for properly, you can use it for life.

Stainless steel blades, typical of mass-produced Western knives, do not require the same attention that *hon-yaki* or *kasumi* knives do. This is probably the type of knife you already have in your kitchen. Once honed, stainless knives dull quickly and cannot keep the fine edge that is easy to maintain with a carbon steel knife. The only advantage of a stainless steel blade is that it does not rust, yet the effort needed to keep a good nonstainless blade from rusting is so small, one wonders what real advantage a stainless blade has. A dull knife demands much more time and effort in the kitchen—that is, you work harder and longer—than with a good, sharp blade.

A brief survey of the principles of cutting with a knife should prove helpful. There are three basic strokes:

1.   Drawing cut (*hiki-giri*): Place the heel of the cutting edge on the material, and cut by lightly pressing down or letting the weight of the knife itself do the work *while* drawing the knife towards you. This cutting motion applies mainly to the long blade of the *sashimi-bōchō* and is used for slicing raw fish for *sashimi* and for cutting cooked foods.

2.   Pushing cut (*oshi-giri*): Push the center of the blade *straight down* to make the cut. This is the way to cut through a sticky cake of *mochi* rice, for example, or how to cut through a thin, crisp sheet of *nori* seaweed without creating ragged edges.

3.   Thrusting cut (*tsuki-giri*): Cut with a *forward* thrusting motion. Cutting a cucumber into julienne strips is a good example. When a *nakiri-bōchō* is used to cut raw foods, this cutting motion is employed.

With all three strokes, the left (or free) hand plays a very important role. Resting on the food being cut, with knuckles guiding the knife (see page 139), it ensures smoothness of strokes and evenness in slice or piece size. Be sure to keep the fingers of the guiding hand curled and the thumb bent out of the way—preservation of fingers is sufficient motive to do this naturally. Hold the material to be cut lightly but firmly and never raise the edge of the blade higher than your knuckles. If the knife is raised too high, not only is it likely that your hand will suffer, it is hard to establish a good cutting rhythm.

There are some slight differences in ways of holding Japanese knives, depending on the type of knife you are working with.

The carver (*deba-bōchō*) is held in two ways.

When boning a chicken or cutting off a fish head or fins, for example, lay your index finger on the back of the knife as shown. With fingers and thumb, grasp the shank quite firmly. This hold stabilizes the wrist and makes for firm, smooth cutting.

To chop bones apart and cut joints, you will have to shift your grip a little. Twine your finger and thumb around the shaft near the blade firmly and make sure that you can move your wrist freely. For jointing, use the bottom of the blade (near the heel); this part of the blade is not as often used and as a result does not become dull as quickly as the point.

The vegetable knife (*nakiri-bōchō* or *usuba-bōchō*) may be held in two ways. One is to hold the shaft with four fingers and thumb just below the blade, and the other is to place your index finger along the front of the blade and the thumb on the back of the blade.

The slicer (*sashimi-bōchō*) is handled in one way. Remember that the entire length of the blade is used for slicing, so the grip has to facilitate a sliding motion of the knife, from the heel to the tip. Place your forefinger lightly on the front side of the blade, as shown, and use the weight of the blade to cut through the material as you draw the knife toward you. With relatively hard or tough material, you may have to exert light pressure.

In all cases, hold the knife lightly, not with a stranglehold grip. Your entire arm should move as a single unit from the shoulder. With the correct movement and rhythm, a knife becomes an extension of your hand, and there is no tension or awkwardness. Chopping from the wrist is tiring, not very neat, dulls the blade, and gives the chopping board a lot of wear and tear.

Two rules of safety should be closely observed. If a knife should happen to slip out of your hand while you are working, stand back and let it fall where it will. To put it simply, a freely falling knife is all blade and no handle. Do not try to grab for the knife.

Second, do not leave knives out while you work in places where they might "pop up" and injure you. Working in a routine, systematic way makes

holding a kitchen cleaver

holding a vegetable knife

holding a *sashimi* slicer

things not only pleasant and efficient, but safe. This means that you should *never* leave your knife where you may cover it from sight with dish towels, recipe cards, or the like. And *never* drop it into a sinkful of dishwater and expect to fish it out later unscathed. Treat your tools and yourself with respect.

Keeping knives sharp does require a little effort. This is no euphemism—the effort is not great. There are three ways to sharpen blades: honing with a whetstone, a grinder, and a steel. Japanese knives are only honed on a whetstone and should *never* be ground on a wheel or "sharpened" with steel. Such treatment may be all right for stainless steel or for other steel of Western kitchen knives, but it is not the correct way to keep a Japanese kitchen knife sharp, *especially* a high-quality, or even middle-quality, knife.

Honing on a whetstone is best for hard steel and may be used for stainless steel knives also. To keep a really fine edge, any kitchen knife should, ideally, be honed before every use. Professional chefs must be rigorous, but you need not go to this extreme. Stainless knives lose their edge quickly and resist honing, whereas a hard-steel edge dulls relatively slowly, if well taken care of, and it is easy to sharpen.

Whetstones are used in the same way East or West, but the grains and natures of whetstones may differ with different steel-forging traditions. In Japan, whetstones are quarried from well-known sites, and the stones may be given the name of the place where they are quarried or be named for color, pattern, etc. Stones are cut into blocks about 3 to 4 inches (8 to 10 cm) wide and 8 to 10 inches (20 to 25 cm) long, with a height of about 2 inches (5 cm). There is a school of thought that Western whetstones are not appropriate for Japanese steel. This is logical, since Japanese whetstones were chosen over the centuries to hone Japanese steel. It is certainly true that if you invest in a "true-forged" (*hon-yaki*) kitchen knife, which costs hundreds of dollars, you should also use the best type of whetstone for such a blade. But, for practical purposes, the finest grain of natural whetstone (or, reluctantly, composition) will serve to sharpen Japanese knives.

Before use, the stone should be immersed in or doused with water. Do not use an oil stone. The stone has to have an even surface. If wear has produced a groove in the stone, use a harder stone to grind down the grooved surface till it is level once again.

Set the stone on a damp towel or damp cutting board to give it a little traction so there is no slippage while you work.

To hone a blade, place the beveled cutting edge of the blade flat onto the moistened stone so that it is in direct contact, as shown below.

Grasp the handle firmly in your right hand, and with the fingertips of your left hand keep the blade firmly in contact with the stone. Push the blade away from you in an arc-shaped sweep. The entire length of cutting edge should be honed at each sweep. Release pressure a bit as you come to the end of the stroke, and pull the blade back to start. This stroking motion appears circular with speed and practice.

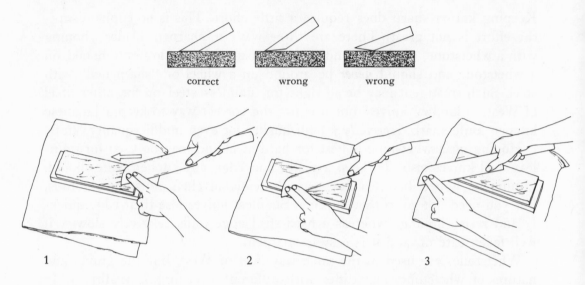

Honing requires that you put your whole body into the movement. It is not something that you do only with your hands and forearms. Stand in front of the stone with one foot in front of the other for a stable position. Use your arms, shoulders, and torso in the honing motion.

Once you have got your knives sharp, keep them that way. Do not store them in a drawer to be jostled around and chipped. Keep knives in a special place—in a special drawer with slots, in a rack, or in a stand.

Where there are good knives, there should also be good chopping blocks. The surface on which you use a knife affects the sharpness of the blade. The best surface on which cutting can be done is wood.

The best chopping blocks are boards with the grain running the length of the board. In Japan, cypress (*hinoki*) wood is the most common material. Willow is also good. There are also plastic boards, which are sanitary and kind on knives, but are not aesthetic. The rigorous Japanese cook will have three boards—for fish, for vegetables, and for "finishing."

Never soak wooden boards to clean them. Wash them quickly with warm water, rinse thoroughly, and wipe dry. Let the wood dry thoroughly; do not store while still damp. Dry your board in the sun occasionally.

Cutting boards should be as large as possible. Boards without legs allow you to use both sides.

Selecting and Cutting Fish, Chicken, and Vegetables

Fresh fish, chicken, and choice crisp vegetables comprise most of the ingredients of Japanese cooking. In fact, vegetables have their own cuisine—under Buddhist influence, an elegant vegetarian cooking called *shōjin ryōri* evolved centuries ago. This subject alone can be treated in an entire book.

Included in this lesson are ways to choose and shop for these foodstuffs. Essentially, this means picking quality—foods that have the best flavor and texture. Westerners eating Japanese food never fail to remark on the beautiful presentation of dishes, and a large part of presentation is in the cutting. This chapter also discusses the cutting techniques for fish, chicken, and vegetables, plus a few points on how to enhance the natural flavor of foods.

Every ethnic cuisine in the West has one or more fish specialties, but no Western nation uses fish to such an extent that it can be regarded practically as a foundation of the cuisine. The Japanese, however, do. And to cook Japanese food it is necessary to know something about fish.

First and foremost, you have to be able to tell whether a fish is really fresh. If the fish is whole, look to see if the scales are intact and not slimy. Scales in old fish drop out easily and become superficially slimy. The gills should be bright red, since a lot of blood is contained in them. If a fish is old, the area around the gills turns whitish and smells of rot. Fish eyes are another indicator—they should be big and clear. Stay away from fish with clouded or bloody eyes. A fish whose belly is hard and elastic will be fresh. Fish begin to decay first in the viscera, and this is the part that turns soft and bad first. Give a fish a few pokes to make sure it is firm. Use your nose too. Fresh fish smell like the ocean; there should be no reek—not even a hint.

These criteria for freshness are the most reliable guide, lacking a great amount of experience, but they are "grandmother's rules" because they apply to whole ungutted fish, which is how fish were displayed in markets years ago. Today, it is often the case that fish are gutted, filleted, and often skinned, ready to be cooked. So judge the overall quality of the fish shop by the whole fish you see, even though that might not be the fish you buy. And, once you find a reliable fishmonger, stick with him. If bad fish should come into your kitchen, let him know—it's the only way he can improve his service.

Learning about fish is quite easy. It just involves a little experience. There are not that many fish commonly available on the market; a bit of directed interest and culinary adventuring in a quiet way will make you conversant with what your trusted fishmonger sells in a relatively short time. It is when your knowledge takes on depth that the excitement starts.

Anyone who has looked into fish names even superficially, or, for that matter, who has purchased fish on the East and West coasts of the North American continent, knows that names of fish approach total chaos. The same fish is known by different names in different places; totally unrelated fish are known by the same name; names and whole groups are mistaken and confused (something called a sole may really be a flounder), and so on. Until some kind of sanity or clarity is established in common fish names, it is very hard to write with authority about fish of other than a limited geographical area. With this heavy qualification, I beg the reader's indulgence.

The fish tables included at the back of the book are very rough indeed but may help show what freedom you have in fish cookery. If a recipe calls for a fish that is either unavailable or too expensive, you can choose a fish with similar characteristics and do just as well. This is especially true when preparing Japanese dishes abroad. For instance, the "true" sea bream, which Japanese prize, is not found off any other shores, but Japanese bream, being a firm-fleshed, lean white fish, may be substituted for by red snapper or porgy or any other lean white fish with estimable results. So, though recipes in this book maintain authenticity and stipulate the correct Japanese fish, by all means use whatever fish is available and appropriate.

The leanness or fattiness of fish of course is a determinant of flavor and also has a bearing on cooking method. Lean saltwater fish have fat contents of only 1 to 5 percent, and most of the fat is in the liver, which is removed in gutting. The flesh is extremely white owing to the low fat, and it is liable to become dry during cooking if moisture is not retained in some way.

Fatty fish have from 5 to 35 percent oil, and flesh of fatty fish ranges from pinkish to blood red, depending on fat content. The flavor of saltwater fatty fish is more affected by season than is the case with white-fleshed fish. A number of factors combine to change fat levels in the flesh, and unless these fish are eaten in season, their flavor is not all it might be. Some very general seasonal comments are included in the table, but the best way to learn about catches is to see what is happening at your fishmonger's from month to month. He cannot help but notice your interest. Talk to him. You will learn a lot.

Freshwater fish are not categorized so easily. Fat content ranges from 1 to 50 percent; for example, river trout is lean, but carp is oily. Even within one species, fat content is not entirely predictable. Season, spawning, region, whether the fish are commercially farmed in restricted waters or caught wild, all contribute to the presence or absence of fat. Some very general tendencies toward leanness or fattiness are noted in the fish table (page 487), but these should be interpreted rather loosely.

All fish are suitable for *sashimi*, if fillets are cut in the proper way and appropriate dipping sauces offered. Japanese do not concern themselves with the possibility of parasites in selecting fish for *sashimi*. Experience has indicated which species can be and which should not be used. If you are concerned about whether a freshwater species can be used for *sashimi*, the United States Department of Agriculture can probably answer your questions.

The shape of a fish tells you how to go about gutting and filleting it. Look at the sketches of the two generalized fish types.

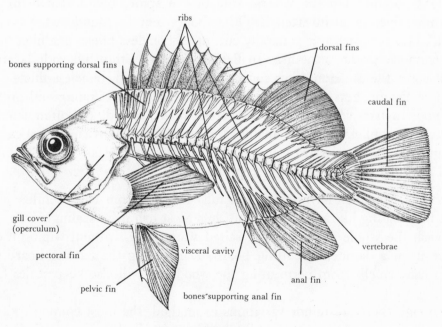

ROUNDFISH

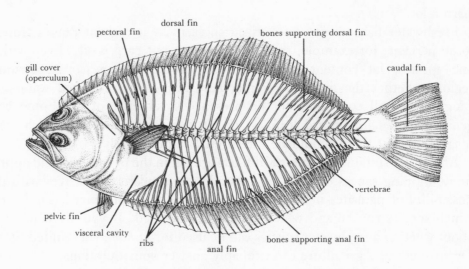

pectoral fin
dorsal fin
bones supporting dorsal fin
gill cover
(operculum)
caudal fin
pelvic fin
visceral cavity
ribs
anal fin
bones supporting anal fin
vertebrae

FLATFISH

With the round-bodied fish, bones stick up from the spine in a single straight column. On the ventral side of the spine, bones radiate in two columns, making an inverted-V. Other bones may be found in the "center line." This sort of fish is generally cut into 2 boneless fillets, one fillet being cut from each side of the fish. In flatfish, relatively thin but wide layers of flesh cover the skeleton. This sort of fish yields 4 thin, boneless fillets.

Most fishmongers will take care of all the chores of scaling and gutting for you. In fact, you can easily buy fresh fillets, boned, and often skinned. Butterfly-cut fillets are also available at many fish markets as a matter of course. Large fish are cut crosswise into 1¼-inch (3½-cm) steaks. But it is just as well to know what to do from step one.

Scaling: Most fish have scales, generally ranging from large coinlike chips to a fine coating like silver dust, and thus most fish need scaling.

Wash the whole fish in lightly salted water, and, without wiping it dry, place it on a dampened cutting board. Dampening the cutting board will keep fishy smells from permeating the wood and will also keep scales from sticking to it.

Though there are minor variations in method, the most common way of scaling fish in Japan might be helpful to anyone who has never scaled a fish. For the experienced, ignore the following; just scale the fish carefully.

Lay the wet fish on the board, its head facing left. With your left hand, grasp the head firmly and raise the fish up off the board slightly so that the body is bowed. With the front edge of a kitchen carver or a sharp-edged Western scaler, scrape the scales away in short strokes from tail to head. It is quite easy around the middle of the body, but care and thoroughness are required around the head, as well as the soft belly, where the flesh is most easily damaged or broken.

Removing gills: Whenever a fish is to be served head and tail intact, the spongy, red-pleated gills must be removed. If you gut the fish through the mouth (*tsubo-nuki* technique below), you will save yourself this step. If not, follow this procedure.

The gill flaps will open automatically if you force open the mouth of the fish. To free the gills, cut the bone under the lower jaw of the fish, as shown. Place thumb and forefinger of your free hand into the opened gill slit on one side and spread apart to make the opening even wider. Holding the gill slit open, insert the tip of the knife and cut the base of the gills, where they are attached to the bone, as shown, and then scrape round the edges of the cavity. Part of the gills will come free. Pin them to the cutting board with the knife tip and lift the fish up; the gills should come away. Rinse the fish.

Gutting: To maintain freshness, fish should have their gills removed and be gutted as soon as possible. There are three ways of removing innards from a roundfish. The usual method anywhere is to make a slit along the underbelly from the anal orifice to the pelvic fin and to scoop out the viscera with your hands. Do not puncture the liver or roe—they are delicacies in themselves. Then, run the tip of the knife along the inside of the cavity along the spine to break blood pockets. Wash the cavity well.

The second method, known as the *tsubo-nuki* technique, is to bring the innards out through the mouth. Use this method for fish that are to be served whole. The body is left intact and will keep its shape very well, whereas belly-slit fish twist out of shape in cooking. This technique can be used only for small fish, no larger than horse mackerel (*aji*).

To gut through the mouth, first sever the bone under the lower jaw, as is done for removing the gills. Take a pair of (throw-away pine) chopsticks, poke one chopstick into the fish's mouth to a point beyond the gills, then insert the other chopstick. Grasp both chopsticks and twist a few complete turns till the gills and innards catch on them, then pull the lot out. Rinse the fish well. It is tricky to gut the fish in this way unless it is absolutely fresh. If there is some question of freshness, decapitate the fish and scoop the innards out through the cut. If the fish has been frozen, the innards might stick to the visceral cavity. Cut along belly to scoop them out. The headless body will still keep its shape nicely while cooking.

The third method is similar to the second in that it does little to destroy the body's basic shape. Make a small incision above one pelvic fin and pull the internal organs out through this small opening. Used with larger fish.

| REMOVING GILLS | TSUBO-NUKI TECHNIQUE |

1. sever bone below jaw

1

2. cut bone inside top of gills

2

3

3. pull out gills with knife tip

1–3. insert chopsticks beyond gills, twist 2 or 3 times, and extract innards together with gills

4. pin down gills and pull fish away

The viscera of flatfish take up only a small amount of space in comparison with roundfish. There are two ways to gut flatfish. The first is as described immediately above: make a small incision behind the gills on the white (under) side of the fish and pull innards out. The second is to decapitate the fish and press the innards out. The first method preserves the shape, the second is a prelude to filleting.

Filleting: Japanese cooks use three fundamental filleting techniques for fish. These techniques take their names from the number of pieces into which the fish is cut. These are:

> *nimai oroshi*, or "two-piece cutting"
> *sanmai oroshi*, or "three-piece cutting"
> *gomai oroshi*, or "five-piece cutting"

In fact, these cutting techniques are very similar to those used in the West. The only absence is of boning roundfish; stuffed, whole, boned fish are not in the Japanese repertoire.

Filleting, but not skinning, may be done several hours in advance of final preparation. Japanese cooks trim fillets and wrap them in damp kitchen toweling and refrigerate. The point is to wrap fillets in something protective and absorbent.

Nimai oroshi ("two-piece cutting"): For roundfish only. Gut through the belly and cut head off. Starting from the head end and placing the knife above the skeleton, cut the entire length of the fish. Use the full blade of a kitchen carver in a gentle drawing motion. Bones will be left in each half of the fish, but one half will have the backbone, while the other will be left with far fewer bones. The fillet with the backbone is good to use for grilling because the skin preserves moisture and the bones help keep the shape and add flavor. In American markets, fish cut this way is sold as "pan-dressed halves."

Sanmai oroshi ("three-piece cutting"): For roundfish. One boneless fillet is cut from each side of the fish, and the skeleton is left as the third piece with little flesh on it (use for stock or deep-fry or grill as a nibble to serve with *sake*). Roundfish range so greatly in body shapes and widths that the basic "three-piece cutting" technique for four representative roundfish types—bream, mackerel, sea bass, and sillago (*kisu*)—are described below.

Bream, or other tight white-fleshed fish, such as grunt and yellowjack, have bodies that are comparatively wide from dorsal to ventral fin but are relatively narrow laterally. The fish is gutted and gilled in the conventional way. For slicing, use a kitchen carver. Fish should be rinsed but patted dry. Cutting board is dampened.

FILLETING SEA BREAM
(*nimai* and *sanmai oroshi* techniques)

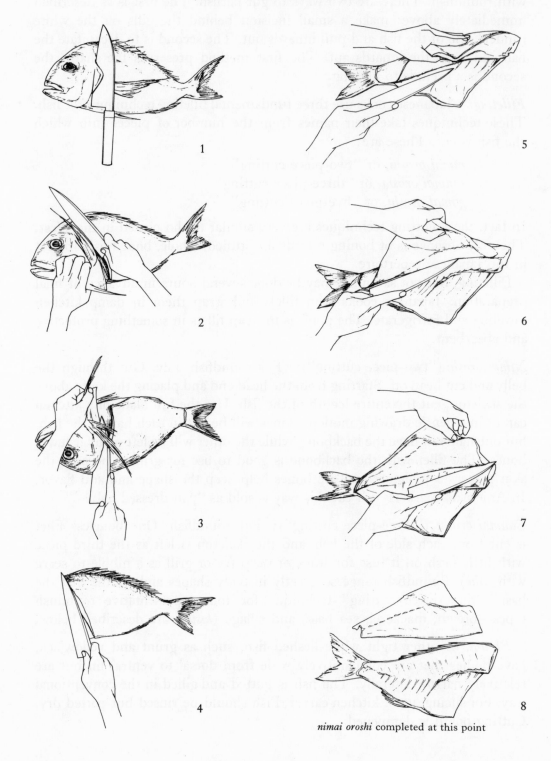

1

2

3

4

5

6

7

8

nimai oroshi completed at this point

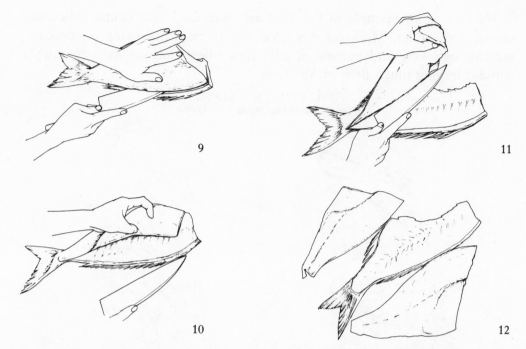

9

11

10

12

1.   First cut away the bone that connects each horny gill flap (operculum). Unless these bones on both sides of the fish are removed, fillets cannot be separated into dorsal and belly parts later.

2–4.   To cut off the head, slide your knife under the bone near the gills, and push the knife forward with your free hand to sever the spine. Turn the fish over and make a second stroke.

5.   With your free hand gently pressing down on the fish to keep it from slipping, start cutting along the belly from the head end and cut through the bones at the back of the visceral cavity (the back of the ribcage).

6.   Use the point of the knife to cut through the hard bones that radiate off the spine above the visceral cavity (the top of the ribcage).

7, 8.   After the hard bones have been cut, using a drawing motion of the knife (do not saw with it or force it into the flesh), continue cutting toward the back and tail. Hold the fillet up and out of the way until it is freed. Lay this first fillet aside. The "two-piece cutting" (*nimai oroshi*) is completed.

9.   To cut the second fillet, turn the fish over, so that the tail is at your left and the back is facing you. Begin cutting from the head end, working the blade as close as you can above the skeleton.

10, 11.   Hold the fillet up as you work, draw the knife blade lightly toward you, and separate the second fillet.

12.   The cutting completed, there are 3 parts—2 fillets and flesh-webbed skeleton.

Mackerel is an example of fish that are "tubular," like young yellowtail, saurel, and mullet. Mackerel is a good fish to start practicing on because, even though long and narrow, it has thick fillets that can be cut quickly without leaving much flesh on the bone.

FILLETING MACKEREL
(*nimai* and *sanmai oroshi* techniques)

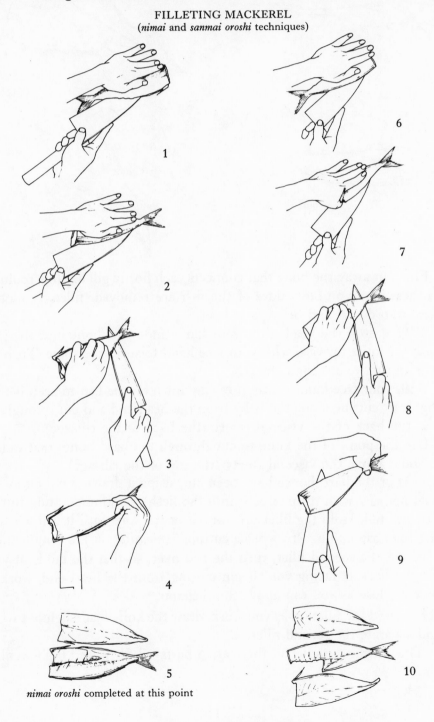

nimai oroshi completed at this point

1.   Place the fish on a dampened cutting board so that the tail is at the left. Use a kitchen carver. Hold it so that your forefinger rests on the back of the blade and your other fingers and thumb are curled round the handle. This grasp gives the wrist stability, but also enough flexibility to make a smooth drawing cut. Your left hand, palm open, should rest on the fish to keep it from moving.

Slice from the belly to the tail, using a drawing motion of the blade. The knife point should reach the center of the spine, and the blade should be at an angle as it cuts back from the visceral cavity to the tail. Lift the fillet up and out of the way as it is cut free.

2.   Reverse the fish so that the tail is on your right and the back now faces you and proceed to cut along the back from the tail to the head end.

3.   Reverse fish again so tail is on your left and back faces you. Cut from head end to tail; blade should go no farther than the spine.

4, 5.   Flip fish over so tail is on your right and belly faces you. Cut from tail to head to free fillet. This completes the "two-piece cutting" (*nimai oroshi*).

6–10.   Turn the fish over and cut the second fillet in the same manner as the first.

Feel the fillets for stray bones and pluck them out with tweezers. Remember to cut off the shallow layer of bones remaining at what was the visceral cavity *at the beginning of each recipe*, not at this point.

Sea Bass. The fillets are separated by pulling the meat from the bones, as compared to the usual cutting.

FILLETING SEA BASS
(*sanmai oroshi* technique)

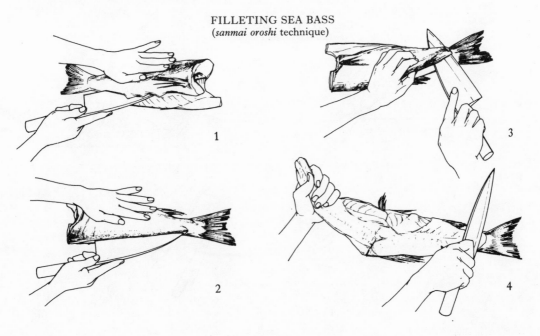

The fish is already decapitated, rinsed, wiped dry, and placed on a dampened cutting board. Use a kitchen carver.

1.   Tail should be at left, belly facing you. Cut from the *bottom* of the visceral cavity to the tail just above the bones until the blade reaches the spine.

2.   Reverse fish so its tail is now on your right and the back is facing you. Cutting just above the bones, slice in as far as the spine, drawing the knife from tail to head.

3.   With the fish in the same position (tail at right), pick up the fillet with your left hand, insert the knife under the meat at the tail, blade horizontal and edge toward the tail, and separate the fillet from the tail.

4.   Grasp the fillet at the tail end, where it has been freed from the bone (much of the fillet is still attached to bones) and firmly pull the flesh away, freeing the fillet.

Turn the fish over and remove a second fillet in the same manner.

Kisu (sillago). Use a long-bladed *sashimi* knife for filleting this small fish that has soft, easily broken flesh.

Cut off the head from behind the gills, slice open belly to gut. Rinse and pat dry.

1.   With the tail end at your left and back facing you, begin from the head end, with the blade horizontal and as close to the spine as possible, and cut through the flesh in one smooth motion. Remove the fillet.

2, 3.   To cut the second fillet, turn the fish over—tail still on left but belly facing you—and proceed in the same manner.

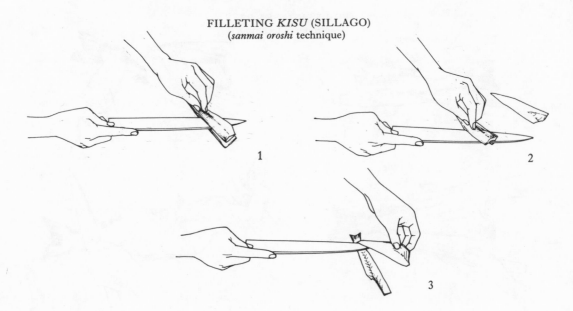

FILLETING *KISU* (SILLAGO)
(*sanmai oroshi* technique)

1

2

3

Gomai oroshi ("five-piece cutting"): For flatfish only. Two boneless fillets can easily be cut from each side of the fish. The four fillets thus cut, plus the flesh-webbed skeleton remaining after filleting, equal five pieces, hence the name "five-piece cutting." In fact, this method of filleting flatfish is almost identical to the one Western chefs use.

You need scale only the brown upper side; the white (bottom) side is nearly scaleless. Gut, rinse, and pat dry.

FILLETING FLATFISH
(*gomai oroshi* technique)

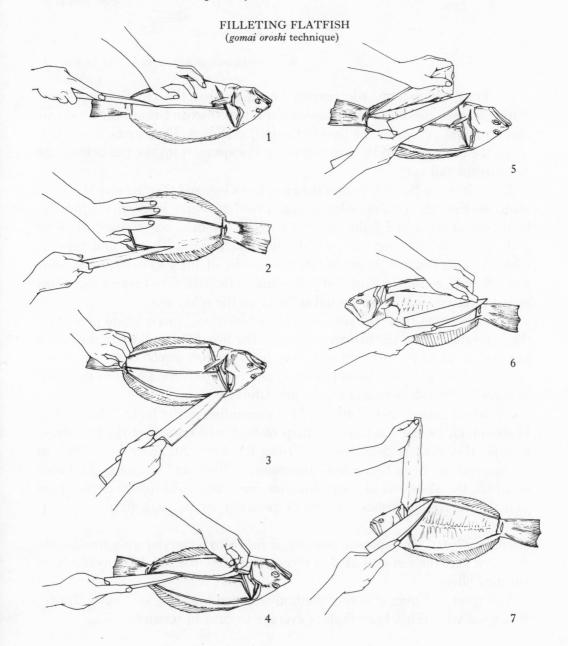

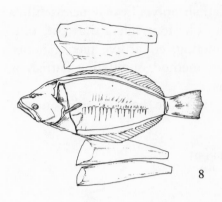 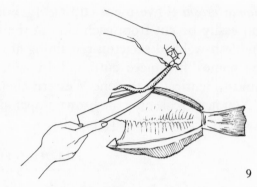

8   9

removing the strip of flesh at the base of the fins

1.   Place the fish on the cutting board so that the tail is facing you. With a kitchen carver make an angled cut across the fish behind the head and also a straight cut across the base of the tail, as shown. Then make an incision along the center line of the fish following the spine, from the cut behind the head to the tail cut.

2, 3.   Reverse the fish so that the head faces you and then reverse the knife blade so that the cutting edge is up. From the first incision behind the head, cut along a line following the base of the fins, but a small distance away from the fins themselves (this distance varies with size and type of flatfish). This distance is greater in the middle of the fish than at the head and tail ends, as shown. Cut along one side to the tail, then reverse fish again so tail faces you and cut from tail to head on the other side.

4, 5.   Starting from the center and head incisions, insert blade point into the left-hand half of the fish and cut away the first fillet as close to the bones as possible. Hold the fillet up and away from the fish as you cut.

6–8.   Reverse fish so head faces you and remove second fillet in the same manner. Turn fish over and repeat procedure.

9.   Many minute bones attach the halolike fins to the body. This is why fillets cannot be cut too close. A strip of flesh will remain at the fin edges; because this flesh is delicious, in *hirame* flounder, cut these bits away, as shown, and use them for *sashimi*, *sunomono*, grilling, and steaming. You may also turn the skeletons of *karei* flounder into deep-fried tidbits or use them to make interesting dishes (FLOUNDER TREASURE SHIPS, page 405).

Skinning fillets: In Japanese cooking, if fish is to be served without skin, for the most part the removal of skin takes place after the fish has already been cut into fillets.

The most common skinning method is called *soto-biki*, or "outer draw." It is used with fish whose flesh is average to firm in texture.

Place fillet *skin down* on a damp cutting board. The tail should be facing you. Use the long-bladed *sashimi* knife. Hold the end of the tail with your free (usually left) hand and make an incision as near to the end of the fillet as possible. When the blade reaches the skin, pull the skin to the left, while the blade at a slight angle moves to the right with a sawing motion, cutting as close to the skin as you can. The aim is to cut away only the skin.

CONVENTIONAL SKINNING METHOD
(*soto-biki* technique)

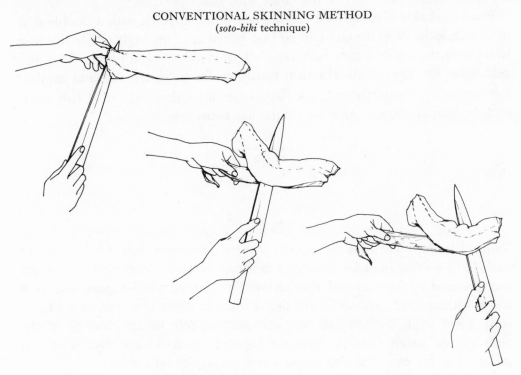

For fish with soft flesh that is liable to break or flake, use another skinning technique, the *uchi-biki*, or "inner draw."

SKINNING DELICATE FISH
(*uchi-biki* technique)

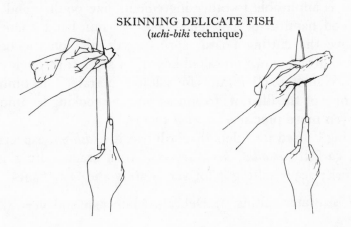

Place fillet skin down on a damp cutting board with the tail away from you. Reach across the fillet and hold the tail edge of the skin with your left hand. With a long-bladed *sashimi* knife, cut just above the skin, pulling the knife toward you. More of the flesh comes away with the skin in cutting this way than with the "outer draw," but soft fillets will remain undamaged.

With the types of raw fish served with skin as *sashimi* or *sushi*, you can soften the skin and improve the color with this operation:

Place fillet skin side up on a cutting board and cover it with a double fold of cheesecloth. Prop up one end so that board is at an angle. Pour scalding water over the covered fish. Remove cloth immediately and plunge fillet into cold water for 30 seconds. Swish it gently in this bath, remove, and pat dry.

Kannon-biraki (butterfly cut): A flap is cut on either side of a fish fillet, shrimp, etc., as shown. This technique has many uses.

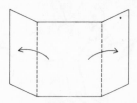

Salting: In Japanese cooking, almost without exception, fish is salted before cooking or grilling in order to extract moisture and any odor. Amounts of salt and timing of salting vary with the fish type. In general, white-fleshed fish takes less salt than fatty fish, and fatty fish are salted some time before cooking, while most white-fleshed fish take salt immediately before cooking or the flesh will be tough. The professional Japanese cook is very rigorous about salting, but for everyday purposes, a few principles will suffice.

Ground sea salt is the best, but regular kitchen salt may be used.

Furi-jio ("hand-sprinkled salt"): The most popular fish-salting technique, and one that is applicable to other ingredients like poultry and vegetables. Take a good handful of salt, and, holding your hand about 14 inches (35 cm) above the cutting board, sprinkle salt first on the board. Then placing fillet skin side down on salted board, let salt sift through your fingers onto the fish. Wait 40 to 60 minutes for salt to penetrate. This timing depends on the thickness of the fillet, its freshness, and the cooking technique. Salting times are given more precisely in each recipe.

Light salting is used for fillets that will become *sashimi*, especially tilefish, sillago, and garfish (*amadai, kisu, sayori*). An average salting is used for white, lean fish; heavy salting is for very watery and fatty fishes.

Tate-jio ("seawater salting"): Delicate white fish and very thinly sliced firm-textured white fish are salted by placing them in a salt-water bath. The solution should be about the same as seawater—about 3.5 percent salt. A convenient formula is 2 Tbsps salt in 1 quart (1 L) water. Let fish soak for 20 to 30 minutes maximum. Remove and pat dry.

For extra-subtle flavor, add a 3-inch (8-cm) square of *konbu* kelp to 1 quart (1 L) water.

Beta-jio or *mabushi-jio* ("salt covered"): Dredging in salt. A good technique for extremely fatty fish, which need much salt. Dredge on both sides about 60 to 90 minutes before cooking and let rest. Wash off salt just before cooking.

Kami-jio ("paper salting"): An exclusively Japanese salting technique used when only a very slight salting is required, mainly when fish is to be served raw as *sushi* or *sashimi*. Japanese traditionally use hand-laid paper (*washi*) for this procedure, but you may use absorbent paper toweling.

Sprinkle the board with an average amount of salt. On it lay a dry sheet of paper. On top of the paper, lay fish, Cover with a second sheet of paper and then salt the paper with an average sprinkling. Let this salted paper "sandwich" stand for 40 to 60 minutes. A slight amount of salt is drawn through the paper into the moist fish, and the result is a subtle background flavor.

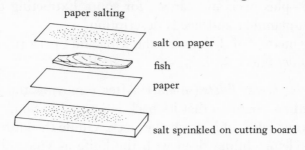

paper salting

salt on paper

fish

paper

salt sprinkled on cutting board

CHICKEN

Chicken (and poultry) did not fall into the Buddhist proscription against the killing of four-footed animals and thus became a part of Japanese cooking.

In Japan, chicken is sold primarily according to age. A 3- to 4-month-old chicken is called *hina* ("infant"). If the bird is allowed to fatten up for a few more months, it becomes a *waka-dori*, "young chicken" (4–6 months). Older than half a year, it becomes an *oya-dori*, "adult." Most home cooks do not buy a whole bird, but generally just the parts they need.

Tender young chickens are preferred for all Japanese cooking methods. White meat of breasts may be briefly boiled—just till pink at the center— cooled, shredded, and tossed in light salads (*aemono*). Because the inner breast fillet (the *sasami*—more about this below) is so tender, fine-textured, and lean, it makes a good *sashimi*; it is often served almost raw in thin slices with a bright-flavored dipping sauce. Likewise, the breast fillet is an elegant ingredient in clear soups. Bones are used for making soup stock; livers, hearts and gizzards are skewered and grilled for YAKITORI.

The meat that is most used comes from the leg. This is thought by the Japanese to be more interesting in taste than the breast. In fact, in disjointing the chicken, the drumstick and thigh are taken off together and kept in one piece. The whole leg is often boned, spread open, and the meat used in that form or cut to fit the recipe. The fine-textured white meat of the inner breast fillets—there are two to every bird—is also appreciated, but its use in Japanese cooking is limited. Measuring about 1 inch (2½ cm) at the widest and about 4 to 5 inches (10 to 13 cm) long, these fillets are called *sasami*, or "bamboo-grass fillets," because their narrow, tapered shape is reminiscent of the leaves of *sasa*, bamboo grass. The breast meat (other than *sasami*), and wings come next in popularity in Japanese cooking.

Disjointing a chicken in Japan involves nothing different or exotic and no detailed description is necessary here. The common method ends up with four usable pieces—two legs (drumstick plus thigh) and two wing and breast pieces—plus neck and carcass for soup. Extracting the *sasami* fillets is probably unfamiliar and needs description.

The method of disjointing the wing and breast relates directly to obtaining the *sasami* fillets, so it is best to start there.

Removing breast fillets (*sasami*): After removing the legs, place the bird on the cutting board so that its back is up, tail to you.

In your left hand, grasp the neck. Guide the knife between the neck meat and skeleton, biting deep with the knife as you follow the contours of the breast bones back from the neck toward the tail. After making this cut, grasp the whole wing securely and pull it firmly and evenly from the carcass. Most of the breast meat on that side of the bird will come off with the wing. Turn the bird and remove the other wing in the same way.

Finally, the only choice meat left on the carcass is the two *sasami*—inner breast—fillets. These are nestled in the hollow of the keellike bone that supports the breast muscles and are attached to it with white stringlike tendons.

The *sasami* fillets have to be detached from the breastbone. To do this, cut through the white tendons that hold them to the bone at either end, then slip your first two fingers under a fillet and run fingers the entire length of the meat; the fillet will be raised up and out of its nestling place. Remove the other fillet similarly.

The tendons must be removed from the fillets because they are tough. Pin the end of the tendon down on the board with your left fingernail (or fork or knife point) and with the body of a knife, scrape the meat off the tendon.

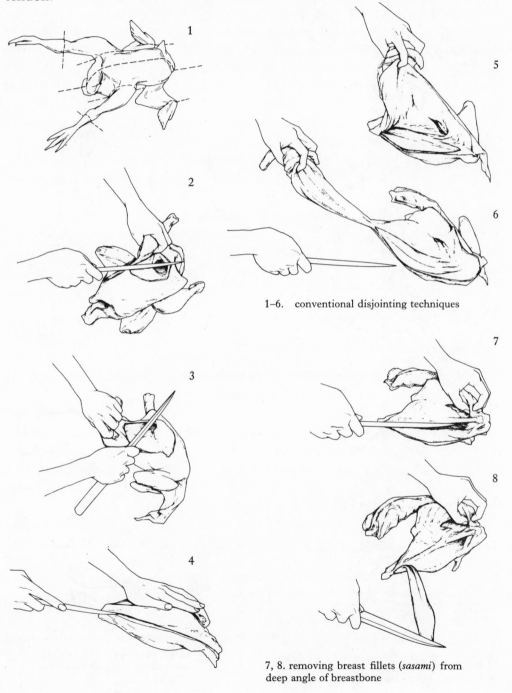

1–6. conventional disjointing techniques

7, 8. removing breast fillets (*sasami*) from deep angle of breastbone

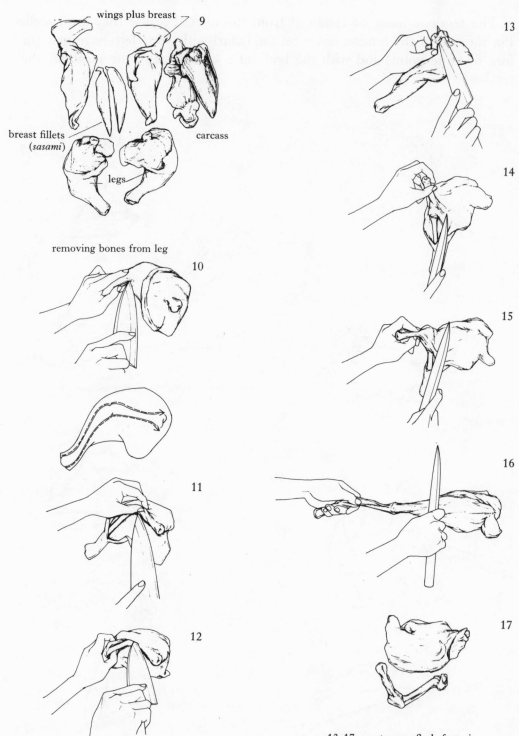

wings plus breast   9

breast fillets (*sasami*)   carcass

legs

removing bones from leg   10

11

12

13

14

15

16

17

10–12. cut along both sides of bone on inside of leg

13–17. cut away flesh from inside of bone and pull away bone from leg

Boning the leg: With a small sharp knife, make an incision down to the bone along the inner side of the leg, as shown. Fold back the flesh to expose the bones and joint.

The joint between drumstick and thigh bones may be cut or left intact before removing bones. The meat of the entire leg can now be spread out in one piece. Remove tendons before using.

Skinning and freshening (shimofuri): The skin of the boned leg and breast meat may or may not be removed, depending on the dish being made. With skin, a dish will be comparatively richer and more "hearty"; without, more refined. Generally, skin can be easily peeled off the cut pieces by hand, if you use a knife to start the work and then sever the skin at the end. Even though this is a hand process, be sure to work gently so as not to tear or deform the meat. If you come to a segment that resists, cut under the skin.

If chicken has been cut, wrapped, and stored in the refrigerator for a day or so, you can remove any chickeny odor with the following *shimofuri*, or "hoarfrost," technique.

Lay the meat flat, skin side up, on a cake rack, in a shallow colander, or the like. Pour boiling water over the meat just till the surface changes to pale white. Turn the meat quickly and douse the other side. Follow this with a cold water bath for a few seconds to prevent cooking. Pat dry.

If you are freshening *sasami* fillets, it is easiest to swish each one individually in a pot of boiling water for a few seconds, remove, rinse in cold water, and pat dry.

As for other poultry in Japanese cooking, duck is generally regarded as too heavy and too overpowering in taste to be eaten often. It appears in one-pot dishes with onions and bean curd and also grilled TERIYAKI style. All fat is avoided, so mainly the breast is used. Duck is always combined with such vegetables as long onions (*naganegi*), with flavors that can stand up to that of the duck.

Chicken is all-purpose and duck eschewed as too fatty, but in Japanese cooking, the real prince of poultry is quail. Though this small bird was once the food of the nobility, it is raised commercially today in Japan. (Quail eggs are also widely used.) The Japanese variety is different from that familiar in North America and Europe. A moderately expensive delicacy, but not out of the range of almost everyone to enjoy once in a while, quail are often grilled with a basting sauce or with salt. Sometimes they are covered with a light *miso* paste before being put over the fire, and they are often dusted lightly with fragrant *sansho* powder. Quail may also be simmered whole in rather strongly flavored soy-based stock.

VEGETABLES

The Japanese art of cutting and slicing vegetables always evokes admiration. Comments of approval slip out of even the most blasé diners with the appearance of tempting morsels—prize vegetables cut and arranged just so—such as lacelike lotus rounds, green cucumber circlets, "tea whisks" fashioned from tiny eggplants, and baby potatoes carefully pared into hexagons, to name just a few. Though vegetable shapes might occasionally seem exotic, all cutting is done with one underlying idea: to use a shape that capitalizes on the nature of the vegetable while enhancing its flavor. It is not so much cleverness or virtuosity as working to find the decorative shape that, while taking advantage of natural form and texture, also heightens flavor so that the whole can be best appreciated. Decorative shapes might be chosen to express the season, annual observances, etc. There are many such conventional shapes, developed over centuries of cooking tradition.

Cut or sliced vegetables are all related to a few fundamental geometric forms. Cutting is not difficult, but it does take a certain amount of practice to get the knack. Peeling a giant white radish (*daikon*) into a single, continuous sheet is good practice for controlling the knife. In fact, at the Tsuji school, aptitude for the kitchen is judged by how well entering students can perform this task.

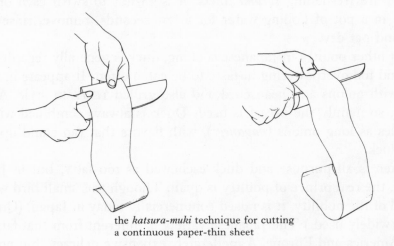

the *katsura-muki* technique for cutting
a continuous paper-thin sheet

This technique is a good place to begin this discussion of the practical points of cutting and slicing vegetables. For this technique, as for most general vegetable work, use a vegetable knife (an *usuba-bōchō* is best; see page 111). Hold the knife so that your index finger is curled above the grip around the back of the blade and your thumb very close to the cutting edge on the front, where it can "guide" cutting. Work is done in midair, not on a board. The secret of mastery is to move the blade backward and forward in a sawing rhythm while turning the radish cylinder with the left hand in coordination with the knife movement. This will take practice, obviously. For uniform thickness, the motion should be smooth and continuous. The knife should not force its way into the radish; rather, the radish should be fed into the knife.

This sheet of radish has many uses. One of them is to make shred-cut radish. Cut sheet into about 8-inch (20-cm) lengths, stack these, then chop stack crosswise into fine shreds. Such crisp radish shreds (or carrot, if *daikon* is not available) are one of the standard beds on which seafood dishes like *sashimi* are served. (Freshen by soaking shreds in cold water with a few ice cubes before serving.) The same technique is used for potato (see page 411).

This crosswise cut for rectangles displays basic knifework. Hold the knife as shown, thumb and three fingers around the grip but with the index finger

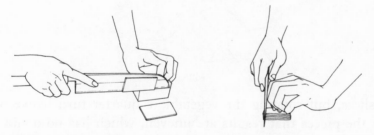

extended on the top half of the front of the blade for control. The blade is *always pushed forward*. The bent knuckles of the left hand, which is guiding the material and knife, are flush with the back of the blade, and the rest of the hand is arched—as if an egg was being held in the hollow of the palm. (The form and position of the guiding hand in cutting is generally the same in every country.)

When chopping, use a light touch. A professional chef prefers a heavy knife and allows the weight of the knife to work for him. No need to exert more force than necessary, or to strangle the food with your guiding hand. Automatic food processors certainly help speed the drudgery of chopping, mincing, and so on, for large quantities of food. For some of the operations below, you may depend on your electric assistant. But in Japanese cooking a food processor is of dubious aid for most family meals.

Rounds, half-moons, and quarter slices: Rounds and half-moons are the natural shape for cylindrical vegetables like giant white radish (*daikon*) and carrots. Bamboo, which is a tapering cylinder, lends itself to quarter slices.

Slice vegetables crosswise for rounds. If half-moons are required, first cut cylinder in half lengthwise, then slice. For quarter rounds, cut the vegetable lengthwise first into halves and then quarters. For efficiency, align two quarters and cut slices together.

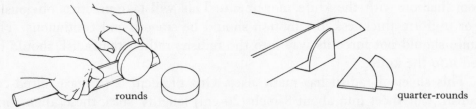

rounds

quarter-rounds

Diagonal slices and *"rolling wedges"*: Used primarily for cutting long and thin vegetables that are neither too soft nor too fibrous, such as long onions (*naganegi*) for SUKIYAKI, or burdock, carrots, and Japanese-type cucumber.

For the diagonal slice, hold the knife at an angle and make diagonal cuts across the vegetable, working your way along the root or stalk.

So-called rolling wedges are made by using the knife in the same way as

rolling wedges

for diagonal slices, but rotating the vegetable a quarter turn between cuts. The faces on the pieces that results are uneven, which has no doubt given rise to the Japanese name for this cutting technique—*ran-giri*, or "disorderly cut." "Rolling wedges" are good for burdock, carrots, and giant white radish (*daikon*) and can be adapted to bamboo for simmered dishes.

Bevel-edged cylinders: For vegetables that will be cut in thick rounds and simmered in large pieces. Turnip, giant white radish (*daikon*), and carrot are typical examples. Edges are beveled for a neater appearance. Straight edges are likely to crumble during simmering.

beveled cylinder

Sphere segments or *wedges (kushigata-giri):* When small round onions are called for, or tomatoes, as they sometimes are in Western-influenced dishes, they may be cut in quarters or in sixths. Cut the vegetable in half lengthwise first, then with the cut face down, slice into quarters or sixths.

sphere segments

"Clapper-cut" rectangles (hyōshigi-giri): Named after the wooden blocks that were clapped together by night watchmen to remind townsmen to tend live charcoal in heating braziers to avoid accidental fires. These vegetable rectangles are typically ⅛ to ⅜ inch (½ to 1 cm) thick; the grain runs lengthwise, the same way that the wood grain on the *hyōshigi* clappers does. Usually applied to fairly dense vegetables—carrot and *daikon*—for simmering, as a cooked garnish in steamed dishes, and the like.

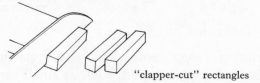

"clapper-cut" rectangles

Rectangles and *julienne strips:* For cutting rectangles (*tanzaku-giri*), the width of the final product is determined by how thickly you cut "slabs" from the original material, as shown. The grain of the vegetable runs in the same direction as the length of the cut shape. Thin rectangles are for vinegared dishes and thicker ones for soups.

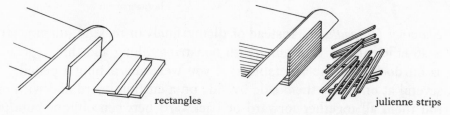

rectangles   julienne strips

For julienne strips, make thin cuts through a stack of thin "slabs."

Cubed, *diced*, and *minced* vegetables are all produced using the same two cutting techniques described immediately above, but taking them one step further and cutting rectangles or strips crosswise, as shown.

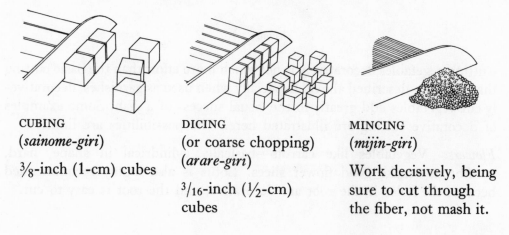

CUBING
(*sainome-giri*)

⅜-inch (1-cm) cubes

DICING
(or coarse chopping)
(*arare-giri*)

3/16-inch (½-cm)
cubes

MINCING
(*mijin-giri*)

Work decisively, being
sure to cut through
the fiber, not mash it.

Thin and *thick squares (shikishi-giri)*: From the vegetable cut a long block with a square cross-section. Slice it crosswise paper-thin for vinegared dishes; for soups, cut more thickly.

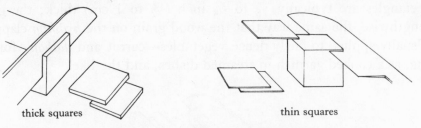

thick squares   thin squares

Hexagonal cutting (roppō-muki): A shape particularly suited to small vegetables that will be simmered, such as small turnips and Japanese field yams (*sato imo*). Both top and bottom of the vegetable are cut flat and then the sides are pared to form a hexagonal shape.

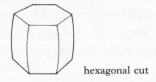

hexagonal cut

Shavings (sasagaki): Instead of dicing finely or making julienne strips, this is an efficient way of dealing with nonstringy, long and thin vegetables such as burdock. Cut the vegetable as if you were sharpening a pencil. To shave several at once, lay them side by side on a cutting board and with one hand roll them all together forward or backward between oblique cuts.

shavings

Cutting vegetables decoratively is not much more effort than the basic cutting that has been described above. Especially when used as garnishes, decoratively cut vegetables add greatly to the visual success of a dish. Some examples of decorative cutting are illustrated here. The possibilities are limitless.

Flowers: Vegetables like carrots—basically cylindrical in shape, hard, nonfibrous—make good flower slices. Lotus is also highly recommended because the holes in the root are decorative, and the root is easy to cut.

Plum blossoms (baika-giri): Work with vegetable sections about 3 inches (8 cm) long. Cut the vegetable into a 5-sided shape, as shown. Make an incision about ⅛ to ¼ inch (½ to ¾ cm) deep lengthwise in the middle of each side. From each edge cut in an arc *toward the bottom* of each incision. It is easiest to work in one direction first and then cut in the opposite direction. When the whole form has been "sculpted" a into plum flower shape, cut slices to the desired thickness. For more petals, increase the number of sides in the basic block shape.

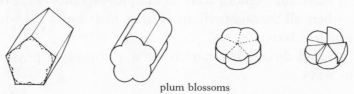

plum blossoms

Cucumber peaks (kiri-chigai): If you can obtain Japanese-type cucumbers, which are about 1 inch (2½ cm) in diameter, the peaks shown make a good all-purpose one-bite hors d'oeuvre or ornamental garnish.

Cut unpeeled cucumber into 1½-inch (4-cm) lengths. Run the knife through the center of a length, as shown, but do *not* cut through the ends. Keeping the center cut parallel to the cutting board, make a diagonal cut halfway through the cucumber up to the center cut. Roll the cucumber over to the other side and make an identical diagonal cut. Separate the two pieces by hand. You can adapt this cutting technique to other vegetables such as *udo*, but cucumber is the best for visual effect.

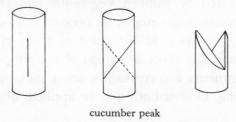

cucumber peak

Cucumber "fans" (senmen-giri): Cut cucumber into 1½-inch (4-cm) lengths. Cut each in half lengthwise, and then trim off rounded sides to form a more rectangular shape. Make lengthwise cuts at narrow, even intervals through all but ¼ inch (¾ cm) at one end. Gently spread open the "fan" and use as garnish. Works best with Japanese-type cucumbers.

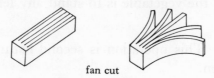

fan cut

Chrysanthemum turnip (kikka-kabu):   See recipe, page 251.

Decorative citron peel: Especially in soups and in steamed dishes, *yuzu* citron rind (or substitute lemon) adds its unique fragrance. Pare off only the top $1/16$ inch, where all the oily perfume is to be had; avoid the white spongy inner peel, which is bitter.

You may pare off dime-sized rounds, or if you peel strips, these can be cut in various ways.

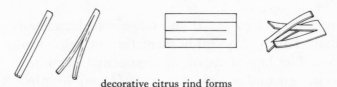

decorative citrus rind forms

Before vegetables are sliced, cubed, cut into rectangles or whatever, they should be thoroughly washed. Use a lot of water.

After vegetables are washed and cut into the desired shape, some sort of intermediate treatment may be required before they are added to the dish in preparation. This is especially true of leafy vegetables and vegetables cut in bite-sized pieces. Grated or minced vegetables, on the other hand, are usually used as is. Excess water might be pressed out of grated giant white radish (*daikon-oroshi*), or the mild bitterness of finely chopped green onion might be washed away, but these are steps of the simplest kind.

The principle treatments for vegetables are a soaking in water or acidic solution and parboiling. One or both may be applied, depending on the vegetable in question.

Water or acidic solution bath (sarasu or aku-nuki):   This soaking is carried out not only to prevent a cut vegetable from turning brown or gray when exposed to air, but also to remove bitterness. It is routinely used with burdock, yams, *udo*, lotus root, and sweet potatoes. For an acidic solution, use about 2 tsps vinegar or lemon juice in 1 quart (1 L) water. Let stand 30 minutes minimum. If the vegetable is to stand any length of time, change water 2 or 3 times.

Parboiling (yugaku):   This operation is second nature to Japanese cooks, since it is done so often.

The heat of simmering water penetrates leafy vegetables and fresh beans rather quickly, so start with water already boiling. Watch vegetables carefully; they should be *barely* tender. If greens simmer too long, their color will darken and flavor will deteriorate. This is particularly true of spinach.

Root vegetables like potatoes are dense, and if they are placed in already simmering water to boil, by the time heat penetrates to the middle, the outer layers will be cooked too much. When whole or in chunks, potatoes and the like (including not only roots and tubers, but any firm, dense vegetable) should be placed in cold water and brought to a simmer to parboil. If sliced, such vegetables are parboiled in already boiling water. Test for tenderness by probing with a fork or skewer, or taste a small sample.

After parboiling, some vegetables (especially leafy greens) are rinsed in cold water to keep retained heat from cooking them further. Greens turn grayish if left to cool to room temperature naturally. Drain as soon as cooled.

Potatoes or root vegetables, Chinese cabbage, and eggplant are best drained and allowed to come to room temperature in the open air.

There is a third method of handling vegetables after parboiling: they can cool in the pot liquor. For example, green peas get wrinkled skins if subjected to a cold water shock, so they should be allowed to cool gradually in the water in which they were parboiled.

In parboiling, a pinch of this or that is often used for various reasons. These are:

Salt: Used not only for seasoning, but also to prevent chlorophyll from breaking down. Keeps greens green.

Vinegar: Used as a "whitener" or "brightener" with such vegetables as lotus root and *udo.* Adds slightly piquant background flavor.

Rice or wheat bran: Two cups in 4 quarts (4 L) water in which bamboo shoot or burdock is being parboiled, and color is made true and clear and bitterness is removed.

Bicarbonate of soda: Used for parboiling fibrous or hard-skinned vegetables such as green peas, large spinach, snow peas. Fibers or skins will be softened, and harsh, metallic tastes will be eliminated. A little goes a long way: ½ tsp in 2–3 quarts (2–3 L) water is plenty. Important: add soda at the last moment—2 or 3 seconds before removing from heat. Vegetables will be pulpy if added too soon.

Burnt alum (yaki myōban): Used with soft vegetables like eggplant to help retain color and shape. A scant tsp in 1 quart (1 L) water is sufficient. Do not cook with alum; soak vegetable in alum solution for 30 to 40 minutes, then drain and cook.

Basic Stock
Dashi

Dashi, Japan's all-purpose soup stock and seasoning, stands figuratively if not literally at the right hand of every Japanese chef. Different varieties of *dashi* lend subtle depth to a wide variety of soups and entrées. *Dashi* provides Japanese cuisine with its characteristic flavor, and it can be said without exaggeration that the success or failure (or mediocrity) of a dish is ultimately determined by the flavor and quality of the *dashi* that seasons it. Making good *dashi* is the first secret of the simple art of Japanese cooking.

Before the age of instant mixes, obviously *dashi* had to be made fresh. This (usually) involved *katsuo-bushi* and *konbu*. The former is dried fillet of bonito (see page 61), and the latter dried giant kelp (page 72). Today, most Japanese home cooks often rely on instant *dashi*, packaged granules that dissolve in hot water, generically called *dashi-no-moto*, or "stock essence." You will probably turn to this instant preparation too, but it is important to understand the traditional method of preparation, for the sake of knowing how to make the highest quality, most delicious *dashi* as well as for the satisfaction of understanding the theory behind this basic stock. While some instant mixes are excellent, and none is bad, nothing compares in subtle flavor and delicate fragrance with *dashi* made from freshly shaved dried bonito.

A stick of *katsuo-bushi* looks like a 6- to 8-inch (15- to 20-cm) long brownish hunk of wood. A bonito yields four fillets, two dorsal and two ventral. These are dried in shade in the open air in a complex process involving many steps and taking six months. One guide in buying a dried fillet is weight in relation to size: the denser the better. Two *katsuo-bushi* struck together should emit a metallic sound. It should have an ash-white coating of mold; green mold means it is too watery, and yellow too acid. For the best flavor, *katsuo-bushi* should be used as quickly as possible. However, it keeps well in a moisture-free container. Store it in a can in a cool, dark, dry place or wrap well in plastic wrap and refrigerate.

The best-tasting *dashi* is made with flakes shaved immediately prior to use. The dried bonito fillet is transformed into pinkish-tan curls or flakes by a shaver that looks like a carpenter's plane fixed above a single-drawer box (in fact, you can use a sharp carpenter's plane). Shaving *katsuo-bushi* takes time and it is an activity requiring a certain amount of skill and practice. Perhaps for these reasons, commercially prepared and packaged flakes (called *hana-katsuo* or *kezuri-katsuo*) are available. These are convenient, and stock made with commercially shaved flakes is good, but does not compare with the flavor and aroma obtained from just-shaved bonito flakes.

Konbu, giant kelp, is the second main ingredient. (Some restaurants ignore the *konbu* and make *dashi* with bonito alone.) The most prized variety of *konbu* is harvested in the subarctic waters off tiny Rebun Island in Hokkaido. Good quality is signified by thick, wide leaves, a dark amber color in the dried product, and a whitish powder encrusting the surface. The whitish powder holds much of the flavor of this seaweed, so the standard practice no matter what the recipe is to wipe it before using with only a few sweeps of a clean damp cloth. Washing this seaweed would dissolve away its flavor.

Lacking any or all of these ingredients, use instant *dashi* for basic stock. There are a number of such instant *dashi* preparations; check directions on jar or packet. Instant *dashi* or *dashi-no-moto* is often sold with dried Chinese foods in American supermarkets.

Of course many substitutes for *dashi* are possible, but without *dashi*, dishes are merely *à la japonaise* and lack the authentic flavor. Chicken stock is only used in Japanese cooking when chicken is the main ingredient of a dish. But the flavor of chicken may be added to *dashi* by making the stock with water in which chicken has been boiled for 10 minutes. Keep all flavors *light*.

Because it has a lovely fragrance, fresh primary *dashi* is best for clear soups. A Japanese clear soup should be thin enough to allow one to clearly perceive the flavors of the other ingredients present. Its bouquet disappears quickly and is lost if the *dashi* is not used immediately. For use as a basic seasoning, however, primary (and secondary) *dashi* made well ahead of time is perfectly fine. Leftover *dashi* may be stored in a sealed bottle in the refrigerator for up to 3 days or may be frozen, but flavor and aroma are lost.

Primary *Dashi*
(Ichiban Dashi) 一番出し

makes 1 quart (1 L);
serves 6 as base for clear soup

1 quart (1 L) cold water
1 ounce (30 g) giant kelp
(*konbu*)
1 ounce (30 g) dried bonito
flakes (*hana-katsuo*)

To prepare: Fill a medium-sized soup pot with 1 quart (1 L) cold water and put in the kelp. Heat, uncovered, so as to reach the boiling point in about 10 minutes. IMPORTANT: Kelp emits a strong odor if it is boiled, so remove *konbu* just *before* water boils.

Insert your thumbnail into the fleshiest part of the kelp. If it is soft, sufficient flavor has been obtained. If tough, return it to the pot for 1 or 2 minutes. Keep from boiling by adding approximately 1/4 cup cold water.

After removing the *konbu* bring the stock to a full boil. Add 1/4 cup cold water to bring the temperature down quickly and immediately add the bonito flakes. No need to stir. Bring to a full boil and remove from the heat at once. If bonito flakes boil more than a few seconds, the stock becomes too strong, a bit bitter, and is not suitable for use in clear soups. If you make this mistake, all is not lost, use the stock as a base for thick soups, in simmered foods, and so on.

Allow the flakes to start to settle to the bottom of the pot (30 seconds to 1 minute). Remove foam, then filter through a cheesecloth-lined sieve. Reserve the bonito flakes and kelp for secondary *dashi*.

Secondary *Dashi*
(Niban Dashi) 二番出し

While primary *dashi* is best suited for clear soups by virtue of its fragrance, subtle taste, and clarity, secondary *dashi* does noble service as a basic seasoning—for thick soups, for noodle broths, as a cooking stock for vegetables, and in many other ways.

makes 3–4 cups

bonito flakes and giant kelp
reserved from primary
dashi

To prepare: Place the bonito flakes and giant kelp reserved from the primary *dashi* in 1½ quarts (1½ L) cold water in a medium-sized soup pot. Place over high heat just until the boiling point, then reduce heat

1½ quarts (1½ L) cold water
⅓-½ ounce (10-15 g) dried bonito flakes (*hana-katsuo*)

and keep at a gentle simmer until the stock is reduced by ⅓ or ½, depending on the flavor desired. This reduction takes about 15–20 minutes.

Add the fresh *hana-katsuo* and immediately remove from heat. Allow the flakes to start to settle to the bottom of the pot (30 seconds to 1 minute), and remove foam from the surface. Filter liquid through a cheesecloth-lined sieve.

Discard the *hana-katsuo* flakes and *konbu*.

Kelp Stock
(*Konbu Dashi*) 昆布出し

Since the flavor and nutrients of giant kelp pass quickly into clear water, it is not actually necessary to subject it to heat to produce a delicate stock. A lengthy soaking, 8 hours or overnight, yields what is considered to be a delicious and subtle liquid. In many homes, this liquid is used in primary *dashi* in lieu of heating the kelp in water—just heat this seaweed liquor and begin the primary *dashi* recipe midway with the addition of the dried bonito flakes. *Konbu dashi* is also the base in preparing sardine stock (below).

makes 1 quart (1 L)

1⅓ ounces (40 g) giant kelp (*konbu*)
1 quart (1 L) cold water

To prepare: Wipe kelp lightly with a damp cloth. Fill a medium-sized bowl with the cold water and add kelp. Let stand at room temperature at least 8 hours, or overnight.

Remove kelp and reserve for use in other recipes.

Sardine Stock
(*Niboshi Dashi*) 煮干し出し

A type of fish stock is made from small sun-dried sardines called *niboshi*. Wooden or basketwork drying pallets on quays, spread full of these tiny silvery fish, are a part of fishing village scenes in Japan. Savory sardine stock is much stronger than bonito *dashi* and makes a very good base for thick and rich *miso* soups (see page 156). It is also often used in broth for *udon* noodles (see page 310). *Niboshi* vary considerably in size; about 2 inches (5 cm) is average. Good-quality *niboshi* should have whole bodies that are relatively straight and well formed.

makes 1 quart (1 L)

1⅓ ounces (40 g) dried small
  sardines (*niboshi*)
1 quart (1 L) cold water or
  cooled KELP STOCK

To prepare: To prevent the stock from being bitter
or sour, pluck off heads and pinch away entrails of
dried sardines.

Place the sardines in 1 quart (1 L) cold water or cooled
KELP STOCK (above) in a medium-sized soup pot and
place over high heat to bring quickly to the boiling
point. Reduce heat and simmer for 7–8 minutes.

Remove from heat and strain through cheesecloth.
Use as required.

Making Soups
Suimono and Shirumono

The entire category of soups is known as *shirumono*; this includes clear soups and "thick" soups; the latter is by far the largest group, and, at one extreme, merges into simmered foods (*nimono*).

Clear soup, commonly called *suimono*—literally "something to drink"— is usually served after the appetizer as the first course in the main body of a full Japanese meal. *Suimono* is so highly regarded that, depending on the formality and length of a banquet, gourmets have contrived that some variety also appear at midpoint in the meal, to refresh the palate in much the same way as a *sorbet* does in the grand French manner. Further, clear soups sometimes appear with the last course—the rice—instead of the usual "thick" soup.

Whenever *suimono* is served, in keen anticipation diners remove the cover from their lacquer bowls—puff, a cloud of fragrant steam rises, and in the clear broth floats an exquisite arrangement, perhaps a pink curl of shrimp nestled near bite-sized slices of translucent winter melon cut into decorative shapes and a sliver of citrus rind set at a jaunty angle. Soups are both simple and a sophisticated aesthetic expression.

Such a clear soup is an impressive prelude to a Western meal. Good clear soup is impressive in its purity and restraint, making a meal unforgettable. One word of caution: because clear soup is so simple and natural, base it on the best and freshest stock and do all you can to insure that the other ingredients are perfect in color and shape.

As a soup genre, *suimono* is made according to a deceptively simple formula: in addition to stock, there are usually three "solid" ingredients to lend flavor and color. The first is a bite-sized piece of fish fillet or part of the fish head (the eye is given to the guest of honor), chicken or egg, a bit of shellfish, a boiled sliced vegetable such as bamboo shoot, or a processed material such as *tōfu* (bean curd). The second is a complement to the first. For example, two julienne strips of boiled burdock goes with the jowl of sea bream, paper-thin squares of seaweed with bamboo shoot, slices of mushroom with shellfish, and so on. The third and final of these "solids" is for fragrance (and is often not to be eaten). These garnishes include trefoil; a tiny, tender sprig of *sansho* pepper leaves (*kinome*); and bright slivers, often decoratively cut, of *yuzu* citron or lemon or other citrus rind. In the lesson recipe below, we see a medallionlike shrimp served forth with wafers of seaweed and a sprig of fragrant *kinome*. Using this formula as a basis, you will be able to adapt and work within the category of *suimono* to suit your own preferences.

Alongside elegant, sparkling clear soups, there is the category of "thick" soups. These appear in many forms, among which are those made from stock and fermented bean paste (*miso*) and those so full of meat or fish or poultry and vegetables that they are like Western stews.

Miso soup is the main dish served in the traditional Japanese breakfast. The origin of this is obscure. *Miso* appears not only at breakfast, but at lunch and dinner in millions of Japanese households daily. *Miso* soup with a bowl of rice, a side dish of pickles, and a mug of scalding hot tea is favorite standard fare.

There are many, many types of *miso*; generally, the white types are "sweet," red ones salty. The darker the color, the saltier the *miso*. (The same is *not* true of soy sauce—beware.) Their textures also are many, from smooth to chunky. Their variety and quality are analogous to the numerous regional wines and cheeses found throughout France, and nearly all can be bases for soup, though they are used constantly in other dishes as well—in dips, toppings and spreads, in dressings, with sautéed and simmered dishes, with grilled dishes and deep-fried foods, to pickle, and even in sweet confections.

No Japanese meal is complete without at least one soup. The simplest meal should consist of *ichijū sansai*, "soup and three [side dishes]," although in times of austerity people make do with "soup and one"—protein-rich *miso* soup and a simmered vegetable.

Japanese soups, both thick and thin, are served in covered lacquer bowls. The wood beneath the lacquer is an effective insulator, so it is possible to hold the bowl in your hands even when the soup is steaming hot.

The soup should be so hot that one has to imbibe quite a bit of air with one's sips to avoid being scalded. This should, however, be done as elegantly as possible, with only a gentle sipping sound and not a great slurping (but, see Noodles, page 306).

My notorious fussiness about soup's being really hot caused the proprietor of one of Tokyo's most celebrated and exclusive restaurants to build an entirely new kitchen for soup alone. The soup used to cool off perceptibly on its brief trip upstairs from the ground-floor kitchen, so another kitchen was built on the second floor in the very center of the building for the soup, which now only takes 30 seconds to reach each of the private dining rooms.

The smaller the establishment, the tastier the food. The old Japanese emperors and shoguns in their sprawling palaces with miles of corridor between kitchen and the exalted presence could never have known the delight of truly fresh, hot, flavorsome food.

Hot soup affects the color of black lacquer over a long period unless the lacquer is of the highest quality (determined by the lacquer refining and also the lacquering processes). The restaurant mentioned above has a splendid collection of lacquer soup bowls over a hundred years old that still look like new. But even inexpensive, undecorated lacquer soup bowls with lids are very durable, and the eventual color change from black to dark brown on the inside due to the hot soup is nothing to worry about. Such bowls are worth having for any soup, because they keep it so nice and hot. They really are a must for Japanese clear soup, since so much of the subtle flavor of *suimono* is lost without a lid. Consommé cups can be made to do, or even large breakfast-size teacups, but whatever you do, avoid the shallow Western soup dish. With a lid, the sooner you cover the bowl after filling, the more flavor and aroma you trap inside. I was served a most delightfully ingenious soup the other day that had two lids, as it were. At the bottom of the lidded bowl were clams and sprigs of bright green seaweed, while floating on the surface of the soup was a paper-thin slice of *daikon* (giant radish) the exact size of the bowl, sprinkled with tiny flecks of real gold foil. Besides keeping in all the sea aroma of the clams, the sheet of radish had absorbed just the right amount of flavor from the soup. You could do the same abroad with a large turnip.

A word of caution: if some time has elapsed and the soup has cooled slightly, a small vacuum may make the lid stick quite tightly. When this happens at a Japanese banquet, do not panic. Just squeeze the bowl itself gently to free the lid. The kind of clear soups that are sophisticated works of art are more often served in restaurants than in the home. *Miso* soup is the home favorite, and every family uses its preferred variety of *miso*. Because of this, people tend to be rather fussy about *miso* soups in restaurants—disappointed if it does not taste like the soup mother makes. So restaurants circumvent this by skillfully blending various *miso* types for their *miso* soup that comes at the end of a formal banquet.

Clear Soup with Shrimp

(*Ebi Suimono*) 海老吸い物

serves 4

garnishes:

**4 medium-sized raw
shrimp**
**1 small piece dried
wakame seaweed**
4 sprigs *kinome*
**(as alternative garnishes,
use coarsely chopped
watercress instead of
seaweed, and slivers of
lemon or lime rind for
the *kinome*)**

seasoned stock:

2½ cups *dashi*
½ Tbsp salt
**1 Tbsp light soy sauce, or
slightly larger amount
of dark soy sauce**

To prepare: Take care of the garnishes first. Shell the shrimp, leaving the tail attached, and devein. Wash, pat dry, salt lightly, and lightly dredge in cornstarch (or *kuzu* starch or arrowroot). Parboil in unsalted water for 2 minutes.

Soften the dried *wakame* seaweed in cold water for 20 minutes. Cut out hard parts and discard, then cut into 1-inch (2½-cm) lengths. (Professional chefs might treat *wakame* in a slightly different way to bring out its bright green color and to insure tenderness: swish it in boiling water for 30 seconds then plunge it into a cold bath before leaving it to soak.)

Wash and pat dry the *kinome* sprigs.

Method: In a medium-sized soup pot bring the *dashi* to a simmer over medium heat. Never boil. Add the salt gradually, dissolving it little by little. Taste and stir frequently. Better to add the salt gradually and to keep tasting than to add too much.

When the *dashi* is salted to desired taste, gradually add the soy sauce. Again, stir and taste. The higher the quality of the *dashi*, the less soy sauce required.

To assemble and serve: Warm individual covered lacquer soup bowls by filling with hot water and letting them stand for 1 or 2 minutes. (In lieu of lacquer, use small or medium-sized deep soup bowls or cups on saucers.) Dispose of hot water and wipe bowls dry.

Attractively arrange a shrimp and a small amount of seaweed in each bowl. Ladle in the seasoned stock carefully so that it does not splash and mark the side of the bowl or disturb the arrangement. Fill bowls ¾ full—no more! Add a sprig of *kinome* to each bowl. Serve immediately.

If there is anything to take note of here, it is the method of seasoning the stock. Salt to taste just *before* adding the soy sauce. Good, naturally fermented soy sauce recommended for Japanese cooking tastes of soy, not of salt, so no compensation has to be made. Moreover, the flavor of soy sauce is fairly volatile and changes if it is heated for too long. In clear soups such as this one, it is the last seasoning to be added.

Clam Consommé

(*Hamaguri Ushio-jiru*) 蛤 潮 汁 (color plate 9)

This unsurpassed clam consommé is an example of a non-*dashi*-based clear soup. The water in which the live clams are gently boiled and coaxed to open becomes a delicately flavored broth. Though clams are plentiful in Japan, choice fresh ones are not inexpensive, and this is definitely soup for an "occasion." In fact, it is often served at Japanese wedding banquets—in the broth in each bowl, the meat of a clam rests in each side of the hinged shell, said to represent the happily joined couple.

serves 4

8 live clams, shells about
  2½ inches long
3-inch (8-cm) length of *udo*
3⅓ cups water
4-inch (10-cm) square giant
  kelp (*konbu*)
salt
yuzu rind
(as alternative ingredients,
  use a piece of parboiled
  asparagus tip in each bowl
  instead of *udo*, and fresh
  rind of lime or lemon for
  the *yuzu*.

To prepare: A large part of the preparation is careful shopping. Choose clams with perfect shells. Strike two together. If the sound is metallic, the clams are most likely still alive. If the sound is dull, the clam is either dead or the shell has been cracked or chipped. Using less than the best clams will result in "smelly" soup.

Cover clams with lightly salted or plain water for 4–5 hours (in summer, 10 hours in water) in a cool, dark place to allow clams to expel sand and dirt.

Gently scrub shells clean under running cold water with a brush. Hinged shells will be used as a garnish.

Udo is a vegetable with a flavor somewhere between celery and asparagus with a hint of fennel flavor. Wash the stalk and cut into pieces 1½ × ½ × ⅛ inches (4 × 1½ × ½ cm). *Udo* is good raw or cooked; here parboil it 1 minute in lightly salted water after cutting.

Outside Japan, *udo* may be difficult to buy, so use 2 parboiled asparagus tips per serving as a substitute.

To cook: Put the unopened clams in about 3⅓ cups of cold water in a medium-sized soup pot together with the giant kelp, already wiped clean with a damp cloth. (Try to use a piece from the base of the leaf for best flavor). Place over medium to high heat and bring to a boil. Remove kelp just before boiling point is reached. Boil until all clams open, then scoop them out of the broth. Remove broth from heat and strain into another pot.

With a paring knife cut the clams from their shells. In clear water wash the shells and gently scrape insides clean. (The clams are cut out of their shells in deference to the diner—this way they will be easy to eat and there will be no embarrassing struggle at the table in dealing with any recalcitrant shell-clinging clams.) Over low heat add salt to strained broth, little by little, tasting frequently. Remove from heat.

To assemble and serve: In each warmed lacquer bowl, place a cleaned, open clam shell (2 halves). Place the meat of 1 clam on each half shell. Over this lay 2 pieces of *udo* (or 2 pieces of parboiled asparagus). For garnish and fragrance, add a sliver of *yuzu* rind (or lemon or lime), about ⅛ inch (½ cm) wide and 1½ inches (4 cm) long. Over this arrangement, carefully ladle the hot broth. Cover the bowls, and serve.

VARIATIONS: This sort of soup is particularly well suited to sweet-fleshed shellfish and fish without strong idiosyncracies, such as sea bream, sea bass, and flathead (*kochi*).

Miso Soup
(*Miso-shiru*) 味噌汁

In many way, *miso* is to Japanese cooking what butter is to French cooking and olive oil to the Italian way (to paraphrase M.F.K. Fisher), and behind *miso*'s omnipresence in the Japanese kitchen lies abundant common sense. Take *miso*-based soups. Not only do they require just a few minutes to prepare (an important criterion for a breakfast food), more important, typical servings provide roughly one-sixth the adult daily requirement of protein.

It is impossible for *miso* soup to be boring. It can be based on any type of *miso*, from salty to sweet, and it is always served with supplementary ingredients and seasonings. In the course of the four seasons, relying on easily available produce and nonseasonal staples, one can make a different *miso* soup nearly every day without repetition.

Below is just one of the seemingly limitless variety of *miso* soups.

serves 4

3⅓ **cups primary *dashi*, or secondary *dashi*, or sardine stock**

To prepare: Make the stock of your choice and assemble the supporting ingredients. *Nameko* mushrooms are available fresh and in cans; they are similar to conventional button mushrooms, but have a slippery

approximately ½ cup
nameko mushrooms (or
2 *shiitake* mushrooms,
sliced)
⅓ cake *tōfu* (bean curd)
4 Tbsps red *miso*
4 stalks trefoil
ground *sansho* pepper

coating. (Substitute *shiitake* mushrooms.) Drain the *tōfu*.

To cook: Soften the *miso* in a medium-sized bowl by adding 2 Tbsps tepid stock and blending with a wire whisk. If you put the *miso* directly into the stock pot, it will not be properly held in solution, and the soup will be full of *miso* pellets.

Gradually ladle the softened *miso* into the stock in a medium-sized pot, simmering over medium heat. (If you want satin-smooth soup, strain the soup from one pot into another.)

When all the *miso* has been added and is dissolved, add the solid ingredients. The *tōfu* can be cut into ½-inch (1½-cm) cubes over the stock pot. Chop the trefoil stalks into small pieces. Keep soup at a simmer a few minutes until the mushrooms and *tōfu* are heated.

Remove from heat just before boiling point. Do not boil—boiling will change the flavor.

To serve: Ladle into individual lacquer bowls, distributing the mushrooms, *tōfu*, and chopped trefoil equally and attractively. Garnish with a shake or two of *sansho* pepper. Cover and serve immediately.

Slicing and Serving Sashimi

In their own countries, Westerners feel no qualms in asking for filet mignon so rare it is "just passed over the fire"—or steak tartare, oysters on the half-shell, or raw clams. But the food best loved in Japan, *sashimi*—sliced raw fish—often seems unbearably exotic, almost bordering on the barbaric, and requiring a great sense of gastronomic adventure and fortitude to down!

But let Westerners roll a slice of choice pink tuna, succulent yellowtail, or cool firm sea bream on their tongues and opinions often change. More than once I have witnessed the conversion of a skeptic as he savors a cut of raw fish in closed-eye delight, as if the fish were rare roast beef. To the surprise of those who do try *sashimi*, they find the taste of fresh, uncooked fish not at all "fishy." It may take a little while for them to overcome their conditioning, but they do quickly see that Japanese fish are a far cry from the opaque and dull-eyed specimens found in too many fish markets abroad.

Freshness, vividness of fish as it were, is essential to *sashimi*. Freshness is such a fundamental concept that it cannot be repeated too often. It encompasses more than the idea of having access to freshly caught fish. Freshness also means fresh in season, for each species is most delectable at a certain time of year, depending on such a variety of factors as changes in sea currents, temperature and climate, foods upon which fish themselves feed, sea levels through which fish run, and spawning times.

Various kinds of tuna, bream, and mackerel are available year round. But the winter months are best for savoring *hon-maguro*—a tuna that many consider the finest—fatty bellied yellowtail, *sawara* mackerel, and tiny "whitebait" (*shirauo*) brought to the table still leaping. From April through June, there is Japan's king of saltwater fish, sea bream (*tai*) as well as *karei* flounder, its great rival in popularity. Firm, distinctive bonito *sashimi* is fresh as a spring day, and "dancing" shrimp take us into the first hot days of the year. High summer is marked by dishes featuring the king of fresh-water fish, carp, as well as by perch and *anago* eel. And who could possibly mourn the passing year as autumn comes with mackerel, various bream, clams, and, when the cold sets in, oysters and *hirame* flounder, to feast on?

Sashimi is the crowning glory of the formal meal. The soup and raw fish are so important that the other dishes are merely garnishes, as it were. But *sashimi*, always arranged on especially beautiful plates, is the showpiece of the chef's skill—both in his knifework and his mastery of the essence of Japanese cuisine. It proves his ability to choose the freshest materials in their seasonal prime and to present them with the utmost artistry.

Sashimi is served early in the meal so its subtle flavor may be enjoyed while one is still hungry and before one's palate is sated with cooked foods. Home meals are usually served all at once, but the *sashimi* should be eaten first, for the same reason.

When serving *sashimi* I urge you to avoid frozen fish. It negates the spirit of Japanese cuisine. Tuna freezes best, and maintains texture well, but the flavor invariably suffers. The availability of frozen tuna is ruining the tradition of Japan's cuisine, alas. Although it is very expensive, everyone wants tuna and things like bream and lobster, wherever they live and whatever the season, despising as low class cheaper fish such as sardines and mackerel. But in small rural fishing ports, rich and poor alike enjoy the catch of the day. How wise they are! The fish in season is always the best—and cheapest. Good fish is not good because it is expensive. It is good because it is in season. Sardines in season are ridiculously cheap, and they are delicious served with grated ginger.

People who live in the mountains should only eat local freshwater fish. It is the tragedy of Japan today that everybody wants the same fare, whether they live in large landlocked cities or in villages by the sea.

I was horrified to find frozen crab served at San Francisco's famed Fisherman's Wharf, where there must be plenty of fresh seafood of one sort or another available. For your *sashimi*, serve only what can be obtained fresh where you live. A *sashimi* course may consist of shellfish alone. The cherrystone clams of America's East Coast are superb, and fresh, uncooked Maine lobsters served in thin slices with lemon, soy sauce, and grated fresh ginger are not only marvelously delicious but in the very best Japanese tradition.

Everything related to the preparation of *sashimi* is done with elaborate care, from obtaining the freshest fish to slicing it, to deciding on appropriate condiments, garnishes, and dipping sauces, and, last but not least, making an attractive arrangement.

Sashimi is usually served on individual shallow dishes (or plates), in slices $\frac{1}{4}$ to $\frac{1}{2}$ inch ($\frac{3}{4}$ to $1\frac{1}{2}$ cm) thick. Five or six rectangular slices rest like fallen dominoes against a high bed of crisp, shred-cut giant white radish. Other garnishes such as the delicate heart-shaped *shiso*, an herb blending the scents of lemon and mint, or a sprig of its tiny lavender-colored buds lend more color and texture to the presentation. Somewhere in the arrangement is a cone of spicy condiment—finely grated pale green *wasabi* horseradish, or pale yellow finely grated fresh ginger root, to name just two of the most popular. *Saké* goes well with *sashimi*, and should always accompany it.

The use of dipping sauces to enhance natural flavor is very important in Japanese cuisine. For *sashimi*, the sauce, basically soy sauce with various flavorings added, is poured into small individual bowls. Using chopsticks, mix some of the spicy condiment with the soy sauce in your dipping bowl. Momentarily rest a slice of raw fish in this sauce en route to your mouth; pop the whole slice in at once and enjoy. Appreciate the tenderness of truly fresh fish, redolent of the sea. Some aficionados put a touch of *wasabi* on the fish itself before dipping it in the sauce. Restaurants always use reduced soy-and-*saké* for *sashimi*.

Another popular way of serving *sashimi* is to cut paper-thin slices and arrange them in a rosette or flower pattern on a platter. Cutting indeed affects flavor: the very same fillet cut into paper-thin slices makes an entirely different impression than when it is served in thicker slices. The sauce appropriate for the thick cut of *sashimi* is not necessarily the best sauce for paper-thin slices—even if both have been cut from the very same fillet. With paper-thin slices, a light yet tangy sauce is required, and the great favorite is a citrus-and-soy-sauce dip called PONZU (page 172). A platter of *sashimi* in a rosette is not without its garnishes—a curl of carrot or cucumber and a leaf of chrysanthemum, as well as the ubiquitous spicy condiments, this time finely grated giant white radish spiked with hot red pepper called RED MAPLE RADISH (page 170) and finely chopped green onions.

Mix the spicy condiments with the PONZU SAUCE in your dipping bowl.

Sea Bream *Sashimi*

(*Tai no Sashimi*) 鯛の刺身 (color plates 9 & 13)

Sashimi is easy to serve at home if a few general things are observed:
Five or six rectangular $\frac{3}{8}$-inch (1-cm) slices usually comprise one serving. Serve in individual shallow dishes or on small plates. Arrange the slices on a bed of finely shred-cut *daikon* (or lettuce or cucumber) and garnish with a sprig of *shiso* buds (or a *shiso* leaf) and a curl of carrot. Place a cone of *wasabi* horseradish on the dish also, to be used as a spicy condiment as desired. Serve TOSA SOY SAUCE (page 170) in individual dipping bowls at the side.

About ⅔ pound (300 g) of paper-thin slices arranged in a rosette on a 10- to 12-inch (20- to 25-cm) platter serves 2. Garnish the platter with some sort of decorative green leaf and, if space permits, also place the spicy condiments on the platter—little mounds of finely chopped green onion and grated RED MAPLE RADISH (page 170). Otherwise pass the condiments separately. Serve with PONZU SAUCE in small individual dipping bowls at the side.

Choosing the fish: Freshness is the key. Buy from a reputable fishmonger and choose fish with bright, clear eyes and red gills, having a clean, seaweedy aroma. The belly should be resilient and you should not be able to push it in easily with your finger. Scales should be firm.

Have the fishmonger scale and gut the fish, or do this yourself immediately after purchase. Wash well to remove blood.

Filleting: Most fishmongers will take care of this chore for you, but it is just as well to know what to do. For sea bream and other firm, white-fleshed fish with bodies wide and long but with a narrow cross-section apply the "three-part slicing" technique (*sanmai oroshi*) described on pages 123ff. Two fillets are cut, one from each side of the fish, and the skeleton is left with quite a bit of meat on it. This is precisely as it should be for *sashimi*—only the best part of the fillet is used. Use the meaty skeleton in other ways.

Skin the fillet according to the *soto-biki* technique described on page 131. Or, if you intend to serve the fish with the skin, soften it and improve its flavor. Place the fillet skin side up on a cutting board and cover it with a double thickness of cheesecloth. Pour on boiling water. Remove the cloth immediately and plunge the fillet into cold water for 30 seconds. Swish gently in the bath, remove, and pat dry. Do not skip the cold-bath step or the flesh will cook slightly.

To prepare: Feel the fillet with your hands to find where bones are embedded. Cut off wafer-thin strips including such bones. Trim off the thin sides to make the fillet more rectangular in shape.

Remove the bones that line the body cavity by a simple, single draw of the knife from the top and just under the bones to the bottom (that is, the belly). This may entail two draws of the knife, but try to keep it to one —not difficult if your knife is as sharp as it should be.

For big fish, halve the fillet by cutting down the center line of the flesh. As the flesh narrows towards the tail, cut away from the center line, being careful to maintain an *equal width* of flesh, as shown.

FILLETING FOR SASHIMI

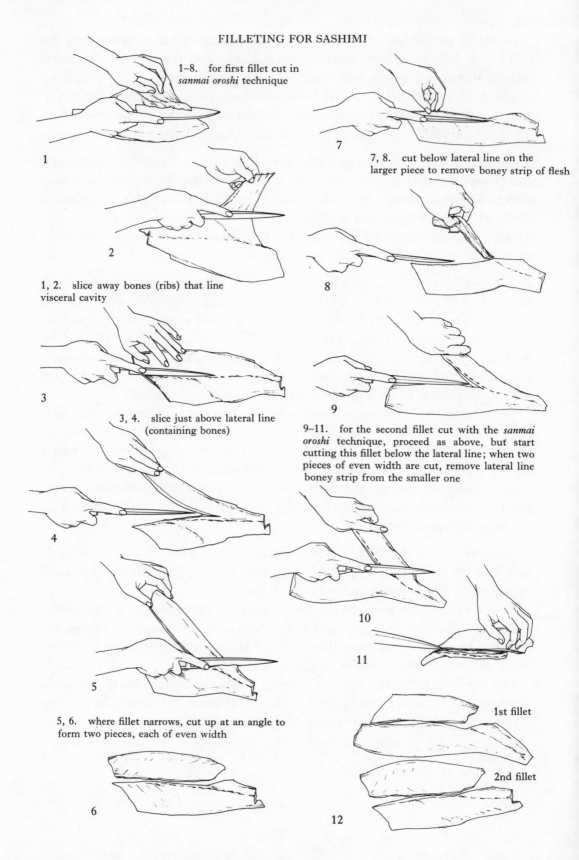

1–8. for first fillet cut in *sanmai oroshi* technique

1, 2. slice away bones (ribs) that line visceral cavity

3, 4. slice just above lateral line (containing bones)

5, 6. where fillet narrows, cut up at an angle to form two pieces, each of even width

7, 8. cut below lateral line on the larger piece to remove boney strip of flesh

9–11. for the second fillet cut with the *sanmai oroshi* technique, proceed as above, but start cutting this fillet below the lateral line; when two pieces of even width are cut, remove lateral line boney strip from the smaller one

1st fillet

2nd fillet

Filleting may be done several hours in advance, but skinning and the following steps must be done just before serving. Refrigerate the fillets wrapped in cotton cloth; such wrapping prevents fish from absorbing the smells of other foods in the refrigerator as well as protects from moisture.

SLICING TECHNIQUES

Rectangular ⅜ inch (1-cm) slices—the *hira-zukuri* cut: All the work up to this point has been done with a kitchen carver, but from this point on use a fish slicer (*sashimi-bōchō*).

Because this cutting technique can be applied to any type of fish, the ⅜-inch (1-cm) slice made with the *hira-zukuri* technique is the most useful of all *sashimi* cutting methods. Place fillet lengthwise on the board, skin side up, the thin side toward you and thick side away from you. Hold the knife so that top of blade is inclined very slightly to the left. Use the knife in a sweeping draw from the base to the tip, cutting through the fillet without force or much pressure.

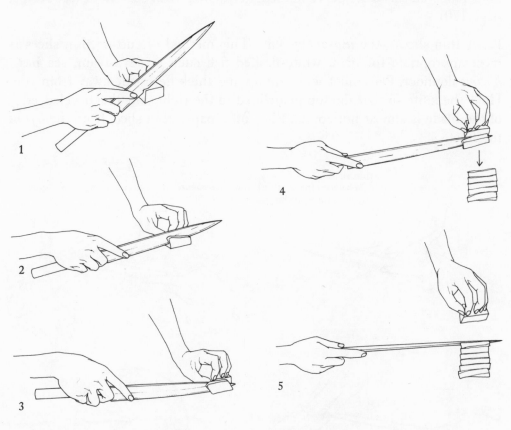

rectangular slices
(*hira-zukuri* technique)

Start slicing at the *right* of the fish. A ⅜-inch (1-cm) slice is standard, but firm-fleshed fish may take as thin as a ⅛-inch (½-cm) slice, and soft-fleshed fish as large as a ½-inch (1½-cm) slice. Your technique will naturally become refined with practice.

Wipe the blade with a moist, clean towel occasionally. Because of the way the knife is held, each slice comes to rest on the blade near the tip. Slide the tip of the blade with the slice attached a few inches to the right, then lay the slice on its right side, as shown. Repeat this procedure of cutting till you have a neat row of "domino" slices.

Transfer one portion (5 or 6 slices) to plate or dish, using chopsticks or your fingers to arrange slices. The dish or plate should be already chilled and garnished with a bed of finely shred-cut giant white radish (*daikon*), lettuce, or cucumber (see below). After placing the row of "domino" slices against the bed of shredded vegetable, arrange other garnishes: sprigs of *shiso* buds and a curl of carrot. Add the cone of spicy condiment, *wasabi* horseradish in this case. Serve immediately. Offer TOSA SOY SAUCE (see recipe, page 170).

Paper-thin slices—the *usu-zukuri* cut: This method of cutting thin slices is most appropriate for firm, white-fleshed fish such as sea bream, sea bass, *hirame* flounder. Place fillet skin side up and thick flesh side away from you. Hold the knife so that the top is inclined to the right and the beveled edge of the blade is almost horizontal. Slice off a paper-thin slice, from the *left* of the fillet.

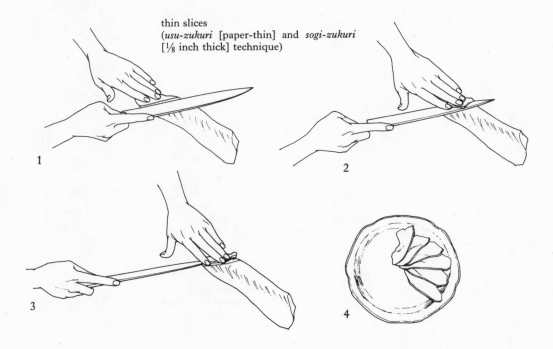

thin slices
(*usu-zukuri* [paper-thin] and *sogi-zukuri*
[⅛ inch thick] technique)

1

2

3

4

The *usu-zukuri* cut is to all fish cutting techniques what the backhand is to racquet sports. You begin cutting from the left of the fillet with the cutting edge of the knife at a very acute angle to achieve a cut across the grain of the flesh. Study the accompanying sketches. The firmer the flesh of the fish, the thinner the slice. The thickest slice is no more than $\frac{1}{16}$ inch ($\frac{1}{4}$ cm). Somewhat thicker slices, called *sogi-zukuri*, are made with the same cutting method.

Because the slices are so thin, transfer each slice immediately to a plate or small serving platter, overlapping the slices slightly to make a rosette. With the fingertips of your free hand, lightly guide each slice as you work to keep it from folding.

Add garnishes to the rosette—a decorative leaf, curl of carrot, and the spicy condiments, in this case, mounds of finely chopped green onion and grated RED MAPLE RADISH (page 170). Serve immediately with PONZU SAUCE (page 172).

Other cutting techniques—*hiki-zukuri*, *kaku-zukuri*, and *ito-zukuri*: A variation of the *hira-zukuri* slice above is the *hiki-zukuri*. The only difference from the *hira-zukuri* technique is that instead of sliding the slices over the board a few inches and laying them in a "domino" row, they are laid in place onto their right side as they are cut. This method is best for easily flaked or broken, soft-fleshed fish, which should be handled as little as possible.

The *kaku-zukuri*, or cube cut, is for fish such as tuna and bonito with thick but soft-fleshed fillets. Slice the fillet lengthwise into $\frac{3}{4}$-inch (2-cm) widths. A single cut is recommended when cutting these strips. Do not separate strips; rotate flesh 90° and cut straight down at $\frac{3}{4}$-inch (2-cm) intervals to form cubes of fish, as shown.

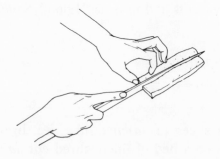 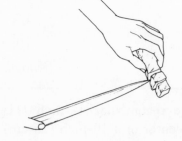

cube cut
(*kaku-zukuri* technique)

The thread cut, or *ito-zukuri*, is for fish with very, very thin fillets, such as garfish (*sayori*) or sillago (*kisu*). Cut at an angle to the length of the fish with the tip of the blade to produce strips about $\frac{1}{16}$-inch ($\frac{1}{4}$-cm) wide and $2\frac{1}{2}$ inches ($6\frac{1}{2}$ cm) long. The angle of cut will vary, depending on the width of fillet. To serve, make a small stack of thread slices, as shown.

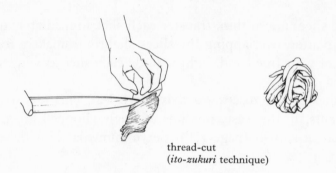

thread-cut
(*ito-zukuri* technique)

Arranging and serving sashimi: With all the care that is taken to use only the best part of the fish for *sashimi*, it is easy to deduce that how *sashimi* looks when it is served is of great importance. *Sashimi*, among all Japanese foods, is for the imaginative eye as well as for the sensitive palate. Many Japanese restaurants and inns earn their reputation not only on the strength of exceedingly fresh fish but also on its presentation in elaborate set pieces. The treasure-ship filled with seafood morsels is the most common motif; this can reach Hollywood spectacular proportions (and expense) and involve intricately carved and modeled vegetable flowers and seascapes; using only sliced fish, chefs create collages of thin slices representing cranes in flight, chrysanthemums, even moon-filled landscapes!

For the home cook with average experience, this sort of elaborate set piece is probably not a goal. One fantasy idea, emulating on an easily done, small scale the extravaganzas of exclusive restaurants and inns, is "Igloo" *Sashimi*.

"Igloo" Sashimi
(*Kamakura*) "かまくら"

Arrange rectangular $\frac{1}{2}$-inch ($1\frac{1}{2}$-cm) slices of *sashimi*, like sea bream, in the center of a 10-inch (25-cm) plate on a bed of finely shred-cut *daikon* and garnish with *shiso* buds. Mold a decorative igloo by firmly packing 6 to 7 cups of shaved ice around the outside of a Japanese tea mug or on-the-rocks glass, and cut away a U-shaped gap for the door on one side. Remove cup or glass and place igloo over the *sashimi* arrangement. Add a cone of pale green *wasabi* horseradish at the door, and serve. To eat, use chopsticks to maneuver the sea bream *sashimi* out the door. See sketches.

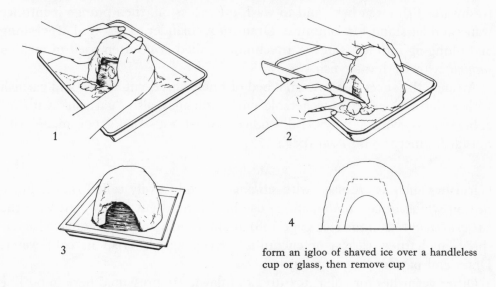

form an igloo of shaved ice over a handleless cup or glass, then remove cup

Trout *Sashimi*
(*Masu no Sashimi*) 鱒の刺身

Because of the difficulty in days of old in transporting fresh ocean fish to inland areas, *sashimi* was made from freshwater fish such as trout and carp. Carrying the concept of freshness to its natural limit, restaurants often keep freshwater fish swimming in tanks until moments before they are to be prepared. This is the assumption we make here—that you will have a leaping 12-inch (30-cm) trout, maybe even one just fly-caught in a clear stream.

On the cutting board cut off the head in one stroke. Gut the fish and wash in cold running water.

Place your free hand on the fish to keep it from slipping while you cut the first fillet. Keep the blade horizontal and use the middle of the blade, cutting just above the skeleton from the head to the tail (use cutting technique for small fish, page 128). Turn the fish over and cut the second fillet in the same way. Quite a bit of flesh will be left on the skeleton, but as a result fillets are practically free of bones. Slice ribcage bones off fillets.

Pluck bones from the center line with tweezers. Skin the fillets using the *soto-biki* technique shown on page 131.

With a fish slicer (*sashimi-bōchō*), cut fillets using the *usu-zukuri* technique described above, into ⅛-inch (½-cm) slices (*sogi-zukuri* cut).

Working efficiently, it takes less than 5 minutes to transform a leaping trout to sliced *sashimi*.

Place *sashimi* in a bowl of cool water and wash to rid it of the "muddiness" freshwater fish often have and to wash off excess oil, then plunge it into ice water and let stand for 1 minute. Drain in a colander. This kind of washing and plunging into ice water is a technique called *arai*, often used in making *sashimi* with freshwater fish.

Arrange the slices in a row on a bed of finely shred-cut *daikon* and garnish with a decorative leaf or vegetable curl. You may also "garnish" with ice cubes! Serve with a tangy, full-bodied KARASHI-SU-MISO SAUCE made with mustard, vinegar, and *miso* (page 172).

GARNISHES

Garnishes such as are used with *sashimi* are collectively called *tsuma*. For a bed on which to lay *sashimi* slices, use finely shred-cut *daikon*, cut with the *katsura-muki* technique (see page 138) or shred on a grater. You may also use shred-cut lettuce, carrot, or cucumber. Keep shreds crisp in cold water. Drain and pat dry before using.

Other garnishes for color, texture, and flavor are presented here in outline form. Some are common and available anywhere. Others are very esoteric, perhaps unavailable outside Japan and maybe hard to find even there, but the purpose of including them is to give a clear picture of authentic presentation of *sashimi*. Even so, the list of *tsuma* here is far from complete.

From the Western garden are carrot, cucumber (peeled and seeded), red radish, sliced or cut decoratively. You may also use small sprigs of parsley, cress, etc., and parboiled young asparagus tips, and okra.

Listed alphabetically, Japanese fresh garnishes include:

benitade—small wine-red sprouts having a slightly tangy aftertaste.

bōfu—eat only the wine-red stem, not the leaves. Cut the stem into quarters by piercing it with a pin just below the leaves and pulling the pin through the stem length. Place in very cold water, and the quartered stems curl like ribbon.

hanatsuki kyūri (flowering cucumber)—yellow-petaled baby cucumbers. Rub with salt, then immerse quickly in a hot bath, then cold. If you find baby cucumbers without flowers, you can make them more decorative by paring the skin from one end, as if sharpening a pencil.

kinome—fragrant, bright green sprigs of the *sansho* plant (see entry, page 85).

shiso—See entry, page 88. Use the green heart-shaped leaves (*ao-jiso*) as is or shred them. Stems of flowers (*hana hojiso*) and seed pods (*hojiso*) and tiny, red-and-green sprouts (*me-jiso*) can also be used to garnish *sashimi*. Separate the seed pods from the stalk at table by running the stalk between chopsticks or fingers over your dipping bowl, and mix the pods with the soy sauce.

udo—See entry, page 96. Peel and shave into curls.

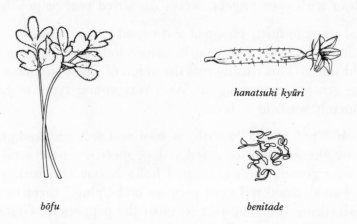

hanatsuki kyūri

bōfu   *benitade*

To be reconstituted:

bakudai—crack pods then soak in tepid tea (*bancha*) with a drop-lid (*otoshi-buta*) for about 20 minutes, or until they break open. Reserve centers and wash in cold water (see color plate 6).

iwatake—translated as "rock moss." Soak in water for 1 day then boil with a pinch of baking soda (see color plate 6).

kiku (chrysanthemum)—fresh flowers may be used as they are. A sheet of dried yellow flower petals must be boiled for about 1 minute, then flavored with salt and vinegar.

Suizenji nori—a dried pond alga from Kyushu. Soak in water to soften. (see color plate 6)

CONDIMENTS

Wasabi horseradish is to *sashimi*, especially strong-flavored fish, exactly what horseradish is to boiled or roast beef. In fact, both share the same fresh sharpness, though fresh Japanese *wasabi* has a stronger "bite." Scrape the green root clean and remove knots with paring knife. Grate in a circular motion on a fine grater (graters discussed on page 104). Pinch the freshly grated *wasabi* into a cone between your thumb and first two fingers and put this dab of pale green paste on the serving vessel.

The "*wasabi*" available dried and powdered and in a moist form sold in a small tube (refrigerate after opening) is not made of true *wasabi* and has a harsher but less sharp taste than the fresh root. Because it loses its fragrance quickly when fresh, grate and use *wasabi* in exact quantities. *Wasabi* is also used in making some types of *sushi*.

Shōga is fresh ginger. Peel rhizome and grate on a fine grater. If the finely grated ginger is too watery, gently press out moisture in a piece of clean cheesecloth or with your fingers. Never use dried root or powder.

Sarashi-negi refers to finely chopped and rinsed green onion. Use any variety of green onion. Chop very fine, wrap in cheesecloth, and gently rinse in a large bowl of cold water. This rinsing rids the onion of slight sliminess and bitterness. Wring gently but thoroughly. With very young types of green onion, or chives, merely wash in a sieve.

Momiji-oroshi, "red maple" radish, is cool and soft-textured grated radish given bite by the addition of dried red peppers. Prepare a piece of giant white radish for grating and make 3 or 4 holes in one end with a chopstick. Seed 3 or 4 small dried red chili peppers and "plug" them into the holes in the radish, using the chopstick to push the peppers in. Grate the whole on a fine grater. The result will be very watery, so gently wring in a piece of clean cheesecloth.

None of these four spicy condiments keeps very well. Prepare only what you will need. Leftovers will have to be thrown away.

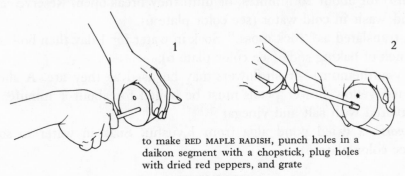

to make RED MAPLE RADISH, punch holes in a daikon segment with a chopstick, plug holes with dried red peppers, and grate

Dipping Sauces

Tosa Soy Sauce
(*Tosa-jōyu*) 土佐醬油

Basically soy sauce with bonito flavoring added, this is the most popular of sauces that accompany *sashimi*. Tosa is the old name of the southernmost area of Shikoku, known for its bonito catch.

1 cup

5 tsps *saké*
3 Tbsps *mirin*
2-inch (5-cm) square giant
  kelp (*konbu*)
1 cup dark soy sauce
3 Tbsps *tamari* sauce
⅓ ounce (10 g; 1 small
  handful) dried bonito
  flakes (*hana-katsuo*)

Mix the *saké* and *mirin* and burn off the alcohol. Wipe the giant kelp with a damp cloth. Put all the ingredients in a bowl and let stand 24 hours. Strain through cheesecloth and store in a cool dark place for 30 days to mature. Keeps 2 to 3 years, but the best flavor occurs after aging from 6 months to 1 year. (This liquid can be strained and used after only 1 day's aging, but only in an emergency.) Should you need a *sashimi* dip at a moment's notice, mix to taste dark soy sauce with *mirin* from which the alcohol has been burnt off.

Sesame Soy Sauce
(*Goma-jōyu*) ごま醬油

makes ½ cup

Toast 2 Tbsps white sesame seeds in a dry frying pan till golden brown and grind to a flaky paste in a Japanese grinding bowl (*suribachi*). Stir well into ½ cup of TOSA SOY SAUCE (or use dark soy sauce plus ½ Tbsp *mirin* from which alcohol has been burnt off).

Plum Soy Sauce
(*Bainiku-jōyu*) 梅肉醬油

makes ½ cup

Rub 2 Tbsps PICKLED PLUM meat (*bainiku*, available canned) through a sieve. Or remove seeds and use the meat of whole red pickled plums (*umeboshi*) and rub through a sieve. Combine 2 Tbsps sieved plum with ½ cup TOSA SOY SAUCE. Mix well and use.

Horseradish Soy Sauce
(*Wasabi-jōyu*) わさび醬油

makes ½ cup

Mix 1 Tbsp finely grated *wasabi* horseradish with ½ cup TOSA SOY SAUCE (or use dark soy sauce).

Ginger Soy Sauce

(*Shōga-jōyu*) しょうが醬油

makes ½ cup

Mix 1 Tbsp finely grated ginger with ½ cup TOSA SOY SAUCE (or use dark soy sauce). Prepare only immediately before using.

Note: In using the two immediately preceding, which include condiments, it is, of course, not necessary to garnish plates with or use any other spicy condiment.

Ponzu Sauce

(*Ponzu*) ぽん酢

Also widely used as a dressing for vinegared foods (*sunomono*) and with one-pot dishes, such as SHABU-SHABU.

about 2½ cups

1 cup lemon juice or combination lemon-lime (in Japan, *sudachi* citron or other very acid citrus fruits are used)
⅓ cup plus 2 Tbsps rice vinegar
1 cup dark soy sauce
2 Tbsps *tamari* sauce
3 Tbsps *mirin*, alcohol burned off
⅓ ounce (10 g; 1 small handful) dried bonito flakes (*hana-katsuo*)
2-inch (5-cm) square giant kelp (*konbu*)

Mix all ingredients and let stand 24 hours. Strain through cheesecloth and mature 3 months in a cool dark place, or refrigerate. Keeps indefinitely, but should be used within 1 year for best flavor.

Mustard-Vinegar-*Miso* Sauce

(*Karashi-su-miso*) からし酢味噌

Also good with boiled pork and certain vegetable dishes.

about 2 cups

miso *base:*

   ¾ cup (220 g) white *miso*
   2 eggs yolks, beaten
   2 Tbsps *saké*
   2 Tbsps sugar
   ½ cup water
1 Tbsp rice vinegar
1 Tbsp powdered mustard
   blended to a paste with
   ½ Tbsp water; let ripen
   1 hour

Blend *miso* with beaten egg yolks, *saké*, and sugar. Thin *miso* mixture with ½ cup water. Put in a double boiler *over* hot water and stir till thick as original *miso.* Remove from heat and cool to room temperature. Refrigerate this base mixture in sealed container. Keeps 3 weeks.

For use: Mix 6 Tbsps *miso* base mixture with 1 Tbsp rice vinegar and ⅓ tsp mustard paste.

There are no hard and fast rules for what dipping sauces to use for what fish, but in general, the lighter the flavor of the fish, the lighter the seasoning. Lemony PONZU goes well with light-flavored, nonoily, white-fleshed fish and preferably when it is cut in paper-thin slices. Thicker-cut white-fleshed fish needs a stronger soy flavor, because the larger volume of the pieces dissipates the lightness of PONZU.

Miso, mixed with vinegar and sometimes mustard, masks the muddiness of freshwater fish, and the vinegar kills parasites. The vinegar also tenderizes octopus.

Grilling and Pan-Frying
Yakimono

It seems reasonable to assume that man's first cooking was done directly over an open flame—what we call grilling or broiling today. In Japanese cooking, simmered and grilled foods constitute the two widest food categories after the preparation of raw fish, which is the biggest category. *Yakimono*, literally "grilled things," includes foods ranging from charcoal-grilled whole fish skewered and set in an S-curve so it seems as if the fish on the plate is poised in the waves, the salt like flecks of ocean foam, to chicken tidbits on short skewers basted in sweet soy sauce, one kebab enough for a few mouthfuls, the perfect food for leisurely conversation and drink. The *yakimono* category also includes pan-fried dishes, such as thick rolled omelettes, because the Japanese verb *yaku* encompasses the meanings of "to grill," "to broil," "to bake" (in oven), and "to pan-fry." The essence of this technique is to cook quickly over such high heat that the outside crisps while the inside remains tender and succulent.

For example, the tastiest portion of *hirame* flounder is the thin strip of flesh attached to that row of tiny bones called the *engawa*, or "veranda," which runs all the way round the fish. This is the muscle that undulates and enables the fish to swim. If skillfully grilled over good charcoal, the skin and tiny bones become deliciously crisp, while the flesh remains tender.

The secret of *yakimono* (grilling) is to stop cooking when the heat has barely reached the center but the outside is crisp. Grilled shrimp should be so crisp on the outside that it crumbles, but the center should be moist. All the degrees of doneness—*au bleu*, rare, medium-rare, and well-done should be present in the same grilled piece of beef. Pork, must, of course, be cooked through. But chicken, like fish, tastes better if "just done" and moist inside.

My favorite grilled dish is the skeleton of any fish that has just been filleted for *sashimi*—say flounder or sea bream—since there is always flesh adhering to the bones no matter how skillful the filleting. Just grilled lightly, that flesh is delicious. *Ayu no shio-yaki* (salt-grilled sweetfish) is another favorite of mine. It is the *pièce de résistance* of Japanese grilled foods. Unfortunately there are no *ayu* in North American rivers. The *ayu*, or sweetfish, is at its prime between May and June. The salt you liberally sprinkle it with gets charred too, and the whole fish is delectable, bitter innards and all. It is one of the few Japanese dishes in which this bitterness is meant to be enjoyed.

There are two kinds of broiling: that done over a direct flame and what might be termed the indirect method. Bonito *tataki* (a *sashimi* variant, in which the surface of the fish fillet is seared) is done in the direct manner to bring out the flavor of the fat under the skin. The traditional way involves just placing the bonito fillet into burning straw, which burns fast and hot. Nothing could be simpler or more direct. Indirect broiling now often makes use of a flameproof mat of some kind, a perforated metal plate, or a pan. Chicken, duck, and some vegetables are best done over the direct heat of the flame. Asparagus is excellent grilled thus and served with lemon and salt; so are onions, both Spanish and green; eggplant is gently slashed, grilled, then eaten with gingered soy sauce.

There are degrees with grilling, of course. Some things are better grilled very lightly, some done to a golden turn, some almost burnt to a crisp. Personal taste is an arbiter too. Some people like mushrooms really charred, while others prefer them lightly done. It mainly depends on the character of the food itself. Grilled bean curd should be well charred on a high heat. YAKITORI (chicken kebabs) too, taste nicer with charred bits among the gold.

In France the diners specify how they want their steak: *au bleu*, *saignant*, *à point*, or *bien cuit*, but in Japan such decisions are left to the chef, who determines what suits each ingredient best.

Yakimono dishes come towards the end of a formal meal, so their volume is never great. Their blacks and golden browns call for chinaware in harmonizing shades. Dark brown pottery, of course, is out.

Direct-flame cooking preserves simplicity and purity of flavor, and is easy and quick. Charcoal broiling or grilling predominates in the history of Japanese cooking; the oven was never developed. Foods that in other cultures might be baked in the dry heat of brick or clay oven are grilled over an open fire in Japan. Even today, most households get along without a large oven that will accommodate a many-pound fowl or a ham or roast. Cooking in Japan is largely a stove-top process. Charcoal grilling is commonly done in restaurants; an average urban home uses appliances that make it possible to use stove-top gas burners as grilling units.

The spirit of a former age, when grilling was done at pit hearths at the center of communal rooms or over charcoal-filled braziers, has yet to be lost. *Robata-yaki*, or "grilled by the fireside," restaurants are extremely popular nowadays. Patrons perch on stools at a bar and order their favorite fresh foods to be grilled. Which leads us to the subject of charcoal.

The Japanese never strive for the aromatic smoky flavor that Americans, for example, associate with charcoal grilling. A charcoal was developed to suit Japanese needs, specifically one that burns smokelessly and odorlessly and emits a very hot heat so foods grill quickly. The best hardwood charcoal, called *Binchō*, is made of oak, which came, traditionally, from Wakayama Prefecture. *Binchō* was named after a wholesale charcoal dealer. This charcoal is so hard and shiny that when poured from its sack it looks and sounds like large obsidian chips. It has such a high kindling point that it must be started with softer pine charcoal. *Binchō* charcoal is expensive, however, and produced only in small quantities, so a commercial grade of mass-produced charcoal is more often used. Or gas or electricity. But *Binchō* charcoal burns for 8 hours, and one batch will cook both lunch and dinner.

A wide range of grilling utensils are available on the Japanese market—skewers of varying lengths and a number of materials, grills of all sizes, mainly designed for fish, but easily used for chicken or whatever. Interestingly, grilling on a turning spit is not part of traditional Japanese cooking. Perhaps it never developed because the foods usually grilled—fish, vegetables, and chicken—were not large and heavy and do not require much time over the fire. There are no sides of beef, no legs of veal or lamb or whole roast kid in Japanese cooking.

In fact, history and geography conspired to lead Japanese to develop a taste for fish, and grilling fish is what is done best.

With chicken, meat of the thigh and leg is preferred for grilling because it roasts moist and tender. Breast alone tends to be dry. Duck is also sometimes grilled, but here the problem is one of excess fat, which must be trimmed off.

Despite the host of vegetables available in Japan and generally used for simmered, deep-fried, or steamed dishes, or as salad ingredients, only a limited number are grilled. Mushrooms are very good, as are eggplant, small green peppers, onions, etc. Bean curd (*tōfu*), which is a vegetable product, is included in the *miso*-anointed subgenre of grilling called DENGAKU (page 192).

Fish and fowl are often marinated before grilling as much for tenderizing as for seasoning. Japanese marinades ordinarily are a combination of *saké*, soy sauce, and *mirin*. Foods are normally marinated only for about 30 minutes, quite a bit shorter than the time it takes for a typical red or white wine and vinegar marinade of Western cooking to do its work. Another point is that

Japanese foods are usually cut into small portions or bite-sized pieces, which reduces both marinating time and grilling time.

Salt is sometimes used alone as a seasoning for *shio-yaki*—"salt-grilled" foods—fish in particular. White-fleshed saltwater fish, lobster, squid, and shellfish as well as small freshwater fish are grilled immediately after proper salting. In the case of fatty fish, like mackerel, salt is used to draw moisture and oil out of the flesh, so such fish is left for a while after salting and before grilling. Red tilefish (*amadai*) is white fleshed but is salted and left to rest like a fatty fish (page 363).

Skewering: The common Japanese method of grilling is to thread foods on skewers and either rest the skewers on braces or lay them on a grill over the fire. Using skewers makes handling and turning easier. Though short bamboo skewers are used for individual chicken kebabs (YAKITORI) and for other small morsels of food, thin stainless steel skewers conveniently come in a number of lengths. Choose an appropriate length for the size of your grill and the type of food you will broil. While foods are grilling, it is always wise to rotate each skewer a few times so food does not cook on and skewers are easy to remove. The grill should be preheated.

In threading food onto skewers, the single most important point is to do it in a way that enhances the look of the final dish. In other words, make the dish as appetizing in form and shape as possible. The Japanese have devised various techniques of skewering foods that allow efficient cooking and an attractive result.

One main object in skewering is to make sure that the side of the fish that is presented to the diner—whether a whole fish, a fillet, or a fillet slice— is not mutilated by skewer holes. In grilling whole fish (the culinary term is *sugata-yaki*, or "form grilling"), skewers must run through the spinal bones yet never pierce one side of the fish. It is this unpierced side that will be seen.

With fillets, skewering must be done crosswise with a number of skewers so the flesh will not flake away and fall down into the charcoal. Skewers are inserted in the flesh underneath the skin of fillets so that the skewer holes are hidden. It is easy to deduce why working with thick fillets is easier than working with thin ones. To make sure that fillets are grilled uniformly, when arranging several pieces on the same set of skewers, thread them on so that the thicker pieces can be grilled over the hottest heat, which is usually in the center of the charcoal fire.

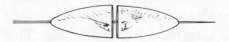

skewer so thick flesh is in hottest part (center) of fire

Grilled fish skin is a real delicacy. The skin of very, very fresh fish shrinks over a fire, and this action can damage the fish's shape, which you have worked to keep in skewering. To keep shrinkage at a minimum, before skewering, slash fillets or fillet slices lightly in one or two places. With a whole fish, prick skin with a needle, allowing condiments to seep in and fat to flow out.

Some fish-skewering techniques:

"Wave skewering" (*uneri-gushi*) applies to ocean fish and is the same as the techniques known as "climbing skewering" (*nobori-gushi*) and "dancing skewering" (*odori-gushi*), which are for freshwater fish. This standard technique is applied to whole fish—whether large or small. It results in fish that look as if they are still actively swimming upstream or against a current. First gut the fish so as to keep the belly intact (see page 121).

Use 2 long skewers for a large fish and begin skewering from the tail. Important: *the skewers go in and come out of the same side of the fish.* For a small fish, a single skewer may be used. Hold the small fish in your left hand and begin skewering just beneath the eye, bring the tip out just below the gill flap, and so on. The tail will stand up smartly if the skewer is made to come through about 2 inches from the end of the tail on the same side that threading was begun.

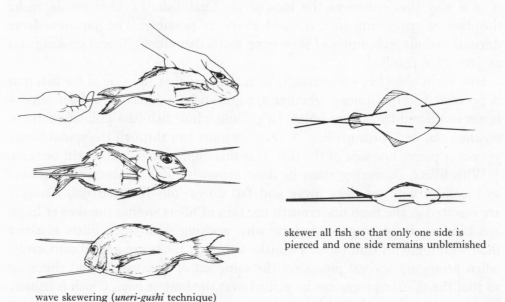

skewer all fish so that only one side is pierced and one side remains unblemished

wave skewering (*uneri-gushi* technique)

When a fish is skewered and ready to be grilled, prick skin a few times with a needle to prevent it from blistering and shrinking, then salt tail and fins heavily, as shown, to keep them from scorching. This is "cosmetic" salting. You may wrap fins and tail with foil after salting.

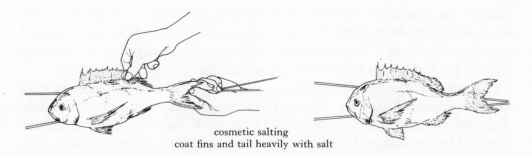

cosmetic salting
coat fins and tail heavily with salt

"Tucked-under skewering" (*tsuma-ore-gushi*). "*Tsuma-ore*" refers to tucking a kimono up to allow oneself freer movement. In Hiroshige's woodblock prints, for example, figures of men as bearers on the mountain highways or as barge workers on riverways are often shown with their kimonos tucked up into their sashes. This term is applied to a skewering technique, used mainly with thin fillets, which by "tucking" adds height to an otherwise flat fillet piece, because the fillet retains the tucked form after being unskewered. This form enhances the appearance of the fish on the serving plate. Tucking also acts to slow the cooking, keeping fillets soft and preventing drying.

There are two ways of tucking fillet pieces on skewers. When only one side is tucked, the technique is called, aptly, "one-sided tucking" (*kata-tsuma-ore*). When both sides of the fillet are treated this way, the skewering technique is "two-sided tucking" (*ryō-tsuma-ore*).

one-sided tucking   two-sided tucking

You may put 2 or 3 pieces of fillet on a set of skewers. Skin is sometimes cross-scored lightly to keep it from shrinking.

As a rule, fish is skewered lengthwise (*tate-gushi*). "Side skewering" (*yoko-gushi*) is used primarily for eel fillets or thin fillets with skin. Also good for whole shrimp and for small whole fish to be grilled in twos or threes. There are many variations of technique, each of which has its own name.

1. The name may refer to the number of skewers—1 skewer is *ippon-gushi*; 2 skewers, *nihon-gushi*, etc.

2. The form of the fish desired after grilling determines technique. An example is the "wave skewering" (*uneri-gushi*) described above.

3. The manner in which the skewers are inserted determines the technique name, such as the *nui-gushi*, "stitch skewering," technique used for squid.

Skewers are pushed in and out at intervals, resembling stitchwork. This stitch skewering helps keep the shape of squid, which tends to shrink and warp during grilling. (A short skewer is inserted diagonally after the primary skewers are in place to help minimize warping.)

4. "Flat skewering" (*hira-gushi*) is used to thread several pieces of fillet on a single set of skewers. Skewers are inserted crosswise, in the middle of the flesh at right angles to the grain of the flesh, because, if some fish are skewered in the *tate-gushi* manner, the flesh easily flakes off and falls into the fire. Cross-score to keep skin from shrinking.

5. The "fan style" (*ōgi-gushi*) allows the skewers to be gripped easily.

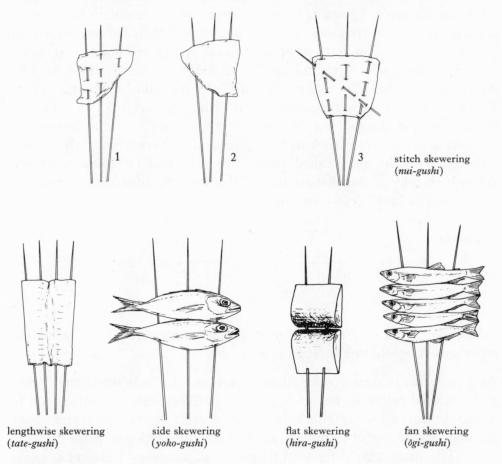

1   2   3   stitch skewering (*nui-gushi*)

lengthwise skewering (*tate-gushi*)   side skewering (*yoko-gushi*)   flat skewering (*hira-gushi*)   fan skewering (*ōgi-gushi*)

The fire: Exposing foods to proper heat is another variable to attend to in grilling. Here is where practice will make perfect. If you place skewers too close to the coals, the food will scorch on the outside and will not be done on the inside. If too far away, it will take too long for the foods to cook, and juices will drip down and evaporate, leaving foods dry and tough.

Try to grill on a fire that is "just right." This usually means starting the charcoal fire about 1½ to 2 hours before cooking time. Coals should be red. If you are using an oven broiler instead of a charcoal fire, the oven should be preheated. Usually, a very hot fire is good for grilling. A rather dangerous but helpful rule of thumb is to hold your hand over the fire. If you cannot count to three before having to withdraw your hand, the fire is right. A less intense heat, however, is best when grilling whole fish than when grilling pieces of fillet so that the outside does not burn before the inside is done. Similarly, less heat is advisable when using basting sauces such as TERIYAKI SAUCE (see page 200) or YAKITORI SAUCE (page 185), which scorch easily.

Basting: Japanese do baste grilling foods, but use a technique that is slightly different from that employed in Western cuisine. First, because the volume of skewered foods is relatively small (that is, no large roasts), basting does not begin till foods are more than half-done, usually when beads of "sweat" form on the skin or flesh of the food being grilled. Whereas butter is often used in Western cooking for basting, it is rarely used in Japanese cooking (except for a small number of pan-fried items like scallops). Japanese are partial to using basting sauces made of sweetened soy sauce. TERIYAKI and YAKITORI sauces are the prime examples. Other foods—particularly vegetables such as green peppers and eggplant—are simply brushed and kept glistening with salad oil or sometimes basted with TERIYAKI SAUCE.

Grilling: Ever conscious of how food will look on a plate, Japanese chefs and home cooks always grill first the side of the food that will face up when served. For a sea bass fillet or boned chicken, this means that the crisp, flavorsome skin will attract the attention of the diner's eye. Grilled first, the skin side is usually "cleaner." This method also keeps juices from dripping through the meat onto the fire. *Turn only once.* Constant turning merely ensures that a maximum amount of natural juice is lost into the fire, creating food-blackening smoke. The less movement over the fire the better—not only in terms of the effects on appearance but on flavor too.

How much, or to what extent, should foods be grilled? A good rule of thumb is to grill the first side till the whole dish is about 60 percent done (beads of pinkish "sweat" will form on the upper side in the case of fish or chicken, and the side facing the fire should be nicely browned). Then turn and grill the "back" side till cooked. Most foods should actually be taken off the grill when almost done because retained heat will finish the required cooking. Chicken should not be cooked until dry—the center should have a pink flush and be moist. Duck may still be rosy in the center. Fish should be light and flaky. Below is a more specific guide:

White-fleshed fish—Because flesh is tight and not very watery, remove from fire when 90 percent done and let retained heat finish cooking.

Fatty-fleshed fish—Because flesh is watery and has a distinct odor, such fish must be thoroughly done over the fire. Do not count on retained heat helping much.

Freshwater fish—Such fish usually taste muddy if underdone. They may be grilled with entrails intact, and should be grilled longer than ocean fish.

Shellfish, lobster, and *squid*—Grill quickly over strong heat to prevent flesh from becoming tough and rubbery.

Vegetables—A strong heat for vegetables with a high water content; medium heat for those that are more fibrous. Baste with salad oil, which is a good heat conductor.

Animal meat—Heat should penetrate through white-fleshed meats (poultry), but red meat may be taken off the fire when medium or rare.

Salt-Grilled Sea Bass
(*Suzuki Shio-yaki*) すずき塩焼き

This basic technique can be used with many kinds of fish. There are 3 principles for success in salt-grilling fish: the skin should be crisp; the flesh should not be overcooked; fish should be served and eaten hot.

4 servings

1¾ pound (800 g) sea bass fillet
12 small green peppers (*ao-tōgarashi*) or 4 small bell peppers
salt
vegetable oil
lemon wedges
PICKLED GINGER SHOOTS
  (*hajikami shōga*)

To prepare: Cut fillets crosswise into 4-inch (10-cm) slices. Salt rather heavily (*furi-jio* technique, page 132). Skewer with the "flat skewering" (*hira-gushi*) described above on page 180. Thread 2 fillets on a pair of skewers.

Wash small green peppers (*ao-tōgarashi*) and cut off stems. If using bell peppers, wash, stem, seed, and cut in half lengthwise. Skewer crosswise, using a pair of skewers.

To grill and serve: Use the hottest charcoal fire and adjust the grill to the optimum cooking distance from the coals. Place skewered fish with skin side facing the fire and grill till 60 percent done, about 5 minutes. The flesh on the upper side of the fillet will begin to bead with pinkish sweat; skin facing the fire will be crisp golden brown.

Turn and continue grilling till done, about 2 minutes more. Rotate each skewer once or twice to keep flesh from sticking.

At the same time, grill the green peppers, basting with oil and turning once. Total grilling time for peppers, about 2 minutes.

Remove skewers and arrange fish on individual plates. Put 3 small green peppers or 2 bell pepper halves on each plate too. Garnish with a wedge of lemon and a PICKLED GINGER SHOOT (*hajikami shōga*). Serve hot.

Bamboo leaves are often used as plate-liners for grilled fish dishes. If a fish is served whole, the head is placed on the left side of the plate (the diner's left). This Japanese convention has its roots in such practical things as convenience of eating for a (right-handed) diner with chopsticks (try drawing a picture of a fish and see which direction it faces). How the fish is going to be presented is something to figure out carefully before skewering it.

Deciding on garnishes is no problem with grilled foods, unless you consider wide selection a problem. Here are just a few of the many foods that make good garnishes.

Acidic garnishes such as vinegared CHRYSANTHEMUM TURNIPS or pink PICKLED GINGER SHOOTS, vinegared lotus root slices or vinegared wafer-thin field yam slices, pickled shallots (*rakkyō*), and the like, are very suitable for grilled fish and beef.

Lemon wedges go well with salt-grilled fish (and dishes pan-fried with a little butter like scallops or abalone).

Good for TERIYAKI dishes (pan-broiled and grilled) and YAKITORI and other "thick" tasting grilled foods are vinegared cucumber slices, pickled radish, grilled green onions, or grilled small green peppers (*ao-tōgarashi*).

In recent years, more and more Japanese dishes are leaving the category of exotic fare eaten occasionally in restaurants and are becoming part of the familiar repertoire of meals cooked at home. *Yakitori*, literally "grilled chicken" —6-inch (15-cm) kebabs of chicken morsels, grilled over live coals and basted with a sweet soy-based sauce—is one of Japan's more popular foods that seems a likely candidate for a permanent place in the multinational cooking of America.

In Japan, though YAKITORI is eaten at home, it is also the ultimate food to go with drink, the product of colorful backstreet stalls with special narrow, long braziers that can accommodate many skewers at once, where office workers scurrying to catch trains home break stride and perch on a streetside stool for a quick beer and YAKITORI and a bit of gossip. Of course, there are also long-established YAKITORI restaurants devoted to nothing but the serious serving of this chicken speciality and its many variations.

The best part of chicken for YAKITORI is leg or thigh. Meat from this part of the bird is more juicy than the fine-textured breast. Chicken livers (washed to eliminate the odor) and even chicken skin are also delicious skewered and grilled as are minced chicken balls and chicken wings. Vegetables are also made *à la yakitori*. The most popularly used vegetables are long onions (*naganegi*; substitute leeks) and green peppers, with mushrooms next in line. With this variety, it is easy to see how versatile YAKITORI is. The version included here is the standard basic one, but this can be expanded as one desires. *Yakitori* is a dish that has possibilities as the main attraction of a barbeque party.

Hosts might be interested to know that the cutting and skewering can be done well in advance, which means that the only last-minute work is grilling the kebabs, an event that guests enjoy watching. An all-Japanese, all do-ahead party menu might include: cold ROLLED OMELETTE, sliced and "tied" with *nori* seaweed (page 203); several kinds of YAKITORI, recipe below; a light vinegared salad; and RICE BALLS (page 440). Fresh fruit for dessert.

Good YAKITORI SAUCE enhances the flavor of grilled chicken morsels. This sauce is available store-bought, but it is easy to prepare a homemade version, which can be kept going indefinitely by adding fresh sauce as the original batch is depleted. Some very fine YAKITORI shops add to the batch this way and keep their sauces going for up to 10 years! These sauces are especially rich and flavorful because, instead of brushing skewered food with sauce over the flame, chefs at these places customarily dip hot, cooked skewered foods into a pot of sauce. (The process is: grill without sauce till 80 percent cooked; dip skewers in sauce; grill again till completely cooked; dip in sauce again; grill again briefly.) The hot juices from the grilling chicken add a flavor background to the original sauce mixture. A glance at the ingredients below will give you some idea of the sweetness of the sauce. It is not quite viscous, but very thick. The roasted chicken leg bone is optional, but it adds flavor.

Yakitori Sauce

(*Yakitori no Tare*) 焼き鳥のたれ

3⅓ cups

bone of one chicken leg
1¼ cups *saké*
½ cup plus 2 Tbsps *mirin*
5½ ounces (160 g) rock sugar
2 cups dark soy sauce
3 Tbsps *tamari* sauce

To prepare: Remove meat from bone. Grill or roast bone till crisp but not scorched.

Combine other ingredients in a medium-sized saucepan and stir well. Add grilled chicken bone. Simmer over low heat till reduced by 20 percent, stirring frequently till rock sugar is dissolved.

Remove from heat, let come to room temperature and strain. Discard bone. Refrigerate tightly sealed in a bottle, or store in a dark cool place.

If you dip skewers into sauce during grilling instead of basting, you should reheat the sauce after every use and simmer for a few minutes to cook out moisture given off by the grilled foods. Allow to come to room temperature and strain before storing. If this step is skipped, moisture from the grilled foods is liable to sour the sauce.

Quick Yakitori Sauce

(*Sokuseki Yakitori no Tare*) 即席焼き鳥のたれ

For one-time use only; throw away leftovers.

7 Tbsps *saké*
¾ cup dark soy sauce
3 Tbsps *mirin*
2 Tbsps sugar

Bring to boil (to eliminate alcohol).

The following recipe for YAKITORI is designed for a small party—indoor or outdoor—taking into consideration the guest(s) who cannot resist just one (or five) more. Skewer the various types of food as shown. Figure on at least 10 skewers per person.

Here are some typical YAKITORI kebab types. Since each ingredient has its own cooking time, it is skewered separately; the onion-chicken combination is an exception.

    small chicken leg (salted; without skewers)
    chicken wing with tip removed (salted; with or without skewer)

halved chicken livers
halved gizzards
squares of chicken skin
long onion and chicken
minced chicken balls
long onion (or leek)
mushrooms
ginkgo nuts
bell peppers
small green peppers

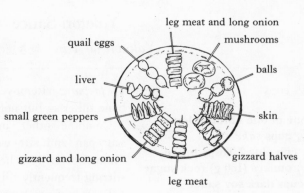

It is convenient to cut all the ingredients into small morsels first, then to do all the skewering at once. You will then be sure to distribute ingredients evenly and have enough of every combination.

For a simpler meal, concentrate on only one kind of kebab—for example, only meat or only livers.

Yakitori

焼 き 鳥 (color plate 16)

4 servings

⅔ pound (310 g) chicken livers
2 pounds (1 kg) boned chicken leg meat (thigh and leg).
8 small bell peppers
5 long onions (*naganegi*) (substitute 7-8 medium leeks)
YAKITORI SAUCE (recipe above)
ground *sansho* pepper
seven-spice mixture (*shichimi*)

improvised *yakitori* grill using bricks

To prepare: Cut livers in half, wash well, and drain.

Bone chicken and remove tendons. Cut chicken meat into 1-inch (2½-cm) pieces.

Seed peppers and cut into 1-inch (2½-cm) squares. Clean long onions (or leeks) and cut crosswise into 1-inch (2½-cm) lengths.

Use disposable 8-inch (20-cm) bamboo skewers made specially for *yakitori* and available at oriental provisions stores, or short stainless steel kebab skewers.

Thread ingredients on skewers, making the varieties indicated above. Arrange on a platter.

To grill and serve: Grill over the hottest coals. You can rest skewers on a conventional grill, but the sketch shows a setup with bricks that allows the cook to turn the skewers without burning fingers.

Put the skewers over the coals without salting. Grill and turn several minutes till juices begin to flow out of the foods. Brush with YAKITORI SAUCE or dip kebabs into sauce and continue grilling. Baste or dip a second time. If you dip food into the sauce, let excess sauce drip back into its pot so it does not drip into the fire and cause flare-ups.

Do not overcook, or food will be dry.

As kebabs are finished, remove to serving platter and let guests help themselves. Let guests sprinkle on some fragrant *sansho* pepper powder or seven-spice mixture (*shichimi*), as preferred. Eat while hot, nibbling along the skewers (or slide pieces off skewer onto individual plates and eat with knife and fork). Eating from the skewer is usual in Japan.

VARIATION: Oven-broiled *yakitori*. If you wish to use your oven broiler instead of a charcoal fire for *yakitori*, just cut the chicken in somewhat larger chunks, because broiler temperature is lower than charcoal and small pieces will become dry.

Yūan-yaki, "Yūan-style grilling," most often involving chicken, but also possible for fish, is simplicity itself. Yūan was a famed tea-ceremony master of the Edo period, and this dish is associated with his name. The name Yūan in any recipe indicates the use of a soy-*saké-mirin* marinade often with lemon, ginger, and long onion (*naganegi*) for flavor. The *saké* in the marinade tenderizes the meat. No salt or dips or seasonings are needed. Serve hot or at room temperature.

Whereas YAKITORI is chicken skewered and grilled (or oven-broiled) in bite-sized pieces with an applied sauce, *Yūan-yaki* entails skewering and grilling a large piece of meat that has been marinated. The bone is removed from a whole chicken leg, and the meat is spread flat and pierced with 3 or 4 skewers.

Yūan-Style Grilled Chicken
(*Tori no Yūan-yaki*) 鶏の幽庵焼き

---

4 servings

2 small whole chicken legs (thigh and drumstick), about ½ pound per leg

marinade (for 1 pound of chicken):
½ cup *saké*
½ cup *mirin*

To prepare: Bone chicken leg by the technique described on page 136. Pull out tendons if necessary. Spread meat out flat and pierce the skin a few times with a fork.

Mix *saké*, *mirin*, and soy sauce and add *yuzu* rind. Marinate meat in this mixture for 20 to 30 minutes. Do not use salt; marinade provides sufficient seasoning for chicken.

½ cup dark soy sauce

3 1-x-½-inch(2½-x-1½-cm) slices of *yuzu* citron rind or lemon rind (optional)

2 stalks long onion (*naga-negi*) (substitute 3-4 medium leeks)

ground *sansho* pepper (optional)

skewer chicken through center of meat

To grill and serve: Skewer each piece of meat with about 3 or 4 long stainless steel skewers, as shown.

Grill, skin side first, over hottest coals for about 7 minutes, or till skin is golden brown. Turn and grill other side, about 3 minutes.

Avoid turning chicken more than once; with frequent turning, the coals will flare up often from dipping juices and fat, and the skin might burn black in spots. Do not overcook; chicken meat at center should be faintly pink.

You may also cook, unskewered, in a preheated oven broiler. Turn only once. Broiling time is about 15–20 minutes total for both sides.

When done, rotate skewers to loosen them from meat and slide out. Cut chicken crosswise into ½-inch (1½-cm) slices and arrange portions of 6 slices or so—skin side up—on individual plates. Garnish with 2½-inch (4-cm) lengths of long onion (or leek), marinated and grilled. Sprinkle with a tiny bit of *sansho* pepper powder if *yuzu* or lemon rind is not added to marinade. Serve hot or at room temperature.

With this dish, no lemon or dipping sauce is necessary because chicken has been seasoned by marination.

In the category of *yakimono*, a rolled-beef dish called *Yawata-maki* perhaps deserves more renown.

Maki means "roll," and *Yawata* refers to a site in the ancient capital of Kyoto where burdock plants grew well. The dish consists of thin slices of marbled beef rolled around strips of burdock and grilled in a long roll. To serve, the long roll is cut into bite-sized rounds.

Burdock is bitter and tough, so it must undergo some sort of preliminary preparation. Here, it is boiled and then marinated in a *dashi*-based liquid for 3 to 4 hours. For extra whiteness, it may be boiled in the milky water resulting when uncooked rice is washed, or in lightly vinegared water (½ Tbsp vinegar in 1 quart [1 L] water). This step may be done well ahead of time. Cut and boiled, burdock will keep refrigerated in water for several days.

Burdock may be a hard ingredient to find outside an oriental market. In Japan, burdock in this dish is often replaced by julienne strips of long onion (substitute green onion). If you use onion instead of burdock, the dish is called *Namba-maki*, Namba being a place in modern Osaka once known for its onion fields.

Beef and Burdock Rolls

(*Gyūniku no Yawata-maki*) 牛肉の八幡巻き

4 servings

4 medium burdock roots, scrubbed well with a stiff brush

burdock marinade:

  1⅔ cup *dashi*
  ½ tsp salt
  3 Tbsps *mirin*
  2 Tbsps light soy sauce

1½ pounds (675 g) prime-quality, well-marbled beef

beef-roll marinade:

  3 Tbsps *saké*
  6 Tbsps *mirin*
  6 Tbsps dark soy sauce

ground *sansho* pepper

To prepare: Burdock may be prepared ½ day ahead of time and refrigerated. Cut roots lengthwise into long julienne strips, compensating for the tapering root shape so all strips are approximately the same thickness. A uniform strip size allows even cooking.

Boil strips till soft in generous quantity of milky water from rice washing or in light vinegar water (½ Tbsp vinegar: 1 quart [1 L] water). Plunge hot burdock into cold water and leave till cool.

Combine ingredients for burdock marinade and let cooled burdock strips marinate for 3 to 4 hours, then pat dry before using.

Have your butcher cut meat into paper-thin slices about 1½ inches (4 cm) wide by 4 inches (10 cm) long, the same as meat for SUKIYAKI.

Lay ⅓ of meat slices side by side with edges overlapping to make a "sheet" of meat. Along the side of the meat "sheet" closest to you, lay about 8 burdock strips in a row. Take care that the diameter of the burdock row is uniform so that the roll will not have bulges. Roll up the meat "sheet" and burdock and tie securely in 3 places. For tying, use white cotton string. This recipe makes 3 long rolls.

Mix beef roll marinade, place tied rolls in baking pan, pour marinade over rolls, and marinate 1 hour, turning rolls a few times. Reserve marinade for basting.

To grill and serve: With 4 or 5 skewers, pierce rolls laterally as shown. Skewer in a fanlike (*ōgi-gushi*, page 180) arrangement so all the skewer handles come together at one end; this makes grilling easier.

Grill over charcoal for about 5 or 6 minutes, grilling the meat medium or well done, as preferred. If meat looks dry, baste occasionally during grilling with reserved marinade.

(Instead of grilling over charcoal, you may broil, unskewered, in a preheated oven for about 7 minutes, turning once. You may also pan-broil, unskewered, in a large heavy skillet with a scant amount of oil over high heat. When surface is cooked, add marinade, deglaze pan, and continue cooking until done.

Twist skewers in place to loosen and then slide the skewers out. Cut off strings, then slice rolls crosswise into ½-inch (1½-cm) lengths. Arrange rounds on individual serving plates garnished with a few greens and serve hot as an entrée. Season with a light sprinkling of fragrant *sansho* pepper powder. No sauce is necessary. Serve with a simmered vegetable dish at the side and a salad for the main part of a substantial meal. Serve at room temperature as hors d'oeuvre.

rolling, marinating, and skewering beef roll

VARIATION: BEEF AND LONG ONION ROLLS (*Gyūniku no Namba-maki*)

Instead of using burdock, replace with strips of long onion (*naganegi*). Amount depends on size of onions; use the sketches in the burdock recipe as a rough guide to the diameter of the vegetable center of the roll. It is not necessary to boil the onions, as is done for burdock, though you may want to rinse onion in cold water, after cutting into strips, to remove slight bitterness. Also omit marination before rolling. Simply cut long onion into strips, rinse, pat dry, and roll in meat "sheet." Proceed with tying, skewering, and grilling of roll as in burdock recipe.

In Japan, besides burdock and long onions some stalky vegetables may do duty in beef rolls. Sometimes used are long strips of parboiled *udo*, a delicate stalk with a light, fennelish flavor, and tender stalks of *fuki*, which tastes like celery. In an American kitchen, you might experiment with parboiled asparagus stalks.

In medieval Japan, public entertainments called *dengaku* were part of agricultural observances and festivals. Among the various forms of dance or acrobatics, dancers known as *dengaku hōshi* cavorted on single short stilts. Small cakes of grilled *tōfu* with *miso* from which a single, flat skewer handle protrudes are somehow reminiscent of the one-stilted *dengaku hōshi*, and thus this *miso*-coated *tōfu* dish took its name.

In the 18th century, DENGAKU in various forms was served along the post stations and rest stops on the several great roads that linked major cities and was also frequently served at tea shops in entertainment quarters. The name came to include vegetables and *konnyaku* grilled and anointed with *miso*.

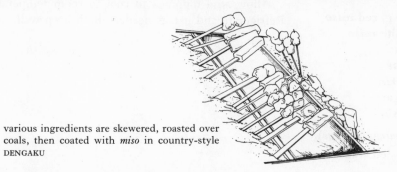

various ingredients are skewered, roasted over coals, then coated with *miso* in country-style DENGAKU

In its 20th-century form, DENGAKU is popular with home cooks. It is easy to make, and with soup, rice, and pickles it provides a filling lunch or good dinner. DENGAKU is very good with *saké*.

Like many things that are based on simple ideas, DENGAKU is extremely versatile. Vegetables may be used in place of bean curd. Vegetables suitable for DENGAKU include: sliced eggplant, large mushrooms, bamboo shoots (boil bamboo till tender, then simmer in seasoned stock, and slice into rounds), *konnyaku* squares (boiled or pan-fried), and green pepper strips. Some seafood also lends itself to this treatment: scallops and such small fish as smelt, or river fish such as *ayu* (sweetfish) and trout.

It is with the *miso* topping, however, that your personal preference has the final say. Below is a basic recipe for the topping, but use this simply as a model. It is perfectly proper to vary the type of *miso* and vary the fragrant seasonings—crushed *kinome* leaves, ground toasted sesame, grated *yuzu* citron rind, ginger juice, and so on.

Besides charcoal broiling, oven-broiling and pan-frying are also possible for DENGAKU.

Dengaku Miso Toppings

田楽味噌

WHITE MISO

¾ cup less 1 Tbsp (200 g) white *miso*
2 egg yolks
2 Tbsps *saké*

To prepare: Put *miso* in top of double boiler, and before putting over hot water blend in egg yolks, *saké*, *mirin*, and sugar. Place over simmering water and gradually add *dashi*. Stir until thick. At the very last moment add *one* of the fragrant seasonings.

2 Tbsps *mirin*
2 Tbsps sugar
7 Tbsps *dashi*

RED MISO

½ cup (150 g) red *miso*
3 Tbsps white *miso*
2 egg yolks
2 Tbsps *saké*
2 Tbsps *mirin*
2 Tbsps sugar
7 Tbsps *dashi*

fragrant seasonings (use one):
  ground toasted sesame
    seeds
  grated rind of *yuzu* citron,
    lime, or lemon
  mortar-ground *kinome*
    leaves
  fresh ginger juice

Dengaku miso is impossible to make in small quantities; it is convenient to prepare these sauces before you start preparing the *tōfu* or while the *tōfu* is being pressed.

Allow *miso* toppings to cool to room temperature. Refrigerate and use as needed. Both keep well.

Bean Curd *Dengaku*
(*Tōfu Dengaku*) 豆腐田楽

For this recipe, "cotton" *tōfu* is the best because it contains less water than "silk" *tōfu*. But any *tōfu* is fragile and tricky to handle without a little practice.

Make both *miso* toppings, using a complementary seasoning in each.

4 servings

2 cakes *tōfu* (bean curd)
white and red DENGAKU MISO
  TOPPINGS (recipes above)

garnishes (choose one):
  white poppy seeds
  kinome sprigs
  toasted white sesame
    seeds
  toasted black sesame seeds

To prepare: Take bean curd out of water in which it has been packed, wrap each cake in a towel, weight lightly (with 1 dinner plate), and let stand at least 1 hour to press out water.

To grill and serve: Cut pressed bean curd cakes into ⅜- × -¾- × -2-inch (1- × -2- × -5-cm) pieces. Skewer each piece with a double-pronged ("pine-needle") skewer, or use two bamboo skewers per piece.

Grill on both sides over hottest charcoal fire for about 3 minutes on each side, till surface is speckled brown and *tōfu* is heated through.

Remove from fire and spread one side with *miso* topping about $1/16$ inch ($1/4$ cm) thick. Use knife to spread topping to edges of *tōfu*. Sprinkle with garnishing seeds, or, if *kinome* sprig is garnish, press it into the topping at center.

Grill the *miso*-topped side only for 1 minute or 2 till thoroughly heated.

Remove to individual plates and serve hot. Eat directly from the skewer.

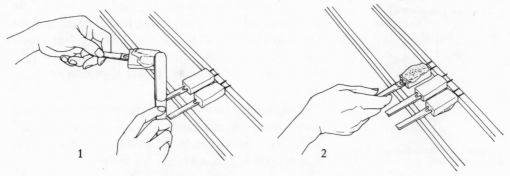

1, 2. apply *miso* toppings to *tōfu* after it has been grilled, then grill topping briefly

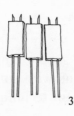

3. two conventional bamboo skewers may be used instead of the special pronged DENGAKU skewers

4. use different garnishes

Although a charcoal fire gives the best flavor, you may also oven-broil (never bake) *tōfu* pieces, unskewered. Pan- or griddle-frying on very high heat is also possible, but deep-frying after dusting with flour is better than pan-frying. With such fried TŌFU DENGAKU, the dish is served immediately after *miso* topping is applied.

The following variation shows how to proceed with vegetables instead of *tōfu*. The mildness of eggplant is harmonious with the deeper flavor of a *miso* topping, and small eggplants—cut in half lengthwise—are perfect in size and shape for this dish. For other vegetables that go well as DENGAKU, see page 191 above.

You can turn DENGAKU into a gala array of different flavors and textures by making both *miso* toppings—one sweet, light, and one dark, salty, red—and use these on all the appropriate ingredients you desire to find and prepare.

Eggplant *Dengaku*

(*Nasu Dengaku*) なす田楽

4 servings

**4-6 small eggplants, or
  2 medium eggplants**
vegetable oil
white and red DENGAKU MISO
  TOPPINGS **(recipes above)**
garnishes (as above)

scored and skewered eggplant
for DENGAKU

To prepare: Wash and dry small eggplants. Leave stems on if eggplants are really tiny, but remove calyx and stem if regular (small) size and cut in half lengthwise. Cross-score cut surface to keep topping from, slipping off. If using larger American eggplant, cut crosswise into rounds ¾ inch (2 cm) thick.

Brush both flesh and skin of eggplant halves lightly with salad oil to keep vegetable from becoming hard and tough over heat. Pierce each half eggplant crosswise with two skewers, if grilling. The eggplant may also be pan-fried in scant oil over high heat or deep-fried.

Grill, broil, pan-fry, or deep-fry till tender, turning once. Apply topping to cut side, as shown; add garnish. Serve immediately. If grilling, you may return *miso*-topped eggplant to heat for toasting.

Scallop *Dengaku*

(*Kaibashira Dengaku*) 貝柱田楽

SCALLOP DENGAKU, is of rather recent creation. It is a good example of a trend in modern Japanese cooking to mix native traditions with some principles and tastes of European cooking, in this case the gratin technique. The dish is oven-baked, not grilled on skewers.

4 servings

1½ pounds (675 g) scallops
salt
vegetable oil
white and red DENGAKU MISO
  TOPPINGS **(recipe above)**
garnishes (as above)

To prepare: Clean scallops by rinsing under cold water and patting dry with paper towels. Salt lightly.

Lightly grease individual casseroles (or shallow baking dish) with salad oil and line casseroles with scallops.

To bake and serve: Cover scallops with *miso* topping in a layer about ⅛ inch (½ cm) thick. Use a knife to spread *miso* topping. Sprinkle on garnishes. Bake about 3 to 4 minutes in a hot oven. Remove from oven and serve immediately. Be careful with timing: if overcooked, scallops toughen. It is enough to cook only the scallops' surface.

Another cooking technique placed in the *yakimono* category includes foil-baking and baking in unglazed earthenware.

Gingami-yaki, literally "foil-grilling," need not be elaborated upon except to say that it is the contemporary version of the age-old practice of wrapping foods in large wet bamboo leaves or putting them in wet paper for cooking in hot ashes, basically similar to the French *en papillote* technique. In Japan, a strong native hand-laid paper was used as a wrapper (it is now very costly). Paper or leaves allow foods to "breathe" as they cook. Today foil is so much more economical than either of these traditional wrappers and it is so available that many home cooks never stop to think about the way foil-baking evolved. They just reach for the roll of foil.

The use of unglazed earthenware for cooking also has a long history. In many cuisines—those of India and China are two that spring to mind—certain foods are packed in wet clay, then "fired" till the clay is baked. The "earthenware" covering is cracked open while still hot, and the contents, nicely cooked in their own juices, are laid bare. In Japan, a 2-piece earthenware vessel called a *hōraku* was developed. It looks like two cymbals sealed rim to rim. In ancient times, such a lidded vessel containing food was sealed with clay or mud and buried in live coals to cook the foods in it.

Whether wrapped in foil or placed in an earthenware *hōraku*, foods are actually steamed by this technique, not broiled. Though this is technically true, in Japan the traditional heat source, live coals, is given precedence, and this method of food preparation is called *mushi-yaki*, "steam-grilling."

The best season for *mushi-yaki* is autumn, when the right ingredients are at their freshest and the steamy warmth emitted by foil pouches brought straight from the fire can be most appreciated. In autumn, fresh mushrooms should definitely be included because they are best at this time of the year. In Japan, the *matsutake*, or "pine mushroom," is the delicacy to include (see page 75). You can use *shiitake* mushrooms instead of the princely (and costly!) *matsutake*, or, going outside the realm of Japanese ingredients, you may use large champignons. Make sure they are firm, white, and fresh.

Whatever type of mushroom you select for steam-grilling, wash *briefly* in running water and then wipe with a damp towel. *Matsutake*, especially, should be washed just briefly, or the flavor is lost. Avoid too much rubbing. Always cut lengthwise into slices about ¼ inch (¾ cm) thick. If slices are too thin, they will become limp in cooking. Large mushrooms and thickish slices are the secret for the best texture and taste when using mushrooms in this sort of cooking.

Mixed Grill in Foil

(*Foiru-yaki*) ホイル焼 or 包み焼き

Use filleted white-fleshed fish of any type—sea bream, sea bass, flounder, sole, and so on—with or without skin, as preferred. Figure on one foil packet per serving. Fish is salted 30 minutes in advance, and vegetables and chicken are salted just before wrapping in foil.

<u>4 servings</u>

1 pound (450 g) sea bass fillets, or fillets of other white-fleshed fish, salted
½ pound (225 g) shrimp
½ pound (225 g) chicken thigh meat
8 large mushrooms (*matsutake*, *shiitake*, or Western-type mushrooms)
butter
1 lemon, sliced thinly
2 Tbsps *saké*

To prepare: Cut large fish fillet crosswise into 4-ounce (115-g) portions, if possible.

Shell and devein shrimp. Leave tails attached. Parboil in lightly salted water till pink, then drain and cool.

Cut chicken into 1-inch (2½-cm) or slightly larger pieces and score each a few·times. This is to make certain that the chicken cooks at the same rate as the fish, which cooks relatively quickly.

Clean mushrooms. Trim off hard *shiitake* stems, but discard only the root end of the *matsutake* stem. Cut lengthwise into slices ¼ inch (¾ cm) thick.

To assemble and grill: The charcoal fire should be at its hottest; coals should be red, and there should be no flame. The hand test for hotness of charcoal is described above, on page 181. (Or, preheat oven to 475°F/250°C).

Butter the centers of 4 12-inch squares of aluminum foil. In the center of each square, place a portion of fish fillet, skin side up. On top and around it arrange shrimp, chicken, and mushroom slices. Top with a pat of butter and a lemon slice. Over each portion sprinkle about ½ Tbsp *saké*.

Fold up into a packet and crimp edges so packet is tightly sealed.

Place on grill above coals and grill for 10 minutes. Do not turn. (Or bake in very hot oven for 15 to 20 minutes.)

To serve: Remove packets from coals (or oven) and place on individual serving plates. Let diners open packets themselves at the table. Serve hot with salt and light soy sauce.

As described above, the lidded earthenware vessel called the *hōraku* or *hōroku* was originally filled with food, sealed with clay or mud, and thrust directly into the hot coals to cook.

Today, of course, such cooking is impractical. The true earthenware, unglazed, easily breakable *hōraku* vessels are still made as a kind of curiosity in two, perhaps three, places. What is passed off as a *hōraku* today is a glazed, often decorated shallow casserolelike thing of the same refractory clay as the *donabe* casserole and made for restaurant use.

A conventional oven's heat is too low for true *hōraku* cooking. This type of earthenware cooking is a fast cooking of delicate foods, not a slow steaming. An oven does not go above 550° F (288° C), while a charcoal fire is in the range of 1470° F (800° C). All the ingredients of a *hōraku* dish have different cooking times, so lacking a large bed of hot coals, the practical way of making this dish is to grill each ingredient separately, then arrange them together on a bed of (preferably hot) beach or river pebbles or rock salt, with a scattering of pine needles. This method makes it easy to use any type of convenient, simple vessel. See color plate 11.

Seafood Platter with Pine Needles
(*Hōraku-yaki*) 焙烙焼き (color plate 11)

---

4 servings

2 small fillets of any white-fleshed fish, salted
8 medium shrimp
8 fresh *shiitake* mushrooms (or large Western-type mushrooms)
pine needles
4 CANDIED CHESTNUTS (recipe, page 461; or bottled)
12 or 24 ginkgo nuts in shells (optional)
rock salt or rounded beach or river pebbles
PONZU SAUCE (see page 172)
lemon slices or wedges

To prepare: Cut each fish fillet in 4 pieces (2 pieces per serving).

Keep shrimp whole, with heads and shells attached. Devein and salt.

Wipe mushrooms and trim.

Wipe pine needles clean of all resin.

To cook: Grill fish, shrimp, mushrooms, and whole candied chestnuts. Roast unshelled ginkgo nuts in dry frying pan.

Roast rock salt in dry frying pan and spread a ¾-inch (2-cm) layer on the bottom of casserole. Or, instead of salt, use pebbles heated in casserole in oven.

On top of the salt, scatter a thin layer of pine needles. On this arrange the fish pieces, skin side up, and then the shrimp, chestnuts, ginkgo nuts, and mushrooms. Scatter on a few more pine needles.

Bring the lidded casserole to the table and dish out with appropriate ceremony. Serve with PONZU SAUCE and lemon wedges.

The reason for including the preceding recipe, even in its emasculated form that has no relation to earthenware cooking, is that it is delicious, decorative, and a concept that can be experimented with by the adventurous cook.

Another good concept, using the same ingredients but with a decorative cooking technique involving a coating of beaten egg white heavily laced with salt, follows. This is a recent innovation that utilizes the dry heat of the oven.

Salt Domes
(Shio Gama) 塩 釜

---

4 servings

4 medium shrimp
2 small white-fleshed fish
  fillets
salt
saké
2 small *matsutake* **or**
  8 medium *shiitake*
  mushrooms
12 or 16 ginkgo nuts, shelled
  and boiled (optional)
1 egg white
¾ cup salt

salt-saturated egg white forms a decorative dome in which delicate ingredients cook

To prepare: Remove heads from shrimp; shell and devein. Leave tails attached.

Cut each fish fillet into thin slices. Separately season shrimp and fish with salt and small amount of *saké*.

Wash mushrooms briefly, pat dry, and notch decorative cross in caps.

Beat egg white until firm but not dry. Add ¾ cup salt and fold in well.

Wrap a single portion (1 shrimp, 2 pieces of fish, 1 mushroom, 3 or 4 ginkgo nuts) in cellophane or baking paper (do not use wax paper or plastic wrap). Sprinkle a baking sheet with salt, place each packet of ingredients on the sheet and, with a rubber spatula, form a dome of salted egg white over each packet.

Bake in a preheated 400°F/205°C oven for about 15 minutes.

Remove white domes to individual plates, garnish with any green leaf from your garden. Serve immediately. Simply break open top of dome, open packet, and eat contents.

In Japanese cooking, skillets are not summarily put aside in favor of charcoal fires and skewers. Many foods that are grilled also can be pan-broiled over high heat in their own fat or with a film of oil in the pan, or quickly browned then lightly sautéed. Since the use of a pan or griddle also is defined by the verb *yaku*, such cooking is a part of the wide *yakimono* ("grilled things") category. Cooking skewered foods over charcoal is the orthodox Japanese method; the use of a pan is something of a stepchild or secondary technique, though often employed. Though many meats may be cooked both ways, some things are strictly skillet food. Omelettes, for instance, depend on skillets for form and can be cooked no other way. Japanese-style omelettes are made in special rectangular skillets.

For pan-broiling and frying the Japanese way, it is important to note that butter is rarely used. Dairy products such as milk, cheese, and butter are not native foods. No matter how inspiring those with Western-trained palates find its flavor, butter does not enhance the already complete range of Japanese seasonings. *Dashi*, soy sauce, *saké*, and the like are the foundations of Japanese seasonings, and have been designed to harmonize perfectly. Butter comes from a different flavor palette. Pan-frying is done with tasteless, odorless oil, used in minimum amounts, which neither adds to nor subtracts from the seasonings. Of course, there are a few exceptions to this general rule: butter may be added in small amounts as a flavoring as in the clam recipe on page 359, but this sort of sautéing is a result of Western influence. And, when butter is used, you will find that the traditional seasonings are omitted.

The various kinds of TERIYAKI are good examples. But a digression is in order to define *teriyaki*. In American-Japanese (and some Western) restaurants one often hears a menu-reader's voice wafting from some table, "What does '*teriyaki*-style' mean?"

As it has come to be known and adapted in the United States, the word *teriyaki* is applied to meat or shellfish, grilled on skewers or pan-broiled, which has been flavored either by marination or by application of a "*teriyaki* sauce." In Japanese cooking, *teriyaki* refers to a sweet soy-sauce-based glaze that is applied in the last stages of grilling or pan-frying to fish, chicken, beef, and pork. *Teri* literally translates as "gloss" or "luster" and describes the sheen of the sauce that goes over the broiled (*yaki*) foods.

There is some choice as to what kind of TERIYAKI SAUCE to use. Simplest of all is to purchase a commercially prepared sauce, the one made by Kikkoman being the most available in the U.S. This is a general all-purpose TERIYAKI SAUCE, and when recipes require a TERIYAKI glaze for basting (or for adding to the skillet in the last minutes of pan-frying), you can use this from the bottle. When using commercial sauce, adjust seasoning(s) to taste.

For homemade TERIYAKI SAUCE, an easy recipe follows. It will keep indefinitely in the refrigerator in a sealed bottle. You may want to make a double batch.

Teriyaki Sauce
照り焼きソース

1⅓ cups

7 Tbsps *saké*
7 Tbsps *mirin*
7 Tbsps dark soy sauce
1 Tbsp sugar

Mix ingredients in a saucepan and bring to a boil over medium heat; boil until sugar is dissolved. Use immediately, or cool, bottle, and store in refrigerator.

In some recipes, like STEAK TERIYAKI on page 370, the TERIYAKI SAUCE is quickly made in the skillet after the pan-frying of the meat.

For fish *teriyaki*, buy fatty fish such as yellowtail, mackerel, fresh tuna, and so on. The flavors of such fish make them particularly well suited to this method of preparation. In Japan, it is easy to buy fillets with skin (which crisps deliciously), but in America, steaks may be more common. Both cuts are acceptable. One technique used with fish that might seem unusual, however, is dousing it with boiling water after frying. This step is practical, not just an overrefinement—the fish is very oily, and rinsing it after cooking lightens the texture and flavor, to which the TERIYAKI SAUCE adds depth. Place cooked fish fillets or steaks in a small, flat sieve or strainer tray, if you have one. A flat vessel is better than the ordinary deep-bowled colander, in which fish is easily broken and damaged.

Yellowtail *Teriyaki*
(*Buri Teriyaki*) ぶり照り焼き (color plate 12)

4 servings

1¾ pounds (800 g) boned yellowtail fillets (with skin) or steaks
salt
4 CHRYSANTHEMUM TURNIPS (see page 251)
4 PICKLED GINGER SHOOTS (*hajikami shōga*) (see page 304)

To prepare: If using fillet, cut crosswise into 4 equal pieces. Steaks should be about ¾ inch (2 cm) thick. Salt fish (*furi-jio* technique, page 132) and let rest at least 30 minutes.

Prepare turnips. Ginger shoots should be on hand. Or, choose other tangy garnishes or even crisp cucumber strips.

To pan-broil and serve: Heat a scant amount of oil in a medium-sized heavy-bottomed skillet. Place over very high heat. Lay in the pieces of fillet (skin side

½ cup TERIYAKI SAUCE (see recipe above)

down) or steaks. Move fish around constantly while frying to keep from sticking. There will be a fair amount of smoke. Turn with a spatula only once. When fish is half done, remove from pan to tray-sieve or colander and pour boiling water over fish to eliminate excess oil.

Return fish to pan with juices still in it. Add TERIYAKI SAUCE. Heat till sauce begins to bubble. Tilt pan and turn slices so fish is well coated with sauce. With spatula remove fish to individual plates. Continue to heat remaining sauce and stir for a minute or so to deglaze pan and give sauce luster. Spoon a few Tbsps of this sauce over the fish on individual plates.

Garnish each plate with one CHRYSANTHEMUM TURNIP and a ginger shoot, or the garnish of your choice. Serve hot as an entrée.

Chicken (as well as pork and beef) may be pan-broiled TERIYAKI style.

Chicken *Teriyaki*
(*Tori no Teriyaki*) 鶏の照り焼き

4 servings

2 chicken legs (thigh and drumstick), boned (see page 136)
vegetable oil
½ cup TERIYAKI SAUCE (page 200)
ground *sansho* pepper (optional)
4 CHRYSANTHEMUM TURNIPS (see page 251)

To prepare: Pierce skin of chicken with a fork to allow sauce to penetrate freely and to avoid shrinkage during frying.

To pan-fry: Over a high flame, heat a scant amount of oil in a large skillet. Lay chicken skin side down in the skillet.

Fry over medium heat, till skin is well browned. Move the chicken in the pan to keep it from sticking to the skillet. When browned, turn and fry, covered, for about 10 minutes.

Remove chicken temporarily from the pan. Over medium heat, into the juices left in the skillet, pour the TERIYAKI SAUCE. Bring liquid to a boil, stirring. After a minute or so the liquid will thicken slightly and take on a luster. Return the chicken to skillet. Continue cooking, over high heat, turning chicken several times so that it is well coated in TERIYAKI SAUCE. Remove from heat when TERIYAKI SAUCE is almost completely reduced, a few minutes at most.

To assemble and serve: Place chicken skin side up on a cutting board and cut crosswise into ½-inch (1½-cm) slices, using the drawing cut (see page 113). Place about 8 slices, skin side up, in a domino or fanlike arrangement, on each individual plate. Sprinkle on a little *sansho* pepper, if desired, and garnish each serving with a CHRYSANTHEMUM TURNIP. Serve hot.

You may, of course, decide on garnishes other than turnips. Some suggestions are: vinegared lotus slices; cocktail onions (in Japan it would be *rakkyō*, a pickled shallot); PICKLED GINGER SHOOTS; cucumber strips, and suchlike. If you want to serve a vegetable with CHICKEN TERIYAKI, you might stir-fry strips of bell pepper for a side dish that will certainly add vibrant color to each plate.

As stated earlier in this chapter, omelettes also fall in the category of *yakimono*. Whereas the French-style omelette is folded after cooking, the Japanese-style omelette is rolled many times in the frying pan during cooking. The result is a cylindrical, loaf- or roll-like omelette, less dense than the creamy Gallic omelette and just as delicious. In fact, the Japanese version is probably best called an egg roll or ROLLED OMELETTE; it is firmly set in its cylindrical shape by letting it stand wrapped in a slatted bamboo mat (*maki-su*) for a minute after being removed from the frying pan. Then it is sliced crosswise into rounds and served hot.

To facilitate making this egg roll, a rectangular frying pan was invented long ago. Most Japanese households are equipped with one, and it is used for nothing but eggs. The rectangular, square-sided pan makes it easy to form a neat, perfectly shaped cylinder, equally thick at the ends and the middle, that can be cut crosswise into rounds without waste at the ends. Lacking such a rectangular pan, the Japanese omelette is close to impossible to make; a conventional omelette will substitute. Japanese rectangular egg pans are made of sturdy materials, often heavy copper. Do not be tempted to experiment with a rectangular cake pan or some other baking tin—they are too thin.

The success of a rolled omelette depends on three things—beating of eggs; temperature of pan; degree of cooking and heating. If eggs are overbeaten, the roll will not be light. The pan temperature must remain constant. Keep the heat about medium-high, so the egg cooks quickly, but not so high that the egg scorches or becomes rubbery. Because heat retained in the roll continues to cook the egg even when removed from the pan, the omelette is done when it is 80 percent cooked and still soft.

The recipe below is for 4 servings, or 2 rolled omelettes about 1 inch (2½ cm) thick and 5 to 6 inches (13 to 15 cm) long. You may mix all the eggs together with the *dashi* stock and other seasonings to get the beating step out of the way at the start, but use only half the mixture to make one roll. Eggs are delicate and difficult to cook to perfection in large quantities.

Rolled Omelette

(*Dashi-maki Tamago*) 出し巻き卵

4 servings (2 rolls)

8 eggs (1⅔ cups)
⅔-¾ cup *dashi* or light
  chicken stock
½ tsp salt
1 Tbsp *mirin* or 1 tsp sugar
1 Tbsp light soy sauce
½ to ¾ cup finely grated
  giant radish (*daikon-
  oroshi*)
few drops light soy sauce
few Tbsps vegetable oil

To prepare: In a bowl, mix eggs just so yolks and whites are roughly mixed but not smoothly combined or frothy. In another bowl, combine room-temperature *dashi* or light chicken broth, salt, *mirin* (or sugar) and light soy sauce. (Sugar must be boiled until dissolved, then *dashi* cooled.)

Pour beaten egg into the *dashi* mixture and fold just till combined. Divide egg-*dashi* mixture in half —each half will make one rolled omelette.

Grate giant white radish and flavor with a few drops light soy sauce.

To fry: Keep *empty* frying pan (Japanese rectangular egg pan) over medium heat till hot. Lightly wipe pan with a cloth swab moistened with oil so only a slight oil film is left. Reserve swab to use again. Test pan to see whether or not it is hot enough for frying by placing a drop of the egg mixture into the center of the pan. It should sizzle. *Maintain the pan at this temperature*, adjusting heat if necessary while making omelette.

When the pan is properly heated, pour ⅓ of egg mixture for one roll into pan and tilt so egg mixture spreads in an even thin layer over the bottom. Break air bubbles formed in the first few seconds after the egg is poured into pan.

When egg sheet starts bubbling around edges and is 70 percent cooked, even though the center top is still runny, tilt pan up and towards you, and with chopsticks or a spatula, roll the egg layer towards you. Leave the roll in the pan. (You may just as correctly tilt the pan away from you and roll egg away from you, continuing till the end with directions opposite to those given here. The direction in which the omelette is rolled makes no difference.)

With the oily swab, oil the pan surface not covered by the omelette roll, then push the omelette back to the just-oiled part of the pan and continue oiling the remaining pan surface. The idea is to oil the entire pan again quickly, without taking the omelette roll out. Reserve oil swab.

Keep the roll at the end of the pan away from you and pour in the second third of the egg mixture. Again, tilt the pan so that the egg mixture covers the bottom of the pan evenly, then briefly lift the edge of the rolled omelette so that the raw egg mixture flows under it too.

When this second pouring of egg mixture begins to set, repeat the rolling operation, using the first roll as the core and wrapping the second sheet of fried egg around it.

Oil the pan again without taking the omelette roll out of the pan. Pour in the last third of the egg mixture and cook and roll in the same way.

Remove from pan and wrap in a bamboo mat. Press gently. A small quantity of brothlike liquid should be given off. If no liquid is forthcoming, the omelette is overdone. Let rest 1 minute in the mat.

To serve: Unwrap omelette roll from bamboo mat and slice crosswise into 2-inch (5-cm) rounds. Place 2 rounds per serving on individual plates and garnish each plate with a mound of soy-flavored finely grated giant white radish.

Serve hot as a side dish for breakfast, a light lunch, or supper.

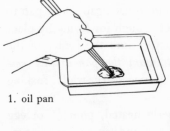

1. oil pan

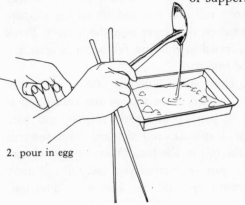

2. pour in egg

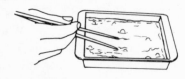

3. break air bubbles

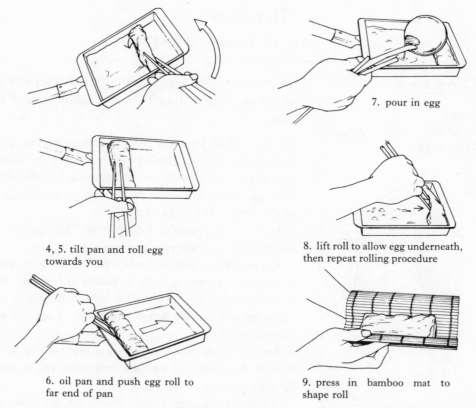

4, 5. tilt pan and roll egg
towards you

6. oil pan and push egg roll to
far end of pan

7. pour in egg

8. lift roll to allow egg underneath,
then repeat rolling procedure

9. press in bamboo mat to
shape roll

Nori seaweed is also a good combination with egg. Lay a sheet of *nori* seaweed over the egg after the first and second pourings and roll with the omelette. The sliced rounds of this omelette have a spiral pattern in the center.

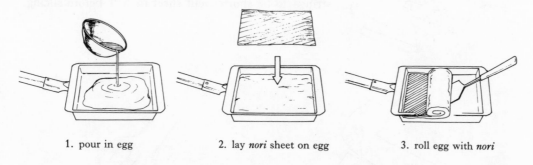

1. pour in egg

2. lay *nori* sheet on egg

3. roll egg with *nori*

In the omelette family is a very thin member, which is extremely versatile. This flat, thin sheet of egg is used somewhat like a crepe for wrapping other ingredients (see SILK SQUARE SUSHI, page 453) and is also cut into threadlike filaments, called "golden strings" (*kinshi-tamago*), and used as a garnish. See the SCATTERED SUSHI recipe on page 448, where the "golden strings" are used to cover a layer of vinegared rice.

Thin Omelette

(*Usuyaki Tamago*) 薄焼き卵

3 7-inch sheets

2 eggs
⅓ tsp salt
2 tsps sugar

To prepare: Mix eggs roughly (do not beat) and stir in salt and sugar. Strain to remove stringy bits of egg white.

To fry: Heat Japanese rectangular egg pan or 7- or 8-inch (18- or 20-cm) skillet over medium heat. Grease pan very lightly with an oil-dampened cloth swab. Test pan for temperature by dropping a bit of egg in in the center. It should sizzle.

Pour ⅓ egg mixture into pan and tilt quickly so egg mixture spreads evenly over the bottom.

Keep over low heat, and when surface of egg mixture is almost dry, use spatula to loosen edges and then insert spatula under a third or half of the sheet and carefully and quickly flip the egg over. Cook for 4–5 seconds more.

Remove from pan and lay on a dry cutting board to cool. Regrease pan and use remaining egg mixture for 2 more thin, flat sheets. Cool.

Do not stack egg sheets while hot or they will stick together. Use whole sheets as wrappers for other ingredients. For "golden string" garnish, slice stack of sheets crosswise into very thin strings. If you wish strings to be shorter, cut sheet in half before slicing.

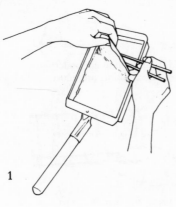

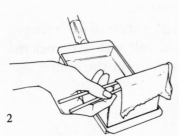

1

2

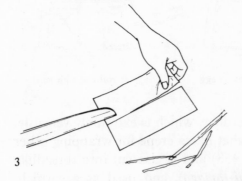

3

4

after removing thin egg sheet from pan, trim off edges and stack cooled sheets (cut stack in half if desired), then slice stack into threads

Steaming
Mushimono

Cooking in a contained, hot, wet atmosphere—steaming—is a technique common throughout the Orient. Steam cooks foods quickly and without loss of flavor, aroma, or nourishment and maintains tenderness as well as tenderizes. Though steaming is a popular technique in Japan, steamed dishes are not as numerous as one might expect. Steaming has both advantages and drawbacks. Unlike simmering, steaming captures all of a food's flavor, but at the same time it may also entrap unpleasant odors. Ingredients must be chosen with care; not all foods steam well. One of its advantages over oven heat is that ingredients do not dry out or toughen, for all their moisture is kept in.

Steaming as a means to cook vegetables has now caught on in America, and if the present interest in emphasizing natural flavor and minimizing loss of nourishment continues, perhaps more and more steamed foods will be found on American menus.

Seafood and chicken are quickly cooked and steam well. Particularly recommended are sea bream, flounder, and salmon, and from the mollusk kingdom, clams and abalone. Though the Chinese fill their tiered steamers with sliced beef, pork, duck, as well as chicken, the Japanese are definitely partial to chicken, which is steamed with a sprinkling of ginger juice and *saké* and eaten with a dipping sauce (which may include finely grated fresh ginger). If very fresh, steamed chicken can be so good it needs no seasoning at all except, perhaps, some roasted salt. Occasionally Japanese recipes are built around ground pork or beef.

Seafood and chicken may be divided into individual portions and steamed in individual serving dishes, together with a vegetable. Both vegetables and meat must be cut to sizes that will cook in the same time. Astringent or bitter vegetables are parboiled in salted water or in *dashi* stock to eliminate the unpleasant quality and give them a mild seasoning.

Justly celebrated for its delicate flavor and texture is hot, savory, steamed egg custard (*chawan-mushi*, page 214 below), undoubtedly Japan's best-known steamed dish. Sliced vegetables and morsels of chicken or fish are embraced in its pale yellow smoothness. In Japan this is served in special lidded cups, and is eaten with a spoon and also chopsticks.

Japanese have a nostalgic regard for *okowa*—steamed dishes made with glutinous rice and served on special occasions. *Sekihan*, RED RICE (page 280), is a favorite that appears on birthdays and other festive occasions. It consists of glutinous rice mixed with *azuki* beans and steamed. A mixture of glutinous and ordinary rice steamed together with green peas or small pieces of raw sea bream, skin and all, is particularly good. The steaming releases delicious juices from the fish, and you eat it with chopped ginger that has been marinated in SWEET VINEGAR (*amazu*, page 242). At a famous Kyoto restaurant, chefs steam glutinous rice dishes with *dashi* rather than plain water. The results are superb. Readers might try using chicken broth. You can serve the broth afterwards as soup.

If there is any rule in steaming, it is to *begin with the steamer full of steam*; the water must be boiling and emitting a good "head" of steam—puffs should come from the steamer lid before any food is put in. If you begin with a cold steamer, foods will become discolored and may remain raw at the center even when the surface is overdone. The result is unappetizing, and raw odors may persist. Steaming means thorough and immediate envelopment in hot mist.

As you will see in looking over the recipes in this chapter and the steamed foods in Part Two, most specify the use of high heat to produce strong steam. To test whether or not a food is cooked, pierce it with a skewer. If the skewer passes easily into the center of the food, it is cooked. With chicken, pierce the thickest part of the meat; if a clear liquid oozes out of the puncture, the meat is done. As with the application of heat to most foods, the object is not to cook the life and soul out of it. Consider the nature of what is being steamed and *keep cooking times as short as possible*. For example, because white-fleshed fish has a low fat content and not much moisture, fish such as sea bream become very dry if oversteamed. The heat penetration with white-fleshed fish should only be 90 to 95 percent. With clams it is about the same. With oily fish such as mackerel, the problem is different. Here the heat has to penetrate 100 percent to eliminate fishiness. Chicken, if very fresh, is best when the meat at center has just turned from pink to white—about 95 percent heat penetration, but steam chicken that is of average freshness to 100 percent penetration. Steamed abalone (small ones) can be used in various dishes, but should not be cooked again later by another method. For tenderness this seafood should be steamed for at least 2 hours.

Keep heat high to steam vegetables. Hot steam preserves their color and texture. The heat should barely penetrate to the heart of broccoli, cauliflower, bell peppers, snow peas, corn, etc. Steaming time is longer on the whole than it takes to parboil the same vegetable. Vegetables like potatoes, squash, and pumpkin are often cut in cubes and require a relatively longer period of steaming. Pierce with a skewer to test if cooked. The rule of keeping cooking time to minimum should be observed with vegetables particularly.

Not all foods, however, are steamed on high heat. Custards or steamed egg concoctions as well as dishes calling for bean curd or ground meat require medium to low heat. Experience will teach you exactly how much heat to use. Too strong a blast of steam makes air bubbles in the materials, which expand, causing pocking and destroying both texture and flavor. On the other hand, lethargic steam—vague lifeless wisps—makes foods sticky and tacky.

Eggs are sensitive, yet it is important that heat penetrate mixtures that include egg. A cloth is often placed on the bottom of the steaming rack to insulate vessels holding a delicate egg mixture. In steaming some especially delicate foods, even the sides of the vessel are insulated by dampened towel or paper. Finally, a paper or foil tent is propped over the top of the vessel. To control the steam, a bamboo skewer is sometimes inserted under the edge of the steamer lid to prop it open and vent off some of the heat.

Because the taste of seasonings added to foods before steaming is either lost in the steaming process or becomes more concentrated, Japanese steamed dishes are put into the steamer unseasoned, but later they are served with a savory topping or dipping sauce. SAVORY CUP CUSTARD is an exception; seasoning to taste is done beforehand, including simmering vegetable ingredients in seasoned stock.

Perhaps of all sauces in the Japanese repertoire, the one most associated with steamed dishes is *gin-an*—SILVER SAUCE. It is a gentle *dashi*-based sauce, thickened with cornstarch or *kuzu* starch (or arrowroot). SILVER SAUCE is a good complement to white-fleshed fish.

Silver Sauce

(Gin-an) 銀あん

1⅔ cups

In a medium-sized saucepan combine the *dashi*, salt, and soy sauce. Bring to a simmer. Dribble *kuzu-*

1⅔ cups *dashi*
½ tsp salt
1 tsp light soy sauce
1½ Tbsps *kuzu* or cornstarch
  mixed with 1½ Tbsps
  water

or cornstarch-water mixture into the simmering liquid and stir over medium heat until thickened.

Flavor additions such as fresh ginger juice, lemon juice, or *yuzu* citron rind can be added at the last moment, depending on the food the sauce is to complement.

Another thickened sauce called *bekkō-an*, or TORTOISESHELL SAUCE, owing to its translucent amber color, accompanies steamed bean curd or potato dishes. The recipe for *bekkō-an* is on page 398.

Two dipping sauces served at the table with *mushimono* are piquant NOODLE DIPPING SAUCE (page 311), the standard accompaniment to noodles, and tart PONZU SAUCE (page 172), which does all-purpose service with a wide variety of foods.

The common steamers in Japan are metal. These consist of a pot for the water, over which fit one or more tiers with perforated bottoms; a cover caps the steam. The most common form of such metal steamers in Japan is square with rounded corners. Round ones are also made.

The Chinese-style steamer must be set over a kettle or wok in which water boils; when the steam is circulating freely, food is placed on the bamboo-slat bottom, usually on a cloth or in vessels, but sometimes directly on the slats. Different foods can be steamed simultaneously in each tier, a way to use the steam and heat most efficiently. When two tiers are used, because steam is stronger in the lower, it may be necessary to exchange the positions of the tiers at some point during steaming, depending on the foods being cooked.

The advantage of this wood-and-bamboo steamer is that the thick wooden hoop and double-woven domed lid act as efficient insulators—little heat is lost compared to other steamer types. The traditional Japanese steamer is square, has many tiers, and is too large to be used in an ordinary modern kitchen.

A conventional Western steamer pot can be used for Japanese-style steaming. Folding stainless steel racks that fit any pot diameter from 5½ to 9 inches (14 to 23 cm) are designed for steaming vegetables and are difficult to use for Japanese cooking.

Using the proper equipment is, of course, the best way to cook, but it is not difficult to improvise a convenient steamer. Use a large covered pot—a stock pot, covered roaster, or the like—and put any racklike device in it that will support and elevate vessels *over* the boiling water. As supports, use inverted heatproof bowls or cups, a long-legged cake rack, or 2 or 3 cleaned tuna cans without ends (see sketch).

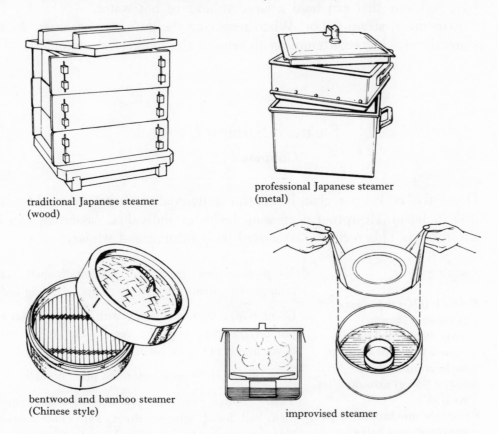

traditional Japanese steamer
(wood)

professional Japanese steamer
(metal)

bentwood and bamboo steamer
(Chinese style)

improvised steamer

To reduce or moderate the circulation of steam, a dampened cloth may be spread across the bottom of one or both steamer tiers. Similarly, a cloth may be stretched over the top tier beneath the lid in order to absorb the moisture that collects and condenses on the underside of the lid. This latter step is necessary with an improvised steamer.

Some of the recipes in this book, like SAVORY CUP CUSTARD (*chawanmushi*; page 214) and EGG "TŌFU" (page 216), can also be cooked in a preheated 425°F/220°C oven in a bain-marie—a large pan containing hot water in which smaller vessels are set to cook. Here, too, some sort of insulation is sometimes necessary so that foods are not heated too strongly, especially insulation for the bottom of the vessel. You can set vessels on folded kitchen towels or rest them on wooden chopsticks to keep them from contact with the hot bottom of the bain-marie. Vessels should always be covered tightly with foil for oven-steaming, unless otherwise stipulated in a recipe.

For any type of steaming, the boiling water should never be allowed to evaporate to less then half its original volume. Replenish with fresh boiling water as necessary, or risk a scorched pot. When choosing a steamer to buy, pick one that can hold a large volume of hot water.

Remember, steam is hot! When removing the lid of any steamer, *let the steam disperse* before attempting to remove the food. Use potholders.

Steamed Salmon Casserole

(*Chiri-mushi*) ちり蒸し

Decorative lidded porcelain bowls (for individual servings) are used for this dish in Japan. Heatproof deep soup bowls or individual casseroles can be substituted. This recipe is associated with autumn and winter.

1 serving

2½-inch (6½-cm) square
    giant kelp (*konbu*)
⅓ cake bean curd (*tōfu*)
⅛ ounce (4 g) *yuba* (dried
    soybean milk skin)
5-ounce (150 g) salmon fillet,
    with skin
1 *shiitake* mushroom, wiped,
    trimmed, and halved
⅓ bunch *enokitake* mush-
    rooms, trimmed and
    washed
3-4 sprigs edible chrysanthe-
    mum leaves (*shungiku* or
    kikuna) or spinach,
    washed and trimmed
5-6 raw ginkgo nuts, peeled
    and sliced (if available)
1 thin slice lemon
2 Tbsps *saké*
PONZU SAUCE **(page 172)**
1 generous Tbsp finely
    chopped green onion
1 generous Tbsp RED MAPLE
    RADISH **(page 170)**

To prepare and steam: In each individual vessel arrange ingredients attractively in the following order:

Giant kelp: Wipe the *konbu* with a damp towel and put on the bottom of the vessel. The kelp imparts flavor and is not to be eaten.

Bean curd: Halve or quarter and place on kelp.

Yuba: Soften *yuba* in tepid water for 10 minutes, then boil for 1 minute, drain, and chop coarsely. Place chopped *yuba* in a mound beside the bean curd cubes.

Salmon: Halve fillet lengthwise then cut into 1½-inch (4-cm) pieces. Salt pieces and place skin side up in vessel.

Mushrooms: Arrange *shiitake* halves over salmon. Keeping *enokitake* in a bunch, also arrange over salmon.

Chrysanthemum (or spinach): Chop into 4-inch (10-cm) lengths. Arrange on top of mushrooms.

Ginkgo nuts: Sprinkle slices over chrysanthemum.

Lemon: Seed and cut into thin slices. Top all ingredients in the steaming vessel with a lemon slice.

Saké: Sprinkle ingredients in steaming vessel with about 2 Tbsps *saké*.

Place uncovered vessels in a hot steamer. Stretch a kitchen towel under the steamer lid to absorb moisture and to keep drops of condensed steam from falling into the food. Cover steamer and steam over high heat for 10 minutes.

To serve: Remove from steamer and serve immediately. This may be served in two ways. 1) Sprinkle PONZU SAUCE (to taste), green onion, and RED MAPLE RADISH over each serving. 2) Make a dip of PONZU seasoned with green onion and RED MAPLE RADISH to taste and dip the steamed foods. Eat with chopsticks or fork and spoon. The broth in the bottom of the steaming vessel is delicious.

Combines well with FIVE-COLOR SALAD (page 425) and ASPARAGUS RICE (page 438).

Snowdrift Tilefish with Silver Sauce
(*Amadai no Awayuki-mushi*) 甘鯛の淡雪蒸し

This looks like an extravaganza, but it is really quite simple, consisting of mushroom-stuffed red tilefish fillets covered with beaten egg white. The word *awayuki* means soft melting snow (*awa* is "foam"; *yuki*, "snow"), but in gastronomic terms it always means beaten egg white. Heatproof bowls with a diameter of about 6 inches (15 cm) are right for individual portions.

1 serving

5 ounces (150 g) red tilefish (*amadai*) fillets, with skin
3-4 dried *shiitake* mushrooms, softened and trimmed (see page 88)
for simmering mushrooms:
¾ cup *dashi*
2 Tbsps *saké*

To prepare: Wash fish fillet and pat dry. Salt lightly on both sides and let stand 40 minutes to 1 hour. Wash again and pat dry.

Cut softened and trimmed *shiitake* mushrooms into ¼-inch (¾-cm) slices. Simmer till well seasoned in mushroom simmering liquid (about 20 minutes).

Place salted fillet on cutting board skin side down and cut two flaps in it, using the butterfly cut (*kannonbiraki* technique, page 132). Then cut fillet in half crosswise.

1 Tbsp *mirin*
2 Tbsps dark soy sauce
½ Tbsp sugar

2 egg whites
pinch salt
1 stalk trefoil (or sliver *yuzu*
citron rind or lemon rind,
or small sprig of fresh
dill), finely chopped
SILVER SAUCE **(see page 209)**

To assemble and steam: Put the larger-looking piece of tilefish into the steaming vessel, skin side down. Open up the butterfly-cut flaps and lay on sliced mushroom. Cover with the other half of fillet, skin side up.

Cover vessel tightly with plastic wrap or foil; this does a better job of keeping out moisture than anything else, including covers made to fit the vessel. Cover steamer and steam over high heat for 15 minutes.

While the fish steams, beat egg whites till just foamy and add pinch salt. (Egg whites should be at or just above room temperature.) Beat to soft-peak stage, not until dry and stiff. Sprinkle beaten whites with finely chopped trefoil (or citrus rind).

Remove fish from steamer, but keep steamer over heat. Uncover steaming vessel and spoon beaten egg white over fish. With a knife or spatula spread egg white to edges of the vessel to seal in the fish. Make little swirls with the spatula to give a decorative effect. Cover again with plastic wrap or foil and return to hot steamer. Steam 2–3 minutes more.

Make the SILVER SAUCE.

Remove steamed "snowdrift" fish from steamer and uncover. Pour on a few Tbsps of SILVER SAUCE. Serve immediately. Eat with chopsticks or forks.

Savory Cup Custard

(*Chawan-mushi*) 茶碗蒸し (color plate 12)

Though the word "custard" evokes images of sweet eggy desserts, this is a delicate, stock-enriched, nonsweet egg custard containing chicken, shrimp, and assorted vegetables. Inventive cooks will be able to come up with any number of variations: you can add anything that complements the taste of the savory custard base, including sliced mushroom, small strips of lemon rind, parboiled carrot slices, or, as Japanese do, parboiled bamboo shoot slices, slices of fish paste (*kamaboko*), or even *udon* noodles.

Attesting to the general popularity of this dish, special lidded *chawan-mushi* cups are available in Japan wherever china is sold. You may safely use heatproof cups or conventional custard cups.

Chawan-mushi is one of the few Japanese dishes eaten with both chopsticks and a spoon. Even though the egg completely sets in steaming, the stock and juices released from various ingredients make the dish a little soupy. In fact, this dish is regarded by many as a soup and is often served as a soup course. In cold months it is brought to table piping hot, and in summer it is very good chilled.

4 servings

2½-3 ounces (70–80 g)
 chicken breast
about 1 tsp *saké*
about 1 tsp light soy sauce
4 small raw shrimp, shelled
 and deveined
1 lily root (*yuri-ne*) (optional)
12 stalks trefoil (or equivalent
 amount of young spinach
 or watercress)
12-16 raw ginkgo nuts,
 shelled and peeled (if
 available)
4 raw chestnuts, peeled and
 sliced

custard:

 4 medium eggs
 2½ cups *dashi* or light
  chicken stock
 ½ tsp salt
 1 Tbsp *mirin*
 1 Tbsp light soy sauce

To prepare: Prepare all the solid ingredients first.

Cut chicken breast into ½-inch (1½-cm) morsels. Marinate in a scant amount of *saké* and light soy sauce for about 15 minutes. Drain; discard marinade.

Blanch shrimp in hot water for 30 seconds, remove, and pat dry. Leave whole, but if very large, slit half-open down the belly, press out flat, and cut in half crosswise (see page 458).

Lily root is worth trying if you can find it. Its shape is somewhat like a flattened garlic bulb, but its flavor is mild and it has a pleasant, delicate texture. Separate bulb into segments and parboil gently in lightly salted water for 4–5 minutes. Drain. Wash trefoil or other greens, pat dry, and chop coarsely.

Shell and peel ginkgo nuts and use whole, if you are able to find fresh ones. Peel and slice chestnuts.

To assemble, steam, and serve: Beat eggs in a medium-sized bowl. In another bowl mix the room-temperature *dashi*, salt, *mirin*, and light soy sauce. This recipe is one in which chicken stock is as good as *dashi*, not just a substitute. Pour stock mixture in a thin stream into beaten egg. Mix well, but do not beat. The surface of the mixture should be free of bubbles or foam. Strain. The seasoned stock mixture should be 3 times the volume of beaten egg, so apply this ratio of 3 : 1 in adjusting this recipe to the number of diners.

Divide the prepared solid ingredients between 4 cups, except for chopped trefoil or greens. Ladle the egg stock mixture into the cups, filling them to about ½ inch (1½ cm) from the top. Add chopped greens.

Cover each cup with plastic wrap or foil and set in a hot steamer. Cover steamer and steam over medium heat for 20 minutes, or place foil-covered cups in a bain-marie and cook in a preheated 425°F/220°C oven for 30 minutes.

The *chawan-mushi* is done when a toothpick inserted in the center comes out clean. The custard should be set but still jiggle freely. The volume of the custard will not increase much. It is overdone if the top is pocked or cracked and tough looking.

Serve hot or chilled and eat with a spoon and chopsticks. If you intend to serve chilled *chawan-mushi*, omit the chicken, which might develop an odor in refrigeration.

Egg "*Tōfu*"
(*Tamago-dōfu*) 卵豆腐 (color plate 10)

Unsweetened egg custard, delicate and smooth. Because it has the consistency of fine bean curd (*tōfu*), this dish has been dubbed *tōfu*, but, in fact, bean curd is not an ingredient.

Serve several 1¹/₂-inch (4-cm) cubes topped with sauce as a side dish, or dice and float in clear soups (*suimono*). The one simple rule to follow in adjusting this recipe for any number is to use twice as much seasoned stock as volume of beaten egg.

The recipe below is for chilled EGG "TŌFU" and cold sauce, but it can just as well be served hot with warmed sauce.

4 servings

6 eggs (about 1¼ cups), beaten
2½ cups *dashi* or chicken stock
1 Tbsp salt
3 Tbsps *mirin*
3 Tbsps light soy sauce

sauce:

  1 cup *dashi*
  3 Tbsps *mirin*
  3 Tbsps light soy sauce
  1 cup (a generous handful) dried bonito flakes (*hana-katsuo*)

finely grated *yuzu* citron or lemon rind

To prepare: Beat eggs gently till yolks and whites are thoroughly mixed. Do not beat to a froth; skim off any foam.

In another bowl, mix the *dashi*, salt, *mirin*, and light soy sauce, making sure the salt is dissolved completely.

Pour the *dashi* mixture into the eggs and stir till mixed. Strain.

To steam: Line an 8-inch (20-cm) square baking pan with foil so that the foil extends over two opposite sides of the pan (see sketch, page 369). Make sure the foil is not wrinkled in the pan bottom. Do not oil or butter. Pour egg mixture into the pan. Put the pan into a bain-marie, resting it on chopsticks or a folded towel so that the bottom of the pan is insulated from the bottom of the bain-marie. Insulate even further by folding more towels around the sides of the mold or by laying 4-ply dampened newspaper strips around it. Cover the mold by gently placing a single sheet of creased foil over the top like a tent. All these measures are to make sure that the delicate custard is cooked only by even mild heat. With too direct or uneven heat, the egg will turn rubbery.

Fill the bain-marie with hot water till water reaches about halfway up the side of the pan. Put this arrangement into a hot steamer and steam on high heat for 3 minutes, then reduce flame to low and continue steaming for 25 minutes. Or cook in a preheated 425°F/220°C oven for 30 minutes. The custard is done when a toothpick inserted into the center comes out clean. Some clear broth will seep out of the hole made by the toothpick. This is correct. It should not be firm and dry, but should jiggle a little if you tap the side of the pan.

Remove the pan from the steamer. If eating it hot, cut and serve immediately. Otherwise, transfer the hot pan to another bain-marie-type arrangement, this one filled with ice-cold water. The cold water should reach all the way up the outside of the mold, but should not run over the top into the custard. Let stand 15 minutes or so, until cool. You can make the custard ahead of time and refrigerate for 1 day (no more) if you plan on serving it chilled.

Sauce: While the custard is steaming, make the sauce. In a medium-sized saucepan bring the *dashi*, *mirin*, and light soy sauce just to a boil. Add dried bonito flakes, and over medium heat bring to a boil again. Remove from heat and immediately strain into a metal bowl through a sieve lined with 2 layers of dampened cheesecloth. If serving sauce hot, use immediately.

Force-cool the sauce by twirling the metal bowl in a larger bowl half-filled with water and ice cubes. Use when sauce is cooled, or cover and refrigerate till serving time.

To serve, hot or cold: Lift out the custard by picking up the two ends of the foil and transfer to a cutting board. Cut into 1½-inch (4-cm) cubes with a knife or spatula. Place 2 or 3 cubes per serving in individual dishes. Top with a few Tbsps of the sauce and garnish with finely grated *yuzu* citron or lemon rind.

Simmering
Nimono

If the quantity of simmered dishes in modern Japanese cooking is any indication, one can conjecture that the first potter in Japan made pots *in order* to simmer food, rather than vice versa. Who can tell? The first Japanese pots are conservatively carbon-dated to 10,000 B.C.! Simmering—putting food into a pot with plain water or flavored liquid and letting this bubble away on a fire—is a technique that can be used with almost every kind of food, which is a reason it is universally practiced. Also, it is a fast and simple way of cooking. Heavy iron soup kettles like those of the West are not used in Japan because tough materials or large hunks needing long stewing are not a part of Japanese cuisine, which is based on the relatively short cooking of young and tender ingredients in their prime.

In Japanese cooking, simmering (*ni*) and broiling (*yaki*) are important categories; the basic Japanese meal consists of soup, raw fish, a simmered dish and a broiled dish. In a recently published encyclopedic work on Japanese gastronomy, no less than fifteen major divisions are listed under *nimono*, "simmered foods." Each of these divisions—and their subdivisions— is characterized by a differently seasoned simmering liquid, from lightly salted water and mild broths to stocks strongly flavored with such ingredients as fermented bean paste (*miso*) or fresh ginger.

Listed alphabetically below are some of the basic Japanese techniques of simmering.

Kara-ni: *Karai* means "salty" or "piquant"; *kara-ni* refers to foods simmered in a half-and-half mixture of *saké* and soy sauce, which gives them a strong flavor.

Kimi-ni: Egg yolk characterizes this simmering technique, especially appropriate for shrimp, scallops, and chicken. Dredge foods in cornstarch, dip into beaten egg yolk, then simmer in *dashi* seasoned with *saké*, *mirin* (or sugar), and soy sauce. When the yolk coating is set, turn heat to low and simmer till tender.

Miso-ni: Fermented bean paste (*miso*) is blended with *dashi*, further seasoned with *mirin* (or sugar), soy sauce, and finely chopped fresh ginger. This piquant mixture also masks strong tastes of oily fish.

Nitsuke: Rendered in the recipes here as "*saké*-simmered." Cook ingredients in a mixture of *saké*, *mirin* (or sugar), and soy sauce. Applies mainly to fish.

Shigure-ni: *Shigure* ("autumn rain") is a conceit for soy sauce. Simmer ingredients in a stock heavily seasoned with soy sauce and often chopped ginger.

Shōga-ni: *Shōga* is ginger, and it is the primary seasoning in this simmering stock.

Yoshino-ni: Simmer materials in *dashi*, seasoned with *saké*, sugar, and soy sauce. After removing solid ingredients from the simmering pot, just before serving, thicken the hot liquid with a constarch-and-water mixture, or use *kuzu* starch (page 94)—the latter is the preferred thickening agent. The best *kuzu* traditionally comes from the Yoshino mountains, hence the name. Good with chicken, shrimp, and clams.

Primary *dashi* is generally used for *nimono*. But this is not an inviolable rule, and just as often as not, especially for routine meals, Japanese turn to secondary *dashi* (page 148) or instant *dashi* powder.

The most common stock seasonings, and the order in which they are stirred into the stock, are: *saké*, *mirin* (or sugar), salt, soy sauce, and fermented bean paste (*miso*). *Saké* is a tenderizing agent, particularly beneficial in simmering fish and poultry.

Mirin, the sweet cooking *saké*, is preferred over sugar for simmering. It is about half as sweet as sugar, but it is not just a substitute for the latter. Experiment with how much *mirin* to use; if used too liberally it can tighten up vegetable fibers and make them tough. Many Japanese burn off the alcohol in *mirin* beforehand in order to get rid of its odor. This is known as *nikiri mirin*.

White sugar is used very moderately, not only for sweetness, but also to palliate subtle bitterness or acidity in many foodstuffs. Avoid using sugar with whitish vegetables such as giant white radish (*daikon*) or lotus root or with green vegetables like beans or spinach because the sugar may blacken in cooking and create a film that adheres to the vegetables. Use *mirin* instead.

The soy sauce commonly available at supermarkets labeled "all-purpose" is, in fact, dark soy sauce.

If you can find both dark and light soy sauces, however, use the dark for seasoning the simmering liquid when the solid ingredients have a simple taste or when materials are to be thoroughly penetrated by seasoned liquid. Use the light when it is important to keep the natural coloring of the solid ingredients. In either case, preserving the soy sauce's aroma is very important; this is why soy sauce is added last.

Preliminary steps: Many *nimono* are cooked in two steps—put into the pot twice, as it were. The parboiling usually involves only water, not a flavored stock, and its purpose is to draw out excess natural moisture and with it, any harsh tastes and rawness, from the ingredients. Ingredients are then put into a seasoned simmering liquid to soak up flavor and complete the cooking. This interrupted cooking technique varies greatly with the ingredient; different ingredients and techniques are discussed below. Sometimes, a combination of cooking methods is employed: sautéing followed by simmering (*itame-ni* technique, see page 396), or deep-frying followed by simmering (*age-ni* technique, see page 382.)

These double-step and combined-method cooking procedures reflect Japanese awareness that foods do not cook on the inside and the outside at the same rate. Using these techniques is one way of gaining more precise control. This same awareness is what stands behind the way Japanese cut materials for cooking in general. Rarely are there large pieces of meat and uncut vegetables. It even influences how materials are put into a pot. No matter how thick a pot, when it is over heat, the metal in direct contact with the heat (usually the center) is hotter than the metal not in contact with heat. This difference in temperature results in different cooking rates at different places in the pot. Therefore, hard-to-cook materials belong in the center, and more delicate ones should be given room at the sides. When simmering solids that are not particularly fragile, shake the pot occasionally so ingredients change place in the pot.

Equipment: The equipment for simmering foods is quite simple. A thick-bottomed pot will not scorch easily and will do a better job of distributing heat evenly than a thin pot. Pot size is determined by the nature and amount of food and by the type of simmering you will be doing. Use a deep pot that holds an ample amount of liquid for materials that require hours on top of the stove. For materials that take only minutes in just a little liquid, use a shallow pot or skillet. A shallow pan is also best for fragile materials, such as delicate fish that crumbles easily.

Indispensable for making *nimono* is an *otoshi-buta*, literally "drop-lid." The usual Japanese drop-lid is of well-dried cypress or cedar wood, with an edge beveled from the bottom and a single shallow "fin" across the top that acts as handle. About ½ inch (1½ cm) smaller than the diameter of the pot in which it is used, a drop-lid floats on the surface of the simmering liquid. Because of this, not only does the lid act to submerge solids to be simmered, thereby ensuring even cooking, but ingredients are not subject to the rolling and tumbling usually encountered with boiling and thus retain their shape. Further, the drop-lid increases the penetration of seasonings into the solid being simmered and decreases heat loss from the liquid surface, thus speeding up cooking time. Even when the heat is high, the only evidence of boiling is a ring of small bubbles between the lid and the pot. Wood, as compared to plastic or metal, is a pleasant material, it does not interact chemically with the food, and a wooden drop-lid is the right weight—not heavy enough to crush materials, but with enough weight to keep the lid firmly on the surface of the liquid and to keep the ingredients underneath from moving about.

Finding a wooden drop-lid outside Japan is a problem. The fact that they are inexpensive and not in demand limits the merchants' motivation to market them. However, they may be used for other cooking besides Japanese. If and when the opportunity presents itself, if, say, you stumble over them at an oriental provisions store or import-export market, buy several different sizes. Impose on friends visiting Japan to buy some, or order them through stores listed here.

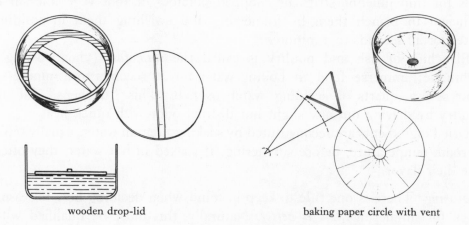

wooden drop-lid   baking paper circle with vent

All is not lost, however, without an authentic wooden *otoshi-buta*. One substitute is aluminum plates; another is circles of paper with center vents. Fold a square of baking paper or kitchen parchment into quarters along one diagonal between corners, then into eighths or sixteenths, and cut along the edge in an arc as shown. Snip off the pointed tip to make a vent. Be sure to cut the circle a bit *bigger* than the pot, so that when you fit the paper down into the pot, the edges will fold up against the sides of the pot. The weight of a wooden lid keeps it pressing down on the liquid, but paper may occasionally have to be nudged downward as the simmering liquid reduces. If the baking paper sticks to the side of the pot, do not worry. It will come off without much effort when the pot is washed. A paper circle does not halt the movement of simmering foods, but serves every other function of a drop-lid.

In lieu of a wooden drop-lid, also try any *flat*, lightweight cover for a pot, saucepan, or skillet. Avoid domed lids with underturned rims.

Double-step cooking; parboiling; blanching: For delicious *nimono*, begin with quality materials, the fresher the better. As mentioned above, most ingredients demand some sort of preliminary cooking after being washed and cut into pieces and before simmering. For example, the rigorous and really scrupulous cook will parboil nearly all vegetables in lightly salted water; this extracts surplus water, making it easier for seasonings to penetrate during the subsequent simmering. (This is the first step of the double-step cooking described above.) Put each green vegetable into *boiling* water, and, when the vegetable is brilliant in color, drain and plunge it immediately into cold water. This cold water bath is called the *irodashi*, or "color-giving," technique. On the other hand, start potatoes and root vegetables in cold water. Dropping them into boiling water is a mistake, for the outside cooks and softens before heat can penetrate to the core. If, however, a recipe calls for thin julienne strips or chopped potatoes or root vegetables, it is sufficient to blanch them by immersing and swishing them in scalding water for 30 seconds to a minute.

Blanching of fish and poultry is called the *shimofuri* ("hoarfrosting") technique: immerse food in boiling water for 30 seconds to a minute or pour several quarts of scalding water over it. This "freshens" fish or poultry by driving out any slight but distinct odor with quick heat.

Dried ingredients are reconstituted by soaking them in water, usually tepid or room temperature, before simmering. If soaked in hot water, they often lose their flavor.

Seasoning: There is one rule to keep in mind when deciding how to season stock for simmering: *less is better*. Naturally, this must be qualified with the principle of matching seasonings with ingredients and the kind of dish you want to make. The fresher and more delicately flavored the ingredients, the more you should strive to capture or bring out fundamental flavors. Use *light* seasoning in the stock. You may rely, for example, only on the stock itself to provide seasoning. For heavy-tasting, robust ingredients or materials that have some odor it is desirable to mask, use an appropriately greater amount of seasoning in the stock. The outline below will guide you when you innovate *nimono* dishes.

Fresh white-fleshed fish and shellfish—Because the flesh is rather firm and not very watery, cook quickly over strong heat in lightly seasoned simmering liquid just till center is heated. Transfer cooked materials to individual plates and spoon on a few Tbsps of remaining simmering liquid. Serve hot or at room temperature. Do not thicken simmering liquid.

Oily (and borderline fresh) fish—These are quite watery, so simmer over medium heat in rather heavily seasoned simmering liquid till heat penetrates thoroughly. To eliminate dominating odors, use *saké*, ginger, or vinegar in the simmering liquid.

Meat and poultry (and squid)—Use medium to heavy seasoning. Cook quickly over high heat, since these materials tend to become rubbery if done too slowly. Remove cooked materials to individual plates, reduce remaining simmering liquid slightly, and stir in a thickening agent or return the cooked materials to the pot to heat in reduced simmering liquid. Serve hot.

Freshwater fish—Blanch, then simmer in heavily seasoned stock (liberal use of *saké*). Long simmering is required to soften bones and remove odor.

Green vegetables—Cook parboiled vegetables like green beans and snow peas quickly in lightly seasoned simmering liquid so that their color does not pale. Drain, spread out, and force-cool in the draft of a fan. Place them in chilled simmering liquid to soak up seasoning flavor. With leafy vegetables, parboil, drain, rinse under cold water (the *irodashi* technique, described above) and then place in chilled seasoned stock (8 parts *dashi*, 1 part *mirin*, 1 part light soy sauce) to add flavor.

Potato and root vegetables—A rather sweet seasoning liquid is appropriate. Simmer over medium heat. Use a circle of baking paper or drop-lid to keep materials from crumbling, especially potatoes.

Serving: Whether all major ingredients are simmered together in one pot or major ingredients are cooked in separate pots, they must be arranged together in individual dishes before serving. Put larger pieces of food at the "back" of the dish and against them lay the smaller, daintier pieces in "front." The principle of arrangement is to make "mountains" at the back, and "water" at the front. Place greens such as snow peas at an attractive angle to provide color accents. Pour on enough simmering liquid to keep ingredients moist over the arrangement, but not so much that ingredients swim.

The most frequently used garnishes are *kinome*, *yuzu* citron rind, and fresh ginger. Because the *kinome* sprigs are eaten as is, choose medium-sized, soft-budded shoots. Soak *yuzu* rind, cut in 3/4-inch (2-cm) lengths, in cold water to diminish bitterness, or, if hard, soak in scalding water for a few seconds. Finely shred-cut the fresh ginger; use with foods that have dominating or strong smells.

Whether you cook them in one pot or combine foods after cooking, maintain harmony by using ingredients that go well together—in flavor, color, shape, and aroma.

Nimono are considered one of the major components of a full-course meal. Simmered vegetables may also be served in small portions as one of several appetizers or as a side dish for an entrée. Midday meals are often built around fish *nimono*.

Saké-Simmered Flounder

(*Karei Nitsuke*) かれい煮付け (color plate 13)

Good for any flatfish (sole, flounder, turbot, halibut, etc.). This recipe has been calculated with one whole fish per serving, but if fish is large, cut crosswise into generous 3-inch (8-cm) wide portions. Serve hot as an entrée. Keeps, refrigerated, up to 2 days. May be reheated in the seasoned broth; if there is not enough broth, moisten with a little *saké*. Also may be served chilled, in which case the broth will jell; good chilled as an hors d'oeuvre or summer entrée.

2 servings

2 fresh flounder, about ½ pound (225 g) each

for simmering:
  7 Tbsps *mirin*
  7 Tbsps *saké*
  ¾ cup *dashi*
  6 Tbsp dark soy sauce
  2 Tbsps light soy sauce
  pinch sugar*
  ***kinome* sprigs**

To prepare: Scale, gut, and wash fish; leave heads and tails intact. Score the top side of the fish (the mottled brown side) with 2 or 3 diagonal slits through the skin about ¼ inch (¾ cm) deep, as shown. These slits will allow the simmering liquid to penetrate the flesh more thoroughly, thus speeding the cooking time and keeping the fish from losing its shape. (Do *not* cross-score. Cross-scoring is sometimes recommended for poaching, which this method is not. Patches of flesh may slough off a very fresh fish if it is cross-scored with *nimono* cooking.)

To simmer: Mix the *mirin* and *saké* in a medium-sized pot, heat, then carefully ignite liquid and burn off alcohol. Next, stir in the *dashi*, soy sauces, and sugar. If only dark soy sauce is available, increase amount to 7½ Tbsps. Bring to a boil.

Lay the fish with slit, dark side up, in boiling stock in the pot. Immediately cover with a drop-lid (*otoshi-buta*) or circle of baking paper with a vent (see page 221). Cook over high heat for about 10 minutes. Cooking quickly over high heat this way keeps the fish delicate. Over low heat the fish will become rubbery and hard. Be sure to cover with a drop-lid or cut circle of baking paper to allow seasonings to penetrate thoroughly and shorten cooking time by reducing heat loss from liquid.

To serve: Carefully lift whole fish from the pot with a spatula or pancake turner and transfer to a plate. Spoon a few Tbsps of remaining simmering liquid over fish. Garnish with a few fragrant sprigs of *kinome.* Eat with chopsticks or knife and fork.

Goes well with TANGY WHITE SALAD (page 421) and FRIED AND SIMMERED FREEZE-DRIED TŌFU (page 399).

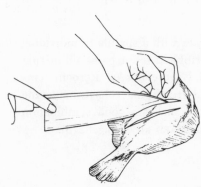

score flatfish before simmering

*Note: The fresher the fish, the less sugar is necessary. With best-quality fish, omit the sugar entirely.

Saké-Simmered Mackerel

(Saba Nitsuke) さば煮付け

The preceding recipe is applicable to white-fleshed fish, and this one is well suited to round-bodied, "oily" fish such as mackerel, herring, shad, etc. A filling lunch with boiled rice and soup.

4 servings

1 fresh mackerel, about
  1 pound (450 g)
¾ cup *saké*
½ cup minus 1 Tbsp *mirin*
⅓ cup dark soy sauce
2 Tbsps shred-cut fresh
  ginger
pinch sugar

To prepare: Scale, gut, and wash fish. Chop off head and tail. Cut two fillets, (*sanmai oroshi* technique, pages 123ff), and cut each fillet in half crosswise to make four pieces in all, one piece per serving.

To simmer: In a medium-sized heavy saucepan heat the *saké* just till simmering. Lay in the mackerel pieces, skin side up. Use high heat to bring the *saké* to a quick boil. Pour over the *mirin* and dark soy sauce, sprinkle over the ginger. Wait for the liquid in the pot to come to a boil between additions. This "staggered" boiling is part of the process of ridding the mackerel of odor. Finally, add the sugar. Cover with a drop-lid (*otoshi-buta*) or cut circle of baking paper (see page 221). Cook over high heat for about 10 minutes. Fish is done when flesh is tender; test with a fork.

To serve: Remove pieces with a spatula to individual plates, skin side up. Dribble a few tsps of simmering liquid over the fish and serve hot or at room temperature. The *saké* and fresh ginger have made the mackerel quite savory; it makes a good combination with hot white rice and MIXED RICE (page 278).

Yellow Flower Shrimp

(*Ebi Kimi-ni*) 海老黄身煮 (color plate 9)

A good example of a *nimono* composed of several main ingredients simmered separately and assembled on serving plates just before the meal. Twisted into "flower" shapes, then glazed with egg yolk, the shrimp are like exotic blossoms and are the main attraction. With the simmered squash and spinach, the dish as a whole is a filling entrée. Ideal as the main course for a festive luncheon.

4 servings

12 medium shrimp

1 small Japanese squash (*kabocha***), or acorn squash, peeled**

½ pound spinach (or green beans), washed and par-boiled (see page 93)

for soaking vegetables:

  2 cups *dashi*

  ¼ cup *mirin*

  ¼ cup light soy sauce

for simmering:

  2½ cups *dashi*

  3 Tbsps *saké*

  6 Tbsps *mirin*

  4 Tbsps light soy sauce

cornstarch

3 egg yolks, well beaten

***yuzu* citron rind slivers**

To prepare: Remove heads, devein, and shell shrimp, but leave tails attached. Slit back of shrimp open and press out flat. Cut a lengthwise slit in the middle, then push the tail through this slit to make a shrimp "flower," as shown. Continue with remaining shrimp.

Cut squash into 2- × -1½-inch (5- × -1½-cm) cylindrical pieces or cut into bite-sized cubes. Put into pot of lightly salted boiling water and boil gently, covered with a drop-lid (*otoshi-buta*) or cut circle of baking paper (see page 221), till just tender. Time varies greatly. Drain and rinse immediately in cold water.

Meanwhile, in a medium-sized pot, combine the ingredients for soaking vegetables and bring just to a boil. Remove half to a medium-sized metal mixing bowl and force-cool by twirling the bowl in a larger one filled with water and ice cubes. Set aside.

Into the hot liquid remaining in the pot, put the drained, boiled squash. Bring to boil and simmer for 7–8 minutes. Allow to cool to room temperature in seasoning liquid. (Ideal soaking time is 2–3 hours, but a shorter soaking is all right).

Soak parboiled spinach in cooled soaking liquid. Reheat before serving. (Cook any substitute green so that the result is a very fresh, crisply cooked, and bright green vegetable.)

To simmer and serve: Mix ingredients for simmering in a medium-sized pot. Bring just to a boil, then turn heat down to a simmer. Brush prepared "flower" shrimp with cornstarch, and, holding each shrimp by its tail, dip into beaten egg yolk to coat.

Still holding the shrimp by the tails, carefully lay into the simmering liquid and simmer gently, uncovered, till egg has set and tails turn a pinky-red. The egg yolk coating should inflate a bit as the shrimp cook; this is why medium shrimp are better for this recipe than large ones, but large shrimp may be cut into attractive-sized pieces after simmering. For frozen shrimp, simmering time is not more than 8 minutes, depending on size; fresh shrimp need only 3 minutes.

Meanwhile, reheat squash and spinach in seasoned stock. Arrange several shrimp, several pieces of squash, and a portion of spinach in each individual dish. Spoon on a few Tbsps of simmering liquid. Serve hot. Garnish with a decoratively cut sliver (see page 144) of *yuzu* citron rind.

Combines well with POTATO-CHICKEN NUGGETS (page 411) and MUSCATS WITH MUSTARD DRESSING (page 423).

1. slice open shrimp through back

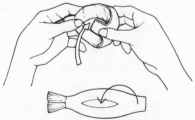

2. push head end through slit

3. keep form full and loose—do not pull ends tight

Deep-Frying
Agemono

Although the technique of deep-frying was originally introduced to Japan centuries ago by Europeans and Chinese, the Japanese have elevated it to its very apogee of refinement. Adjusting the method to suit the differing textures of various ingredients, Japanese chefs produce marvels of airy lightness that trap, with a minimum of cooking, the natural flavors of fresh seasonal foods.

Deep-frying in Japan has become an art that depends so much on specialized expertise in both cooking and serving that one can only savor it to real advantage in restaurants that do nothing else. The time element is especially crucial. Full-course restaurants avoid these dishes because too much time elapses between kitchen and diner. Ideally, deep-fried foods in the Japanese manner should be eaten seconds after cooking, which is only possible if they are cooked before you as you sit at a counter.

Modern domestic kitchen-dining rooms—especially those with counters near the stove—provide ideal conditions for Japanese-style deep-frying at home, but preclude the cooking member of the family from actually sitting down with the others. He or she, however, can quite enjoyably snack while frying and serving.

The reason Japanese fried foods are so light is twofold: great care is taken with the temperature of the oil, and great restraint is exercised in blending the batter. One must force oneself to leave the egg, water, and flour batter looking decidedly unmixed. The very act of dipping the materials in actually completes the mixing. The morsels pass through the batter ingredients roughly in an egg-water-flour sequence, since most of the flour is still floating on the water and the egg lies at the bottom of the bowl. This rudimentary combining procedure is what "does the trick."

While TEMPURA—batter-coated deep-frying—is Japan's most celebrated example of *agemono*, it represents only one of three frying methods. Some foods are best deep-fried just as they are, to preserve color and shape; some are lightly dusted with flour only. Flatfish lend themselves to this treatment, and I remember an outstanding taste experience I once had. *Wakasa-garei*, tiny dabs caught in the Bay of Wakasa, provided minuscule fillets, which were served raw. Then the bones were dredged with flour and deep-fried— first over a low heat and then over high till golden brown—until they were like crisp cocktail crackers. I ate them with salt and lemon. This can be done with any soft-boned flatfish (see FLOUNDER TREASURE SHIPS, page 405).

A detailed discussion of Japanese deep-frying techniques inevitably begins with the oil. Care is essential in its selection and handling.

Oil: Pure vegetable oil is recommended for deep-frying. A highly refined blend of various vegetable oils is light in color and has neither strong taste nor odor. *Tempura* oil, which is available in bottles or cans at oriental provisions stores, is a blended vegetable oil too, but it is not highly refined. *Tempura* oil is darker in color than refined vegetable oil and has a distinct flavor due to the presence of sesame seed oil, one of its major ingredients. Other vegetable oils—corn, peanut, or safflower, for example—give good results, but are expensive, and, besides, a carefully blended oil gives better results than oil of a single type. Do not attempt to deep-fry using heavy animal fats or olive oil. These mask the flavors of foods.

Japanese TEMPURA restaurants have their own house oils. Chefs are inclined to rely on sesame oil as a sort of base, but since this oil is too thick and heavy alone, every chef blends it, according to his own recipe, with soybean oil and rapeseed oil. The blend of oil also directly affects the appearance of fried food and has influenced regional taste. TEMPURA deep-fried a light gold conforms to the Tokyo idea of what TEMPURA should look like. Snowy-white TEMPURA is what epicures expect in Osaka.

Temperature: Foods are not all deep-fried at the same temperature; each recipe here clearly stipulates the temperature required. If the oil is not hot enough, the food will absorb quite a lot of oil and become heavy and "fatty." If the oil is too hot, while the outside frizzles black, the inside will still be raw. The importance of oil temperature cannot be overstressed. Generally speaking, meat and fish are fried quickly at a high temperature to retain moisture and tenderness. Vegetables are fried at a lower heat.

Experienced Japanese chefs may test oil temperature by pressing one long, wooden kitchen chopstick down to the bottom of the oil-filled pot to feel the reaction of the oil on the chopstick shaft. But this is certainly not a reliable technique for the home cook, who probably deep-fries only occasionally. For cooks without a deep-fat thermometer or an automatically controlled deep-fryer, the temperature of hot fat may be judged by the way a few drops of batter react in the oil.

300°F/150°C—two or three globules of batter dropped into hot oil stay at the bottom of the pot and do not rise.

320°F/160°C—drops of batter begin to rise as soon as they touch the bottom of the oil-filled pot.

340°F/170°C—drops of batter sink only part way down into the hot oil and float up to the surface quickly.

350°F–360°F/175°C–180°C—drops of batter do not sink into the hot oil at all, but skitter about on its surface.

Once oil has been heated to the required temperature, *keep it at that level.* For the same reason that you cannot roast or bake in an oven whose temperature fluctuates, you cannot deep-fry successfully with oil that is repeatedly being cooled and reheated while cooking proceeds.

There are a few general rules to follow to keep the oil at a relatively constant temperature while foods are being deep-fried. First, *deep-fry foods in small quantity* so the pot is never crowded. Introducing large amounts of food at once suddenly lowers oil temperature, so *never put an amount of food whose total area covers more than ⅓ of the oil surface into the deep-frying pot.*

Foods should be close to room temperature when they are lowered into hot oil. Frozen or thoroughly chilled foods shock the hot oil and lower its temperature drastically. The preferred source of heat is gas because gas responds quickly. Electricity may be convenient, but it is slow.

Oil quantity, equipment, recycling: Two notions about deep-frying—that great quantities of oil are required and that the oil may not be reused—are widespread and largely false. The *depth of oil in the pot should be twice or more than twice the thickness of the food items being deep-fried.* Just make sure all surfaces of the food in question have good exposure to the hot oil for even frying. For example, to deep-fry the stuffed crab shells in the STUFFED CRAB recipe on page 407, which are about 2 inches (5 cm) thick, 4 to 5 inches (10 to 13 cm) of oil are required in the pot. This rule also relates to keeping a constant oil temperature—do not introduce foods thicker than ½ the oil depth. On the other hand, it is generally advisable to deep-fry with an oil depth of no less than 3 inches (8 cm).

Besides deciding on how much oil to use, you will also have to decide on what kind of pot to put it in. The electric, automatically controlled deep-fryers that have made their way into many kitchens are a convenient luxury, but any flat- and thick-bottomed pot, saucepan, or skillet of appropriate size will do very well. The thick bottom keeps heat evenly distributed. A Chinese wok is convenient for certain kinds of deep-frying, but is not good for Japanese cooking. The rounded shape results in different oil temperatures at the sides and in the center, which makes the wok difficult to control and use for delicate foods and batters.

Deep-frying oil can be stored and used again. First, after all food has been removed, heat oil and stir lightly so that any moisture introduced into the oil by foods is evaporated. Then, while the oil is still warm (but not too hot), pass it through a paper filter into a container with an airtight lid. Seal and store in a dark, cool place. Do not refrigerate.

Always check used oil to make sure it has not become sour or stale. It will take on a darker color with every use. You may "top up" old oil with fresh oil (half and half), but such refreshening is not effective for more than 2 or 3 times at most. By that time the oil will have deteriorated in color, luster, and taste and should be discarded. The older oil is, the more likely it is to froth and foam, thus making it impossible to fry light and crisp foods.

Techniques: Foods for deep-frying, whether they are dredged in flour, dipped in batter, or fried without any coating at all, should be as dry as possible so that oil will not spatter. In fact, Japanese have categorized *agemono* according to the type of coating used. These categories are:

Su-age, or "naked frying." As the name clearly states, food is deep-fried without first being dredged in flour or dipped in batter. Since, in this case, the food absorbs oil on direct contact, the *su-age* technique is not very suitable for soft or watery materials. The best foods for this method are those whose color and shape are important and should not be masked by a coating. Examples of such foods are: small freshwater fish, green beans, small eggplants, sliced lotus root, sweet potatoes, and Irish potatoes. The oil temperature for *su-age* is on the low side—about 320°F/160°C.

Kara-age originally meant "Chinese frying" (唐揚), but *kara* (空) also means "empty" (without batter), so it is thought of as meaning "dry frying." The food to be deep-fried is dusted or dredged in flour, *kuzu* starch, or cornstarch. The flavor of a food is not markedly changed by the hot oil because the food is cooked through the thin outer coating, which seals the surface. Representative *kara-age* foods are: flatfish, rock trout, chicken, and bean curd (*tōfu*). After dredging with flour or starch, shake off any excess and let food rest for a while so that coating will "set." Ideally start deep-frying at a low temperature (320°F/160°C) and gradually but rather swiftly raise the temperature to around 340°F/170°C, so that by the end of the few minutes it takes to cook an item, the coating is a warm golden brown.

Koromo-age, or "batter frying." In order to be light, batter is always loosely mixed and lumpy, not blended until smooth. A smooth batter becomes heavy, sticky, and masks the flavor of food. The most typical example of this method of deep-frying is TEMPURA. For batter-dipped vegetables, the ideal temperature is from 300°–320°F/150°–160°C, and for fish, from 340°–360°F/170°–180°C. Skim the surface of the oil periodically to keep it free of batter that rolls off the food.

Seasoning: In methods other than TEMPURA, most foods are seasoned in advance of being deep-fried by either light salting or marination, but the flavors of many deep-fried foods, particularly the light-flavored ingredients of TEMPURA, are enhanced by a simple seasoned dipping sauce in a small dish at the side in which tangy, spicy condiments such as finely grated *daikon* and a dab of finely grated fresh ginger are mixed. Some deep-fried foods, for instance the DEEP-FRIED EGGPLANT in the recipe immediately following, are put in individual bowls and then covered with a hot light sauce just before serving. Still other deep-fried dishes are garnished merely with a wedge of lemon at the side of the plate, to be squeezed over the food as desired, sometimes with a tiny dish of freshly ground, toasted sea salt to dip food into.

Serving: Deep-fried foods are served on individual plates or on small woven bamboo trays on top of which a single folded sheet of white paper is arranged. In Japan, this paper is a machine-made version of *washi*, the beautiful smooth but soft, resilient yet strong paper that Japanese have made by hand for over a millennium. The idea of using *washi* to line serving plates is both practical and aesthetically pleasing. *Washi*-type paper absorbs excess oil, and this rich paper ornaments a dish brightly yet quietly. The sketch shows some ways that paper may be folded. As you can see, it is folded at a slight angle, off-center, to create an asymmetrical balance and to catch the eye for a brief moment. (A small caution. Avoid folding paper in the reverse of the standard fold shown. This is for occasions connected with bereavement.)

Obviously, it requires special effort to locate *washi*-type paper outside Japan. Plain, single- or double-ply white paper dinner napkins will do; in fact, any plain, white, absorbent paper will work. Avoid any colored decoration or embossing on the napkins; the less texture the better. While paper towels for the kitchen are oil absorbent, they look too raggedy to use in this way for a meal that is a real occasion.

conventional fold

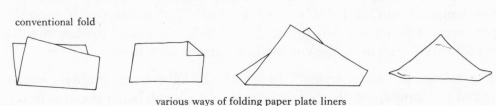

various ways of folding paper plate liners

Deep-Fried Eggplant

(*Beinasu Iridashi*) 米なすいりだし

An example of the simplest type of deep-frying, *su-age*—without dusting with flour or dipping in batter.

Buy plump eggplants, around 4½ inches (11½ cm) long. After being cut in half lengthwise and deep-fried, the boatlike eggplant halves are lightly covered with thickened sauce. Handsome and good.

If only the very large eggplants are available, cut flesh into strips. Deep-fry strips and serve with hot sauce ladled over them. Since part of the pleasure of this dish is to enjoy the shape of the eggplant, perhaps it is worth waiting to get the smaller size.

4 servings

2 eggplants, 4½ inches (11½ cm) long (½ eggplant per serving)
oil for deep-frying

sauce:

1¼ cups *dashi* (or chicken broth)
5 Tbsps *mirin*
5 Tbsps light soy sauce
2 tsps cornstarch dissolved in 1 Tbsp water
1 tsp fresh ginger juice (see page 70)

garnishes:

¼ cup or more dried bonito thread-shavings (*ito-kezuri katsuo*, or substitute conventional dried bonito flakes (*hana-katsuo*)
¼ cup or more finely shred-cut toasted *nori* seaweed (optional)
¼ cup or more finely chopped green onion (optional)

To prepare: Wash eggplants and cut off stems. Cut in half lengthwise, cut deeply around the circumference of the eggplant, about ⅛ inch (½ cm) from skin, then deeply score the exposed flesh in about ¾-inch (2-cm) squares, as shown, but not so deeply that the purple skin of the vegetable is pierced. This scoring makes the eggplant easier to cook and eat, and makes pockets to catch sauce.

(If you are using large eggplant, peel and cut flesh lengthwise into 3-inch (8-cm) long strips, about ½ inch (1½ cm) square. With fork tines, perforate each strip in a few places to make frying quicker.)

To deep-fry: Bring a generous amount of oil to low heat (about 320°F/160°C, or slightly higher) in a heavy-bottomed pot or deep-fryer. The oil should not be very hot because eggplants are full of water and at higher temperatures they not only spatter in deep-frying but also discolor.

Slip eggplants into hot oil, scored side down, 2 halves at a time (3 or more halves if the pot is big). It is better to deep-fry in several batches, both to keep oil at constant temperature and to have vegetables freely floating in the oil. Deep-fry approximately 6 to 7 minutes, till skin is brilliant purple and exposed flesh golden. Turn once, when about 70 percent cooked. Remove and drain on absorbent paper toweling. Keep hot.

To assemble: While eggplant is deep-frying, combine

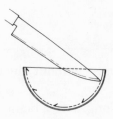

cut eggplant half around circumference and across the flesh

sauce ingredients in a pot and simmer. Just before serving, add cornstarch-and-water mixture, stir till thickened, and, finally, for fragrance, mix in 1 tsp of fresh ginger juice. Prepare garnishes of dried bonito thread-shavings and (optional) *nori* seaweed and green onion.

Place 1 eggplant half in each individual dish. Spoon over a few Tbsps of thickened *dashi* sauce. Garnish with bonito thread-shavings—and with *nori* seaweed and green onion if desired. Serve as an entrée, and eat with a spoon.

If deep-frying strips of eggplant in lieu of halves, place 5 or 6 strips in each individual dish, cover with a few Tbsps hot *dashi* sauce, and add garnish(es).

Combines well with GRILLED SQUID WITH SESAME (page 364) and GREEN BEANS WITH SESAME-MISO DRESSING (page 420).

VARIATIONS: Small fish and vegetables such as asparagus, sweet potato, Irish potato, green beans, small green peppers, lotus root, etc. can be treated in essentially the same way as the eggplant halves in the recipe above. Deep-fry uncoated ingredients in low-temperature oil, drain, arrange on dish—with or without a thickened hot *dashi* sauce—with shredded, grated, or chopped garnishes whose flavors complement that of the main ingredient.

Deep-Fried Marinated Chicken

(*Toriniku Tatsuta-age*) 鶏肉竜田揚げ

Representative of basic "dry frying" (*kara-age*), even though the chicken is marinated beforehand.

Tatsuta, after which this dish and other marinated deep-fried dishes take their name, was a site in the ancient capital of Nara famed for its maples. The color of these bite-sized morsels—reddish with soy sauce marination—is somehow poetically associated with the red of maple leaves.

The use of fresh ginger with chicken is as common in Japanese cooking as the use of thyme with poultry is in European cooking. Soy sauce, which penetrates the chicken meat during marination, burns rather easily, so watch carefully for scorching as you deep-fry the chicken.

4 servings

2 pounds (900 g) boned chicken

marinade:

6 Tbsps *saké*
3 Tbsps light soy sauce
1 Tbsp fresh ginger juice
2 Tbsps very finely chopped green onion
oil for deep-frying
1 cup flour

To prepare: Cut chicken into generous bite-sized pieces, with skin.

Mix ingredients for marinade in a bowl, add chicken pieces, and mix thoroughly with your hands. Marinate 30 minutes.

To deep-fry: Bring a generous amount of oil to medium temperature (340°F/170°C) in a heavy-bottomed pot or deep-fryer. Drain the marinade from the chicken and dust the chicken lightly with flour. Use your hands to toss and coat individual pieces thoroughly. Let coated chicken rest for 2-3 minutes.

Slide chicken into hot oil, a few pieces at a time. Turn and separate individual pieces as they deep-fry. Skim the oil occasionally. As the chicken is finished, remove and drain on absorbent paper toweling. Keep hot.

To serve: Place 6 to 8 bite-sized pieces of deep-fried chicken on a sheet of folded white absorbent paper (see above) on individual plates or small bamboo basketwork trays.

Combines well with BEATEN EGG SOUP (page 346) and TEA-WHISK EGGPLANTS (page 416).

Tempura

天ぷら (color plate 16)

The classic "batter-fried" food in Japan is TEMPURA, which is no stranger to the West. What is not well known about this so-called typical Japanese dish is that in actual fact it was introduced, or at least devised, centuries ago by Europeans living in Japan—the Spanish and Portuguese who established missions in southern Japan in the late sixteenth century. The dish caught on with the Japanese, who added the thin, delicately seasoned dipping sauce with grated *daikon* mixed in. By now TEMPURA has passed so thoroughly into native cooking that its origin is almost forgotten.

While TEMPURA remains an exclusive domain of TEMPURA specialty restaurants, it is also easy enough to make at home with very good results. In its higher forms it is a food reserved for special occasions, in its more pedestrian forms, simply a good meal. Whatever the purpose of the meal, to feast or to feed, in making TEMPURA the cook should observe three points

—fresh ingredients, oil at a constant temperature, and *lumpy* batter. The reasons behind using the freshest fish and vegetables available are self-evident. Keeping oil at a constant, proper temperature means even frying, and precise control, and light food, as discussed in detail above. But perhaps *lumpy* batter as a *sine qua non* for good TEMPURA requires further explanation.

With TEMPURA, the goal is to achieve a lacy, golden effect with the deep-fried coating, not a thick, armorlike pancake casing. To avoid a heavy, oily-tasting coating, do the opposite of all that you would do to make good pancakes. *Make the* TEMPURA *batter just before you are ready to begin deep-frying.* Do not let the batter stand. In fine TEMPURA restaurants, for instance, batter is made in small batches as orders come in. TEMPURA *batter should never be mixed well.* It should *not* be smooth and velvety. It should be only loosely folded together (with chopsticks, which are not an efficient tool for mixing and hence the perfect utensil for this job). The marks of good TEMPURA batter are a powdery ring of flour at the sides of the mixing bowl and a mix-ture marked with lumps of dry flour.

Important. *Make sure all foods to be coated are thoroughly dry* (pat dry with toweling if necessary) *and then dredge lightly in flour* (except *nori*, *shiso* leaves, and knotted trefoil). This flour coat allows the batter to adhere well to the food.

Depending on how much lacy, golden coating you like on your TEMPURA, you may adjust the coating technique and the consistency of the batter. If you like a thick coating, make a thick batter using slightly less ice water than in the recipe below. Much batter will adhere, and the coating will be thick. For the thinnest coating possible, make a thin batter by using more ice water than indicated below and gently shake dipped items over the batter bowl so excess batter returns to the batch.

Seasonal fish and vegetables are used in TEMPURA. The ingredients for TEMPURA in the recipe below are only a few of the many, many common ingredients that lend themselves to this treatment. Shrimp; squid; small whole fish like perch, smelt, and goby; white-fleshed saltwater fish; eggplant; green beans; onion rings; sweet potato slices; bell pepper strips; mush-rooms—the list could go on for several pages. Chicken, beef, and pork, however, are not usually prepared as TEMPURA because of their relatively heavier, identifiable taste. Chicken and pork are deep-fried in other ways (see other recipes in this chapter), and beef is often given a more highlighted preparation, say, in SUKIYAKI.

Soup and pickles accompany TEMPURA. Beverages should be *saké*, beer, or tea. Hot rice and more pickles conclude the repast.

4 servings

4-8 medium shrimp
6-inch (15-cm) piece raw
squid
4-8 small sillago (*kisu*)
fillets, or fillets of small
white-fleshed fish
2-3 medium onions
4-5 inches (10-13 cm) lotus
root
4-8 *shiitake* mushrooms or
white mushrooms, wiped
and trimmed
1-2 sweet potatoes
4-8 *shiso* leaves
15-16 stalks trefoil

dipping sauce:

1 cup *dashi*
⅓ cup *mirin*
⅓ cup light soy sauce

1 cup grated giant white
radish (*daikon-oroshi*)
few tsps finely grated fresh
ginger

batter:

2 egg yolks
2 cups ice water
2 cups sifted flour

oil for deep-frying

tie three trefoil stalks into a knot and
cut off stalks about 1½ inches (4 cm)
below knot

To prepare: Shell and devein shrimp, but leave tails attached. Chop off the tips of shrimp tails and gently press out moisture from shrimp with the flat of the knife tip. To prevent shrimp from curling as they are deep-fried, make a few deep incisions along the belly, as shown, and then lightly tap across each shrimp with back of knife blade.

Cut squid into 1½-inch (4-cm) squares, then cross-score the outer, smooth side of each piece lightly.

Use the *sanmai oroshi* technique (pages 123 ff) for sillago or other small fish, but in this case stop the knife at the base of the tail and cut off and remove the central bone as close to the tail as possible. The result is 2 fillets attached to a tail. This may be tricky, and is mainly decorative anyway; it is no disaster if the fillets have no tails. Clean and pat dry sillago fillets. If you are using fillets of a large white-fleshed fish, remove bones and cut fillets crosswise into bite-sized pieces.

Pierce onions with toothpicks then cut into rounds, as shown, to keep rounds from falling apart into rings.

Scrape lotus root and slice into rounds. Place immediately in weak vinegar-water to prevent discoloration.

If mushroom caps are very large, cut in half.

Peel sweet potato and slice crosswise into rounds. Wash and pat dry *shiso* leaves.

Hold 3 or 4 trefoil stalks together and tie into a knot just below leaves. Trim off stalks about 1½ inches (4 cm) below knot.

Prepare the dipping sauce by combining ingredients over heat and bringing just to a boil. Keep warm.

Grate radish and ginger.

To deep-fry: Make the batter in 2 batches, the first batch *just* before you are ready to begin deep-frying, as you are waiting for the oil to heat. In a mixing bowl, lightly beat 1 egg yolk, then pour in 1 cup of ice water and give this a *few* strokes. Add 1 cup sifted flour all at once. Stroke a few times with chopsticks or fork, just till ingredients are loosely combined. The batter should be very lumpy. If you overmix, the batter will be sticky and the coating will turn out oily and heavy. Mix the batter with the least amount of movement. Make the second batch of batter as the first is used up.

The oil should be fairly hot, about 340°F/170°C. Test by dropping a tiny bit of batter into the oil; it should descend slightly beneath the surface of the oil, then be buoyed up to the surface, the oil gently bubbling round its edges.

When you begin to deep-fry, set up the area around the heating unit like an assembly line: a tray or several trays of foods to be fried, a container of flour for dipping, and the batter bowl at your left; the hot oil pot at center; the rack for draining and skimmers and chopsticks and slotted spoons, at right. Try to arrange the physical layout and your timing to serve the *tempura immediately* after frying, but if you cannot, keep foods hot.

Each food item progresses through the assembly line in this way: use fingers to dip food in flour, shake off excess, then dip in batter; lay or slide coated material in hot oil and deep-fry till golden, around 3 minutes, turning in the oil for even cooking. Retrieve with slotted spoon or cooking chopsticks and briefly drain before transferring to serving plate. Skim the surface of the oil occasionally to keep it clean. Stir batter once or twice as you work, to keep it from separating.

Begin with vegetables, then move on to shrimp and fish or other foods that need a higher oil temperature.

There are exceptions to this flour- and batter-coating process—*shiso* leaves, *nori* seaweed, and knotted trefoil are not dipped in flour and are batter-coated on the "back" side only. If these were completely covered with batter, their color or texture would be lost.

a toothpick keeps an onion slice from falling apart

score shrimp across the belly, then tap with back of knife to eliminate curling while frying

To serve: A bar-type arrangement that allows you to serve diners directly from the stove or from a deep-fryer at a sideboard is ideal for *tempura*. Diners should be provided with a plate or bamboo tray lined with absorbent paper on which *tempura* is placed as it is done. If, on the other hand, you have to bring the deep-fried food from kitchen to table, arrange 8 or 10 pieces of *tempura* (2 shrimp, 2 fish, and several vegetables) on paper-lined plates or trays and serve that way.

At the table, pour hot dipping sauce into a small bowl, mix in grated *daikon* and a bit of grated ginger, if desired. Dip *tempura* in this sauce and eat.

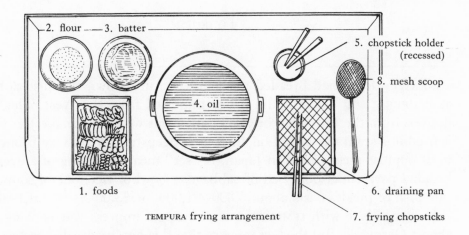

2. flour —— 3. batter

5. chopstick holder
(recessed)

8. mesh scoop

4. oil

1. foods

6. draining pan

TEMPURA frying arrangement

7. frying chopsticks

The flour-based batter for TEMPURA is not by any means the only coating for deep-frying. Japanese have developed coatings made with an interesting assortment of other ingredients. These are collectively known as *kawari-age*, or "variation frying." *Kawari-age* are a rather recent innovation in Japanese cooking, built on the tradition of deep-frying, particularly on TEMPURA.

Clean and prepare the same kinds of seasonal fish and vegetables as you would for TEMPURA. Dredge in flour, quickly dip into just barely beaten egg white (5–10 strokes of a fork for a very fresh egg), then roll or pat on one of the variation coatings and deep-fry at a slightly lower temperature than for TEMPURA. Some of these coatings are delicate and are liable to burn, so take care. Too much depends on the nature of the coating and the food coated to be able to give any specific temperature rules.

The coatings you might use fall into several broad categories:

Noodles: Fine egg *sōmen* noodles, chopped into ¼-inch (¾-cm) lengths. You may also use chopped *harusame* filaments, which puff out white and wild. If you can find green-tea buckwheat noodles (*cha-soba*), the result is very attractive. In Japanese, this has been dubbed *matsuba-age*, or "pine-needle frying."

Seeds and nuts: White sesame seeds, thinly sliced almonds, chopped walnuts, crushed macadamia nuts, and crushed cashews.

Sea vegetables: Use any of several types of *nori* seaweed, or *wakame*-type or *konbu*-type seaweed. Chop finely or cut into very thin strips with scissors.

Starches, flours, and meals: You may use crushed rice crackers (*sembei*); glutinous rice meal (*Dōmyōji-ko*), toasted; dried *mochi* rice cake flavored with a brush of soy sauce and crushed; or *kuzu* starch granules.

For a meal that is both fun and gorgeous, choose 5 different coatings—for example, egg noodles, sesame seeds, almonds, and two types of seaweed—and cover only large shrimp. Serve 5 differently coated shrimp on a paper-lined plate and garnish only with ½ small lemon or lime. Offer salt and soy sauce. If you prefer dipping sauce, serve regular TEMPURA DIPPING SAUCE and omit lemon; garnish plate with mound of grated *daikon*. These coatings look good, taste even better, and are practically guaranteed to impress just about anyone. This dish is known as FIVE-COLOR SHRIMP (*Ebi Goshiki-age*).

Tonkatsu
とんかつ

TONKATSU, deep-fried breaded pork cutlet, is in its own way just as famous as TEMPURA; and like tempura it was imported from the West. This dish is derived from the European breaded cutlet, but whereas the Western version is fried in a scant amount of oil, this one is deep-fried. TONKATSU is one of the most popular meat dishes in Japan. A "set" meal consisting of a deep-fried breaded pork cutlet on a bed of cabbage, a bowl of rice, one of soup, and a side dish of pickles costs about ¥800–¥1,000, or $3.00–$4.00 (in 1980).

In comparison with TEMPURA, this dish might impress you as being heavy, almost Germanic. But the fact remains that this *kawari-age* dish is very much a daily food and is inexpensive as well as filling. Done well, with pork loin or tenderloin, it can be very good indeed. TONKATSU is accompanied by a thick sauce, based on Worcestershire sauce, which is available in bottles, or you can use the dipping sauces recommended below. It is commonly laid against shredded raw cabbage, which acts as a salad.

4 servings

4 slices pork loin or
tenderloin, about ½ inch
(1½ cm) thick and
4-6 ounces (115-180 g)
freshly ground black pepper
salt
flour
2 eggs, lightly beaten
2 cups fresh or dried bread
crumbs
oil for deep-frying
shredded cabbage
lemon wedges (optional)
commercially prepared
tonkatsu sauce, or a
combination of the
following mixed to taste:
ketchup
Worcestershire sauce
dark soy sauce
prepared mustard
saké

To prepare: In a few places slash the fat rimming one side of the loin cutlet to keep meat from curling when deep-fried. Salt lightly then grind fresh pepper over both sides. Dredge lightly in flour. Dip into beaten egg and then press into breadcrumbs.

To deep-fry: Bring about 3 inches (8 cm) of oil to about 350°F/175°C in a heavy-bottomed pot or deep-fryer. Lay 1 or 2 cutlets in the hot oil. Deep-fry till golden brown, about 5 to 7 minutes, turning them in the oil once or twice. Skim the oil periodically. Briefly drain cutlets on absorbent paper. Cut pork crosswise at ¾-inch (2-cm) intervals into bite-sized slices that are easy to manage with chopsticks. If you plan on eating *tonkatsu* with knife and fork, do not bother to cut it at this point.

To serve: Against a generous half-plateful of shredded cabbage, arrange cutlet slices as if cutlet was whole. Garnish with a wedge of lemon, if desired. The sauce may be poured from a small ewer into a small bowl to be used as a dip, or it may be poured over the cutlet and cabbage.

Japanese Salads
Sunomono and *Aemono*

Sunomono, literally "vinegared things," and *aemono*, "dressed things," may be loosely described as the equivalents of salads. *Sunomono* and *aemono* are generally served in small portions in elegant bowls or small dishes at the side. The vinegared or dressed ingredients are chosen to complement the main dish in taste, color, and texture.

There is great scope for creativity in these Japanese-style salads. You can make all sorts of interesting combinations. The natural acidity of fruit such as kiwi fruit, strawberries, peaches, or the flavor of persimmon, and even avocado, heightened with rice vinegar and lemon and seasoned with a drop of soy sauce, go beautifully with chopped clams, scallops, oysters, and other shellfish.

Minute portions of assorted *sunomono* or a few kinds of *aemono*, merely a taste of each, are often served before the start of a meal to accompany hot *saké*, when guests are seated. If the dinner is formal, the more elaborate or rare the ingredients the better. Before the meal, these tiny "salads" are called *sakizuke*, *zensai*, or *tsukidashi*. Sometimes, however, "vinegared things" or "dressed things" are eaten at the end of the meal, before the rice.

"Vinegared things," *sunomono*, embrace a wide range of ingredients: practically any vegetable, raw and crisp or parboiled and cooled, and many kinds of fish or shellfish, fresh from the sea or sometimes grilled, steamed, or fried, then cooled. The ingredients are tossed with or sprinkled with a thin vinegary or lemony dressing.

The word *aemono* in fact translates as "combined," "composed," or "harmonized things." The vehicle for harmonizing ingredients is a dressing, so, in effect, *aemono* are "dressed things." They likewise consist of several raw or cooked (then cooled) vegetables or fish or poultry. The *aemono* category technically includes *sunomono*, since vinegar is a dressing; strictly, the two are not separate categories, but for purposes of simple identification, one might say that *aemono* dressings tend to be thicker than vinegar-based dressings. There are any number of exceptions; this is a convenient generalization, not a rule. In general, *aemono* dressings are based on pureed bean curd (*tōfu*), toasted and ground sesame, or *miso* (bean paste). Sometimes egg yolk is used. *Aemono* dressings usually include rice vinegar, but merely as one of several seasonings, not as a base. The table below of the most typical dressings should give a clear idea of what and how *sunomono* and *aemono* are composed. After you make these dressings a few times according to recipe, make adjustments to suit your own taste. *Sunomono* and *aemono* are flexible ideas, not dogma.

The amount of dressing you use—whether vinegary or thick—is critical to the success of the dish. Too much, and the taste and texture of the vegetables or fish is lost, drowned. Too little, and the taste is incomplete, as if the cook had to answer the telephone while adding seasonings and forgot to finish the job. Generally speaking, for 4 servings, it is safe to use 5 Tbsps vinegary dressing or 6 Tbsps thick dressing.

Two important points for the success of these dressed salads are: 1) *never* to use warm ingredients (*escabeche* is the only exception). Everything must be cooled or chilled, depending on season and ingredients. 2) All ingredients must be thoroughly dry before dressing is added.

Five Basic Vinegar Dressings

NAME	INGREDIENTS	PROCESS
Two-Flavors Vinegar (*Nihaizu*) 二杯酢 makes 1⅓ cups	½ cup rice vinegar 2 Tbsps dark or light soy sauce ⅔ cup *dashi* or water	Mix vinegar with soy sauce and thin to taste with *dashi* or water. Keeps indefinitely refrigerated.
Three-Flavors Vinegar (*Sanbaizu*) 三杯酢 makes 1⅓ cups	1½ Tbsps sugar (or *mirin*) ½ cup rice vinegar 2 Tbsps dark or light soy sauce ⅔ cup *dashi* or water	Mix in a saucepan over medium heat. Dissolve sugar in (or mix *mirin* with) vinegar and add soy sauce, then stir in *dashi* to taste. Bring just to a boil, remove from heat, and cool to room temperature. Keeps indefinitely refrigerated.
Sweet Vinegar (*Amazu*) 甘酢 makes 1 cup	½ cup rice vinegar 2½ Tbsps sugar (or *mirin*) ½ cup *dashi*	Dissolve sugar in (or mix *mirin* with) vinegar and add *dashi* or water. Bring just to a boil, remove from heat, and cool to room temperature. Keeps indefinitely refrigerated.

NAME	INGREDIENTS	PROCESS
Ponzu Sauce (*Ponzu*) ポン酢 This is also a popular dipping sauce for *sashimi* and one-pot dishes (*nabemono*).	recipe on page 172	
Plum Vinegar (*Bainiku-zu*) 梅肉酢 makes ⅔ cup	⅔ cup PICKLED PLUM (*umeboshi*) meat 1 Tbsp rice vinegar 2 tsps *mirin* 3 Tbsps *dashi*	Pickled plum meat (known as *bainiku*) is sold canned, or cut off the meat of pickled plums (*umeboshi*). Rub plum meat through a sieve with the back of a wooden spoon to puree, then add vinegar and *mirin*. Stir in *dashi* as desired to thin and smooth dressing. Keeps indefinitely refrigerated.

Eleven Vinegar Dressing Variations

NAME	INGREDIENTS	PROCESS
Tosa Vinegar (*Tosa-zu*) 土佐酢 makes ¾ cup	1 cup NIHAIZU or SANBAIZU (see above) ⅙–⅓ ounce (5–10 g) (roughly 1 cup) dried bonito flakes (*hanakatsuo*)	In a saucepan bring NIHAIZU or SANBAIZU just to a boil. Add bonito flakes and stir over heat till thoroughly soaked, about 30 seconds. Remove from heat and strain immediately. Discard flakes. Let dressing cool to room temperature. Keeps indefinitely refrigerated.
Egg Yolk Vinegar (*Kimi-zu*) 黄身酢 makes about ¾ cup	2–3 egg yolks ½ cup NIHAIZU, SANBAIZU, or AMAZU (see above)	Beat yolks lightly. Put vinegar dressing in the top of a double boiler, and over boiling water gradually stir in the beaten yolk; continue stirring until mixture becomes creamy. Remove from heat and cool to room temperature. Does not keep.
Ginger Vinegar (*Shōga-zu*) 生姜酢		Add about 1 Tbsp finely grated fresh ginger to ½ cup room-temperature NIHAIZU or SANBAIZU (see above).

NAME	INGREDIENTS	PROCESS
Yoshino Vinegar (*Yoshino-zu*) 吉野酢 Mountainous Yoshino is known for its fine *kuzu* starch (similar to arrowroot) and also for cherry blossoms. makes ½ cup	½ cup NIHAIZU, SANBAIZU, or AMAZU (see above) 1 Tbsp *kuzu* starch or cornstarch, mixed with 1 Tbsp water	Heat the vinegar dressing in a saucepan over medium heat. Slowly add the *kuzu*- or cornstarch-and-water mixture, stirring over heat just till the dressing has thickened. Allow to come to room temperature and use cooled. Does not keep.
Sesame Vinegar (*Goma-zu*) 胡麻酢 makes ½ cup	½ cup white sesame seeds ½ cup NIHAIZU or SANBAIZU (see above)	Toast sesame seeds. Transfer to a *suribachi* (Japanese grinding bowl, see page 105) and grind till flaky and pastelike. Stir in the NIHAIZU or SANBAIZU (which should be at room temperature). Keeps about 2 weeks refrigerated.
Radish Vinegar (*Mizore-zu*) みぞれ酢		Add about ¼ cup grated giant white radish (*daikon-oroshi*) to ½ cup room-temperature NIHAIZU or SANBAIZU (see above). Does not keep.
Yuzu Citron Vinegar (*Yuko-zu*) 柚香酢		Add 1 Tbsp *yuzu* citron juice (or juice of lemon or lime) to ½ cup room-temperature NIHAIZU or SANBAIZU (see above).
Kinome Vinegar (*Kinome-zu*) 木の芽酢		Grind a few *kinome* sprigs in a *suribachi* (Japanese grinding bowl, see page 105) and mix in about ½ cup room-temperature NIHAIZU or SANBAIZU (see above). Very fragrant. Use immediately.
Nanban Vinegar (*Nanban-zu*) 南蛮酢		Add 2 seeded dried red peppers and 1 lightly charred long onion (*naganegi*) or 2–3 lightly charred green onions to about ½ cup NIHAIZU or SANBAIZU (see above). Heat in a saucepan till simmering. This is one of the few dressings used hot. Do not eat red peppers, though you may use them for color. Keeps 3–4 days when used to marinate food (such as deep-fried fish), but prepare just before using.

NAME	INGREDIENTS	PROCESS
Horseradish Vinegar (*Wasabi-zu*) わ さ び 酢		Add slightly less than 1 tsp finely grated *wasabi* horseradish to ½ cup room-temperature NIHAIZU or SANBAIZU (see above). Mix just before serving because grated *wasabi* quickly loses its flavor and bite.
Mustard Vinegar (*Karashi-zu*) か ら し 酢		Add slightly less than 1 tsp mustard paste to ½ cup room-temperature NIHAIZU or SANBAIZU (see above). Make just before serving because the mustard flavor is short-lived.

Six Basic Thick Dressings for *Aemono*

NAME	INGREDIENTS	PROCESS
Okara Dressing (*Unohana*) *Okara* is what is left when *tōfu* is made (see page 60). makes about 1 cup	1 cup *okara* 1 egg yolk 1 tsp salt 2 Tbsps rice vinegar 1 Tbsp sugar	Puree *okara* by rubbing it through a sieve with the back of a spoon. Lightly beat egg yolk and mix with *okara*. Mix in other ingredients, blending well with each addition. Place mixture in double boiler and stir over boiling water until dressing is thick and smooth, remove from heat, and let cool to room temperature. Use on same day as made.
Sea Urchin Dressing (*Uni*) As delicious as this dressing is, do not waste fresh sea urchin on it. Eat fresh sea urchin raw! Here, use bottled, salty sea-urchin, available at many oriental food stores. Fresh or jarred, sea urchin is expensive, but well worth the indulgence. makes about ⅓ cup	1 egg yolk 1½ ounces (40–50 g; ⅓ cup) bottled sea urchin 2 tsps *mirin* 2 tsps *saké*	Beat egg yolk lightly. Rub sea urchin through a sieve with the back of a spoon to puree. Blend in lightly beaten egg yolk and *mirin* and *saké* till smooth. Must be used on the day it is made.

NAME	INGREDIENTS	PROCESS
Sesame Dressing (*Goma*) makes ¼ cup	4 Tbsps white sesame seeds 2 tsps dark or light soy sauce 3 Tbsps *dashi* 1 Tbsp *mirin*	Toast sesame seeds then grind in a *suribachi* (Japanese grinding bowl, see page 105) till flaky and paste-like. Add other ingredients and blend well. Dressing should be creamy. Prepare just before using.
White Dressing (*Tōfu*) Mashed or pureed *tōfu* (bean curd) gives this dressing its color and creamy consistency. See the TANGY WHITE SALAD recipe on page 421 for a slightly more complex version. Amount depends upon size of *tōfu* cake	1 cake *tōfu* (bean curd) 1–2 Tbsps white sesame seeds 1 Tbsp sugar ½ Tbsp salt	Press bean curd (see page 58) for 30 minutes. Rub pressed *tōfu* through a sieve with the back of a spoon or mash well in a bowl. Toast sesame seeds then grind in a *suribachi* (Japanese grinding bowl, see page 105), till flaky and pastelike. Add sugar and salt, then add the pureed or mashed bean curd to the crushed sesame seed in the *suribachi* and blend well. Dressing should be thick and creamy. Keeps 1 day refrigerated.
White *Miso* Dressing (*Shiromiso*) makes about 1 cup	1 egg yolk ¾ cup white *miso* 2 Tbsps *saké* 1 Tbsp sugar 1 Tbsp *mirin* (*dashi*)	Beat egg yolk lightly, add to *miso*, blend until smooth, and stir in other ingredients one by one. Place in a double boiler over medium heat and blend well. Remove from heat and allow to come to room temperature. May be thinned to taste with *dashi*. Keeps 2 weeks refrigerated. When cool, any number of garnishing ingredients—such as *kinome* sprigs—may be added. Other suggestions are: *yuzu* citron (or lemon or lime) rind; sesame seeds; green *nori* seaweed (*ao-nori*) flakes; and *sansho* pepper powder.
Red *Miso* Dressing (*Akamiso*) makes about 1 cup	¾ cup red *miso* 3 Tbsps *dashi* (or *saké* or *mirin*, just enough to make the dressing smooth) 2 Tbsps sugar 2 tsps light soy sauce	Blend *miso*, sugar, and soy sauce. Cream *miso* mixture with *dashi* or *saké* or *mirin*. You may flavor with toasted and ground sesame seed or *sansho* pepper powder. Keeps 1 month refrigerated.

Vegetables, fish, or poultry for *sunomono* and *aemono* often need some sort of preliminary attention before being cut and mixed with a sauce. Fish and shellfish may be marinated in a vinegary solution or pressed between kelp sheets for flavor. Very small fish may be grilled, unseasoned, over a hot fire. Chicken is broiled or *saké*-steamed. Vegetables are salted or parboiled. Depending on the type of vegetable, the parboiling may be done in seasoned stock to add a background flavor.

Here are some *sunomono* suggestions, including both garnishes and dressings. Serve in small portions in small dishes or bowls as appetizers, to complement an entrée, or before rice at the end of a Japanese meal. Mix before eating to blend flavors.

Salmon roe mixed with an equal volume of finely grated *daikon* with SWEET VINEGAR (*amazu*).

Raw oysters on the half-shell, a dab of grated *daikon* on each, with PONZU.

Lightly cooked crabmeat, parboiled spinach, a dab of finely grated fresh ginger, and SANBAIZU.

Parboiled shrimp, shred-cut celery, and EGG YOLK VINEGAR (*kimi-zu*).

Boiled octopus and thin-sliced cucumber (rubbed with salt) with MUSTARD VINEGAR (*karashi-zu*).

Julienne strips of carrot and cucumber with SWEET VINEGAR (*amazu*).

Vinegared Crab
(*Kanisu*) か に 酢 (color plate 12)

Fresh crab is, of course, best in winter.

4 servings

6 ounces (180 g) boiled or steamed crab meat (or a 4½-ounce [130-g] can crab meat), chilled
½ cup SANBAIZU **(page 242)**
2 tsps fresh ginger juice
1 cucumber (½ American cucumber, peeled and seeded)

To prepare: Pick over crab meat, discard cartilage, shred finely.

Finely slice cucumber and soak in salted water (2 Tbsps salt in 1 quart [1 L] water) for 15 minutes. Squeeze to drain. Cucumber slices should be limp.

Make SANBAIZU dressing and mix with ginger juice to taste.

To serve: Divide crab meat and sliced cucumber into 4 portions and place in small individual dishes. Spoon on 2 Tbsps of gingery SANBAIZU. Serve chilled. Mix thoroughly before eating.

VARIATION: You may also use cold, thinly sliced steamed abalone, or cold, flaked, poached white-fleshed fish.

Vinegared Octopus

(*Sudako*) 酢 だ こ

Octopus tentacles, boiled pink and tender, are the feature of the next *sunomono* recipe. Japanese home cooks usually purchase octopus already boiled at the fishmonger's, where it is displayed along with the fresh catch in a refrigerator case. As an intriguing digression, however, it is interesting to see how octopus is handled from the very start.

If you can pick and choose a fresh octopus, select one about 1½ pounds (675 g). This weight is ideal for tenderness, and the size is just right aesthetically. The tentacles of 1½-pound octopuses are about 1 inch (2½ cm) in diameter, perfect for slicing into thin, attractive rounds.

Japanese tenderize this creature by kneading it in a bath of finely grated giant white radish (*daikon-oroshi*) or in salt. Finely grate 1 whole *daikon* (about 4–6 cups) to knead a 1½ pound (675 g) octopus.

First, push the body sac inside-out through the orifice in the head. Cut away innards, the eyes, and the beak, and discard. Plop the inside-out octopus into the grated giant radish in a large bowl and knead vigorously and thoroughly, squeezing the tentacles through your hands to "degrease" them. The radish will become gray. This is a messy but satisfyingly therapeutic job. This tenderizing-cleaning step takes about 5 minutes or a bit longer. After its radish treatment, the octopus should have a fresh, oceany smell. Wash well, and return head to its proper form.

Carefully plunge the whole octopus into a large pot filled with lightly salted boiling water and 1 Tbsp dark soy sauce. When you submerge the octopus in the water, hold it with a long chopstick or hook by the orifice in the head so that the tentacles are hanging down, ready to coil up neatly when they come into contact with the hot water. Plunge octopus into the water 2–3 times and then cook for 5–6 minutes uncovered, on medium heat. The skin will change from steel gray to a warm red-pink. The meat remains white. Remove from the boiling water, and hang octopus with a hook inserted into the head orifice. Letting the octopus cool slowly makes it tender.

4–6 servings

2 tentacles from 1½-pound (675 g) octopus, cooked briefly as described above
juice of 1 *yuzu* citron or lemon
½ cup SANBAIZU (page 242)

To prepare: Octopus should be chilled. Slice tentacles crosswise on the diagonal into ⅛-inch (½-cm) thick ovals (or cut into bite-sized pieces).

To serve: Arrange 5 or 6 slices per serving in small individual dishes. Pour about ½ tsp *yuzu* citron or lemon juice over each serving, then spoon over a few tsps SANBAIZU. Serve as a side dish or appetizer.

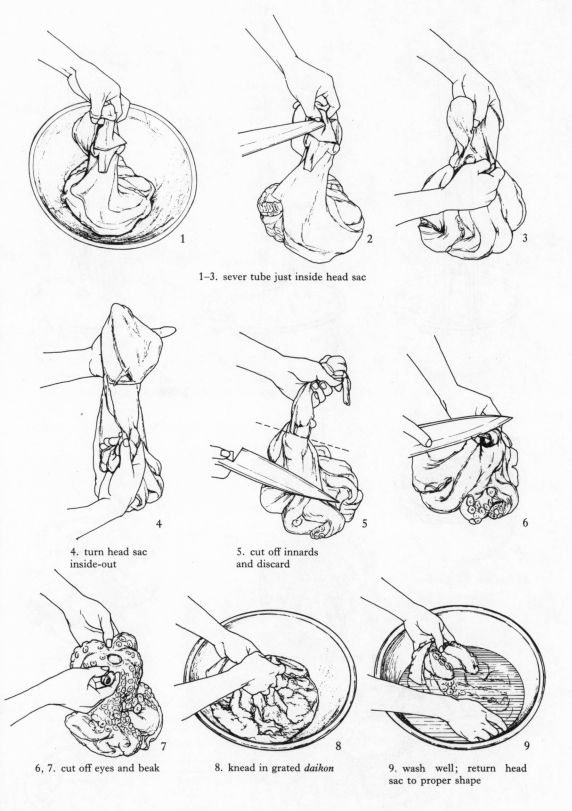

1–3. sever tube just inside head sac

4. turn head sac
inside-out

5. cut off innards
and discard

6, 7. cut off eyes and beak

8. knead in grated *daikon*

9. wash well; return head
sac to proper shape

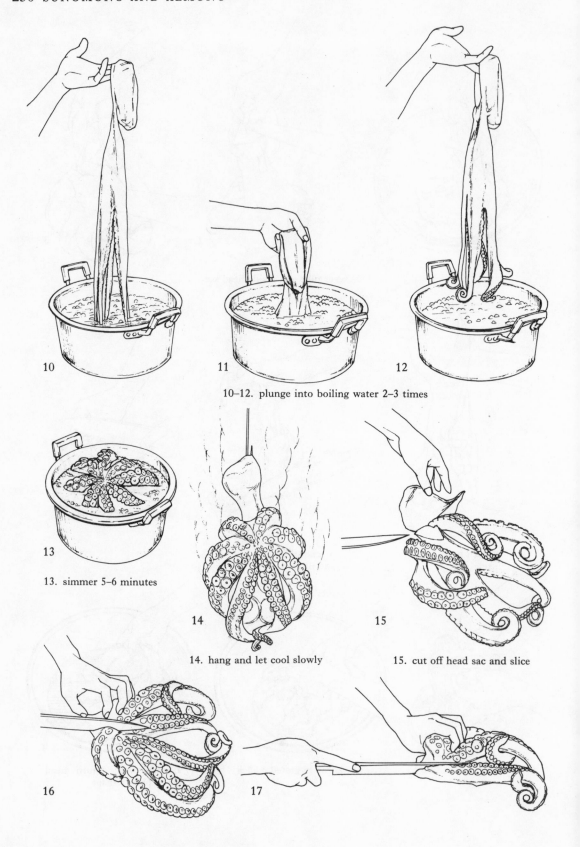

10–12. plunge into boiling water 2–3 times

13. simmer 5–6 minutes

14. hang and let cool slowly

15. cut off head sac and slice

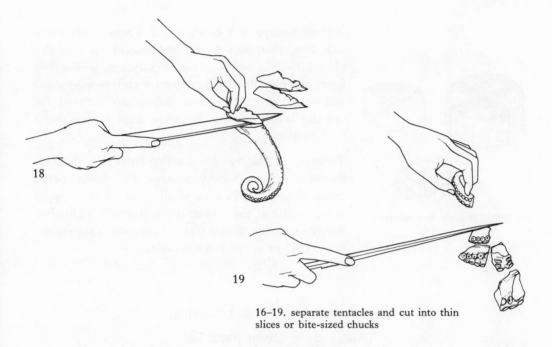

18

19

16–19. separate tentacles and cut into thin slices or bite-sized chucks

VARIATION: You may also use cold, thinly sliced steamed abalone, or cold, flaked, poached white-fleshed fish.

Chrysanthemum Turnip

(*Kikka Kabu*) 菊花かぶ (color plate 11)

This do-ahead dish is practically effortless, but the easy decorative cutting technique transforms turnips into blossoms. Serve this "chrysanthemum" vegetable as a tangy appetizer or garnish for any grilled food.

4 servings

6 medium or, small turnips
1 tsp salt in 1 quart (1 L) water
2-inch (5-cm) square giant kelp (*konbu*)
1 cup SWEET VINEGAR (see page 242)
½ tsp finely chopped, seeded red pepper

To prepare: Trim and peel the turnips and cut off tops level. Rest a turnip on its flat top on a cutting board between two bamboo skewers. Cross-score as deeply and as finely as possible. The skewer guards will keep the knife from cutting all the way through. Cut each turnip into 4 to 6 pieces.

Put cut turnips in salt water in which the kelp (*konbu*) has been left to soak. Let soak 20 minutes, then remove and squeeze out excess water by hand, one by one.

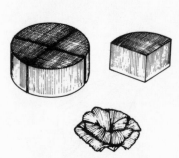

cut turnip as finely as possible

Place turnips in a bowl, add 2 Tbsps SWEET VINE-GAR, toss, then squeeze out and discard vinegar. Replace turnips in bowl, sprinkle lightly with seeded and finely chopped dried red pepper (or chili powder), and add SWEET VINEGAR to cover. Refrigerate, covered, for one day before serving. Keeps at least 1 week under refrigeration.

To serve: Drain vinegar dressing from each chrysanthemum turnip. Gently separate the flower petals (with chopsticks). Place a small piece of red pepper at the center of the flower. Serve in small, individual dishes or on the dinner plate at the side of the entrée. Serve cold or at room temperature.

Shellfish with *Miso* Dressing

(*Nuta*) ぬ た (color plate 12)

For this *aemono*, raw cockles are preferred, but any little shellfish may be used, with the exception of oysters, which are so delicate they are liable to be turned to pulp in this sort of salad. You may even try sliced raw white-fleshed fish.

The variety of green onion that Japanese use for this dish is called *wakegi*. Use the youngest, mildest green onions you can find.

In making this dressing, the amount of *miso* used is crucial. If too much is used, the dressing will be too heavy. Use *miso* judiciously.

4 servings

1 bunch green onions (*wakegi*)
salt
raw or boiled cockles (*torigai*) or other shellfish, 3-4 large ones per serving
5-6 Tbsps (100 g) WHITE MISO DRESSING **(see page 246)**
½ tsp mustard paste (see page 78)
2 Tbsps rice vinegar
5 Tbsps *dashi* (or light chicken broth)
splash of light soy sauce

To prepare: Plunge the whole green onions in boiling water for about 30 seconds to soften them. Remove, drain, and sprinkle lightly with salt. On a dry cutting board roll out green stalks with a rolling pin or pestle to extract as much water as possible. Do not roll or crush the white part. Cut green onions crosswise into 1½-inch (4-cm) lengths.

Parboil shellfish and drain; cool and cut into bite-sized pieces, if necessary.

Put the MISO DRESSING in a *suribachi* (Japanese grinding bowl, see page 105) or large mixing bowl. Add the mustard and mix till well blended and smooth. Add the liquid ingredients little by little, mixing well between additions. Consistency will be somewhat like mayonnaise.

1 Tbsp *saké* (optional)
few Tbsps *benitade* sprouts
(see page 168), if available

To serve: Place neat mounds of green onion into individual, small deep dishes. Place portions of shellfish on the green onion. Spoon on about 1½ Tbsps seasoned WHITE MISO DRESSING. Garnish with a pinch of red *benitade* sprouts. Serve immediately as first course or as a complement to an entrée. Mix with chopsticks or fork before eating.

Another way of serving is to toss the boiled shellfish and green onion in the dressing in a large bowl and then serve in individual portions in small dishes. Add garnish to each portion.

Goes well with anything except noodles.

Spinach with Sesame Dressing

(*Hōrensō no Goma-Ae*) ほうれん草ごまあえ

The first taste of this dressing is like delicately roasted peanuts. Perhaps it is the soy sauce that brings this flavor out. The ingredient to be careful about in this dish is sugar. Do not add too much.

4 servings

1 pound (450-g) fresh spinach, washed and parboiled (see page 93)

dressing:
  4 Tbsps white sesame seeds
  1 tsp sugar
  2 tsps dark soy sauce
  3 Tbsps *dashi*

To prepare: Make the dressing first. Toast sesame seeds (see page 86), then put hot seeds into a large *suribachi* (Japanese grinding bowl, see page 105) and crush with a pestle. Add sugar. Stir with pestle. Add the soy sauce and *dashi*. Mix with relatively great speed and strength, almost a whipping action, to blend well. Taste and add more sugar, if you think it is necessary, mixing thoroughly after this addition.

Chop parboiled spinach into 1½-inch (4-cm) lengths. Put the parboiled, chopped spinach in the dressing in the *suribachi*. With a very light touch, use a pestle to mix the spinach and dressing. The spinach should be *very slightly* bruised to allow sesame dressing to penetrate. Do not crush.

To serve: Place single portions (¼ of total) of spinach in the center of small, deep dishes. Serve at room temperature.

Goes well with anything.

One-Pot Cooking
Nabemono

Friendship and conviviality are the keynote of *nabemono*, the communal one-pot meals served both at home and in restaurants and perennially popular with foreigners and Japanese alike. When one Japanese says to another: "Come and have some *sukiyaki*," this invitation expresses his desire to become friends. It means: "I like you well enough to dip chopsticks with you in the same pot."

The word *nabe* means simply "pot," and *nabemono*, "things-in-a-pot." This category of food includes all one-pot dishes cooked at the table. Diners themselves do their own cooking, choosing what they like from platters overflowing with raw ingredients and cooking it in a communal pot of broth.

This friendly, warming way of eating seems to have been spawned in cold climates. Witness the convivial fondue of Switzerland. The Japanese one-pot meal probably derives from the soup kettle that used to hang over the central open hearth—the *irori*—in the old farmhouses of Japan's snow country, and became popular in the urban climates of Tokyo (Edo) and Osaka perhaps as early as two centuries ago. The cold regions of China, too, had their one-pot communal dish, known in the West as Mongolian hot-pot and adopted by the Japanese about a century ago. Now immensely popular, this Japanese modification is known by the intriguing name *shabu-shabu*.

The *nabemono* setup may look elaborate, but all the food is fresh and simple —freshly cut vegetables and slices of firm-fleshed fish, chicken, or well-marbled beef; squares of *tōfu* (bean curd) and mounds of *shirataki* (filaments made from the devil's tongue starch)—all arranged beautifully on a platter with the same care, almost, that one would expect of a flower arrangement. This sort of dish puts into practice the Japanese culinary principle of eating the freshest food just lightly cooked and beautifully presented. On the table is a cast-iron pot or earthenware casserole, filled with broth, set on a gas ring or some other kind of heating unit. The meal begins, and with chopsticks everyone slides morsels of fresh food into the pot, fishes them out just as they are cooked, usually a minute or so, and dips them in a seasoned sauce in individual dipping bowls.

Whether the ingredients are from a small kitchen garden or a local market or are more elaborate items devised by exclusive restaurants, *nabemono* dishes, together with a soup, a vinegared vegetable or light salad (*sunomono* or *aemono*), and a bowl of hot white rice, make a grand banquet. For a dinner party of 6 (or more), *nabemono* are ideal, easy on the host because everything can be prepared ahead of time. You can arrange platters of ingredients, cover with plastic wrap, and refrigerate till time to use. Moreover, since portions are adjustable, it is easy to accommodate an extra guest or two (though 6 is a comfortable number to gather round a single communal pot). Entertaining this way is also extremely convivial. Everyone gets involved, and conversation never seems to lag as, with amiable flourishing of chopsticks (or fondue forks), each diner samples the plenty of the host's table.

There are a few rules to follow in preparing *nabemono*.

1. Use twice the volume of vegetables as fish and meat. This is for aesthetic as well as nutritional reasons.

2. Choose ingredients that harmonize in flavor. For example, with light-flavored fish such as cod or sea bream, use vegetables of a similar lightness such as Chinese cabbage, etc. With fatty fish such as tuna or yellowtail, use meaty, flavorsome mushrooms (*matsutake*, if available) and savory vegetables such as green onions, trefoil, and so on. Avoid using celery, since its flavor and aroma tend to dominate other foods as it cooks.

3. The timing of the cooking of each ingredient is also important, so cut vegetables and fish or meat into pieces of such a size that the overall cooking time will be equal. Root vegetables such as potatoes, giant white radish (*daikon*), and turnips should be parboiled, since they require a relatively long cooking time. You may want to scald or parboil leafy green vegetables such as Chinese cabbage and spinach, to get rid of excess water in the former, and to eliminate harsh flavor in the latter.

4. Certain ingredients such as chicken exude fats and create scum when they are simmered. Such ingredients should be parboiled ahead of time so that the stock in the communal pot does not become foam-flecked. In any case, it is a good idea to keep a suitable spoon or ladle at the table to skim the broth occasionally.

The classic *nabemono* stock is water flavored by a 4-inch (10-cm) square of giant kelp (*konbu*). Remove the kelp from the pot just before the water comes to a boil. Remember, all the ingredients lend their flavors to the broth in the pot (which is why, in fact, *nabemono* are started with the simmering of pieces of fish or meat), so you do not want to begin with stock that is too highly flavored. For some one-pot dishes, chicken stock is very good; this is indicated when appropriate in the following recipes.

Nabemono often are accompanied by a selection of dipping sauces and spicy condiments. These are set on the table in small pitchers or small bowls, and diners mix whatever they like in individual dipping bowls. Typical are PONZU SAUCE (essentially, lemony soy sauce), RED MAPLE RADISH (grated giant white radish and a small quantity of hot red pepper combined to give a pleasant kick), finely chopped green onions, finely chopped *shiso* leaves, and crumpled, toasted sheets of *nori* seaweed. For SUKIYAKI, hot meat or vegetables are dipped into egg.

So common are *nabemono* dishes that the majority of Japanese households are equipped with a portable gas ring. For those outside Japan, an appropriate source of heat—something to keep the pot simmering at the table for the duration of a 2-hour meal—may require some innovation. An alcohol or canned-heat burner (the bottom of a chafing dish or fondue set) can be used, but to bring the stock up to a healthy simmer, you will probably have to start the pot at the kitchen stove then bring it to the burner at the table. A decorative but bothersome alternative is to set up a small charcoal brazier at the table. A portable electric coil can also be employed. Mongolian hot-pots (*huo-kuo*, or *hōkō-nabe* in Japanese), whether charcoal or electric, are excellent and decorative.

A good substitute utensil is the electric skillet. If you have one of these convenient utensils, no other special equipment is necessary, and you can cease worrying whether or not you have cooking pots attractive enough to use at the table and concentrate on the food.

The traditional vessels in which *nabemono* are prepared should not be ignored. Perhaps the most versatile is the *donabe*, an earthenware casserole easily recognizable by its thick pottery walls and substantial, no-nonsense shape. It is good for any *nabemono* except SUKIYAKI because it diffuses heat well. A *donabe* can be placed directly over heat (and can also be used in an oven). Its function need not be limited to the cooking of Japanese foods.

Donabe are extremely good value for their cost, at least in Japan, and come in small, one-portion sizes, in medium sizes, or in a large size holding a couple of quarts (liters). The diameter of the casserole is the gauge by which to judge how many persons can eat from the communal pot with ease: a 7-inch (18-cm) casserole serves 1; a 10-inch (25-cm) casserole serves 3 to 5; and a 12-inch (30-cm) casserole serves 6 to 8. With over 8 guests, it is advisable to set up 2 portable heat sources and bring 2 pots to the table.

While the lid of the *donabe* is always glazed inside and out, only the inside of the body is glazed. The clay used for *donabe* is very porous and refractory, allowing the pot to take the shock of direct heat. For this reason, despite its heavy appearance, a *donabe* is fragile and must be properly tempered before its first use.

First be sure that the outside, unglazed surface is completely dry. This is important. Then fill the *donabe* with water and place it over low heat for 1 hour. There is no need to temper the lid, since it is glazed all over. Some advise washing only the glazed inside of the pot after enjoying *nabe-mono* dishes to avoid getting the outside, especially the unglazed bottom, wet. This is an old wives' tale. You may wash the whole thing, but take care that the unglazed exterior is *thoroughly* dry before using on direct heat. You can wash *donabe* in a dishwasher, but load the machine carefully so that the *donabe* does not jiggle against other pots and pans. It resists heat well, but is not so strong with knocks and bumps.

Donabe are good for one-pot cookery because the earthenware holds and conducts heat evenly. On the other hand, remember to heat and cool this vessel gradually, because sudden changes in temperature are liable to strain the pottery and produce cracks. If, over time, your *donabe* should develop a hairline crack, try to seal it by cooking rice or gruel in the vessel; this usually effects binding.

If you do not have a *donabe*, you could use a *flameproof* ceramic casserole. Take care. Stoneware casseroles, which are good in an oven, will *not* take a direct flame and will crack.

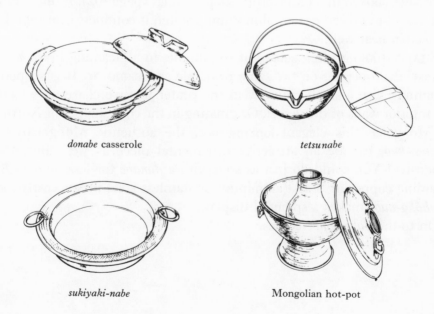

donabe casserole

tetsunabe

sukiyaki-nabe

Mongolian hot-pot

In Japan, the *tetsunabe*, or iron boiling pot, is also frequently used for dishes cooked with a lot of thin broth. *Tetsunabe* come with a wooden (usually cedar) lid and bucket-style handle because they have traditionally been hung over the hearth. These iron pots are associated with farmhouse fare. They should be tempered and treated as cast-iron skillets are.

Besides the ever-serviceable *donabe* (and *tetsunabe*), there are also *sukiyaki-nabe* and *hōkō-nabe*. Sukiyaki is perhaps the best-known one-pot Japanese dish in the West; the word "sukiyaki" is even defined in Webster's. Sukiyaki is prepared in a round, flat-bottomed, cast-iron pan. This skillet is especially thick at the bottom in order to conduct and maintain even heat. This sort of iron skillet is often used for dishes requiring only a scant amount of liquid, so some *sukiyaki-nabe* have slight depressions in the center to collect rich juices. *Sukiyaki-nabe* often do not have conventional handles, but in such cases they may have rings at the side, or some other device for gripping, to facilitate setting at the table. A skillet 10 inches (25 cm) in diameter serves 3 to 4; a 12-inch (30-cm) pan, 5 to 6; and a 14-inch (35-cm) pan, 7 or 8 diners.

Temper and treat the *sukiyaki-nabe* as you would a good cast-iron frying pan. Do not use harsh cleaners on it; remove any metallic taste or oil traces in a new *sukiyaki-nabe* by washing well in water then boiling water and left-over vegetables or tea (*bancha*) leaves in it. Do not rub it with oil before storing, for the oil may turn rancid. To avoid rust, just keep it dry.

As a substitute for a *sukiyaki-nabe*, use a heavy cast-iron frying pan or an electric skillet. Stainless steel pans, while easy to care for, cook food quickly and thus increase the danger of burning or cooking dry; you could use them for dishes cooked in a lot of broth such as ODEN (page 402). A thick aluminum pan is a last choice because aluminum, though it conducts heat rapidly, does not retain heat well.

SHABU-SHABU is often served at restaurants in a gleaming brass *hōkō-nabe*, a vessel that operates on the same principle as a samovar. It is shaped like a doughnut with a small chimney in the center for live charcoal, which heats the interior walls of the vessel. Originating in the cold steppes of North China or Mongolia, this elegant looking pot, the authentic Mongolian hot-pot or *huo-kuo*, can be an attractive ornamental piece as well. But, they are expensive! You could do just as well with a *donabe* for less money. Still, in gleaming copper or brass (aluminum or stainless steel in less costly models), the *hōkō-nabe* makes a splendid display.

On to the *nabemono* recipes.

Fish One-Pot

(*Chirinabe*) ちりなべ (color plate 12)

With raw seafood such as used in *sushi* and *sashimi*, the age and quality of the fish is immediately evident to the diner (some devotees claim they can tell where fish are caught), but in this recipe the fish is cooked, and you need not be as sensitive to the hours of a fish's freshness as you would if it were destined for use as *sashimi*. Still, choose fresh fish over frozen. Keep in mind, too, that cultivated fish from marine farms are greasier, fattier, and softer fleshed than fish caught in the open seas. In the recipe that follows sea bream is used, but cod, sea bass, rock cod, plaice, or any firm-fleshed white fish is good.

Chirinabe utilizes chunks of fish—skin and bones and all. The broth in which the fish and accompanying vegetables are simmered will be deeply flavored. (Boneless fillets are used in the one-pot dish known as *sukinabe*, in which the ingredients are cooked in seasoned *dashi*.) Use the fish head too; the delicate flesh around the jowls and eyes is delicious and is reserved for the guest of honor. If these parts are offered to you, you need not eat the eyeballs, just the meat around them.

The raw fish and fresh vegetables are brought to the table arranged on a large platter, and guests cook whatever they like in a kelp-flavored broth kept at a simmer over a portable heating unit. *Chirinabe* is eaten together with tart PONZU SAUCE and spicy condiments in individual dipping bowls. As a final course, offer hot white rice or make *zōsui* (see EGG AND RICE recipe, page 442) with cooked rice and the broth in the pot and serve in individual bowls. In restaurants, *zōsui* is commonly served as a final course for *chirinabe*.

6 servings

2½ pounds (675 g) firm-fleshed white fish such as sea bream, or 6 ½-pound (225-g) fillets, with skin
6 leaves Chinese cabbage
1 bunch spinach (optional), washed and parboiled (see page 93)
1 bunch edible chrysanthemum leaves (*shungiku* or *kikuna*), washed and trimmed (see page 64)

Fish: Scale and gut fish; cut off fins and tail. Reserve tail if you want to use it to decorate the serving platter. Cut off the fish head and, cutting through the top of it, split the head in half and cut each half into pieces, as shown. Cut the body into 2 fillets (*nimai oroshi* technique, page 123).

For the freshest flavor, blanch all fish pieces in boiling water for about 5–6 seconds then plunge immediately into a bath of cold water. Remove and pat dry.

Cut the fish fillets crosswise into 2-inch (5-cm) chunks. Wrap fish and refrigerate till time to arrange platter.

2 bunches *enokitake* mushrooms
6 4-inch (10-cm) lengths
dried gourd strips
(*kampyō*), softened
(see page 71), optional
2 cakes *tōfu* (bean curd)
6-10 small pieces of wheat
gluten (*fu*)
1 medium carrot, scraped
PONZU SAUCE (see page 172)

spicy condiments:

½ cup finely chopped
green onion
½ cup grated giant white
radish (*daikon-oroshi*)
RED MAPLE RADISH (see
page 170)

4-inch (10 cm) square giant
kelp (*konbu*)

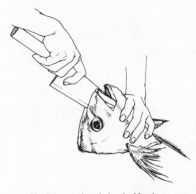

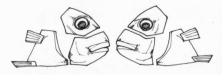

split bream head in half, then cut
into the three pieces shown

Chinese cabbage: Trim bottom of a Chinese cabbage
and separate 6 whole leaves. (Use the rest of the cabbage in another recipe.) Wash and parboil leaves in a
large pot in a generous amount of water. Parboil about
2–4 minutes, or until cabbage leaves are tender. Drain,
salt lightly, and pat dry. To facilitate rolling the leaves,
soften the hard, thick veins of the cabbage by lightly
pounding with the flat of a large knife, or pare away
a lateral section of the thick stem, as shown. Lay 2
leaves on a bamboo mat (*maki-su*), their length parallel
to the bamboo slats. (Instead of a bamboo mat you
can use a slatted place mat or heavy kitchen towel.)
The leaf edges should overlap, and the stem ends of
the 2 leaves should lie in opposite directions so that
the cylinder of rolled leaves will be of uniform thickness. Lay parboiled spinach (for stuffing if desired)
in an even row about 2 inches (5 cm) from the edge of
the mat.

To roll, lift the edge of the mat closest to you with
your thumbs and roll the cabbage (and spinach)
tightly to form a cylinder. Press for a few minutes in
the mat, unwrap, then cut into 1½-inch (4-cm) rounds.
Refrigerate, covered, till you are ready to assemble
the platter.

Edible chrysanthemum leaves: If sprigs are extremely
long, cut in half for easier handling when cooking.

If edible chrysanthemum leaves are not available,
use young and tender turnip greens or watercress
(or spinach, if you are not already using it in the
cabbage rolls). Do not use parsley or celery, both of
which are too strong in flavor.

Enokitake *mushrooms:* Cut off the spongy root cluster
about 1½ inches (4 cm) from the bottom. Separate
each bunch into thirds, and tie each individual portion
with a 4-inch (10-cm) length of softened gourd strip
(*kampyō*). If dried gourd strips are not available,
do not separate *enokitake* bunches into portions, but
simply arrange on the platter in large bunches; when
the time comes to simmer them, separate portions
from the bunch. The dried gourd strips are mainly
aesthetic, not functional. If *enokitake* mushrooms are
unavailable, use whatever fresh mushrooms you can
obtain, either whole or sliced.

Bean curd: Cut cakes into sixths.

Wheat gluten (fu): Wash briefly under running cold water, then set to soak in tepid water for about 5 minutes. Squeeze and drain.

Carrot: Slice into ¼-inch (¾-cm) rounds. Decorative carrot slices may be made either by stamping out each round with a small metal cutter (cherry blossom, maple leaf, and other such shapes are made in Japan) or by whittling the entire carrot length into the shape of your choice (a heart, for example) and then slicing cross-sections. Parboil slices briefly, plunge into cold water, and drain.

Prepare the sauce and spicy condiments.

To assemble the platter: With a bit of practice it will take you only 5 minutes to arrange the ingredients on a large platter—a round 18-inch (45-cm) one is ideal—if you have prepared them all as instructed above.

Make the platter look like a version of the horn of plenty. It should celebrate abundance. Decoratively arrange fish head and tail (if you have saved it). See color plate 12.

Place all of one kind of ingredient together, but consider the balance of color throughout. Chrysanthemum leaves are bushy, so you can use such greens as cushions and lay other ingredients over them.

Depending on the ingredients you use and the number of people you are serving, it may be necessary to prepare two platters. In this case, you can make a main platter to serve first, and a second platter to pass around later in the meal.

Cooking at the table: Wipe the giant kelp (*konbu*) with a damp towel to clean. Slash it a few times so that its flavor will be released. Put the *konbu* into the *donabe* casserole and fill ⅔ full with water. Bring just to the boiling point and remove *konbu*. (You may do this either in the kitchen on the stove or on the heating unit on the table.) Begin the main course by first putting the head and the bonier parts of the fish into the pot to enrich the stock.

After 2–3 minutes, place enough of all ingredients in the pot to feed all the diners. When this first round is finished, replenish pot with more fresh ingredients.

Do not leave cooked ingredients in the pot. Remove anything that is well cooked after each round.

Each diner helps himself, using chopsticks (or fondue forks). In theory, you transfer food from the serving platter to the pot with serving chopsticks and retrieve morsels as they cook with your own chopsticks. In practice, however, fussy rules are ignored. While waiting for the first few pieces of fish to simmer, each diner should help himself to PONZU SAUCE and spicy condiments and mix these in his dipping bowl.

Add more hot water or *konbu* stock to the broth during the course of the meal to maintain an adequate quantity of liquid and density of flavor. Again, remove anything that seems overcooked.

Eat whatever you like, in the order you like, till you are satisfied or the platters are depleted. Rice and a side dish of pickles are usually served as a final course.

Chicken One-Pot
(Mizutaki) 水 た き

Especially good for the winter months, this one-pot dish is begun at the kitchen stove and then assembled for final simmering and mixing of flavors in a *donabe* at the table. *Mizutaki*, literally "water-simmered," is the poultry version of CHIRINABE, the preceding recipe. Chicken is substituted for fish, and chicken stock for kelp broth, but otherwise the recipes are similar. As an economical meal-only-for-the-family-on-a-busy-weekday-night, this is an ideal way to use chicken necks, backs, and wings.

The dish is made by cutting up and preboiling young fryers, skin, bones, and all, then simmering the chicken in a casserole and adding vegetables (*via* a beautifully arranged platter). *Mizutaki* is usually dipped in PONZU SAUCE in which such spicy condiments as finely chopped green onion and RED MAPLE RADISH are mixed to taste. This main dish is followed by a course of rice and mild pickles.

6 servings

1 fryer, about 2½ pounds (1¼ kg)

Chicken: Use a whole chicken, or thighs and breasts, or necks, backs, and wings. Chop into 2-inch (5-cm) pieces—skin, bones, and all. Place in a colander and pour over several quarts (liters) of boiling water to rid the meat of any chickeny odor.

4-inch (10-cm) square giant kelp (*konbu*)
6 leaves Chinese cabbage
12 *shiitake* mushrooms, wiped and trimmed
1 medium carrot, scraped
1 ounce (30 g) dried *harusame* filaments
1 bunch trefoil stalks (or substitute spinach or watercress), washed and trimmed

spicy condiments:

PONZU SAUCE **(see page 172)**
4-6 Tbsps RED MAPLE RADISH **(see page 170)**
4-6 Tbsps finely chopped green onion
slivers of *yuzu* citron or lemon rind

Place chicken pieces in a large pot, add the square of giant kelp (*konbu*), which has been wiped clean with a damp towel and slashed in a few places to help release flavor. Fill pot with 4 to 5 quarts (4 to 5 L) water. Bring to a rolling boil over high heat. Remove *konbu* just before water reaches boiling point. Immediately reduce heat so the contents of the pot are kept at a simmer. Cook for about 20–30 minutes; remove chicken pieces as soon as they are cooked. Skim off foam as it forms on the surface.

Strain broth and let it cool to room temperature. Chicken should be kept moist with some of the broth. Reserve remaining broth for use in the casserole at the table. (If chicken is done ahead of time, refrigerate meat in broth after it is at room temperature.)

Chinese cabbage: Trim bottom of a Chinese cabbage and separate 6 whole leaves. (Use the rest of the cabbage in another recipe.) Wash and parboil whole leaves till tender, about 2–4 minutes, in ample water in a large pot. Drain, salt lightly, and pat dry. Using a bamboo mat, roll cabbage leaves and cut into rounds as described in the preceding recipe.

Shiitake *mushrooms:* Notch decorative crosses in the caps. If large, cut caps in half.

Carrot: Slice into rounds about ¼ inch (¾ cm) thick. To make decorative slices, cut rounds with small metal cutters (cherry blossom, maple leaf, etc.) or whittle entire carrot into desired shape and then slice. Parboil slices briefly, plunge into cold water, and drain.

Harusame *filaments:* Soak in hot water for 1 minute, then wash in cold water to remove any starch. They will become somewhat whiter as a result.

Trefoil: Cut stalks into convenient lengths, or substitute spinach leaves or watercress sprigs.

Prepare PONZU SAUCE and spicy condiments as indicated. Place chopped green onion in a piece of cheesecloth, wash in cold water, then wring gently.

To assemble the platter and cook at table: Use a round 18-inch (45-cm) platter and arrange the vegetables attractively. The chicken should remain in the broth, not on the platter. The table should be set with individual dipping bowls, a couple of small servers of PONZU SAUCE, and dishes filled with spicy condiments. At each place set either chopsticks or fondue forks.

Fill a *donabe* casserole ¾ full of reserved chicken broth. Place the *donabe* on a portable heating unit at the table. Heat till broth is simmering, and add chicken and vegetables. Simmer ingredients till thoroughly heated and tender, a few minutes at most. Dip food into PONZU SAUCE mixed with spicy condiments. Let everyone help himself to whatever he likes, or serve portions with a ladle as food is cooked.

VARIATIONS: Many, many different kinds of vegetable ingredients can be used in *mizutaki*, for example, half-moon rounds of bamboo shoot, diagonally cut lengths of green onion or leek, 1½-inch (4-cm) squares of grilled bean curd (*yakidōfu*), to name just a few.

Shabu-Shabu
しゃぶしゃぶ

The name *shabu-shabu* imitates the sound you make as you gently swish your chopstick-held morsels of raw meat in the steaming broth. Meat cooks quickly in boiling water, and these paper-thin slices are done in a few seconds, so the secret is not to lose them in the broth. Vegetable ingredients, however, usually take a little longer time, so they are cooked according to the "drop-and-retrieve" method used in most other *nabemono* dishes.

Make the sauces and spicy condiments listed below and let each diner mix them at will in his own dipping bowl. This is part of the fun of eating *shabu-shabu*—everyone can create the flavor(s) he desires. The sauces— citron-based PONZU SAUCE and one based on toasted ground white sesame seeds—are used separately. The spicy condiments complement either sauce.

Start the meal with an appetizer, then proceed to the *shabu-shabu* with the flameproof casserole set on a heating unit on the table. Just as fish is cooked first in FISH ONE-POT to develop the flavor of the broth, in this dish, start with the meat. When all the meat and vegetables are finished, you may drink the broth, lightly salted, from cups. Noodles may be added to the broth in the casserole and served in hot broth to each diner. With this dish Japanese drink hot *saké*, cold beer, or hot green tea. If you want to drink wine, choose a dry red. For dessert, offer everyone a choice piece of fruit or a simple sherbet or ice.

In Japan, *shabu-shabu* is a great party dish, served at home on real occasions, in part because the high-quality beef required is expensive. But, East and West, this dish is a treat that guests will long remember. Serve in a *donabe* casserole or a Mongolian hot-pot.

6 servings

2 pounds (900 g) prime-quality, well-marbled beef or lamb
12 *shiitake* mushrooms, wiped and trimmed
6 long onions (*naganegi*), or 8-10 green onions
6 leaves Chinese cabbage
1 bunch edible chrysanthemum leaves (*shungiku* or *kikuna*), washed and trimmed
2 cakes *tōfu* (bean curd)
6-10 small pieces wheat gluten (fu)
8 ounces (225 g) bamboo shoot
PONZU SAUCE **(see page 172)**
SESAME SAUCE **(see below)**
1 cup grated giant white radish (*daikon-oroshi*)
½ cup finely chopped green onion
4-inch (10-cm) square giant kelp (*konbu*)

Meat: Buy sirloin for beef SHABU-SHABU, or lamb loin rib. In either case, the meat should be well marbled, so it will be tender when cooked in boiling water.

Have your butcher cut the meat into paper-thin slices, thinner even than SUKIYAKI slices. This might be difficult to do at home, even with frozen meat.

You may have to cut each slice in half crosswise, depending on size. Individual slices should measure about 8×3 inches (20×8 cm). This makes a convenient one-bite size. Do not simmer slices so large that they are unwieldy as cooked morsels.

Shiitake *mushrooms:* Notch decorative crosses into the caps. If extremely large, cut caps in half.

Long onions (or green onions): Cut diagonally into 1½-inch (4-cm) lengths.

Chinese cabbage: Trim bottom of a Chinese cabbage and separate 6 whole leaves. (Use rest of head in another recipe.) Wash, then parboil whole leaves till tender, about 2–4 minutes, in ample water in a large pot. Drain, salt lightly, and pat dry. Using a bamboo mat, roll cabbage leaves (optional), and cut into rounds, as described in the recipe for FISH ONE-POT, above, or just use leaves without rolling.

Edible chrysanthemum leaves: If sprigs are extremely long, cut in half for easier handling when cooking.

Bean curd: Cut bean curd into 1½-inch (4-cm) squares when platter is arranged.

Wheat gluten (fu): Soak for about 5 minutes in tepid water. Squeeze out moisture and use.

Bamboo shoot: If using canned bamboo, wash thoroughly (remove bitter, limelike deposit between interior ridges), parboil, and cut into half-moon slices about ¼ inch (¾ cm) thick. If you have been able to obtain raw bamboo, cook it as described on page 56.

Prepare sauces and spicy condiments. Both sauces will keep refrigerated for 2 or 3 days, so they can be prepared well in advance, but they are best prepared just before serving. The green onion can be chopped a few hours ahead of time and refrigerated, but the grated white radish must be prepared immediately before serving.

To arrange the platters: Arrange some of all ingredients on 18-inch (45-cm) round platters in the spirit of munificence that this dish deserves.

Arrange the slices of meat attractively so that each slice can be easily picked up with chopsticks or fondue fork; a clump or wad of slices is unappetizing, and slices are difficult to extricate from such a tangle. Arrange vegetables on a second platter in the same way, or arrange one for meat only and one for vegetables only. It takes 5 minutes to arrange the platter if all ingredients have been prepared.

Cooking at the table: Put a 4-inch (10-cm) square of giant kelp (*konbu*) in a large *donabe* casserole or *hōkō-nabe* (Mongolian hot-pot). Wipe it first with a damp cloth to clean, and slash it in a few places to release flavors. Fill the *donabe* or hot-pot ⅔ full of fresh water. (In the event that kelp is unavailable, make a light court bouillon with Chinese cabbage, carrot, fresh mushrooms, etc.)

Bring just to a boil, remove kelp just before boiling point is reached, then simmer gently for 3 to 4 minutes. Do this either on the kitchen stove, transferring the pot to the heating unit on the table at the last minute, or on the table heating unit itself.

Each diner should have chopsticks or a fondue fork. Since there are two dips, you should have two dipping bowls available for each diner. (Chances are, however, that only one will be used.) Either spicy condiment is mixed into PONZU SAUCE to taste, but finely chopped green onion only is added to SESAME SAUCE. Each diner picks up a piece of meat from the serving platter and swishes it to and fro, *shabu-shabu*ing, in the simmering broth till the red meat becomes pink. Rarer meat is also delicious. Diners may alternate between meat and vegetables.

Occasionally skim the broth to keep it clear of foam.

When meat and vegetables have been finished, ladle the broth into bowls and serve lightly salted with a bit of chopped onion.

Sesame Sauce
(*Goma-Dare*) ごまだれ

Do not confuse this with SESAME SOY SAUCE (page 171).

makes 2½ cups

3 ounces (85 g) white sesame seeds
¾ cup *dashi*
6 Tbsps dark soy sauce
2 Tbsps *mirin*
1 Tbsp sugar
1-2 Tbsps *saké*

In a dry, heavy frying pan, toast or parch the white sesame seeds over medium heat till golden brown. They burn easily, so keep the seeds moving by shaking the pan, also using a dry spoon to stir the seeds occasionally as they brown. Be careful: the time difference between golden brown and burnt is not very great!

Transfer warm toasted seeds to a *suribachi* (Japanese grinding bowl, see page 105) and grind with pestle till flaky. Add the remaining ingredients, and dilute with *dashi* (either chilled or room temperature), mixing well between additions. Use a rubber spatula to blend and smooth sauce.

May be stored in a tightly sealed container in the refrigerator for up to 3 days, but best when just made. Stir before serving, in case some of the sesame has settled to the bottom.

Sukiyaki Osaka-Style
(*Osaka no Sukiyaki*) 大阪のすきやき

SUKIYAKI does not have a long history. It is the Japanese one-pot cookery method applied to beef—a food that was not a part of the Japanese diet before the 1860s. Beef-eating was introduced when Western diplomats and traders began to establish residence in Japan. The first cows slaughtered in Japan were for the tables of Western residents. Japanese had been taught for centuries that eating meat ran counter to Buddhist law, which forbade the killing of four-footed animals. But, after a hesitant start, the Japanese added beef to their culinary repertoire. SUKIYAKI became a very popular dish after the Meiji period (1868–1912), when the Japanese were experimenting with all things foreign. The origins of the name *sukiyaki* are obscure. The character used for *suki* means "plow"; *suki* is also a homonym for "like, to be fond of." There are many theories as to the origin of the name. One common explanation is that at first beef was not a popular food and the Japanese of the time did not want to use their everyday pots to cook the stuff. Instead beef was cooked on a plow—thus the name and the fact that today still a special, shallow cast-iron pan is used for SUKIYAKI. True or not (probably not), the story is good enough to have survived.

6 servings

2 pounds (900 g) sirloin beef, well marbled
6 green onions
1 bunch trefoil
10-12 *shiitake* mushrooms, wiped and trimmed
2 cakes grilled bean curd (*yakidōfu*)
½ pound (225 g) *shirataki* filaments
12 small pieces wheat gluten (*fu*)

sauce:
    2 ounces (60 g) beef suet
    3 Tbsps sugar
    several cups water (or half water and half *saké*)
    ½ cup *saké*
    ½ cup dark soy sauce
6 eggs

Beef: Have your butcher cut well-marbled sirloin beef into very thin slices.

Green onions: Cut diagonally into 1½-inch (4-cm) lengths.

Trefoil: If stalks are very long, cut in half so lengths are more manageable with chopsticks or forks.

Shiitake *mushrooms:* Notch decorative crosses on the caps. If very large, cut in half.

Grilled bean curd: Buy grilled bean curd (*yakidōfu*), or use any type of bean curd (*tōfu*) available. Cut into 1½-inch (4-cm) squares as you arrange the platter.

Shirataki *filaments:* Parboil for 1–2 minutes, uncovered, and drain. They will be somewhat whiter as a result of parboiling.

Wheat gluten (fu): Soak for about 5 minutes in tepid water. Squeeze gently and drain.

Arrange all these ingredients attractively on one or two large platters.

Cooking at the table: Put the empty *sukiyaki* pan or large cast-iron skillet over the heat source (or use an electric skillet) at the table. Start to melt suet in the pan over medium heat, using long chopsticks (or a fondue fork) to move it around so the entire pan bottom is well greased. The fat should smoke slightly. Quickly sprinkle about 3 Tbsps of sugar over the bottom and continue moving the fat in the pan (it should not be entirely melted yet). The sugar will caramelize, turning brown and sticky. At this point, add about ½ cup water (or half water and half *saké*). There will be some sputtering (but this helps entertain guests). Add *saké*, stir; add dark soy sauce, stir. Begin the cooking by laying a few slices of beef into the pan. The beef should take about 1 minute to cook. Add more beef, switch to vegetables—including *shirataki*, *tōfu*, and *fu*—then alternate back to beef. Each diner should put into the pan whatever he or she likes. Add water (or half water/half *saké*) to the pan occasionally, as the sauce is reduced. The ingredients should not swim in the sauce; the liquid should just keep the pan bottom covered.

Set each place with an individual dipping bowl into which an egg has been broken. This alone is the dipping sauce. (If you serve a whole egg at each place, which is attractive, provide a saucer or some vessel for the empty shells.) Each diner mixes the egg with chopsticks or fork. As with the other *nabemono*, long-handled fondue forks are best for anyone who is a little shy about using chopsticks, but dinner forks will do in a pinch.

Before eating, dip cooked meat and vegetables into the egg; the thin coating of egg "cooks" on as soon as it is in contact with the hot food. There is no other garnish or relish. To end the meal, serve hot cooked rice, mild pickles, and Japanese tea as a final course. Serve hot *saké* or cold beer up to the rice course.

VARIATIONS: The so-called Tokyo style of *sukiyaki* involves making simmering sauce beforehand—combining the water (or stock), *saké*, sugar, *mirin*, and soy sauce and bringing this mixture to a simmer in the pan before adding beef.

Rice

Gohanmono

Rice is a beautiful food. It is beautiful when it grows—precision rows of sparkling green stalks shooting up to reach the hot summer sun. It is beautiful when harvested, autumn gold sheaves piled in diked, patchwork paddies. It is beautiful when, once threshed, it enters granary bins like a cataract of tiny seed-pearls. It is beautiful when cooked by a practiced hand, pure white and sweetly fragrant.

Rice is the staple of staples. Not only is it a dish in itself, rice is a necessary ingredient in many other common Japanese foods. Fermented, it is *saké*, the well-known Japanese liquor. The thick, sweet lees of *saké* are present in many dishes. Rice bran adds flavor to pickles. The grain also makes a delicate vinegar, which is just being discovered by the West and one day may be found on the staple shelf of any Western kitchen.

Historically, rice was a measure of wealth. The worth of medieval fiefs was counted in terms of a rice volume unit, the *koku*, roughly equivalent to 5 bushels (this value actually fluctuated greatly). Even after the beginning of a strong cash economy, samurai were paid their stipends in *koku* of rice. Today, when the Japanese grow all the rice they need and much more, it is hard to convince farmers to plant anything other than rice. It is not only government rice crop subsidies that lead them to single- and double-crop with modern high-yielding strains. Rice has been planted through the millennia, and the cycle of its growth and harvest is a part of the unchanging rhythm of the seasons. Just as the mountains in the background of every Japanese scene change mood depending on the time of day and whether the light is that of summer, autumn, winter, or spring, so, too, with the rice paddies in the foreground. Rice, like mountains, is part of Japan.

Regardless of how many other dishes are served, a Japanese feels he has not really eaten unless there is rice. At restaurant banquets the rice is not served until after the succession of various fish, poultry, meat, and vegetable dishes, when it completes the meal together with *miso* soup and pickles. But in ordinary homes, rice is central to the meal, and any fish, poultry, meat, or vegetable dishes are basically "luxuries"—tasty side dishes (*okazu*). It is not uncommon in times of austerity, and in poor households, for the rice, *miso* soup, and pickles to constitute the entire meal.

The rice that tastes the best is *shinmai*, or "new rice," on the market in autumn, fresh from harvest. This first rice is moist and tender and requires less water in cooking than last year's shelf-dried stuff. Perhaps with more than a twinge of nostalgia, city residents send to their home provinces in autumn to order a few kilograms of new rice, and normally taciturn people carry on and on about which province on which sides of which mountains with how much rainfall and what sort of growing season and planted in which variety yields the very best rice in Japan. Rice can be a subject of old memories, of regional pride, and of all manner of expert knowledge.

Short-grain rice is the type Japanese prefer, and is best for the nature of Japanese cuisine. The Japanese like full, plump-grained rice that, while tender and moist when cooked, is firm enough to get your teeth into (tea ceremony rice is cooked stickier than normal) and clingy enough to be picked up in small mouthfuls with chopsticks. The kind of rice preferred by the Japanese is quite different from that which most English and Americans have been conditioned to think is good. Perhaps it is the influence of Indian curry, but a great many people in the West seem to have the idea that rice should be rather dry and separate-grained when cooked. So Western cooks use mostly long-grain types and relegate the short-grain variety to rice croquettes, patties, and puddings. Nonetheless, short-grain rice is readily available everywhere. There is excellent short-grain rice in America. The types known as Blue Rose and Kokuho Rose are thought by some to be as good as (some claim, better than) Japanese rice.

Knowing the Western bias against short-grain rice, I made an interesting experiment once. I had invited the chef from Harry's Bar in Venice to Japan, and I asked him to make a risotto. I told him we had many varieties and grades of short-grain rice in Japan and asked him to select the one best for his recipe from a large variety of samples from all over Japan. I had simply numbered each one, so he had no idea of how they were rated here. He boiled the different kinds and sampled each one, and finally said, without any hesitation at all, "This is it!" It was *sasa-nishiki*, the rice we rate the very highest quality of all! We may not be far wrong in considering Japan a rice paradise.

In America some packages of white rice bear on their labels the terms "converted" or "unconverted." Converted rice is processed so that the nutrients and vitamins taken out during the polishing are put back in during a subsequent steaming step. Unconverted rice has been merely polished: the lost nutrients are not reintroduced. The term "enriched" is sometimes used for converted rice (though "unenriched" does not seem to have caught on). With due recognition of the effort to return lost vitamins to refined foods, it is still true that converted or enriched rice tastes pasty in comparison to plain white rice. If you seek the full nutritional value of the grains, use brown rice.

The character ✳ is read *kome* and applies to *uncooked* rice. When you go to the rice merchant's in Japan, you always ask for *okome* (this noun always has the honorific "*o*" prefix, for obvious reasons). As soon as it is cooked, however, *okome* is no longer *okome*, it is either *meshi*, *gohan*, or *raisu*.

In Japanese, brown rice is called *genmai*, literally "dark rice." In an ordinary pot it takes longer for heat and moisture to penetrate these grains than polished grains; brown rice takes three times longer to cook, uses twice as much water, and exercises one's jaw muscles more than white rice. It also has a deeper, nuttier flavor than white rice, besides containing all the vitamins and nutrients that nature bestowed. Brown rice is available in healthfood stores and most oriental provisions stores.

There is also an intermediate category, which is slowly receiving attention in Japan. This is *haiga-mai*, literally "rice-germ rice." As the name states, this is rice in which the germ has been kept in the grain—by incomplete polishing. Cooking time is about the same as for polished white rice; its flavor is somewhere between brown and white rice; it has much greater nourishment than white rice and also does not need so much washing.

Glutinous rice (mochi-gome) makes sticky rice suitable for a number of special foods. Japanese always boil white or brown rice. The term "boil" is not quite accurate, but will do for the discussion here. There are no native dishes requiring that rice be baked or fried. (Fried rice is Chinese.) But glutinous rice is soaked in cold water then steamed rather than boiled. Among its two most popular uses are RED RICE (page 280, below) and *mochi*, glutinous rice-paste cakes. Many sweet confections are also made with glutinous rice (pages 462–69).

Cooked and dehydrated rice, sold as "instant" or "minute" rice, seems now to be one of the most familiar types of rice in America. Most instant rice sold in the U.S. is long grain, although some short-grain instant types may be available in oriental food shops. But for Japanese cooking use it only in a real emergency, or, better, do not use it at all. Texture and flavor are insipid, and it cooks pasty on the outside and raw on the inside.

Boiling rice can be very simple, or it can be carried to complex extremes. Today rice is made daily in practically every Japanese household in an automatic electric or gas rice cooker. The automatic rice cooker, an appliance developed in the postwar period, makes perfect rice every time. Put washed rice into the cooker, add water (there are usually measurement marks in the cooker for water and rice volume), cover, and turn on. Automatic controls take over cooking, reducing heat at exactly the right moment, and, in some models, the rice is kept warm till needed. Cookers come in various sizes, from tiny ones holding only a few cups to immense, gas-fed ones for institutions. Rice cookers are sold in the United States at some oriental provisions stores.

It is in the select restaurants serving Japanese *haute cuisine* that rice cooking is elevated to a complex art. There, one chef is responsible for nothing but boiling rice. The rice is probably obtained by special agreement with a rice dealer in a certain area chosen for fine rice, who, in turn, might have a special agreement with a certain group of farmers. Rice for special uses might come from different areas. The rice cook washes the rice in a stone sink, puts the grains in a flanged iron rice pot with heavy wooden lid of ancient origin, uses only fresh well water for cooking, and carefully tends a wood-fed stove, always adjusting the embers to control the heat. It is said that it takes 20 years to acquire enough experience to make truly perfect rice. This may be an exaggeration, but who can judge? What such folklore demonstrates is the high place that rice enjoys.

For everyday purposes, assuming you do not have an automatic rice cooker, let the recipe below for making boiled rice in a pot guide you.

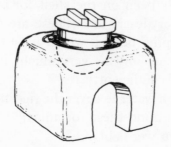

old-fashioned Japanese cooking stove
with large rice pot

automatic rice cooker
(gas or electric)

Boiled Rice
(*Gohan*) 御飯

Allow ½ cup uncooked rice per serving. Short-grain rice expands about 75 percent in cooking, long-grain rice even more.

Whether using an automatic rice cooker or boiling rice in a pot, always wash rice 30 minutes to 1 hour beforehand and let it drain in the open air in a colander. To wash, put rice in a large bowl and set it in the sink for convenience. Cover rice with cold water from the tap and stir quickly with your hands for about 30 seconds, till the water becomes milky. Never let the rice stand in this milky water. The milkiness comes from powdered bran and polishing compound, which is exactly what should be washed away. Pour off milky water and wash again with fresh water from the tap. Repeatedly wash this way till water is *almost* clear. It takes about 5 minutes of washing, pouring off, and washing to clean rice sufficiently. The penalty for rice washed too hastily is "smelly" rice. Stir more gently in later washings than at first in order not to bruise grains. The grains, absorbing more and more water with every washing, become tenderer. (There is another common method of letting rice rest for 1 hour or more in the water you will cook it in. The colander-draining technique is thought to result in better flavor.)

Put the rice in a tight-lidded, heavy and deep pot. Use a pot that is neither too large nor too small for the quantity of rice you are cooking. Cooked in too large a pot, the rice will be dry, perhaps even scorched. Cooked in too small a pot, the rice will be tacky.

It is difficult to prescribe an exact formula for the size of pot and the amount of water to use in cooking rice because there are so many variables. Assuming that our interest is only in short-grain rice, we still must consider whether it was grown in a flooded paddy or dry field, whether the rice is newly harvested or whether it has already been on the shelf for some time, whether the climate is hot and muggy or desert dry. These are all factors that the rice chef, with a many-year training period, would have no trouble in dealing with. And, they need not bother anyone very much. For family meals, a medium-sized, heavy saucepan is sufficient.

As a general but flexible rule, use enough water to cover the rice in a proper-sized pot by 1 inch (2½ cm), or keep in mind these formulas:
with rice of Asian origin (usually grown in wet fields)—
   1⅕ cups water to 1 cup dry rice, or 1 cup water to 1 cup washed rice;
with rice of American or European origin (usually grown in dry fields)—
   1¾ cups water to 1 cup dry rice.
Short-grain rice is less absorbent that long-grain rice, and new rice requires less water than old rice. In cooking only a few servings of rice, use more water to keep rice from getting too dry. If, when hard pressed for time, you cannot let the rice stand before cooking, add a bit more water than you would normally use. Only experience and your own taste can be your ultimate guide. You may decide to cook rice in broth or stock instead of water in order to obtain a particular flavor.

To cook, place rice in tightly covered pot over medium-high heat till water just boils. Then turn heat up to high, and let water come to a vigorous boil;

the lid might bounce from the pressure of the steam. A white, starchy liquid will bubble from under the pot lid. When this starchy bubbling ceases, reduce heat to low and cook till all the liquid is absorbed by the rice. *Do not* lift the cover off the pot during cooking.

Turn off the heat (do not take pot off burner) and let rice stand, covered, 15 to 20 minutes before fluffing. During this interval, the grains are allowed to "settle," and the cooking process is completed by the heat retained in the rice and the walls of the pot. With a wooden paddle or spoon, fluff the rice with a sideways, cutting motion. Stretch a kitchen towel underneath the pot lid to catch moisture, then return lid to pot. Let stand till ready to serve.

Serve in individual rice bowls. In Japanese households, hot rice is customarily not served directly from the pot, even though today the design of the automatic rice cooker has induced some people to do this. The traditional practice is to bring the rice to the table in a covered wooden container or tub of suitable size and to serve into individual bowls with a slightly concave wooden paddle. For some reason custom dictates that each serving be made in two paddlefuls, even when only a little is served. In any case it is considered vulgar to fill the bowls too full. The more refined the banquet, the smaller the servings of rice. Wooden rice tubs (usually cedar or cypress) are best because they absorb moisture and keep the rice warm. The lacquer containers one sees are luxury items made for decorative effect. They are used in inns and restaurants and are not as practical as the wooden tubs.

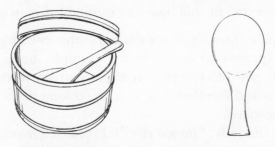

wooden tub for cooked rice and rice paddle

To repeat the cardinal rules of rice-making:
1. Wash rice 30–60 minutes before cooking and let drain in colander.
2. Use a heavy, tight-lidded pot of the right size.
3. Adjust the amount of liquid used for boiling to fit the rice you are cooking.
4. Do not remove the lid of the pot while cooking.
5. Let rice "settle" in covered pot for 15 to 20 minutes after heat is turned off (keep pot on burner) before fluffing.

If you are making a large quantity of rice at once, you should alter the technique described above slightly. Place washed rice into a hot pot with water *already boiling*. Stir once and cover tightly. Bring to a boil again (over high heat), then follow the conventional technique as described above.

A crusty brown scorch on the bottom of the rice is no catastrophe, in fact, some people do this on purpose. (A black, smelly burn, however, will probably make all the rice smell burnt and make it unusable.) In Japanese families there is always someone (maybe everyone) who loves to snack on scorched rice, called *okoge*—literally, "scorch." Some people like its crunchiness so much that they deliberately scorch rice to use in making RICE BALLS (page 440) or TEA-AND-RICE (page 442).

When the word *meshi* (飯) or *gohan* (御飯) appears in the name of a recipe, it means that the main ingredient is rice. The Chinese character (飯) shared by both these words in its widest sense means, not cooked rice, but "food" and "livelihood." But, when Japanese look at this character and say either *meshi* or *gohan* (the latter is honorific), they mean boiled rice. In the Japanese mind, sustenance and rice are one and the same.

Funnily enough, the Japanized English word *raisu* only applies to boiled rice when it is served as a side dish on a flat plate with non-Japanese-style food. Otherwise, with typical Japanese foods, when it is served in a rice bowl or another kind of traditional bowl, plain rice is always *meshi* or *gohan*. *Gohan-mono*, "rice dishes," are flavored and sometimes cooked together with other things such as vegetables and fish. Since the main types of rice dishes are all represented in this book, an outline list is helpful:

1. *Takikomi-gohan* (literally, "rice cooked with something else"). Various ingredients (precooked or raw)—for example, beans or chestnuts— are put in the pot with raw rice, or added partway through the cooking, and all are cooked together. Foods with cooking times longer than rice must be precooked.
2. *Maze-gohan* (literally, "mixed rice"). Precooked ingredients are mixed into the cooked rice during the "settling" period. However, the flavor of fresh greens such as *shiso* is destroyed by heat, so they should be stirred into hot rice at the last minute.
3. *Okowa* originally referred exclusively to plain steamed glutinous rice, but today this word refers to *sekihan*, RED RICE (page 280 below); white steamed glutinous rice has another name.
4. *Okayu* is rice gruel. There are many types of rice gruel, and these are discussed on page 443 in the basic recipe. *Okayu* is the single case in which rice is cooked in an uncovered pot. It is usually cooked over rather strong heat, but if you want a stickier rice, cook slowly over low

heat. *Okayu* is usually salted after cooking, whereas plain boiled rice is not salted at all and most other rice dishes are salted at the beginning.

Zōsui is similar to gruel, but whereas *okayu* is made from scratch, from uncooked rice, *zōsui* is made from already cooked rice. For everyday purposes, this is a rather fine distinction.

5. *Sushi-meshi*: vinegared rice used for *sushi*. *Sushi* plays such an important part in what the Japanese eat that the entire next chapter is devoted to it alone. The chapter begins with a discussion of how to make vinegared rice, page 290.

Sea Bream and Rice

(*Tai Meshi*) 鯛めし

This dish, a robust lunch or satisfying dinner, combines a whole grilled fish and boiled rice. This is a double virtue—it is easy to prepare and elegant in appearance. *Tai-meshi* is traditionally brought directly from the stove to the table in an earthenware *donabe*-type casserole (see page 103). A 10-inch (25-cm) casserole serves 2 to 4, and a 12-inch (30-cm) casserole serves 6 to 8. Naturally, adjust the amount of fish for the numbers you are serving, and increase or decrease other ingredients accordingly. The recipe below, cooked in a 10-inch (25-cm) earthenware *donabe*, serves 3 generously.

3 servings

1 whole sea bream or sea bass, about 8 inches (20 cm) long

2½ cups short-grain rice, washed

3⅓ cups *dashi* (or chicken broth)

1 tsp salt

2 Tbsps dark or light soy sauce

few drops *mirin*

Fish: If sea bream or sea bass is not available, sea trout or salmon may be used.

Scale and gut fish, but keep head and tail intact. Skewer as shown on page 178 (*uneri-gushi* technique.) Salt lightly on both sides. Grill over a medium-hot charcoal fire or broil in preheated oven. Grill on both sides, turning once, until almost done, about 8 minutes on each side, depending on strength of heat and thickness of fish. If fish skin blisters, bubbles, and bursts with oil, you are lucky—you have very fresh fish.

You can grill the fish ahead of time and then assemble with other ingredients in the flameproof casserole an hour before serving. If, on the other hand, you are in a hurry and want to speed up the grilling, you can do this efficiently by covering the fish with a V-shaped tent of water-dampened kitchen parchment, a thick layer of water-moistened newspaper, or heavy-duty foil.

To assemble and cook: Put washed rice into 10-inch (25-cm) earthenware casserole (or an appropriate, lidded casserole that can take direct flame). Add *dashi*, salt, soy sauce, and *mirin*, and stir. Place the grilled fish in the center (the stock will cover it by half).

Cover with tight-fitting lid. Cook in the same manner as BOILED RICE (page 273). Remove from heat and let stand 10 to 15 minutes, undisturbed. (Even though the fish has been grilled, it is not overcooked. Simmering with the rice drives its flavor into the rice.)

To serve: Bring casserole to the table as is. The host or hostess should show off the finished dish, since it is quite attractive. The server then flakes the fish, removes bones, mixes fish with rice, and finally spoons fish and rice into individual bowls.

Flaking the cooked fish is very easy. The fish should be tender, well cooked, and hot, so the flesh easily separates from the bones. Use chopsticks or a fork to flake the top side of the fish in the casserole. Remove skeleton, then flake the remaining flesh.

Goes well with a clear soup, a vinegared vegetable, fresh fruit, and green tea. Drink cold beer or dry white wine, if desired.

VARIATIONS: You may add vegetables—a few Tbsps chopped trefoil; 1 tsp finely grated fresh ginger; *dashi*-and-soy seasoned mushrooms; and the like.

Mixed Rice

(*Gomoku Meshi*) 五目めし

Gomoku literally means "five things," and this rice casserole is traditionally made with a variety of five ingredients. In the Osaka dialect, this dish is called *kayaku gohan*, "variety rice."

4 servings

2 ounces (60 g) boned chicken meat

To prepare: Cut chicken into bite-sized pieces, with or without skin, as preferred, but do not use bones.

Cut burdock using the pencil-shaving (*sasagaki*)

1 small burdock root, well
scrubbed with a stiff brush
½ small carrot, scraped
½ cake thin deep-fried bean
curd (*aburage*)
⅓ cake *konnyaku* (devil's
tongue jelly)
3⅓ cups short-grain rice,
washed

for cooking rice:
4 cups *dashi* (or chicken
broth)
½ tsp salt
4 Tbsps *mirin*
3 Tbsps light soy sauce
3 Tbsps dark soy sauce

technique (see page 142). Place in cold water immediately to prevent discoloration.

Finely dice carrot.

Remove excess oil from fried bean-curd cake (*aburage*) by pouring on scalding water. Drain, wrap in a kitchen towel or strong paper toweling, and gently squeeze out excess oil. Cut both fried bean curd cake and *konnyaku* into julienne strips.

To assemble and cook: Use an earthenware casserole (*donabe*, see page 103), a heavy lidded pot, or an electric or gas rice cooker. Place washed rice and solid ingredients into casserole or pot.

In a bowl, mix the ingredients for cooking rice (*dashi*, salt, *mirin*, soy sauces). Check and correct seasoning. Pour over rice and vegetables in casserole. Do not stir. Cover casserole or pot.

Cook rice with the same technique used for BOILED RICE, page 273 above. However, this rice mixture scorches easily, so carefully watch and adjust the heat.

To serve: If you have used an attractive casserole, serve family style at the table. Or, in the kitchen, put rice into deep, covered *donburi*-style bowls (page 108 for sketch) or deep soup bowls. Serve hot.

Combines well with DRENCHED RADISH (page 395) and SAKÉ-SIMMERED MACKEREL (page 225).

VARIATIONS: Here are a few ideas: grilled, flaked white-fleshed fish such as cod or sea bream instead of chicken; quarter-moon slices of bamboo shoot or shredded *shiitake* mushrooms instead of burdock.

Chestnut Rice
(*Kuri Gohan*) 栗ご飯 (color plate 11)

In late September in Japan, large shiny brown chestnuts come on the market. This dish is as autumnal in Japan as pumpkin pie is in America. With a hot clear soup and a dressed vegetable (*aemono*) to start, followed by a meat or fish entrée, this rice and a side dish of pickles make a marvelous supper on a cool fall night.

Westerners might think of chestnuts as a sweetish roasted snack, or as a glazed candy, but salt is used as a seasoning here, so the flavor of the nuts is transformed into something entirely different.

This recipe should prove worth the search for fresh chestnuts in season.

4 servings

15 large fresh chestnuts
½ tsp salt
4 cups water
3⅓ cups short-grain rice, washed

To prepare chestnuts: Carefully shell chestnuts and remove the thin inner skin. You need a very sharp paring knife for this (see page 64).

Chestnuts, especially the large size grown in Japan, are hard to eat whole, so cut chestnuts into quarters or sixths. Try to avoid making a pile of chestnut bits and crumbles—these will disintegrate when cooked. Rinse pared, cut up chestnuts in cold water to remove starch. Drain.

To assemble and cook: Use an earthenware casserole, a heavy pot with tight-fitting lid, or an electric or gas rice cooker.

Dissolve the salt in the water, then pour over rice in cooking vessel. Add chestnuts, cover, and cook in the same manner as BOILED RICE (page 273). Let stand, covered, 10 to 15 minutes before serving. Serve hot in individual rice bowls. No garnish is necessary, but make sure a few chestnut pieces are shown off to good advantage in every rice bowl.

Red Rice
(*Sekihan*) 赤 飯 (color plate 15)

Popular for festive occasions, particularly weddings and birthdays. This dish consists of barely cooked *azuki* beans (see page 328) steamed with glutinous rice, then sprinkled lightly with toasted black sesame seeds. It keeps very well.

Sekihan is usually served at room temperature. It is often packed into small, individual lunch boxes. In traditional Japanese homes, bowls of *sekihan* are set as offerings before the small family shrines for the ancestors, too, on days of festivity. *Sekihan* takes the place of plain boiled white rice, so when *sekihan* appears, everyday rice does not.

Please note that *sekihan* requires glutinous rice (*mochi-gome*). Glutinous rice is also used to make *mochi* rice cakes, which, though now a year-round food, finds particular prominence on the New Year's menu.

Glutinous rice should be soaked and steamed, not boiled. If you boil glutinous rice as you do ordinary short-grain rice, though not inedible, the result is dense and greasy.

4 servings

1 cup dry *azuki* beans
5 cups glutinous rice
(*mochi-gome*)
liquid reserved from boiling
beans
black sesame seeds
few Tbsps lightly salted
water

Beans: Soak beans in water 3–4 hours, then parboil for 5–6 minutes in a generous amount of boiling water. Rinse in clear cold water. This boiling and rinsing is actually a thorough way of washing beans.

Put parboiled beans in pot and cover with approximately 1½ quarts (1½ L) of cold water. Bring to a boil, uncovered, over medium-high heat, and boil for about 10 minutes or till water becomes reddish. Test to see whether the beans have been boiled enough by mashing a bean between your fingers and tasting it. The bean should be not quite tender—barely cooked—somewhat crisp, and should taste raw. Do not overcook beans at this stage because they will be steamed again later with the rice.

Drain, reserving the reddish water in which beans were boiled. Let both beans and water come to room temperature naturally, uncovered. Refrigerate beans, covered with a damp towel, till time to steam. This step can be done a day ahead of time.

Rice: Wash the glutinous rice as you would ordinary rice (above, see page 273). Then put in a pot with the room-temperature, reddish water in which the beans were boiled and let stand for 24 hours, or overnight. This tints rice pink. Drain tinted rice.

To steam: Use a steamer in which the beans and rice can be evenly spread in a fairly thin layer of 1 to 1½ inches (2½ to 4 cm). A bamboo steamer is recommended, but you can improvise, using a high-legged colander inside a large pot or a similar setup. (See page 210 for a discussion of steaming utensils.) (If, for one reason or another, you have to fall back on boiling as the cooking method rather than steaming, use 10–20 percent glutinous rice in a mixture with ordinary rice.)

Mix beans and rice, making sure distribution of each is even. Spread out evenly on damp cheesecloth in the steamer.

Steam over high heat for 20 minutes, after which

time you should lift the lid of the steamer and sprinkle a small amount of the salt water over the rice several times. The rice should be transparent and a little hard —it is half-cooked. Re-cover and continue steaming over high heat 15–20 minutes more.

To serve: Toast black sesame seeds very lightly in a dry frying pan. If sesame seeds are already toasted, just reheat. Serve rice and beans hot or at room temperature in individual rice bowls, sprinkled with toasted black sesame seeds mixed with a little salt.

Goes well with BEATEN EGG SOUP (page 346) and SALT-GRILLED SEA BASS (page 182).

A *donburi* is a deep-footed bowl, usually of porcelain, about 6 inches (15 cm) in diameter at the lip, about twice as large—to hold twice as much—as a standard rice bowl. *Donburi* are lidded. When people say *"donburi,"* they mean what goes into the bowl as well as the bowl itself. As a food, a *donburi* is hot boiled rice with a topping of meat, fish, egg, or vegetables, colorful garnishes and spicy condiments, if desired, and a few Tbsps of *dashi*-based sauce added at some time in the making to flavor the rice.

Donburi is not an old dish. The idea was concocted only about a hundred years ago as the new, faster pace of Meiji-period life—characterized by top hats and bustles, trolleys and two-story brick buildings, gaslights, railways, and steamships—brought "convenience foods" into demand. *Donburi* is still a popular lunch, snack, or bite-on-the-run. Falling in the same general category as noodles (*udon* and *soba*, pages 305–314), *donburi* is one of Japan's original fast foods. The number of *donburi* chains has grown at a phenomenal rate in Japan's urban centers, and *donburi* chain restaurants have even started appearing outside Japan.

How do you recognize a *donburi*-type dish on a Japanese menu? The last syllable *don* is the signal. For example, *tendon* is an abbreviation for *tempura donburi*, and *katsudon* stands for *tonkatsu donburi* (PORK CUTLET ON RICE). The recipes for these two extremely popular *donburi* dishes are on pages 444 and 445.

Toppings for *donburi* can be practically anything, so you can see why this dish is a practical and tasty way of using leftovers. Put chopped or sliced leftovers into a modest amount of *dashi*-based sauce, as in the *oyako donburi* recipe below, heat and pour onto rice in a bowl. Some ingredients you might try using are: pork, beef, chicken, fried bean curd (*aburage*), or pieces of

TEMPURA (leave whole). Add slivers of green onion. Generally, toppings for noodles are equally good on rice.

In Japan it is "not done" to eat plain white rice alone in a *donburi* bowl —it appears greedy and gluttonous. To fill a large *donburi* bowl with boiled rice is to give one person more than a just portion. *Donburi* bowls are for *donburi*, and rice bowls are for rice alone. Large, deep Western-style soup bowls may be used for *donburi*.

The main categories of rice dishes in Japanese cuisine—*sushi*, *gohanmono*, and *donburi*—have been introduced. No day passes in Japan without rice in one of these forms being eaten.

The following is a recipe for one of the commonest *donburi*. Made with chicken and egg, it rejoices in a whimsical name that literally means "parent and child."

Chicken-'n-Egg on Rice
(*Oyako Donburi*) 親子丼 (color plate 15)

4 servings

6-8 cups hot cooked rice
4-5 eggs
¼ pound (115 g) chicken
2 long onions (*naganegi*)
  or 4 green onions

sauce:
  2½ cups *dashi* or chicken
    stock
  6 Tbsps dark soy sauce
  3 Tbsps light soy sauce
  3 Tbsps sugar

To prepare: Boil plain white rice, following the basic recipe on page 273.

Mix (do not beat) eggs in a bowl lightly with chopsticks or fork and set aside.

Cut boned chicken (with or without skin, as preferred) into ¼-inch (¾-cm) pieces. The chicken should be raw, but if the purpose of making the dish is to use leftovers, cooked chicken is fine, as is thin-sliced raw or cooked pork or beef. The flavor is best if you start with raw meat.

Wash and clean onions. Cut diagonally into 1-inch (2½-cm) lengths.

To cook: Combine ingredients for sauce in a medium-sized saucepan. Bring to a gentle boil over medium heat. Add chicken and simmer, uncovered, for 5 minutes. Add onion and simmer 1 minute longer. Correct seasoning, if necessary.

Stir the eggs and pour gently in a steady stream around the chicken in the simmering sauce. Let the egg spread naturally. *Do not stir.* Keep heat at medium high till the egg starts to bubble at the edges. At this point, stir once. The egg will have almost set but will still be a little runny. Keep in mind that the high temperature of the rice over which the egg will be placed will do the final cooking. Do not let the egg cook hard.

To assemble and serve: Put portions of hot rice, 1½ to 2 cups, into individual *donburi* bowls, or use deep soup bowls. With a large spoon, scoop a portion of the egg topping and sauce and place on rice. Sauce will seep down into rice, but the dish will not be soupy. Serve immediately. With this meal-in-a-bowl, serve hot green tea. Goes well with a clear soup.

Beef Bowl

(*Gyūdon*) 牛 丼

The single item served by some of Japan's fast-food chains.

4 servings

6-8 cups hot cooked rice
½ pound (225 g) thin-sliced beef
2 long onions (*naganegi*) or 1 medium round onion
3 Tbsps salad oil
sauce:
  1 cup water
  ⅓ cup dark soy sauce
  ⅓ cup *mirin*
2 Tbsps fresh ginger juice (see page 70)

To prepare: Boil plain white rice, following the basic recipe on page 273.

Have the butcher cut the beef into paper-thin slices. Cut slices into 2-inch (5-cm) lengths.

Cut long onions diagonally in 1-inch (2½-cm) lengths or slice round onion.

To cook: In a large frying pan (or wok), heat about 3 Tbsps vegatable oil over high heat. Stir-fry the onion for a few minutes till soft. Add beef slices and continue stir-frying for another minute or so till meat is no longer red. Add sauce and continue stir-frying for another minute. Remove from heat and stir in ginger juice.

To assemble and serve: Put portions of hot rice, 1½ to 2 cups per serving, into individual *donburi* bowls or large deep soup bowls. Cover rice with stir-fried beef and onions. Moisten with a few Tbsps sauce. Cover and serve immediately. Good with green tea.

Sushi Varieties

If asked to name their favorite Japanese food, many a foreign enthusiast would unhesitatingly reply: "*Sushi*!" *Sushi* marries the flavor of vinegared rice to the clean flavor of fresh raw fish and shellfish. The rice is deftly shaped into bite-sized "fingers," seasoned with a dab of zesty *wasabi* horseradish, and covered by a strip of choice seafood.

Like TEMPURA and eel, the expert preparation of *sushi* takes years of practice; therefore these foods when prepared at home, or even in high-class full-course restaurants, cannot compare with that served in specialty shops that serve nothing else.

Running a *sushi* restaurant requires not only skill in cooking the rice and shaping the "fingers" with their luscious toppings, but also perhaps even greater skill in buying and handling the seafood itself. Molding the rice "fingers" looks easy but is remarkably difficult. They say that when done properly, all the rice grains face the same way. You do not squeeze the rice into wads—you merely invite the grains to cling with just the right amount of pressure. The dexterity needed in this operation is a good example of the skills that underlie the simplicity of the whole art of Japanese cooking.

But first and foremost with *sushi*, the fish must be exceptionally fresh. The optimum time to visit a *sushi* restaurant is at noon. Many people drop in at *sushi* shops for an early evening, or even worse, a late night snack, since it did not use to be considered a full meal. The real connoisseur, however, knows that lunch is the best time for *sushi*, for it is nearest to the time the fish arrives fresh from the market. And he takes care to patronize a *sushi* shop with the highest standards. There is a great temptation to put in the refrigerator what was not sold today and save it for tomorrow. By that time it is second grade, and by the day after that the fish has acquired the flaccid look of hospital patients.

Good *sushi* is exorbitantly expensive: twice the price of the best Kobe beef. Take prime tuna—not the frozen variety, but that caught in Japanese waters: just one fish costs 4 or 5 million yen wholesale, so the succulent *toro* portions would fetch 4 or 5 thousand yen for 100 grams, barely enough for 8 *sushi* "fingers" (4 servings)! Frozen tuna fits the average pocketbook, and although it is a far cry from the exquisite taste experience of the fresh commodity, it is the only frozen fish I can condone—together with, perhaps, squid. But how much better—and infinitely more in keeping with the spirit of Japanese cuisine—to eat fresh fish in season; *hamachi* (yellowtail), for instance, remarkably resembles the *toro* of tuna.

There is nothing quite like the atmosphere of a first-rate *sushi* establishment. Behind the ice-cooled glass shield backing the bar-type white Japanese-cypress counter is displayed a dazzling array of varied fish fillets and shellfish with the unmistakable bloom of pristine freshness upon them. Behind stand the *sushi* master and his assistants busy serving their customers, but not too busy to greet you as you enter with a hearty, resounding "Welcome!" Their cheerful pleasantries mingle with their quick, clean knife strokes and deft hand movements. Someone never fails to keep you constantly supplied with a mugful of piping hot green tea, plenty of *gari* (VINEGARED GINGER slices), and a clean damp cloth.

The ginger is for refreshing the palate between orders—all seafood except for the thick, succulent omelette. A pair of *sushi* "fingers" comprises one serving or order, and you may order *sashimi* (raw fish) alone without the rice if you wish. You order what takes your fancy as you go along. If you want another beverage as well as the hot tea, hot or cold *saké* is available, and beer, and usually other things as well.

Chopsticks are provided, but many aficionados use their fingers, which is easier. When you pick up a "finger" of *sushi*, turn it over so that the fish is on the bottom, and dip the fish side in the saucer of soy sauce. If you dip the rice side, the "finger" will break up. Eat the *sushi* in one or two bites. Already seasoned fish such as *anago* eel should not be dipped in the sauce.

Certain fish appear only in season, but below is a short list of fish and shellfish generally available in Japan.

akagai—ark shell (a ribbed clam with red meat)
anago—a type of sea eel (boiled in seasoned stock then grilled; a thick, sweet sauce is brushed on just before serving)
aoyagi—round clam (trough shell)
awabi—abalone
chū-toro—pinkish tuna meat of "middle" fattiness
ebi—shrimp (boiled)
hamachi—young yellowtail (*buri* is the adult)

hirame—flounder

ika—squid

ikura—salmon roe (a strip of toasted *nori* seaweed circling the finger of rice forms a nest for the roe)

kohada or *konoshiro*—a medium-sized gizzard shad

maguro—red meat of tuna (usually the first raw fish that Westerners take to, quite similar to rare steak in taste). Excellent *maguro* may be had in cities on the East Coast that are close to the rich Atlantic tuna-fishing grounds.

odori—"dancing" (that is, live) shrimp

shako—gray mantis shrimp (boiled)

shime-saba—vinegared mackerel

tako—octopus (boiled)

tamago—thick omelette sweetened with sugar and *mirin*, cut in slices and served on rice. Not fish or seafood, but nonetheless a stock item in every *sushi* shop.

toro—"white" prime tuna; the fattiest cut

uni—sea-urchin roe

Though oysters are used in many Japanese dishes, they are not used for *sushi*. Their flavor does not go especially well with vinegared rice, and they are much too fragile to use as a topping.

There is no set rule about the order in which to eat *sushi*, but many people begin with tuna (*toro*, *chū-toro*, or *maguro*—any one of the three magnificent tuna cuts) and end with either egg *sushi (tamago)*, which is quite sweet, or *nori-maki* (NORI-ROLL SUSHI).

Japanese love *sushi* so much that a special, aficionado's vocabulary has developed. At a *sushi* restaurant, you do not ask for soy sauce as *shōyu*, but, rather, as "purple," or *murasaki*. Every shop has its own house sauce, made by reducing soy sauce or thicker *tamari* sauce over heat with *saké*, *mirin*, bonito flakes and so on. The resulting sauce is darker and thicker than regular soy sauce, so the name *murasaki* seems appropriate. When you finish your meal, do not ask for tea as *ocha*, but as *agari*, meaning "finished." (Now you are ready to complete your meal with tea). VINEGARED GINGER slices, normally called *sushōga*, meaning "vinegared ginger," are instead called *gari*. *Wasabi* horseradish is merely abbreviated to *sabi*. Occasionally, because of its strength, it is called *namida*, "tears."

Sushi originated as a way of preserving *funa*, or crucian, a kind of carp. The fish was salted and allowed to mature on a bed of vinegared rice, after which the rice was discarded. Before long vinegared rice came to be eaten together with the fish, and many different combinations and ways of serving them evolved. The kind of *sushi* described so far in this chapter, served in *sushi* restaurants throughout Japan, is called *nigiri-zushi* ("hand-shaped *sushi*") to distinguish it from the other varieties, but the word *sushi* alone commonly is used to refer to this kind—the jewel in the multifarious *sushi* crown.

Nigiri-zushi is representative of Tokyo food. The reasons for this might relate to the fact that Tokyo—or Edo as the city was known before 1868— is situated on a bay that was once rich in seafood of all kinds. No doubt influenced by the bountiful catch of their wide, placid bay, the people of Edo always knew the taste of truly fresh fish and craved it.

The rice merchants and entrepreneurs of Osaka, the financial capital of the country, developed *oshi-zushi*, "pressed *sushi*." For *oshi-zushi*, vinegared rice is packed into a mold and covered with marinated (sometimes boiled) fish. When unmolded, the resulting loaf of *sushi* is cut into bite-sized pieces.

These two types of *sushi* today are served throughout Japan, alongside another popular type of *sushi* called *maki-zushi*, "rolled *sushi*." For *maki-zushi* and its variations, narrow strips of seafood or crisp strips of vegetable or pickle are arranged on a layer of vinegared rice, which has been spread on a sheet of toasted *nori* seaweed, and the whole is rolled. The roll is cut into rounds convenient for serving.

When you are at a *sushi* restaurant and money is short but craving is great, order a kind of *maki-zushi* called *nori-maki*, or NORI-ROLL SUSHI. There is a lot of rice, and the ingredients rolled into the center do not have to be the visually perfect specimens required for *nigiri-zushi*.

Nori-maki is served in many Japanese restaurants in the U.S. because other ingredients besides raw fish can be rolled into the center, if the supply of fresh fish is uncertain. The fact that some Japanese restaurants abroad serve only *maki-zushi* has had the effect of leaving an impression that *sushi* is only *maki-zushi*. One aim of these pages is to show how wide a food category *sushi* is.

One very simple type of *sushi*, made in all Japanese kitchens, is *chirashi-zushi*, or "scattered *sushi*." *Chirashi-zushi* requires neither the manual dexterity of hand-formed *nigiri-zushi*, nor the special mold that some types of pressed *sushi* do. *Chirashi-zushi* is simply seafood and vegetables in or on vinegared rice. The standard Tokyo version (recipe on page 448) calls for bite-sized pieces of fresh seafood to be strewn over the top of a bowlful of vinegared rice, while ingredients are mixed with the rice in the Osaka version. Shredded thin omelette and chopped seasoned mushrooms may be used for *chirashi-zushi*.

Chirashi-zushi without raw seafood often makes its appearance in lunch boxes. It is taken on picnics or is often sold on railway platforms as *eki-ben*, Japan's delightful "station lunches." Station lunches are not exclusively *chirashi-zushi*, but many are. Stations may be known for the type of *eki-ben* sold there as well as for the unique container in which the lunch is sold.

There are other kinds of *sushi* that are also regarded as picnic, lunch, or snack food. These fall mainly into the category of *maze-zushi*, "mixed *sushi*," because the vinegared rice has been tossed with chopped seafood and vegetables. Usually such mixed rice is used as a sort of stuffing. Two examples of mixed *sushi* are *Inari-zushi* and *fukusa-zushi* (SILK-SQUARE SUSHI). *Inari-zushi* consists of deep-fried bean curd pouches (see page 400) stuffed with mixed vinegared rice. For *fukusa-zushi*, a square of paper-thin omelette is used to wrap mixed vinegared rice, just as silk squares (*fukusa*) are customarily used for wrapping presents or precious articles in Japan. See the recipe on page 453.

No matter whether it is hand-packed, mold-pressed, or rolled in seaweed, for *sushi* to be *sushi* there is one constant ingredient—vinegared rice. Vinegared rice is a little harder and "chewier" than plain boiled rice because rice for *sushi* is cooked with a little less water than the usual boiled rice. *Sushi* restaurants usually cook large quantities of rice, starting with hot rather than cold water; this technique also affects the consistency of the rice. Quick cooling while tossing is the real key to making good SUSHI RICE (*sushi-meshi*). It helps produce the desired "chewiness" and gives rice a glossy sheen —these are the qualities that people who know *sushi* insist upon.

Tossing is traditionally done in a large, handsome vessel called a *hangiri*, which is nothing more than a shallow wooden tub made of Japanese cypress (*hinoki*) and (usually) hooped with copper. Here again, as with so many traditional Japanese utensils, material and form are beautifully related to function: the wood absorbs moisture from the hot rice and makes the rice-cooling even quicker; moreover, the *hangiri* shape allows rice to be spread in a thin layer to cool, and thus also grains are not mashed during tossing. *Hangiri* are expensive, even in Japan, and not an everyday utensil. Use any wide and shallow tub or even a clean plastic wash basin. Avoid anything made of metal; it might make the vinegar react and an unpleasant taste might develop. Use a rice paddle, a flat wooden spoon, or wooden spatula for tossing.

Sushi Rice
(Sushi-meshi) すしめし

The flavor of *sushi* rice varies somewhat with the seasons. In summer a little more vinegar is used. Adjust the flavor of the rice as you like.

3⅓ cups short-grain rice, washed
4 cups water
3-inch (8-cm) square giant kelp (*konbu*)

dressing:
  5 Tbsps plus 1 tsp rice vinegar
  5 Tbsps sugar
  4 tsps sea salt

To prepare: Put rice in heavy-bottomed medium-sized pot or rice cooker and add the 4 cups water.

Wipe kelp (*konbu*) clean with a damp cloth. You may slash kelp with a knife in a few places to enable flavors to be released more completely. Place kelp on top of rice in water.

Cover and heat over medium heat just until the boiling point. When just boiling, remove kelp and discard. Cover tightly, boil over high heat for 2 minutes, then turn heat down to medium and boil for 5 minutes. Reduce heat to very low and cook for 15 minutes or till all water has been absorbed. Turn off heat and let stand (on burner), with pot lid wrapped in a kitchen towel, 10 to 15 minutes.

Have the vinegar dressing prepared. Dissolve the sugar and salt in the vinegar over low heat. Force-cool to room temperature by placing hot vinegar mixture in a metal bowl and twirling the bowl in a bath of water and ice.

To toss rice: Using a flat wooden spoon or proper rice paddle, spread the hot rice in a thin layer in a wide and shallow wooden or plastic bowl—some convenient substitute for a *hangiri* tub. To keep the grains separate, toss rice with horizontal, cutting strokes. This lateral motion will also keep grains from being bruised or mashed. While tossing, sprinkle vinegar dressing generously over the rice. You may not have to use all the vinegar dressing. Be careful not to add so much liquid that the rice becomes mushy.

At the same time that you are tossing the rice, cool it quickly and thoroughly with a hand-fan (or a folded newspaper). Get someone else to stand by and do this. A helper is more sensible than juggling the spoon and fan by yourself. The tossing and fanning takes about 10 minutes. Taste to test whether the rice is room temperature.

To keep vinegared rice from drying out, when it has cooled to room temperature, place in a container and cover with a damp cloth. Vinegared rice should be eaten the same day it is prepared; it does not keep more than 1 day. It should *not* be refrigerated. Leftovers, if there are any, unfortunately cannot be stir-fried Chinese-style to make fried rice.

1, 2. pour on vinegar mixture as you spread rice

3. use only a sideways cutting motion when mixing and tossing *sushi* rice

4. cool rice with fan as you toss it

Normally, the tossing of vinegared rice is not one of the things you see being done behind the counter if you go to a *sushi* restaurant. The rice tossing done by professionals —the *sushi* master or one of his juniors sweeping through the rice and air with paddles, and a cluster of apprentices furiously fanning—is pure theater. It is too bad this tossing is not done when everyone can see it, but this performance usually occurs before shop hours.

Nigiri Sushi
(*Nigiri-zushi*) にぎりずし (color plate 15)

Although *nigiri-zushi* attempted at home cannot compare with that served in specialty *sushi* restaurants, it is a challenge, fun to make, and the results are rewarding. *Sushi* is good food, and there is a sense of accomplishment in making it, even if the professionals, obviously, will do better.

Nigiri-zushi make wonderful hors d'oeuvres or can be served as a first course. *Sushi* also makes an excellent one-course lunch. Until you have had practice making it a few times, it seems wisest to limit *nigiri-zushi* to one or two kinds of fish at one time or serve one type of fish-topped *nigiri-zushi* and a vegetable-filled ROLLED SUSHI (*nori-maki*) in combination. *Nigiri-zushi* cannot be prepared very much in advance; serve as soon as possible.

8 servings (about 4 dozen pieces)

4 cups *sushi* rice
2 pounds (1 kg) fillet(s) of tuna, squid, or sea bream (one or all), without skin
1 Tbsp finely grated *wasabi* horseradish

tezu ("*hand-vinegar*"):
2 tsps rice vinegar
6 Tbsps water

soy sauce
thin-sliced VINEGARED GINGER (*sushōga* or *gari*) (see page 304, below)

To prepare: Make the *sushi* rice according to the recipe on page 290.

Obtain the freshest fish fillets or shellfish, unsliced, of the same cuts and quality as for *sashimi* (see page 159).

With a sharp knife, cut fillets crosswise at a slight angle into slices about $\frac{1}{8}$ inch ($\frac{1}{2}$ cm) thick (with tuna, $\frac{1}{4}$ inch [$\frac{3}{4}$ cm] thick is best). The *sushi* cut is very similar to cutting *sashimi* (see pages 163ff). Wrap in a kitchen towel, but do not refrigerate. Assemble with rice "fingers" as soon as possible.

To assemble: Mix the "hand-vinegar" in a cup or small bowl and use to moisten your hands to keep rice from sticking while you work.

Dip fingers into "hand-vinegar" and rub palms together. Pick up about $1\frac{1}{2}$ Tbsps vinegared rice and shape into a roughly rectangular form (or "finger") about $1\frac{1}{2} \times \frac{3}{4}$ inches (4×2 cm).

Place rice across the first joint of the fingers of one hand (the right hand for right-handed people) and form roughly by clenching that hand. With index and middle fingers of right hand, press and form rice into a more defined and firm shape, as shown, turning rice over so that all sides receive equal pressure. Do not squash or mash the rice; the pressure should be firm but gentle. Smear a dab of grated *wasabi* horseradish in the center of a slice of fish and press fish and rice "finger" together, as shown. The fish should cover the top of the "finger." (No *wasabi* is used for egg *sushi*.)

As a cocktail party hors d'oeuvre, arrange on a tray to be passed among guests. Put a small dish of soy sauce on the tray for dipping, and supply cocktail napkins to offer along with the *sushi*. Guests should pick up *sushi* with their fingers.

If serving as a course at a sit-down dinner, place 5 or 6 pieces of *sushi* per serving on individual plates. Serve immediately. Offer soy sauce (usually mixed with 20 percent *mirin*) for dipping and vinegared ginger slices to refresh the palate. Goes well with clear soup.

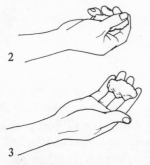

1. moisten your hand with hand vinegar and pick up a small amount of rice

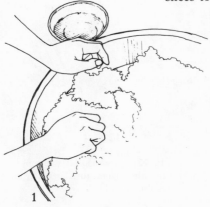

2, 3. press rice into a wad (do not mash it)

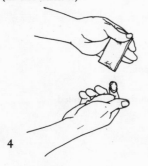

4, 5. pick up a slice of fish with your other hand and spread a dab of *wasabi* on it (rice "finger" is concealed in fist of right hand)

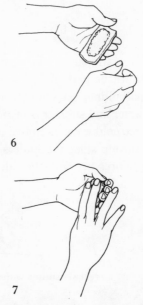

6, 7. place rice on fish slice and press firmly with index and middle fingers

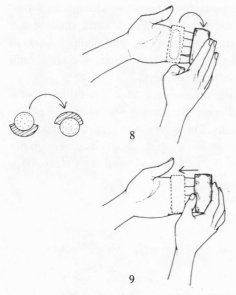

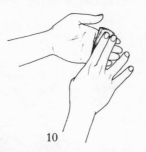

8, 9. roll *sushi* over so fish faces up and return to former position on palm

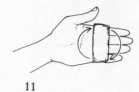

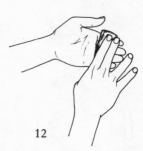

10–12. press *sushi* with index and middle fingers, turn around, and press again

skewer shrimp with a toothpick to keep from curling when boiled

VARIATION: SHRIMP NIGIRI-ZUSHI

Shrimp must be parboiled. Use medium to large shrimp. To keep shrimp from curling during parboiling, skewer with a toothpick as shown. Drop into lightly salted simmering water and simmer over medium heat for about 3 minutes, till just pink and firm. Plunge into cold water. Remove toothpicks, remove shell, but leave tail attached. Devein. Cut the shrimp along the underside about ¾ of the way through and then gently flatten out. Apply pressure with the side of a knife to flatten even more.

BATTERA SUSHI takes its name from the Portuguese word for ship (*bateira*). The pressed *sushi* itself was seen as a fanciful form of ship. Formerly gizzard shad (*konoshiro*) was used instead of mackerel, and this fish surmounted the rice with its tail intact. It was this tail that evoked the image of a galleon.

The three-piece cypress-wood *oshiwaku*, or "push frame," used to make BATTERA SUSHI, looks like a large oriental puzzle. How does this device work? While pushing the wooden lid down over the vinegared rice in the mold with your thumbs, with your fingertips lift the 4-sided body of the mold up and over the top. A rectangular block of packed, molded rice is left neatly on the traylike bottom piece. In a sense, you have "pushed" the vinegared rice through the mold. An *oshiwaku* is useful if you make this *sushi* often, and it is a decorative item in the kitchen, but it is not essential. Instead of an *oshiwaku*, you can use a pan with a removable bottom, a stainless spring-form pan, or, if you have utensils for French cooking, you can even innovate with a stainless *forme sans fond*.

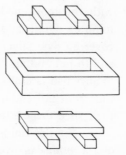

three-piece wooden BATTERA SUSHI
mold (*oshiwaku*)

Mackerel is used in the recipe below, but any deep-flavored fish—sea bream, sea bass, herring—will do. Or use thin-sliced smoked salmon, thinly sliced cooked or smoked chicken, prosciutto ham (*crudo*) or 1/8-inch (1/2-cm) thick sweet omelette (see page 203).

You may be surprised to find that aspidistra (*baran*; also known as the cast-iron plant) leaves are called for in the recipe. The leaves are cut into rectangles to line the bottom of the mold. The object is to put a thin layer of "waxy" substance between the wooden bottom of the mold and the layer of fish, which is put in first, to keep the fish from sticking to the wood. The waxy layer is peeled off the molded *sushi* without disturbing its shape. Using aspidistra leaves is the traditional Japanese way of tackling the problem. Lacking aspidistras in your garden, use a banana leaf, or any thin, wide leaf of a nontoxic plant. Wax paper is just as easily used, as is aluminum foil, but leaves are more rewarding to use, if for no other reasons than that they are traditional and they are leaves.

BATTERA SUSHI can be made some hours in advance—a good picnic food. Cut the loaves into 1-inch (2½-cm) pieces just before serving. Serve with or without soy sauce for dipping.

Battera Sushi

(*Battera-zushi*) ばってらずし (color plate 15)

---

4 servings, 2 loaves about 6 x 2 x 1½ inches (15 x 5 x 4 cm)

4 cups *sushi* rice
1 mackerel, about 1½ pounds (675 g)
4-inch (10-cm) square giant kelp (*konbu*)
marinade:
  ¾ **cup rice vinegar**
  4-5 Tbsps water
  1 Tbsp sugar
  1 Tbsp light soy sauce
several aspidistra (or other nontoxic) leaves (or wax paper)
1 tsp finely grated *wasabi* horseradish (optional)
tezu ("*hand-vinegar*"):
  1 tsp rice vinegar
  3 Tbsp water
2 8-inch (20-cm) squares *shiraita konbu* ("white sheet" *konbu*) (optional)
for simmering shiraita konbu:
  6 Tbsps water
  6 Tbsps rice vinegar
  1 Tbsp light soy sauce

To prepare: Make the *sushi* rice according to the recipe on page 290.

Scale, gut, and fillet (*sanmai oroshi* technique, pages 123ff) the fish, then bone the fillets. Salt both sides of fillets generously and let stand 3–4 hours. Wash and then wipe fillets with a towel. Moisten *konbu* with marinade first, place fillets in the marinade, and cover with the moistened kelp like a blanket. Marinate 10 minutes. Drain and pat dry. Remove thin epidermal covering over silvery skin by pulling it off from head end to tail and also remove any remaining bones.

Slice fish laterally as shown into 3 equal thicknesses. Cut from tail end with a sawing motion across fillet, then slice diagonally into 1½-inch (4-cm) widths.

To cut the lining for the mold, place the bottom of the *oshiwaku* over the waxy side of the aspidistra leaf (or wax paper). With a knife, cut along the edge to make a lining to fit the mold. (Or trace and use scissors.) Make as many linings as the number of loaves you intend to make.

(Optional) For a garnish that adds an interesting complementary taste, you may use *shiraita konbu* to cover the tops of the loaves. Simmer these thin kelp sheets flat in a large pan in the simmering liquid for 20 minutes. The kelp will become pliant and a translucent light green color. Let it cool in the liquid. Drain. Lay flat on a cutting board and cut sheets somewhat larger than the lining of the mold. The *shiraita konbu* should overlap the fish and extend over the rice a little.

To assemble: Line the bottom of the mold with the cut piece of "waxy" sustance you have choosen—leaf, wax paper, or foil. Place a diagonal strip of fish, *skin side down*, in one-half of the mold; place strip of fish without skin to fill the other half of the mold, as shown.

Try to make the arrangement as neat as possible because this will become the loaf top. Make sure that the layer of fish has uniform thickness (use any extra flesh to fill in thin spots).

(Optional) With your index finger, smear a thin film of *wasabi* horseradish on the fish fillets in the mold. Make sure there are no large deposits, or mouths will be set aflame.

Next, fill the mold to overflowing with *sushi* rice. The rice should stand about ¼ inch (¾ cm) above the sides of the mold. Mix the "hand-vinegar" and moisten your hands slightly to keep rice from sticking. With your hands, press the rice down firmly into the mold. Make sure there are no air pockets.

With the "hand-vinegar," lightly moisten the inside surface of the mold top.

Place it over the rice-filled mold and press with strength, using even pressure. With thumbs holding the top stationary, use your fingertips to lift the body of the mold up and through the top, as shown.

Run a wet knife or spatula under the top to make sure no rice sticks. Then remove the top of the mold. Peel off and discard aspidistra leaf or wax paper, then drape on the cut sheet of simmered *shiraita konbu*.

Cut loaves into 1-inch (2½-cm) thick pieces and serve immediately, or wrap whole loaf in a kitchen towel, but serve the same day.

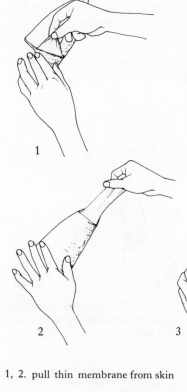

1, 2. pull thin membrane from skin

3–5. place fillet skin side down and slice into 3 equal thicknesses

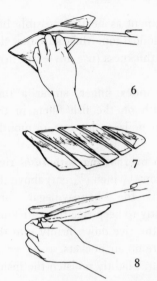

6–8. cut fish into diagonal slices about half the width of the mold interior

9. place leaf, wax paper, or foil in mold

10, 11. lay one slice with skin (skin side down) and one skinless slice side by side in mold and spread thin film of *wasabi* on fish

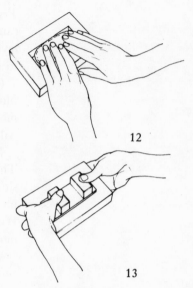

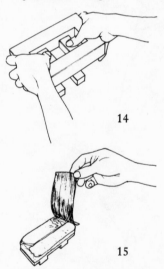

12, 13. fill mold to overflowing with rice, place on mold lid, and press with strength

14, 15. lift mold rim up and off, then reverse *sushi* and remove base and leaf

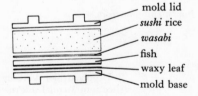

mold lid
sushi rice
wasabi
fish
waxy leaf
mold base

VARIATION: PRESSED SUSHI (*Oshi-zushi*)

For a very simple version, use the same ingredients as for BATTERA SUSHI, but put the *sushi* rice in the mold first and pack it lightly. Then remove the mold lid and lay on a thin layer of fish or shrimp (or boiled chicken cut into thin slices or ham or omelette). Cover with a sheet of wax paper and press with the mold lid. Before removing from the mold, run a knife around the edge to keep rice from sticking. Once removed, cut *sushi* into ½-×-2-inch (1½-×-5-cm) bars with a wet sharp knife. Arrange on a platter and serve. This is a good method to use with spring-form pans or other improvised molds. But, for the most compressed, most compact *sushi*, the "reversing" method in an *oshiwaku* mold, as described in the recipe for BATTERA SUSHI, is recommended.

Maki-zushi is the general name for all *sushi* that is rolled. *Nori* seaweed is the most common; such *nori-maki* can be thick or thin, depending on how many ingredients are used for the core. Thick *nori-maki* is 2 inches (5 cm) in diameter and contains about 4 or 5 core ingredients. Typical ingredients are: seasoned sliced mushroom, freeze-dried bean curd (*Kōya-dōfu*), gourd shavings (*kampyō*), thick omelette cut in strips, parboiled trefoil.

Thick or thin, *nori-maki* are usually rolled in a bamboo mat (*maki-su*) to pack the roll firmly. The exception is *temaki sushi*, a "thin" rolled *sushi* that is rolled by hand and eaten as made. If you do not have a bamboo mat, use an undyed, flexible place mat.

Nori, called purple laver in some English texts, is commercially cultivated in Japan on vertical frames set in tidal shallows. The harvested seaweed is dried in large, thin sheets. It is then cut into standard-sized, 6½-x-8-inch (17½-x-20½-cm) sheets and sold 10 sheets to a package. Once packaged *nori* is opened, it should be kept in an airtight container to keep it crisp. *Nori* has a "front" side and a "back" side. The "front" side is the smoother, shinier one, and this attractive, glossy side should be used on the outside of rolled *sushi*. The rough, textured side (the "back") is the side on which the ingredients are laid before rolling. Always toast *nori* by passing the "front" side only over a flame or burner till crisp.

Dried *nori* seaweed is an essential ingredient for *nori-maki*. *Kampyō*, or dried gourd strips, almost ranks the same way. *Kampyō* might not be the first thing you find in oriental provisions stores, but if you can get it, *kampyō* will make the inner core of your *nori-maki* subtly sweet.

Packaged dried gourd strips look like skeins of thick, cream-colored ribbon. *Kampyō* is shaved from the pith of the bottle calabash, and 90 percent of Japan's *kampyō* comes from the countryside around Utsunomiya, about 2 hours north of Tokyo.

Another often-used ingredient in *nori-maki* is *Kōya-dōfu*, or freeze-dried bean curd (see page 60). *Kōya-dōfu* is soaked in hot water then simmered in seasoned stock.

Though grated *wasabi* horseradish is used in most types of *nigiri-zushi*, it is not used with most *nori-maki* except the types of thin rolled *sushi* made with cucumber called *kappa-maki* (see recipe below) and with tuna.

Nori-Roll *Sushi*
(*Nori-maki*) のりまき (color plate 15)

4 servings, 2 rolls about
6 x 2 inches (15 x 5 cm)

4 cups *sushi* rice
2 cakes *Kōya-dōfu* (freeze-
dried bean curd), softened
(see page 60)

for simmering Kōya-dōfu:
   1⅔ cups *dashi*
   2 Tbsps sugar
   1 Tbsp light soy sauce
   ½ tsp salt

6 large dried *shiitake*
mushrooms, softened and
trimmed (see page 88)

for simmering mushrooms:
   ½ cup *dashi*
   3 Tbsps light soy sauce
   1 Tbsp sugar
   1 Tbsp *mirin*

2 ounces (60 g) dried gourd
strips (*kampyō*), softened
(see page 71)

for simmering kampyō:
   1⅔ cups *dashi*
   4 Tbsps dark soy sauce
   1 tsp sugar

6 stalks trefoil
2 standard sheets *nori*
seaweed

To prepare: Make the *sushi* rice according to the recipe on page 290.

The 3 major dried ingredients—*Kōya-dōfu*, *shiitake*, and *kampyō*—are seasoned by simmering in separate stocks. This can be done ahead of time.

In a small saucepan, bring ingredients for simmering *Kōya-dōfu* just to a boil over high heat. Add softened *Kōya-dōfu* and reduce heat to low. Simmer until liquid is almost gone (about 20 minutes). Remove from heat and let softened bean curd cool in remaining liquid. Bean curd should absorb seasoned liquid. Cut each piece of *Kōya-dōfu* into 6 strips.

Cut softened mushrooms into ⅛-inch (½-cm) slices. In a small saucepan bring ingredients for simmering mushrooms just to a boil over high heat, then add mushroom slices and simmer over low heat for 15 minutes, until the simmering liquid is almost totally reduced and mushroom slices are well flavored.

In a small saucepan, bring ingredients for simmering dried gourd shavings (*kampyō*) just to a boil over high heat. Add softened gourd shavings and simmer for 20 minutes, till soft, then drain. Cut in 6-inch (15-cm) lengths.

Parboil trefoil for 30 seconds. Pat dry.

To assemble: Just before rolling *sushi*, toast the *nori* seaweed by passing the shiny side over a high flame. The color of the *nori* will change from brownish-black to dark green. Without toasting, the *nori* will be gummy, hard to chew, and without much flavor.

tezu ("*hand-vinegar*"):

1 tsp rice vinegar
3 Tbsps water

Place one sheet of toasted *nori* shiny-side down on a bamboo mat (*maki-su*; see page 102), as shown.

Spread the *sushi* rice in a ⅜-inch (1-cm) layer over ¾ of the *nori* sheet closest to you. First moisten your hands with the "hand-vinegar" to keep the rice from sticking to your hands as you work. Using about 2 cups *sushi* rice, spread the rice with your fingertips.

Next, lay the core ingredients across the center of the rice. Lay the strips of *Kōya-dōfu* end to end all the way across the sheet. Place *shiitake* mushroom slices, several lengths of *kampyō*, and trefoil stalks on top of the *Kōya-dōfu* strips.

To roll, hold the line of ingredients firmly in place with your fingertips, and with your thumbs push up and turn the end of the bamboo mat, as shown. The edge of the *nori* sheet nearest you should be lifted over to meet the far edge of the sheet.

Gently but firmly press the bamboo mat around the roll for about 30 seconds to shape it. The art of making this kind of *sushi* is getting the core ingredients at the very center of the roll; this is what takes practice.

To unroll, place on a flat surface (usually a cutting board, because cutting is the next step) so that the edge of the *nori* is on the bottom.

To serve: Usually the roll is cut in half crosswise and each half into 4 pieces. Use a wet knife, and clean it between cuttings. Do not saw through the roll. Arrange the slices on a platter or individual plates with cut sides up to show off the centers.

Always offer VINEGARED GINGER slices as a garnish. The basic recipe is included below. Serve without a dipping sauce.

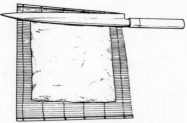

1. place *nori* sheet on bamboo mat; weight down edge of *nori*

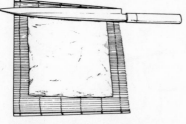

2

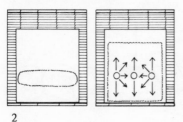

3

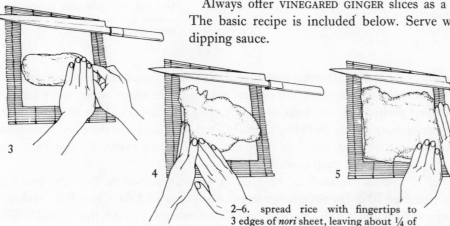

4

5

2–6. spread rice with fingertips to 3 edges of *nori* sheet, leaving about ¼ of sheet uncovered

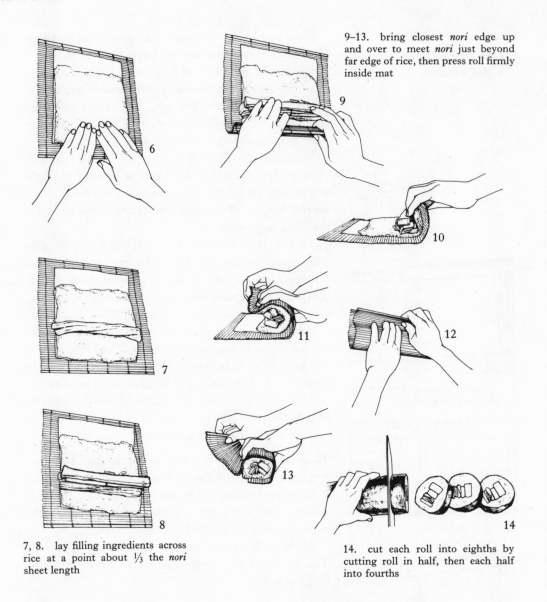

9–13. bring closest *nori* edge up and over to meet *nori* just beyond far edge of rice, then press roll firmly inside mat

7, 8. lay filling ingredients across rice at a point about ⅓ the *nori* sheet length

14. cut each roll into eighths by cutting roll in half, then each half into fourths

There are any number of ingredients that go well in thick *nori-maki*. Do not limit yourself only to what is described above. Add fresh seafood—with the recipe above, use 4 ounces (115 g) of white-fleshed fish, raw tuna, or shrimp. The tuna does not have to be the most attractive cut; remove sinews and chop coarsely. Parboil shelled and deveined shrimp in seasoned stock just till pink and firm (2 cups *dashi*, 2 Tbsps sugar, 1 Tbsp light soy sauce, and ½ tsp salt), and chop coarsely.

Instead of *Kōya-dōfu* (freeze-dried bean curd), you can substitute thin omelette cut into strips (see page 206). Do not simmer in stock as you would the *Kōya-dōfu*. Also use julienne strips of cucumber. The classical ingredients are always good, but small kitchen adventures may be rewarding. Try local or seasonal things as fillers for ROLLED SUSHI.

Cucumber *Sushi* Roll

(*Kappa-maki*) かっぱ巻

To explain the name of a highly popular, thin type of ROLLED SUSHI called *kappa-maki*, we have to turn to tales of old. In Japanese folklore, *kappa*s are water sprites with saucer-topped heads that always must be filled with water or the *kappa* looses his strength. It is believed that the favorite food of *kappa*s is cucumbers, so cucumber-filled ROLLED SUSHI has been dubbed *kappa-maki*. It is also called *kyūri-maki*, "cucumber roll."

With the recipe for *kappa-maki* as a model, you can expand on the theme of thin *sushi* rolls. For entertaining, make thin rolls filled with only a single ingredient, such as cucumber, gourd shavings (*kampyō*), omelette, raw tuna, *shiso* leaves (chop leaves coarsely first), or *takuan* pickles cut in strips.

The method of rolling thin *sushi* rolls is exactly the same as described above for the thick type in the recipe for NORI-ROLL SUSHI.

4 servings

4 cups *sushi* rice
1 Japanese cucumber (or ½ Western-type cucumber, peeled and seeded)
2 standard sheets *nori* seaweed

tezu ("*hand-vinegar*"):
   1 tsp rice vinegar
   3 Tbsps water
1 Tbsp finely grated *wasabi* horseradish

To prepare: Make the *sushi* rice according to the recipe on page 290.

It is not necessary to peel or seed Japanese cucumbers. Clean and cut into julienne strips about 4 inches (10 cm) long. With Western-type cucumbers, use only the crisp flesh between the rind and core.

To assemble: Just before rolling *sushi*, toast *nori* seaweed (see page 80). Cut toasted *nori* sheets in half crosswise. Place ½ sheet of *nori*, shiny-side down, on bamboo mat (*maki-su*; see page 102).

Moisten hands with "hand-vinegar" and spread about 1 cup of *sushi* rice over the ¾ of the sheet closest to you in a layer about ⅛–¼ inch (½–¾ cm) thick.

With your index finger, smear a thin line of grated *wasabi* horseradish across the center of the rice.

Lay julienne strips of cucumber along the *wasabi* horseradish. Make sure that the distribution is even so that the roll will not be lumpy.

Roll the ingredients in the bamboo mat as described in the recipe immediately preceding to make a firmly packed cylinder. Use remaining ingredients to make 3 more rolls.

To serve: Cut the roll into 1-inch (2½-cm) rounds. Use a sharp knife and wipe it clean with a damp cloth between slicings. (Cut straight down through the roll, then pull the knife towards you.) Serve with soy sauce as dipping sauce.

HAND-ROLLED SUSHI (*Temaki-zushi*)

Without using a bamboo mat, you can produce almost the same sort of *sushi* by hand rolling. But because hand-rolled *sushi* is not as firmly or evenly packed as the kind rolled in a mat, the hand-rolled type is eaten as is, without being cut into bite-sized rounds.

The procedure for hand-rolled *sushi* is the same as for the mat-rolled kind. Roll gently, using the fingers and palms of both hands. Eat immediately, without cutting. *Temaki* really is not the sort of food that is brought around on a platter or served on a plate. In Japanese *sushi* shops, *temaki* are made to order between rounds of *nigiri-zushi*, and rolls are simply passed across the counter from master to patron without much ceremony. You may use soy sauce as a dipping sauce, if desired.

Vinegared Ginger

(*Sushōga* or *Gari*) 酢生姜 または ガリ

2 cups

½ **pound (225 g) fresh ginger root**
2 tsps salt

marinade:

1 cup rice vinegar
7 Tbsps water
2½ Tbsps sugar

Clean ginger knobs well with damp cloth. Sprinkle lightly with salt and leave for 1 day.

Mix marinade in crockery bowl, making sure sugar is dissolved. Drain the ginger, then pickle in marinade for 7 days. Keeps in covered container in refrigerator at least several months. The ginger will turn pinkish in the vinegary marinade.

Cut into paper-thin slices along the grain. Set a small mound on every individual plate. Two Tbsps per person throughout the course of *sushi* meal is about average. Eat with fingers.

PICKLED GINGER SHOOTS

If you come across ginger shoots *ha-shōga*, you can also make a delicious garnish out of them by more or less following the principles in the recipe for VINEGARED GINGER. Separate shoots and clean. Pour scalding water over the shoots, but *do not parboil*. Parboiling will make the shoots limp. Fill an old pickle jar or relish jar with hot marinade and stand shoots up in the jar. The shoots will turn pinkish and be ready in 3–4 hours. You can keep the marinade almost indefinitely, adding new shoots every time you take vinegared ones out. These vinegared shoots are known as *hajikami shōga* ("bashful ginger") and are usually served with grilled fish.

Noodles
Menrui

Noodles have a long history in Japan, and though they are in a category all by themselves and are not part of formal Japanese cuisine, more noodles are probably consumed in Japan daily than any other dish. They are, in fact, the original Japanese fast food—quick to make, easy to eat, and cheap.

Working people in Japan have been conditioned not to spend much time over meals, and noodles are a dish that must be eaten fast, while the noodles still have that tooth-resistant texture the Italians call *al dente* and before they become limp in the piping hot broth.

Besides the traditional forms of Japanese noodles, several Chinese varieties are popular in Japan too, for noodles are important in the diet of China, Southeast Asia, and Korea as well as Japan. In fact, modern research indicates that noodles and *pasta* in general are of Asiatic origin, but whether they were introduced into Italy by Marco Polo is open to question.

Noodles in Japan can be divided into two distinct types: the buckwheat noodles associated with Tokyo and northern Japan and the wheat noodles of Osaka and southern Japan. I was born in Tokyo, and when I first went to Osaka as a young reporter, the first thing that struck me was the pallor of their noodle broth and the way you could see the noodles so clearly in it. I had always heard Osaka people were stingy, so I just assumed they used less soy sauce. Later I found out it was because they use *usukuchi* (light) soy sauce, which is just as flavorsome but lighter in color than the Tokyo variety. I thought they were being mean, too, with their green onions, using the tough green portion we throw away in Tokyo. But I discovered that the Osaka onions—unlike the variety I used in Tokyo cooking, which are mostly white—are mostly green. But then everything seemed so different, although the cities are only 372 miles (600 kilometers) apart. The accent—even the words used. For instance, they refer to eels in Osaka as *mamushi*, the name we give to poisonous vipers up north!

Japan's noodles vividly exemplify this cultural division between north and south. *Soba*, cold-climate buckwheat noodles, are at their best in Tokyo and the north, and are mainly eaten there, while *udon*, those made of wheat, flourish from Osaka right down to southernmost Kyushu. Historically, buckwheat noodles are the older.

Oddly enough, the buckwheat variety claims more connoisseurs and sparks more controversy than *udon*, although aficionados of both kinds like to savor noodles *al dente* and eat them plain, with just the broth and nothing else. In the case of the cold buckwheat noodles served in summer, real connoisseurs hardly add any broth at all. In the urban sophistication of seventeenth-century Edo (now Tokyo), eating cold *soba* with a lot of broth came to be considered boorish and a sign that the eater was a country bumpkin and did not appreciate good noodles. But a well-known humorous anecdote —part of the traditional repertoire of the old variety theater raconteurs— belies the logic of this taboo. It depicts a *soba* devotee on his deathbed expressing a lifelong yearning just once to eat a dish of cold *soba* absolutely swimming in tasty broth!

The word for buckwheat noodles, *soba*, is a homonym of the word *soba* meaning "near." The Japanese love plays on words, and when one moves into a new home it is customary to present one's new neighbors with buckwheat noodles, calling them *hikkoshi soba*, "we've moved near you." The last thing eaten on New Year's Eve is traditionally *soba*, when it is called *toshi-koshi soba*, "the year is passing," but there is no pun here.

Udon and *soba* are easy to make at home. *Sōmen* (vermicelli) and *cha-soba* (green-tea-flavored buckwheat noodles) are available in the U.S., and the broth is sold canned, so it is possible to enjoy real, authentic Japanese noodles abroad.

Like sipping piping hot Japanese soup, to really enjoy noodles, one must imbibe them fast with a cooling intake of breath. To do this involves a decided sucking sound, which easily deteriorates into a slurp. But no one minds in Japan, since the whole point of noodles is to eat them fast while they are very hot. Noodles are just too hot to eat in puckered silence, so you have to open your mouth a bit wider than necessary to accommodate the slippery pasta and suck in with a fair amount of gusto. For a Westerner, picking up the knack of noodle-eating may depend on how quickly he or she can abandon the taboo on noise in eating. I know how hard it is for those trained to eat noiselessly. My own daughter finds it almost impossible to eat noodles properly, having been trained at an English boarding school. But eating noodles too quietly can be mistaken in Japan for a lack of enjoyment of this food.

Noodle shops abound in Japanese cities—from small stalls to nationwide chain noodle restaurants, each shop boasting the same garish plastic sign and brightly lit interior. In tiny hamlets with only one public eatery, noodles are prominent on the menu hanging on the wall. In the last half of the 1970s, the great boom of dried-noodles-in-the-cup rolled over the Japanese islands. Such "cup noodles" have appeared on the Western market under a variety of names. These just-add-water-and-wait-3-minutes styrofoam "meals" are mentioned here only as an example of the versatility of noodles. Actually, instant noodles are mostly of the *ramen* type, which are Chinese, not Japanese in origin.

Of course, the same kind of noodle is not used for every noodle recipe. The differences between the members of the noodle family are not so much their shapes as their ingredients and how the noodles are made. There are four basic types of noodles made from wheat flour and one from buckwheat.

The characteristics of noodles are related to the flour type used for noodle dough. Flour rather rich in gluten—either all-purpose or bread flour—is used for wheat noodles.

Udon: A round or flat, flour-salt-and-water white noodle. If you are not able to find *udon* noodles, try making them yourself with the recipe below. Homemade noodles are always better than store-bought.

Kishimen: A wide and thick, flat, white flour-salt-and-water noodle, differing from *udon* only in its larger size and its shape.

Hiyamugi: A fine white noodle used specifically in cold dishes.

Sōmen: A very fine white noodle, made from a hard-wheat dough slightly moistened with cottonseed or sesame seed oil. Superficially, *hiyamugi* and *sōmen* are hard to tell apart. There is also a type of *sōmen* called *tamago sōmen*, identifiable by its warm yellow strands, enriched with egg yolk.

Soba (buckwheat) noodles are thin and brownish gray in color. When served as a course in itself, boiled *soba* is arranged on a bamboo lattice set in a square bamboo or wooden frame. One interesting kind of *soba* is made with the addition of powdered green tea. It is easily recognizable by its appealing green color and memorable for its subtle flavor and is called, naturally enough, "green-tea *soba*"—*cha-soba*.

When home-made, *soba* and *udon* doughs are kneaded vigorously for a long time to activate the gluten in the flour. This makes the dough adhesive and pliant so the noodles never break apart in boiling. Important: practically all recipes calling for *udon* noodles can be made with *soba* noodles.

Homemade Japanese Noodles

(*Teuchi Udon* or *Soba*) 手打ちうどん，そば

Using only all-purpose white flour, the result is *udon*-type noodles; *soba* noodles are made with buckwheat flour and wheat flour at a ratio of about 4 buckwheat to 1 wheat. These noodles can be frozen. Cook after defrosting.

4 pounds (1¾ kg)—6 servings

1¾ cups water (about)
3⅓ Tbsps salt
2 egg yolks (optional)
**8⅓ cups (2¼ pounds or
1 kg) all-purpose flour**

To prepare: Dissolve salt in cold water. (If using eggs, beat yolks, mix with water, then dissolve salt in this mixture.) Make a well in the center of the flour and gradually work in the liquid with your hands to make a stiff dough. This recipe is based on standard Japanese flours. Adjust the amount of liquid to the flour you use. Knead vigorously until dough is smooth and soft but firm—"like your earlobe," is the traditional Japanese guide. Cover with a damp kitchen cloth and let rest 8 hours in winter or 3 hours in summer for the best results, but 2 hours are adequate.

On a flour-dusted board or pastry cloth, roll out dough in an even width (a rectangular shape, *not* a round) till ⅛ inch (½ cm) thick or slightly thinner, as shown. Sprinkle sheet of rolled-out dough with flour and fold as shown. Cut with a sharp knife or cleaver across the folded sheet into ⅛-inch (½-cm) strips. After cutting, insert a long chopstick or long skewer into the center fold and shake out the strands.

Udon noodles can be frozen or will keep refrigerated for 3-4 days in a closed container. *Soba* are more delicate—the flavor does not keep well. See below for cooking directions.

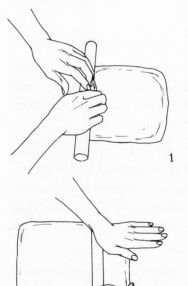

1

2

1, 2.   roll out dough in a rectangular (not round) shape

3

3.   fold rolled-out dough so that a chopstick can be inserted into the center fold

4

5

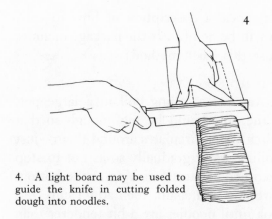

4. A light board may be used to guide the knife in cutting folded dough into noodles.

5. insert a chopstick or skewer into the center fold and shake out noodles

Besides *udon*, *soba*, and *sōmen*, which are the three most commonly used Japanese noodles, there are others, which are not noodles. *Harusame* ("spring rain") is made from various starches and comes in the form of fine, translucent filaments. *Shirataki* ("white waterfall"), a transparent, ropy, gelatinous filament often used in SUKIYAKI or other one-pot dishes, is made from the starchy root of the devil's tongue plant, *konnyaku*. Both *harusame* and *shirataki* are made by an extrusion process, not cut with a knife. They are often called vermicelli, an unfortunate misnomer. They do not fit any Western category, so they are called filaments in this book—not the best word, but adequate.

As mentioned above, the instant noodle preparations gaining worldwide attention are the result of Japanese ingenuity, but the type of noodle is Chinese and is not a part of Japanese cuisine. Like fried rice, fried noodles (*yakisoba*), too, are Chinese, not Japanese, though part of the ambience of every Japanese festival (as is cotton candy).

There are two places to look for noodles in a Japanese store: dried noodles are on the grocery shelf; both fresh uncooked and cooked ones are in the refrigerator case. You may at first feel overwhelmed by the wide selection of packaged noodles to chose from (this is certainly true in Japan), but merely pick out the basic kind of noodle you want—*udon*, *sōmen*, *soba*, or whatever. There are many regional variations, and manufacturers often specialize in one noodle for which they have become famous. There are thus any number of different *soba*s or *udon*s, etc. Outside Japan, the variety is less, and the choice is easier.

Cooked noodles do *not* freeze well and must be used within 1 or 2 days of purchase; uncooked fresh *udon* noodles keep 2 weeks refrigerated and also freeze well; dried noodles keep indefinitely. Manufacturers of fresh cooked noodles in Japan often include concentrated noodle broth (to be mixed with hot water) and other seasonings in plastic packets, in cans, or in some form.

Before going on to some noodle recipes, a description of how to cook both freshly made and dried noodles will be helpful. If the package includes its own directions, follow them, or use this basic method:

TO COOK FRESH AND DRIED NOODLES

Bring about 2 quarts (2 L) unsalted water to a rolling boil in a large pot. There should be enough water and the pot should be big enough so that the noodles are not crowded and boiling water circulates around them—just as with any pasta. Add noodles to boiling water gradually so as not to stop the boiling entirely. Stir slowly to keep noodles from sticking to the bottom of the pot. Let water come to a full rolling boil again, then add 1 cup cold water. Repeat this 3–4 times, and cook until noodles are a bit tenderer than *al dente*. To test, remove a strand from the boiling water, run it under cold water, and bite into it. The noodle should be cooked through to the center (no hard core), but still quite firm. Test frequently to avoid overcooking. Drain noodles in a colander and rinse under cold running water, rubbing vigorously with the hands to remove surface starch.

To reheat cooked noodles, place in a colander or deep, handled sieve and plunge into a pot of boiling water just until heated. Separate strands by shaking the colander or sieve.

Noodles, if not served floating in a mild broth, are almost always eaten with a slightly stronger-flavored dipping sauce. Since both the broth (*kake-jiru*), literally "soup for pouring on," and dipping sauce (*tsuke-jiru*), freely rendered, "soup on the side" are standard recipes, they are included here. Take time to master the noodle broth (*kake-jiru*), for its flavor naturally affects the flavor of the whole dish, and an overseasoned broth as well as an insipid one can dim the experience of good noodles, homemade or otherwise.

Noodle Broth

(*Kake-jiru*) かけ汁

Used with *udon* and *soba* noodles. This recipe is a general guideline—change it to your taste.

8 cups

8⅓ cups *dashi*
2 tsps salt
3 Tbsps dark soy sauce
3 Tbsps light soy sauce

To prepare: In a large pot, bring *dashi* just to a boil over medium-high heat, and season with other ingredients. Remove and strain. Keep at a low simmer and use hot. You may prepare this noodle broth in advance, cool to room temperature, then refrigerate in a covered container in which it will keep up to 3 days.

2 Tbsps sugar
2 Tbsps *mirin*

When making broth to use with *soba* noodles, increase the quantity of dark soy sauce to taste.

Noodle Dipping Sauce
(*Tsuke-jiru*) つけ汁

Primarily for *soba* noodles.

3 cups

2½ cups *dashi*
½ cup plus 2 Tbsps dark soy sauce
4 Tbsps *mirin*
1 tsp sugar
1 ounce (30 g) (about 3 cups, loose) dried bonito flakes (*hana-katsuo*)

To prepare: In a medium-sized pot, mix all ingredients except bonito flakes and bring just to a boil over medium-high heat. Stir in the bonito flakes and immediately remove from heat. Wait about 10 seconds, till flakes are thoroughly soaked, and strain. Let liquid cool to room temperature to use.

You may prepare this dipping sauce in advance. In a covered container, it will keep several months refrigerated.

Noodles in Broth
(*Kake-udon*) かけうどん

This is one of the simplest noodle dishes. It consists of hot *udon* noodles in a deep bowl, almost covered with tasty broth, garnished with finely chopped green onion. A lunch or a filling snack.

4 servings

1 pound (450 g) dried *udon* noodles
4 generous Tbsps finely chopped green onion
4-6 cups NOODLE BROTH (see page 310)
seven-spice mixture (*shichimi*)

To prepare: Boil dried noodles according to directions on package, or follow the recipe above on page 310. Drain in a colander and rinse well with hands under cold running water to remove surface starch. Reheat cooked noodles by putting noodles in a colander or deep sieve and plunging into boiling water until heated.

Make NOODLE BROTH according to recipe immediately above, page 310. Keep at a simmer.

Rinse finely chopped green onion in a square of cheesecloth in cold water to rid onion of slight bitterness. Gently wring cloth with green onion to eliminate moisture.

To assemble and serve: Divide hot noodles into portions in warmed noodle *donburi* bowls, or large, deep soup bowls. Garnish with about 1 Tbsp finely chopped green onion. Ladle over 1 to 1½ cups simmering NOODLE BROTH (*kake-jiru*) and serve.

Sprinkle on seven-spice mixture (*shichimi*) to taste. Eat noodles with chopsticks or fork.

VARIATIONS: NOODLES IN THICK BROTH (*Ankake Udon*)
Prepare noodle broth as in previous recipe, and while simmering add 3 Tbsps *kuzu* starch or cornstarch mixed with 3 Tbsps water. Stir until broth thickens. Ladle hot thickened broth over noodles and garnish with 1 Tbsp chopped green onion and a slice of *kamaboko* (fish paste).

FOX NOODLES (*Kitsune Udon*) (color plate 14)
Noodles and broth are prepared in the usual manner. Calculate ½ cake thin deep-fried bean curd (*aburage*) per serving. Simmer *aburage* in a mixture of 8 parts *dashi* or water, 6 parts dark soy sauce, 2 parts *mirin*, 1 part sugar until most of liquid is absorbed. Top noodles with seasoned *aburage* and garnish with chopped green onion.

Noodles in a Basket

(*Zaru Soba*) ざるそば (color plate 14)

These chilled buckwheat noodles are traditionally served on basketwork "plates" or in square bamboo boxes with slatted bottoms, accompanied by a cup of clear, strong, cold dipping sauce. Sharp *wasabi* horseradish and finely chopped green onion are mixed into the dipping sauce as desired. A perfect meal for a hot and humid summer day, this is a universal favorite, and every region has its own way of serving it.

4 servings

½ **pound (225 g) dried buckwheat noodles (soba)**
2-3 cups NOODLE DIPPING SAUCE **(see page 311)**
about ¼ cup finely shred-cut, toasted *nori* seaweed

spicy condiments:

1 tsp grated *wasabi* horseradish

To prepare: Boil dried noodles in a large pot full of water, following package directions, or follow recipe on page 310. Remove noodles, plunge into cold water, then wash noodles briskly with the hands to eliminate surface starch. Drain and divide among 4 baskets (or ordinary plates, as long as the noodles are well drained).

Combine the ingredients for the NOODLE DIPPING SAUCE (page 311) in a medium-sized saucepan and bring to a simmer. Strain into a metal mixing bowl and force-cool by swirling that bowl in a larger one filled with water and ice cubes. Chill in refrigerator.

5 Tbsps finely chopped
  green onion
4 Tbsps grated giant
  white radish (*daikon-
  oroshi*)

noodle baskets (*zaru*)

Toast sheet of *nori* seaweed (see page 80) then cut the desired amount of fine shreds with scissors. Prepare spicy condiments. Rinse the finely chopped green onion in cheesecloth in cold water to eliminate bitterness.

To serve: Sprinkle *nori* shreds on each serving of noodles. Serve the dipping sauce in individual small bowls. Place spicy garnishes in serving dishes and let each diner help himself.

To eat, mix a dab *wasabi* horseradish and about 1 Tbsp of finely chopped green onion or grated *daikon* into the dipping sauce. Pick up noodles, dip into sauce, and eat. Chopsticks are the best implement to use here, but forks will work.

Noodles in the Pot

(*Nabeyaki Udon*) なべ焼きうどん

Nabeyaki udon is essentially a one-portion version of NOODLE SUKIYAKI (page 435). Use small flameproof casseroles. Hearty food for a cold day.

4 servings

1 pound (450 g) dried *udon*
  noodles
4 medium shrimp
1 cake fish paste (*kamaboko*)
  (optional)
4 fresh or dried *shiitake*
  mushrooms
12 stalks trefoil
4-6 cups noodle broth (*kake-
  jiru,* see page 310)
4 eggs

To prepare: Boil noodles as directed on package or follow basic directions given above on page 310. Rinse well with hands under cold water to remove surface starch.

Clean, shell, and devein shrimp, but leave tails attached. Cut *kamaboko* into slices about ¼ inch (¾ cm) thick. If using fresh *shiitake* mushrooms, just trim stems and notch caps with a decorative cross. If dried mushrooms are used, soften (see page 88) and trim, then notch caps and simmer in the same mushroom seasoning liquid as in SCATTERED SUSHI, TOKYO STYLE, page 448. (If mushrooms are very large, cut in half.) Wash trefoil and pat dry.

Prepare NOODLE BROTH according to recipe on page 310, above. Keep at a simmer.

To assemble and serve: Divide noodles into portions, placing them in the bottom of small casseroles. On top of the noodles arrange the other ingredients—shrimp, *kamaboko* slices, and trefoil. Ladle about 1 to 1½ cups hot NOODLE BROTH into each casserole. Cover casseroles and bring liquid to a boil over medium heat (about 4–5 minutes). With the back of a spoon, make a small nest in the noodles, crack open an egg, and gently drop raw egg into the nest. Re-cover and simmer until egg is cooked but yolk is soft. Do not cook egg until hard.

Serve immediately. Eat with chopsticks, or fork and spoon, or Chinese-style porcelain spoon.

VARIATIONS: Any number of other ingredients may be added: bite-sized pieces of chicken; green onions diagonally cut into 1½-inch (4-cm) lengths; and fresh spinach or edible chrysanthemum leaves instead of trefoil (avoid using both these greens together). If you use spinach or chrysanthemum, add to the casserole only after the broth has already begun to boil gently.

Pickling Vegetables
Tsukemono

Pickles are a vast domain in Japanese cuisine. There is a seemingly endless variety of both delicate and strong pickled foods, preserved in all sorts of ways, and they play an important role in the dietary life of the people. Rice and pickles are to the Japanese what bread and cheese are to the English, and French bread and wine to the French.

Pickling began in ancient times as a means of preserving food, and over the years pickles became an important part of the Japanese meal—in many cases the only food served besides rice. *Miso* soup, rice, and pickles were looked upon as a hearty repast, and in the northern provinces they still consume mounds of pickles for *oyatsu*—afternoon tea.

Now that prosperity reigns, however, young people have begun to think of pickles as an optional item on the menu, often dispensing with them altogether. But for the older generation, no meal, be it humble or a banquet, is complete without its final pickles, rather like dessert (or cheese) to the Westerner. Some pickles are said to aid digestion, especially of fried foods.

As a young impecunious reporter twenty-two years ago, I used to have very little money left at the end of the month, and the last five or six days I would eat in the company canteen, where one could get a large bowl of rice for 10 yen (then 36 cents) and a small one for half that. Strong yellow radish pickle (*takuan*) and chopped green onions were free. The onions were meant as a garnish for noodles, but I would buy a bowl of rice and cover it with both radish pickle and onions, flavored with lots of soy sauce—also free!

The special, characteristic "taste of home," exemplified by *miso* soup made from the local variety of fermented bean paste, is even more pronounced in the homemade pickle. For centuries, every home in Japan has had its stone-weighted pickle barrel, each with its very own characteristic flavor of rice-bran mash imparting a nostalgic aroma to the pickles. Nostalgic, that is, as far as the family members are concerned, but sometimes an aroma slightly repellent to others—especially visitors with fussy palates. Rice bran, the most common pickling medium, is quick to pick up surrounding odors, and home bran-mash tends to smack of the dank earth beneath the floorboards—the only convenient place in most houses for keeping the barrel, which must be stored somewhere dark and cool.

Pickles made professionally became increasingly popular for this very reason. Prepared in neutral mediums free from any "house" odors, storebought pickles were not only safe to offer guests, but gave rise to a nationwide competitiveness in producing pickles that are a specialty of each locality. Every region has its own celebrated kind of pickle, artistically packaged and sought after as elegant gifts to bring back from travels.

But you need not journey from region to region to taste the local specialties. Just wander through the food floor in any urban department store—usually the basement—to view and sniff. Barrels, crocks, jars, and cases are filled with pickles of every color and shape made from just about everything in Japan that is pickleable: some tightly packed in salty brine, others embedded in brown yeasty mash. The mixture of aromas surrounding the pickle counters is an experience in itself.

Vegetables most commonly pickled in Japan are Chinese cabbage, *daikon* radish, radish greens, cucumber, and eggplant. Eggplant—at its best from September to October—is the jewel in the pickle crown, so much so that the Japanese have a time-honored saying: "Feed not autumn eggplant to your daughter-in-law."

Kyoto is celebrated for its tasty vegetables of all kinds, and hence its pickles, especially *senmai-zuke*, paper-thin slices of giant turnip radish pickled with kelp to give it sweetness. There is almost no limit to what you can use. Western vegetables such as cauliflower, celery, and pimiento all make delicious pickles. During the war in Japan, when food was very scarce, we even pickled watermelon rind.

Fish and meat are pickled as well as vegetables, but the only fruit that is pickled almost stands in a category by itself. The *umeboshi*, or pickled "plum," was originally considered a medicine because of its healing and soothing properties in all kinds of stomach disorders. Added to gruel (*kayu*), it is the Japanese mother's cure-all. One or two *umeboshi* with a cup of tea after a meal refreshes the palate.

Pickled Plums

(*Umeboshi*) 梅干し

Though Japanese *ume* are usually called plums, they are, in fact, a species of apricot (*Prunus mume*; the common apricot is *Prunus armeniaca*). This is the same fruit used for PLUM LIQUEUR (page 470), but whereas the liqueur uses the fruit when it is hard and green, for pickling it should have turned yellow but not yet be sweet. This occurs in about mid June. Common apricots can be used as a substitute, and the same principles apply. There are as many variations in making *umeboshi* as there are villages in Japan. Here is one.

2-quart (2-L) jar

2¼ pounds (1 kg) *ume*,
    yellow but not sweet
½ cup *shōchū* (often sold as
    "white liquor")
¾ cup salt (200 g)
2⅕ pounds (1 kg) clean
    pebbles in cheesecloth
    bag, used as weight
2-quart (2-L) canning jar,
    sterilized
1 pound (450 g) red *shiso*
    leaves (green *shiso* will
    not substitute)
⅓ cup salt
½ cup *shōchū*
½ cup sugar

To prepare: Wash *ume* carefully, taking care not to injure or bruise. Wipe each fruit dry with a cloth. Place in bowl and add ½ cup *shōchū* and ¾ cup salt. Mix well. Place in jar. Put weight (pebbles in bag) on fruit, cover, and let rest 2–3 days. Liquid will increase.

Wash red *shiso* leaves and pat dry (the easiest way to do this is while leaves are still on the plant; wash entire plant). Place *shiso* leaves (stems removed) in bowl and add ⅓ cup salt. Knead leaves in salt vigorously. A dark liquid will be given off, and the leaves will greatly reduce in volume. Discard dark liquid.

Add 1 cup of the liquid from the *ume* jar to the kneaded *shiso* leaves. Gently knead leaves in this liquid, place leaves and liquid in jar and spread out on top of fruit. Replace weight, cover, and store in a cool, dark place about 1 month or more, until late July or early August, when you are sure of having 3 or 4 continuous days of hot, dry weather.

On a bright, clear day, remove fruit from liquid (keep liquid in jar) in the morning and sun-dry fruit all day. Squeeze liquid out of *shiso* leaves and dry those also. That evening, return fruit and leaves to liquid in jar. Repeat this drying procedure for 2–3 days. This enhances flavor and color and increases the life of the pickles, but is not necessary. When returning fruit to jar on the last day of drying, add ½ cup *shōchū* and ½ cup sugar gradually as plums go into jar. Place *shiso* leaves on top of plums, cover (do not weight), and let mature in a cool, dark place one more month. The pickled fruit is ready to eat in early September. Keeps indefinitely.

Pickling is done in various traditional ways. Some vegetables are pickled in a rice-bran mash, while others are treated in salt or rice vinegar or fermented bean paste (*miso*). Some are pickled under pressure—containers with pressure lids and weights are among Japanese pickle-making utensils. One kind of pickled sliced cucumber, which is very easy to make at home, takes only an hour to ripen in juices extracted from the vegetable itself by salt, while another kind—the famous *takuan* radish pickle—is perhaps better store-bought than homemade because it takes several months to ripen, all the while emitting a high odor.

Wheat bran is just as good for pickling as rice bran. Oatmeal—and even cornflakes—may be used as pickling media. Japanese pickles also vary in degree of "ripeness."

Use the pickle recipes below as models: they demonstrate the basic principles behind four very common pickle-making methods:

pickling in rice-bran mash (*nukamiso-zuke*)
pickling in dry rice bran (*nuka-zuke*)
salt-pickling (*shio-zuke*)
vinegar-pickling (*su-zuke*)

Do not be slavish about using only the vegetable ingredients listed below. Freely substitute the vegetables you would like to taste as pickles. You will find that most vegetables can be pickled in one of the ways demonstrated here if you apply the fundamental method.

Once you have started making any rice-bran mash pickle, you are committed to a brief daily attendance on the pickle crock: the rice-bran mash has to be stirred, or "disturbed," every 24 hours. It takes about 10 days for the mash to ripen, during which time your efforts are preparatory, without pickles. Thereafter, your mash crock will yield pickles daily, and the mash can, with the proper attention, last indefinitely, like a yoghurt culture.

To start, you need a fair-sized stoneware crock or glass vessel, deep and not too wide. A new Japanese wooden pickle tub, if you can find one, is perfect, but expensive! Even a small lidded plastic pail works well. In case you are shopping in Japan or in a Japanese provisions store, a *tsukemono-ki* is convenient—this is a plastic container with a screw-top pressure lid or a straight-sided crock that has a heavy stoneware drop-lid that fits down into the container. But such *tsukemono-ki* are small and do not produce large quantities of pickles. With a pickle-making tub or crock or bucket, a wooden drop-lid is weighted with a heavy stone. A round granite river or beach stone is excellent for this use. In the first recipe that follows, a weight is unnecessary. In Japan, rice bran is commonly sold at rice shops (*kome-ya*)—just ask for *nuka.* In the West, in oriental provisions stores or natural foods stores, it is sold packaged on the same shelf as grains and flours and is labeled either "rice bran" or "*nuka*." Any kind of vegetable may be pickled in the yeasty medium of rice-bran mash.

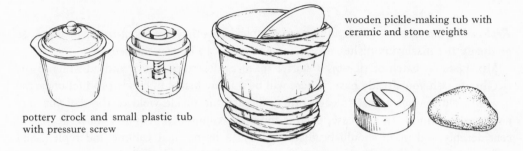

wooden pickle-making tub with ceramic and stone weights

pottery crock and small plastic tub with pressure screw

Rice-Bran Mash Pickles

(*Yasai no Nukamiso-zuke*) 野菜のぬか味噌漬け

to start the mash

4 pounds (1¾ kg) rice bran (*nuka*)

1 pound sea salt (or crushed rock salt)

1-2 Tbsps powdered mustard

½ cup beer

3 cups water, boiled and cooled

3 small dried red peppers, seeded

4-inch (10-cm) square giant kelp (*konbu*)

peel of 2 apples

½ tsp reduced iron (*kangentetsu*) (optional)

To prepare: Make sure the rice bran is absolutely dry. You may want to dry it briefly, stirring it in a large dry frying pan over medium-low heat for a few minutes. Do not brown or scorch it. Put in pickle crock.

Kneading the bran with your hands, mix in the salt, mustard, beer, and water. Mix well after each addition.

By the time you have mixed in the water, the bran will be pastelike. Tuck in red peppers, *konbu*, and apple peel, making sure they are distributed evenly through the mash. Add reduced iron (optional).

With one hand, dig deep into the mash and insert a few vegetables (these will not be eaten and need not be fresh), such as a leaf or two of Chinese cabbage, at the bottom of crock. Insert 2 or 3 more vegetables or leaves at other levels—that is, one in the middle, another nearer the top. Put lid on crock and place crock in a cool, dark place.

Let the vegetables pickle for 24 hours, then extract them and throw them away. Replace them with new vegetables (again, these need not be fresh). Follow this routine for 10 days. On the eleventh day, you can start making pickles to eat. At this time extract and discard apple peel. If, out of curiosity, you taste the vegetables pickled in the first few days, you will discover that they are "raw" tasting and very, very hot.

Keep crock in the cool and dark. Summer is a good time to make rice-bran mash pickles because the mash ferments quickly and vegetables are quickly pickled.

Replenishing the mash: Mash adheres to the pickles as they are taken from the crock, so gradually the mash diminishes in volume and needs to be replenished.

Mix ¼ to ½ batch of rice-bran starter mash as described above and add this to the rice-bran mash you already have. There will be a 1-day hiatus in pickle production as the new and old mashes adjust to each other: discard the pickle yield of the day you mix new mash with old. In any case, even if the mash volume seems not to have decreased considerably, old mash should be discarded by ½ its original volume and replenished with starter mash every 30 days from the start of edible pickle making.

Making pickles: Japanese vegetables commonly used are Chinese cabbage, eggplant, cucumber, green peppers, and so on. Wash vegetables and pat dry. With Chinese cabbage, cut off the bottom of the head, then gently separate leaves by hand, or cut base of head into quarters and then continue the cuts by gently pulling apart the quarters by hand. This way, the more delicate upper part of the leaves will not be unnecessarily shredded. With cucumber, eggplant, green peppers, etc., use whole or cut into large chunks. You can pickle 1 kind or several kinds of vegetables at once if your container is big enough. Vegetables should not be packed in the crock so closely that they are touching; all should be surrounded by about a ¾-inch (2-cm) layer of mash.

Before inserting vegetables into mash, rub with salt. This is not only for taste and color; it also allows mash flavor to penetrate the vegetables more easily—that is, it speeds up the pickling process. Bury completely in mash. Put lid on crock and keep in a dark cool place. Pickles will be ready in 24 hours.

What happens if you leave the vegetables in the mash to pickle for longer than 24 hours? If the mash is rather salty, there is no problem. In fact, there are some who love "old" pickles (*furu-zuke*). But the absolute maximum, with regard to time, is 1 month.

To serve, extract the day's yield and wash off sticky rice bran under cold running water. Pat dry. Chop or slice. Serve family style in a shallow bowl set at the center of the table, or set out in individual portions in small dishes at every place. The pickles arrive with hot rice as one of the final courses of the meal. You may season pickles with a few drops of soy sauce, if desired. Eat with chopsticks or fork.

Cabbage in Dry Rice Bran

(*Kyabetsu no Nuka-zuke*) キャベツのぬか漬け

This pickle takes a month to ripen. Use any sort of cabbage—green, red, or Chinese cabbage—or giant white radish (*daikon*) dried in the open air for

2 to 3 weeks, or turnips or rutabagas may be used. Use whole, or cut large vegetables into chunks that fit in your pickle crock.

1 head cabbage
4 pounds (1¾ kg) sea salt or crushed rock salt
4 pounds (1¾ kg) rice bran (*nuka*)
3 small dried red peppers, seeded
4-inch (10-cm) square giant kelp (*konbu*)

To prepare: Core cabbage, wash, and pat dry. Cut head into sixths or eighths.

Lay a section of cabbage in the bottom of the pickle crock. Next, sprinkle on a layer of sea salt or crushed rock salt. Cover with rice bran and continue with layers of cabbage, salt, and rice bran. In the process, tuck in at random the seeded red peppers and piece of dry *konbu*. Continue layering this way till you have used up all the cabbage (or other vegetable). Make sure to finish with a layer of rice bran. Place the drop-lid on the bran layer and weight it. A clean, round stone is the usual weight for pickle tub or crock. Set aside in a cool dark place and let ripen 30 days.

If the crock has a rather close-fitting lid and it is weighted, the pickles will keep during the cooler seasons of the year for 2 to 3 months. Summer is questionable.

To serve: Remove the quantity of pickles you need, wash off adhering rice bran under cold running water, pat dry, and chop or slice into bite-sized pieces. Serve family style or in individual pickle dishes. You may season with a few drops of soy sauce, if desired.

Takuan pickling is very similar to *nuka-zuke* pickling. *Takuan*, a great favorite of many, is a pungent, yellow pickle made from giant white radish (*daikon*). The 17th-century Buddhist priest Takuan is said to have invented and introduced this item into the Japanese diet. Even today, the sharp smell of *takuan* wafts around monastery kitchens just as fragrant incense does around the altars. Hot rice with *takuan* is as common on Japanese tables as bread and butter in America.

To make *takuan*, large just-harvested *daikon* are hung in the cool, dry, autumn shade for 2 or 3 weeks, prepickled in salt, then finally pickled in dry rice bran and salt. *Daikon* are prepared for *takuan* only once a year; the pickle takes 2 to 3 months to ripen and keeps until the next year.

Salt-Pickled Chinese Cabbage

(*Hakusai no Shio-zuke*) 白菜の塩漬け

Excellent for cucumber. Peel, slice lengthwise, and seed large cucumbers.

20 pounds (10 kg) Chinese cabbage
4 pounds (2 kg) sea salt

To prepare: Cut off the bottoms of cabbages and with your hands gently separate heads into lengthwise sections (sixths or eighths). Wash sections under cold running water and pat dry.

Sprinkle salt on each section and rub in salt by hand, lay cabbage in the crock, packing it in tightly, (one convenient method is to alternate cabbage tops with bottoms). Arranging the sections this way also ensures that each layer will be of uniform depth. Sprinkle a generous handful of salt over each completed layer of cabbage. Continue packing in layers. End with a thick layer of salt.

Cover with a drop-lid and weight. Remove to a cool dark place. Within 24 hours, a ring of water should appear around the edges of the lid. This is a sign that the pickling process is underway. Let stand, undisturbed, 2 or 3 more days before eating. The maximum amount of time these pickles can stand in the brine before spoiling is approximately 2 to 3 months during the cool part of the year. In summer, they are a little more difficult to keep without refrigeration.

To serve: Remove the quantity of pickles you need from the crock, wash well under running water. Squeeze out extra moisture by pressing tightly in your hands. Do not wring. Chop coarsely and serve in individual pickle dishes in a mound. Serve with rice course. You may season with a few drops soy sauce, if desired.

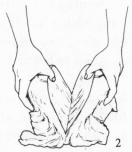

1, 2. cut base of Chinese cabbage into quarters and pull apart by hand

3. sprinkle layer of salt in bottom of pickle tub or crock

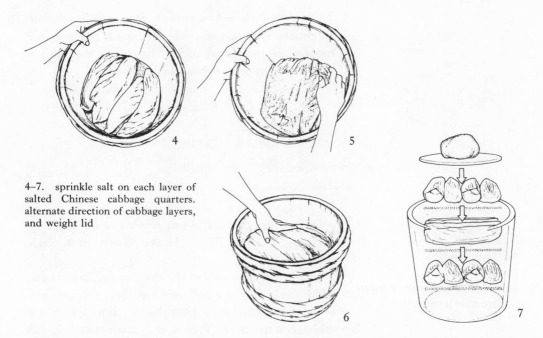

4–7. sprinkle salt on each layer of salted Chinese cabbage quarters. alternate direction of cabbage layers, and weight lid

Note: This method of salt-pickling also works particularly well with mustard greens.

Quick Turnip Pickles

(*Kabu no Sokuseki-zuke*) かぶの即席漬け

An example of "instant" salt-pickling. It takes only an hour for these pickles to ripen, and they will keep, covered, in the refrigerator for the better part of a week. Also appropriate for cucumber sliced in thin wafers. Peel and seed large cucumbers.

12 medium turnips
5 heaping Tbsps salt
4-inch (10-cm) piece giant kelp (*konbu*)
1-inch (2½-cm) square *yuzu* citron or lemon rind

To prepare: Cut off greens from turnips and reserve. Wash turnips, peel, then cut into very fine julienne strips. Wash greens, dry, then chop finely.

Put turnip strips with finely chopped greens into a bowl and sprinkle with salt. Table salt is fine. Knead with your hands and mix thoroughly to draw water out of vegetable. In less than a minute, a fair amount of liquid will be produced. Discard this liquid.

Add the dry *konbu* and a 1-inch (2½-cm) square *yuzu* citron or lemon rind. Let stand, lidded and with a light weight, 1 hour at room temperature.

To serve: Pick out a portion from the bowl with chopsticks or fork and shake off liquid. Arrange in a mound on individual pickle dish. You may season with a few drops of soy sauce, if desired.

Vinegar-Pickled Cabbage
(*Kyabetsu Su-zuke*) キャベツ酢漬け

¼ **head cabbage**
5 **cups rice vinegar**
2 **Tbsps salt**
4-5 **Tbsps sugar**
2 **cups water**
1-**inch (2½-cm) square** *yuzu*
   citron or lemon rind

To prepare: Core and wash cabbage, pat as dry as possible with a towel. Cut into about 1- × -2-inch (2½- × -5-cm) chunks. Place chunks loosely in a pickle crock.

In a saucepan combine the rice vinegar, salt, sugar, and water. Bring to a boil over high heat, stirring once or twice. Immediately pour boiling liquid over the cabbage in the crock. Tuck in the *yuzu* citron or lemon rind. Cover immediately with a drop-lid and weight it. Remove to a cool dark place and wait 2 days before eating.

To serve: Cut or chop chunks into bite-sized pieces. Serve family style or put individual portions into small dishes. Season with a few drops soy sauce, if desired. Keeps refrigerated 1–2 months.

Sweets and Confections
Okashi

Fruit is the "dessert" in a Japanese meal. The Western practice of serving a sweet confection as the last course of the meal does not exist in Japan. If, however, the meal is a formal one, after it is over, sweets are served with whisked, powdered tea (*matcha*, the tea ceremony tea) to complement the flavor of the tea itself. But rather than being a part of the meal, these sweets are, properly speaking, detached from it.

Normally, sweets—more properly, tea-sweets (*chagashi*)—are served with *bancha* or *sencha* leaf tea, or, on formal occasions, a tea-sweet is eaten before drinking tea ceremony tea. Such tea-sweets, whatever their ingredients may be, are made to resemble flowers, fruits, and other shapes evocative of the season.

Today, Western confections—cakes, pies, chocolates, candies, cookies—served with black tea or coffee have by and large replaced their Japanese counterparts, at least in the cities.

There are three general categories of Japanese sweets:

1. "Raw" confections (*namagashi*): As the name implies, such sweets are ones that do not preserve well. This category includes delicate, fresh jellies and pastes and doughs made of various starches or *mochi*, formed into "dumplings," often in combination with sweet bean paste. Confections included here in this category are, for example, OHAGI, CHERRY BLOSSOM MOCHI, and RED-BEAN JELLY.

2. "Semiraw" confections (*han-namagashi*). These confections are made to keep longer than the "raw" ones and are often associated with a region of Japan and contain ingredients special to that region. The various kinds of *yōkan* (see page 463), but not the lighter *mizu-yōkan* (RED-BEAN JELLY), and types of *manjū* (steamed "buns" with usually a sweet bean paste filling) are in this category, which is quite large. In this book, SWEET BEAN "GONGS" is an example.

3. "Dry" confections (*higashi*): The sweets in this catetory come closest to what one would call candies. In this category also are nonsweets, such as rice crackers (*senbei*) flavored with salt, soy sauce, *miso*, and the like.

A BRIEF HISTORY OF JAPANESE SWEETS

It was long the custom in Japan to eat two meals a day, and, in between, to eat fruit, either fresh or dried. Pears, peaches, apricots (*ume*), apples, strawberries, and grapes have all been eaten since earliest days. Dried persimmons are the most common type of dried fruit. The word for confectionery in Japanese—*kashi*—derives from the word for fruit, *kajitsu*, and once referred only to fruit. Almost the same Chinese character is used in both cases, and its pronunciation, *ka*, is identical. The *shi* in *kashi* means "seed."

The confections introduced to Japan from the Asian continent in the Nara period (645–781) were known as "Chinese fruit" at the time. They were the precursors of Japanese sweets (*wagashi*) and consisted of ground grains or soybeans, salted, kneaded, and fried in oil.

Sugar was also introduced into Japan in the Nara period. It is said to have been first shipped over in 754 by the famous Chinese Buddhist priest Ganjin. The sugar of those days was black, and was made by boiling and drying the juice of sugar cane. But for centuries sugar was a luxury used only occasionally by members of the aristocracy as a cure for chest conditions. It was not until the Muromachi period (1392–1572) that sugar was used by more than a tiny segment of the population, and not until the Meiji period (1868–1912) that its use spread among the common people.

In the Heian period (782–1184), confections came to be served at various ceremonies and feasts and were used as offerings to both Shinto gods and Buddhist deities. To this day, in the vicinity of many temples and shrines, sweets special to the locality are still made according to the forms and methods handed down from centuries past, a vestige of this Heian period custom.

What were offerings to the gods and deities in the Heian period became food exclusively for the upper classes in the following centuries. And, as the tea ceremony developed and flourished, such confections came to be eaten with tea and to find their way into the kitchens of the common people.

The Momoyama period (1573–1615) is the time when European desserts such as sponge cake and cookielike and candylike sweets, made of sugar, eggs, and flour, were brought into Japan by the Portuguese and Dutch traders who dropped anchor at Hirado and Nagasaki in Kyushu. These Western desserts were known as "southern barbarian sweets" (*namban-gashi*) and had a considerable influence on Japanese confectionery.

Chocolate, however, was not introduced into Japan until after 1868, in the first years of the Meiji period. Until this time, only sweets that complemented the flavor of green tea were the ones to catch on in Japan.

In the eighteenth and nineteenth centuries, Japanese sweets split into two general types. Confections made in Kyoto, the imperial capital, reflected the refinement of this ancient city and its emphasis on understatement. The sweets made in Edo (now Tokyo), the shogunal capital, displayed the vigor and "townsman" culture of that urban center. Both regional types split further into high-class or quality confectionery, known simply as *wagashi*, and popular or cheap sweets, *dagashi*. These distinctions still exist.

The majority of ordinary Japanese sweets contain sweet bean paste—*an*. Consequently, the quality of the sweet bean paste largely determines the quality of the sweets.

On a few occasions in the year, sweet bean paste might be made at home, for example, at the spring and autumn equinoxes, when OHAGI (page 462) is eaten, and in winter for the warming qualities of good ZENZAI (page 464). Otherwise, *an* is made by Japanese confectioners, whose professional cooks prepare *an* according to the special recipe of their shop or region. Most neighborhoods, in fact, have their local confectioner(s), where fresh, seasonal confections are sold.

Sweet bean paste is made by boiling some types of beans, usually *azuki* beans (red beans). Sweet pastes may be made of sweet potatoes and other materials as well. There are two types of sweet red-bean paste—the smooth, pureed type is known as *koshi-an*, and the "chunky" type, known as *tsubushi-an*. The latter has the beans either intact or partially crushed. Pureed *an* also may be made from an instant, powdered form of *an* called *sarashi-an*.

Pureed Sweet Red-Bean Paste

(*Koshi-An*) こしあん

makes 2 cups (450 g)

1 cup (180 g) *azuki* beans
1½ cups sugar
pinch salt

To prepare: Wash *azuki* beans and place in large saucepan full of water. Bring just to a boil, then drain and discard water.

Add 5 cups water to pan containing beans and bring to boil rapidly. When water starts boiling, reduce heat to low, cover pot, and simmer beans slowly till soft.

When beans are soft, pour pot water into a bowl. Place a sieve over the bowl, pour beans onto the sieve mesh and mash (the palm of your hand is excellent for this job) so that the pulp is strained through into the water but the bean skins remain on the sieve.

Pour the watery pulp mixture into a cotton bag. Squeeze out all the water. What remains in the bag is unsweetened, pureed *an*.

Put the unsweetened *an* in a saucepan. Add sugar, place over low heat, and stir with wooden paddle or spoon, using only a back-and-forth stroke. If the paste is stirred with a circular motion, it will lose its luster. When the paste is nearly as thick as *miso*, turn off the heat. Add salt and mix well.

Instant Pureed Sweet Red-Bean Paste
(*Koshi-An made with Sarashi-An*)インスタントこしあん

makes about 4 cups (480 g)

1 cup (144 g) *sarashi-an*
1½ cups water
1½ cups sugar
pinch salt

To prepare: Place *sarashi-an* in a bowl, add a generous amount of boiling water, and leave for a while to eliminate any odor resulting from the dehydration process.

When the solid *an* has settled to the bottom of the bowl, remove and discard the liquid above it, being careful not to disturb the fine puree.

Add boiling water once again, leave for a while, then pour mixture into a cotton bag and squeeze out moisture.

Remove *an* from the bag and place in a saucepan with the sugar. Over low heat, stir mixture until thick but still softer than *miso*. Add pinch of salt and stir.

Chunky Sweet Red-Bean Paste
(*Tsubushi-An*) つぶしあん

makes 2 cups (450 g)

1 cup (180 g) *azuki* **beans**
1 cup sugar
pinch salt

To prepare: Wash beans and place in large saucepan full of water. Bring just to a boil, then drain and discard water.

Add about 3 cups water to beans in pan and simmer over medium heat, covered, until beans are very soft.

Add more water when necessary to prevent dehydration, but water should be almost entirely reduced when beans are done. (At this point, the beans are simply boiled *azuki* and can be used in any recipe that needs this ingredient.)

Add sugar and stir with wooden paddle or spoon over low heat. The beans are so soft that some will disintegrate while stirring. You want a thick mixture in which the beans are half-crushed. Add the salt and mix well. The bean paste should be softer than *miso*.

Tea and Saké

As everybody knows, green tea (*ocha*) and *saké* (so-called rice wine) are the national beverages of Japan.

A great deal has been written about the history of tea, a drink that originated in China several thousand years ago and eventually spread throughout the world. The Chinese name for it is *ch'a*, and many a British Tommy who served in neighboring India still calls his afternoon drink a "cuppa char." It is the South China dialect version *t'e* that gave birth to the word "tea" —pronounced "tay" on its introduction into just pre-Queen Anne seventeenth century England. Alexander Pope observed in his famous rhyme about the royal palace of Hampton Court:

> Here thou, great Anna! whom three realms obey,
> Dost sometimes counsel take—and sometimes tea.

Tea became known in Japan around the eighth century, long before it was exported from China to Europe. The Japanese adopted the standard Chinese name but customarily preface their *cha* with an honorific *o*, which now conveniently distinguishes their "green" tea from *kōcha*, the name given to the "black" tea drunk almost everywhere in the world, and also in Japan.

It is strange that it should be in these two island nations, England and Japan—half a globe apart—that this Chinese beverage should have taken its strongest hold. In England the tea ritual is a deep-seated part of the daily routine and almost a religion, while in Japan it *is* a religion—the vehicle of the spiritual discipline of Zen Buddhism's *chadō*, the Way of Tea—as well as being an indispensable part of everyday life.

There are many kinds of green tea in Japan. The sort that is freely dispensed at restaurants and drunk in offices and factories at breaktime is not the sort that is served to guests at home, and so-called guest tea is not the sort whisked to a froth in the tea ceremony.

When tea was first brought to Japan, it was regarded as a medicine and a stimulant. Its use was limited primarily to the priesthood and the aristocracy

—to those with access to the court. In this early era, leaves were crushed and packed into forms to make bricks, like the brick tea used in Mongolia and Russia today. To make tea, the brick was scraped, and shavings were dropped into water, which was then vigorously boiled. A far cry from the dictates of powdered tea, for which water that is too hot will ruin the entire effort.

It appears that cultivation of tea plants on a large scale failed in these early centuries, so tea remained an exclusive novelty. The beverage was reintroduced in its powdered form (*matcha*) in the twelfth century, when it was brought back with Japanese monks returning from China, where they had been studying Buddhism. By this time, Japanese agricultural techniques were advanced enough to include tea cultivation, and tea flourished at the same rate as Zen. Powdered tea was used mainly by priests as a stimulant—to keep them awake during all-night prayer. Very slowly, rules and etiquette evolved, many elements of tea drinking being rooted in the precepts of Zen. Tea drinking in the contemplative style spread gradually to the aristocracy and the warrior class.

In the late sixteenth century, leaf tea—*sencha*, in fact—was imported from China. It was simpler to make than powdered green tea and relatively economical, so this sort of tea became popular among townsmen and commoners. At the same time, the ritual of *matcha*-style tea-making became a cultural institution, and the Way of Tea was regarded as basic cultural training for the upper classes.

Japanese tea is "green," whereas the teas of India and China and the type that is generally drunk in the West are "black." With a very few variations in agricultural techniques, the tea bushes of Japan are the same as the tea bushes grown in the hills behind Colombo or in the shadow of the Himalayas in Darjeeling. What makes Japanese tea green and other Asian teas black is the processing.

In Japan, once leaves are picked, they are immediately steamed. If tea is not given this treatment, an enzyme in the leaf ferments and the leaves turn black. This steaming process is one the Indians and Sri Lankans (formerly Ceylonese) do not follow. But if the enzyme is destroyed, the leaves stay green, and the result is green tea.

Japanese tea can be divided into two major categories: leaf tea and powdered tea. For leaf tea, steamed tea leaves are crumbled while still moist; as they dry they twist into shredlike particles on average about ¼ inch (¾ cm) long. For powdered tea, steamed leaves are dried flat and later ground into a fine, light, green dust.

Leaf tea is the most ordinary drink. It is quick to make, and brewing requires very little skill. Powdered tea is more expensive, and whisking it into the proper frothiness is not as easy as making everyday tea. Powdered tea (*matcha*) is the drink of the tea ceremony, which involves a complex ritual and etiquette. It also may be enjoyed simply as a beverage.

If you visit a traditional teashop in Japan, you will see that leaf tea is available in numerous grades at varying prices. All leaf tea falls into one of the following broad grades. Price further depends on the quality of the leaf within each grade.

Bancha (番茶), so-called coarse green tea, is the lowest grade, but it is the tea that is consumed in the greatest quantities. In restaurants, *bancha* in handleless mugs (*yunomi*) is always served free of charge when patrons take their seats—something to sip while reading the menu—and fresh tea is poured once the meal is underway. In factory and in office, *bancha* is the beverage that employees drink at breaktime—there are even *bancha* vending machines. *Bancha* is also popular at home because of its economical price.

> For *bancha* for 4 to 5: Warm a large teapot with hot water, empty it and put about 3 rounded Tbsps of *bancha* leaves into the pot. Add about 3 cups freshly drawn *boiling* water. Let steep about 2 to 3 minutes, then pour into warmed mugs. Drain the pot to the last drop (if left to steep too long, the leaves make the tea bitter). Strain or not, as you like. Most Japanese teapots have an internal strainer at the base of the spout, but this varies in effectiveness. If more tea is required, you may use the leaves for a second batch. After that, discard soaked leaves and use fresh.

Bancha is often described as coarse because it is made from larger, more mature leaves than any other tea, and leaves are cut to include even stems. The poorer the grade of *bancha*, the more dried stems and twigs in the tea. Coarse green tea is often roasted to heighten flavor. Such tea is known as *hōji-cha* (焙じ茶, literally "roasted tea"), and the leaf is ebony brown. *Hōji-cha* brews a tawny brown beverage with a deep smoky taste that is different from the yellowish, slightly astringent tea that plain *bancha* yields. *Hōji-cha* is palatable when cold, but green *bancha* turns bitter when it cools.

You can toast green *bancha* at home to make *hōji-cha*. Place dry leaves in a dry, heavy-bottomed frying pan and toast over high heat till browned and aromatic, about 2–3 minutes for ½ cup leaves. Shake the pan constantly to keep leaves from scorching.

Another type of *bancha* is *genmai-cha* (玄米茶), or "rice tea." This sort of tea consists of *bancha* mixed with grains of roasted and popped rice. It is not difficult to recognize *genmai-cha*; the popped rice looks like miniature popcorn in a green bed of leaves. *Genmai-cha* is brewed exactly as *bancha* is. It has a slightly nutty flavor owing to the presence of the rice.

Most *bancha* is good to drink with meals because it complements the taste of food (not so much attention has to be paid to the taste of this sort of tea itself). At the same time it refreshes the palate. *Bancha* is even drinkable alongside *saké*. It is customary to serve cups of both during long banquets.

Sencha (煎茶), literally "infused tea," is good, medium-grade green tea. The leaves that go into *sencha* are tenderer and younger than those used for *bancha*. The leaf-picking has been done with greater care so that there are no stems or twigs. Naturally, *sencha* is more expensive and better than *bancha*; it is "guest tea."

Sencha is appreciated and is not drunk as a thirst-quencher like *bancha*. It is made and served in smaller quantities—in special small pots (*kyūsu*)—and drunk from small handleless pottery or porcelain cups. *Sencha* is found as the complimentary drink only at exclusive restaurants with free-spending clientele (most likely *sushi* shops, because *sencha* tastes very good with raw fish dishes). In offices or factories or places of business, *sencha* is offered to visitors of note. In homes, it is often brewed to impress visiting relatives. There is also a *sencha* ritual, but it is not as celebrated as the powdered tea (*matcha*) ceremony.

Sencha for 4 to 5: Warm a small teapot (*kyūsu*) with hot water, empty it and put about 2 rounded tsps of *sencha* leaves into the pot. Pour in about 1 cup hot water that has been allowed to drop from the boiling point to about 175°F (80°C). (Remove water from the heat and allow to stand a bit to reach this lower temperature.)

Let tea steep for 1 minute. First pour a little tea into each warmed cup, repeat this procedure again, then "fill" each cup. Do not fill cups brim full; the proper level is about ⅔ cup. Drain the pot to the last drop. If more tea is required, you may use the leaves a second time.

Gyokuro (玉露), or "jewel dew," is the best leaf tea. Young buds of ancient bushes are coaxed into extreme tenderness by special growing techniques. In early spring when buds first appear, each old bush is enclosed in a slatted bamboo blind so that the sun's rays are shut out. Leaves are picked about 2 weeks after this enclosure, when they are about ¾ inch (2 cm) long; no second or third picking is carried out. The result of enclosing the bushes is fewer leaves; this, plus the single picking means a small crop. Rare and expensive, *gyokuro* is extremely fragrant and tender. Even more than *sencha*, this tea is drunk a little at a time purely for its flavor; it is not meant to slake thirst. The first taste of highly aromatic *gyokuro* might seem a bit strong, but it mellows on the tongue. If this tea is brewed in water that is too hot, it will taste strong and sour. Dried *gyokuro* leaves are long and thin "needles," about ½ inch (1½ cm) long, with a clear, uniform deep green color. No stems or other plant particles should be present in the dried tea. Like *sencha*, *gyokuro* is brewed in small quantities in small pots (*kyūsu*) and served in small handleless cups.

Gyokuro for 4 to 5: Warm a very small teapot (*kyūsu*) with hot water, empty it and put about 5 heaping tsps *gyokuro* leaves into the pot. Pour in about ½ cup hot water that has been allowed to drop from the boiling point to about 120°F (50°C)—this temperature is warm, not hot. (Remove water from the heat and allow to stand to reach the temperature desired.)

Let tea steep for about 1½ minutes. Disturb the leaves in the pot by rocking the teapot once or twice. Pour into warmed small teacups. Drain the pot to the last drop. If more tea is required, you may use the leaves a second time, but add water that is slightly *hotter* than that used for the first infusion.

The other major category of tea is powdered tea, known as *matcha* (抹茶) or *hiki-cha* (碾き茶). Both names mean roughly the same thing—"pulverized tea." There are grades of powdered tea, but the grade distinctions are best left to the connoisseur: it is enough to know that powdered tea is the famous ceremonial beverage, drunk only on occasion, whipped to a frothy green in individual teabowls.

Matcha (or *hiki-cha*) is ground from the same tender leaves that are cultivated for *gyokuro*, the finest of all the leaf teas. Instead of crushing the steamed, fresh-picked leaves and letting them curl into tight shred-like shapes, the steamed leaves are dried flat. Traditionally, the dried whole leaves were sealed in airtight containers to preserve them, being ground to a very fine powder with special mortar and pestle only as needed. But tea-grinding is a laborious task, and these days *matcha* is commercially ground.

Matcha is made by the portion, not by the pot. Volumes have been written on the Zen-oriented art and philosophy underlying the making of powdered tea, so let the following suffice as a brief description of the actual process:

Warm a Japanese teabowl, or large bowllike cup, with hot water. At the same time, rest the bamboo tea whisk in hot water so that the green color of the tea will not soak into the bamboo pores and stain the whisk.

Empty and dry the teabowl. Put about 2 level tsps of powdered green tea into the bowl and pour in about ½ cup hot water. Beginning slowly, then gaining speed, whip the tea into a frothy green with the tea whisk. This tea may be made thick and frothy or thin and liquidy, as one desires, by using more or less powdered tea, judging the amount needed from the start.

A sweet of some sort—a red-bean-paste cake, a "dried" candy (*higashi*), or one of the numerous confections made for tea—usually precedes tea drinking to complement the somewhat dry, slightly bitter flavor of the tea. A serving of whisked *matcha* is drunk in several long sips (usually 3), tea-bowl held in cupped hands, till the entire portion is consumed.

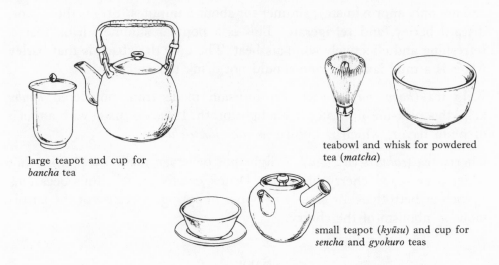

large teapot and cup for
bancha tea

teabowl and whisk for powdered
tea (*matcha*)

small teapot (*kyūsu*) and cup for
sencha and *gyokuro* teas

Neither sugar nor milk nor lemon is served with Japanese tea. Leaf and powdered teas are drunk plain. Sweet cakes are usually served with or before tea, however, to complement the drink. In fact, many Japanese sweets were invented precisely to go along with green tea. Most such tea sweets do not combine well with, say, milk, soft drinks, or coffee.

The secret in making good Japanese tea is to pay attention to the water temperature and to steeping time. If water is hotter than required, it destroys the tea flavor. If the steeping is too long, the taste of the tea will be so strong that your lips will pucker. Never sprinkle tea leaves into a water-filled pot and attempt to boil tea—this is the recipe for certain failure.

Japanese teas are sometimes iced. Roasted *hōji-cha* is all right at room temperature, and barley water is customarily chilled (an infusion of roasted barley—a summer drink). Even *gyokuro* may be steeped in room-temperature water in summer.

Loose tea and powdered tea should be purchased a little at a time. Stored in airtight containers in a cool, dark, dry place, tea keeps fresh a few months. Green tea in teabags, the form in which Japanese tea too often appears abroad, gets stale quickly. However, loose tea freezes well and can be kept in the freezer for about a year. Let leaves come to room temperature before brewing; it only takes about 10 minutes for a few Tbsps to thaw.

Several other beverages have the suffix "tea" (*cha*) attached to their names, but they are infusions made with things other than tea.

Barley water (*mugi-cha*; 麦茶). Roasted barley can be brewed to make a refreshing chilled summer drink. To about 2 quarts (2 L) boiling water, add about ½ cup roasted barley (these amounts depend on many factors and are only approximate); simmer for about 5 minutes. Strain the liquor, discard barley, and refrigerate. This is a popular summer drink that is refreshing and effectively combats heat. The only drawback is that barley water is a mild laxative; one should not drink too much.

Kelp tea (*kobu-cha*; 昆布茶). An infusion made from powdered *konbu* kelp, this pick-me-up tastes like a light broth. It also is made with a touch of plum flavor, which is known as *ume kobu-cha*.

Cherry tea (*sakura-yu*; 桜湯). A light hot beverage made by pouring hot water over salted cherry blossoms. Drunk chiefly on felicitous occasions —such as betrothals, or simply in honor of spring—because of the auspicious symbolism of the cherry.

SAKÉ

Saké, pronounced "sah-ké" (*ke* as in "ken"), and generally given the honorific prefix *o*—especially in polite conversation—is both the name of Japan's national alcoholic beverage *and* the general word for all alcoholic drinks. The more precise term for Japan's so-called rice wine is *Nihon-shu*, "Japanese sprits."

Saké is probably Japan's most ancient beverage. Stories of how this drink of the gods was first brewed are part of myth, and even today *saké* has a profound role in native Shinto belief. In households, tiny cups of *saké* are set before domestic shrines at festive times and on certain days. In the Shinto wedding rite, by which most couples are joined, it is the exchange of cups and drinking of *saké* that seals the marriage.

The *saké* that the Japanese of antiquity knew is certainly not the same as the clear beverage (15–17 percent alcohol) that is produced today. Reserved for nobles and priests in the ninth and tenth centuries, *saké* was thick and milky or yellow in color. Even in the late eighteenth century and early nineteenth century, when the brewing process had been greatly refined, the alcoholic content was quite low. Only in the last two hundred years, with peace, the growth of the country's economy, and the rise of a merchant class and an urban culture did *saké* become the universal drink.

It is difficult to describe *saké* to those who have never seen or drunk it.

First of all, it is fragrant and colorless. Its taste is . . . well . . . its own. Government agencies abroad do not know quite how to categorize it: under U.S. tariff laws, imported *saké* is taxed as a wine (its 15–17 percent alcohol content is similar to the 10–14 percent alcohol content of grape wines), but internal revenue taxes it like a beer, presumably because the raw material —grain—and method of fermentation are analogous to those used in making beer. If wine is defined as the product of fermentation of fruit sugars, then *saké* certainly is not a wine.

For good *saké*, there are two requirements: high-quality rice and pure water. Though *saké* is made throughout the Japanese archipelago, it is widely held that some places are better than others for *saké* production—Nada near Kobe, for instance, where fresh rivers tumble through granite canyons of the Rokko Mountains, or Fushimi, near the rich Kansai rice bowl, also with sources of pure water, or Akita, where high-quality rice is produced.

Saké is made by inoculating steamed white rice with a special mold (*kōji kabi*; *Aspergillus oryzae*), allowing fermentation to occur, and then refining. It takes about 45 to 60 days to produce *saké*, from start to finish. And, there is no aging period involved; *saké* is good to drink as soon as it is made, and some think that it is best within 3 months of bottling.

Saké has no vintage years. It is best drunk within the year it is bottled. Aging in no way enhances the flavor. In fact, *saké* may well be described as alive, because any number of harsh conditions can "kill" it. Heat and sunlight can destroy good *saké*, so store full bottles in a cool, dark place. And, since it is a fermented product, not a distilled liquor, once a bottle is opened, it should be drunk reasonably quickly.

All *saké* sold in Japan is government graded for taste, color, and aroma regardless of place of origin. The grades are:

tokkyū	特級	special class
ikkyū	一級	first class
nikyū	二級	second class

There is also a "super-special" category called *chōtokkyū* (超特級), but this is not usually found on the market. Strange to say, these grades are entirely arbitrary! *Nikyū saké* may be quite good; second class does not necessarily mean inferior quality. Because the production volume for the highest classes of *saké* is predetermined, some very good *saké*, typically that produced in small quantities by small local manufacturers, is ranked as *nikyū*. *Saké* also comes sweet and "dry"—*ama-kuchi* (甘口) and *kara-kuchi* (辛口). The sensitivity required to distinguish between these two involves a small amount of experience and the opportunity to compare types.

Relative sweetness or "dryness" is the main thing to consider when you buy *saké* in Japan. The best *saké*, made from the finest rice and purest water, is somewhat sweet in its natural state. Making it "dry" is an artificial process.

As to the bewildering choice of brands, it is impossible to say which one is best. Some restaurants have two or three available, but the best establishments normally serve but one—that which the proprietor likes best himself. *Saké* exported to the United States and other countries is dependable medium-grade liquor. Japan is eager to find a market abroad for its *saké*, and brewers have chosen their export *saké* with care.

Saké comes in several standard-sized bottles. The 1.8-liter (half-gallon; *isshō*) size may look huge, but if you are at all familiar with Japanese-style entertaining and Japanese cooking, you will understand why this is the most popular size of all. If you are buying *saké* for the first time or only for kitchen use, the 25-ounce (720-mL; *yon-gō*) bottle, about the size of a wine bottle, and the 30-ounce (900-mL; *go-gō*) size are convenient.

The pattern of *saké*-drinking among the Japanese may not be exactly what you expect. A bottle of *saké* is not taken out every time a meal is served. In some countries in the West, wine is an inseparable part of the meal. A wine should harmonize with the food, and must be selected carefully and from experience.

Saké presents no such problems of connoisseurship. The variety of grades and flavors does not approach the bewildering complexity of wine. Besides complementing Japanese food, *saké* is also enjoyed for itself. It is drunk at such typical male gatherings as company parties or with colleagues stopping off for a drink on the way home; it may be a before-dinner cocktail or a nightcap; but most often it is accompanied by something to eat, whether a quick nibble or something more elaborate. Like cocktail snacks, many special side dishes—called *saké no sakana* or *otsumami*—have been devised to nibble while *saké*-imbibing.

Saké is sometimes drunk cold but more often warmed in serving bottles called *tokkuri* before being poured out into small cups (*sakazuki*). Made of

two *saké* bottle and cup styles

stoneware or porcelain, some small *tokkuri* are often mistaken by non-Japanese for bud vases. *Saké*-serving sets, with a pair of *tokkuri* and a number of small cups (the Japanese number is 5, though export sets may have 6), are sold in most Japanese goods shops at reasonable prices. Otherwise use liqueur glasses.

To warm *saké*, put the *tokkuri* in a hot water bath over a very low flame. It will be sufficiently heated in several minutes to 108–122°F (42–50°C). For "dry" *saké*, the optimum temperature is 108–113°F (42–45°C), and for sweet *saké*, 113–122°F (45–50°C). Such fine differentiation is mainly of abstract interest—few people pay much attention. But some experience is necessary to judge the right temperature of *saké*. Perhaps the best test is to drink a bit.

Heating *saké* does nothing to its chemical composition—it does not make it stronger or weaker. What it does is release the bright rice fragrance. And, being close to body temperature, the alcohol in warmed *saké* is absorbed quickly into the blood. Heated *saké* that has cooled loses its flavor and can only be used for cooking. Warmed *saké* is the most popular form of this beverage. Cool *saké* is often poured out from cask, barrel, or bottle and served in small square cedarwood boxes (a premodern unit of measure); such *masu-zaké* comes with a small mound of salt on one corner of the box and is drunk like tequila, all in one go.

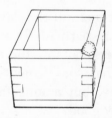

salt accompanies *saké* served in small wooden measures (*masu-zaké*); a taste of salt before drinking brings out the sweetness of the *saké*

With *saké* cups normally being small—a sip or two at the most—when drinking goes on, there is a lot of pouring and toasting to be done. There are, in this regard, a few points of *saké* etiquette: Take note of how your drinking companions are progressing, and when their cups are drained, offer to pour for them—this is, according to the Japanese view, only common courtesy. When *saké* is offered to you (by your companions who have kept an eye on the level of your cup), *hold* your cup to receive the *saké*. It is rude to allow your cup (or beer glass) to be filled without your acknowledging the courtesy by holding the cup (or glass). Finally, it is marginally impolite to refuse *saké* when the bottle is proffered (especially by a superior), though you may indicate that you want only a few drops. If, however, you have reached your limit or do not wish to drink, then decline firmly but in the spirit of the occasion.

A few drops of *saké* (a milliliter to be precise) is one Calorie. *Saké* is sugary and contains several amino acids. Its sweetness and its food-softening properties (the amino acids) make *saké* a principal Japanese seasoning, like salt or soy sauce. No special grade of *saké* is necessary—you can cook with the same kind of *saké* you drink. See page 85 for a brief discussion of *saké* as a seasoning.

Besides *saké*, another Japanese alcoholic drink often available abroad is *shōchū* (焼酎), literally "fiery spirits"—a distilled spirit made from sweet potatoes or rice, or millet, or molasses, or etc. Its alcohol content is usually 20, 25, or 35 percent, though some local brews go as high as 45 percent (90 proof). It may be heated like *saké* or drunk cold, but it is most often used as a beverage outside meals. *Shōchū* is considered a low-class drink, and so one type now goes under the euphemism "white liquor" for use at home to make fruit liqueurs with the addition of sugar and fresh fruit or berries (see page 470).

Obviously *saké* is the alcoholic beverage best suited to go with Japanese cooking, just as wine is indispensable to French cooking. But if you are not in the mood for *saké*, then beer or whiskey will do. In fact, the number of customers at traditional Japanese restaurants in Japan who order beer or whiskey continues to grow.

Whiskey is always taken with water and ice, never straight, since drinks that are too strong in taste or aroma kill the flavors of delicate foods. The light and mild types of Scotch are particularly suitable for Japanese dishes, and the Japanese whiskey distillers, notably the Suntory people, have made a point of producing whiskey that complements Japanese cuisine. Almost any dish goes well with whiskey, but among the recipes included in this book, the following are especially good.

BEEF AND BURDOCK ROLLS	any hearty ONE-POT DISH
BEEF SASHIMI	POTATO-CHICKEN NUGGETS
CHILLED PORK SLICES	SAKÉ-STEAMED ABALONE
DEEP-FRIED MARINATED CHICKEN	SHABU-SHABU
DEEP-FRIED MIXED KEBABS	SHRIMP WAFERS
FLOUNDER TREASURE SHIPS	SOYBEANS IN THE POD
GINGER PORK SAUTÉ	STEAM-SIMMERED OCTOPUS
GRILLED CHICKEN ROLLS	SUKIYAKI
GRILLED SQUID WITH WITH SESAME	TEMPURA
GRILLED WHOLE SHRIMP	TEPPAN-YAKI
HORSE MACKEREL ESCABECHE "NANBAN"	TERIYAKI of any kind
KAMABOKO SLICES	YAKITORI
ODEN	YŪAN-STYLE GRILLED CHICKEN

Part Two

Part Two

✳ Part Two Contents ✳

❀ Soups ❀
Suimono and Shirumono

Clear Chicken Soup
(Tori no Suimono) 鶏の吸もの (color plate 11)

An attractive soup—based on chicken stock—with plenty of eye appeal.

4 servings

¼ pound (115 g) frying
  chicken (small thighs or
  backs and wings)
10 cups water

first broth seasoning:
  ¾ tsp salt
  1 Tbsp light soy sauce

second broth seasoning:
  ½ tsp salt
  2 tsps light soy sauce

about 10 sprigs edible chrysanthemum leaves (*kikuna*
  or *shungiku*) (or 2 medium
  sprigs spinach)
4 fresh *shiitake* mushrooms,
  wiped and trimmed
1 small carrot, scraped
4-8 okra pods, washed and
  caps removed

for simmering vegetables:
  1 cup reserved broth
  ¼ tsp salt
  1 tsp light soy sauce

Chicken: Gently boil the chicken, uncovered, in 10 cups of water until the liquid is reduced to 5 cups (about 1½ hours). After the first 10 minutes, remove about 1 cup of broth to be used separately for heating the vegetables. Skim the broth in the pot periodically and add more water if necessary. Season with ¾ tsp salt and 1 Tbsp soy sauce when liquid is reduced. (While the broth is cooking, prepare the vegetables to be heated.)

Strain the broth and keep hot. Remove and discard chicken skin and bones. Cut meat into bite-sized pieces. Season strained broth with ½ tsp salt and 2 tsps light soy sauce.

Vegetables: Wash and coarsely chop the chrysanthemum, or parboil spinach (see page 93) and chop coarsely. Notch a decorative cross on the top of each mushroom cap. Slice the carrot into ¼-inch-thick (¾-cm) rounds and cook in a small amount of boiling salted water till tender; drain. Rub salt onto the okra to remove the down, then parboil in lightly salted water about 1 to 2 minutes. Drain, but do not rinse in cold water. Cut into ¼-inch (¾-cm) rounds. Place these vegetables in a small pot with the cup of reserved broth and heat just before serving.

To assemble: Put two pieces of chicken meat into each individual soup bowl. Alongside the chicken, attractively arrange a few lengths of chrysanthemum (or spinach), a mushroom, and slices of carrot and okra. Use chopsticks or a slotted spoon to transfer the vegetables from the heating pot to the bowls.

Ladle the hot chicken broth over the arranged ingredients and garnish with a thin slice of lemon and finely chopped green onion. Serve immediately.

Combines well with SCATTERED SUSHI, OSAKA STYLE (page 449) and GREEN BEANS WITH SESAME-MISO DRESSING (page 420).

Beaten Egg Soup

(*Kakitama-jiru*) かき玉汁

The Chinese have a similar soup known in Chinese restaurants the world over as Egg Drop Soup. This is possibly Japan's most popular clear soup, and it goes well with any meal. It is easy to make and nourishing and tasty, with its tang of ginger and egg filaments floating in suspension.

4 servings

5 cups *dashi* (or light chicken or beef stock)
1 tsp salt
½ tsp light soy sauce
splash *saké*
2 tsps cornstarch, mixed with 2 Tbsps water
2 eggs, beaten
½ tsp fresh ginger juice (or finely chopped lemon rind or green onion)
4 stalks trefoil (*mitsuba*), cut into 1-inch (2½-cm) lengths (or substitute 1 sprig either watercress or parboiled fresh spinach)

To assemble and serve: Bring the *dashi* just to a boil over high heat, then simmer while seasoning to taste with the salt, soy sauce, and *saké*. Reduce heat to low.

With the heat on low, stir in the cornstarch-and-water mixture. Stir for 30 seconds or so till thick and smooth and raise heat to bring the soup to a high simmer. Never let it boil.

Slowly pour a thin stream of beaten egg in a spiral over the entire surface of the soup. Do not stir immediately, but let the egg start to set, about 30 seconds to 1 minute. Stir soup gently and constantly with a wire whisk for another minute or so to allow the egg to separate into threadlike filaments.

Finally, add the ginger juice and trefoil and remove from heat immediately. Pour into individual soup bowls, garnishing each with a bit of trefoil from the soup. Serve immediately.

VARIATION: Use ½ cake *tōfu* (bean curd), cut into ½-inch (1½-cm) cubes. Add after the egg and let simmer till heated (about 30 seconds) before adding the ginger juice and trefoil.

Green Onion and Tuna Soup

(*Negi-ma-jiru*) ねぎま汁

In times past, before the succulent, buttery *toro* portions of raw tuna became so popular with aficionados—and consequently very expensive—*sushi* shops used to serve this part of tuna in a soup simmered with tangy green onions.

4 servings

1 pound (450 g) raw tuna
   (fattiest parts are best)
10 green onions
4 cups *dashi*
¾ tsp salt
1 Tbsp light soy sauce
seven-spice mixture
   (*shichimi*)

To prepare: Cut the raw tuna crosswise against the grain into slices about ¼ inch (¾ cm) thick, and then cut the slices into 1-inch (2½-cm) pieces. Lay tuna pieces in a colander and pour boiling water over them (or plunge into boiling water); immediately rinse under cold water.

Cut the green onions diagonally into 1½-inch (4-cm) lengths.

To cook and serve: In a medium-sized pot combine the *dashi*, salt, and soy sauce and bring to a simmer. Add the tuna, and simmer, just on the verge of boiling (but do not boil), for about 2 minutes. Add the onion and stir. Immediately remove from heat.

Ladle into soup bowls and sprinkle with a scant amount of seven-spice mixture (*shichimi*). Serve immediately.

Pureed Corn Soup

(*Tōmorokoshi Surinagashi-jiru*) とうもろこしすり流し汁

The freshly crushed corn lends an exotic flavor to this novel soup—a tasty meeting of East with West. Refreshing in summer served very cold, like vichyssoise, but serve it piping hot in winter.

4 servings

1 cob fresh corn (or 1 cup
   frozen packaged corn)
5 cups *dashi* (or light chicken
   stock)
½ tsp salt
½ tsp light soy sauce
3 Tbsps white (or red) *miso*

To prepare: Cook the corn on the cob, covered, in lightly salted boiling water for 1 minute. (Heat frozen packaged corn till half-cooked, which may take several minutes.) Strip kernels from the cob and chop coarsely on a cutting board. Grind to a paste in a mortar or *suribachi* grinding bowl (or use a food processor), then press through a sieve with the back of a wooden spoon. Discard pulp in sieve. (You may use canned corn, but

¼ tsp mustard paste (see page 78)

½ cake *tōfu* (bean curd), cut in ½-inch (1½-cm) cubes

the soup is designed to take advantage of the flavor of fresh corn.)

To cook and assemble: Rapidly bring the *dashi* just to a boil, then simmer while seasoning to taste with the salt and light soy sauce. Soften the *miso* with a few Tbsps of *dashi* from the pot, then mix in and stir. Stir in the pureed corn and bring to a simmer. Add the mustard paste, stirring well. Add the bean curd cubes and cook just till *tōfu* is heated (do not break cubes). Serve immediately.

Combines well with CHILLED PORK SLICES (page 390) and VINEGARED CUCUMBER (page 423)

VARIATIONS: Instead of using *tōfu*, substitute either bite-sized pieces of grilled *mochi* (glutinous rice cake) or eggs. The chewy rice is a good combination with the corn. Dribble beaten egg into the simmering soup, or break eggs directly into the boiling soup and serve one such poached egg in each individual soup bowl, ladle the soup over, and serve immediately. To eat with poached egg, break the egg yolk (with your chopsticks), stir around vigorously in your bowl, then begin.

Chunky Vegetable Soup

(*Noppei-jiru*) のっぺい汁

A chunky soup as substantial as stew. The word *noppei* refers to the smooth, thickened broth enfolding bite-sized vegetable chunks. When available and in season, vegetables such as small mild onions, zucchini, cucumber, and cauliflower may also be used. If you use vegetables with dominating odors, such as celery and Brussels sprouts, be sure to parboil them first.

4–6 servings

¼ pound (115 g) frying chicken thighs

1 cake *konnyaku* (devil's tongue jelly)

6-8-inch (15-20-cm) length giant white radish (*daikon*)

2 small carrots

To prepare: Bone and cut the chicken into ¾-inch (2-cm) squares, with skin. Tear the *konnyaku* into 1-inch (2½-cm) pieces with your hands; the rough edges allow the broth flavor to penetrate. Wash, skin, and peel the vegetable ingredients as required. Use the *ran-giri* cut for the giant white radish and carrot (see page 140).

If whole or in chunks, quarter bamboo shoot lengthwise then cut in ⅛-inch (½-cm) slices.

2 cups sliced bamboo shoots
(see page 55)

4-6 fresh *shiitake* mushrooms, wiped, trimmed,
and quartered

4-6 new potatoes, halved

1 cake thin deep-fried *tōfu*
(*aburage* or *usuage*), cut
into 1-inch (2½-cm) squares

5 cups *dashi* (or light chicken
or beef stock)

1 tsp salt

1½ Tbsps light soy sauce

3 Tbsps cornstarch, mixed
with 3 Tbsps water

To cook: Place the chicken, all the vegetable ingredients, and fried *tōfu* in a medium-sized soup kettle. Pour in the *dashi* to cover. Bring to a boil, reduce heat, and simmer for 30 to 40 minutes, uncovered. Add a cup or so more *dashi* if the soup is greatly reduced by simmering. Skim off fat periodically. When solid ingredients are just tender, add salt then light soy sauce, seasoning to taste. Pour in the cornstarch-and-water mixture and stir until thickened. Serve immediately. No garnish is necessary.

Combines well with YELLOWTAIL TERIYAKI (page 200) and QUICK TURNIP PICKLES (page 323).

Thunder Soup

(*Kaminari-jiru*) 雷汁

A thunderingly good soup of bean curd and traditional vegetables vigorously fried then simmered. When the bean curd is crumbled into the hot oil it crackles and sputters like a violent electric storm—hence the name. The traditional ingredients may be varied as whim and availability dictate, but the basic character of this soup is determined by the *tōfu*. While bean curd in its natural state goes well with the strong flavor of *miso* soup, it is too bland and watery for some broths unless the liquid is first removed, here by frying. The drier the curds, the better they absorb the broth.

4–6 servings

1 cake *tōfu* (bean curd)

2 carrots, sliced in ¼-inch-
thick (¾-cm) half-moons

1 medium burdock root,
cut into "pencil" shavings
(see page 142)

6-8 new potatoes, peeled and
sliced

2-3 cakes thin deep-fried *tōfu*
(*aburage* or *usuage*), cut
into julienne strips

To prepare: Drain the *tōfu* and wrap in a clean kitchen towel to absorb moisture. Clean and cut all the vegetable and solid ingredients as described. (Put the burdock shavings in cold water to keep them white.)

To cook: Cover the bottom of a large heavy pot with vegetable oil and apply high heat till very hot: a drop of water should skitter across the surface of the hot oil. Squeeze the cake of *tōfu* through your fingers and into the hot oil. Reduce heat to medium-high. With a long-handled wooden spoon stir constantly till the water in the *tōfu* has evaporated and the *tōfu* is like rather dry scrambled eggs.

6-8 fresh *shiitake* mushrooms wiped, trimmed,
and sliced
1 cake *konnyaku* (devil's
tongue jelly), cut into
julienne strips
1-inch (2½-cm) knob fresh
ginger, peeled and cut
into paper-thin slices
1 green onion, cut diagonally
into 1½-inch (4-cm)
lengths
vegetable oil
5 cups *dashi* (or light chicken
or beef stock)
1 tsp salt
1 Tbsp light soy sauce
½ Tbsp dark soy sauce
2 tsps cornstarch, mixed
with 2 Tbsps water
(optional)

Add a few more Tbsps vegetable oil. When this oil
becomes very hot, add all the vegetable ingredients at
once *except* the ginger and green onion, and stir-fry
over high heat till all ingredients are cooked but still
crisp, about 3 to 4 minutes.

Pour in hot *dashi*, stir, and add the ginger slices.
Rapidly bring to a boil, then simmer while seasoning
with salt, light soy sauce, and dark soy sauce. Simmer
about 20 minutes. (To make a thick broth, pour in the
cornstarch-and-water mixture during the last 5 minutes
of the 20-minute simmering. Stir constantly until
thickened.) Add green onion at the last moment and
stir. Serve immediately.

Combines well with GINGER PORK SAUTÉ (page 369)
and ROLLED OMELETTE (page 203).

Ozōni

お雑煮

Ozōni is to Japanese New Year what turkey is to American Christmas and
Thanksgiving, and also, like turkey, it is good prepared any time of the year.
Traditionally, it is the main food served on New Year's morning after the
toast with *otoso*, spiced *saké*. It is, in fact, a delightfully filling hot soup with
a variety of ingredients, as its name, meaning "simmered miscellany,"
implies. But the word *ozōni* mainly evokes a picture of *mochi* rice cakes in
some kind of soup, for these two are the only constants in the many varieties
of *ozōni* that have developed throughout the islands.

4 servings

½ pound (225 g) boned
chicken, leg and breast,
with skin
4 medium shrimp
2-inch (5-cm) length giant
white radish (*daikon*)
1 medium carrot

To prepare: All the ingredients from the chicken to
chrysanthemum may be cut and parboiled separately
some hours in advance and combined with the stock
to heat just before serving.

Slice the chicken on the diagonal into thin pieces
and sprinkle lightly with salt. Blanch in lightly salted
water till whitish, about 2 minutes. Drain.

Shell, devein, and wash shrimp; leave tails attached.

8 sprigs edible chrysanthemum leaves (*shungiku*
or *kikuna*)
3⅓ cups *dashi*
½ tsp salt
½ tsp light soy sauce
4 *mochi* cakes (2 x 1½ inches
[5 x 4 cm])
4 1½-x-¼-inch (4-x-¾-cm)
pieces *yuzu* citron rind.

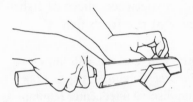

daikon hexagons

decorative cut for *yuzu* rind

Boil in lightly salted water till just firm and pink, about 3 minutes. Plunge into cold water to cool.

Pare length of radish into a hexagonal shape, then cut into slices about ¼ inch (¾ cm) thick. Hexagons make up the tortoiseshell pattern, and the tortoise is the symbol of longevity. Parboil in lightly salted water till almost tender, about 15 to 20 minutes. Drain.

Peel the carrot and cut into ¼-inch (¾-cm) rounds. Parboil in lightly salted water till almost tender, about 10 minutes. Drain.

Parboil chrysanthemum leaves in lightly salted water till almost tender. Rinse under cold water, gently squeeze out excess water, and chop coarsely. Divide into 4 small mounds.

To cook and serve: In a soup pot, bring the *dashi* just to a boil. Turn down heat to keep at a simmer, then stir in salt and light soy sauce and adjust seasonings to taste.

Meanwhile, grill the *mochi* rice cakes over a charcoal fire or use an oven broiler. Turn, making sure the cakes do not burn. When the surface is crisp and a mottled brown, pierce with a fork or toothpick in several spots to allow soup to penetrate.

Remove hot grilled *mochi* cakes to individual deep soup bowls. Place a mound of chrysanthemum next to each cake and add chicken, shrimp, radish hexagons, and carrot rounds. Carefully ladle on the simmering soup, making sure that all the ingredients are represented in every bowl. Add a thin section of *yuzu* rind, decoratively cut and folded, as shown. Eat hot. Use chopsticks (but forks or spoons will do). Best served in lacquer bowls, but any small, elegant, deep bowls can be used.

Combines well with CRUSHED BURDOCK WITH SESAME DRESSING (page 427) and YELLOWTAIL TERI-YAKI (page 200).

❀ *Sashimi* ❀

Yellowtail Lemon *Sashimi*

(*Hamachi-Remon Tsukuri*) はまちレモン造り (color plate 13)

Lemon goes well with fish such as yellowtail (*buri* or *hamachi*) and mackerel (*saba*). Its tartness counteracts their oiliness, while its fragrance effectively masks the fishiness of sillago (*kisu*), scallops, oysters, shrimps, etc. In this elegantly simple presentation, lemon slices are tucked between slices of fish, exerting an astringent effect that enhances the flavor of the fresh fish.

8–10 servings

**1 young yellowtail, about
  2¼ pounds (1 kg)**
2 or 3 lemons
**sprigs of *shiso* buds or
  shiso leaves**
carrot curls
**finely grated *wasabi*
  horseradish**
TOSA SOY SAUCE **(see page 170)**

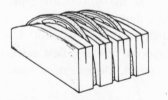

fish fillet is alternately cut completely through and scored ⅓ through, then lemon slices are inserted

To prepare: Clean, gut, and cut the fish into two boneless fillets (*sanmai oroshi* technique, pages 123ff), without skin. Cut off and discard fillet center (containing bones).

Since the purpose of the dish to is blend the taste of fresh lemon and fresh fish, thin slices of lemon are tucked between slices of fish. Place fish skin side up on the cutting board. Alternately score and slice entirely through the flesh crosswise at intervals of ⅛ inch (½ cm).

Cut lemon in half lengthwise and seed. Cut off ends of lemon, then cut into 1/16-inch (¼-cm) slices.

To assemble and serve: Insert a lemon slice between the fish slices. Arrange 5 lemon-filled pieces on a plate as one serving and garnish with *shiso* buds (or leaves), and carrot curls. Add cone of grated *wasabi* and serve with TOSA SOY SAUCE.

Combines well with STUFFED CRAB (page 407) and BEATEN EGG SOUP (page 346).

VARIATION: Cut the fillets into paper-thin slices. Arrange about 9 1/16-inch (¼-cm) half-moon lemon slices along the edge of a single-serving plate and, partially covering the lemon, arrange about 12 paper-thin slices of fish in a rosette. Garnish with chrysanthemum leaves (not to be eaten), flowering miniature cucumber, *iwatake*, and *benitade* (page 168), or other decorative garnishes. For a spicy condiment, use finely chopped green onion. Serve with PONZU SAUCE (see page 172). This is just a simpler way of serving the fish—like setting out thin slices of smoked salmon with lemon as done in the West.

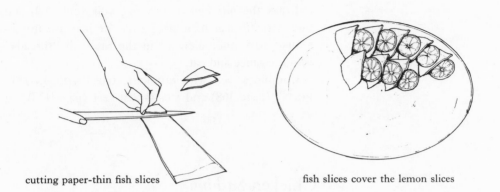

cutting paper-thin fish slices   fish slices cover the lemon slices

Kisu (Sillago) *Sashimi*

(*Kisu Konbujime*) きす昆布じめ

Wrapping fish in moistened giant kelp (*konbu*) qualifies as a sort of marination, and this adds subtle depth of flavor to raw seafood. *Kisu* is a common Japanese fish, but does not appear in Western seas, at least according to all the references consulted for this book. Any delicately flavored seafood that can be cut into thin "threads" (using the *ito-zukuri* technique, page 166) may be served this way: river trout, sea bass, whiting, shrimp, crab, oysters, clams, and fresh abalone are all delicious.

4 servings

4 sillago, 8 inches (20 cm) long
salt
2-inch (5-cm) square
"white sheet" giant kelp
(*shiraita konbu*)
1 Japanese cucumber (or ½
large Western cucumber,
peeled and seeded)
4 sprigs *shiso* buds (or
1 sprig watercress)
2 green onions, finely
sliced diagonally
4 raw egg yolks or poached
eggs (optional)
HORSERADISH SOY SAUCE
(see page 171)

To prepare: Clean, gut fish, and cut boneless fillets, with skin. Place fillets in salt water (1 cup water: 1 tsp salt) with the square of "white sheet" kelp and let stand 10 minutes. Remove from water, wrap fish in water-moistened kelp, and refrigerate 3 hours.

After marination, remove skins from fillets with your fingers or by the *sotobiki* technique (see page 131).

With the tip of a sharp knife, cut fillets into thin, thread-like pieces on the diagonal (the *ito-zukuri* technique, page 166).

To assemble and serve: Cut cucumber crosswise into 2½-inch (6½-cm) lengths, then again slice lengthwise into shreds. Mix cucumber shreds with fish "thread" slices in individual serving dishes and arrange in a mound. Garnish with *shiso* buds (or watercress) and small mounds of finely sliced green onion. Put raw egg yolks (or whole poached eggs) in the same dish or into small individual dipping bowls.

Break the poached or raw egg yolk (optional) and mix with HORSERADISH SOY SAUCE, or just use HORSE-RADISH SOY SAUCE alone. Dip the raw fish "threads" into the sauce and eat.

Combines well with CHICKEN LOAF "WIND-IN-THE-PINES" (page 368) and MUSHROOM RICE (page 438).

Chicken *Sashimi*

(*Toriwasa*) 鶏わさ

In Japan, this is a popular way of eating chicken.

Best suited for chicken *sashimi* is the fine-textured breast fillet called *sasami*. These fillets (two per bird) run parallel with the breastbone—one on either side—and are shaped like *sasa* (bamboo-grass) leaves, hence the name *sasami*—literally, "bamboo-grass meat." Turn to page 135 for directions on how to extract fillets from whole breasts. The advantage of *sasami* is that it has the best texture and is most easily cut into uniform, attractive slices. Take care to remove tendons first. Any part of the breast may be used, however (without skin). Slice thinly across the grain of the meat.

4 servings

8 *sasami* fillets or ½ pound (225 g) chicken breast meat without skin
1-2 Tbsps finely grated *wasabi* horseradish
½ cup TOSA SOY SAUCE (see page 170) or dark soy sauce
½ sheet *nori* seaweed, toasted and cut into julienne strips (optional)

To prepare and serve: Swish whole *sasami* fillets in boiling hot water for about 30 seconds, just till flesh becomes frosty white. This technique is used to refresh the meat, banishing odors. To arrest cooking and cool, plunge fillets into a cold water bath, then immediately remove to a towel and pat dry.

Lay fillets on dry cutting board. Using a long-bladed (*sashimi*) knife, cut diagonally across the meat (with the blade vertical) to make thin slices.

Mix grated *wasabi* horseradish and soy sauce together in a medium-sized bowl. Add sliced chicken and toss with your hands.

Place each portion (the equivalent of 2 *sasami* fillets or 2 ounces breast) in an individual dish. Julienne strips of toasted *nori* may be sprinkled over the chicken as a garnish (optional). Serve at room temperature as an appetizer or with a clear soup to begin a meal.

Beef *Sashimi*

(*Gyūniku no Sashimi*) 牛肉の刺身

One Japanese answer to Steak Tartare. Here the raw beef is very briefly grilled first in the manner of a traditional recipe for bonito.

4 servings

1 pound (450 g) choice
  lean sirloin, tenderloin,
  or fillet of beef
salt
½ large Western cucumber,
  peeled and seeded (or a
  2-inch [5-cm] length of
  mountain yam [*yama no
  imo*], if available)
4 *shiso* leaves

spicy condiments:

  4 Tbsps finely grated giant
    white radish (*daikon-
    oroshi*)
  4 Tbsps RED MAPLE RADISH
    (see page 170)
  4 Tbsps finely chopped
    green onion
  4 tsps finely grated fresh
    ginger
  4 *shiso* leaves, finely cut
  4 tsps finely grated *wasabi*
    horseradish

PONZU SAUCE **(see page 172) or**
soy sauce

To prepare: Trim any fat and sinew off the beef. Salt to bring juices of the meat to the surface. Quickly grill both sides over the hottest charcoal fire or use oven broiler to sear. Plunge the meat in ice water to cool, then pat dry.

Cut cucumber into thin half-moons. Or, if you can find the long mountain yam (*naga imo*), peel, cut in half lengthwise and slice into paper-thin half-moons.

Prepare spicy condiments as suggested at left. For recipes, see page 170. Prepare PONZU SAUCE (page 172), if this is your choice for dipping sauce.

To serve and eat: Cut the washed, seared meat against the grain at a slightly oblique angle to make very thin (about 1/8-inch [½-cm]) slices. Place 1 whole *shiso* leaf on each plate and on this attractively arrange 1 portion of beef slices, in a rosette or other pattern. Garnish with a few cucumber or mountain yam half-moons. Place the spicy condiments in small quantities on each plate or serve in small dishes. Provide separate small dipping bowls or saucers for the PONZU SAUCE or soy sauce. Add spicy condiments of your choice to sauces and dip in beef slices.

Combines well with SAVORY CUP CUSTARD (page 214) and SAVORY OKRA (page 420).

❋ Grilled and Pan-Fried Dishes ❋
Yakimono

Grilled Whole Shrimp
(Ebi Onigara-yaki) えび鬼殻焼き

The Japanese name for this dish is "demon shrimp"—because the flesh turns bright red like the *oni* (demons) of folklore, and also because of the firm crispness of the charcoal-grilled shells. The word *oni* (demon) traditionally indicates hardness and masculinity, while *hime* (princess) indicates feminine softness. This recipe is designed to make the most of the tastiest part of the shrimp—the flesh immediately under its shell. The shells of small shrimp crisp tastily over hot charcoal and may be eaten, but those of larger shrimp usually must be peeled off.

4 servings

8 large live (or frozen) shrimp
¼ head lettuce
1 lemon, quartered
4-6 peeled miniature cucumbers (substitute celery or half-done Kosher dills cut into ¼-x-2-inch [¾-x-5-cm] pieces, or use 4-6 cherry tomatoes)

sauce:

⅔ cup *saké*
1 cup *mirin*
½ cup dark soy sauce

To prepare: Chop off the shrimp head just before the eyes to dispose of whiskers and tip of snout, as shown. Leave the shell, tail, and legs intact. Cut deeply through the head and shell along the back (be careful not to cut shrimp in half), then press open flat and devein with the tip of a small knife.

Skewer sideways (*yoko-gushi*, page 180), using 3 long metal skewers for 2 to 4 shrimp.

In a small pan, heat *saké* and *mirin* to eliminate alcohol, add soy sauce, then reduce by half over low heat.

To grill and serve: Place shrimp over hottest charcoal fire, shell side down, for 2 minutes, then turn. When both sides have been grilled halfway, brush on the sauce; turn and grill a little more, till the sauce is rather dry and has formed a glaze. (Or cook in an oven broiler.)

To serve, remove skewers and cut each shrimp in half crosswise. Arrange 4 halves against a bed of lettuce on an individual plate and garnish with lemon quarter and peeled miniature cucumber (or a substitute). Serve immediately, and eat by hand, peeling off the shells as you eat.

Goes well with SEA BREAM STEAMED WITH BUCKWHEAT NOODLES (page 375) and CLAM CONSOMMÉ (page 155).

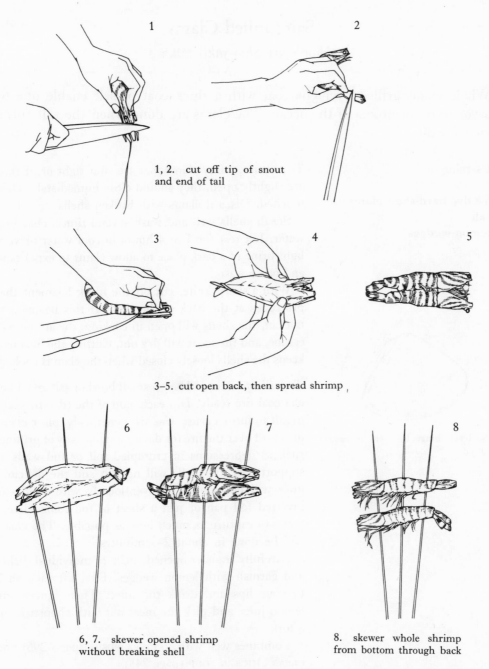

1, 2. cut off tip of snout
and end of tail

3–5. cut open back, then spread shrimp

6, 7. skewer opened shrimp
without breaking shell

8. skewer whole shrimp
from bottom through back

VARIATION: Splitting the shrimp open and grilling them as above is fine for both live and thawed frozen shrimp, but live shrimp taste even better when salt-grilled without splitting open. Trim the whiskered snout as above and devein, then use 3 long metal skewers to pierce the shrimp sideways (see sketches). Sprinkle with a moderate amount of salt, then grill, turning a few times over a very hot fire, about 5 minutes total. Use no sauce. Cut into bite-sized pieces and serve with lemon quarters and garnish.

Salt-Grilled Clams

(*Hamaguri Shio-yaki*) 蛤塩焼き

Whole clams grilled over charcoal with a thick coat of salt enable one to savor fully the aroma of the ocean. The clams are done when the salt turns snowy white.

1 serving

**6-8 live hard-shell clams
salt
lemon wedges**

the black hinge ligament is easily cut off

To prepare: Buy clams that are shut tight or, if they are slightly open, they should close immediately when touched. Discard clams with broken shells.

Scrub shells well and wash several times, changing water. Let rest for 3 or 4 hours in cool water or very light brine in a dark place to allow clams to expel sand and other waste.

With a sharp knife, cut off the black ligament that protrudes at the back of the shell. If this ligament is not cut, the shells will open in cooking, the aroma will escape, and the meat will dry out. Cutting the ligament keeps the shells loosely closed when the clam is cooked.

To grill and serve: Have a small bowl of salt and a hot charcoal fire ready. Dip each side of the (damp) shells in salt to form a crust. Use salt generously, place clams on a grill over the fire (or devise a stable way of grilling, such as depressions in crumpled foil or foil wads as supports) so the shells will not tip and the delicious juice will not run out. Cover loosely with a lid—an inverted foil pan or just a sheet of foil folded like a tent—to capture as much heat as possible. The clams will be done in about 2–3 minutes.

Carefully transfer opened shells to individual dishes and garnish with lemon wedges. First lift each shell to your lips and drink the juice. Then squeeze on lemon juice and pick the meat out with chopsticks or a fork.

Combines well with BATTERA SUSHI (page 296) and CLEAR CHICKEN SOUP (page 345).

Butter-Fried Clams

(*Hamaguri Bata-yaki*) 蛤バター焼き

Fresh clams are fried in butter after being lightly dusted with cornstarch and dipped in egg yolk to keep in the juice. Chopped trefoil or grated lemon or citron rind may be added to the egg.

1 serving

4-6 medium live hard-shell clams
cornstarch (or *kuzu* starch)
1 egg yolk, beaten with pinch of salt
2 Tbsps vegetable oil
2 Tbsps butter
lemon wedges

To prepare: Before shucking, let clams rest in cool water or light brine in a dark place for 3 or 4 hours to expel sand and grit.

Cut off the black ligament protruding outside the hinge, open shells, and cut out the clam meat. Set aside the best shells (2 shells per serving) to serve cooked clams in. Gently press clams dry in a clean towel.

To fry: Lightly dust clams on both sides with cornstarch. Dip clams lightly into the beaten egg yolk.

Rub a thin layer of vegetable oil over the bottom of a frying pan and heat over low heat. Lay in clams and move them over the bottom of the pan to oil them and then *turn once only*. After turning, add the butter. Fry, uncovered, another 1 minute or until clams brown a little. Total frying time is 1–2 minutes.

To serve: Carefully cut clams in half if large and arrange meat in opened shells on a flat plate. Garnish with lemon wedges and serve immediately.

Combines well with ASPARAGUS RICE (page 438) and VINEGAR-PICKLED CABBAGE (page 324).

Stuffed Foil-Baked Salmon

(*Sake Sarada Tsutsumi-yaki*) 鮭サラダ包み焼き

This succulent dish is a descendant of foods cooked in either paper (*en papillote*) or bamboo leaves. The stuffing is a type of potato salad. Sea bass, sea bream, yellowtail, and trout are all good done this way.

4 servings

2 salmon fillets with skin,

To prepare: Salt both sides of the fillet pieces then let rest 1½ hours. Pluck out stray bones with tweezers. Place each fillet piece skin side down on cutting board,

each about 9 ounces (250 g),
cut in half crosswise

salt

salad-stuffing:

3 potatoes, peeled
½ medium carrot
½ medium onion, thinly
sliced
1 Japanese cucumber, thinly
sliced (½ Western cu-
cumber, peeled, seeded,
and thinly sliced)
½ cup mayonnaise
freshly ground black
pepper

butter
4 12-inch (30-cm) squares
of aluminum foil
1 lemon, cut in thin slices
4 or 8 small fresh *shiitake*
mushrooms, wiped and
trimmed

cut two wings in each piece, using the butterfly cut (*kannon-biraki* technique, see page 132).

While salted pieces of fillet rest, prepare the stuffing—essentially a potato salad. Cut potatoes in fourths lengthwise. Boil with carrot pieces of the same size until just soft. Drain, salt, and heat over high heat, uncovered, to evaporate moisture. A film of potato starch will form on pot bottom when done. Chop potato and carrot into ¼-inch pieces.

Separately salt the onion slices and cucumber slices and let stand 15 minutes; then press any moisture out of each. Both these ingredients should be very limp. Combine potatoes, carrots, onions, and cucumber with mayonnaise and add freshly ground pepper last. (Add no salt.)

To assemble and cook: Preheat oven to very hot (475°F/250°C). Butter the center of 4 12-inch-square (30-cm) sheets of foil. Form a small handful of salad-stuffing into a ball and place in the center of a sheet of greased foil. Press down and mold into a rectangular shape. Cover with a piece of fillet as shown, making sure the flaps enclose the stuffing on two sides. Top the fillet with a pat of butter, a slice of lemon, and one or two mushrooms. Fold the foil into a pouch, making sure to seal ends tightly, but do not disturb the arrangement of the stuffed fish. Make 4 pouches.

Bake in hot oven 15 minutes. Do not turn the pouches.

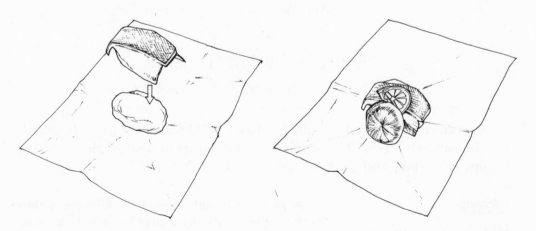

cover stuffing with fish fillet, add other ingredients, and wrap with foil

To serve: Serve hot from the oven on individual plates, each with a nonedible decorative leaf (anything seasonal from your garden) softening the presentation. Either fold the foil back in the kitchen or let everyone open his own foil packet at the table.

Combines well with GRILLED MUSHROOMS WITH PONZU SAUCE (page 425) and EGG "TŌFU" (page 216).

Pan-Broiled Salmon
(*Sake Nanban-yaki*) 鮭南蛮焼き

4 servings

4 salmon steaks, ¾ inch
  (2 cm) thick
oil
2 Tbsps butter
2 Tbsps rice vinegar
2 Tbsps *mirin*
1 Tbsp dark soy sauce
1 cup finely chopped green
  onion
1 lemon, quartered

To fry: Salt the salmon (see *furi-jio* technique, page 132).

In a large frying pan heat a scant amount of oil and fry both sides of the salmon steaks for a few minutes over high heat. (This will produce a lot of smoke.) Discard oil in pan, add the butter (in several pats), and as soon as the salmon is coated with butter, remove to individual plates with a pancake turner or spatula.

Into the buttery liquid and glaze that remains in the frying pan, add the rice vinegar, *mirin*, and dark soy sauce. Stir over high heat about 1 minute. Add the finely chopped green onion and stir just till well mixed. Spoon this green onion sauce generously over the salmon steaks and serve immediately. Garnish each plate with a lemon quarter.

Combines well with DRENCHED RADISH (page 395) and SOUSED SPINACH (page 429).

Stuffed Red Tilefish
(*Amadai Kenchin-yaki*) 甘鯛けんちん焼き (color plate 11)

This stuffing is typically oriental. The name *kenchin* is used for any combination of chopped ingredients (usually vegetables) that includes bean curd. (The egg is merely to bind the stuffing.) Bean curd, which goes well with most things, blends particularly well with the delicate flavor of this fish.

4 servings

kenchin *stuffing:*

1 cake *tōfu* **(bean curd)**
⅓ **carrot, scraped**
**12 ginkgo nuts, chopped (or
3 Tbsps green peas)**
**1 medium burdock root,
scrubbed with a brush**
**3 large dried cloud-ear
mushrooms, softened
(see page 65)**
vegetable oil
5 eggs, beaten
salt

**red tilefish fillet with skin,
12 ounces (340 g) or larger**
cornstarch
aluminum foil

glaze:

¼ **cup** *mirin*
¼ **cup dark soy sauce**

4 pink PICKLED GINGER SHOOTS
(*hajikami shōga***)**
lemon wedges

To prepare: Make the *kenchin* stuffing first. Drain bean curd and wrap in a clean towel for 1–1½ hours to extract as much moisture as possible. Rub through a sieve to puree.

Slice, separately parboil, then finely dice or chop carrot, ginkgo nuts, and burdock root. Keep burdock in cold water to prevent discoloring. Chop softened cloud-ear mushrooms to match the size of the other chopped ingredients.

Lightly coat the bottom of a large frying pan with vegetable oil. Over medium heat add the pureed bean curd and sauté lightly. Gradually add all the chopped vegetable ingredients and sauté till heated. Turn the heat on low and add the beaten egg. When the egg begins to thicken, stir with a wooden spoon to "scramble." Add salt, keep stirring. When egg mixture is about half cooked, remove from heat.

Spread the stuffing evenly on a broad surface (such as a cookie sheet) to cool. Do not let the stuffing cool naturally, but force-cool it with the draft from a fan to bring it to room temperature quickly.

To stuff and bake: Place fillet skin side down, remove stray bones with tweezers, and cut two wings with the butterfly cut (*kannon-biraki* technique, see page 132). Dust the inside of the fillet lightly with cornstarch, then lightly pack *kenchin* stuffing between fillet wings.

Fold a rather large piece of heavy cooking foil in two and grease with vegetable oil. Place oiled foil over stuffed fish and invert; the fish will now be skin side up, with stuffing beneath. Fold the sides of the foil up around the fish like a pan, as shown.

Place on a pan or cookie sheet and bake uncovered in a hot preheated oven at 475°F/245°C for 15 minutes. Five minutes before it is finished brush on the *mirin*-soy-sauce glaze rather generously.

To serve: Open foil and with a very sharp knife cut stuffed fish into ½-inch (1½-cm) slices. Arrange 2 or 3 slices on individual plates, garnish with pink PICKLED GINGER SHOOTS and lemon wedges, and serve hot.

Combines well with RICE WITH GREENS (page 440) and CLEAR SOUP WITH SHRIMP (page 154).

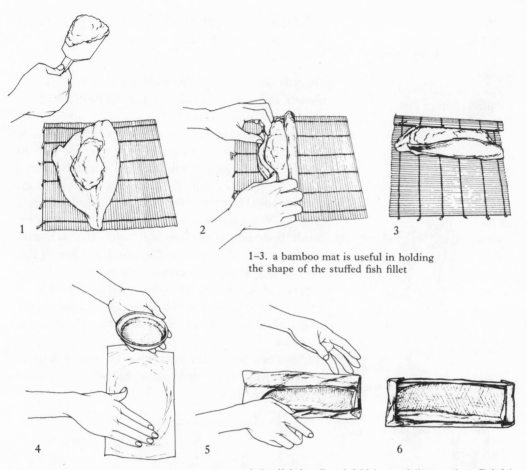

1–3. a bamboo mat is useful in holding
the shape of the stuffed fish fillet

4–6. lightly oil and fold heavy foil around stuffed fish

Grilled Red Tilefish "Wakasa"

(*Amadai Wakasa-yaki*) 甘鯛若狭焼き (color plate 13)

This tasty way to prepare a rather watery, delicately flavored fish originated
in olden times when it was necessary to salt it for its journey to the capital,
Kyoto, from its habitat in Wakasa Bay. Grilled over charcoal, the skin
—complete with scales—is pleasantly crisp and the flesh tender.

6 servings

**1 red tilefish, about 2
    pounds (1 kg)**
salt

To prepare: Cut fish into 2 fillets with the *sanmai
oroshi* technique (pages 123ff); let skin, scales, as well
as fins behind gills remain. With tweezers remove stray
bones from the fillets. Salt moderately on both sides
and let stand 2 hours. Wash well and pat dry, then hang

sauce:

  ½ **cup** *saké*
  ½ **cup light soy sauce**

lettuce
2 lemons, quartered
6-8 pink PICKLED GINGER SHOOTS
  (*hajikami shōga***)**

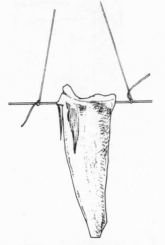

use a long metal skewer to hang
fish fillet

each fillet on a long metal skewer inserted through the front end, as shown. Hang in a cool dry place for 24 hours.

To grill and serve: Cut each fillet into 3 pieces. Skewer them as shown so that grilling takes about the same time for each piece.

Place over hottest charcoal fire and grill skin side first for 5 minutes. Loosely cover the raw side with an inverted foil pie pan, or foil folded in a tent, or even a couple of layers of wet newspaper, to direct as much heat as possible to the fish. Turn and grill about 3 minutes. When the flesh just becomes lightly browned, brush flesh side then skin side with the *saké*-soy-sauce mixture and grill until sauce dries. Repeat this basting 2–3 times. The skin should be browned.

Serve, skin side up, on individual plates next to or on lettuce and garnish with a lemon quarter and a pink ginger shoot or two. The crisp skin (with scales) can be eaten.

Combines well with FLOUNDER IN THE WOODPILE (page 374) and eggplant or cucumber RICE-BRAN MASH PICKLES (page 319).

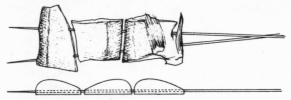

fillet pieces should be skewered so that each
piece grills evenly

VARIATIONS: This rather unusual method of preparation also works well with sea bream and sea bass, but these fish must be scaled.

Grilled Squid with Sesame

(*Ika Goma-yaki*) いか胡麻焼き

Squid freezes well, and frozen squid is inexpensive and available. But the longer this pleasant seafood is exposed to direct heat, the tougher and more rubbery its flesh becomes, so use a very, very hot charcoal fire and a brief cooking time. Black sesame seeds look handsome on the pearly white flesh and contribute a delicate nutty flavor.

4 servings

4 pieces squid, 5 inches (13 cm) long, cleaned and skinned
salt
2 egg whites
2-3 Tbsps black sesame seeds
4 spears asparagus, trimmed
sesame-salt (with black sesame)
1 lemon, cut into ¼-inch (¾-cm) slices

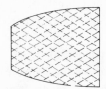

score outside in fine diagonals and inside in wider intervals lengthwise

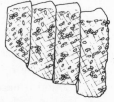

cut squid in bite-sized pieces after grilling

To prepare: Diagonally cross-score the outside (shiny, smooth side) of the squid as shown to a depth of about 1/16 inch (¼ cm) at ⅛-inch (½-cm) intervals. Score the inside (dull side) with straight incisions at about ¼-inch (¾-cm) intervals along the length of the piece as shown. The scoring keeps the flesh tender.

Use three long skewers per piece. Squid shrinks when grilled, so beginning from an edge of the inside, skewer in and out at 1½-inch (4-cm) intervals as if sewing (the *nui-gushi* technique, page 179). To keep the squid from curling as it cooks, insert a short bamboo skewer at about a 45° angle to the long metal skewers (necessary if flesh *not* scored; optional otherwise).

Salt the inside of the skewered squid, then paint the cross-scored outside with egg white. Sprinkle immediately with black sesame seeds.

To grill and serve: Have a charcoal fire at its hottest or have the oven broiler hot. Cook squid over as intense a heat as possible; grill the sesame-sprinkled side first. Grill about 2 minutes, till about ¾ done. Turn and grill the other side another minute. Turn only once. If broiling in an oven, do not cook more than 5 minutes total, for both sides. Do not pan-broil.

Brush asparagus with oil, and grill. Only a very brief grilling is necessary. Sprinkle with sesame-salt when done.

To remove skewers from squid, place on a cutting board with the sesame-sprinkled side up and press down on the squid lightly but firmly. With your other hand slowly rotate each skewer and keep rotating it as you draw it out. This keeps the flesh intact and makes the skewers easy to draw out.

Cut into pieces about 1½ inches (4 cm) long (just the right size to eat with chopsticks).

Arrange 5 pieces or so on each individual serving plate. Garnish with grilled asparagus and lemon slice. Serve immediately.

Combines well with STEAMED SALMON CASSEROLE (page 212) and CHESTNUT RICE (page 279).

VARIATION: MARINATED AND GRILLED SQUID (*Ika Mirin-yaki*)
For the same amount of squid as above, marinate in 7 parts *mirin*, 3 parts dark soy sauce, and a dash ginger or lemon juice for 30–40 minutes. Skewer and grill as above.

Grilled Chicken Rolls

(Toriniku Yawata-maki) 鶏肉八幡巻き

In ancient times Yawata, near Kyoto, was famous for its tender burdock. Traditionally this recipe calls for eel fillets wrapped around strips of burdock root; it is a typical summer delicacy—the season when both eels and burdock are at their best. But chicken makes a tasty and convenient variation, and instead of burdock, you may use fresh asparagus or parboiled celery.

4 servings

2 **medium burdock roots, scrubbed with a brush**

marinade:

1½ cups *dashi*
1 tsp salt
3 Tbsps *mirin*
2 Tbsps light soy sauce

2 **whole chicken legs (thighs attached to drumsticks)**

sauce:

1 cup *saké*
1 cup *mirin*
1 cup dark soy sauce

4 **pink** PICKLED GINGER SHOOTS **(hajikami shōga) (or small amount of your choice of pickles)**

To prepare: Cut burdock into narrow strips 8 to 9 inches (20 to 23 cm) long. Boil in lightly vinegared water till tender, which step also bleaches the burdock. Mix marinade and add burdock strips. Marinate 3 to 4 hours. Discard marinade when finished.

The legs of a 3-pound (1⅓-kg) fryer are perfect for this dish. (Use the breast and wings in another dish.) Bone both legs (technique on page 136).

Spread the meat flat open, and trim edges. Make 3 cuts (or use scissors) all the way through from meat (not skin) side as shown, then turn 180° and make 2 cuts between the first 3, also as shown. The object is to cut the meat to make one long strip. If you pick the meat up at one cut end, the entire piece now "unravels" in a long skinny strip.

To assemble: Hold 4 to 5 lengths marinated burdock against the side of a long metal skewer. Wind the strip of chicken, skin side out, neatly around the burdock, adding more burdock strips as necessary. Make a roll of chicken-and-burdock about 8 or 9 inches (20 or 23 cm) in length. If the cutting of the chicken has been less than perfect, bind the weak spots on the roll with clean cotton string. If you have not found it necessary to bind weak points along the roll, tie at 2-inch (5-cm) intervals anyway to keep the roll from breaking. Bind both ends securely with string, but do not trim the ragged ends of the roll until cooking is done. Draw out the skewer.

Using the meat of one leg per roll, make 2 such rolls, then skewer each roll as shown.

To grill: Place over the hottest charcoal fire. Grill each side 3 minutes, then start brushing with sauce.

(Begin with the sauce when the meat is about half cooked.) Each side should get 2 or 3 more minutes exposure to heat, with 2–3 more sauce-brushings—10 minutes total.

Remove from fire, remove skewers, give the rolls a 90° turn, and reskewer. Return to the fire and grill the uncooked sides in the same way but only for 6 or 8 minutes total. Brush on sauce as before. This way the roll grills evenly.

To serve: Remove skewers and let stand a minute or so to "set." Cut off and discard ragged ends and string. Cut the roll into pieces about 1 inch (2½ cm) long. Arrange 3 or 4 pieces attractively on individual plates with round face up. Garnish with a PICKLED GINGER SHOOT or small quantity of substitute pickle and serve immediately.

Combines well with SOYBEANS IN THE POD (page 471) and VINEGAR-PICKLED CABBAGE (page 324).

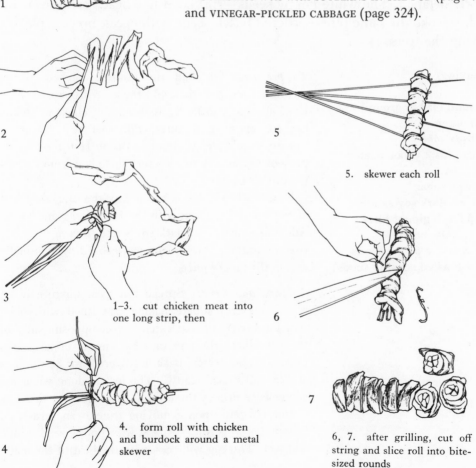

1

2

5

5. skewer each roll

3

1–3. cut chicken meat into one long strip, then

6

4. form roll with chicken and burdock around a metal skewer

4

7

6, 7. after grilling, cut off string and slice roll into bite-sized rounds

VARIATION: Preheat oven to very hot (500°F/260°C). Marinate the rolls for 40 minutes in the sauce, then wrap each in a greased sheet of aluminum foil; twist ends of foil tightly. Bake for 20 to 25 minutes. Remove from foil and cut and serve as above.

Note: The sauce is a basic *teriyaki* type. Once mixed, it will keep under refrigeration for a long time. To keep it fresh, add fresh ingredients now and then and occasionally boil it to eliminate moisture given out by foods marinated in the mixture. Cool to room temperature before refrigerating.

Chicken Loaf "Wind-in-the-Pines"
(*Toriniku Matsukaze-yaki*) 鶏肉松風焼き

The name of this recipe typifies the poetry in everyday Japanese life. The soft whisper of the boiling kettle in the tea ceremony has associations with the wind blowing through the pine groves that border many a picturesque shore in Japan. The white poppy seeds—sprinkled like beach sand over this dish—evoke the same pine-bordered beach scene with ocean breezes playing among the trees.

4 servings

1 pound (450 g) ground chicken
3 Tbsps *saké*
1 egg plus 2 yolks, beaten
¼ tsp salt
2 Tbsps sugar
3 Tbsps dark soy sauce
1 tsp fresh ginger juice
1 egg yolk, beaten
2 tsps white poppy seeds (or toasted sesame seeds)

To prepare: Put half the ground chicken into a medium-sized pot, then add the *saké*. Cook over high heat, stirring constantly to keep the chicken broken up, for about 2 minutes, till meat turns whitish. Spread in colander to drain and cool. Half the meat is precooked this way to keep the whole loaf from shrinking during baking.

In a bowl, with your hands mix the uncooked half of the ground chicken with the beaten egg and yolks. Add salt, sugar, and dark soy sauce, mixing well between additions. Mix in the pan-cooked meat. Finally mix in the ginger juice.

To bake and serve: Spread the meat mixture in an 8-inch (20-cm) square baking pan lined with oiled (not buttered) foil that extends over opposite sides of the pan. Place the pan in a bain-marie or large pan filled with hot water. Bake, uncovered, for 30 minutes at 425–450°F/220°–230°C. The loaf is done when the center is as firm as the meat at the edges.

Immediately upon removing from oven, brush on beaten egg yolk and sprinkle with poppy seeds while still wet. The egg will cook with the heat of the loaf.

the ends of a foil lining in a baking pan can be used to lift out the finished dish

Run the blade of a knife between the hot pan and meat, then lift out the foil with the loaf and place on a cutting board. Cut the loaf into 1-inch (2½-cm) squares. Carefully transfer squares to individual plates. One serving is 4 squares. Serve hot or at room temperature.

Combines well with SEAFOOD IN CITRON SHELLS (page 430) and ASPARAGUS WITH MUSTARD DRESSING (page 424).

Ginger Pork Sauté

(*Butaniku Shōga-yaki*) 豚肉しょうが焼き

4 servings

8 large fresh *shiitake* mushrooms, wiped and trimmed
oil
4 pork loin cutlets, ¼ inch (¾ cm) thick
2 Tbsps *saké*
1 Tbsp *mirin*
1 Tbsp dark soy sauce
1 Tbsp fresh ginger juice

To prepare: Cut mushrooms at a slight angle into ⅓-inch (⁴/₅-cm) slices.

To cook and serve: Heat a scant amount of oil in a frying pan and fry pork cutlets over high heat till lightly browned on one side. Turn heat to low and cook, uncovered, about 2 minutes. Turn, and cook other side the same way till done. Remove from pan and keep warm.

Pour all but 2 Tbsps of fat from the pan, and while the skillet is still hot mix in the *saké*, *mirin*, dark soy sauce, and ginger juice. Stir over medium heat for 2 minutes to deglaze, then add the mushroom slices. Cook, stirring, 1 minute.

Quickly slice each cutlet crosswise into 1-inch (2½-cm) widths and arrange on individual plates (1 cutlet per serving). If not using chopsticks, the slicing is unnecessary. Spoon sauce and mushrooms over meat and serve immediately.

Combines well with DEEP-FRIED TŌFU (page 412) and VINEGARED CUCUMBER (page 423).

VARIATIONS: Use very thinly sliced lean pork or cutlets thicker than ¼ inch, but adjust cooking time and quantity of sauce. The basic recipe may also be applied to beef and to chicken.

Steak Teriyaki

(Gyūniku Teriyaki) 牛肉照り焼き

Teri means "glossy luster," and the secret is to achieve this effect by reducing the sauce without overcooking the meat.

4 servings

4 sirloin steaks, about
 1 inch (2½ cm) thick and
 6-8 ounces (180-225 g) each
salt
2 Tbsps vegetable oil
4 Tbsps *saké*
3 Tbsps *mirin*
2 Tbsps dark soy sauce
mustard paste (see page 78)

To pan-broil: Salt the meat lightly on both sides to extract juices.

Heat a scant amount of oil in a large frying pan and brown on one side, covered, over high heat, about 3 minutes. Turn once only. While the meat is frying on the second side, splash on the *saké*. Cover the pan and fry for another 2 or 3 minutes. This browning will produce quite a lot of smoke; the meat will be seared on the outside and will be quite rare on the inside.

Remove steaks to a side plate. Over heat add the *mirin* and dark soy sauce to the meat juices in the pan (this forms the *teriyaki* sauce). As soon as meat glaze is dissolved, return the steaks to the pan to coat with the sauce, about 30 seconds on each side.

To serve: Cut the steaks across the grain into ½-inch (1½-cm) slices. This slicing is necessary only for eating with chopsticks. Arrange on individual plates. Spoon over some of the *teriyaki* sauce. Garnish with a dollop of prepared mustard.

Combines well with ASPARAGUS WITH MUSTARD DRESSING (page 424) and BEATEN EGG SOUP (page 346).

Grilled Eggplant

(Yakinasu) 焼きなす (color plate 10)

Japan's small eggplants are delicious grilled over hot charcoal until the skin is charred, when you plunge them momentarily into cold water so the peel comes off easily. You can eat the flesh hot with ginger and soy, or lemon. They are also served chilled in summer, with the same seasonings.

4 servings

8-10 small eggplants, about
 4 inches (10 cm) long

To prepare: Brush the eggplants with vegetable oil and prick the skin in a few places with a toothpick to enable heat and oil to penetrate.

vegetable oil
dark soy sauce
1 Tbsp finely grated fresh
   ginger and 1 Tbsp ginger
   juice (or lemon wedges
   and lemon juice)

To grill and serve: Grill eggplants about 5 inches (13 cm) from the hottest charcoal fire. Grilling takes about 15–20 minutes, depending on heat and thickness of eggplants. Turn frequently until eggplants are wrinkled and the skin is fairly well charred; you should be able to feel that the skin has separated slightly from the inner pulp.

Remove from grill, plunge into cold water, peel, and discard the charred skin. Use 2 grilled eggplants per serving, either whole or cut into bite-sized pieces. Place on individual plates, pour about 1 Tbsp soy sauce and a bit of ginger (or lemon) juice over the eggplant, and garnish with a cone of grated ginger (or lemon wedge). Serve immediately.

Goes well with CHILLED FINE NOODLES (page 457).

VARIATION: With large eggplant, cut into ¼-inch (1¼-cm) rounds or "steaks," brush with oil (including skin), and broil on a greased baking sheet in a preheated broiler for 5 minutes. Turn with a pancake turner and broil the uncooked side—another 2 or 3 minutes. Serve seasoned with soy sauce and ginger juice and garnished as above. Eggplants of any kind are very versatile and can be baked, sautéed, stir-fried, deep-fried, and boiled.

Foil-Cooked *Enokitake* Mushrooms

(*Enokitake Mushi-yaki*) 榎茸蒸し焼き

A succulent way to prepare those intriguing little white mushrooms that look like bundles of long, thin matches.

4 servings

2 bunches *enokitake*
   mushrooms
12-inch (30-cm) square of
   aluminum foil
1 Tbsp butter
1 thin lemon slice, seeded
kinome sprigs

To cook and serve: Wash *enokitake* mushrooms and cut off and discard spongy root. Drain.

Butter the center of a 12-inch (30-cm) square of heavy-duty aluminum cooking foil and in the middle place mushrooms, keeping them bunched. Top with butter and lemon (salt, if butter is not salted). Add a few sprigs of *kinome* as a fragrant garnish.

Fold foil carefully into a loose packet so that no juices can escape. Bake in a preheated oven at 475°F/245°C (high heat) for 5 minutes (or cook over a hot charcoal fire).

Remove packet to a plate and serve immediately, folding back the foil and inviting diners to help themselves. Individual foil packets can also be made with ½ bunch of *enokitake* each.

Combines well with DEEP-FRIED KEBABS (page 418) and CLEAR SOUP WITH SHRIMP (page 154).

Teppan-yaki
鉄板焼き

In restaurants specializing in this dish, the *teppan*, "iron sheet," is either an entire counter made into an immense griddle or a large griddle incorporated into the center of a table around which the diners sit cooking the seafood, chicken, lean red meat, and sliced vegetables. At home, you may use an electric griddle, an electric frying pan, or a heavy skillet on a heating unit at the table.

8 servings

8 large fresh shrimp
1 pound (450 g) chicken
 meat, boned
2½ pounds (1125 g) sirloin
 or tenderloin beef
2 5-inch (13-cm) pieces of
 squid
2 medium onions
8 fresh *shiitake* mush-
 rooms, wiped and
 trimmed
½ pound (225 g) bean
 sprouts (mung beans)
2 bell peppers

sauces and condiments:
 PONZU SAUCE (see page 172)
 SESAME SAUCE (see page
  267)
 finely grated giant white
  radish (*daikon-oroshi*)
 RED MAPLE RADISH (see
  page 170)

To prepare: You can clean and trim the ingredients to be grilled a number of hours in advance, refrigerate each separately, then arrange on a platter just before serving time.

Shrimp: Remove heads and shells, but leave tails attached. Devein and wash.

Chicken: Cut boned chicken into 2-inch (5-cm) squares. Leave skin on, but pierce with fork prongs a few times to keep it from shriveling while cooking.

Beef: Cut steak crosswise into ¼-inch (¾-cm) strips.

Squid: Score on both sides (crosswise on one side, and lengthwise on the other) to keep meat from curling over heat. Cut in half lengthwise, then crosswise into strips 1 inch (2½-cm) wide.

Onions: Insert toothpick to keep rings together, and cut crosswise into ¼-inch (¾-cm) thick rounds.

Mushrooms: Notch decorative crosses into caps of mushrooms.

Bean sprouts: Wash, pick over, and drain.

Bell peppers: Seed and cut lengthwise into quarters.

Prepare sauces and condiments and refrigerate.

To cook and serve: Set the table with the griddle unit

**finely chopped green
 onion
lemon wedges
salt (only for seafood)**

a toothpick keeps an onion slice from falling apart

at the center. Individual place settings should consist of a plate and a dipping bowl at the side in which to mix the sauces and condiments.

Bring the platter of ingredients to the table. Sauces should be in small ewers or servers, condiments in small bowls to pass.

Heat the griddle to high. Rub with a scant amount of salad oil (or use a combination of salad oil and suet). Lay the food on, a few pieces at a time, and cook, turning, till done. You may turn the heat down to medium, once cooking has started. None of the ingredients takes longer than 7 or 8 minutes to cook, so do not make them tough by overcooking. Everyone can cook his own favorites using his own chopsticks or fork, but with the bean sprouts one person might preside with a pancake turner. The only ingredients eaten with salt and lemon juice, instead of being dipped into one of the sauces, are shrimp, squid, or other "bloodless" sea creatures.

Sauce and condiment combinations:

PONZU SAUCE with finely chopped green onion and
   RED MAPLE RADISH
SESAME SAUCE with finely grated giant white radish and
   finely chopped green onion
salt with squirt of lemon (for seafood)

VARIATIONS: Other possible ingredients: sliced pork, thin lamb chops, oysters, clams in the shell, scallops, sweet potato rounds, Japanese long onions or green onions cut diagonally, and for many but not everyone, sliced garlic.

❀ Steamed Dishes ❀
Mushimono

Flounder in the Woodpile
(*Hirame Shiba-mushi*) 鮃柴蒸し

The word *shiba* means "brushwood," and in this dish, julienned vegetables and long thin *enokitake* mushrooms are arranged around fish fillets like wood laid for a fire.

4 servings

1 pound (450 g) *hirame* flounder fillet(s)
salt
1 bunch *enokitake* mushrooms, trimmed
3-4 fresh *shiitake* mushrooms, wiped and trimmed
⅓ medium carrot, scraped
1 bunch trefoil (*mitsuba*) stalks only (substitute asparagus or green beans cut into julienne strips)
1 egg white, lightly beaten with a fork
saké
SILVER SAUCE (see page 209)
finely grated giant white radish (*daikon-oroshi*) seasoned with a dab of finely grated *wasabi* horseradish

To prepare: Lightly salt the fillets on both sides and let rest 1 to 1½ hours. Wash well and pat dry. Remove skin (use the *soto-biki* technique, page 130) and cut the fillets crosswise into 4 equal pieces.

(If the fillets are thin and you want to make the dish appear to have more volume, first cut each whole fillet into a regular shape, reserving thin sections and trimmings. Then, cut flaps or wings into the trimmed fillet with a butterfly cut [*kannon-biraki* technique, see page 132]. Cut crosswise into individual portions. Use the reserved parts and trimmings as a stuffing for the butterfly-cut pieces.)

Scrape and clean vegetables. Cut the carrot and *shiitake* mushrooms into julienne strips about 1½ inches (4 cm) long. Cut the trefoil stalks (or julienne strips of asparagus or green beans) into 1½-inch (4-cm) lengths. (With green beans, parboil julienne strips for 30 seconds.)

Toss all the cut vegetables in a large mixing bowl, salt lightly, and toss again. Wait a few minutes for the salt to penetrate. Then add lightly beaten egg white and toss so that all ingredients are well coated.

To assemble and steam: Steam in individual heatproof bowls. Lay in a piece of fillet, sprinkle with about 1 Tbsp of *saké*, arrange julienned vegetables on the fish like the spokes of a wheel.

Cover with plastic wrap or foil, sealing the edges tight. Even if the steaming bowls have their own covers, use the plastic wrap or foil because these materials allow a good, tight seal.

Place sealed bowls in a hot steamer. Cover. Steam 10 minutes over high heat.

Make the SILVER SAUCE (directions on page 209) while the fish and vegetables are steaming.

To serve: Remove the bowls from the steamer, uncover, and top with hot SILVER SAUCE. Garnish with a small cone of grated giant white radish (*daikon-oroshi*) into which a dab of finely grated *wasabi* horseradish has been mixed. Serve immediately.

Combines well with SCATTERED SUSHI, OSAKA STYLE (page 449) and BEATEN EGG SOUP (page 346).

VARIATIONS: Use fillets of any white-fleshed fish: sea bream, sea bass, and yellowtail, for example. You may use a piece of giant kelp (*konbu*) on the bottom of each steaming vessel for flavor, as in the recipe for SEA BREAM STEAMED WITH CHESTNUTS (page 376).

Sea Bream Steamed with Buckwheat Noodles
(*Tai no Shinshū-mushi*) 鯛の信州蒸し (color plate 13)

The Shinshū region—the forested mountain spine of Japan's main island—has always been known for its buckwheat noodles (*soba*). The subtle flavor of the buckwheat pleasantly permeates delicate white-fleshed fish such as bream when the two are steamed together.

4 servings

1 sea bream, about pound
  (450 g)
salt
¼ pound (115 g) dried
  green-tea buckwheat
  noodles (*cha-soba*) or
  regular buckwheat
  noodles (*soba*)
4-x-6-inch (10-x-15-cm)
  piece of giant kelp
  (*konbu*)
saké

To prepare: Scale, gut, and clean the fish, then cut into boneless fillets, with skin. Lightly salt both sides; let rest 40 minutes to an hour. Wash and pat dry.

With its skin side down on the cutting board, make two wings in each fillet, using the butterfly cut (*kannon-biraki* technique, see page 132). Cut each fillet in half crosswise.

While the salted fillets are resting, boil the noodles according to the directions on page 310.

Wipe the giant kelp (*konbu*) with a damp cloth. Cut into four pieces. The seaweed is for flavor and is not to be eaten.

sauce:

  1⅔ cups *dashi*
  6 Tbsps *mirin*
  6 Tbsps dark soy sauce
  1 cup (loose) dried bonito
    flakes (*hana-katsuo*)

finely chopped green onion
1 sheet toasted *nori*
  seaweed, cut into fine
  shreds

To assemble and steam: Steam in individual heatproof bowls. First lay a piece of giant kelp in each bowl. On that, in a mound, arrange one portion of drained green-tea noodles. Over this, lay a piece of fish fillet, skin side up, flaps hugging the mound of noodles. Splash about 1 Tbsp *saké* on the fish.

Cover with plastic wrap or foil, sealing the edges tight. Even if the steaming bowls have their own covers, use plastic wrap or foil because these materials allow a good, tight seal.

Place sealed bowls in a hot steamer. Cover. Steam over high heat for 10 minutes.

To make the sauce: While the fish is steaming, in a medium-sized saucepan combine the *dashi*, *mirin*, and dark soy sauce over high heat and bring to a boil. Stir in bonito flakes, and strain immediately. Discard bonito flakes.

To serve: Remove the bowls from the steamer, uncover, and top with hot sauce. Garnish with finely chopped green onion and fine shreds of toasted *nori* seaweed. Serve immediately.

Combines well with STUFFED CRAB (page 407) and SEAFOOD IN CITRON SHELLS (page 430).

Sea Bream Steamed with Chestnuts

(*Tai no Tamba-mushi*) 鯛の丹波蒸し

A dish for the autumn season when sea bream are at their best, and when large, lustrous chestnuts come onto the market from Tamba, an ancient name still used for a district not too far from the former imperial capital of Kyoto.

4 servings

1 sea bream, about
  1½ pounds (675 g)
salt
12 raw chestnuts, shelled
  and peeled (see page 64)

To prepare; Scale, gut, and clean fish, cut into boneless fillets, with skin. Salt lightly on both sides, wrap and refrigerate for 1 hour. Wash and pat dry.

Cut fillets crosswise but at a slight diagonal into portion-sized pieces about 2 inches (5 cm) wide. Score the skin in the direction of the scales 2 or 3 times on each piece to avoid shrinking during steaming.

12-16 ginkgo nuts, shelled
and peeled (optional;
substitute ¼ cup green
peas)
1 bunch trefoil (*mitsuba*)
(or substitute ½ bunch
spinach, parboiled)
4-x-6-inch (10-x-15-cm)
piece giant kelp (*konbu*)
saké

SILVER SAUCE:

2 cups *dashi*
½ tsp salt
1 Tbsp light soy sauce
4 Tbsps *saké*
2 tsps cornstarch, mixed
with 2 tsps water
few drops fresh ginger juice
or lemon juice (optional)
in place of either ginger
or lemon juice, garnish
with sprig of *kinome* or
slivers of *yuzu* citron
rind

Slice peeled chestnuts into paper-thin rounds. Wash sliced nuts under cold running water to remove starch. Drain well.

Use fresh, shelled and peeled ginkgo nuts. Canned ginkgo nuts are not satisfactory; substitute green peas if fresh nuts are unavailable.

Chop trefoil stalks (or parboiled spinach) into 1½-inch (4-cm) lengths.

Wipe the giant kelp with a damp cloth. Cut into 4 pieces. The kelp is to impart flavor during steaming and is not to be eaten.

To assemble and steam: Steam in individual heatproof bowls. First lay a piece of giant kelp in each steaming bowl. On this place a piece of fish, skin side up. Sprinkle on raw chestnut slices and add 3–4 ginkgo nuts (or a few peas). At the side lay in a neat mound of trefoil (or parboiled spinach).

Over this arrangement splash about 1 Tbsp *saké*.

Cover with plastic wrap or foil, sealing the edges tight. Even if the steaming bowls you are using have their own covers, use the plastic wrap or foil instead because these materials allow a good, tight seal.

Place sealed bowls in a hot steamer. Cover. Steam 15 minutes over high heat.

To make the sauce: While the fish is steaming, in a medium-sized saucepan heat the *dashi*, then season with salt, light soy sauce, and *saké*. Bring to a simmer.

Just before serving, stir the cornstarch-and-water mixture and pour it into the hot liquid, stirring till thickened. At the very last moment, so as to preserve the fragrance, stir in the fresh ginger juice or lemon juice.

To serve: Remove the bowls from the steamer, uncover, and top with thickened SILVER SAUCE. If the sauce has been made without ginger juice or lemon juice, you may garnish the bowls with fragrant slivers of *yuzu* citron rind or sprigs of *kinome*.

Combines well with TROUT SASHIMI (page 167) and CLEAR SOUP WITH SHRIMP (page 154).

VARIATIONS: Use sea bass, salmon, or trout.

Steamed Salmon and Roe

(*Sake no Oyako-mushi*) 鮭の親子蒸し

Like the popular CHICKEN-'N-EGG ON RICE (page 283), this dish also bears the whimsical Japanese name *oyako*, "parent and child."

4 servings

1 pound (450 g) boneless
  and skinless fillet of
  salmon (defrosted is
  fine)
oil
4 Tbsps salmon roe
2 Tbsps *saké*
1 cup grated giant white
  radish (*daikon-oroshi*)
½ egg white, lightly
  beaten
pinch salt

sauce:

  1 cup *dashi*
  2 Tbsps light soy sauce
  3 Tbsps *mirin*
  2 Tbsps vinegar
  2 tsps cornstarch, mixed
    with 2 tsps water

1 lemon, quartered

To prepare and steam: Salt the salmon (see *furi-jio* technique, page 132) and cut into large bite-sized pieces. Lay the pieces in a lightly oiled, hot frying pan and fry over medium heat till heat penetrates thoroughly, about 3 minutes total for both sides. Turn carefully to keep pieces from crumbling. Remove to a colander and rinse with boiling water. Immediately place pieces in 4 individual vessels for steaming.

In a bowl, with your fingers mix the roe in 2 Tbsps *saké* (this cleans the roe); then discard this liquid. Remove excess water from grated radish by squeezing it gently in cheesecloth. Fluff squeezed radish and then mix in the beaten egg white and salt. Finally, toss the roe with the radish. Spoon over the salmon pieces in the steaming vessels.

Cover vessels tightly with plastic wrap or foil and steam over high heat for 5 minutes.

To assemble and serve: While steaming the main ingredients, make the sauce. In a medium-sized saucepan combine the *dashi*, soy sauce, *mirin*, and vinegar and bring to a boil. Pour in the cornstarch-and-water mixture and stir until thickened. Remove from heat.

Remove vessels from the steamer and uncover. Spoon the thickened sauce over the roe-radish-salmon and the squeeze the juice of a quarter lemon over each portion. Serve immediately. Eat with spoons or forks.

Goes well with CRAB-AND-TŌFU BALLS IN BROTH (page 413).

Saké-Steamed Abalone

(*Awabi Saka-mushi*) 鮑酒蒸し (color plate 10)

This recipe is impossible unless a small species of imported abalone is available frozen. Abalone are well protected in U.S. waters, and small ones necessary for this dish cannot be gathered. The tenderized abalone steaks sold in the U.S. (frozen, usually) are not appropriate for this recipe, though some kind of creative adaptation is certainly possible. The subtle flavor and tenderness of the traditional dish makes inclusion of the classical recipe worthwhile, even if for many readers it must remain a study piece.

3 servings

1 about 3-inch (8-cm) fresh
   abalone, in its shell
salt
approximately 4 Tbsps
   saké

sauce:

   green innard from the
     abalone
   1 Tbsp mayonnaise
   1 tsp lemon or ginger
     juice
   1 Tbsp *dashi*
   ½ tsp dark soy sauce

1

1. keep abalone shell level in steamer

To steam: While the abalone is in its shell, salt the exposed meat fairly generously (this is its foot). With a stiff scrubbing brush, rub the salt in; the salt acts as a cleaner and will become quite gray. Rinse well in running cold water.

Run a knife between the shell and the meat, but not so deeply as to separate the two. Pour *saké* generously over the meat and between meat and shell.

Steam, covered, for 2 or 3 hours over moderate heat to tenderize meat. Cool.

To assemble: Cut the cooled abalone out of the shell. Trim off the dark fringy portion around the edge of the foot and the innards. Discard all this except a 1-inch (2½-cm) or so intestinal tube packed with green stuff (the green is the pure and tender seaweed on which the abalone feeds).

Cut the abalone into ⅜-inch (1-cm) thick slices diagonally across the grain.

Rub the green innards through a sieve. In a bowl, blend with the other sauce ingredients.

To serve: Use as an hors d'oeuvre or as a first course. Serve at room temperature in small individual dishes with a small amount of thick sauce on the side.

Combines well with KISU (SILLAGO) SASHIMI (page 353) and GREEN BEANS WITH SESAME-MISO DRESSING (page 420).

2   3   4

2–4. cut steamed abalone into thin slices.

Steamed Chicken in Seasoned Broth

(*Toriniku Shio-mushi*) 鶏肉塩蒸し

4 servings

1 pound (450 g) chicken
thighs
salt
6 Tbsps *saké*

broth:

½ cup broth reserved
from the steaming pan
1 Tbsp dark soy sauce
2 Tbsps lemon juice

To prepare and steam: Score the skin side of the meat fairly deeply to allow the *saké* to penetrate the meat and to steam easily. Lay skin side up in a pan, salt lightly, and splash on 6 Tbsps *saké*.

Place the pan, uncovered, in a hot steamer. Steam 15 to 20 minutes on high heat.

To assemble and serve: Cut the hot steamed chicken meat into bite-sized pieces and arrange in individual serving dishes. Discard bones.

Reserve the broth from the steaming pan and strain. Add dark soy sauce and lemon juice to the broth, mix, and adjust seasonings. Spoon over the chicken pieces and serve immediately. No garnish.

Goes well with CRAB-AND-TŌFU BALLS IN BROTH (page 413).

VARIATION: COLD STEAMED CHICKEN WITH SESAME SAUCE

sesame sauce:

2 Tbsps sesame paste or
white sesame seeds,
toasted and ground to a
flaky paste (see page
86) (or smooth peanut
butter)
2 Tbsps *dashi* or chicken
stock
1 Tbsp dark soy sauce
¼ tsp sugar
pinch salt
¼ Tbsp lemon juice

Prepare and steam the chicken exactly as above. Bring to room temperature and refrigerate. Before serving, slice into ¼-inch (¾-cm) thick slices and arrange on individual plates. Top with a few Tbsps sesame sauce and serve. No garnish.

For the sauce, mix sesame paste or toasted and ground seeds (or peanut butter) with the *dashi* (or chicken broth) till smooth, then blend in other ingredients.

❋ Simmered Dishes ❋
Nimono

Simmered Mackerel with Radish
(*Saba Oroshi-ni*) 鯖おろし煮

A good way to prepare any oily fish. Plentiful and relatively inexpensive in Japan, mackerel is popular, but if you can obtain yellowtail instead, all the better. Do not add the grated radish until the end, to preserve its aroma. Like lemon, the piquant radish counteracts the oiliness of the fish. It also gives substance to the broth, as in the dip for TEMPURA, enabling each morsel of fish to be amply coated with succulent sauce. This is an everyday family dish, not fancy fare.

6 servings

1½ pounds (675 g) mackerel fillets, with skin
1 cup *saké*
3 Tbsps fresh ginger, cut into fine "needle" shreds
½ tsp salt
2 Tbsps light soy sauce
2 Tbsps *mirin* (or 1 scant tsp sugar)
1 cup *dashi*
1½ cups finely grated giant white radish (*daikon-oroshi*)
1 Tbsp finely chopped green onion
seven-spice mixture (*shichimi*)

To prepare: With tweezers, remove any bones from fillets, then cut into pieces about 3 inches (8 cm) long. You may lightly fry the fish, dusted in flour, in a scant amount of very hot oil to eliminate any smell if *absolute* freshness is in question.

To cook: Place the *saké* and ginger in the bottom of a wide saucepan and mix. Lay in the fish, skin side up. The pieces may touch, but must not overlap. Bring to a boil over high heat, reduce heat to simmer, then cover with a drop-lid (*otoshi-buta*, see page 107), which rests directly on top of the fish, to keep fillets intact. Simmer about 10 minutes.

Mix the salt, light soy sauce, and *mirin* with the *dashi*, pour gently over the fish, and simmer, uncovered, until the broth is reduced 50 percent.

Spread the grated white radish over the fillets and then sprinkle on the chopped green onion. Replace the drop-lid and simmer again for 1–2 minutes.

Carefully transfer the fillets with a spatula to individual shallow bowls, taking care that the radish and chopped green onion blanketing the fish do not fall off. Spoon a bit of the sauce from the pan over the top. Serve immediately with a small cellar or shaker of seven-spice mixture.

Combines well with CHINESE CABBAGE AND DEEP-
FRIED TŌFU (page 398) and SOUSED SPINACH (page 429)

Fried Cod in Broth

(*Tara no Age-ni*) たらの揚げ煮

4 servings

1½ pounds (675 g) fillet of
  cod (or other firm white-
  fleshed fish), with skin
flour
oil for deep-frying

for simmering:

  1⅔ cups *dashi*
  4 Tbsps *mirin*
  1 Tbsp sugar
  2 Tbsps dark soy sauce
  1 Tbsp *saké*

finely chopped green onion
finely grated fresh ginger

To prepare: Cut fillet(s) into 2-inch (5-cm) pieces.
Blanch in boiling water for 30 seconds, then wash
thoroughly in cold water. Pat dry and dust both sides
with flour.

Deep-fry at a low temperature (320°F/160°C) for 5
minutes, several pieces at a time, till lightly browned.
Turn pieces once only. Drain on paper towels.

To simmer and serve: Combine the ingredients for
simmering, bring to boil quickly, then reduce heat till
liquid is simmering. As soon as the cod is drained,
gently slide the deep-fried fish into the simmering
liquid. Spoon the hot liquid over the top of the fish, if
necessary, to make sure the fish is well seasoned by the
hot stock; cooking time is about 10 minutes.

Carefully remove fish to individual bowls. Ladle over
a generous amount of simmering stock, but not so much
as to make the cod appear to swim. Garnish with finely
chopped green onion and the finely grated fresh ginger.
Serve immediately.

Goes well with BEAN CURD DENGAKU (page 192).

Saké-Simmered Herring

(*Nishin no Nitsuke*) にしんの煮つけ

A flavorsome recipe for fillets of herring with bean curd in a sauce of *saké*
and soy. In Kyoto they use dried herring—claiming it is even tastier—and
call the dish *Migaki Nishin no Nimono*.

4 servings

2 herring, about 10 ounces
  (285-g) each

for simmering:

  ½ cup *saké*

To prepare: Scale and gut fish, and cut boneless
fillets, with skin. Blanch fillets in boiling water for 30
seconds, then wash thoroughly in cold water and drain.

To simmer and serve: Pour the *saké* into a medium-
sized frying pan and place over medium heat. When it

½ cup *mirin*
1 cup *dashi*
½ cup dark soy sauce
3-inch (8-cm) square giant
  kelp (*konbu*)

2 cakes *tōfu* (bean curd)
1 generous Tbsp shred-cut
  fresh ginger

reaches a simmer, add the other ingredients for simmering, including the piece of giant kelp. Reduce heat to low.

Add the fillets, skin side up, and cover with a drop-lid (*otoshi-buta*) or circle of baking paper with a vent (see page 220). Simmer, just on the verge of a boil, over *low heat* till the liquid just covers the bottom of the pan, 20 to 30 minutes.

Remove from heat and cut each fillet crosswise into thirds. With a pancake turner remove from the pan to individual dishes, 3 pieces per serving.

Remove kelp from pan and discard. Cut each cake of bean curd into sixths, and place these in the liquid that remains. Cook 1 minute or so over medium heat till the bean curd is thoroughly heated. Spoon the hot liquid over the bean curd. Remove bean curd carefully with a pancake turner or spatula to the bowls with the herring. Pour the remaining liquid into the bowls in equal portions.

Garnish with shred-cut fresh ginger. Serve hot or at room temperature.

Goes well with EGG "TŌFU" (page 216).

VARIATIONS: The bean curd is used to lend its texture and its innocent taste, but you may use a wide variety of "clear-tasting" parboiled vegetables instead, such as giant white radish (*daikon*), turnip, burdock (*gobō*), and so on.

Steam-Simmered Octopus

(*Tako Yawaraka-ni*) たこやわらか煮 (color plate 10)

Tenderizing octopus is a problem. Greek fishermen are said to bash the poor creature against seaside rocks ninety-nine times before tossing it in the pot. In Japan, the secret lies in first kneading the octopus in grated radish (*daikon-oroshi*), then steam-simmering it in stock, then allowing the steamed octopus to rest 8 hours.

Simmering the broth inside a steamer prevents evaporation that would intensify the seasoning and harden the octopus. The quantity of the broth remains constant, and so does the flavor. Moreover, you do not need to worry about the broth boiling away, even with the heat full on. The result is very tender octopus with its skin perfect. A word of advice: large octopuses are tough, so choose one about 2½ pounds (1¼ kg) in weight. At the midpoint, tentacles should be no more than 1½ inches (4 cm) in diameter.

This is good as an entrée and also delicious served with drinks.

4 servings

2¼-3½-pound (1-1½-kg) octopus
1 giant white radish, finely grated (2 Tbsps salt may be substituted, though salt toughens the flesh)

for simmering:
  8 cups *dashi*
  1 cup *saké*
  7 Tbsps sugar
  2 Tbsps *mizuame* (wheat-starch syrup), if available
  5 Tbsps light soy sauce
  ½ cup *tamari* sauce

2-inch (5-cm) square giant
about 1 cup (loose) dried bonito kelp (*konbu*) flakes (*hana-katsuo*)
kinome sprigs or shred-cut fresh ginger

To prepare: Turn the octopus's saclike body inside out by pushing it through the opening in the sac and cut off and discard all internal organs, the eyes, and the beak. Also chop off and discard the wispy ends of the tentacles (see sketches, pages 248–49).

Knead the entire octopus vigorously in grated giant white radish for 5 minutes. This cleans the octopus of a gelatinous epidermal covering and also tenderizes the flesh. Discard the grated radish, which will have turned gray. Wash the octopus well, and return head sac to original position.

With a long cooking chopstick or wooden spoon handle inserted into the head-sac opening (or some kind of hook used in the same way), plunge the octopus into a large pot of gently boiling water 2 or 3 times and swish it around until the tentacles curl, about 2–3 minutes. The color of the skin changes to a deep pink. Hang the octopus to drain and cool. The curled tentacles will relax somewhat, making handling easier.

Cut off the head sac and cut tentacle section into 4 pieces, each piece with 2 tentacles.

Mix the ingredients for simmering. Put the octopus pieces into a 6-quart (5¾-L) pot or heatproof container and cover with the liquid for simmering. After wiping the giant kelp (*konbu*) with a damp towel, add to the pot. Put the dried bonito flakes in a small cheesecloth bag and add bag to pot; the bag is to keep the simmering liquid from becoming scummy.

Place a drop-lid (*otoshi-buta*) or a circle of baking paper with a center vent (see page 220) directly on the octopus. Cover the pot or heatproof container securely with cooking foil.

Put the whole into a steamer (or improvise as shown on page 211) and steam over high heat for 1½ hours or until tender. Prick with a toothpick to test for tenderness. Remove from heat, and allow to come to room temperature naturally, then let rest 8 hours.

To assemble and serve: Cut tentacles into 1½-inch (4-cm) lengths. Cut the meat of the head into diamond shapes of about the same size. Strain the liquid in which the octopus was steam-simmered. Discard the kelp and bonito flakes. Put 5 or 6 octopus pieces into medium-sized deep dishes and ladle a few Tbsps simmering liquid on top. Garnish either with a sprig of fragrant *kinome* leaves or with fine shreds of fresh ginger. Serve immediately.

Combines well with GRILLED CHICKEN ROLLS (page 366) and VINEGARED CUCUMBER (page 423).

Chikuzen Chicken

(*Iridori* or *Chikuzen-ni*) いり鶏又は筑前煮

This specialty of Chikuzen Province, now Fukuoka Prefecture in northern Kyushu, consists of chicken and vegetable pieces stir-fried and then simmered in a little highly flavored broth until the liquid is gone. It may be kept for a few days and reheated.

4–6 servings

1 pound (450 g) boned chicken thighs, with skin
4-6 fresh *shiitake* mushrooms, wiped and trimmed
2 medium carrots
3-4 inches (8-10 cm) medium bamboo shoot, washed
1 medium burdock root, scrubbed with a brush
1 cake *konnyaku* (devil's tongue jelly)
vegetable oil
1 cup *dashi*
2 Tbsps sugar
3 Tbsps light soy sauce
2 Tbsps dark soy sauce
2 ounces (60 g) snow peas, parboiled

To prepare: Cut the chicken into ¾-inch (2-cm) cubes. Scrape, peel, or trim the vegetables as required and cut into rolling wedges (the *ran-giri* technique, see page 140). Cut *konnyaku* into chunks the same size as vegetables. Keep cut burdock in water to avoid discoloration.

For excellence in flavor, parboil each of the vegetables separately in lightly salted water, rinse under cold water, and drain. The parboiling is optional.

To cook and serve: Heat 1 or 2 Tbsps oil (use as little oil as possible) in a medium-sized pot over high heat till very hot and add the chicken first, then the *konnyaku*, mushrooms, carrot, bamboo shoot, and burdock in that order. Stir-fry, using a wooden spoon, about 3 minutes, till all ingredients are well coated with hot oil and partially done.

Pour the *dashi* over the fried meat and vegetables to barely cover. Bring to a boil over high heat and add the sugar and soy sauces (if you do not have light soy sauce, use a total of 6 Tbsps of dark soy sauce). Cover with a drop-lid (*otoshi-buta*) or circle of baking paper with a vent (see page 220), and simmer till reduced by approximately 30 percent. Remove from heat. Mix in parboiled snow peas for color just before serving.

Serve hot or at room temperature in individual bowls, making sure the variety of ingredients is attractively represented in each dish.

Goes well with GRILLED SQUID WITH SESAME (page 364).

Chicken and Chinese Cabbage

(*Tori Jibu-ni*) 鶏じぶ煮

There are two entertaining theories as to how this dish came by its name: one that the simmering liquid sounds like *jibu-jibu-jibu* as it bubbles; the other that it was created by a man called *Jibu*emon. Grated ginger may be used instead of *wasabi* horseradish, but the latter is traditional.

4 servings

12 ounces (340 g) boned chicken, with skin (thigh recommended)
flour
6 leaves Chinese cabbage

for simmering:

1 cup *dashi*
4 Tbsps light soy sauce
4 Tbsps *mirin*
1 Tbsp sugar

finely grated *wasabi* horseradish or ground *sansho* pepper

To prepare: Cut boned chicken into 2-inch (5-cm) pieces and brush thoroughly with flour.

Carefully separate whole leaves from the head of Chinese cabbage and parboil in a large pot in ample lightly salted water (about 3–4 minutes); drain well.

Lay out each leaf and cut into 2½- × -1-inch (6½- × -2½-cm) strips as shown—first cut the leaf crosswise, then lengthwise. If the stem is very thick, slice off a thin layer. Transfer the cabbage strips to a medium-sized pot.

To cook and serve: In a second medium-sized pot mix the ingredients for simmering. Bring to a boil over medium heat and simmer for about 2 minutes.

Pour ⅔ of this very hot simmering liquid directly over the cabbage in the first pot. Place on medium heat immediately and gently boil cabbage strips for approximately 10 minutes, uncovered, stirring occasionally. Be careful not to break up leaf pieces.

In the second pot, in which ⅓ of the simmering liquid remains, lay the flour-brushed chicken pieces. Place over medium to high heat. Shake the pot frequently to keep the chicken moving. The meat will absorb most of the liquid within 7 to 10 minutes. Do not cover.

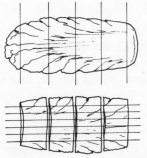

cut Chinese cabbage into strips
as shown

Remove the two pots from heat. Arrange mounds of Chinese cabbage on small, individual plates or dishes. On these, cushion pieces of chicken (¼ of amount cooked), skin-side up. Pour 1 Tbsp or so of simmering liquid from the cabbage pot over the cabbage and chicken. Garnish with a small cone of grated *wasabi* horseradish or a pinch of ground *sansho* pepper. Serve immediately.

Goes well with BAMBOO RICE (page 439) or THUNDER SOUP (page 349).

Chicken Balls in Sauce

(*Torigan-ni*) 鶏丸煮

These chicken balls are delicious served either with this sauce or in a clear soup made with primary *dashi*. As soon as they are cooked, place them immediately in individual serving bowls and cover them with the thick, hot sauce—or with *dashi*, if you are serving soup—to keep the flavor in.

4 servings

balls:

10 ounces (300 g) ground chicken

2½ ounces (70 g) white-fleshed fish fillet, without skin

2 eggs, beaten

1 tsp salt

2 Tbsps *saké*

3 Tbsps dark soy sauce

1 Tbsp fresh ginger juice

2 Tbsps sugar (optional)

2-inch (5-cm) square giant kelp (*konbu*)

for simmering balls:

2½ cups *dashi*

½ cup *saké*

⅓ cup *mirin*

2 Tbsps light soy sauce

2 Tbsps cornstarch, mixed with 2 Tbsps water

To prepare: Make and boil the chicken balls ahead of time.

Work the ground chicken to a fine, smooth texture with a pestle in a *suribachi* (Japanese grinding bowl, see page 105), or use a food processor. Add the fish fillet in small quantities while working the mixture, and continue till smooth. Gradually add the beaten egg, mixing well between additions. Season with salt, *saké*, soy sauce, ginger juice, and sugar. The sugar is less for taste than for tenderizing the meat and may be omitted. The chicken mixture will be somewhat runny.

To make a light broth in which to boil the chicken meat balls, wipe the giant kelp (*konbu*) clean with a cloth and put in a pot with 8 cups water. Bring just to a boil, then reduce heat to a gentle simmer.

Make chicken balls as instructed below and place them in the kelp broth one by one as they are formed.

To form balls, pick up a fistful of the chicken mixture with one hand and clench it (thumb on the outside). Gradually squeeze your hand closed, exerting the most pressure with your little and ring fingers— a small ball of ground chicken will be forced out be-

kinome sprigs, or finely shred-cut fresh ginger, or thin strips of *yuzu* citron rind

tween your thumb and first finger. Scoop the ball off your hand with a teaspoon as shown (dip spoon in water frequently to prevent sticking) and drop each ball into the light broth. The balls will sink to the bottom.

After forming the chicken balls, raise the heat and gently boil, uncovered, for 7 to 8 minutes, till slightly more than half-done—the balls will come floating to the top. Simmer for 2 to 3 minutes, lightly pressing balls with back of spoon or ladle. Remove boiled chicken balls to a colander and drain. Discard boiling liquid and kelp.

To simmer and serve: In a medium-sized pot, mix the ingredients for simmering, bring just to a boil, then reduce heat and simmer. Add the boiled chicken balls and simmer just till heated through, about 4 minutes, covered with a drop-lid (*otoshi-buta*) or circle of baking paper with a vent (see page 220).

Just before serving, remove drop-lid and dribble in cornstarch-and-water mixture. Stir gently for about 1 minute over medium-low heat till the liquid thickens.

Serve in deep individual dishes, 6–9 chicken balls per serving. Carefully transfer the balls to the bowls, arrange attractively, then cover with a few Tbsps of hot, thickened sauce. Garnish with sprigs of *kinome*, or ginger shreds, or *yuzu* citron rind. Serve immediately.

Combines well with GRILLED RED TILEFISH "WAKASA" (page 363) and GRILLED MUSHROOMS WITH PONZU SAUCE (page 425).

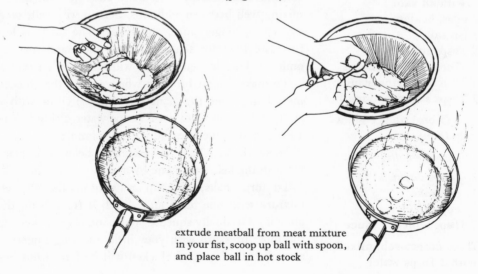

extrude meatball from meat mixture in your fist, scoop up ball with spoon, and place ball in hot stock

VARIATIONS: Add other vegetables to the ground chicken, such as sautéed minced onion, diced parboiled carrots, and so on. You may also serve the chicken balls along with another ingredient such as slices of (independently) simmered giant white radish (*daikon*) or turnips.

Nagasaki-Style Braised Pork

(*Buta Kaku-ni*) 豚角煮

It was in Nagasaki—almost the only port open to foreign trade for 250 years—that meat dishes first made their appearance in Japan, where Buddhism forbade the slaughter of four-legged beasts. The influence of Chinese cuisine is still strong in Nagasaki. It takes practically two days to prepare this dish, but the pork becomes so tender that it literally melts in your mouth.

6 servings

2½ pounds (1¼ kg) raw slab bacon (or fatty plate boiling beef)
vegetable oil
2½ cups *okara* (bean curd "lees," see page 60) (or substitute the water from washing rice, or rice or wheat bran)
2 3-inch (8-cm) knobs fresh ginger, peeled then crushed

for simmering pork:

3⅓ cups *dashi*
1 cup *saké*
2 Tbsps *mirin*
6 Tbsps dark soy sauce
6 Tbsps sugar

12 pearl onions, peeled
18 snow peas

for simmering vegetables:

1¼ cups *dashi*
2 Tbsps *mirin*
2 Tbsps light soy sauce

The morning of Day One: Cut the pork into pieces about 1 × 2½ inches (2½ × 6½ cm). Coat the bottom of a large frying pan very lightly with vegetable oil, then fry pork over very high heat for about 10 minutes. Turn frequently so all sides are well browned. Turn out into colander and run under hot water to remove excess oil.

Fill a large pot (about 5–6 quarts [5–6 L]) ¾ full of water and add the *okara* (or bran) and crushed knobs of ginger. Add the pork. The liquid should cover the meat. Cover with a drop lid (*otoshi-buta*) or a circle of baking paper with a center vent (see page 220) and simmer over low heat for at least 5 or 6 hours, until very tender. Add water to the pot if necessary; meat should be kept covered with liquid.

When tender, turn the meat out into a colander, discarding the rest of the contents of the pot. With your hands, gently rub off *okara* sticking to the meat and rinse under cold running water to clean thoroughly.

Put the meat into the pot for the second time and cover with water. Bring to a boil and simmer 30 to 40 minutes. This second simmering is to eliminate all odor of the *okara*. Rinse meat again under cold running water and then refrigerate in a sealed container. The meat will look rather gray and shriveled.

Day Two, about 1 hour before serving time: Bring pork to room temperature. Combine the ingredients

2 Tbsps mustard paste (see page 78)

for simmering the pork and pour into a large pot. Add the pork; the meat should be covered by liquid. Bring to a quick boil, then reduce heat and simmer gently, covered with a drop-lid or paper circle for 30 or 40 minutes.

During this time, peel the onions and slash the bottom of each bulb with a cross to allow heat to penetrate quickly. Parboil onions in lightly salted water until translucent, wash in cold water, then simmer for 2 to 3 minutes in a medium-sized pot with ¾ of the liquid for simmering vegetables. Discard liquid.

Parboil snow peas in lightly salted water for 2 or 3 minutes, wash in cold water, then simmer till heated through in a small pan in ¼ of the mixture for simmering vegetables. Discard liquid.

To serve: In deep, medium-sized dishes (or small bowls), place one or two pieces of pork, then arrange 2 onions and 3 snow peas with the pork. Garnish the pork with a dab of mustard and serve.

Combines well with FIVE-COLOR SALAD (page 425) and CHUNKY VEGETABLE SOUP (page 348).

Chilled Pork Slices

(*Butaniku no Hiyashi-chiri*) 豚肉の冷やしちり

A dish adapted from Chinese cuisine. Good for summer parties.

4 servings

2 Japanese long onions (*naganegi*) (or 3 leeks), cut into 3-inch (8-cm) lengths
3½-inch (9-cm) knob fresh ginger, peeled and cut into 2 or 3 chunks
½ tsp salt
1-pound (450-g) block fat-topped pork loin or bacon
PONZU SAUCE **(see page 172)**
finely chopped green onion

To cook: Fill a large pot with 2 quarts (2 L) cold water and add onion pieces, fresh ginger chunks, salt, and the meat block. The water should cover the meat.

Gently boil, covered with a drop-lid (*otoshi-buta*) or circle of baking paper with a vent (see page 220) for 2½ hours. Plunge cooked meat into cold water, let stand until cool, then refrigerate meat, still in the water, until chilled.

Meanwhile, make the PONZU SAUCE and prepare spicy condiments. Wrap the finely chopped green onion in cheesecloth, wash to remove bitterness, and gently wring out water.

finely grated fresh ginger
RED MAPLE RADISH **(see page
170)**

cut chilled pork into thin slices

To serve: Remove pork from chilled water, pat dry, and cut the meat against the grain into very thin slices, about $1/16$ inch ($1/4$ cm) thick. Arrange on a platter in a rosette pattern, putting spicy condiments in the center to garnish. Provide individual dipping bowls to mix the PONZU SAUCE and condiments. Dip the thin-sliced meat into sauce and eat.

Combines well with DEEP-FRIED EGGPLANT (page 233) and VINEGARED CUCUMBER (page 423).

VARIATION: Instead of serving the pork sliced thin, cut into pieces $1/4$ inch ($3/4$ cm) thick. In this case, PONZU SAUCE will be too light. Drizzle a mustard-based sauce (1 Tbsp prepared Japanese mustard paste [see page 78] mixed with 2 Tbsps dark soy sauce and the juice of $1/4$ lemon) on top of the arranged slices. No spicy condiments are necessary. A dip of SESAME SOY SAUCE (page 171) is another possibility.

Boiled Beans

(*Nimame*) 煮　豆

This recipe calls for dried soybeans, but you may substitute any medium-sized dried beans you wish. Do not use fresh beans, because they are too moist. This dish will keep for a few days.

6 servings

**1 pound (450 g) dried soy-
beans**
2 medium carrots, scraped
**4-inch (10-cm) square of
giant kelp (*konbu*)**

for simmering:
  2½ cups *dashi*
  1 tsp salt
  3 Tbsps sugar
  2 Tbsps light soy sauce
  3 Tbsps dark soy sauce

The day before: Soak dried beans in 3 to 4 times their volume of cold water and let stand 24 hours. Discard beans that float.

To cook: Discard soaking water, and gently boil soaked beans in fresh water, uncovered, for 10 minutes, or just till the smell of raw beans disappears. (The water soybeans soak in becomes bitter, so soybeans must be boiled in fresh water. This is not true of many other beans, which may be boiled in the water in which they have soaked.) Drain and wash under cold water.

Cut carrots into thin rounds or half-moons. Parboil in lightly salted water, rinse under cold running water, and drain.

With a very sharp knife (a large knife is easier to use) cut giant kelp (*konbu*) into flakes, about $1/4$ inch ($3/4$ cm) or so square.

In a medium-sized pot, mix all the ingredients for simmering. Add carrot slices, *konbu* flakes, and boiled soybeans. Simmer, covered, with a drop-lid (*otoshi-buta*) or circle of baking paper with a vent (see page 220) for 30 minutes, or until tender. Stir occasionally. Simmering liquid should be almost entirely reduced by the end of the cooking time.

To serve: Serve—hot or cold—3 or 4 heaping Tbsps in small dishes.

Combines well with YELLOWTAIL TERIYAKI (page 200) and SAVORY CUP CUSTARD (page 214).

Burdock or Carrot *Kinpira*

(*Kinpira Gobō* or *Ninjin*) きんぴら午旁又はにんじん

A popular vegetable dish. The concentrated flavors of soy and *saké* give this dish a piquancy suggestive of Kinpira, a strong and dashing mythical hero of old Japan. Carrot may be effectively substituted for burdock.

6 servings

1 medium burdock root, scrubbed with a brush, or 3 medium carrots
few Tbsps vegetable oil

for simmering:
  2 Tbsps *saké*
  2 Tbsps dark soy sauce
  1 scant Tbsp sugar

¼ tsp red pepper flakes (*ichimi*) or seven-spice mixture (*shichimi*)

To prepare and cook: Cut burdock in shavings as if sharpening a pencil (the *sasagaki* cutting technique, see page 142). Keep cut burdock in water to avoid discoloration. (Scrape carrots and cut into 2-inch [5-cm] julienne strips.)

Coat the bottom of a frying pan with a few Tbsps oil, heat, and add vegetable. Stir-fry over high heat till vegetable begins to soften (about 3 minutes). Add the *saké* to the pan, stir in the soy sauce and sugar, and continue stir-frying over medium heat till the liquid has been almost completely reduced. Stir occasionally to keep the vegetable from sticking to the pan. Flavor to taste with red pepper flakes or seven-spice mixture.

To serve: Serve hot or at room temperature. Either serve family style in a large dish or in small individual dishes during the rice course. This dish also is a fine companion for *saké*. Keeps one week, refrigerated in a sealed container.

Combines well with CHICKEN-'N-EGG ON RICE (page 283) and MISO SOUP (page 156).

VARIATIONS: *Konnyaku* (devil's tongue jelly)—rub cake with salt, lightly pound, wash, and cut into thin 1-inch squares.

Lotus root (*renkon*)—scrape surface, cut into thin rounds, then quarter the rounds. Till ready to use, keep cut lotus root in water with a drop of vinegar to whiten it.

Minced meat—for a different effect, you may also use ground meat (pork, beef, chicken) together with the vegetable. Use ¼ pound (115 g) and fry with the vegetable.

Potatoes Simmered in *Miso*

(*Jaga-imo Miso-ni*) じゃがいも味噌煮

Jaga-imo, the common Japanese name for the Irish potato, is short for *Jagatara-imo*, "Jakarta potato." Introduced from Java by the early Dutch traders, they are also sometimes called *barei-sho*, "horse-bell potato" from the resemblance of little round new potatoes to the small ball-shaped bells on Japanese pack-horse bridles.

4 servings

5 medium potatoes
2 cups *dashi*
6 Tbsps white (or 4 Tbsps red) *miso*
4 pods okra, washed and trimmed (or 12 pods snow peas; tender green peas, or French-cut green beans may also be used)

To prepare: Peel potatoes and cut into quarters (into sixths, if large Idaho potatoes). Parboil in slightly salted water till tender but not flaky, then drain well.

In ½ cup of the *dashi*, soften the *miso* and strain through a sieve.

To cook and serve: Into a medium-sized pot put the remaining 1½ cups *dashi* and the parboiled potatoes. Heat over medium heat till simmering.

Add the strained, softened *miso*. Mix. Cover with a drop-lid (*otoshi-buta*) or circle of baking paper with a vent (see page 220) and simmer or *gently* boil for 20 minutes.

Parboil okra in lightly salted water for 2 or 3 minutes, rinse in cold water, then cut into ¼-inch (¾-cm) rounds. (Parboil substitutes in lightly salted water until almost tender, then rinse in cold water.)

To serve, use a slotted spoon to transfer portions (5 potato pieces per serving) to deep individual dishes, then top with a few Tbsps of the hot *miso* liquid. Garnish with okra rounds (or substitute) and serve immediately.

Combines well with SAKÉ-SIMMERED MACKEREL (page 225) and SALT-PICKLED CHINESE CABBAGE (page 322).

Potato Tumble

(*Jaga-imo Nikkorogashi*) じゃがいも煮っころがし

Good homely fare. The pot should be shaken and the contents tumbled about when the simmering liquid is almost completely reduced—thus its name.

4 servings

**4 medium Idaho potatoes
   (3, if large)**
1 medium onion
1 package *ito-konnyaku*
   **(devil's tongue jelly in
   "thread" form)**
**4 fresh *shiitake* mushrooms,
   wiped and trimmed**
**1 medium burdock root,
   scrubbed with a brush**
**¼ pound (115 g) thin-sliced
   very lean pork (or beef),
   or 4 very small chicken
   drumsticks**
vegetable oil

for simmering:

   2½ cups *dashi*
   4 Tbsps sugar
   6 Tbsps dark soy sauce

To prepare: Peel potatoes and cut into 1½- to 2-inch (4- to 5-cm) chunks. Quarter the onion. Parboil the *ito-konnyaku* for 1 minute, drain, and chop coarsely. Chop the mushrooms, burdock, and pork coarsely. (Keep cut burdock in water to avoid discoloration.)

To cook and serve: In a large pot, heat a few Tbsps oil over high heat. Add all the solid ingredients at once and stir-fry until the meat is white, about 3 minutes.

Add the simmering liquid. Simmer, covered with a drop-lid (*otoshi-buta*) or circle of baking paper with a vent (see page 220), for 30 minutes, till the simmering liquid is almost completely reduced, then shake pot to evenly coat the ingredients with liquid.

Ladle into individual bowls, making sure all the ingredients are represented and attractively arranged, and serve hot. No garnish.

Combines well with SPINACH WITH SESAME DRESSING (page 253) and MISO SOUP (page 156).

Radish with White Miso Sauce

(*Furofuki Daikon*) 風呂ふき大根

A warming winter dish and probably the most popular way of serving *daikon*.

6 servings

**1 giant white radish
   (*daikon*)**
**2-inch (5-cm) square of
   giant kelp (*konbu*)**
pinch salt

To prepare: Peel the radish and cut into rounds (or half-moons) from ¾ to 1 inch (2 to 2½ cm) thick.

To make a light broth, put kelp square and water in a medium-sized pot, bring to simmer, and add a pinch of salt. Add the radish rounds or chunks, cover with drop-lid (*otoshi-buta*) or circle of baking paper with a vent (see page 220), and gently boil about 40 minutes

sauce:

⅔ cup (200 g) sweet white
  miso
3 Tbsps *saké*
2 Tbsps *mirin*
1 Tbsp sugar
1 egg yolk
½ cup *dashi*, if necessary

choose one for fragrance:

3 tsps grated *yuzu* citron
  or lemon rind, put in a
  tea strainer and rinsed
  briefly (½ tsp per serving)
pinch chopped *kinome*
  leaves
3 tsps finely grated fresh
  ginger
pinch seven-spice mixture
  (*shichimi*)
pinch ground *sansho*
  pepper

kinome sprigs

or so, until the radish becomes slightly translucent.

Meanwhile, make the sauce. In the top of a double boiler, soften the *miso* by gradually mixing in the *saké* and *mirin*. Add the sugar and mix in the egg yolk. Cook over boiling water till creamy thick, about 2 minutes. If the sauce is too thick, dilute with *dashi*. Remove from heat. Add one of the fragrant ingredients. *Yuzu* rind is most "authentic" because it is in season during the cold months.

To serve: With a slotted spoon, transfer 2 or 3 pieces of boiled vegetable from the pot to each deep individual dish. Top with 1 or 2 Tbsps sweet white *miso* sauce and garnish with a sprig of *kinome*. Serve hot.

Combines well with BEEF AND BURDOCK ROLLS (page 189) and FOIL-COOKED ENOKITAKE MUSHROOMS (page 371).

VARIATIONS: Instead of giant white radish (*daikon*), use other mild-tasting root vegetables with a similar texture such as turnips, swedes (rutabagas), parsnips, kohlrabi, or experiment with firm-fleshed potatoes.

Drenched Radish

(*Daikon Fukume-ni*) 大根含め煮 (color plate 12)

6 servings

1 giant white radish
  (*daikon*)
salt

for simmering:

2½ cups *dashi*
1 tsp salt
2 tsps light soy sauce
splash of *mirin*

kinome sprigs (optional)

To prepare: Peel the radish and cut into rounds (or half-moons, if very large) between ¾ to 1 inch (2 to 2½ cm) thick. So that they keep their shape and to add visual interest, bevel the edges of the rounds as shown (next page).

Heat water in a medium-sized pot, salt lightly, and gently boil the radish rounds, covered with a drop-lid (*otoshi-buta*) or circle of baking paper with a vent (see page 220), about 40 minutes or so, till the radish becomes slightly translucent. Drain.

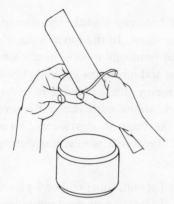

To cook and serve: In a medium-sized pot mix the ingredients for simmering. Bring just to a boil and add the cooked radish rounds. Simmer, covered with a drop-lid or paper circle, for another 30 minutes over medium heat.

To serve, transfer one or two pieces of vegetable to each deep individual bowl and ladle on simmering liquid. Garnish with *kinome* sprigs.

Goes well with DEEP-FRIED MARINATED CHICKEN (page 234) and SHELLFISH WITH MISO DRESSING (page 252).

VARIATIONS: Instead of giant white radish (*daikon*), use turnip (exactly as above); squash or pumpkin (peel and use quite a bit more soy sauce for simmering); zucchini (peel, but leave in large pieces so it is not simmered to a bodiless pulp).

Spicy Eggplant

(*Nasu Itame-ni*) なす炒め煮

One of the many tasty ways of preparing this delightful vegetable. Eggplant just simmered in broth becomes soggy, but frying it first firms the skin and improves the flavor.

4 servings

**8 small eggplants, about
4 inches (10 cm) long**
about ¾ cup vegetable oil
**2 dried red peppers,
seeded**

for simmering:

1⅔ cups *dashi*
1 Tbsp *mirin*
4 Tbsps sugar
2 Tbsps dark soy sauce

To prepare: Cut the eggplants in half lengthwise and score with fairly deep diagonal cuts, as shown, so that seasonings can easily penetrate. Cut each half into 2 pieces crosswise.

To cook and serve: In a medium-sized pot heat a few Tbsps vegetable oil until hot, add the scored eggplant quarters, and stir-fry with chopsticks or a wooden spoon. Add the red peppers and continue stir-frying. Add more salad oil as necessary; the eggplant will absorb the oil quickly, but try to use as little oil as possible. There should be no puddle of oil in the pan. The eggplant will be done in about 7 minutes—the skins will turn a more brilliant, vivid purple, and the flesh will be semisoft.

At this point pour in the *dashi*, stir, and add the *mirin*, sugar, and dark soy sauce. Cover with a drop-lid (*otoshi-buta*) or circle of baking paper with a vent (see page 220) and simmer over medium heat for 10 minutes

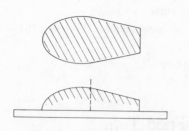

score eggplant halves as shown then cut in half

or slightly longer, till the liquid is reduced somewhat. Unfortunately, the bright purple color disappears with the simmering.

Serve in individual deep dishes; one portion is 8 eggplant quarters (2 eggplants). Arrange so that the skin faces up. Pour a few Tbsps of the simmering liquid over and serve. It should be emphasized that the simmering liquid is an integral part of such dishes and *must* accompany the solid food. Discard the red peppers.

Combines well with CHICKEN TERIYAKI (page 201).

VARIATION: To use large eggplants, pare off skin and cut flesh into 3- × -1½-inch (8- × -4-cm) rectangles. Deep-fry before simmering in seasoned stock.

Mushroom Relish

(*Shiitake Kara-ni*) 椎茸辛煮

The term *kara-ni* refers to the method, that is, "to simmer until strongly seasoned"; the seasoning is a half-and-half mixture of *saké* and soy sauce. The flavor of vegetables simmered in *saké*-and-soy-sauce till the liquid is almost entirely reduced is quite piquant. Because of its saltiness, usually this dish is served in small portions to go along with hot white rice.

6 servings

7 ounces (200 g) fresh *shiitake* mushrooms, wiped and trimmed (any type of mushroom is fine)
½ cup *saké*
½ cup dark soy sauce

To prepare and cook: Cut mushrooms into ⅛-inch (½-cm) slices.

Mix the *saké* and soy sauce in a medium-sized pot and add the sliced mushrooms. Cover with a drop-lid (*otoshi-buta*) or circle of baking paper with a vent (see page 220) and gently simmer over low heat till the liquid is almost completely gone. As the liquid reduces, stir from time to time to keep the mushrooms from sticking to the pot.

To serve: Serve hot or at room temperature. Either serve family-style, in one large dish, or in small individual dishes. Keeps 1 to 2 months refrigerated in a sealed container.

Combines well with RICE BALLS (page 440) and ODEN (page 402).

VARIATIONS: *Enokitake* mushrooms—trim off the spongy root-webs and cut stems about 2½ inches (6½ cm) below the thick cluster of tiny caps.

Small green peppers (*ao-tōgarashi*)—cut off the stems of these slender 2½-inch (6½-cm) pods.

Any vegetable that will hold its shape after long simmering.

Chinese Cabbage and Deep-Fried *Tōfu*
(*Age-dōfu Hakusai-ni*) 揚げ豆腐白菜煮

Served piping hot, this simple dish is a family favorite. The substantial "meatiness" of the fried *tōfu* goes well with the delicacy of Chinese cabbage.

4 servings

10 leaves Chinese cabbage
4 cakes thick deep-fried
  bean curd (*atsuage*)
1 cup *dashi*
2 Tbsps light soy sauce
1 Tbsp sugar

To prepare: Separate whole cabbage leaves from the head and parboil for 3 minutes to soften slightly. Cut into 2-inch (5-cm) lengths, then chop coarsely.

Cut deep-fried bean curd into 1-inch (2½-cm) squares.

To cook and serve: Put the *dashi* into a medium-sized saucepan. Bring to a simmer over medium heat and add the Chinese cabbage. Stir in the light soy sauce and sugar. Add the deep-fried bean curd squares. Simmer all ingredients together for about 2 minutes, uncovered. Ladle simmering liquid over bean curd several times.

Carefully remove cabbage and bean curd from the pan and arrange attractively (cabbage as a bottom layer, bean curd squares on top) in individual dishes. Pour on a few Tbsps of the simmering liquid and serve immediately. No garnish.

Combines well with VINEGARED OCTOPUS (page 248).

Tortoiseshell *Tōfu*
(*Tōfu Bekkō-ni*) 豆腐べっこう煮

The thick, translucent amber simmering liquid poured over squares of white bean curd reminds one of glossy tortoiseshell, and hence the intriguing name of this recipe. Any kind of *tōfu* is all right, but if you can obtain the delicate "silk" *tōfu* you will have a special treat.

2 servings

2 cups *dashi*
   (or light chicken
   stock)
½ Tbsp sugar
2 Tbsps *mirin*
2 Tbsps dark soy sauce
pinch salt
1 cake *tōfu* (bean curd),
   pressed for 1 hour (see
   page 58); do not press
   "silk" *tōfu*
3 Tbsps cornstarch, mixed
   with 3 Tbsps water
kinome sprigs or finely
   shred-cut fresh
   ginger

To cook and serve: Mix the *dashi*, sugar, *mirin*, and dark soy sauce in a medium-sized pot and bring to a boil. Turn down to a simmer and gradually add salt, tasting often.

Cut the bean curd cake into quarters and carefully slide them into the pot. Be careful to keep liquid at a simmer—higher heat will break up the bean curd. Ladle the liquid over the top and sides till the bean curd is heated thoroughly, about 4 minutes.

With a pancake turner, remove the bean curd pieces to deep individual dishes (2 pieces per serving). Keep the pot on the heat and add the mixture of water and cornstarch to the simmering liquid. Stir until thickened, about 1 minute. Ladle the thickened sauce over the heated bean curd. Garnish with a sprig of *kinome* or very finely shred-cut ginger. Serve immediately, and eat with teaspoons instead of chopsticks.

Combines well with SAKÉ-SIMMERED FLOUNDER (page 224) and GREEN BEANS WITH SESAME-MISO DRESSING (page 420).

Fried and Simmered Freeze-Dried *Tōfu*

(*Kōri-dōfu Age-ni*) 凍り豆腐揚げ煮 (color plate 14)

Because the technique of freeze-drying *tōfu* is said to have been devised over eight centuries ago by Buddhists at a monastery on remote Mt. Kōya (southeast of Kyoto), freeze-dried *tōfu* (*kōri-dōfu*) is more often than not called *Kōya-dōfu*. Reconstituted, *Kōya-dōfu* has a somewhat spongy, fine-grained texture and an extremely pleasant flavor—it is also a good source of protein.

4 servings

8 cakes freeze-dried bean
   curd (*kōri-dōfu*), 2½ inches
   (6½ cm) square
oil for deep-frying

for simmering:
   3⅓ cups *dashi*
   4 Tbsps sugar
   1 tsp salt

To prepare: Reconstitute the freeze-dried bean curd by letting the cakes stand in very hot water (180°F/ 80°C) in a bowl for 3 to 5 minutes. Cover with a drop-lid to keep the *tōfu* submerged. Turn *tōfu* once in the hot water.

Pour off the hot water and replace with tepid or cold. Place each cake of *tōfu* between your palms and gently press out the hot water and milky liquid. Repeat this process, changing water each time, until no milky discharge remains. Press once more, then cut into quarters.

4 Tbsps light soy sauce
finely grated fresh ginger

To cook and serve: In a medium-sized, heavy saucepan, heat about 2 inches (5 cm) of deep-frying oil. Bring the oil to a medium temperature (340°F/170°C).

Slide the reconstituted *tōfu* into the oil. The cakes should float, and there should be no great hissing, frying sound. They are done when the beige color of the cakes turns golden brown and the edges begin to crisp—bubbles will appear round the edges of each piece. Turn gently to fry both sides. Remove and drain on absorbent paper.

In a medium-sized pot, mix the ingredients for simmering. Stir, bring to a boil, turn down to a simmer, and adjust seasonings. Add the fried *tōfu* and simmer, covered with a drop-lid or circle of baking paper with a center vent (see page 220), for about 15 minutes.

To serve, use a pancake turner to transfer pieces of *tōfu* to individual dishes. Spoon over a few Tbsps of the hot liquid from the pot. Top with a cone of freshly grated ginger, and serve immediately.

Combines well with STUFFED FOIL-BAKED SALMON (page 359) and ROLLED OMELETTE (page 203).

Gold Purses
(Fukuro) ふくろ

These little bags of fried bean curd—resembling the purses of old used to hold gold coins and other treasure—whet one's appetite with curiosity as to the vegetables within. Sometimes included in ODEN (page 402) fare.

4 servings (8 pouches)

4 cakes thin deep-fried bean curd (*aburage* or *usuage*), 6 x 3¼ x ⅜ inches (15 x 8 x 1 cm), or 2½-inch (6½-cm) square ready-to-stuff pouches (see color plate 7)
⅓ ounce (10 g) dried gourd shavings (*kampyō*), softened (see page 71)
⅛ giant white radish (*daikon*)

Pouches: Scald the deep-fried bean curd with boiling water and wrap in a clean kitchen (or paper) towel to eliminate excess oil.

With the large (6-inch [15-cm] length) size of *aburage*, cut in half. With smaller sizes, trim off one edge only. Pull apart gently at the center to make a pouch, or bag, as shown.

Cut softened gourd shavings into 8 5-inch (13-cm) lengths. These are to tie the pouches. Chop any remaining cooked *kampyō* and add to vegetables below.

Vegetables: Peel the giant white radish and carrot and cut into large chunks. Boil each separately in lightly

⅓ medium carrot
1 cake *tōfu* (bean curd),
   drained and pressed for
   30 minutes (see page 58)
8 dried *shiitake* mushrooms,
   softened and trimmed
   (see page 88)

for simmering:

   2 cups *dashi*
   6 Tbsps *mirin*
   6 Tbsps dark soy sauce

1, 2. the large size of thin deep-fried *tōfu* may be cut in half to form pouches

salted water till just tender, drain and cool, then dice finely.

Dice pressed bean curd. Dice softened *shiitake* mushrooms.

Toss all the vegetables and *tōfu* together in a large bowl till well mixed.

To stuff and cook: Fill the deep-fried bean curd pouches ¾ full of mixed vegetables. Tie closed with a 5-inch (13-cm) length of softened gourd strip (or use giant kelp [*konbu*] cut into strips, or secure with toothpicks.)

Mix the *dashi*, *mirin*, and soy sauce together in a wide pot and bring to a boil. Place stuffed pouches in the pot, being careful to keep them upright. Cover with a drop-lid (*otoshi-buta*) or circle of baking paper with a vent (see page 220). Simmer gently over medium heat for 30 minutes.

To serve: Carefully remove pouches from the pot and place on individual plates, 2 per serving. Spoon over a few Tbsps of the simmering liquid. Eat hot with knife and fork.

These pouches may also be eaten at room temperature. They can be made ahead of time and refrigerated up to 3 days. Reheat before serving.

Combines well with CHICKEN TERIYAKI (page 201) and CHRYSANTHEMUM TURNIP (page 251).

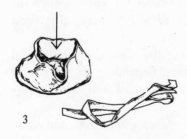

3–5. stuffed pouches are tied with gourd strips

VARIATIONS: The only limit to the stuffings possible for these pouches is your own taste and imagination. Some typical Japanese ingredients are burdock (*gobō*), ginkgo nuts (*ginnan*), glutinous rice cake (*mochi*), chopped gourd shavings, some other possibilities are lotus root (*renkon*), green peas, *udo* stalks, sesame seeds (*goma*), and so on.

Oden

おでん

A great favorite, especially popular in winter, served in small restaurants and also by vendors pushing steaming, roofed carts. The later, darker, and colder the night, the more welcoming the sight of the *oden* man's lantern and the more appetizing his stew. This dish originated in the Kantō area surrounding Tokyo Bay, once rich in tiny seafood, and began as fish dumplings eaten with *miso*. These dumplings were served on bamboo skewers and came to be known as *dengaku* (see pages 191ff), after an ancient dance. This was soon shortened to just *den* and given the honorific *o*.

In Osaka they call it Kantō "Stew" (*Kantō-Daki*) and use mainly processed ingredients, such as *kamaboko* (fish paste) and *satsuma-age*, cooking them separately and fast to preserve their individual flavors. In Tokyo, however, they include raw ingredients and simmer everything over a very low heat for a long time. The secret of good *oden* is to combine things that give flavor with things that absorb—fish products with radish, bean curd, or potato. Kelp and bonito stocks are traditional, and fresh chicken stock may be used, but *never* commercial chicken bouillon preparations.

6 servings

1 cake *konnyaku* (devil's tongue jelly)
salt
1 giant white radish (*daikon*)
1 turnip
6 cakes *ganmodoki* (a type of deep-fried bean curd) or grilled bean curd (*yakidōfu*)
6 hard-boiled eggs, shelled
4 *chikuwa* (fish paste rolls)
2 cakes *kamaboko* (fish paste)
6 cakes *satsuma-age* (deep-fried *kamaboko*)

To prepare: Rub *konnyaku* with salt, lightly pound and wash, then cut into triangles about ½ inch (1 cm) thick with sides about 2½ inches (6½ cm).

Peel the giant white radish and cut into 1-inch (2½-cm) rounds or half-moons, depending on size of the root. Boil in water to cover till tender (when the radish can be easily pierced with a toothpick). Treat the turnip in the same way.

Pour boiling water over the *ganmodoki*, drain, and cut into halves or quarters, depending on the size of the cake (just cut grilled bean curd into 1-inch [2½-cm] cubes).

Cut the fish products—*chikuwa*, *kamaboko*, and *satsuma-age*—into 1½-inch (4-cm) pieces. Leave egg whole.

To cook and serve: Use a large, flameproof earthen-

for simmering:

4 cups chicken stock
4 cups *dashi*
¾ cup light soy sauce
¾ cup *mirin*
2 tsps salt

serve one, some, or all of the following:

mustard paste (see page 78)
seven-spice mixture (*shichimi*)
red pepper flakes (*ichimi*)
ground *sansho* pepper

ware pot (*donabe*, see page 103) which disperses slow, constant heat throughout the walls of the vessel, or any wide and not very deep cooking pot.

Heat the chicken stock and *dashi* over low heat. When simmering, add the soy sauce and *mirin*. Finally, little by little add salt, tasting often, till flavor suits you.

Add the *konnyaku* and *daikon* first, then the other ingredients in the order listed. The last are the fish products. Simmer on a very low heat at least 90 minutes. Do not cover. Be sure to use enough stock—the ingredients at the beginning of the simmer should almost float. By the time the *oden* is ready to serve, the broth should be reduced by ⅓ at least and should be medium dark, about the color of hotcake syrup.

This is a community dish, so bring the pot to the center of the table for everyone to help himself family style. Individual bowls are placed at each setting. Pass small dishes (or shakers) of spices. Mustard is the orthodox spice with *oden*.

Oden keeps well for 2 days. On the second day, reheated, it often tastes richer than on the first day.

VARIATIONS: Instead of fish products (*chikuwa, kamaboko, satsuma-age*), you may substitute meatballs made of mixed ground beef and pork. Use ¾ pound (340 g) mixed ground meat, ½ shredded onion, 1 beaten egg, 2 tsps flour, and ⅔ tsp salt. Mix, form into ¾-inch (2-cm) meatballs and deep-fry in medium-temperature oil (350°F/180°C) for 4 to 5 minutes.

In addition to fish products or meatballs, you may used parboiled small chicken legs or pieces of chicken.

Other vegetables that are often used in *oden* are squash, pumpkin, and potatoes. Peel, parboil, and cut into large chunks. Mild-flavored root vegetables such as rutabaga (swedes) and kohlrabi may be use, but avoid red beets.

As far as *tōfu* products are concerned, do not limit yourself only to *ganmodoki*. Any kind of deep-fried *tōfu* is suitable, or use fresh bean curd cakes cut into 1-inch (2½-cm) cubes.

There is a whole spectrum of *oden* ingredients made by professional *oden* ingredient makers in Japan. Some of these are packaged and may find their way to Japanese food stores outside Japan. There seems to be an unending effort to create original *oden* things, and the *oden* fancier in Japan is always on the alert for a good new flavor or texture. But such baroque flavor creations appear and disappear and only emphasize the goodness of a simple *oden* made with the basic ingredients.

❋ Deep-Fried Dishes ❋
Agemono

Deep-Fried Fillet of Trout

(Masu no Agemono) 鱒の揚げもの (color plate 11)

River fish such as trout are delightful to eat served with vegetables in a thick vinegar sauce. Scoring the flesh helps to dispel any "fishiness," and the vinegar also serves to counteract it.

4 servings

2 rainbow trout, 6-8 ounces
    (180-225 g) each
flour
4 snow peas, washed and
    strings removed
2 cups sliced bamboo shoot
    (see page 55)
½ medium carrot
5 dried *shiitake* mushrooms,
    softened and trimmed
    (see page 88)
3 Tbsps salad oil
2½ cups *dashi*
2 Tbsps vinegar
2 Tbsps sugar
2½ Tbsps dark soy sauce
oil for deep-frying
2 Tbsps constarch, mixed
    with 2 Tbsps water

To prepare: Clean and gut the trout and cut 2 boneless fillets, with skin, from each (*sanmai oroshi* technique, pages 123ff). Score the inside of the fillets with shallow straight cuts at ¼-inch (¾-cm) intervals as shown to allow heat and flavoring to penetrate quickly, to cut through any small bones that might remain, and to keep it from curling in the hot oil. Just before deep-frying, brush both sides of the fillet with flour.

Clean, scrape, and trim the vegetables as necessary. Use snow peas whole. Slice the other vegetables into 1½- × -¼-inch (4- × -¾-cm) slices, about the same size as the snow peas; this is to equalize cooking time.

In a large or medium-sized frying pan, heat the salad oil and stir-fry all the vegetables at once. When the vegetables are thoroughly coated with hot oil and begin to soften (about 2 minutes), add the *dashi*. Stir and add the vinegar, sugar, and dark soy sauce. Simmer, uncovered, for 3 minutes, till the *dashi* has reduced somewhat. Remove from heat. (Do *not* add the cornstarch-water mixture yet.) Meanwhile, deep-fry the fish fillets.

To deep-fry and serve: Bring 2 to 3 inches (5 to 8 cm) of oil to medium heat (340°F/170°C) in a heavy-bottomed pot or deep-fryer. Deep-fry flour-dusted fillets, two at a time, for about 2 minutes, till skin is crisp. The flesh should *not* be fried completely dry.

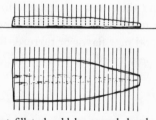

trout fillet should be scored deeply

Remove with a slotted spoon and drain on absorbent paper toweling.

Return vegetables to medium heat, simmer, and add cornstarch-and-water mixture to the simmering liquid. Stir till the liquid thickens, about 1 minute.

Serve in individual dishes, or deep plates. Place 1 fillet in each dish and cover with the vegetables in thick, hot sauce, making sure that vegetables are evenly distributed. Serve immediately.

Combines well with TANGY WHITE SALAD (page 421) and MUSHROOM RICE (page 438).

VARIATIONS: Use other fish fillets—salmon, bass, carp, sea bream, various flatfish, etc.—or even very lean pork. Substitute mild-tasting vegetables as desired.

Flounder Treasure Ships
(*Karei Rikyū Funamori*) かれい利久舟盛り (color plate 13)

Sen no Rikyū, the celebrated tea master of old, gave his name to the use of sesame in cooking for the tea ceremony. In this masterpiece of a dish, sesame-coated, deep-fried flounder morsels are served as the treasure cargo on crisp, edible "boats." The treasure ship rides on "waves" of fried, foam-white *harusame*.

Take care to follow directions on oil temperature. The treasure ships need to be done first at a moderately low temperature, then the fish morsels and garnishes are deep-fried when the temperature has been raised.

<u>4 servings</u>

4 *karei* flounders (or any small flatfish), 8-10 ounces (225-285 g) each
flour
2 egg whites, lightly beaten
7-8 Tbsps white sesame seeds
1 sheet *nori* seaweed
fine egg noodles (*tamago sōmen*), cut in 10-inch (25-cm) lengths
8 small green peppers (*ao-tōgarashi*), or 1 bell pepper, cut in ½-x-3-in (1½-x-8-cm) strips

To prepare: Clean and gut the fish, leaving heads and tails attached. Cut 4 fillets, with skin, from each fish (2 per side), using the *gomai oroshi* cutting technique illustrated on page 129. Take care to keep the skeletons intact; deep-fried, these are the "treasure ships" in which fillets are served.

With a brush, lightly dust both sides of fillets and skeletons with flour. Place a thin layer of sesame seed on a plate. Brush the inner side of each fillet (not the skin side) with beaten egg white and while still wet press fillet into the sesame seed to coat the fish.

With a sharp knife or kitchen scissors cut the *nori* sheet into rectangles about ⅜ × 1¼ inches (1 × 3 cm). Hold 10 to 12 dry noodles in a bunch and bind them

oil for deep-frying
1 ounce (30 g) "spring rain"
filaments (*harusame*)
salt
lemon wedges

wrap lengths of fine noodles in the
middle with *nori*, then cut through
center to form noodle whisks

together by wrapping a seaweed rectangle, moistened with egg white, around the middle, as shown. Let rest for a few minutes till seaweed is dry, then using a very sharp carving or heavy knife, cut the noodles through the center of the *nori* band. (In hot oil, this spreads open into a whisk.) One bundle decorates each serving.

Wash, then trim stems from the small green peppers, and with the tip of a paring knife make a few small slits in each pod so that they do not burst open in the hot oil.

To deep-fry: Fill a heavy-bottomed pot or deep-fryer with at least 5 inches (13 cm) of oil and heat to low, about 320°F/160°C. Deep-fry the skeletons, one at a time, about 10 minutes, till all moisture has been cooked out of the bones. If skeleton is large, fry twice to make the bones edible. Holding the skeleton by the tail, slide it into the hot oil. It is done when no more watery bubbles fizz around the edges and when it has achieved an even brown color. Remove and drain on paper toweling.

Increase heat to bring the oil to a higher temperature, about 350°F/180°C. First fry the egg-noodle bundles, one by one. Holding a single bundle with long wooden chopsticks (or tongs) just below the seaweed, dip into the hot oil and swish gently till the noodles fan out, about 30 seconds.

Deep-fry the sesame-coated fillets next, about 3 at a time. Slide fillets into the oil at the side of the pot, sesame-coated side down, skin side up. Turn frequently in the oil. The fillets will be done in about 3 minutes—the sesame golden brown, skin crisp, but flesh should still be moist. Remove and drain on paper toweling.

Deep-fry the small green peppers (or bell pepper strips) about 1 minute, till pods are shiny green. Remove and drain on paper toweling.

Finally, deep-fry, a handful at a time, as many "spring rain" filaments as are needed for "waves" in the serving arrangement. These noodles expand wildly, so a good handful should cover the entire surface of the fryer with puffed noodles about 30 seconds after being dropped into the hot oil. Remove with a slotted spoon and drain on paper toweling. Salt lightly.

To assemble and serve: On individual dinner plates, place a sheet of folded absorbent paper and arrange on that a sea of "waves" of salted white "spring rain." On this, place a deep-fried skeleton, taking care that the eye side faces up. Arrange four fillets, sesame-coated sides shown to advantage, on the midsection of the fish, that is, where the fillets have been cut away. Garnish with a noodle whisk, 2 small green peppers, and a wedge of lemon.

Serve hot with a small dish of salt into which lemon juice has been squeezed. Dip fillets into the lemon-salt.

Everything is edible. The crisp framework is particularly good.

Combines well with RED-AND-WHITE VINEGARED SALAD (page 429) and BEATEN EGG SOUP (page 346).

Stuffed Crab

(Kani Kōra-age) 蟹甲羅揚げ

An elegant Japanese deep-fried version of *crabe farcie*. An extra advantage is that all the basic work can be done ahead of time. Serve one crab per person, unless the crabs are very large, in which case, they may be cut in half before stuffing to serve two.

<u>6 servings</u>

6 live hard-shell or soft-shell crabs, about 6 ounces (170-180 g) each
flour

kenchin *stuffing:*
  ⅕ medium carrot
  8 ginkgo nuts (or substitute ¼ cup green peas)
  1 medium burdock root, scrubbed with a brush
  3 dried cloud-ear mushrooms, softened
  2 cakes *tōfu* (bean curd)
  2 eggs, beaten

To prepare: Clean and boil the whole crabs in lightly salted water for about 20–30 minutes, depending on type and size of crab. Remove meat from the shells and legs; flake the meat.

Scrub the empty shells with a brush, rinse, and dry. Dust insides with flour and set aside, ready to stuff.

Make *kenchin* stuffing as described in STUFFED RED TILEFISH, page 361, using ingredients listed here. Mix in the crabmeat. Salt to taste.

Spoon the stuffing into the flour-dusted shells until it is level with the edges of the shell. Do not overstuff. Sprinkle flour over the top. If a shell is very large, cut it in half with a cleaver before stuffing.

Paint the stuffing (not the shell) with the beaten egg. While still wet, sprinkle a rather thick layer of fresh breadcrumbs over the egg-coated stuffing. At this point

salt
1 egg, beaten
1 cup fresh breadcrumbs
oil for deep-frying
3 lemons, quartered

you may interrupt preparation and refrigerate or freeze.

To deep-fry and serve: Half fill a heavy-bottomed pot or deep-fryer with oil and gradually heat to medium, about 340°F/170°C.

Prepared stuffed crabs should be at room temperature. Hold the shell at the side and slide it into the heated oil, stuffing side up. Fry till golden brown, submerging the shell so that the top browns. It takes about 5 minutes, in all. It is not necessary to turn the shell. Remove with a slotted spoon and drain on paper toweling. Fry only 2 shells at a time.

Decoratively fold sheets of absorbent white paper and place on individual plates to absorb excess oil. Place one of the stuffed shells on each plate. Garnish with quartered lemon and serve hot.

Combines well with SIMMERING TŌFU (page 436) and SALT-GRILLED CLAMS (page 358).

VARIATIONS: Instead of stuffing shells, you may simply make croquettes by rolling the stuffing into balls or short cylinders and coating with bread crumbs. In lieu of shells, you may substitute any number of "skins"—thin crepes, paper-thin omelette sheets (see page 206), store-brought skins for spring rolls, and so on.

Large clam shells may also be used, filled with the same crab stuffing.

Shrimp Wafers
(*Ebi Senbei*) えびせんべい

These large, crisp wafers are best eaten as a hot hors d'oeuvre, but are good if kept for a later occasion. When cool, pack in a moisture-proof container for a week. The oily taste will disappear, leaving only the delicious sea aroma of shrimp.

6 servings

12 medium shrimp
cornstarch
oil for deep-frying
salt

To prepare: Shell and devein the shrimp, cut off tails. Press the shrimp down on a cutting board, back facing up. With a sharp knife open up shrimp with a butterfly cut (*kannon-biraki* technique, see page 132).

Dust both the cutting board and shrimp with cornstarch. Pound the shrimp lightly with a rolling pin to spread it. Sprinkle shrimp with cornstarch occasionally.

Turn frequently. When shrimp has spread a great deal and is about ⅛ inch (½ cm) thick, roll it out like pastry dough until paper thin and you judge that it can get no thinner. A few holes or tears do not matter. It is impossible to give precise rules for when to cease pounding and to start rolling—a few trials are the best teacher. This is not as hard as it may seem, but the first attempts should be done carefully.

To deep-fry and serve: Heat 2 to 3 inches (5 to 8 cm) of oil in a medium-sized, heavy-bottomed pot to about 300°F/150°C, very low temperature. Deep-fry flattened shrimp one by one till crisp, about 1 minute. Skim the top of the oil occasionally. Drain shrimp on paper toweling. Salt lightly.

Serve hot or at room temperature. If hot, use folded absorbent paper on flat plates, two shrimp per portion, or serve family style in a paper-lined basket. Good as a side dish or hors d'oeuvre.

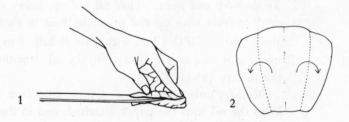

1, 2.   open up shrimp with butterfly cut

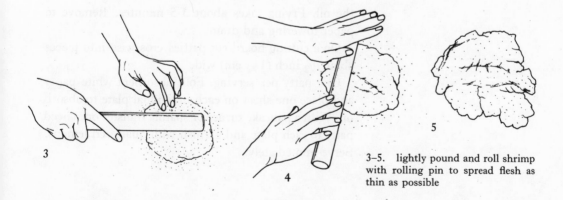

3–5.   lightly pound and roll shrimp with rolling pin to spread flesh as thin as possible

VARIATIONS: Use scallops or fillets of white-fleshed fish.

Deep-Fried Chicken Patties

(*Tori-Minchi Kara-age*) 鶏ミンチ唐揚げ

Instead of minced chicken, these patties can be made with pork or beef, but Japanese prefer the more delicate flavor of chicken, white-fleshed fish, or shrimp for this recipe.

4 servings

½ pound (225 g) ground chicken
1 green onion, finely chopped
    or
2 fresh *shiitake* mushrooms, wiped, trimmed, and finely chopped
1 tsp finely grated fresh ginger
1 Tbsp *saké*
1 tsp dark soy sauce
baking paper
oil for deep-frying
1-2 lemons, quartered

To prepare: Work the ground chicken to an even finer texture in a *suribachi* (Japanese grinding bowl, see page 105), or use a food processor. Add the finely chopped vegetable. Blending with a rubber spatula, add grated ginger, *saké*, and dark soy sauce. Adjust seasoning.

On each of 4 10-inch (25-cm) squares of baking paper, spread the seasoned minced chicken with a spatula into rectangular patties, about 3 by 6 inches (8×15 cm) and slightly over ¼ inch (¾ cm) thick. Dust lightly with flour.

To deep-fry and serve: Half fill a deep, heavy skillet or deep-fryer with oil and gradually heat to medium, about 340°F/170°C. (Test with a small ball of minced meat; it should sink halfway into the oil then float to the surface quickly.)

Deep-fry only one patty at a time. Slip each patty in to the oil with the paper attached, and in the first 30 seconds of frying, gently shake the patty free and draw the paper out. Fry till golden brown, submerging the patty to brown the top instead of turning it over in the oil. Frying takes about 3-5 minutes. Remove to paper towering and drain.

On a cutting board cut patties crosswise into pieces about ½ inch (1½ cm) wide

One patty per serving. Fold absorbent white paper and place one sheet on each individual plate to absorb oil. With a pancake turner or spatula transfer one sliced patty to each plate and garnish with quartered lemons. Serve immediately.

Potato-Chicken Nuggets

(*Toriniku Barei-age*) 鶏肉馬鈴揚げ (color plate 10)

In both appearance and flavor, these deep-fried morsels of chicken wrapped in thin, crisp potato are elegant. The secret lies in rinsing the paper-thin potato well to remove the starchy juice, which darkens the potato when fried and prevents it from becoming really light and crisp. These are delicate.

4 servings

2 large potatoes
½ pound (225 g) boned
  chicken thigh meat
salt
flour
oil for deep-frying
2 lemons, quartered

To prepare: Peel potatoes and pare into cylinders. With a *very* sharp knife, cut each cylinder into one thin, continuous sheet (the *katsura-muki* cutting technique, see page 138). Roll up the sheet. If making such sheets is too difficult, then cut potatoes into very fine julienne strips about 2 inches (5 cm) long.

Salt the chicken lightly, then cut the chicken meat, skin and all, into strips, about 1½ × ½ inches (4 × 1½ cm).

On a dry cutting board, unroll about 2½ inches (6½ cm) of potato sheet, as shown. Brush the side facing up with flour. Cut a length of chicken the size of the potato sheet width, roll chicken in potato sheet and continue rolling until potato is 2–3 layers thick, cut potato roll from sheet, and secure roll with a toothpick. Brush the outside of the roll with flour. Repeat till all chicken is used.

If you are using julienne potato sticks instead of the potato sheet, lightly coat meat with TEMPURA BATTER (see page 235) and pat on a covering of potato strips. Deep-fry immediately.

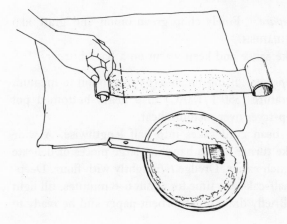

roll chicken strip in 2–3 turns of flour-dusted potato sheet, then secure roll with toothpick

To deep-fry and serve: Half fill a heavy-bottomed pot or deep-fryer with oil and gradually heat to medium, about 340°F/170°C. (Test with a piece of potato; it should sink to the pan bottom then quickly rise to the surface.) Deep-fry until light gold, turning the potato rolls in the oil (long wooden cooking chopsticks are recommended when frying delicate things). Fry about 3 or 4 rolls at a time. It takes about 4 minutes to fry a roll. Remove and drain on paper toweling.

(For parties, you may slowly deep-fry the rolls ahead of time in *low* temperature oil (325°F/165°C) to cook. Just before serving, deep fry in very *hot* oil to heat the rolls to the center and to brown the potato.)

Fold sheets of absorbent white paper and place on individual plates or in small baskets. Arrange 3 rolls per serving on plates or in baskets in a pyramid (2 on bottom, 1 on top), garnish with lemon quarters and serve hot as an hors d'oeuvre.

VARIATIONS: Instead of chicken use shrimp, squid, or fillet of white fish.

Deep-Fried *Tōfu*

(*Agedashi-Dōfu*) 揚げ出し豆腐

The ingredients are very simple and there is no new twist to the deep-frying technique, but the flavor is sophisticated.

4 servings

4 Tbsps finely chopped green onion, rinsed (see page 170)

¼ cup RED MAPLE RADISH (see page 170)

sauce:

   1⅓ cups *dashi*
   2 Tbsps light soy sauce
   2 Tbsps *mirin*

oil for deep-frying

To prepare: Finely chop green onion and grate RED MAPLE RADISH.

Make sauce and keep warm on a back burner.

To deep-fry: Bring 3 inches (6½ cm) of oil to medium temperature (350°F/180°C) in a heavy-bottomed pot or deep-fryer over medium heat.

Cut bean curd cakes into half lengthwise. A wide pancake turner makes handling large pieces of delicate *tōfu* much easier. Dredge *tōfu* lightly with flour. Deep-fry 1 half-cake at a time for about 6–8 minutes, till light gold. Briefly drain on absorbent paper and be ready to

2 cakes *tōfu* (bean curd), pressed for about 30 minutes (see page 58)
2-3 Tbsps flour

serve almost immediately. Keep surface of oil clean by skimming off any foam and particles.

To serve: Transfer hot half-cakes of *tōfu* to individual dishes. If desired, use folded absorbent paper to line the dishes. Provide small dipping bowls at the side for the hot sauce. Put the hot sauce in a small pitcher or gravy boat and the spicy condiments in small dishes.

To eat, pour the thin, hot sauce into the dipping bowl and mix in spicy condiments as desired. Dip the deep-fried bean curd into sauce before eating.

Combines well with SALT-GRILLED SEA BASS (page 182) and CHRYSANTHEMUM TURNIP (page 251).

VARIATIONS: Serve with a thickened hot *dashi* sauce and choose other garnishes with some freedom, for example, finely grated fresh ginger or dried bonito thread-shavings (*ito-kezuri-katsuo*).

Deep-fry the bean curd as above and drain briefly. Place *tōfu* in individual dishes. Dissolve about 1 Tbsp cornstarch (or *kuzu* starch) in 1 Tbsp water and pour into simmering sauce in a saucepan; stir over heat till thickened. Pour a few Tbsps thickened hot sauce over each portion of deep-fried bean curd cubes and garnish with ginger, dried bonito, and finely chopped green onions.

Crab-and-*Tōfu* Balls in Broth

(*Kani-Dōfu Iridashi*) かに豆腐炒り出し

---

4 servings

*crab-and-*tōfu* balls:*
   1½ cakes *tōfu* (bean curd)
   1 cup fresh cooked, frozen, or canned crabmeat
   1 egg, beaten
   ¼ tsp salt
   1 Tbsp light soy sauce
   2 Tbsps finely chopped green onion
   1 Tbsp finely grated fresh ginger
oil for deep-frying

To prepare: Drain and press bean curd (see page 58), then rub through a sieve. Flake crab and pick out cartilage.

Combine bean curd and crabmeat in a bowl, and with your hands mix in the beaten egg. Add salt and light soy sauce, mixing well with hands after each addition. Finally mix in finely chopped green onion and finely grated fresh ginger.

To deep-fry: Fill a pot or deep-fryer with 2 to 3 inches (5 to 8 cm) of oil and heat to 320°F/160°C. To form balls, use the clench-in-the-hand method illustrated on page 388 (CHICKEN BALLS IN SAUCE). Gently drop the balls into the hot oil as you form them and deep-fry sauce:

1 cup *dashi*
4 Tbsps *mirin*
4 Tbsps dark soy sauce
1 cup grated giant white
   radish (*daikon-oroshi*)

for about 5 minutes, till golden. Turn balls to ensure even browning. Remove and drain on absorbent paper. Keep warm.

For the sauce, combine *dashi*, *mirin*, and dark soy sauce in a medium-sized saucepan and bring to a boil.

To serve: Arrange 8 to 10 deep-fried balls per serving in a pyramid on paper-lined individual plates. Use a green leaf (even one from the garden) to decorate the plate. Serve the hot sauce in separate dipping bowls. Either mix the grated giant white radish into the sauce in the kitchen just before bringing to the table or serve it separately and let guests mix the amount of radish they prefer in their own dipping bowls.

Combines well with CHICKEN TERIYAKI (page 201) and SHELLFISH WITH MISO DRESSING (page 252).

Deep-Fried *Mochi* in Broth

(*Agemochi Iridashi*) 揚げ餅炒り出し

Mochi cakes are deep-fried and enlivened by a hot broth flavored with grated radish. A warming dish.

4 servings

8 pieces *mochi* (glutinous
   rice cake), each about
   2¼ x 1½ x ⅜ inches (6 x
   4 x 1 cm)

sauce:

   1½ cups *dashi*
   ½ cup *mirin*
   ½ cup dark soy sauce
oil for deep-frying
½ cup grated giant white
   radish (*daikon-oroshi*)
2 Tbsps finely chopped
   green onion

To prepare: It may be necessary to cut the *mochi* into the size specified; the size of *mochi* cakes is not standardized.

Mix the ingredients for the sauce in a medium-sized saucepan and heat till simmering. Keep hot.

To deep-fry and serve: Half fill a heavy-bottomed pot or deep-fryer with oil. Heat to a moderately low temperature, about 320°–330°F/160°–165°C. Slide in pieces of *mochi*, no more than six at a time, and deep-fry till golden, about 5 minutes. Turn and move the *mochi* pieces throughout the frying; they will inflate in the hot oil. Remove and drain on paper toweling.

Serve hot in small, deep individual dishes. Arrange 3 deep-fried squares in a pyramid (2 on bottom, 1 on top). Pour a small ladleful of hot stock over the *mochi*. Top with a generous Tbsp of grated radish and garnish with green onion.

Deep-Fried Stuffed Eggplant

(*Nasu Hasami-age*) なすはさみ揚げ

There are two ways of preparing this dish, and both versions are given below. With small eggplants, the vegetable is partially cut in quarters lengthwise and the stuffing is wedged in. It is then deep-fried with only a dusting of flour. In the second method, appropriate for larger eggplants, the vegetable is cut into slices, and the stuffing spread between them. Batter is used to bind this layered arrangement together during deep-frying.

I: 4 servings

4 small eggplants, about 4 inches (10 cm) long
flour

stuffing:

½ **pound (225 g) ground chicken**
pinch salt
1 Tbsp dark soy sauce
1 Tbsp *sake*

sauce:

2 cups *dashi*
½ **cup** *mirin*
1½ **cups dark soy sauce**

oil for deep-frying
½ **cup grated giant white radish (***daikon-oroshi***) or 1 heaping Tbsp finely grated fresh ginger**

II: 4 servings

4 small eggplants, about 4 inches (10 cm) long (or 1 or 2 large eggplants)
flour

stuffing:

same as above

batter:

1 egg yolk
⅓ **cup ice water**
1 cup sifted flour

Method I

To prepare: Wash eggplants and keep stem and calyx intact. Quarter each eggplant lengthwise, cutting to within ¾ inch (2 cm) of the calyx.

Before combining the stuffing ingredients, smooth the ground chicken to an even finer texture by working it in a *suribachi* (Japanese grinding bowl, see page 105), or use a food processor. Mix in the seasonings. Brush cut surfaces of eggplant with flour.

To stuff, hold the eggplant open with one hand and pack in the stuffing with fingers to reach the innermost crevices. Dust with flour (optional).

Combine the sauce ingredients in a medium-sized saucepan, heat to a simmer, then keep hot.

To deep-fry and serve: Bring 3 to 4 inches (8 to 10 cm) of oil to medium heat (340°F/170°C) in a heavy-bottomed skillet or deep-fryer. Deep-fry stuffed eggplant, 2 at a time, for about 4 minutes, till exposed stuffing is golden and the skin of the eggplant is a vivid purple. Remove with a slotted spoon and drain on aborbent paper toweling.

Cut each eggplant into a few pieces crosswise and place in individual bowls, stuffing exposed. Ladle on the sauce and serve hot. Top with a generous Tbsp of grated giant white radish, a cone of grated ginger, or both.

Method II

To prepare: Cut off tops of eggplants and cut lengthwise into slices about ½ inch (1½ cm) thick, as shown. (With very large eggplants, cut crosswise into rounds.)

sauce:

same as above

oil for deep-frying

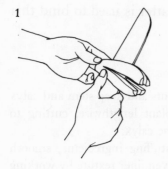

1

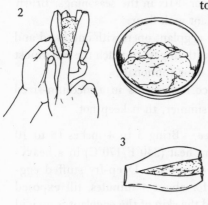

2

3

1-3. whole small eggplants are stuffed after being cut in quarters

Prepare both stuffing and sauce as above.

Brush cut surfaces of eggplant with flour; stuff the eggplant slices as if making a sandwich, as shown. Stuffing should be about ¼ inch (¾ cm) thick. Dust stuffed eggplant slices lightly with flour on both sides.

In a large mixing bowl, lightly beat the egg yolk. Add ice water and give the mixture a few strokes with a whisk (or long wooden chopsticks). Add the sifted flour all at once, and mix lightly. The batter should be lumpy (overmixing means sticky, oily-tasting batter).

To deep-fry and serve: Prepare oil as above.

Dip the flour-dusted, stuffed eggplant slices into the batter to coat. Deep-fry, 2 or 3 at a time, until batter is light gold (about 3 minutes). Turn the eggplant in the hot oil. Skim the surface of the oil from time to time.

When golden, remove and drain on paper towels.

Serve hot in individual dishes. Place 2 or 3 deep-fried stuffed eggplant "sandwiches" in each dish and top with a small ladleful of hot sauce.

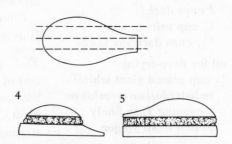

4

5

4, 5. slices of both small and large eggplants may be stuffed like a sandwich

Tea-Whisk Eggplants

(*Chasen-Nasu Su-age*) 茶筅なす素揚げ (color plate 13)

Success with this dish depends first of all on finding very small, round (not skinny) eggplants, no longer than 3 inches (8 cm). The eggplants are cut and twisted in such a way that they are reminiscent of the bamboo whisks used in the tea ceremony. Utilizing the shape, color, and flavor of the eggplant, this dish is as delicious as it is novel.

You may serve this as a vegetarian entrée on a bed of puffed "spring rain" filaments with deep-fried small green peppers as described below, or, in a Western-style meal, as a side dish with grilled meat or fowl.

4 servings

8-12 eggplants, no more than 3 inches (8 cm) long
8-12 small green peppers (*ao-tōgarashi*)
1 ounce (30 g) "spring rain" filaments (*harusame*)
2 cups TEMPURA DIP (see page 237)
1½-2 Tbsps finely grated fresh ginger
lemon wedges
oil for deep-frying

deeply score small eggplant from *bottom to top*, using heel of knife blade

To prepare: Wash vegetables, trim off eggplant and green pepper stems.

With a *very* sharp knife, deeply score the eggplant from bottom to just below the stem at $\frac{1}{16}$-inch ($\frac{1}{4}$-cm) intervals, as shown. This a bit tricky; care and patience (and maybe a razor blade if you do not have a very sharp knife) are recommended.

Pierce the small green peppers with a fork so that they will not explode in the hot oil. If small green peppers are not available, substitute okra or greenbeans.

Mix TEMPURA DIP and keep warm till serving time. Prepare grated ginger and lemon wedge garnishes.

To deep-fry: Bring about 4 inches (10 cm) of oil to about 340°F/170°C (medium temperature) in a heavy-bottomed pot or deep-fryer.

Begin by deep-frying the *harusame* filaments. It takes only 10 to 20 seconds for them to puff up in the hot oil. Remove immediately and drain on absorbent paper toweling. The puffed filaments are the bed against which the vegetables are displayed. Deep-fry several handfuls.

Keep the oil at 340°F/170°C. Lightly wipe the eggplants with a damp towel, then deep-fry scored eggplants a few at a time, for about 3–4 minutes, till purple skin becomes very brilliant. Skim off foam and impurities as deep-frying progresses. Remove eggplants and drain briefly on paper toweling.

Deep-fry the small green peppers in the same way. The peppers will brighten considerably in color.

To serve: Holding the scored and fried eggplant at the top, press it down squarely and twist so that the scorings separate and a "tea-whisk" shape is achieved.

Arrange a small bed of puffed "spring rain" at the back of a small plate. Against the bed lean 2 or 3 "tea-whisk" eggplants and a few green peppers. Place a small cone of finely grated ginger to one side and a few wedges of lemon. Pour hot TEMPURA DIP in a small bowl at the side.

Squeeze lemon over vegetables and eat, or mix grated ginger in TEMPURA DIP and dip vegetables in that sauce before eating.

Combines well with DEEP-FRIED MARINATED CHICKEN (page 234) and VINEGARED CRAB (page 247).

Deep-Fried Mixed Kebabs

(*Kushi-age*) 串 揚 げ (color plate 17)

In Japan, this dish is served in specialty restaurants offering anything up to thirty varieties of skewered delicacies. You sit at a bar while aproned chefs deep-fry the skewered foods you order. In front of you is a pottery dish with compartments for the dipping sauces and garnishes. A plate of shredded cabbage, over which one pours a little *tonkatsu* sauce (page 240) is the standard salad. (Sometimes the cabbage is broken or cut into 2-inch (5-cm) squares and diners dip pieces into salt as they eat.) On the bar may be containers filled with small whole green onions to munch between skewers. Here is a simple home version of this dish. Use a fondue pot at the table, but cook no more than four skewers at once to keep the oil temperature constant.

4 servings

½ pound (225 g) small shrimp or 8 large shrimp, shelled and deveined

1 pound (450 g) sirloin or tenderloin beef, cut into paper-thin slices (as for SUKIYAKI), rolled and cut into 1-inch (2½-cm) lengths

12 quail eggs, hardboiled and shelled (canned are good)

1 can crabmeat, drained, cartilage removed, and meat wrapped in thin fillet of white-fleshed fish

To prepare: Clean and cut the ingredients and precook those that require it. Skewer on 8-inch (20-cm) bamboo skewers, using only about 4½ inches (11½ cm) of the skewer length for the food.

Dust skewered ingredients with flour and paint with beaten egg yolk. Roll in breadcrumbs. Arrange on a large platter or tray. You may garnish this with portions of shredded cabbage (or broken cabbage pieces) that make the salad for this meal.

To cook and eat: Bring at least 4 inches (10 cm) of vegetable oil (or lard, or oil and lard mixture) to 330–350°F/170–180°C. Cook skewered food in hot oil till golden brown, turning in the oil, about 4 minutes. Skim surface of oil occasionally. Remove and drain for a minute or so before eating. Dip into sauces or condiments as desired, or sprinkle with lemon juice. Eat off the skewer.

8 large fresh mushrooms (any kind), wiped and trimmed

2 bell peppers, seeded and cut into 1½-inch (4-cm) squares

½ pound (225 g) pork loin, cubed, skewered with onion quarters

1 pint fresh oysters

1 eggplant, salted and sliced

for breading:

flour

4-5 egg yolks, beaten

dried or fresh bread-crumbs

oil for deep-frying

sauces and dips:

tonkatsu sauce (see page 240)

ketchup

Worcestershire sauce

prepared mustard

salt (especially for seafood)

lemon wedges

salad:

1 head cabbage, shredded or broken into bite-sized pieces

2 bunches green onions

Preparation of kebabs in color plate 17.

(l to r) 1. spread marmalade on bread and roll with beef. 2. spread mustard on bread, roll with asparagus, add ham, continue rolling; cut roll into 1-inch lengths. 3. slit peeled pearl onion along one side, remove center of onion through slit, insert hard-boiled quail egg in onion center through slit, and cut in half. 4. fill holes in lotus root slices with seasoned minced pork. 5. bite-sized piece of beef steak. 6. cut chicken breast fillet (*sasami*) into thin slices and roll with 1-inch lengths of green onion. 7. skewer ½ large raw shelled shrimp, 1-inch length of asparagus, and 1-inch square of ham attractively as shown. 8. make slit in center of 2-inch piece of salmon steak and stuff slit with WHITE MISO DRESSING (page 246) flavored with a bit of finely grated *yuzu* citron rind. 9. roll thinly sliced salmon with 1-inch length of asparagus. 10. roll a sillago fillet with a toasted and shelled ginkgo nut. 11. skewer a sillago fillet in the "two-sided tucking" style (page 179). 12. sandwich a thin slice of ham between two squid strips and skewer in an S curve. 13. using the *katsura-muki* technique (page 138), cut 1-inch asparagus length into a spiral, then roll with a strip of squid. 14. score one side of squid piece, cut into strips, and roll with *nori* seaweed. 15. one scallop. 16. one shrimp. 17. shelled crab claw.

❋ Salads ❋
Sunomono and *Aemono*

Green Beans with Sesame-*Miso* Dressing

(*Sandomame Goma-Miso Ae*) 三度豆胡麻味噌あえ

The *ingen* (green or string bean) was introduced from China in olden times. Fascinated by its triple yearly harvest, the Japanese popularly dubbed it the "three-times bean" (*sandomame*). A light cooking and then dressing with sesame paste and *miso* makes this often dull vegetable both interesting and delicious. The same dressing goes well with many vegetables, and this dish goes well with most foods.

4 servings

1 pound green beans, strings removed

dressing:

4 Tbsps (80 g) red *miso*
2 Tbsps white sesame seed, toasted and ground (see page 86)
1½ Tbsps sugar
1 Tbsp *mirin*

To prepare: Chop or snap beans into 1¾-inch (4½-cm) lengths. Cook, covered, in lightly salted boiling water until barely tender. Rinse in cold water and drain.

Make the dressing. Add the red *miso* all at once to freshly ground sesame in the *suribachi* (grinding bowl) and mix with the pestle. Add the sugar and *mirin* and mix with the pestle or a rubber spatula. The dressing will be rather coarse in texture.

To assemble and serve: In a medium-sized mixing bowl combine the beans and the sesame-*miso* dressing and mix until beans are well coated.

Serve at room temperature in neat mounds in individual dishes.

Savory Okra (cold)

(*Okura Wasabi-jōyu*) オクラわさび醤油

4 servings

20 pods okra, washed and trimmed

To prepare: Boil okra gently, uncovered, in lightly salted water till bright green, about 2 minutes. Rinse under cold running water and drain. Cut okra on the diagonal into ¼-inch (¾-cm) thick pieces.

salt
at least 1 tsp grated *wasabi*
  horseradish
2 Tbsps dark soy sauce
1 Tbsp *mirin* (alcohol
  burned off)

Mix grated *wasabi* with the dark soy sauce and *mirin* (or see page 171 for another version of HORSERADISH SOY SAUCE). Blend well.

To serve: Serve at room temperature or chilled in individual shallow dishes. Arrange a mound of okra in the center and spoon over a scant amount of HORSERADISH SOY SAUCE dressing. Mix well before eating.

Combines well with FRIED COD IN BROTH (page 382) and BOILED BEANS (page 391).

Tangy White Salad
(*Shirazu-Ae*) 白酢あえ (color plate 14)

The basis of the creamy thick dressing for this salad is *tōfu*, pureed and seasoned and enriched with sesame paste. This is a typical Japanese use of bean curd. The vegetables and dressing may be prepared ahead of time but must *not* be mixed together until just before serving. Any *tōfu* dressing is fragile, so be sure to refrigerate.

4 servings

6-8 dried *shiitake* mushrooms, softened and trimmed (see page 88)

for simmering mushrooms:
  1⅔ cups *dashi*
  3 Tbsps dark soy sauce
  2 Tbsps *mirin*
  1 tsp sugar

1 Japanese cucumber (or ½ large Western cucumber, peeled and seeded)
salt
½ medium carrot, scraped
½ cake *konnyaku* (devil's tongue jelly)

for simmering carrot and konnyaku:
  1⅔ cups *dashi*

To prepare solid ingredients: None of the vegetables is used raw: all are prepared with deep-penetrating seasonings that complement the taste of the "white" dressing.

Slice mushrooms thinly. Combine liquid for simmering mushrooms in a small saucepan, heat, add sliced mushrooms and simmer, uncovered, over medium-low heat till the liquid is almost totally reduced. Drain and cool to room temperature.

Cut cucumber into paper-thin slices (or use food processor). Marinate in lightly salted water (½ Tbsps salt to 1 cup water) to cover for 20 minutes. After marination, squeeze the cucumber wafers with your hands to extract as much water as possible. Squeeze, do not wring.

Cut the carrot lengthwise into paper-thin slices (about 1½ × ¼ inches [4 × ¾ cm]). Parboil, covered, in a small amount of water for a few minutes till almost tender and bright orange. Rinse in cold water and drain.

Parboil *konnyaku* for 2 to 3 minutes, drain and cool.

½ tsp salt
2 tsp sugar
2 Tbsps dark soy sauce
4 ounces (115 g) chicken breast fillets (optional)

WHITE DRESSING:

1 cake *tōfu* (bean curd), boiled for 1-2 minutes then pressed (see page 58) and cooled
2 Tbsps sesame paste or white sesame seeds
1½ Tbsps sugar
1 Tbsp light soy sauce
½ Tbsp rice vinegar
½ Tbsp *mirin*

garnish with one:

finely chopped *shiso* leaf
cone of finely grated fresh ginger
grated rind of *yuzu* citron (or lemon)
sprig of *kinome*

Cut into pieces about the same size as the carrot slices.

Combine seasonings for carrot and *konnyaku* in a small saucepan, heat and add the two solid ingredients. Simmer 3 to 4 minutes over medium-high heat, stirring frequently so that the seasonings penetrate thoroughly. Allow carrot and *konnyaku* to come to room temperature in the seasoning liquid. Discard the liquid.

Optional: Blanch the chicken breast fillets by swishing them around in gently boiling water for 20 to 30 seconds. Remove, drain, and cut diagonally into slices about ⅛ inch (½ cm) thick. (Or use boiled white chicken meat.)

At this point, you may put all seasoned vegetables (and chicken) into a mixing bowl, cover tightly with plastic wrap, and refrigerate until 1 hour before serving, at which time these ingredients should be removed from the refrigerator and allowed to come to room temperature.

To prepare white dressing: Rub drained, pressed *tōfu* through a sieve to puree.

Put sesame paste into a mixing bowl and add pureed *tōfu*. If using sesame seeds, toast and grind into a flaky paste (see page 86), then add pureed *tōfu* and mix.

Add the sugar, light soy sauce, vinegar, and *mirin*, mixing between additions. You may make this dressing ahead of time and refrigerate.

To assemble and serve: Pour the white dressing over the vegetables (and chicken) in the mixing bowl and toss lightly so that all ingredients are lightly coated. Transfer little mounds of the salad to small individual dishes. Garnish with one of the ingredients listed. Serve at room temperature.

Combines well with YŪAN-STYLE GRILLED CHICKEN (page 187) and BEATEN EGG SOUP (page 346).

VARIATION: For less tanginess, omit the vinegar from the dressing ingredients and the recipe will be plain *shira-ae*, White Salad.

Vinegared Cucumber

(*Kyūri no Sumomi*) きゅうりの酢もみ

4 servings

**4 Japanese cucumbers
(or 2 Western cucum-
bers, peeled and seeded)
salt**

SANBAIZU SAUCE:

   1 cup rice vinegar
   1 cup *dashi*
   4 Tbsps dark soy sauce
   2 Tbsps sugar
(Use this recipe for SANBAIZU
SAUCE, **or use** NIHAIZU SAUCE,
recipe on page 242)

To prepare: Cut cucumbers into paper-thin slices (or use food processor).

Spread out on a large wooden cutting board and sprinkle with a moderate amount of salt. Knead about 1 minute. A fair amount of water will be given off. Transfer cucumber to a medium-sized mixing bowl. Do not wash.

In a medium-sized saucepan combine all the ingredients for the sauce and bring just to a simmer. Force-cool by pouring hot sauce into a metal bowl and twirling that bowl in a larger one filled with water and ice cubes.

To assemble and serve: Pour slightly more than half the sauce over the salted cucumber. Gently squeeze cucumber with your hands. Pour off excess sauce from the cucumber and discard. Finally, pour remaining sauce over the cucumber. If you add sauce to cucumber only once, the mixture will become watery.

Transfer small mounds of cucumber drenched with sauce to small individual dishes. Serve at room temperature. This goes well with everything.

VARIATION: CUCUMBER AND SEAWEED IN SANBAIZU SAUCE. Proceed exactly as above, but add trimmed and softened lobe-leaf seaweed (*wakame*). Soak dried *wakame* in tepid water 30 minutes. Scald in hot water, then plunge into cold water to improve texture and color. Trim off hard parts with a knife and chop coarsely. Wrap in a kitchen towel to extract moisture. Toss with the salted cucumber before adding SANBAIZU SAUCE.

Muscats with Mustard Dressing

(*Masukatto Karashi-Ae*) マスカット辛子あえ

A good sweet-and-piquant appetizer. Mustard, surprisingly, goes well with the refreshing bouquet of juicy muscat grapes. Unless you enjoy peeling grapes, use only large varieties.

4 servings

1 pound (450 g) muscat
grapes, washed and
stemmed

dressing:

   1 tsp powdered mustard
   mixed to a paste with
   ½ tsp hot water
   1 tsp white *miso*
   2 Tbsps *dashi* or chicken
   stock
   few drops light soy sauce

To prepare: Peel the grapes, discarding the skins. Slice in half and extract seeds with the tip of a paring knife or pointed chopstick.

Blend mustard paste with the white *miso* till smooth. Add the *dashi* and mix well. Finally add the soy sauce to taste.

The grapes and the dressing can be prepared separately in advance and tossed together at the last minute.

To assemble and serve: Put grape halves in a medium-sized mixing bowl and pour on the dressing. Toss gently but well.

Serve in small, deep individual dishes, at room temperature or slightly chilled.

Goes well with SEA BREAM SASHIMI (pages 160ff).

VARIATIONS: Use other table varieties of grapes, for example the pale green Thompson seedless. Experiment with melon balls, or fresh pineapple wedges, cherries, or various berries. Sweet apples are good, first sprinkled with lemon juice to prevent discoloring.

Asparagus with Mustard Dressing
(*Asuparagasu Karashi-Ae*) アスパラガス辛子あえ

---

4 servings

20 spears asparagus,
trimmed (and pared, if
necessary)
salt

dressing:

   2 tsps powdered mustard
   mixed with 2 tsps water
   1 egg yolk
   1 tsp dark soy sauce

To prepare: Cut asparagus spears into 1½-inch (4-cm) lengths.

Parboil in lightly salted water. Remove while still crisp and rinse in cold water to improve color.

Prepare the mustard in a large mixing bowl. Beat in the egg yolk and mix well. Add the soy sauce and mix. (You may add flavor to the dressing by including ¼ cup *ito-kezuri-katsuo* [dried bonito thread-shavings] after finishing with the dressing and before adding the asparagus.)

Put the asparagus in the large mixing bowl with the dressing. Toss.

To serve: Serve in small individual dishes. Arrange asparagus lengths in a neat pyramid. Serve at room temperature.

Combines well with BAMBOO RICE (page 439) and CLEAR CHICKEN SOUP (page 345).

Grilled Mushrooms with *Ponzu* Sauce
(*Yaki-Shiitake Ponzu-Ae*) 焼き椎茸ポン酢あえ

When using *shiitake* mushrooms, be careful not to overcook them or their subtle aroma will disappear and they will dry out. Good as a cocktail snack or as a garnish with grilled or deep-fried dishes.

4 servings

12 large fresh *shiitake* mushrooms, wiped and trimmed

for "instant" PONZU **(*or see page* 172)**
  4 Tbsps lemon juice
  4 Tbsps dark soy sauce splash *mirin*

1 Tbsp finely chopped, green onion, rinsed (see page 170)

To prepare: Salt mushrooms lightly. Grill stem side first, then cap side, over a hot charcoal fire for no longer than 5 minutes total. To pan-broil, cook both sides of mushrooms in a frying pan over medium-high heat in a scant amount of oil for about 3 minutes total. (Oven broiling does not give good results.)

Mix the PONZU SAUCE (see page 172 for a slightly more elaborate version) and stir in the finely chopped green onion.

To assemble and serve: The mushrooms must be served really *hot*. As they come off the grill or out of the pan, cut mushrooms in half. One serving is six halves; serve in small individual dishes and top each with 1 Tbsp of PONZU SAUCE.

Combines well with TEMPURA ON RICE (page 444).

Five-Color Salad
(*Goshiki Namasu*) 五色なます

Though their dressings are about the same, five colorful ingredients make this a more vivid dish than TANGY WHITE SALAD (page 421). The vegetables in this dish, however, are not seasoned. Instead of the dried persimmon (a winter delicacy in Japan) you may substitute almost any dried fruit, such as apricots, figs, or prunes.

The vegetables and dressing can be prepared separately a day ahead of time and tossed just prior to serving. Be sure to refrigerate the dressing if prepared ahead of time; the *tōfu* spoils easily.

4 servings

2-3 dried persimmons
⅕ giant white radish (*daikon*), peeled

To prepare: Cut the dried fruit into julienne strips.
Cut the radish and carrot into julienne strips. Quarter green beans lengthwise then cut into 1½-inch (4-cm) lengths. Parboil each vegetable separately—radish and

½ medium carrot, scraped
¼ pound (115 g) green
   beans, strings removed
4-6 fresh *shiitake* mushrooms, wiped and trimmed
for the WHITE DRESSING, see
   page 422, but increase
   amount of rice vinegar
   to 1 Tbsp

carrot for 2 minutes, green beans for 3 minutes—in lightly salted water, then rinse in cold water.

Grill mushrooms briefly and slice thinly.

Combine dried fruit and vegetables in a mixing bowl.

To assemble and serve: Pour the WHITE DRESSING over the dried fruit and vegetables and toss so that all ingredients are lightly coated. Serve at room temperature in neat mounds in small individual dishes.

Goes well with SHRIMP WAFERS (page 408).

Abalone and Kiwi Fruit Salad

(Mushi-Awabi to Kiwi no Aemono) 蒸し鮑とキウィのあえもの

An example of Japanese culinary ingenuity. The fragrant tang of this novel fruit now imported in quantity from New Zealand combines particularly well with tender steamed abalone.

4 small servings

2½ ounces (70 g) steamed
   or canned abalone
2 kiwi fruit
1 tsp light soy sauce
juice of ¼ lemon

To prepare: If fresh, steam the abalone according to the directions on page 378 and trim and discard black "fringe" and innards. Canned abalone is fine. Cut abalone into julienne strips.

Skin the kiwi, cut in half lengthwise, then cut into thin half-moon slices.

To assemble and serve: Put the kiwi half-moons into a mixing bowl and crush with the back of a spoon. The fruit should become somewhat pulpy, but individual slices should still be definable If the kiwi is not quite ripe and the flesh is hard, use a *suribachi* (Japanese grinding bowl, see page 105) for this step.

Add the abalone strips to the kiwi and toss. Sprinkle on the soy sauce and lemon juice and toss.

Serve in small portions in small dishes or cups.

Combines well with GRILLED RED TILEFISH "WAKASA" (page 363).

VARIATION: Shred grilled squid and use instead of abalone.

Crushed Burdock with Sesame Dressing
(*Tataki Gobō*) たたき午旁

Pounded burdock root marinated in vinegar and seasoned with sesame makes an appetizing dish to enjoy with hot rice or just with *saké*. This is one of the foods traditionally made for the long New Year holiday, when cooking is taboo. Foods eaten then are also chosen for their propitious names, and the word *tataki* (pounded, beaten) also means "joy aplenty."

4 servings

4 medium burdock roots, scrubbed with a brush
vinegar

for simmering:

1¼ cups *dashi*
2 Tbsps *mirin*
2 Tbsps light soy sauce
½ tsp salt

sesame dressing:

3 Tbsps white sesame seeds, toasted and ground (see page 86)
1½ Tbsps *dashi*
1 Tbsp sugar
2 Tbsps vinegar
½ Tbsp light soy sauce

Burdock: With the side of a heavy knife (or a mallet or bottle), pound the burdock so that the roots are flattened somewhat and fibers are exposed. Cut the crushed roots into pieces about 1½ inches (4 cm) long and about half the thickness of a pencil. Put in cold water with a small amount of vinegar and let stand for 1 hour. Rinse several times in cold water.

Put burdock into a pot and cover with fresh water. Bring to a boil and boil gently, uncovered, for 3 or 4 minutes. Drain and plunge in cold water.

In a medium-sized saucepan mix the ingredients for simmering. Add the boiled burdock and simmer for 2 or 3 minutes. Allow to cool in the seasoning liquid and do not remove burdock from liquid until time to use. Discard liquid.

Sesame dressing: Add the other seasonings to the freshly ground sesame in the grinding bowl (*suribachi*), mixing well between additions.

To assemble and serve: Add the prepared burdock to the dressing in the *suribachi*. Mix well with the pestle to ensure that the dressing penetrates the burdock. To allow flavors to mature, wait 1 day before eating. Keeps 1 week refrigerated in a sealed container.

Serve in little mounds in individual small dishes at room temperature. No garnish.

Goes well with either DEEP-FRIED MARINATED CHICKEN (page 234) or CRAB-AND-TŌFU BALLS IN BROTH (page 413).

VARIATION: Instead of basing the dressing on sesame seed, you may use sesame paste (or butter), peanut butter, or walnut paste. Do not attempt to toast crushed walnuts as you do sesame seed; they will become bitter.

Horse Mackerel Escabeche *"Nanban"*

(*Aji Nanban-zuke*) 鰺南蛮漬け

The early Spanish and Portuguese missionaries who arrived in 16th century Japan via South Asia were called *nanban-jin* ("southern barbarians"). It was they who introduced red peppers, so dishes using these hot, bright vegetables generally have the word *nanban* in their names.

4 servings

southern barbarian marinade:

½ cup less 1 Tbsp rice
   vinegar
⅔ cup *dashi*
2 Tbsps *mirin*
1½ Tbsps light soy sauce
2-3 small dried red
   peppers, seeded
10 green onions or 1
   medium round onion

8 small horse mackerel,
   3-4 inches (8-10 cm) each
salt
flour
oil for deep-frying

Marinade: In a medium-size saucepan, mix the vinegar, *dashi*, *mirin*, light soy sauce, and seeded peppers and bring just to a boil. Remove from heat.

Grill green onions until scorched (the onions should have touches of black char), then cut into 1½–2-inch (4–5-cm) lengths. (If conventional onion is used, slice into ¼-inch [¾-cm] rounds and sauté until soft.) Add onion to the mixture in the saucepan.

Fish: Use whole fish or fillets with skin, as you like. For whole fish, scale, gut, and clean the fish, leaving heads on or off as you prefer. Salt lightly on both sides and let stand for 15 minutes. Wipe off salt and brush both sides of the fish with flour. Deep-fry in 2 to 3 inches (5 to 8 cm) of low-temperature (320°F/160°C) oil for about 5 minutes, or till golden. Drain briefly on paper toweling. While still hot place in a shallow pan.

Bring the sauce to a simmer and immediately pour over the hot, deep-fried fish. Marinate refrigerated for 1 to 2 days. This should be sufficient time for the bones of a small fish to soften completely. (With fillets, starting with the marinade at room temperature, marinate in the refrigerator for 3 to 4 hours.)

To serve: Briefly drain marinated fish and place on individual serving plates. Garnish with some of the onion and the red pepper (the latter for color only, not to be eaten). Serve chilled.

Combines well with GRILLED EGGPLANT (page 370) and ROLLED OMELETTE (page 203).

VARIATIONS: Adjust the amount of sauce you make to fit the size of the fish. Also suitable for this method of preparation are fresh sardines, smelt, and small sea bream (the latter are excellent). Try chicken breast fillet too.

Red-and-White Vinegared Salad

(*Kōhaku Namasu*) 紅白なます

This colorful salad of "red" and white vegetables is made for festive occasions and tastes best after it has been allowed to ripen for 2 or 3 days in the refrigerator. In fact, this will keep up to 2 weeks refrigerated in a tightly sealed container.

<u>6 cups</u> (about 12 servings)

1 8-inch (20-cm) length of giant white radish (*daikon*) (about 4 cups when sliced)
2 medium carrots (about 2 cups when sliced)
1 tsp salt
¾ cup SWEET VINEGAR (*amazu*, see page 242)
1½-inch (4-cm) square giant kelp (*konbu*)

To prepare: Scrape giant white radish and carrot. Cut both vegetables into narrow, very thin rectangles, about 1½ × ½ inches (4 × 1 cm).

Put strips in a large mixing bowl and sprinkle with salt. Wait 5 minutes, then knead thoroughly with hands till radish strips are soft and translucent. (Carrot strips will retain original color and crispness.)

Quite an amount of water will be extracted by salt-kneading. Gather the kneaded radish and carrots in both hands, and over the sink firmly but gently press out all the water you can. Transfer to a clean bowl and add ¼ cup SWEET VINEGAR. Mix thoroughly with hands, press out vinegar lightly, and discard vinegar. Then add remaining ½ cup SWEET VINEGAR, mix, add *konbu* to vegetables, cover, and refrigerate. In an emergency, you may serve after 30 minutes, but the proper flavor does not begin to develop for 1 day or so.

To serve: Serve cold or at room temperature. This dish is really all-purpose. Eat it in small 2- to 3-Tbsp portions at the beginning of the meal as an appetizer, or at the end of a Japanese-style meal with the rice course like pickles. With fried or broiled entrées in particular it makes a good side dish—again, in very small portions.

Soused Spinach

(*Hōrensō no Ohitashi*) ほうれん草のお浸し (color plate 9)

Spinach in Japan is picked when it is young and tender. Also, it is prepared so tastily that it has always been a children's favorite. Here, after the preliminary parboiling and rinsing, it is allowed to soak up the pleasant flavor of lightly seasoned stock. This dish goes well with almost everything.

4 servings

1 bunch spinach, trimmed, washed, and parboiled (see page 93)

seasoning liquid:
1¼ cups *dashi*
pinch salt
1 tsp *mirin*
3 tsps light soy sauce

⅓ cup *ito-kezuri-katsuo* (dried bonito thread-shavings) or substitute ordinary dried bonito flakes (*hana-katsuo*)

To prepare and assemble: Chop parboiled spinach into 2-inch (5-cm) lengths.

In a medium-sized pot, rapidly bring *dashi* to a boil, then reduce heat and simmer. Add the salt, *mirin*, and soy sauce. Transfer liquid to a metal mixing bowl and force-cool by swirling this bowl around in a larger bowl filled with ice and water.

Add the spinach to the force-cooled, seasoned *dashi* and mix. Refrigerate 5 to 6 hours.

To serve: Place ⅓-cup portions of chilled spinach in small dishes. Pour remaining chilled stock over spinach. Garnish with a large pinch of thread-shaved dried bonito or conventional dried bonito flakes.

VARIATION: This same technique is successful with any mild green vegetable.

Seafood in Citron Shells

(*Yose Namasu*) 寄せなます

Each *yuzu* citron is like a gilded chalice holding morsels of pink shrimp and other seafood delicacies in aspic. This conversation piece is as delicious as it is decorative. Moreover, it can be made the day before a party and refrigerated.

4 servings

4 to 8 fresh shrimp, depending on size
¼ pound (115 g) abalone, steamed or canned (or crab)
6-inch (15-cm) square of squid
4 large *yuzu* citron

aspic:
1½ Tbsps gelatin
2½ cups *dashi*
pinch salt

To prepare: Attend first to the seafood ingredients.

Shell and devein shrimp, but leave tails attached. Boil gently in lightly salted water just till pink and firm to the touch. Plunge into cold water until cool, and drain. If small, leave whole. If large, cut crosswise into halves or thirds. The point is to cut everything into bite-sized pieces.

Slice steamed or canned abalone into thin 1-inch (2½-cm) squares. Boiled crab will substitute for abalone.

Cross-score the outside (the shinier and smoother side) of the squid as shown in the recipe on page 449. Cut into 1- × -½-inch (2½- × -1½-cm) strips. Immerse in boiling water for about 30 seconds so that the strips

1 tsp light soy sauce
1 Tbsp *yuzu* juice

sprigs of *kinome*

curl and the "pinecone" cross-scoring pattern opens up. Remove and plunge into cold water to cool.

To fill the yuzu: Cut off the top of the *yuzu* about a quarter of the way down from the stem, as shown. Scoop out all pulp and membrane from both parts. Put pulp in cheesecloth (it is very loose, and seeds are many), squeeze out juice, and reserve.

Into the hollowed-out skins, place bits of shrimp, abalone, and squid. Fill, but do not pack, the shells.

Soften gelatin in a small amount of water. In a saucepan, mix the cold *dashi*, salt, and light soy sauce, and bring to a boil. Add the softened gelatin and remove from heat. The gelatin should dissolve immediately. Add the *yuzu* juice. Strain through a fine sieve and cool.

Carefully ladle the cooled liquid into the shells, not quite to the brim. Place a sprig of *kinome* decoratively in each filled shell. Cover with the *yuzu* tops and refrigerate at least 2 hours.

Serve on chilled individual plates. Uncover and set the lid at a jaunty angle against the fruit.

Goes well with STUFFED RED TILEFISH (page 361) and SALT-GRILLED CLAMS (page 358).

VARIATIONS: The possibilities are almost endless for filling citrus fruit shells with food in aspic, but seafood of various kinds blends best with the *dashi* aspic and fragrant rind. Add a small dollop of fresh salmon roe or other fish roe at the top of the fillings, so it can be seen in the aspic. A *very* light chicken stock, barely salted, works well.

Note: With its "single-portion" size and delicate fragrance that complements most Japanese ingredients, hollowed-out *yuzu* make perfect vessels for chilling aspic dishes or for steaming foods. If *yuzu* is unavailable, use other citrus fruits—small, blanched grapefruit might be easiest, or thin-skinned oranges, also blanched. In Japan, two other citrus fruits that might find their way to the table in this way are *natsumikan* and *hassaku*.

❋ One-Pot Dishes ❋
Nabemono

Cod and Cabbage Casserole
(Tara Chirinabe) 鱈ちりなべ

Cooked at the table, this is an attractive and convivial way to enjoy the delicate natural flavor of cod with typical Japanese vegetables and bean curd.

6 servings

2 pounds (900 g) cod fillets, with skin
6 leaves Chinese cabbage
½ pound (225 g) spinach
10 sprigs edible chrysanthemum leaves (*shungiku* or *kikuna*) (optional)
6 large fresh *shiitake* mushrooms, wiped and trimmed
6 Japanese long onions (*naganegi*) (or 8 leeks)
2 cakes grilled bean curd (*yakidōfu*)
PONZU SAUCE (see page 172)

spicy condiments:

about 6 Tbsps finely chopped green onion
2 lemons, quartered
about 6 Tbsps RED MAPLE RADISH (see page 170)
about 4 Tbsps finely grated fresh ginger

4-inch (10-cm) square giant kelp (konbu)

To prepare: All fresh ingredients, sauce, and spicy condiments may be prepared several hours in advance and refrigerated until serving time.

If fish is whole, scale, gut, and cut into boneless fillets, with skin. Remove any fine bones with tweezers. Cut fillets crosswise into 1-inch (2½-cm) slices. Lay pieces in a colander and pour boiling water over them. Rinse in cold water and drain. Wrap in a kitchen towel and refrigerate till time to arrange the platter.

Parboil the whole Chinese cabbage leaves. Rinse under cold water, and trim thick stem sections to make each leaf roughly the same general thickness. Wash, trim, and parboil spinach (see page 93). Pat Chinese cabbage leaves dry and form into spinach-stuffed rolls (see page 260). Wrap each roll in plastic or a clean kitchen towel and refrigerate.

Cut the tough stem ends off the chrysanthemum sprigs, wash, and drain. Cut each sprig in half. Cut each mushroom in half. Wash long onions (or leeks) and cut diagonally into 1½-inch (4-cm) lengths.

Refrigerate grilled bean curd in a bowl of water to cover.

Make PONZU SAUCE and prepare enough of the spicy condiments to generously serve the number of diners. Refrigerate in separate containers, covered.

To assemble, serve, and eat: Arrange the fish and vegetable ingredients on 1 or 2 platters, cutting the stuffed cabbage rolls into 1-inch (2½-cm) lengths and the bean curd cakes into sixths.

In the kitchen, fill an earthenware casserole (*donabe*, see page 103) or iron pot ¾ full of water. In it place the piece of giant kelp (*konbu*)—slashed a few times with a knife to release essential flavors.

Set the casserole on a heating unit at the table. Bring the water just to a boil on high heat. Bring out the platter(s) of vegetables and fish. Everyone should have his own dipping bowl for the PONZU SAUCE and spicy condiments.

To begin the meal, put pieces of fish into the stock first, then add vegetables and *tōfu* and simmer till just tender. While waiting for the fish to cook, diners help themselves to the PONZU SAUCE and spicy condiments and mix them in their dipping bowls. Eat the vegetable ingredients in any order. Add water to the casserole occasionally to maintain the ¾-full level. Serve boiled white rice any time during the meal.

VARIATIONS: This type of one-pot cooking is delicious with any firm, white-fleshed fish, including swordfish, shark, haddock, and plaice. Also suitable are squid, large shrimp, and clams.

An alternate sauce and spicy condiments combination is as follows:

peanut sauce:
  6 Tbsps pure peanut butter (without sweetening or seasoning)
  ½ Tbsp sugar
  ½ Tbsp vinegar
  1 Tbsp dark soy sauce
  1¾ cups *dashi* or chicken stock
spicy condiments:
  red pepper flakes (*ichimi*)
  lemon quarters
  finely chopped green onion

To make the sauce: Work the peanut butter in a *suribachi* (Japanese grinding bowl, see page 105), and gradually mix in other ingredients, blending and then diluting the mixture with *dashi* till the sauce is smooth. If made ahead of time, stir well before using to make sure the peanut butter has not settled to the bottom. Add spicy condiments as desired.

Note: PONZU and peanut butter sauces can be served at the same time. Just be sure that no one puts grated ginger or RED MAPLE RADISH into the peanut sauce—the flavors do not mix well.

"River Bank" Oyster Stew
(*Kaki Dote-nabe*) かき土手なべ

A one-pot dish cooked at the table. The inside rim of the casserole is coated all round with thick *miso*, resembling the earthen bank (*dote*) of a river, which gradually is dissolved in the simmering stew.

6 servings

**1 quart (1 L or 1 kg)
shucked large oysters
1 generous Tbsp salt
3 Japanese long onions
(naganegi) (or 4 leeks)
3 bunches edible chry-
santhemum leaves
(shungiku or kikuna),
trimmed and washed
2 bunches enokitake
mushrooms, washed and
trimmed
6 fresh shiitake mush-
rooms, wiped and trim-
med
¼ head Chinese cabbage
6 Tbsps (100 g) red miso
6 Tbsps (100 g) white miso
1 Tbsp mirin
½ cup cold dashi
3-x-5-inch (8-x-13-cm)
piece giant kelp (konbu)
1 quart (1 L) dashi
6 eggs (optional, for dip)**

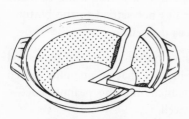

donabe casserole showing distribution and thickness of *miso*

To prepare: All the seafood and vegetables can be prepared a few hours ahead of time.

To clean and "whiten" the shucked oysters, mix thoroughly with your hands in a big bowl with 1 generous Tbsp salt or wash in well-salted water. Carefully rinse oysters one by one in running cold water and drain.

Cut long onions (or leeks) diagonally into 1½-inch (4-cm) lengths. If very thick, halve or quarter lengthwise.

Separate chrysanthemum sprigs into groups of uniform size.

Cut off spongy *enokitake* mushroom root. Leave in small bunches.

Notch decorative crosses into caps of *shiitake* mushrooms, or, if large, cut in half.

Cut the ¼ head cabbage crosswise into 1½-inch (4-cm) lengths. The volume of cabbage will decrease by 80 to 90 percent in cooking.

To assemble and serve: Using a fork or the back of a spoon, mix the two types of *miso* together. Add 1 Tbsp *mirin* and about ½ cup cold *dashi* to soften the *miso*; mix well. With a rubber spatula, spread the paste over the upper inside of a 9- or 10-inch (23- or 25-cm) earthenware casserole (*donabe*, see page 103) or skillet in a smooth layer about ¼ inch (¾ cm) thick, as shown.

Bring the casserole to the heating unit at the table.

Score the giant kelp (*konbu*) a few times with a knife so that its flavors will be released during cooking. Place the giant kelp in the casserole, then pour in 1 quart (1 L) of room-temperature *dashi*.

Bring the *dashi* quickly to a boil, then reduce heat to medium. The other ingredients may now be added to the simmering stock in whatever order you and the diners desire. (The *miso* does not melt with heat and run into the stock, each diner scrapes *miso* into the hot stock as he desires during the meal.) Take care not to overcook oysters or they will be tough.

Add *dashi* and more oysters or other ingredients as desired.

No sauce accompanies this dish, but cooked morsels may be dipped in beaten egg; if you wish, set each place with a dipping bowl and a fresh, raw egg.

Noodle *Sukiyaki*

(*Udon-Suki*) うどんすき

This opulent dish is especially popular in Osaka. The variety of ingredients, good *udon* noodles, and a flavorsome broth give noodles a surprising glamour. This is also fun to eat.

If *udon* or *soba* noodles are not available, make your own. Homemade noodles are always better than the dried and packaged (see page 308 for recipe). Different types of round or flat pasta can be used, but Italian noodles obviously do not taste like the Japanese.

With this hearty dish, cooked noodles are arranged on a platter and are then covered by other ingredients, which are eaten first. The noodles are "uncovered" as the meal comes to its close. Rice is not served; the noodles provide the starch. If you think your guests or family will be really hungry, prepare an extra platter of noodles.

6 servings

1 pound (450 g) dried *udon* noodles
2 cakes deep-fried bean curd (*atsuage*)
4 cakes *ganmodoki* (see page 60)
1 cake *kamaboko* (fish paste)
½ cup sliced bamboo shoot
2 fillets *anago* eel (if available), grilled
4 shrimp, parboiled
8 stalks trefoil (*mitsuba*)
12 fresh *shiitake* mushrooms, wiped and trimmed
6 pieces *mochi* (glutinous rice cake)
4-inch (10-cm) length medium giant white radish (*daikon*), boiled and cut into ½-inch (1½-cm) thick rounds
1 pound (450 g) spinach, parboiled (see page 93)

To prepare: Cook the dry noodles according to the basic recipe on page 310. Do not overcook; *udon* easily becomes mushy. Wash well in cold water, rubbing with your hands to eliminate surface starch. Drain well.

Line the platter with noodles, then arrange the other ingredients on top as you prepare them. These ingredients will soon hide the noodles from sight.

Some ingredients are available packaged and all that needs to be done is to cut them into bite-sized pieces. (If neither type of deep-fried bean curd is available, use grilled bean curd, *yakidōfu*.) If the bamboo shoot is whole, clean and cut into half-moon slices about ¼ inch (¾ cm) thick. If fresh, prepare as described on page 56.

Grill *anago* eel and cut into 6 pieces. Clean, devein, and boil shrimp till just pink; leave tails attached.

Cut trefoil stalks into halves or thirds. Notch decorative crosses into mushroom caps, or cut mushrooms in half if large.

If time allows, bake the *mochi* cakes so that they swell a bit, about 5 minutes in a moderate oven. Cut them into 1½-inch (4-cm) squares, depending on their size when purchased. (*Mochi* is not available in a standard size.)

Since the *daikon* radish takes about 40 minutes to

1 pound (450 g) chicken
   thigh meat, cut into
   1½-inch (4-cm) squares,
   with skin

broth:

   2 quarts (2 L) *dashi*
   ½ cup *mirin*
   1 cup dark soy sauce
   2 tsps salt

spicy condiments:

   4 Tbsps finely grated fresh
      ginger
   5-6 Tbsps finely chopped
      green onion
   seven-spice mixture
      (*shichimi*)
   lemon wedges or juice

cook, it has to be done ahead of time. Cut parboiled spinach into 2-inch (5-cm) lengths.

To cook and serve: Put the *dashi* and other broth ingredients into a *donabe* (see page 103) or other large, flameproof casserole and bring to a simmer over medium heat. This can be done on the kitchen stove and then the casserole can be brought to the table cooking unit, or the heating can be done at the table unit itself. When broth is simmering, begin to cook, starting with seafood ingredients.

Each diner should have an individual dipping bowl to be filled with broth from the casserole at the start of the meal, so have a ladle at the table. Diners add spicy condiments to the broth in their dipping bowls as desired. Ingredients are done as soon as heated through and tender.

Add thin *dashi* to the casserole as the meal progresses to keep broth from becoming too thick. When you think the broth is well flavored, add noodles to casserole. Eat noodles when heated.

As with all one-pot cooking, chopsticks are the ideal implement, but forks and spoons can be used.

Simmering *Tōfu*

(*Yudōfu*) 湯豆腐 (color plate 14)

The Kyoto temple that claims to have devised this Zen food centuries ago still serves it there daily to the general public in beautiful surroundings. The quintessence of Kyoto-style cooking—simplicity and purity of taste—this dish is popular throughout Japan and is an ideal supper for an autumn or winter evening, simmered at the table.

6 servings

spicy condiments:

   finely chopped green
      onion
   finely grated fresh ginger
   RED MAPLE RADISH (see
      page 170)

To prepare: The main part of the dish is cooked at the table, so chop and grate the spicy condiments first; make enough to give each diner a portion of about 1 generous Tbsp.

Next, make the sauce. In a medium-sized saucepan combine the *dashi*, soy sauce, and *mirin*. When the liquid just reaches the boiling point over medium-high heat, reduce heat so that the liquid simmers and then

ito-kezuri-katsuo (dried bonito thread-shavings) or ordinary dried bonito flakes (*hana-katsuo*)

sauce:

**1 cup *dashi*
½ cup dark soy sauce
1 Tbsp *mirin*
handful of dried bonito flakes (*hana-katsuo*)**

**4-inch (10-cm) square of giant kelp (*konbu*)
3 cakes *tōfu* (bean curd)**

improvised SIMMERING TŌFU pot, with vessel for sauce in center

stir in the bonito flakes. As soon as the flakes are soaked (about 1–3 seconds), strain the hot liquid into another pot. Discard bonito flakes. Keep hot on the stove till time to eat.

To cook and serve: Set an earthenware casserole (*donabe*, see page 103) or iron pot ¾ full of cold water on a heating unit at the table. Wipe the giant kelp with a damp cloth and slash it a few times so that essential flavors will be released in cooking. Drain the bean curd cakes and cut each one into sixths. Carefully put bean curd into the cold water.

Over medium heat bring the liquid to a simmer. Do not use a high flame because bean curd hardens and becomes crumbly when overcooked. As soon as the *tōfu* squares are heated, gently remove with a slotted spoon to diners' individual bowls.

While the *tōfu* is heating, each diner should be served a bowl containing hot sauce into which he mixes the spicy condiments of his choice.

Combines well with VINEGARED CRAB (page 247) and SAKÉ-SIMMERED FLOUNDER (page 224).

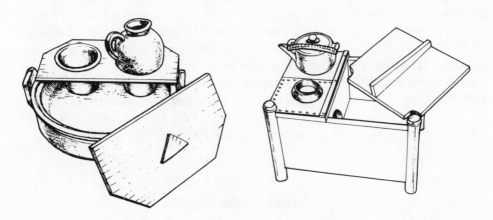

two SIMMERING TŌFU sets; the right one is made like a miniature Japanese bathtub and is heated by charcoal

❀ Rice Dishes ❀
Gohanmono

Asparagus Rice

(*Asuparagasu Gohan*) アスパラガスごはん

4 servings

8 spears fresh asparagus, trimmed (and pared if necessary)
salt
6 ounces (180 g) boned chicken leg or breast
3⅓ cups short-grain rice, washed

liquid for boiling rice:

    4 cups *dashi*
    2 Tbsps light soy sauce
    1 Tbsp dark soy sauce
    2 Tbsps *saké*
    1 tsp salt

1 heaping Tbsp fresh ginger cut into fine "needle" shreds

To prepare: Cut asparagus spears into 1½-inch (4-cm) lengths, then halve the center length (and quarter the lower length), if thick. Salt lightly and let rest 20 minutes.

Cut the chicken into ½-inch (1½-cm) cubes.

To boil and serve: Put washed rice in a heavy, tight-lidded pot or rice cooker. Mix the liquid for boiling rice and pour over the rice. Stir in the chicken cubes and ginger slivers. Cover and bring to a boil over medium heat, then raise heat to high and cook till most of the liquid is absorbed. Reduce heat to very low, lay the salted asparagus pieces on top of the rice, and cook, covered, till all liquid is absorbed (about 10 minutes).

Turn off heat, line underside of pot lid with a clean kitchen towel, cover and let stand 10 to 15 minutes before serving.

To serve, gently mix the asparagus pieces into the hot rice with a rice paddle or wooden spoon. Serve in individual bowls. Pull out and arrange a couple of asparagus pieces on top of each serving.

Mushroom Rice

(*Shiitake Gohan*) 椎茸ごはん

4 servings

5 large fresh *shiitake* mushrooms, wiped and trimmed
salt

To prepare: Salt mushrooms lightly and grill whole over a charcoal fire or use oven broiler to cook surface. When cooled, cut into ¼-inch (¾-cm) thick slices.

Pour boiling water over the deep-fried bean curd, drain, place between paper towels and press with hands. Cut into ¼-inch (¾-cm) squares.

1 cake thin deep-fried
  bean curd (*aburage* or
  usuage)
3⅓ cups short-grain rice,
  washed

liquid for boiling rice:

  4 cups *dashi*
  1 tsp salt
  2 Tbsps light soy sauce
  1 Tbsp dark soy sauce
  1 Tbsp *saké*

To boil and serve: Put washed rice in a heavy, tight-lidded pot or rice cooker. Mix the liquid for boiling rice and pour over the rice. Stir in the deep-fried bean curd pieces. Cover and bring to a boil over medium heat, then raise heat to high and cook till most of the liquid is absorbed. Reduce heat to very low, lay the sliced mushroom on top of the rice and cook, covered, till all the liquid is absorbed (about 10 minutes).

Turn off heat, line underside of pot lid with a clean kitchen towel, cover, and let rest 10 to 15 minutes before serving.

To serve, with a rice paddle or wooden spoon gently mix the mushrooms into the boiled rice. Serve in individual rice bowls. Pull out and arrange a couple of mushroom slices on top of each serving.

Note: The point of using deep-fried bean curd is to include an ingredient with some oil or slight fattiness. You may use chicken instead.

Bamboo Rice
(*Takenoko Gohan*) 筍ごはん (color plate 9)

A food for spring, when bamboo shoots poke their heads out of the earth.

4 servings

½ pound (225 g) bamboo
  shoots
½ pound (225 g) boned
  chicken leg, with skin
3⅓ cups short-grain rice,
  washed
liquid for boiling rice:

  4 cups *dashi* (or chicken
    stock)
  1 tsp salt
  2 Tbsps light soy sauce
  2 Tbsps *saké*

½ sheet toasted *nori*
  seaweed or sprigs of
  kinome

To prepare: Halve the (canned) bamboo shoots lenthwise and wash well. Cut into thin half-moon slices or ⅛-×-⅛-×-1½-inch (½-×-½-×-4-cm) sticks. Wash again and drain. Parboil bamboo for 1 minute or so, then immediately rinse in cold water. Drain. (If you are starting with raw bamboo, see page 56 for directions on preparation.)

Cut the chicken leg meat into ½-inch (1½-cm) cubes, parboil for 1 minute, then wash in cold water to eliminate excess fat. Drain.

To boil and serve: Put washed rice into a heavy, tight-lidded pot or rice cooker. Mix the liquid for boiling rice and pour over rice. Stir in the bamboo and chicken. Cover and bring to a boil over medium heat, then raise heat to high and cook till most of the liquid is absorbed. Reduce heat to very low and cook, covered, till all the liquid is absorbed (about 10 minutes). Turn off heat, line underside of pot lid with a kitchen towel, cover and let rest 10 to 15 minutes before serving.

To serve, gently fluff the rice with a rice paddle or wooden spoon and serve in individual bowls. Garnish with crumbled toasted *nori* seaweed or fragrant sprigs of *kinome*.

Rice with Greens
(*Nameshi*) 菜めし

Hot white rice mixed with radish (*daikon*) greens is a dish to greet the arrival of spring.

4 servings

½ cup finely chopped raw greens of giant white radish (*daikon*)
½ tsp salt
5 cups hot cooked short-grain rice (see basic recipe on page 273)

To prepare and serve: Wash and drain greens and finely chop. Put into a large mixing bowl and sprinkle with the salt. With your hands, crumple and knead the greens till limp and a bit watery, 1 or 2 minutes. Discard excess liquid.

Mix the chopped, salted greens into 5 cups of hot white rice with a rice paddle or wooden spoon. When well mixed, serve in individual rice bowls.

VARIATIONS: Prepare mustard or turnip greens in the same way. Particularly good are leaves of green *shiso*, which only need to be cut crosswise into thin strips and then mixed with hot rice.

Rice Balls
(*Onigiri*) おにぎり (color plate 15)

Japan's traditional sandwich equivalent. *Nigiri* means "clenched," and to make good rice "balls" takes practice. You must press the rice only just hard enough to keep the grains lightly but firmly together, without squashing them, which hardens the rice. *Onigiri* are usually triangular, often oval, and only sometimes spherical. At the core is concealed some tasty morsel such as a pickled plum (*umeboshi*), a small piece of salted salmon, a little salted cod roe (*tarako*), or a few bonito flakes. The "balls" are tastiest when wrapped in toasted *nori* seaweed. Normally a picnic item, *onigiri* may be served at home as a variant to the usual bowl of rice, and leftover "balls" are nice grilled (without *nori*) and seasoned with soy sauce.

for 8–10 triangles:

5 cups hot cooked short-grain rice

4 sheets dried *nori* seaweed

fillings:

dried bonito flakes (*hana-katsuo*) moistened in soy sauce

salted salmon, grilled

salted cod roe (*tarako*), grilled

PICKLED PLUMS (***umeboshi***)

2 Tbsps black sesame seeds, toasted

To prepare: Wash and cook the rice as usual, according to the recipe for plain white boiled rice on page 273. *Onigiri* are made while the rice is still hot.

Meanwhile, toast the *nori* sheets by passing them over a flame and cut sheets crosswise into 1-inch (2½-cm) widths.

Prepare the fillings you desire. Douse bonito flakes with soy sauce to moisten throughly. Grill salted salmon and break into small pieces, about ½ × ¼ inch (1½ × ¾ cm). Grill cod roe. Pit pickled plums; if extremely large, cut plum meat into several pieces.

Toast the black sesame seeds in a dry frying pan.

To form triangles: When handling the hot rice, keep your hands moistened with salty water to season the rice slightly and to keep it from sticking to your hands.

Place a handful of rice (about ½ cup) across the bent fingers of the left hand. Make an indentation in the rice and tuck in one of the fillings—about 1 tsp of soy-doused bonito flakes; 1 tsp of cod roe; a few flakes of salmon; or a whole pickled plum. Use your index finger, middle finger, and thumb as shown to mold the triangular shape, about 2½ inches (6½ cm) high and 1 inch (2½ cm) thick. Continue molding to cover the fillings. The main thing is not to make the rice too salty and to avoid packing it too hard or too loosely.

Set the rice triangles down on their bases and cover each with a strip of *nori* seaweed, shiny side out, like the roof of a cottage, as sketched. The *nori* can be applied in a number of ways.

If the triangular shape is difficult to make, you can mold and pat the rice into an oval and wrap the seaweed around the middle. In this case, sprinkle one or both ends with sesame seeds.

Eat with fingers, of course.

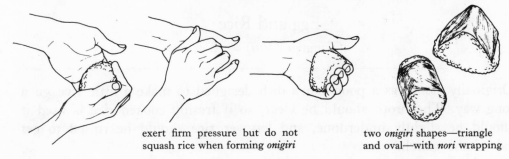

exert firm pressure but do not squash rice when forming *onigiri*

two *onigiri* shapes—triangle and oval—with *nori* wrapping

Tea-and-Rice
(Ochazuke) お茶づけ

The traditional Japanese meal ends with a bowl or two of rice followed by ordinary green tea. Pouring some tea over the rice, with a little *nori* seaweed crumbled in, started as an informal home custom but proved so good that it came to stand alone as a delicious dish with various ingredients added, and is enjoyed by one and all. The recipe below is for a rather grand version of this simple fare.

1 serving

1 cup hot cooked short-grain rice (see recipe, page 273)
2 ounces (60 g) raw sea bream or any other white-fleshed fish
finely grated *wasabi* horseradish
½ sheet *nori* seaweed
1 cup hot Japanese green tea (bancha, see page 332)

To assemble and serve: Place hot rice in a large individual rice bowl. Cut raw sea bream against the grain into paper-thin strips and arrange on top of the rice (or similarly arrange other ingredients—pickles, roe, etc.). Grate *wasabi* horseradish and place in a small mound on the fish. Toast *nori* seaweed by passing it over a flame and cut into shreds or crumble it and sprinkle over the fish and rice. Pour hot tea on rice. Serve immediately. Mix with chopsticks (or a spoon) as you eat.

VARIATIONS: There are many varieties of *ochazuke*, depending on the ingredients used to top the rice. The most typical and traditional types are: *nori-chazuke* (with dried, toasted *nori* seaweed), *tai-chazuke* (with flaked white fish), *sake-chazuke* (with bits of salted salmon), *maguro* or *sashimi-chazuke* (with raw, lean tuna), *tarako-chazuke* (with grilled, salted cod roe), and *tsukemono-chazuke* (with pickles). (There are also many dried, packaged toppings, which are just sprinkled on the rice and reconstituted by hot tea.) In using leftover cold rice, the usual combination is with pickles or *nori*, presumably because these ingredients are found at any time in any Japanese kitchen.

Note: *Wasabi* horseradish is not served with all varieties of *ochazuke*.

Egg and Rice
(Tamago Zōsui) 卵 雑 炊

Originally *zōsui* was a poor man's dish designed to make a little rice go a long way. The broth should be clear, so if freshly cooked rice is used it should be slightly underdone, and leftover rice should be rinsed to get rid of the starch.

4 servings

5 cups *dashi* (or light chicken stock)

2 tsps salt

4 Tbsps light soy sauce

2 Tbsps dark soy sauce

4 Tbsps *saké*

5 cups hot or cold cooked short-grain rice (see basic recipe on page 273), preferably slightly undercooked

4 medium eggs, beaten

use one:

  4 Tbsps finely chopped green onion

  12 stalks trefoil (*mitsuba*), cut into 1½-inch (4-cm) lengths

  1 Tbsp fresh ginger juice

To prepare and serve: The description here is for a single, large vessel, but it is easily adapted to individual vessels, if you have flameproof ones. This dish ideally requires a vessel that can be both put on the stove and brought to the table. Use an earthenware casserole (*donabe*, see page 103). A flameproof ceramic vessel or a heavy kettle will do.

Mix the *dashi*, salt, soy sauces, and *saké* in the cooking vessel and gradually bring to a boil. (At this point, add optional ingredients as suggested in VARIATIONS, below. Simmer till these ingredients are well heated.)

Stir in the slightly undercooked rice. If you are using leftover cooked rice, put in a colander and run cold water over the grains to eliminate stickiness. Drain and stir into the hot liquid. Bring the whole to a simmer over medium heat.

Immediately dribble the beaten egg over the rice in the seasoned stock. Cover and remove from heat, then stir. Add the finely chopped green onion, or trefoil stalks, or fresh ginger juice, and stir. Serve immediately. Let each diner help himself. Use spoons to eat.

The secret of this dish is to eat it while the eggs are still quite runny.

VARIATIONS: You may add almost any vegetable or meat (or a combination of several) to lend both extra flavor and color. For example, raw thinly sliced carrot; sliced mushrooms; coarsely chopped spinach; or parboiled cubed chicken.

White Gruel
(*Shira-gayu*) 白 が ゆ

When your digestion is upset and you are out of sorts, every Japanese knows the answer is *okayu*, "gruel." This most pleasant and easily digested porridge is made by cooking white rice in a lot of water. The most common proportions of rice to water are 1:7, 1:10, and 1:15. This recipe uses the 1:7 formula. Seasoned, and with dried bonito flakes, egg, or vegetables added, it makes a filling meal at any time.

1 serving

1 cup short-grain rice, washed

To prepare: Put the washed rice in a large pot or rice cooker and pour in the water (7 times the volume of rice). Quickly bring to a boil over high heat. Then reduce heat to low and cook without stirring till the

7 cups water
1 tsp salt

rice is very soft and a thick gruel has formed. (Or, cook over high heat, stirring occasionally.) For a 1- or 2-portion batch, this takes at least 40 minutes. Stir only at the very end, when adding the salt.

To serve: Serve hot from the stove as soon as possible in rice or soup bowls. Eat with spoon or chopsticks.

While WHITE GRUEL is often served plain, it is also common to add one other ingredient at the center of the individual bowl. This is then stirred into the dish before eating.

Some additional ingredients are:
—pickled plum (*umeboshi*), which is the most common
—unbroken, raw egg yolk
—thickly whisked powdered green tea (*matcha*)
—dried bonito thread-shavings (*ito-kezuri-katsuo*) moistened with a few drops of soy sauce
—sliced *shiitake* mushrooms, seasoned by simmering in small amounts of *dashi*, soy sauce, and *saké*
—crumbled or shred-cut toasted *nori* seaweed
—thick *dashi* sauce (*bekkō-an* sauce, see page 398) with finely shred-cut or grated fresh ginger

VARIATIONS: SOYBEAN GRUEL (*Daizu-gayu*)
Proceed exactly as for WHITE GRUEL, but add ½ cup dried toasted soybeans per portion. Toast the dried soybeans in a dry frying pan over high heat to crack the skin open. Put in with the rice at the very start. Only a small amount of fresh ginger juice is used as a seasoning.

TEA GRUEL (*Cha-gayu*)
Make a thin tea with 3 Tbsps Japanese green tea leaves (*bancha*) and 7 cups water. Use the thin tea in place of water for gruel. Proceed exactly as for WHITE GRUEL.

NARA GRUEL (*Nara no Cha-gayu*)
Proceed exactly as for WHITE GRUEL, adding ½ cup dried toasted soybeans and substituting the thin green tea (*bancha*) for the boiling water, as in the preceding variation. This special digestive was invented by monks in the ancient capital of Nara.

Tempura on Rice
(*Tendon*) 天　丼

Almost as popular as PORK CUTLET ON RICE, but the price of shrimp precludes this being quite everyday fare.

4 servings

6-8 cups hot cooked short-
 grain rice
8 medium fresh shrimp
flour

batter:
 1 egg yolk
 1 cup ice water
 1 cup sifted flour

oil for deep-frying
12 stalks trefoil (*mitsuba*)
 with leaves (or substitute
 4 pieces *nori* seaweed,
 about 1½ x 3 inch [3 x 7
 cm])

sauce:
 1¼ cups *dashi*
 6 Tbsps dark soy sauce
 6 Tbsps *saké*
 2 Tbsps sugar

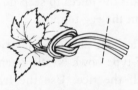

tie three trefoil stalks into a knot and
cut off stalks about 1½ inches (4 cm)
below knot

To prepare: Boil plain rice according to the recipe
on page 273.

Cut off shrimp heads; shell and devein shrimp, but
leave tails attached. Score across the underside then
tap across the back of the shrimp with the inverted
knife blade; this keeps shrimp from curling in the hot
oil.

Dredge with flour, then dip into TEMPURA BATTER
of egg, water, and sifted flour (see page 237).

Deep-fry the shrimp, 2 at a time, in a generous
amount of hot oil (350°F/180°C), till a very light gold,
turning often, about 4 minutes. (For frozen shrimp,
use oil that is slightly less hot.) Remove with a slotted
spoon, drain, and keep hot.

After the shrimp, deep-fry the trefoil leaves—3
stalks to a portion. Hold 3 stalks together and tie the
stems into a knot just below the leafy part, as shown.
Cut off the bottoms of the stems. Dip only stems, not
leaves, into the batter, then slide into the hot oil. Deep-
fry till batter is light gold, about 1 minute. Remove
with a slotted spoon and drain. Keep hot.

In a small pan combine ingredients for the sauce
and over high heat bring just to the boiling point. Keep
at a simmer.

To assemble and serve: Put a single portion of hot rice,
1½ to 2 cups, into a *donburi*-type bowl. On top,
arrange 2 deep-fried shrimp and 1 deep-fried knot
of trefoil. Spoon 2–3 Tbsps of hot sauce over the whole
and serve immediately.

Pork Cutlet on Rice

(*Katsudon*) カ ツ 丼

Breaded and deep-fried pork cutlet (*tonkatsu; ton* is "pork," *katsu* is the
Japanization of "cutlet") in one form or another probably fills more stomachs
daily than any other single dish in Japan except probably noodles. It is on the
menu of most ordinary restaurants and, of course, there are *tonkatsu* specialty restaurants as well. The version of cutlet on rice here is the most popular
one. Small pork chops without bone or pork tenderloin "steaks" may be used
if cutlets are not to be had.

4 servings

6-8 cups hot cooked short-grain rice
4 6-ounce (180-g) pork loin cutlets (pork tenderloin steaks or chops without bone)
salt and pepper

for breading:
   6 Tbsps flour
   2 eggs, beaten
   2½ cups fresh or dry breadcrumbs

oil for deep-frying

onion-and-egg topping:
   1 small onion
   2½ cups *dashi*
   7 Tbsps *mirin*
   3 Tbsps light soy sauce
   3 Tbsps dark soy sauce
   4 green onions, cut into 1½-inch (4-cm) lengths
   6 eggs, beaten

To prepare: Boil plain rice according to the recipe on page 273.

Pound cutlets with a mallet or bottle to flatten slightly. Slash fat at edge of cutlets to keep the meat from curling during deep-frying. Salt and pepper both sides.

Dust with flour, dip in beaten egg, and coat both sides thickly with dry or fresh breadcrumbs. Let rest 2 or 3 minutes before deep-frying.

Heat a generous amount of oil in a heavy-bottomed pot or deep-fryer to medium temperature (340°F/170°C), and deep-fry cutlets one at a time, turning once, till golden brown, about 6 minutes each. Remove, drain on absorbent paper, and cut crosswise into ½-inch (1½-cm) slices. Keep hot.

Meanwhile slice onion into rounds or half-moons and, in a large frying pan in a scant amount of oil, sauté onion over high heat till transparent and soft. Add the *dashi*, *mirin*, and soy sauces to the pan. Bring to a simmer. Add the green onion lengths.

Finally, pour the beaten egg over the simmering onions. Stir when the egg begins to set. The egg is done while still a little runny and juicy. (Do not cook egg until hard and dry!) You want the juices to seep down into the rice in the bowl from the egg topping.

To assemble and serve: Put a single portion of hot rice, 1½ to 2 cups, into a *donburi*-type bowl. Neatly arrange a sliced cutlet to cover half the rice. Use the fried onion-and-egg "topping" to cover part of the cutlet and the rest of the rice. Use all the liquid. Serve immediately.

Minced Chicken, Shrimp, and Egg on Rice
(*Soboro Donburi*) そぼろ丼

Because this *donburi* (see page 282) can be eaten at room temperature, it often fills lacquered lunch boxes. The major ingredients are all chopped or crumbled, then fried with seasonings (the word *soboro* means "finely crumbled"); they are arranged on top of the rice in a box or bowl to present an appealing and colorful display.

4 servings

6-8 cups hot cooked short-grain rice

chicken:

½ pound (225 g) ground chicken
3 Tbsps *saké*
1 Tbsp dark soy sauce
1 Tbsp sugar
few drops fresh ginger juice

shrimp:

8 ounces (225 g) finely chopped fresh or frozen small shrimp
2 Tbsps *saké*
1 Tbsp *mirin*
¼ tsp salt

eggs:

4 eggs, beaten
¼ tsp salt
1 Tbsp *saké*
1 Tbsp light soy sauce
1 Tbsp sugar

sauce for rice:

1 cup *dashi* or (chicken stock)
4 Tbsps dark soy sauce
½ Tbsp sugar

sprigs of *kinome* or sliced red pickled ginger (*beni-shōga*)

To prepare: Boil plain rice according to the recipe on page 273.

Put ground chicken into a frying pan and mix in all seasonings except the ginger juice. Put over high heat and cook, stirring constantly to keep the chicken separated and "crumbled." When the chicken is done and has turned whitish, mix in the ginger juice. Spread in a colander to drain and cool.

Cook the shrimp just till pink, then spread in a colander to drain and cool. Scramble eggs in frying pan till somewhat dry and similar in texture to the fried ground chicken.

In a small saucepan, mix the sauce ingredients for the rice. Over high heat bring just to a boil, then remove from heat.

To assemble and serve: Put a single portion of rice, 1½ to 2 cups, into a *donburi*-type bowl (or Japanese-style lunch box). Dribble over it some of the hot sauce to moisten the rice. Each of the "crumble-fried" main ingredients should cover ⅓ of the surface, as shown. Garnish with *kinome* sprigs or red pickled ginger slices.

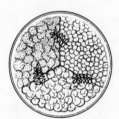 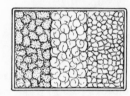

two arrangements for
MINCED CHICKEN, SHRIMP, AND EGG ON RICE

❀ Sushi ❀

Scattered *Sushi*, Tokyo Style
(*Chirashi-zushi*) ちらしずし東京風

Instead of pressing each morsel of raw fish or other tidbit onto individual "fingers" of vinegared rice, this variety of *sushi* consists of a generous bed of rice upon which appropriate ingredients are artistically strewn. Usually packed in a shallow lacquerware box.

4 servings

5 cups prepared *sushi* rice
12 dried *shiitake* mush-
    rooms, softened (see
    page 88)

for simmering mushrooms:
    ½ cup *dashi*
    ¼ cup dark soy sauce
    ¼ cup *mirin*
    1½ Tbsps *saké*

4 large shrimp
4 pieces squid, about
    3 inches (8 cm) square
8 ounces (225 g) fresh raw
    tuna (or substitute sea
    bass, yellowtail, crab)
16 snow peas
1 whole egg plus 3 yolks
2 Tbsps grated *wasabi*
    horseradish
sliced pickled ginger
    shoots (*hajikami shōga*)
sprigs of *kinome*

To prepare: Prepare vinegared SUSHI RICE according to the recipe on page 290.

Mushrooms: Simmer softened mushrooms in the mushroom simmering liquid for 15 minutes to season them. Remove from heat and let mushrooms rest in simmering liquid for 2 hours if possible. Drain. Cut the best-looking 8 mushrooms into halves. Chop the remaining 4 coarsely to be mixed with the SUSHI RICE.

Shrimp: Wash well and boil for a few minutes till just pink and firm. Plunge into ice water to chill. Shell and devein, leaving tail attached. Slit open lengthwise along the underside, spread shrimp flat on a cutting board, then cut in half diagonally (see page 458).

Squid: Cross-score the outside (the shinier, smoother side) of the flesh at intervals of about ⅛ inch (½ cm) as shown. The scoring should be made diagonally into the flesh, not vertically. Slice into 1½-inch (4-cm) widths. Dip into boiling water for about 10–30 seconds (depending on thickness of squid) to make the pieces curl, forming the "pine-cone" (*matsukasa*) effect. Plunge into a bowl of cold water; drain.

Raw tuna: Slice crosswise against the grain into ¼-inch (2-cm) slices.

Snow peas: Parboil in lightly salted water, wash under cold running water, and drain.

Egg: Beat the whole egg with the yolks and strain.

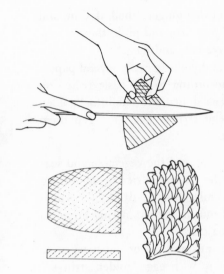

diagonally score outside of squid to form the "pinecone" effect

Make a paper-thin omelette sheet as described on page 206. When cool, fold and cut into thin threads.

Grate *wasabi* horseradish and slice commercially pickled pink ginger shoots into paper-thin slices.

To assemble: Toss the cool vinegared rice with the coarsely chopped *shiitake* mushrooms and lightly pack into a lacquered box (or use any shallow decorative bowl). On top of the rice, spread a covering layer of yellow egg threads. On top of the egg, artfully "scatter" (*chirasu*) the rest of the ingredients—*shiitake* halves, split halved shrimp, "pine-cone" squid, raw tuna slices, snow peas. In one corner, place a mound of *wasabi* horseradish and the pickled ginger. Tuck in garnishing sprigs of *kinome* here and there.

This dish can be prepared ahead of time, but *do not* refrigerate. It should be eaten at room temperature.

Goes well with KISU (SILLAGO) SASHIMI (page 353).

VARIATIONS: Do not limit yourself to the ingredients listed above. Other suggestions are: carrots—sliced, parboiled, and simmered in *dashi*, soy sauce, sugar, and *saké* to season; bamboo shoots—sliced into half-moons, parboiled, and simmered in *dashi*, soy sauce, sugar, and *saké* to season.

Scattered *Sushi,* Osaka Style

(Chirashi-zushi) ちらしずし大阪風 (color plate 15)

As in the Tokyo version above, the mixed rice is covered with a layer of shredded egg. Because there is no raw fish, there is no need to use grated *wasabi* horseradish, and since the rice is moistened and seasoned with the *dashi*-soy mixture, this dish does not call for soy sauce on the side.

4 servings

5 cups prepared *sushi* **rice**

for simmering mushrooms and kampyō*:*

   1½ **cups** *dashi*
   4 Tbsps *mirin*
   1 Tbsp sugar
   3 Tbsps dark soy sauce

To prepare: Prepare vinegared SUSHI RICE according to the recipe on page 290. Put the cooled rice into a mixing bowl, ready to toss with other ingredients.

Mix the *dashi, mirin,* sugar, and soy sauce in saucepan and bring just to the boiling point; add the softened mushrooms and gourd shavings. Simmer till the vegetables are well seasoned and about 2–3 Tbsps of the liquid remain. Drain and cool. Dice mushrooms and chop gourd shavings. Reserve remaining simmering liquid to moisten and color the rice later.

6 dried *shiitake* mush-
rooms, softened and
trimmed (see page 88)
½ ounce (15 g) dried gourd
shavings (*kampyō*),
softened (see page 72)
1 ounce (30 g) sliced red
pickled ginger (*beni-
shōga*)
4 medium shrimp
1 egg plus 3 egg yolks,
beaten
sprig of *kinome*
sliced red pickled ginger
(*beni-shōga*)

Coarsely chop red pickled ginger. Shell, devein, and wash shrimp. Boil till just firm and pink, then plunge into cold water. Remove tail, and dice.

Use the beaten egg and yolks to make several paper-thin omelette sheets according to the basic recipe on page 206. Fold sheets as shown and cut into "golden strings." Shake the egg strings loose to keep them from sticking together.

To assemble and serve: Spread the vegetable and seafood ingredients over the vinegared rice in the mixing bowl. Toss lightly. While tossing, dribble in small amounts of the cooled mushroom simmering liquid to moisten and color the rice.

Put the mixed rice into a bowl or Japanese-style lunch box. Cover thickly with egg "golden strings." Garnish with a sprig of *kinome*. Put a small mound of pickled ginger slices on top at the side.

Goes well with CLAM CONSOMMÉ (page 155).

Grilled Saury Pike *Sushi*

(*Kamasu no Yakime-zushi*) かますの焼きめずし

The long-snouted saury pike is in season in September; the delicate flavor of its soft white flesh is best brought out by marination.

4 servings

4 cups prepared *sushi* rice

marinade:

  ½ cup water
  ¼ cup vinegar
  ½ tsp sugar
  1 tsp light soy sauce

4 saury pike, 8 inches (20 cm)
long
few tsps dark soy sauce
mixed with a few drops
fresh ginger juice

To prepare: Prepare vinegared SUSHI RICE according to the recipe on page 290.

Mix marinade and pour into a 10-inch (25-cm) pan.

Scale and gut the fish. Cut boneless fillets, with skin (2 fillets per fish; *sanmai oroshi* technique, pages 123ff). Salt lightly. Lay fillets in the marinade and marinate 10 minutes.

To grill and assemble: Remove fillets from marinade and pat dry. Using about 5 long metal skewers, skewer the fillets crosswise (*yoko-gushi* technique, page 180). Lightly grill the skin side only to soften it (or use oven broiler), 1 to 1½ minutes. Cool slightly and then remove skewers.

If the fillets are thick, cut one flap or wing into the meat, like a half-butterfly cut (*kannon-biraki* technique, see page 132). This is to make thick fillets better suited to being rolled.

Take 1 cup of cooled vinegared rice and with your hands firmly press into a rectangular block, as shown. The rice should be firmly packed, but not mashed.

Lay 2 fillets skin side down in the center of a cotton cloth or cheesecloth spread over a bamboo mat (*maki-su*). On top of the fillets lay the block of rice, as shown. Use the bamboo mat to roll the fish and rice and again firmly press. Unroll, and with a very sharp knife slice into 1-inch (2½-cm) lengths.

To serve: Place 5 pieces or so per serving on individual plates and sprinkle with the soy sauce and ginger juice mixture. Serve lightly chilled.

Goes well with CLEAR SOUP WITH SHRIMP (page 154).

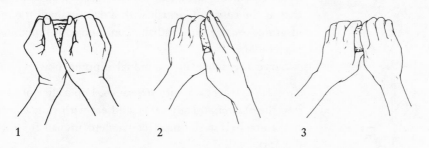

1.   2.   3.

1–3.   press firmly to form block of *sushi* rice

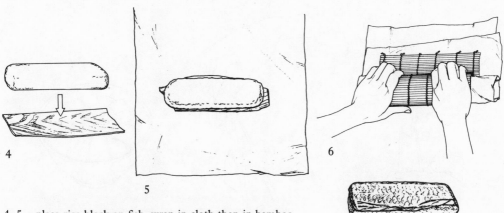

4.   5.   6.   7.

4, 5.   place rice block on fish, wrap in cloth then in bamboo mat, and press to form rectangular stick of *sushi*

Tuna *Sushi* Bowl

(*Tekka Donburi*) 鉄 火 丼

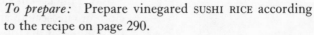

A bed of vinegared *sushi* rice cradles morsels of succulent raw tuna, red as *tekka*—molten iron.

4 servings

6-8 cups prepared *sushi* rice
1 pound (450 g) lean (red)
  raw tuna
⅓ cup dark soy sauce
1 Tbsp finely grated
  ***wasabi* horseradish**
soy sauce

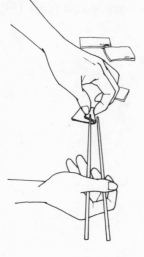

To prepare: Prepare vinegared SUSHI RICE according to the recipe on page 290.

Marinate the tuna in the dark soy sauce for 30 minutes to 1 hour, turning a few times. Drain and cut crosswise against the grain and at a slight angle into slices measuring about 1×2 or 2½ inches (2½×6½ cm) and about ⅛ inch (½ cm) thick. These measurements are approximate. Cut the tuna as you like.

To assemble and serve: Put a single portion of rice, 1½ to 2 cups, into a deep *donburi*-type bowl. On top of rice, arrange the tuna slices in a rosette pattern; finish by curling a few slices into a rosebud and putting that at the center. Garnish with a dab or small mound of grated *wasabi* horseradish. Continue with remaining ingredients.

Serve soy sauce in individual dipping bowls.

To eat: Mix *wasabi* into soy sauce. Dip a slice of tuna into the *wasabi* and soy sauce and eat with rice. Chopsticks are by far the most convenient utensil for this, but forks will do.

a rosebud of tuna slices can be formed to place in the center of the finished dish

Silk Square or Tea-Silk *Sushi*

(*Fukusa-* or *Chakin-zushi*) ふくさ又は茶巾ずし

Since the days of 10th century courtiers, squares of silk called *fukusa* have been used to wrap gifts and precious articles. Here, the same rice used for SCATTERED SUSHI, OSAKA STYLE is wrapped in an omelette so thin and delicately colored that it reminds one of luxuriously textured tawny-gold silk. This kind of *sushi* is actually a combination of SCATTERED SUSHI, OSAKA STYLE, because fish and vegetables are tossed with the vinegared rice, and of ROLLED SUSHI (*maki-zushi*), because of the omelette skin. Serve for lunch or a light supper. *Fukusa-zushi* can be made several hours ahead of time and left, covered, at room temperature till needed.

4 servings (8 pieces)

4-5 cups prepared *sushi* rice same ingredients as
SCATTERED SUSHI, OSAKA STYLE **up to and including shrimp**

for "silk square" omelettes:

6 eggs
3 Tbsps sugar
¼ tsp salt
vegetable oil

either

1 sheet *nori* seaweed

or

8 stalks trefoil (*mitsuba*), parboiled
VINEGARED GINGER **slices (optional)**

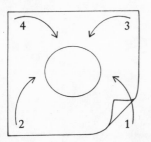

fold the omelette wrapper in the order shown

To prepare: Make vinegared SUSHI RICE according to recipe on page 290.

Prepare the same mixed rice as in SCATTERED SUSHI, OSAKA STYLE, but without "golden strings" of egg. Cool to room temperature.

"Silk square" omelettes: Beat eggs with sugar and salt in mixing bowl. Using an oil-dampened paper towel, lightly coat the bottom of a 9-inch (23-cm) frying pan with vegetable oil. Heat oiled pan on medium heat till a drop of water flicked on its surface skitters and evaporates quickly.

Pour ⅛ of beaten egg into hot pan, tilting pan so egg covers bottom in a very thin layer. Cook over medium heat, till top begins to look firm, then turn over with pancake turner or fingers and cook other side for another few seconds. Slide omelette out of the pan onto a large plate. Grease pan between omelettes. Repeat procedure to make 8 omelette sheets. Stack omelettes, and, when at room temperature, trim stack edges to form a square.

To assemble: Mold about ½ cup mixed rice into a flattened round form and place in the center of one omelette square. The rice should be firmly yet lightly packed—it should neither crumble nor be mashed. Bring up the corners of the omelette in the order shown and form a neat packet.

Toast the *nori* seaweed over a medium flame. With scissors, cut lengthwise into ¼-inch (¾-cm) wide ribbons. Tuck the *nori* ribbons around the *sushi* as a garnish to make the "package" look complete. Or tie the package with parboiled trefoil stalks, as you would with string.

To serve: Place 2 *sushi* packets on every plate. Serve with vinegared ginger, if desired. Eat with chopsticks or fingers.

Goes well with CLEAR SOUP WITH SHRIMP (page 154).

VARIATIONS: Add bamboo shoot or lotus root. Simmer each in separate *dashi*-based stocks for seasoning before chopping finely and tossing with vinegared rice. Lotus goes especially well with vinegary flavors.

❁ Noodles ❁
Menrui

Moon Noodles
(Tsukimi Udon) 月見うどん

Tsukimi literally means "viewing the moon," an allusion to a genteel Japanese pastime in autumn and to the whole raw egg in the center of the dish—a full moon surrounded by "clouds" of noodles. Often those newly introduced to Japanese food decline raw egg when it appears. If it is any comfort, raw egg in Japanese cuisine is often used in such a way that the heat of a dish cooks it lightly. If you break the yolk with chopsticks or fork, then mix the egg into the hot broth, the result is similar to egg-drop soup. Use either *udon* or *soba* noodles.

4 servings

1 pound (450 g) dried *udon* noodles
4-5 cups NOODLE BROTH (see page 310)
1 cake *kamaboko* (fish paste) about 6 inches (15-cm) long (optional)
4 eggs
4 Tbsps finely chopped green onion
seven-spice mixture (*shichimi*) or red pepper flakes (*ichimi*)

To prepare: Boil dried noodles as directed on package, or follow basic directions given on page 310. Wash well with the hands under cold water to remove surface starch. Drain well.

Prepare NOODLE BROTH according to the recipe on page 310. Keep at a low simmer.

If using *kamaboko*, cut into slices about ¼ inch (¾ cm) thick.

To assemble and serve: Reheat noodles by putting individual portions in a deep, handled sieve and immersing in boiling water till hot. Place noodles in warmed deep bowls. Ladle about 1 to 1¼ cups hot noodle broth over each mound of noodles. If including *kamaboko*, arrange 2 or 3 slices at the side of the noodles in each bowl. With the back of a large spoon, make a nest in the center of the noodles in each bowl. Crack open an egg and gently drop the whole raw egg into the nest. Garnish with about 1 Tbsp finely chopped green onion. Serve immediately. Each diner may season to taste with seven-spice mixture (*shichimi*) or red pepper flakes (*ichimi*). Best eaten with chopsticks, but fork and soup spoon work.

Noodles with Chicken and Green Onions
(Tori Nanba Udon) 鶏難波うどん

The name Nanba in this recipe indicates the use of green onions. Nanba, a well-known part of the modern Osaka metropolis, was once largely onion fields. Using *soba* noodles instead of *udon*, you will make what is called *Tori Nanba Soba*.

4 servings

1 pound (450 g) dried *udon* noodles
1 pound (450 g) chicken meat, boned and skinned
6-8 green onions
4-5 cups NOODLE BROTH (see page 310)
ground *sansho* pepper

To prepare: Boil dried noodles as directed on package, or follow basic directions given on page 310. Wash well with hands under cold water to remove surface starch. Drain well.

Cut chicken into ¾-inch (2-cm) squares.

Cut onions into 2-inch (5-cm) lengths, then halve or quarter lengths.

Prepare NOODLE BROTH according to the recipe on page 310. Bring broth to a gentle boil and add chicken pieces. Simmer about 10 minutes, till chicken is tender. Skim off any foam. Add onion and continue simmering another 1 minute, till onion is partially cooked. Stir occasionally.

To assemble and serve: Reheat noodles by putting individual portions in a deep, handled sieve and immersing in boiling water till just hot. Place noodles in warmed deep bowls. Ladle about 1 to 1¼ cups hot noodle broth over each portion. Arrange pieces of chicken and onion on the noodles. Serve immediately. Season to individual taste with *sansho* pepper. Eat with chopsticks or with fork and soup spoon.

Tempura Noodles
(Tempura Soba) てんぷらそば

The flavor of buckwheat noodles and *tempura* go well together, but *soba* noodles can just as well be replaced by *udon* noodles. A great lunch.

4 servings

1½ pounds (675 g) dried buckwheat noodles (*soba*)

To prepare: Boil dried noodles as directed on package, or follow basic directions given on page 310. Drain and wash well under cold water, rubbing with hands to eliminate surface starch.

12 pieces shrimp *tempura*
4-5 cups NOODLE BROTH
  (see page 310)
yuzu citron or lemon rind
seven-spice mixture
  (*shichimi*)

Make TEMPURA BATTER and deep-fry shrimp following the TEMPURA recipe on page 235. You need not be tied exclusively to shrimp *tempura*; make whatever kind you like—seafood or vegetables. Set *tempura* aside on absorbent paper to drain thoroughly. Keep it warm.

To assemble and serve: Reheat noodles by putting each portion in a handled sieve and immersing in boiling water, just long enough to heat. Drain well and place in warmed deep bowls. Place a few pieces of hot *tempura* on noodles and ladle 1 to 1¼ cups hot noodle broth over noodles and *tempura*. Garnish with slices of *yuzu* citron or lemon rind, about 1 inch (2½ cm) long and ¼ inch (¾ cm) wide. Serve immediately. Have a shaker or cellar of seven-spice mixture (*shichimi*) on the table so each diner can season noodles to taste.

Chilled Fine Noodles with Shrimp and Mushrooms
(*Hiyashi Sōmen*) 冷やしそうめん (color plate 14)

A widely popular summer meal, normally garnished with just chopped green onions. The addition of shrimp and mushrooms is a rather extravagant extra. The fine noodles (*sōmen*) should not be soft and limp. Do not boil them too long, and add cold water from time to time while boiling.

4 servings

¼ pound (115 g) fine wheat
  noodles (*sōmen*)
4 large shrimp
4 dried *shiitake* mush-
  rooms

for simmering mushrooms:
  2 Tbsps dark soy sauce
  2 Tbsps *mirin*

12 stalks trefoil (*mitsuba*)
  (or substitute watercress)

dipping sauce:
  1 cup *dashi*
  ½ cup *mirin*
  ¼ cup dark soy sauce

To prepare: Boil noodles according to directions on the package, or follow the recipe on page 310. Drain in a colander and wash well with your hands under cold running water. Let rest in cold water.

Cook shrimp in gently boiling water till they just turn pink and are firm to the touch. Cool in a bowl of cold water. Shell and devein, leaving tails attached. Slit lengthwise along the underside of the body almost all the way through, then flatten the shrimp out on the cutting board and cut in half crosswise on the diagonal, as shown (next page).

Soak the dried *shiitake* mushrooms in 1¼ cups of water until soft (about 3 hours) in a medium-sized saucepan; then add 2 Tbsps dark soy sauce and 2 Tbsps *mirin* and heat. Simmer with a drop-lid or vented paper circle (see page 220) till the liquid is almost com-

small handful of small dried shrimp

about 1 Tbsp finely grated *wasabi* horseradish
about 2 Tbsps finely chopped green onion

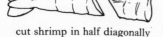
cut shrimp in half diagonally

pletely reduced (about 20 minutes). Remove from heat; allow to come to room temperature. Trim stems if necessary, and cut mushrooms in half.

Parboil trefoil stalks (without leaves) for a few minutes in lightly salted water. Rinse well under cold running water and drain. Chop stems into 1½-inch (4-cm) lengths.

Prepare garnishes of grated *wasabi* horseradish and finely chopped green onion (wrap chopped onion in cheesecloth, rinse in cold water, and squeeze to remove bitterness).

Dipping sauce (best made the day before): Combine the *dashi, mirin,* dark soy sauce, and small dried shrimp in a medium-sized saucepan and simmer over medium heat for 5 minutes. Do not strain. Force-cool by pouring hot liquid into a medium-sized metal mixing bowl and twirling that bowl in a larger one filled with water and ice cubes. When room temperature, refrigerate.

To assemble and serve: Use individual glass dishes for the noodles, if you have them. Use thumb and first two fingers to pick up a "mound" of noodles and transfer several such "mounds" to each glass bowl. Gently pour in about ½ cup ice water at the side of each individual bowl and tuck in a few ice cubes around the sides of the noodle arrangement. Top noodles with 2 shrimp halves, 2 mushroom halves, and a small bunch of trefoil stems.

Serve the dipping sauce in separate small individual bowls. Pass the spicy condiments in small bowls so each person can take what he likes.

To eat, add spicy condiment(s) to dipping sauce in small bowl; pick up bunches of noodles and dip into sauce. Chopsticks are best for noodles, but forks work.

VARIATION: FINE NOODLES WITH SHRIMP AND MUSHROOMS IN BROTH (*Nyū-men*)
This first cousin of *Hiyashi Sōmen* (above) is served hot. The ingredients are essentially the same, but the dipping sauce is replaced by a hot broth with egg.

Prepare fine noodles, shrimp, mushrooms, and trefoil as above. Drain noodles.

In a medium-sized saucepan bring 2 cups *dashi* and 1 Tbsp light soy sauce to a simmer. Add the boiled, drained *sōmen* noodles. Heat thoroughly, stirring occasionally.

Dribble 1 beaten egg over the simmering liquid in the saucepan. Stir till egg is almost set and more or less coats the noodles.

Divide among four serving bowls, apportioning the hot liquid as well. Top with halved shrimp, halved mushrooms, and bunch of trefoil stems as above.

Garnish with a few slivers of *yuzu* citron or lemon rind.

Serve hot.

Sea Bream and Fine Noodles

(*Tai-men*) 鯛めん

A summer specialty of the Seto Inland Sea; this is when sea bream is at its best and Japanese fine noodles (*sōmen*) are traditionally eaten chilled. But you can serve this hot if you wish. The fine *sōmen* noodles go equally well with sea bass, any flatfish, crab, and large shrimp.

4 servings

¼ **pound (115 g) fine wheat noodles (*sōmen*)**

1 **sea bream fillet with skin, 8-10 ounce (225-285 g)**

sauces:

cold:

2 **cups** *dashi*

1 **cup** *mirin*

½ **cup dark soy sauce**

handful of dried shrimp

or

hot:

2½ **cups** *dashi*

½ **tsp salt**

1 **tsp light soy sauce**

finely chopped green onion

RED MAPLE RADISH **(see page 170)**

To prepare: Boil dried noodles according to the directions on the package, or follow the recipe on page 310. Drain in a colander and wash well under cold running water.

Salt-grill the sea bream according to the *shio-yaki* technique described on page 182. When partially cool, slice into 4 pieces crosswise on the diagonal.

Make one of the sauces whose ingredients are listed at left. Combine the ingredients in a medium-sized saucepan and heat. Force-cool the hot sauce by pouring the hot liquid into a medium-sized metal mixing bowl and twirling that bowl in a larger one filled with ice water. The hot sauce is used just as it comes from the stove.

Prepare spicy condiments. Wrap chopped green onion in cheesecloth and rinse in cold water to remove bitterness. Make the RED MAPLE RADISH according to the recipe on page 170.

To assemble and serve: Divide the noodles among 4 serving bowls. Pour the sauce over—either hot or cold. Top with a piece of grilled sea bream, skin side up. Serve hot or cold. Just before serving, place spicy condiments in neat cones on the fish itself.

❀ Sweets ❀
Okashi

Sweet Potato Puree (and "Chestnuts")

(Satsuma-imo Kinton) さつまいもきんとん

A sweet confection delicious with hot green tea and particularly attractive molded into "chestnuts." A popular New Year delicacy.

4 servings

3 medium sweet potatoes

syrup:

> **1⅔ cups (300 g) granulated sugar**
> **2 cups water**

3 egg yolks
pinch salt

To prepare: Peel the sweet potatoes and cut crosswise into ½-inch (1½-cm) rounds. Wash and let stand in cold water for at least 30 minutes (but preferably 1 day) to remove bitterness, changing the water frequently.

Boil in ample water over high heat, covered with a drop-lid (*otoshi-buta,* see page 220), till tender, or steam until tender. Drain and cool.

Make the syrup. In a medium-sized saucepan combine the sugar and water. Bring to a rolling boil over high heat, then boil for 3 minutes, removing any foam from surface. Cool to room temperature before using. This can be done ahead of time.

To cook: Rub the cooled potato through a sieve to puree (or mash and puree by any method you like).

Blend potato, syrup, and egg yolks in the top of a double boiler (a large pot over low flame may be used, but the potato mixture scorches easily). *Stir constantly.* Add pinch salt. When done, the potato mixture will be rather thick, but fluffy (like mashed potatoes). There are too many variables to allow a helpful time estimate for cooking the potato mixture. Allow to come to room temperature before refrigerating.

To serve: Serve, hot or at room temperature, in a big bowl family style. Eat with spoons or forks.

Or, serve as elegant molded "chestnuts"—1 or 2 per serving on decorative plates. To make "chestnuts," pat room-temperature potato puree into small balls, about 1½ inches (4 cm) in diameter. Place one in center of a cotton napkin, gather up the ends of the cloth, and gently wring the ball of potato (some liquid will be forced out). Unwrap to reveal a molded "chestnut." Garnish at the top with a tiny dab of red pickled plum paste (red *umeboshi* paste) or dip the tip of a toothpick into tart red jam or diluted liquid red food coloring and tint the top of the "chestnut." Eat with dessert forks or spoons.

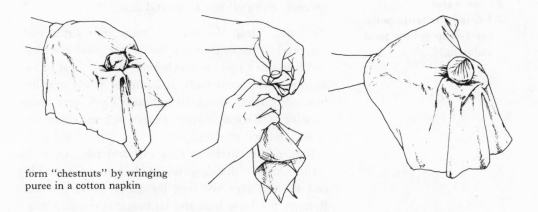

form "chestnuts" by wringing puree in a cotton napkin

VARIATIONS: CHESTNUT KINTON—Exactly as above, but mix in whole or crumbled CANDIED CHESTNUTS before adding the egg yolks. (A good way of using chestnuts that break in the making of CANDIED CHESTNUTS; see recipe below.) Excellent for festive occasions.

GREEN TEA KINTON—Exactly as above, but whisk 2 Tbsps powdered green tea (*matcha*) with boiling water (see page 334), cool, and add when the potato mixture has cooled or just before serving.

Candied Chestnuts

(*Kuri Ama-ni*) 栗甘煮

Associated with the months of September and October, when chestnuts are choicest, this is the Japanese version of *marrons glacés*. The cooking time is short, but the total preparation takes three days. The addition of a little wine or sherry to the syrup makes an interesting variation.

This is by far the simpler of Japan's two candied chestnut recipes. In *shibukawa-ni* (not included in this book) the chestnuts are cooked with their astringent inner skin intact and are therefore more natural-looking, but the technique is extremely complicated.

4 servings

**1 pound (450 g) raw chest-
nuts, shelled and peeled
(see page 64)**

syrup:

**1⅔ cups (300 g) granulated
sugar
2 cups water
2-3 dried gardenia pods
(or 1 drop yellow food
coloring)**

To prepare: Cut the bottom of each peeled chestnut off flat and trim body into an attractive hexagonal shape. Soak the chestnuts in cold water for at least 30 minutes to remove bitterness (but preferably 1 day, changing the water frequently).

Make the syrup. In a medium-sized saucepan combine the sugar and water and bring to a boil over medium heat. Boil until syrup is reduced about 10 percent. Skim off any foam and cool.

To cook: Drop the raw chestnuts into water with the cracked gardenia pods (or yellow food coloring) and bring to a boil over high heat. Reduce heat to low as soon as the water boils, and simmer gently over low heat till tender, about 20 minutes. Cool nuts under running cold water, taking care not to break them, and drain. Discard gardenia pods.

Return the chestnuts to a pot and pour over the syrup. Cover with a drop-lid (*otoshi-buta*, see page 220) and simmer over low heat for about 10–15 minutes. Remove pot from heat and let contents come to room temperature. Do not refrigerate. Let the chestnuts rest in syrup 24 hours.

On the second day, simmer over low heat again, just as on the first day. Let cool, and leave out overnight.

To serve: Serve at room temperature on the third day. Remove chestnuts from the syrup with a slotted spoon and place 2 or 3 on a small individual plate or dish. Eat with dessert forks or spoons. The chestnuts are sweet enough and do not need to have syrup from the pot poured on them.

Ohagi

お は ぎ (color plate 15)

Where Europe and America have chocolate truffles and nut bars, in the world of Japanese sweets there is *ohagi*. This confection is basically a glutinous rice center around which is a layer of sweet red-bean paste (*an*), or vice versa. It takes its name from *hagi*, the willowy bush clover of autumn. The season-conscious Japanese used to serve this sweet only during the celebration of the Autumn Equinox.

12 balls

1 cup glutinous rice
1 cup short-grain rice
¼ tsp salt
lightly salted water (to dampen hands)
2⅔ cups (800 g) PUREED **or** CHUNKY SWEET RED-BEAN PASTE **(see pages 327-28)**
6 Tbsps *kinako* **(roasted soybean flour) mixed with 4 Tbsps superfine granulated sugar**
pinch salt

cross-section of OHAGI ball, showing proportion of rice center to bean coating

To prepare: Combine rices, wash, and boil according to the recipe on page 273, but with a little less water. After the rice has been removed from heat and has rested for 5 to 10 minutes, uncover and lightly salt the top. Mix. Then with a wooden pestle or large wooden spoon, mash the rice till the grains are half-crushed. While the rice is still warm and malleable, form into balls as described below.

To form the balls:
Type 1: Dampen your hands with salted water and pat hot rice into spheres or ovals about the size of golf balls. Cover with a thin outer layer of room-temperature SWEET RED-BEAN PASTE (*an*; either pureed or chunky, as you prefer), about ⅛ inch (½ cm) thick.
Type 2: Use a small round or oval of SWEET RED-BEAN PASTE (*an*) as a core, cover with a ¼-inch (¾-cm) layer of hot rice, and roll in sweetened soybean flour (*kinako*).

There are no exact sizes for *ohagi*—size depends on personal taste.

To serve: Serve one of each type of *ohagi* on a small dessert plate. Eat with dessert forks. Goes well with hot Japanese or Chinese tea.

Red-Bean Jelly

(*Mizu-Yōkan*) 水羊羹

A firm yet delicate sweet served chilled. It is the lighter, summer version of the standard, traditional tea sweet called *yōkan*, which is made of the same ingredients—SWEET RED-BEAN PASTE, sugar, agar-agar, and water—and cooked slowly to the consistency of fudge. The thick *yōkan* may be made of a variety of basic ingredients besides red beans. Brown sugar, *konbu* kelp, persimmons, and chestnuts, to name but a few, all make delicious *yōkan*.

8 servings

1 stick agar-agar (*kanten*), soaked (see page 54)
2¼ cups cold water
sugar (optional)

To cook: Rinse the soaked agar-agar thoroughly and squeeze out excess water. Tear into small pieces, place in the 2¼ cups of water in a saucepan and cook over medium heat. Do not stir until the agar-agar is dissolved. Then skim any foam off the surface and stir frequently until the liquid is reduced by 10 percent.

2⅓ cups (700 g) PUREED
SWEET RED-BEAN PASTE
(see page 327)
pinch salt

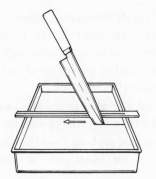

a chopstick can be used to guide cutting across a pan

The finished confection should be delicate and subtle. Strain liquid and return to pan. Add SWEET RED-BEAN PUREE; increase heat to high and boil for 3 minutes, stirring constantly with a wire whisk. Remove from heat.

Put the hot mixture into a medium-sized metal mixing bowl. Force-cool the mixture and keep the bean puree evenly distributed and in solution by twirling the mixing bowl in a larger bowl filled with water and ice cubes. Take care! Agar-agar solidifies quickly, at a higher temperature than gelatin. As soon as it starts to thicken, but while it is still runny, pour into mold.

For a mold, use a 9-inch (23-cm) square baking pan; or use individual dessert dishes.

Cover with plastic wrap and set in a pan or other vessel filled with about ½ inch (1½ cm) ice and water. Refrigerate.

Though the dish can be served about 2 hours after refrigeration, since it is fragile, agar-agar is best when allowed to set overnight in the refrigerator.

To serve: Run a knife around the sides of the pan. Use chopsticks to guide the cutting of the jelly, as shown. After cutting the squares, use a spatula or pancake turner to transfer 1 or 2 squares to each chilled dessert plate. Eat with dessert spoons or forks.

VARIATION: Use 1½ Tbsps gelatin instead of agar-agar. Soften gelatin in cold water, then dissolve over heat in 2¼ cups water. *Do not boil*—high heat weakens gelatin's power to jell. A gelatin *mizu-yōkan* does not have the same delicacy as the agar-agar confection, but is good. Use any convenient container for a mold; dip mold in hot water to remove jelly.

Zenzai
ぜんざい

This traditional favorite, a sort of chunky sweet soup served over pieces of toasted *mochi*, is a delicious pick-me-up on blustery winter days and can be a delicate, sophisticated dessert, as well as something to look forward to at teatime.

8-10 servings

4 cups (900 g) boiled red beans (*azuki*; see page 328)
3 cups water
1½ cups (300 g) sugar
1 or 2 1½-x-2½-inch (4-x-6½-cm) pieces *mochi* (glutinous rice cake) per serving; there is no standard unit in which *mochi* is sold

To cook: In a large pot combine the boiled beans, 3 cups water and 1½ cups sugar. Simmer over medium heat till thick but still liquid. Keep hot.

Grill both sides of the *mochi*, turning frequently, over a charcoal fire (or use oven broiler) until crisp and mottled brown. The cakes will puff up to about twice their size as they are toasted.

To assemble: Put 1 or 2 pieces of grilled *mochi* in a small, deep bowl. Add about ½ to ¾ cup of hot red-bean "soup." Eat *mochi* with chopsticks and drink red-bean "soup" from the bowl.

VARIATIONS: This basic confection can be made as subtle or sweet or as thick or thin as you wish simply by varying the amounts of water and sugar. A drop of liqueur, a bit of citrus rind garnish, or a brush of nutmeg or spice can give it yet another dimension. The thinner and pureed versions of this recipe are known as *oshiruko*.

Sweet Bean "Gongs"
(*Dora-yaki*) どら焼き

One of the most popular Japanese sweet snacks is the filled bun known as a "gong" (*dora*)—a sandwich of two small pancakes with a filling of CHUNKY SWEET RED-BEAN PASTE (*an*). Warm, burnished gold in color and perfectly round like the oriental gongs, the cakes are made by street vendors in two identical molds, one for each side, but you can easily make them in a small frying pan or on a griddle in your kitchen.

5 filled "gongs"

3 eggs, beaten
⅔ cup (150 g) sugar
1 Tbsp *mizuame* (wheat-starch syrup) or light corn syrup
1½ cups (180 g) all-purpose flour
1 tsp baking powder
⅔ cup water
oil

To make the pancakes: In a mixing bowl, beat the eggs, sugar, and *mizuame* (or light corn syrup) till whitish and stringy. Stir in the flour in several additions. Mix the baking powder into the water, then stir the water into the batter in several additions. Beat well. The batter should be smooth.

Many batters profit from resting a number of hours before cooking, but not this one. For good results, you may add only half the water, let batter rest for 20 minutes, then mix in the remaining water and cook immediately.

1 cup (300 g) CHUNKY
SWEET RED-BEAN PASTE
(see page 328)

Wipe the pan with an oil-dampened paper towel. Heat and pour $1/12$ of the batter from the tip of a spoon into the pan. The pouring spoon should be close to the pan, not at any height above it. Cook over very low heat, about 5 minutes, and turn when bubbles appear on the upper surface. Turn only once. Cooking the second side will take only half as long as the first. Cool. Do not stack. Re-oil the pan for every pancake.

To assemble and serve: Have the SWEET RED-BEAN PASTE (*an*) already prepared (see page 328). Spread one pancake with about $1/4$ inch ($3/4$ cm) sweet bean paste and cover with a second pancake. Assemble the sandwiches so that the best-looking browned sides of the pancakes are on the outside. Wrap in wax paper.

Goes well with Japanese green tea or black tea.

cross-sectioned and finished "GONG"

Cherry Blossom *Mochi*

(*Sakura-Mochi*) 桜　　餅

Pink-tinted balls of sweetened glutinous rice with sweet red-bean paste centers, wrapped in edible, brined cherry leaves. This teatime confection is associated with the season when cherry trees bloom. Even if you decide not to eat the leaves, their lingering fragrance gives this confection a special ambience. If you are unable to obtain the leaves, which is likely, just proceed without—the pink-tinted rice balls are appealing by themselves.

12 servings; about 24
$1\frac{1}{2}$-inch (4-cm) balls

2 cups glutinous rice
red food coloring
2 Tbsps sugar
pinch salt
$2\frac{1}{2}$ cups (750 g) CHUNKY
or PUREED SWEET RED-
BEAN PASTE **(see**
pages 327-28)
salt-preserved cherry
leaves (or substitute
vine leaves in brine)

To prepare: Wash glutinous rice repeatedly, until water is clear. Put rice in bowl with ample water and add 1 drop red food coloring to tint the rice a delicate pink. Let rest in colored water 3 hours. Drain, then steam rice 40 minutes, until quite tender. Pour a small amount of water over glutinous rice 3–4 times while steaming.

Put hot, steamed rice in a large bowl. Add 2 Tbsps sugar and pinch salt and mix. Crush rice with pestle or back of spoon until rice grains are roughly cut in half. (This should be quick and easy to do.) Spread out in a thin layer on a nonstick jelly-roll pan or on baking paper.

cherry leaf wrapping and finished
CHERRY BLOSSOM MOCHI

(If you dry this rice, it will look like small, clear crystals. Store in a tight-lidded container. You may also purchase the dried, processed, uncolored glutinous rice preparation called *Dōmyōji-ko*. For 2 cups of *Dōmyōji-ko*, mix with 2 Tbsps sugar and a pinch salt in a bowl. Tint 2 cups boiling water with 1 drop red food color and pour over *Dōmyōji-ko*. Cover bowl tightly and allow all the water to be absorbed. Fluff with wooden paddle or spoon, then spread on a nonstick jelly-roll pan or on baking paper, as above.)

To assemble and steam: Have the SWEET RED-BEAN PASTE already prepared (see recipes, pages 327–28). If you can purchase the salted cherry leaves at a Japanese food-store (doubtful), to separate them, place them briefly in hot water, then drain. Vine leaves in brine are available canned or bottled at Middle Eastern food shops. Vine leaves will do in a pinch, but do not have the associations or ambience of the cherry.

Roll about 1⅔ Tbsps sweet red-bean paste into a ball. Dampen hands and roll this over the hot tinted rice. The rice should adhere to the bean paste. Pack the rice around the bean paste till about the size of a golf ball, perhaps a little larger. Flatten the ball slightly, then wrap the ball with a drained cherry leaf, shiny side in, as shown. Arrange in a steamer and steam over high heat for 10 to 15 minutes.

Serve at room temperature. Eat with fork or pick up with fingers. Eat the cherry leaf if you like. Many people enjoy the briny leaf flavor contrasting with the sweet confection.

Mitsumame

みつ豆

A year-round sweet snack, particularly nice in summer, this dish consists of small cubes of agar-agar jelly topped with fresh fruit, chilled syrup, and succulent little maroon-colored beans called *saru-endo* (monkey peas). The beans are available canned, but they are not essential. The complete *mitsumame* is also available canned, with all ingredients packed separately and ready for assembling, but the homemade dish with fresh fruit is easy to make and worth the effort.

6 servings
<u> </u>

1 stick agar-agar (*kanten*)
   (or substitute about 1½
   Tbsps gelatin)
2¼ cups water
2 Tbsps sugar

syrup:
   1 cup sugar
   2 cups water

3 tangerines, in segments
3 peaches, sliced
   (or the equivalent amounts
   of canned fruit)
lemon juice
¼ to ½ cup juice from
   fruit, if canned
small can *saru-endo*
   (monkey peas)

To cook: Tear the agar-agar into pieces and soak in ample water for several hours. Wash thoroughly and squeeze out excess water. Place in a large pot with the 2¼ cups water and cook over low heat. Do not stir till agar-agar is dissolved. Then, skim any foam off the surface and stir frequently until liquid is reduced by 10 percent. Add 2 Tbsps sugar and dissolve. Remove from heat, strain, and pour into an 8-inch (20-cm) square baking pan lined with foil extending over opposite sides (see sketch, page 369). Let come to room temperature and refrigerate, covered, overnight.

(If using gelatin instead of agar-agar, soften powdered gelatin in ½ cup cold water; place this over low heat until gelatin dissolves. Do not boil. Add sugar and stir over medium heat till sugar is dissolved.)

For the syrup, stir water and sugar in a medium-sized saucepan over high heat till liquid boils and all sugar is dissolved. Remove from heat, let come to room temperature, then chill.

To assemble and serve: Peel and slice fruit, if fresh. Sprinkle a little lemon on the peaches to prevent discoloring. If fruit is canned, drain well but reserve canning syrup and mix some of it with the sugar syrup.

Cut the jelly into ½-inch (1½-cm) cubes, using chopsticks to guide the cutting (see page 464 for sketch). Then, first running a knife between pan and jelly, lift out the foil lining and use a serving spoon or pancake turner to transfer equal portions of cubes to 6 dessert dishes.

Top jelly squares with fruit and syrup, and 1 Tbsp or so of monkey peas, if you have them. Return to refrigerator to chill briefly.

You may also serve this family style in a large bowl with a ladle.

VARIATIONS: Many different kinds of fruit can be used. Canned fruit cocktail is often employed. Dried fruit is suitable too—for example, prunes. You can use canned pineapple rings cut into wedges.

With a scoop of vanilla ice cream on the side, this dish is called Cream *Mitsumame*. With a dab of sweet bean paste (*an*), it becomes *an-mitsu*. You may also add 1 Tbsp liqueur to the syrup—a fruit brandy or perhaps the PLUM LIQUEUR on page 470. Raisins or currants will substitute for the monkey peas, if you cannot find the latter.

Abe River Mochi

(Abe-Kawa Mochi) 安倍川餅

Grilled *mochi* moistened and rolled in sweetened soybean flour (*kinako*) is a popular and filling confection, simple to make. It originated centuries ago at an inn on the Abe River near a ford where tired travelers between Kyoto and Edo (old Tokyo) used to stop for refreshment.

4 servings

1 cup *kinako* (roasted
   soybean flour)
½ cup sugar
pinch salt
2-x-2½-inch (5-x-6½-cm)
   pieces *mochi* (glutinous
   rice cake)

To prepare: Mix the *kinako* with the sugar and salt.

To assemble: Grill the *mochi* over a charcoal fire (or use oven broiler), turning often till both sides are crisp and mottled brown. The *mochi* will about double in size as it is grilled.

Dip the grilled *mochi* into hot water to moisten the surface and then immediately roll in the sweetened *kinako*. Serve immediately on individual plates. Eat with dessert fork.

Uji Ice

(Uji-Gōri) 宇治氷

Uji, a pleasant small river town just south of Kyoto, is famous for its tea. Young leaves of the aged Uji tea plants—steamed, dried and ground to a fine powder—provide the high-quality powdered tea (*matcha*) for the tea ceremony. This powdered green tea, mixed with a syrup and poured over a pyramid of shaved ice, makes a simple and elegant dessert.

4 servings

green-tea syrup:
  1 cup water
  2 cups (400 g) sugar
  **1 Tbsp powdered green
    tea (*matcha*)**
8 cups shaved ice

Syrup: Combine the sugar and water in a saucepan, place over high heat, and stir till sugar is dissolved. Simmer gently till liquid reduces by 20 percent. Allow to come to room temperature. Stir the powdered tea into the room-temperature syrup. You may refrigerate green-tea syrup, but stir before using.

To assemble: Apportion shaved ice into sherbet cups or dessert bowls, packing lightly into pyramid shape. Spoon the green-tea syrup over and serve immediately.

VARIATIONS: Use vanilla ice cream instead of shaved ice. Or use plain yogurt mixed with sugar and powdered tea to substitute for green-tea syrup.

❀ Miscellaneous ❀

Kamaboko Slices
(Itawasa) 板わさ

Kamaboko, fish paste, figures prominently in Japanese cuisine, and is made from squid, *hamo* eel, and white-fleshed fish ground into a very fine paste, rubbed several times through a sieve, then formed into semicylindrical loaves shaped like Quonset (or Nissen) huts. (They are called *kamaboko* huts in Japanese.) The finest-grade *kamaboko* loaves used to be molded and slowly steamed and grilled on fragrant cedar boards (*ita*), hence the name of this dish—*itawasa*. The *wasa* is short for *wasabi*. Slices of high-grade fish paste with *wasabi* horseradish and soy sauce make a pleasant appetizer.

4 servings

1 cake high-quality
  kamaboko (fish paste)
1 tsp grated *wasabi*
  horseradish
2 Tbsps soy sauce

To prepare and serve: Cut the *kamaboko* crosswise into slices about ⅓ inch (⅞ cm) thick. Arrange 4 or 5 slices on a plate, with a bamboo leaf or other decorative green—even lettuce—as decoration. Grate the *wasabi* horseradish and put a small mound on each plate. Serve soy sauce in small individual dipping bowls. Mix the *wasabi* with the soy sauce to taste and use as a dip. Eat chilled or at room temperature.

Plum Liqueur
(Umeshu) 梅　酒

Japanese *ume* never ripen well. They tend to fall off the trees during the humid rainy season, to which they have given the poetic name *tsuyu*, the "Plum Rains." This tight-fleshed, unripe green fruit appears in every market in late May and early June, and a liqueur is made from them in countless Japanese homes annually. A pleasant drink at any time, it is particularly nice in summer over crushed ice or with water as a long drink, and Japanese also value its medicinal qualities for soothing stomach and intestinal disorders. Young, green apricots are a good substitute, though the result is a little sweeter than the *ume* drink (see also PICKLED PLUMS, page 317).

for 2 quarts (2 L)

2¼ pounds (1 kg) green
 ume (or apricots)
1½ pounds (650-700 g)
 rock crystal sugar (*not*
 granulated)
2 quarts (1.8 L) 70 proof
 shōchū (rice or potato
 spirits; now often
 marketed as "white
 liquor") or gin

To assemble: Remove stems and wash *ume* well. Dry carefully, one by one and let stand in the sun for an hour or so, turning fruit occasionally to make sure they are absolutely dry.

Place *ume* and sugar in alternate layers in a large glass jar and add liquor. Seal tightly. Store in a dark, cool place without disturbing the bottle for 3 months (about the time it takes for the sugar to dissolve). The liqueur is drinkable at this stage, but tastes even better when matured for at least a year. Keeps indefinitely. Eat the fruit too.

VARIATIONS: For a liqueur that takes only a week to 10 days to mature, use orange or lemon segments, or hulled strawberries. Any tart fruit works. Berries of any kind are excellent. Various herbs and spices also can be used, but proportions are a matter of personal taste.

Soybeans in the Pod
(*Edamame*) 枝　豆

Young soybeans in their fuzzy green pods appear in the market from mid-June to October. Delicious with drinks and fun to eat, surprisingly they have not yet been "discovered" by the West. *Eda-mame* means "branch beans," and they are sold as bunches of stalks with the pods attached. These beans are as addictive as peanuts, potato chips, or popcorn, but contain a lot of protein. A 3½-ounce (100-g) serving of soybeans-in-the-pod provides 40 percent of the adult daily protein requirement.

3–4 servings

1 bundle (about ½ pound
 [225 g]) young green
 soybeans on the stalk
 (about 4 cups of pods)
2 Tbsps salt

To prepare: Separate pods from the stalks. To be extremely helpful to guests, trim off the stem end so that the beans are easily squeezed out of the pods between the lips.

Put bean pods in a large mixing bowl. Sprinkle generously with salt. With your hands mix and rub the beans with the salt thoroughly. Let stand 15 minutes. This will improve the color of the beans and make it unnecessary to salt the boiling water.

To cook: Bring an ample amount of water to a boil in a large pot. Add beans and boil over high heat 7–10 minutes. Some like a firmer bean and prefer a shorter cooking time. Taste a bean or two toward the end of the cooking time and remove to a colander immediately when done. Do not overcook. Rinse under cold water if you like. Serve hot or at room temperature.

To eat: Finger food. Serve in baskets or bowls. Squeeze the pods with your lips to press the beans into your mouth. Provide containers for discarded pods. The flavor fades quickly; beans must be eaten the day they are cooked.

Appendices

Oriental Food Shops and Sources

ALABAMA

Ebino Oriental Foods
323 Air Base Blvd.
Montgomery 36108

Oriental Super Market #1
3480 Springhills Avenue
Mobile 36608

ARIZONA

Oriental Food Store
408 West Main
Jacksonville 72076

Stern Brokerage Company
310 South 4th Street
Phoenix 95040

CALIFORNIA

NORTH

ABC Fish & Oriental Food
1911 Portrero Way
Sacramento 95822

A. Dong Market
6001 Eldere Creek Road
Sacramento 95814

Alpha Beta Mkt #573
919 Edgewater Blvd.
Foster City 94404

American Fish Mkt
1790 Sutter St.
San Francisco 94115

Asahi Market
5616 Thornton Ave.
Newark 94560

Asahi Ya
229 East Alpine Avenue
Stockton 95009

Asia Food Market
2000 Judah Street
San Francisco 94122

Asian Products Corp.
St. Francis Square, No. 39
Daly City 94015

Ban Do Market
503 E. 2nd Ave.
San Mateo 94401

Brother Discount Market
620 Pacific Ave.
San Francisco 94133

Calif Flower Co-Op
415 East Market St.
Salinas 93901

First Food Market
4454 California Street
San Francisco 94118

Central Fish Co.
1535 Kern Street
Fresno 93706

Chong Kee Jan Co.
838 Grant Ave.
San Francisco 94108

Diablo Oriental Food
2590 N. Main St.
Walnut Creek 94596

Dobashi Company
240 E. Jackson St.
San Jose 95112

Easy Food Co.
299 Castro St.
Mountain View 94040

El Rancho Meat Market
2665 Geneva Ave.
Daly City 94014

Food Center Market
1912 Fruitridge
Sacramento 95822

Gene Wah & Co.
391 8th Street
Oakland 94607

Golden Crown Trading Co.
870 Old San Francisco Rd.
Sunnyvale 94086

Happy Produce
1240 Solano Ave.
Albany 94706

Ho Chin Co.
5069 Freeport Blvd.
Sacramento 95822

Hong Kee Co.
385 8th St.
Oakland 94607

Hong's Market
300 Carmel Ave.
Marina 93933

International Market
2019 Fillmore Street
San Francisco 94115

Jacks Food Center
519 E. Charter Way
Stockton 95206

Jing Keung Trading Co.
1230 Stockton St.
San Francisco 94133

Jin Moon Co.
724 Jackson St.
San Francisco 94133

Keiko Oriental
3417 Chestnut Avenue
Concord 94519

Kenson Trading
1251 Stockton Street
San Francisco 94133

Kiely Market
1074 Kiely Blvd.
Santa Clara 95051

Korean Market
1915 San Pablo Ave.
Oakland 94612

Lee's Food Store
1988 Homestead Rd.
Santa Clara 95050

Lee Sing Company
2424 16th Street
Sacramento 95818

Lee Yuen Grocery Store
1131 Stockton St.
San Francisco 94105

Lucky Dollar Market
825 B Street
Hayward 94541

Lucky Stores-Gemco #4
1701 Marina Blvd.
San Leandro 94577

Manley Produce Co.
1101 Grant Ave.
San Francisco 94133

Marina Oriental Food Mkt.
215 Reservation Rd.
Marina 93933

Mei Heung Co.
2030 10th Street
Sacramento 95814

Metro Food
641 Broadway St.
San Francisco 94133

Miko's Japanese Foods
524 Tuolumne
Vallejo 94590

Musashi Oriental Food
962 West El Camino Real
Sunnyvale 94087

Nakagawa
306 C Street
Marysville 95901

Nishioka Fish Market
665 N. Sixth St.
San Jose 95112

Nomura Market
29583 Mission Blvd.
Hayward 94544

Noris
1119 West Texas
Fairfield 94533

Oakland Market
378 8th St.
Oakland 94607

Ocean Trading Co.
823 Jackson Street
San Francisco 94133

The Omodaka
115 Clement Street
San Francisco 94118

Oriental Food Fair
10368 San Pablo Ave.
El Cerrito, 94530

Oriental Food Store
9189 Kiefer Blvd.
Sacramento 95826

Oriental Market
413-B San Antonio Rd.
Mountain View 94040

Oriental Store
3443 El Camino Real
Santa Clara 95051

Orient Grocery
337 8th Street
Oakland 94612

Pacific Food Center
1924 4th Street
San Rafael 94901

Pacific Grocery
1125 Stockton St.
San Francisco 94133

Pajaro Valley Fish Market
114 Union St.
Watsonville 95076

Parade Food Store
145 Jackson St.
Hayward 94544

Pusan Market
1125 Webster Street
Oakland 94607

Quong Wor Food Co.
725 Webster St.
Oakland 94607

K Sakai Co. (Uoki)
1656 Post Street
San Francisco 94115

Safeway Store #592
7th & Cabrillo St.
San Francisco 94118

Safeway Store #785
850 La Playa
San Francisco 94121

Sam Yick Co.
389 8th Street
Oakland 94607

Santos Market
245 E. Taylor St.
San Jose 95112

Sanwa Market
2122 Cabrillo St.
San Francisco 94121

Save Mart #3
6045 N. El Dorado St.
Stockton 95207

Senator Fish Market
2215 10th St.
Sacramento 95818

Star Fish Market
320 S. El Dorado St.
Stockton 95203

Sunrise Grocery
400 Pearl Street
Monterey 93940

Sun Tung Lee
1351 Powell St.
San Francisco 94133

Sun Wong Kee
333 S. Hunter Street
Stockton 95203

Super Save Market
39 W. Chatterway
Stockton 95206

Suruki
140 Boothbay
Foster City 94404

Tai Wah Grocery
395 Eighth St.
Oakland 94607

Takahashi Company
221 S. Claremont St.
San Mateo 94401

Tim's Market
310 7th Street
Oakland 94607

Vickie Oriental Food
157–8 Parker Street
Vacaville 95688

Wahing Trading Co., Inc.
718 Franklin Street
Oakland 94607

Wakis Fish Market
1335 S. Lincoln St.
Stockton 95206

Wee Wah Trading Co.
1248 Stockton St.
San Francisco 94133

Wing Fat Lung Co.
945 Stockton St.
San Francisco 94108

Wing Lung Co.
1947 Grove St.
Berkeley 94704

Wing Wo Trading Co.
670 Broadway
San Francisco 94133

Wing Yuen Co.
1122 Grant Ave.
San Francisco 94133

Wo Soon Produce Co.
1210 Stockton St.
San Francisco 94133

Yaohan C/O Ug Acct Dept.
P.O. Box #2767
Fresno 93745

SOUTH

Albertson's #603
2505 Via Cameo
Montebello 90640

Albertson's #626
2280 Atlantic Boulevard
Monterey Park 91754

Albertson's #668
3443 S. Sepulveda Blvd.
Los Angeles 90034

Albertson's #1905
4700 Cherry Ave,
Long Beach 90807

Alpha Beta-SCD #29
241 E. 17th Street
Costa Mesa 92627

Alpha Beta-SCD #32
6991 Lincoln Ave.
Buena Park 90620

Alpha Beta-SCD #47
421 N. Atlantic Blvd.
Monterey Park 91754

Alpha Beta-SCD #56
2120 S. Bristol
Santa Ana 92704

Alpha Beta-SCD #129
1500 W. Willow
Long Beach 90806

Alpha Beta-SCD #131
18901 Colima Rd.
Rowland Heights 91745

Alpha Beta-SCD #132
2740 W. Olympic Blvd.
Los Angeles 90006

Alpha Beta-SCD #133
420 S. Alvarado St.
Los Angeles 90057

Alpha Beta-SCD #159
1122 E. Broadway
Glendale 91205

Alpha Beta-SCD #170
2551 N. Ventura Rd.
Port Hueneme 93041

Alpha Beta-SCD #171
5420 La Palma
La Palma 90620

Alpha Beta-SCD #183
13321 Artesia
Cerritos 90701

Alpha Beta-SCD #197
131 W Carson St.
Carson 90745

Alpha Beta-SCD #200
5520 Sunset Blvd.
Hollywood 90028

Alpha Beta-SCD #202
10772 Jefferson Blvd.
Culver City 90230

Alpha Beta-SCD #218
20125 Pioneer Blvd.
Lakewood 90715

Alpha Beta #107
1035 Harbison Ave.
National City 92050

Alpha Beta #117
3350 Palm
Imperial Beach 92032

Alpha Beta #123
1860 Coronado Ave.
San Diego 92154

Ai Hoa Market
860 N. Hill St.
Los Angeles 90012

Aloha Grocery
4515 Centinella Avenue
Los Angeles 90066

Aloha Market
900 West Main Street
Santa Maria 93454

Asahi Company
660 Oxnard Blvd.
Oxnard 93030

Bangkok Market
2849 Leonis Blvd.
Vernon 90058

B. C. Market
711 North Broadway
Los Angeles 90012

Boys Markets, Inc. #5
3670 Crenshaw Blvd.
Los Angeles 90016

Chinese Vegetable Center
709 N. Hill St.
Los Angeles 90012

D. H. Market
848 N. New High St.
Los Angeles 90012

Diho Market
720 S. Atlantic Blvd.
Monterey Park 91754

Do Re Mi Grocery Mkt.
9520 Garden Grove #1
Garden Grove 92644

East-West Food Center
3300 W. 8th St.
Los Angeles 90005

Ebisu Market
18940 Brookhurst St.
Fountain Valley 92708

Eiko Shoten
6082 University Ave.
San Diego 92115

Enbun Co. #2
124 Japanese Village
Los Angeles 90012

Far East Market
8848 Lankersheim Blvd.
Sun Valley 91352

Food City Mkt.
2305 S. Garfield Ave.
Monterey Park 91754

Foods Co. #3
17500 Crenshaw Blvd.
Torrance 90504

Foods Co. #4
2655 Pacific Coast Hwy.
Torrance 90505

Foods Co. #13
15505 Normandie Ave.
Gardena 90247

Foods Co. #17
8936 Glenoaks Blvd.
Sun Valley 91312

Foods Co. #19
15202 Hawthorne Blvd
Lawndale 90260

Foods Co. #21
16100 Lakewood Blvd.
Bellflower 90706

Fujiya Market
601 N. Virgil Ave.
Los Angeles 90004

Fukuda's
2412 S. Escondido Blvd.
Escondido 92025

George's Fish Market
1018 W. Main St.
Santa Maria 93454

Granada Market
1820 Sawtelle Blvd.
Los Angeles 90025

Hankook Mkt.
3121 W. Olympic Blvd.
Los Angeles 90006

Home Food Basket
843 Guadalupe St.
Guadalupe 93434

Hughes Market #1
12836 Ventura Blvd.
Studio City 91604

Hughes Market #2
14440 Burbank Blvd.
Van Nuys 91404

Hughes Market #4
16940 Devonshire St.
Granada Hills 91344

Hughes Market #5
15120 Sunset Blvd.
Pacific Palisades 90272

Hughes Market #6
3075 San Fernando Rd.
Los Angeles 90065

Hughes Market #8
14620 Parthenia St.
Panorama City 91402

Hughes Market #9
11361 National Blvd.
Los Angeles 90064

Hughes Market #10
21431 Devonshire Blvd.
Chatsworth 91311

Hughes Market #11
6657 Laurel Canyon Blvd.
N. Hollywood 91606

Hughes Market #12
1100 N. San Fernando Rd.
Burbank 91504

Hughes Market #13
10400 N. Sepulveda Blvd.
Mission Hills 91340

Hughes Market #14
3501 Saviers Rd.
Oxnard 93031

Hughes Market #15
330 N. Atlantic Blvd.
Monterey Park 91754

Hughes Market #16
606 Lincoln Blvd.
Venice 90291

Hughes Market #17
690 E. Holt Ave.
Pomona 91766

Hughes Market #20
30019 Hawthorne Blvd.
Palos Verdes Pen 90274

Hughes Market #21
22333 Sherman Way
Canoga Park 91303

Hughes Market #22
12021 W. Washington Blvd.
Los Angeles

Hughes Market #23
18300 Van Owen
Reseda 91335

Hughes Market #24
9040 Beverly Blvd.
Los Angeles 90048

Hughes Market #26
5311 Santa Monica Blvd.
Holywood 90046

Hughes Market #28
2909 Rolling Hills Rd.
Torrance 90505

Hughes-El Rancho Mkt. #43
320 W. Colorado Blvd.
Pasadena 91105

IDA Company
339 East First Street
Los Angeles 90012

Jay's Market
4000 W. Pico Blvd.
Los Angeles 90019

Jim's Market
688 W. Baker St.
Costa Mesa 92626

John's Market
14924 S. Western Ave.
Gardena 90249

Jon-son Market #1
2432 Brooklyn Avnue
Los Angeles 90033

Kal's Supermarket
606 South Vermont Ave.
Los Angeles 90005

Korea Food Store
3110 East 16th St.
National City 92050

Kowloon Market
750 N. Hill St.
Los Angeles 90012

Kwan Lee Lung Company
801 N. Hill St.
Los Angeles 90012

Kwong Hing Lung Company
2600 South San Pedro St.
Los Angeles 90011

Los Angeles Korean Grocer
2571 W. Olympic Blvd.
Los Angeles 90006

Lucky Stores. Inc. #426
3456 Sepulveda Blvd.
W. Los Angeles 90034

Lucky Stores, Inc. #427
1635 S. San Gabriel Blvd.
San Gabriel 91776

Lucky Stores, Inc. #435
110 East Carson
Carson 90745

Lucky Stores, Inc. #446
1820 W. 182nd St.
Torrance 90504

Lucky Stores, Inc. #457
855 North Wilcox
Montebello 90640

Lucky Stores, Inc. #463
133 W. Avenue 45
Los Angeles 90065

Lucky Stores-Gemco #478
2169 Redondo Beach Blvd.
Gardena 90247

Lucky Stores, Inc. #487
950 E. 33rd St.
Long Beach 90807

Lucky Stores-Gemco #632
5750 Mesmer Ave.
Culver City 90230

Man Wah Super Market
758 New High St.
Los Angeles 90012

Market Basket #55
11766 Wilshire Blvd.
W. Los Angeles 90025

Market Basket #67
3210 E. Anaheim
Long Beach 90804

Market Basket #87
2520 Glendale Blvd.
Los Angeles 90039

Market Basket #113
2201 S. Atlantic
Monterey Park 91754

Market Basket #128
160 N. Lake Ave.
Pasadena 91106

Market Basket #135
13321 E. South St.
Cerritos 90701

Market Basket #144
7600 Edinger Ave.
Huntington Beach 92646

Market Basket #146
5810 Downey Ave.
Long Beach 90805

Market Basket #154
1040 North Western
San Pedro 90732

Market Basket #159
2727 N. Grand
Santa Ana 92701

Market Basket #161
1421 E. Valley Blvd.
Alhambra 90801

Market Basket #173
10255 Magnolia
Riverside 92502

Market Basket #174
9091 Garfield Ave.
Fountain Valley 92708

Market Basket #175
833 S. Western Ave.
Los Angeles 90005

Modern Food Market
318 East Second Street
Los Angeles 90012

Modern Food Market
601 West Anaheim Street
Wilmington 90744

Motoyama Market
16135 S. Western Ave.
Gardena 90247

New Meiji Market
1620 W. Redondo Beach
Gardena 90247

Nippon Foods
2935 West Ball Road
Anaheim 92804

Olympic Market
3122 W. Olympic Blvd.
Los Angeles 90006

Omori's
2700 N. Santa Fe
Vista 92083

Orange Market
13120 Brookhurst Blvd
Garden Grove 92643

Oriental Grocery
418 Island Ave.
San Diego 92101

Orion Market
3420 W. 8th St.
Los Angeles 90005

Park Store
705 6th Ave.
San Diego 92101

Pioneer Foods #3
4317 Benverly Blvd.
Los Angeles 90004

Pioneer Foods #2
1601 N. Vermont Ave.
Los Angeles 90027

Plow Boys Market
11869 East Carson
Hawaiian Garden 90715

Poong Nyon Food Co.
1042 S. Western Ave.
Los Angeles 90006

Ralph's Groc. Co. #158
5400 Beach Blvd.
Buena Park 90621

Ralph's Groc. Co. #162
3660 Nogales St.
West Covina 91790

Ralph's Groc. Co. #3
7257 Sunset Blvd.
Hollywood 90046

Ralph's Groc. Co. #4
1010 South Western
Los Angeles 90019

Ralph's Groc. Co. #25
4641–5 Santa Monica
Los Angeles 90029

Ralph's Groc. Co. #32
3456 West Third Street
Los Angeles 90020

Ralph's Groc. Co. #37
2205 Rosecrans Blvd.
Gardena 90249

Ralph's Groc. Co. #44
12057 Wilshire Blvd.
Los Angeles 90025

Ralph's Groc. Co. #77
21740 Hawthorne Blvd.
Torrance 90503

Ralph's Groc. Co. #153
10201 Reseda Blvd.
Northridge 91324

Safe & Save Market
2040 Sawtelle Blvd.
West Los Angeles 90025

Safeway Store #35
3461 West Third Street
Los Angeles 90005

Safeway Store #127
4520 Sunset Blvd.
Los Angeles 90027

Sakae Oriental Grocery
4227 Convoy St.
San Diego 92111

S & N Food Market
2600 E. 1st St.
Los Angeles 90033

Sang Rok Soo Grocery
4027 W. Olympic Blvd.
Los Angeles 90019

Senri Market
111 N. Lincoln Ave.
Monterey Park 91754

Shi's Fish Mart
9896 Garden Grove Blvd.
Garden Grove 92641

Spot Store Inc.
15212 S. Western Ave.
Gardena 90249

Thriftimart #61
804 W. Beverly Blvd.
Montebello 90640

Thriftimart #77
4030 Centinella Blvd.
West Los Angeles 90025

Valley Oriental Market
15331 Parthenia St.
Sepulveda 91343

Van Nuys Oriental Market
13723 Oxnard St.
Van Nuys 91401

Viet Hoa Supermarket
211 Alpine St. #1
Los Angeles 90012

Von's Groc. Co. #2
1311 Wilshire Blvd.
Santa Monica 90403

Von's Groc. Co. #8
3334 W 8th St.
Los Angeles 90005

Von's Groc. Co. #10
1020 S. Crenshaw Blvd.
Los Angeles 90019

Von's Groc. Co. #14
1260 W. Redondo Beach Blvd.
Gardena 90247

Von's Groc. Co. #15
3644 W. Santa Barbara Ave.
Los Angeles 90008

Von's Groc. Co. #48
163 S. Turnpike Road
Santa Barbara 93105

Von's Groc. Co. #75
1129 Fair Oaks Ave.
South Pasadena 91030

Von's Groc. Co. #77
3118 S. Sepulveda Blvd.
Los Angeles 90034

Von's Groc. Co. #85
820 N. Western Avenue
San Pedro 90731

Von's Groc. Co. #87
124 N. Western Avenue
Los Angeles 90004

Von's Groc. Co. #90
5922 Edinger Avenue
Huntington Beach 92646

Von's Groc. Co. #100
9860 W. National Blvd.
Los Angeles 90034

Von's Groc. Co. #101
1040 Coast Village Road
Montecito 93103

Von's Groc. Co. #102
956 W. Sepulveda
Harbor City 90710

Von's Groc. Co. #105
4365 Glencoe Ave
Marina Del Rey 90291

Von's Groc. Co. #109
3855 State Street
Santa Barbara 93105

Von's Groc. Co. #152
155 W. California Blvd.
Pasadena 91100

Williams Bros. #15
1650 Grand Ave.
Arroyo Grande 93420

Woo Chee Chong #1
633 16th Street
San Diego 92101

Woo Chee Chong #2
1415 Third Ave.
Chula Vista 92011

Woo Chee Chong #3
4625 Convoy Street
San Diego 92111

Yamamoto Bros.
314 Wilmington Blvd.
Wilmington 90744

Yee Sing Chong Company
960 North Hill Street
Los Angeles 90012

COLORADO

Ann's Oriental Grocery
315 Arvada Street
Colorado Springs 80906

Granada Fish Market
1275 19th Street
Denver 80202

Havana Oriental Market
812 S. Havana Street
Aurora 80012

Kim Young Oriental
1444 Chester Street
Aurora 80010

Pacific Mercantile Grocery
1925 Lawrence St.
Denver 80202

Park's Oriental Market
229 N. Academy Blvd.
Colorado Springs 80909

Pear Garden
1835 Arapahoe Street
Denver 80202

CONNECTICUT

China Trading Co.
271 Crown St.
New Haven 06510

East/West Trading Co.
68 Howe Street
New Haven 00511

Kim's Oriental Foods & Gift
202 Park Road
W. Hartford 06119

Young's Oriental Grocery
243 Farmington Ave.
Hartford 06105

DELAWARE

Oriental Grocery
1705 Concord Pike
Wilmington 19803

FLORIDA

Au's Oriental Foods
2505 N. Pace Blvd.
Pensacola 32505

Misako's Oriental Foods
129 New Warrington Road
N. Pensacola 32406

Oriental Food & Gift
1531 S. Dale Mabry Hwy.
Tampa 32801

Oriental Food Store
4559 Shirley Ave.
Jacksonville 32210

Oriental Imports
1118 S. Orange Ave.
Orlando 32801

Oriental Market
1202 S. Dale Mabry Hwy.
Tampa 33609

Stubbs Oriental Food
807 East Ave.
Panama City 32401

Tomiko's Oriental
441 Bryn Athyn Blvd.
Mary Esther 32569

Yates Brothers Produce
4601 Haines Rd.
St. Petersburg 33710

GEORGIA

Asian Supermarket
2581 Piedmont Rd. Birdview
Atlanta 30324

Dong A Oriental Food
3331 Buford Hwy.
Atlanta 30260

The Eastern Connection
1837–9 Cobb Parkway S.
Marietta 30062

Makoto
1067 Oaktree Rd.
Decateur 30033

Oakland Park Oriental
2031 S. Lumpkin Rd.
Columbus 31903

Oriental Food & Gift Ct.
3656 Buena Vista Rd.
Columbus 31907

Oriental Market
2306 Lumpkin Rd.
Augusta 30906

Oriental Trading
8415 Cresthill Ave.
Savannah 31406

Prince Oriental
960 Prince Ave.
Athens 30606

Satsuma-ya
5271-B Buford Hwy.
Doraville 30340

Seafood & Oriental Market
528 Main Street
Forest Park 30050

IDAHO

Albertson's Inc.
Box 20
Boise 83707

Yuko's Gift
688 N. Holmes Ave.
Idaho Falls 83401

ILLINOIS

Ah Joo Oriental Food
9210 N. Waukegan Rd.
Morton Grove 60053

Co-Op Super Market
1526 East 55th Street
Chicago 60615

Diamond Trading Co.
913 W. Belmont Ave.
Chicago 60657

Dong A Food Store
3264 N. Clark St.
Chicago 60657

Far East Co.
2837 N. Western Ave.
Chicago 60618

Far East Food Co.
105 S. Fifth St.
Champaign 61820

Far East Ort'l Food
1524 Grand Ave.
Waukegan 60085

Furuya & Company
5358 N. Clark St.
Chicago 60640

Ginza & Co.
315 E. University
Champaign 61820

Golden Country Store
2422 Wentworth Ave.
Chicago 60616

Golf Oriental Food
9142 Golf Road
Des Plaines 60016

Hisaya's Oriental Food
112 Homestead
Ofallon 62269

Jasmine Mart
1773 Bloomingdale Rd.
Glendale Heights 60137

Korea Market
2606 W. Lawrence Ave.
Chicago 60625

Kyotoya Corp. Food & Craft
1182 S. Elmhurst
Mt. Prospect 60056

Lee Wah Co.
2246 S. Wentworth Ave.
Chicago 60615

Lin's International Inc.
1537 S. State St.
Chicago 60605

Lucky Oriental Food
4550 North Clark St.
Chicago 60640

Mayjean Co.
1806 Irving Park Road
Hanover Park 60103

New Quon Wah
2515 Wentworth Ave.
Chicago 60616

New Way Trading, Inc.
3328 North Clark St.
Chicago 60657

Northwest Oriental Food Mart
570 E. Algonquin Road
Des Plaines 60016

Oriental Treasure Center Inc.
675 N. Cass Ave.
Westmont 60559

Quon Wah Co.
2241 Wentworth Ave.
Chicago 60616

Schaumburg Oriental
710 E. Higgins Road
Schaumburg 60195

Seoul Oriental Food
5531 N. Clark St.
Chicago 60640

Skokie Oriental
3922 Dempster
Skokie 60076

Star Market
3349 N. Clark St.
Chicago 60657

Sun Hing Co.
2239 S. Wentworth Ave.
Chicago 60616

Wah May Food Prods. Co.
2401 South Wentworth Ave
Chicago 60616

Yenching Oriental Grocery
6421 N. Western Ave.
Chicago 60645

York Food Stores
3240 N. Clark St.
Chicago 60657

INDIANA

Asia Oriental Market
2400 Yeager Rd.
W. Lafayette 47906

IOWA

Jungs Oriental Food Store
913 E. University Ave.
Des Moines 50316

Lucky Dragon, Inc.
319 East Main St.
Ottumwa 52501

Tokyo Foods
1005 Pierce Street
Sioux City 51105

LOUISIANA

Korea House
Rt. 5 Box 268
Leesville 71446

Korea House
615 Orange St.
New Orleans 70130

Oriental Merchandise Co.
2636 Edenborn Ave.
Metairie 70002

MARYLAND

Arirang House
7918 Georgia Ave.
Silver Spring 20910

Asia House
1576 Annapolis Road
Odenton 21113

Diskor
8476 Piney Branch Rd.
Silver Spring 20903

Far East House
33 W. North Ave.
Baltimore 21201

The Fortune Cookie
1749 Rockville Pike
Rockville 20852

Fumi Oriental Mart
2102 Veirs Mill Rd.
Rockville 20852

Gourmet's Delight
8775 N. Cloudleap Ct.
Columbia 21045

Holiday Mart
Rt. 04 Box 12
Smithsburg 21783

New Seoul
1555 Rockville Pike
Rockville 20852

The Oriental House
409 E. 32nd St.
Baltimore 21218

MASSACHUSETTS

Joyce Chen Unlimited Inc.
172–174 Massachusetts Ave.
Arlington 02174

Mirim Trading Co. Inc.
152 Harvard Ave.
Allston 02134

See Sun Co.
36 Harrison St.
Boston 02111

Sun Sun Co.
34 Oxford St.
Boston 02111

Tung Hing Lung
5 Hudson Street
Boston 02111

Yoshinoya
36 Prospect Street
Cambridge 02139

MICHIGAN

House of Wong
519 W. Grand River
E. Lansing 48823

Mt. Fuji Oriental Foods
22040 West 10 Mile
Southfield 48075

Oriental Food Store
18919 W. 7 Mile Rd.
Detroit 48219

MINNESOTA

International House
75 W. Island Ave.
Minneapolis 55401

Kim's Ort'l Grocery
689 N. Snelling Ave.
St. Paul 55104

Oriental Plaza
24 Glenwood Ave.
Minneapolis 55403

United Noodle Corp.
2015 East 24th Street
Minneapolis 55404

Vietnam & Hong Kong Int'l.
419 West Broadway
Minneapolis 55411

MISSOURI

Kim's Mart
6692 Enright
St. Louis 63130

King's Trading Inc.
3736 Broadway Street
Kansas City 64111

Oriental Center
925 Demun Ave.
Clayton 63105

West Quon Wah
1651 South Grand
St. Louis 63104

NEBRASKA

Oriental Market
611 N. 27th Street
Lincoln 68503

Oriental Trading Co.
10525 J Street
Omaha 68127

NEVADA

Oriental Food
953 E. Sahara E-31
Las Vegas 89104

Tokyo-Plaza Shopping Center
3344 Kietzke Lane
Reno 89502

NEW JERSEY

Aki Oriental Food Co.
1635 Lemoine Ave.
Fort Lee 07024

Asian Food Market
217 Summit Ave.
Jersey City 07306

Daido International
1385 16th Street
Fort Lee 07024

First Oriental Company
284–286 Fairmont Ave.
Jersey City 07306

Miyako Oriental Foods
490 Main St.
Ft. Lee 07024

Sam Bok-Linwood Shop.Cent.
3012–18 Edwin Ave.
Ft. Lee 07024

Teri Lee
225 Maywood Ave.
Maywood 07607

NEW MEXICO

Fremont Fine Foods
556 Coronado Center N.E.
Albuquerque 87110

Yonemoto Bros.
8725 Fourth Street N.W.
Albuquerque 87114

NEW YORK

AC Gift
2642 Central Ave.
Yonkers 10710

Ajiya Mart
41–75 Bowne St.
Flushing 11354

Chinese American Trading Co.
91 Mulberry Street
New York 10013

Chinese Commercial Center
83–85 Bowery St.
New York 10002

Five Continental Foods
80–19 Broadway El
Elmhurst 11373

Global Food
80–06 Roosevelt Ave.
Jackson Heights 11372

Golden Pacific Development
199 Centre Street
New York 10013

Harumi
318–320 W. 231 St.
Bronx 10463

Jack Yuen Trading Co.
56 E. Broadway
New York 10002

Kam Kou Food Corporation
7–9 Mott St.
New York 10013

Kam Man Food Products
200 Canal Street
New York 10013

Katagiri Company
224 East 59th St.
New York 10022

Kim's Oriental Grocery
4311 E. Genesee St.
Dewitt 13214

Kim's Oriental Shoppe
1649 Central Ave.
Albany 12205

Koramerica Co. Inc.
127 West 43rd St.
New York 10036

Kwong Ming Intl. Trading
2 Mott St. Room 508
New York 10013

Lam's Trading Inc.
25 Division St.
New York 10002

Lee's Oriental Foods
11 Pullman Ave.
Rochester 14615

Main St. Foods Inc.
41–54 Main St.
Flushing 11355

Meidiya
18 N. Central Park Ave.
Hartsdale 10530

New World Corporation
103–37 Queens Boulevard
Forest Hill 11375

Nippon Do
82–69 Parsons Blvd.
Jamaica 11432

Oh Bok Oriental Mart
1772 Forest Ave.
Staten Island 10302

Oriental Groc. & Prd. Center
2460 Nesconset Hi-Way
Stonybrook 11790

Queens Oriental Food & Gift
81–02 Broadway
Elmhurst 11373

Sam Bok
42–27 Main St.
Flushing 11355

Seoul Oriental Foods
83–28 Broadway
Elmhurst 11373

Shin Shin Market
142–01 38th Ave.
Flushing 11355

Sun Lung Sang
19 Catherine St.
New York 10013

Sunnyside Oriental Foods
47–01 Queens Blvd.
Sunnyside 11104

Tanaka & Company
326 Amsterdam Ave.
New York 10023

Tokyo Sales Corp
142 W. 57th St.
New York 10019

Tomon
5678 Mosholu Ave.
Bronx 10471

Universal Trading Co.
Confucius Plaza 9 Bowery
New York 10002

W & H Industries Corp.
41–05 Union St.
Flushing 11355

Wing Fat Company
35 Mott Street
New York 10013

Wing Lee Lung Food Fair
50 East Broadway
New York 10002

Wing Woh Lung Company
50 Mott Street
New York 10013

C. T. Yang
2830 West Henrietta Rd.
Rochester 14620

NORTH CAROLINA

Asia Market
1325 Buck Jones Road
Raleigh 27606

Oriental Food Mart
803 N. Main St.
Spring Lake 28390

OHIO

Dayton Oriental Foods
812 Xenia Ave.
Dayton 45410

Kim's Mart
1400 Beaverton Dr.
Dayton 45429

Oriental Food & Gifts
500 W. Main St.
Fairborn 45324

Soya Food Products Inc.
2356 Wyoming Ave.
Cincinnati 45214

OKLAHOMA

Japan Imported Foods
808 N. W. 6th Street
Oklahoma City 73106

OREGON

Albertsons #505
5415 S. W. Beaverton-
Hillsdale Hwy.
Portland 97221

Albertsons #506
2595 S. W. Cedar Hills Blvd.
Beaverton 97005

Albertsons #543
15810 S. E. McLoughlin Blvd.
Milwaukie 97222

Albertsons #544
12060 S. W. Main
Tigard 97223

Fred Meyers
7404 N. Interstate
Portland 97217

Fred Meyers
100 N. W. 20th Pl.
Portland 97209

Fred Meyers
777 Kings Blvd.
Corvallis 97330

Fred Meyers
7700 S. W. Beaverton-
Hillsdale Hwy.
Portland 97225

Fred Meyers
11425 S. W. Beaverton-
Hillsdale Hwy.
Beaverton 97005

PENNSYLVANIA

Asia Products Corp.
226 N. 10th St.
Philadelphia 19107

Euro-Asian Imports
5221 E. Simpson Ferry Rd.
Mechanicsburg 17055

Hong Kee
935 Race St.
Philadelphia 19107

Imported Food Bazaar
2000 Market Street
Camp Hill 17011

Lun Chong Grocery Inc.
934 Race St.
Philadelphia 19107

Oriental Food Mart
909 Race St.
Philadelphia 19107

Oriental Food Store
502 Tilghman Street
Allentown 18102

The Oriental Ltd.
804 South 12th St.
Philadelphia 19147

Sambok Market
1737 Penn Ave.
Pittsburgh 15222

RHODE ISLAND

East Sea Oriental Market
90–92 Warren Ave.
E. Providence 02914

Persimmon Oriental Market
University Heights Shop. Cn.
Providence 02906

SOUTH CAROLINA

Chieko Hardy
226 Jamaica St.
Columbia 29206

Oriental Food & Gift
4252 Rivers Ave.
N. Charleston 29405

Yum's Oriental
1717 Decker Blvd.
Columbia 29206

SOUTH DAKOTA

Kitty's Oriental Food
P.O. Box 347
Box Elder 57719

TENNESSEE

Import Shop
1775 Fort Henry Dr.
Kingsport 37664

Park & Shop Oriental
3664 Summer Ave.
Memphis 38122

TEXAS

Asiatic Imports
821 Chartres
Houston 77003

Chung Hing Co.
815 Chartres
Houston 77003

Dockee Import Inc.
817 Chartres
Houston 77003

Eastern Foods
8626–1/2 Long Point
Houston 77055

Eastern Steamer Supply Co.
3143 Produce Row
Houston 77023

Edoya Oriental
223 Farmer Branch
Dallas 75234

First Oriental Market
904 St. Emanuel
Houston 77003

International Grocery
3103 Fondren
Houston 77063

Japanese Grocery
14366–B Memorial Dr.
Houston 77079

Joon Aug Grocery
1427 Gessner
Houston 77055

Jung's Oriental Food
2519 N. Fitzhugh
Dallas 75204

Kazy's Food Mart
9191 Forest Lane #7
Dallas 75243

Kobawoo Oriental
5732 Cedar Springs
Dallas 75235

Ko-Ko's Oriental Food
8001 Bangor Dr.
Fort Worth 76116

Korea House
9331 S. Gessner
Houston 77047

Korea Super Market
6427 Bissonnet
Houston 77074

Nippon Daido Int'l
11138 Westheimer
Houston 77042

Tachibana
4886 Hercules Ave.
El Paso 79904

Taroco Foods Corp.
1103 Chartres
Houston 77003

World Food Co.
1759 W. 34th St.
Houston 77018

UTAH

Oriental Mini-Mart
1786 West 5300 South
Roy 84067

Sage Farm Market
1515 South Main
Salt Lake City 84115

VIRGINIA

China Grocery Inc.
3509 S. Jefferson Street
Baileys Crossroad 22041

Oriental House
7816 Richmond Hwy.
Alexandria 22306

Super Asian Market
2719 Wilson Blvd.
Arlington 22201

Tokyo Market
5312 Va. Beach Blvd.
Virginia Beach 23462

Top Meat Market
1537 North Quaker Lane
Alexandria 22302

WASHINGTON

Albertsons #429
11625 68th Ave. So.
Seattle 98178

Albertsons #450
2755 77th Ave. So.
Mercer Island 98040

Albertsons #545
11808 N. E. 4th Plain Blvd.
Orchards 98662

Albertsons
157 North Town Shop. Cen.
Spokane 99207

Lucky Store #387
6040 Empire Way So.
Seattle 98118

Public Warehouse Mart
West 3330 Central Ave
Spokane 99208

QFC #807
4547 Univ. Village Plaza
Seattle 98105

R & R Food Center
East 628th-9th Ave
Spokane 99204

Rosauars River Ridge Center
West 4507 Wellsley
Spokane 99205

Safeway Stores, Inc. #221
West 2101 Wellsley
Spokane 99205

Safeway #435
9250 Rainier Ave. So.
Seattle 98118

Safeway #472
3903 Factoria Mall
Bellevue 98006

Safeway #496
15000 24th Ave. N. E.
Redmond 98052

Umajimaya
519 6th Ave. So.
Seattle 98104

Umajimaya-Bellevue
15555 N. E. 24th
Bellevue 98007

Villa Thriftco
10110 Gravelly Lake Dr. S. W.
Tacoma 98499

WASHINGTON, D.C.

Da Hua Foods Inc.
617 I Street NW
20001

House of Hanna
7838 Eastern Ave.
20012

Mikado
4709 Wisconsin Ave NW
20016

Suey Sang Lung
604 H St. NW
20001

Wang's Co.
800 7th St. NW
20001

WISCONSIN

International House of Foods
440 W. Gorham St.
Madison 53704

K. P. Oriental Grocery & Gift
321 N. 27th St.
Milwaukee 53208

Oriental Shop
618 South Park St.
Madison 53715

Peace Oriental Foods
4250 W Fond du Lac Ave.
Milwaukee 53216

—CANADA—

BRITISH COLUMBIA

Canada Safeway #118
1300 Lonsdale
North Vancouver, B. C.

Fairway Market
272 Gorge Rd.
Victoria, B. C.

High Low Stores
10345 King George Hwy.
Whalley, B. C.

IGA Stores
4469 Kingsway
Burnaby, B. C.

Mihamaya
392 Powell St.
Vancouver, B. C.

Shimizu Shoten
349 East Hasting St.
Vancouver, B. C.

Stongs Supermarket
4326 Dunbar St.
Vancouver, B. C.

Super Valu #141
555 6th St.
New Westminster, B. C.

Super Valu #140
1020 Park Royal
West Vancouver, B. C.

Super Valu #130
4567 Lougheed Hwy.
Burnaby, B. C.

Woodwards
Oakridge Shopping Center
Vancouver, B. C.

Woodwards
Coquitlam Centre
Port Coquitlam, B. C.

ALBERTA

Allwest Supermarket
5720 Silverspring Blvd N.W.
Calgary, Alberta

Calgary Co-Op #9
2520 52nd St. N. E.
Calgary, Alberta

Canada Safeway #271
3915 50th Ave. S.W.
Calgary, Alberta

Canada Safeway Stores Ltd.
11715 108th Ave.
Edmonton, Alberta

Edmonton Co-op #3
17010 90th Ave.
Edmonton, Alberta

IGA
5105 17th Ave. S. E.
Calgary, Alberta

IGA
Northtown Mall
Edmonton, Alberta

Super Valu #1634
Kingsway Garden Mall
Edmonton, Alberta

Woodwards Stores Ltd.
3850 98th St.
Edmonton, Alberta

Woodwards Stores
Chinook Shopping Centre
Calgary, Alberta

ONTARIO

Chinamart Trading Co.
210 Spadina Ave.
Toronto, Ontario

Dundas Union Store Ltd.
173 Dundas St. West
Toronto, Ontario

Fairway Trading Co.
9 Byward Market
Ottawa, Ontario

Furuya Trading Co. Ltd.
460 Dundas St. West
Toronto, Ontario

Imported Oriental Foods
270 North Cumberland St.
Thunder Bay, Ontario

Iwaki Japanese Food Store
2627 Yonge St.
Toronto, Ontario

JLW Far East Trading Corp.
1445 University West
Windsor, Ontario

Kealson's Ltd.
2501 Eglinton Ave. East
Scarborough, Ontario

Luen Fung Trading Co.
2469 Stevanage
Ottawa, Ontario

Nakanishi Japan Food Store
465 Somerset St. West
Ottawa, Ontario

Pan Asia Food
5420 Maingate Dr.
Mississauga, Ontario

Sambok Grocery Store
2437 Finch Ave. West
Toronto, Ontario

Sandown Market
221 Kennedy Rd.
Scarborough, Ontario

Sanko Trading Co.
221 Spadina Ave.
Toronto, Ontario

Wing Lee Co.
442 Dundas St. West
Toronto, Ontario

Yanagawa Japanese Foods
639 Upper James St.
Hamilton, Ontario

QUEBEC

Leong Jung Company Ltd.
999 rue Clark
Montreal, Quebec

Miyamoto Provisions
382 Victoria Ave.
Montreal Westmount, Quebec

NEW BRUNSWICK

House of Juliet Ltd.
606 Albert St.
Fredericton, New Brunswick

NOVA SCOTIA

Rose Marie Oriental Gourmet
1532 Queen St.
Halifax, Nova Scotia

Seasonal Japanese Fish Chart

FISH	BEST MONTH(S)	AVAILABLE MONTHS	POOR MONTH(S)
anago eel	Dec.	rest of year	
bonito (*katsuo*)	May	March, April, June-Oct.	Nov.-Feb.
clams (*hamaguri*)	Nov.	rest of year	
crab (*kani*)	Dec.	rest of year	
hirame flounder	Dec., Jan.	rest of year	
horse mackerel (*aji*)	May	rest of year	
karei flounder	Jan.	remaining months	Aug.
mackerel (*saba*)	Oct., Nov.	rest of year	
octopus (*tako*)	Dec., Jan.	rest of year	
red tilefish (*amadai*)	Dec.	rest of year	
saury pike (*kamasu*)	Oct.	remaining months	Jan.
sea bass (*suzuki*)	July, Aug.	rest of year	
sea bream (*tai*)	May	rest of year	
sea trout (*masu*)	May	Feb.-April, June-Aug.	Sept.-Jan.
shrimp (*ebi*)	Oct.	rest of year	
sillago (*kisu*)	May	rest of year	
squid (*ika*)	Aug.	remaining months	April
tuna (*maguro*)	Aug.	rest of year	
yellowtail (*buri*)	March	rest of year	

FISH GENERALLY AVAILABLE IN UNITED STATES MARKETS
THAT CAN BE USED IN JAPANESE COOKING

	general type	*common names*
SALTWATER: Lean:	flatfish	petral sole (West Coast) Greenland turbot Dover sole (West Coast) flounder (also lemon sole and fluke) Pacific halibut (West Coast)
	cod	whiting haddock Atlantic pollock Atlantic cod cusk
	snapper (good as a substitute for Japanese sea bream)	red snapper
	porgy (name for the North American sea bream, but not the same species as in Japan)	scup sheepshead (East Coast)

	croaker (also called drum,
	because of the noise it makes)
		red drum
		white sea bass
		spotted sea trout (also weakfish and
		    kingfish)
		California corbina (also Peruvian
		    corvina)
		spot
		Atlantic croaker

	rockfish (coloration from pearly pink to near red)	ocean perch redfish (sometimes incorrectly labeled in markets as sea bream)
	sea bass	white perch (East Coast) giant black sea bass (West Coast) grouper (warm waters) striped bass black sea bass

	general type	*common names*
	tilefish monkfish (ugly as sin, but has very tasty, lobsterlike meat)	
SALTWATER: Fatty:	salmon (summer and fall)	sockeye salmon (also red salmon) pink salmon Atlantic salmon
	smelt	surf smelt (also whitebait) candlefish (also eulachon, West Coast)
	herring (winter, through late spring)	herring
	mullet	striped mullet black mullet
	bluefish (winter through summer)	
	tuna	albacore Pacific bonito
	mackerel	Atlantic mackerel Spanish mackerel
	swordfish	
	silverside (late summer)	Atlantic silverside West Coast grunion
	eel (best in autumn in U.S.)	
	pompano (mid autumn to mid spring)	
FRESHWATER: (may be either fatty or lean, depending on species, food, and environment)	carp (best in winter)	
	whitefish	lake whitefish chub lake herring

general type	common names
trout (leanish)	lake trout
	brown trout
	brook trout
	rainbow trout
sunfish	small- and large-mouthed bass
	bluegill (also called bream)
	crappie
perch (lean)	walleye ("pike")
	yellow perch
	northern "pike"
rainbow smelt (lean)	

Calories and Weights of Some Japanese Foods

The sources used to obtain this information were not always consistent, but since these Calorie tables are continually being revised, inconsistencies are natural. Entries marked with an asterisk * are ordinarily used in such small quantities that the calorie figures are included for interest only.

FOOD	CALORIES IN ½ lb	WT. OR VOL. CONTAINING 100 CALORIES	WT. PER CONVENIENT VOL. UNIT
agar-agar (*kanten*)	0 Cal		1 stick weighs about ⅓ oz (8–10 g)
azuki (red beans)			
dried	734 Cal	1 oz (31 g)	1 cup weighs about 6½ oz (180 g)
boiled	491 Cal	1⅗ oz (46 g)	
bamboo shoots (*takenoko*)			
fresh boiled	81 Cal	9¾ oz (278 g)	
canned	45 Cal	17½ oz (500 g)	a 15-oz can contains about 2 cups sliced shoot
bean paste, sweet red (*an*)			
"chunky," see *azuki*, boiled			
powdered, instant (*sarashi-an*)	785 Cal	1 oz (29 g)	
pureed (*koshi-an*)	304 Cal	2½ oz (74 g)	1 cup weighs about 10½ oz (300 g)
bonito, raw	83 Cal	2½ oz (73 g)	
*bonito flakes, dried (*katsuo-bushi*)	808 Cal	1 oz (28 g)	1 cup flakes weighs ⅖–⅝ oz (12–18 g)
bracken (*warabi*)	81 Cal	10 oz (288 g)	
burdock root (*gobō*)			
boiled	187 Cal	4⅘ oz (138 g)	1 medium root weighs about 7 oz (200 g)
chestnuts (*kuri*)			
raw or boiled	353 Cal	2 oz (56 g)	
chicken breast fillet (*sasami*)			
raw	248 Cal	3⅕ oz (91 g)	
chikuwa	281 Cal	4 oz (118 g)	1 piece weighs about about 4 oz (115 g)

FOOD	CALORIES IN ½ lb	WT. OR VOL. CONTAINING 100 CALORIES	WT. PER CONVENIENT VOL. UNIT
Chinese cabbage (*hakusai*)			
raw	27 Cal	24 oz (688 g)	1 medium head weighs 2–6⅔ lbs (1–3 kg)
chrysanthemum, edible (*shungiku* or *kikuna*)			
raw	47 Cal	1 lb (455 g)	1 bunch weighs (11–14 oz (300–400 g)
boiled	54 Cal	14½ oz (417 g)	
clams, hard-shell (*hamaguri*)			
raw	158 Cal	5½ oz (156 g)	1 clam of 2¾ in (7 cm) diam weighs about 1½ oz (40–50 g) with shell
broiled	180 Cal	4⅜ oz (125 g)	
crab (*kani*)			
boiled	about 182 Cal	4⅓ oz (124 g)	
cucumber (*kyūri*)			
raw	25 Cal	2½ lbs (1125 g)	1 medium cucumber weighs 3–3½ oz (80–100 g)
pickled in rice-bran mash	38 Cal	1¾ lbs (813 g)	
daikon (giant white radish)			
raw or boiled	43 Cal	15⅓ oz (438 g)	1 raw root 16–20 in (40–50 cm) long weighs 1¾–2¼ lbs (800 g–1 kg)
pickled in rice-bran mash	70 Cal	11¼ oz (321 g)	
takuan pickle	90 Cal	8¾ oz (250 g)	
daikon leaves			
raw	45 Cal	7⅖ oz (213 g)	
eel, *anago*			
raw	374 Cal	2⅖ oz (69 g)	1 eel 9¾ in (25 cm) long weighs 1 oz (30 g)
steamed	475 Cal	1⅗ oz (47 g)	
eel, *unagi*			
broiled	682 Cal	1 oz (30 g)	
eggplant (*nasu*)			
raw or boiled	41 Cal	17½ oz (500 g)	1 medium eggplant weighs 3 oz (80 g)

FOOD	CALORIES IN ½ lb	WT. OR VOL. CONTAINING 100 CALORIES	WT. PER CONVENIENT VOL. UNIT
pickled in rice-bran mash	63 Cal	12½ oz (357 g)	
eggs, quail	356 Cal	2⅕ oz (63 g)	1 egg weighs about ⅓–⅖ oz (10–12 g)
flounder, *hirame* raw	209 Cal	3⅓ oz (94 g)	1 20-in (50-cm) fish weighs 2¼ lbs (1 kg)
flounder, *karei* raw	230 Cal	3⅖ oz (98 g)	
boiled	257 Cal	3 oz (88 g)	
broiled	324 Cal	2⅖ oz (69 g)	
flour, glutinous rice	806 Cal	1 oz (29 g)	1 cup weighs 5 oz (144 g)
fuki (coltsfoot) raw or boiled	21 Cal	2½ lbs (1125 g)	
ganmodoki	432 Cal	2 oz (56 g)	1 4½ in (12-cm) diam piece weighs 5 oz (140 g)
ginger, fresh (*shōga*) *raw	70 Cal	7 oz (200 g)	1 thumb-sized knob weighs about 1 oz (30 g)
pickled	79 Cal	10 oz (285 g)	
ginkgo nuts raw	387 Cal	2 oz (58 g)	1 cup weighs 3⅓–4 oz (96–120 g)
*gourd strips, dried (*kampyō*)	524 Cal	1½ oz (43 g)	1 39-in (1 m) length weighs about ⅙ oz (5 g)
harusame (sweet potato starch)	797 Cal	1 oz (28 g)	
horse mackerel (*aji*) raw	322 Cal	3 oz (88 g)	1 small fish weighs about 2½ oz (70 g); medium, about 4⅕ oz (120 g); large, about 7 oz (200 g)
boiled	374 Cal	2 oz (60 g)	
broiled	435 Cal	1⅘ oz (52 g)	
kamaboko (fish paste)	221 Cal	4 oz (118 g)	1 cake measuring 5 × 2¾ × 1½ in (13 × 7 × 4 cm) weighs 12 oz (350 g)
kinako (roasted bean flour)	959 Cal	⅘ oz (24 g)	1 cup weighs about 3⅓ oz (96 g)

FOOD	CALORIES IN ½ lb	WT. OR VOL. CONTAINING 100 CALORIES	WT. PER CONVENIENT VOL. UNIT
konbu kelp, all types	0 Cal		
konnyaku (devil's tongue jelly)	0 Cal		1 average cake weighs 9 oz (250 g)
kuzu starch	781 Cal	1 oz (30 g)	1 cup weighs about 3¾–6 oz (108–170 g)
lily root (*yuri-ne*) boiled	284 Cal	2⅝ oz (81 g)	
lotus root (*renkon, hasu*) boiled	153 Cal	5⅝ oz (163 g)	1 "link" about 4½–6 in long (11–15 cm) weighs 2½–3½ oz (70–100 g)
mackerel (*saba*) raw	527 Cal	3 oz (88 g)	1 fish about 1 ft (30 cm) long weighs about 21 oz (600 g)
boiled	470 Cal	1⅝ oz (48 g)	
broiled	497 Cal	1⅔ oz (45 g)	
mandarin oranges (*mikan*) fresh	90 Cal	8¾ oz (250 g)	
canned	153 Cal	5¼ oz (150 g)	
mirin (sweet cooking *saké*)	531 Cal	about 3 Tbsps	1 Tbsp weighs about ⅗ oz (18 g)
miso (bean paste) (salty) red	351 Cal	2¼ oz (64 g)	1 Tbsp salty *miso* weighs about ⅔ oz (18 g)
(salty) light	356 Cal	2¼ oz (63 g)	
"sweet"	400 Cal	2 oz (56 g)	
hatchō type (very dark)	405 Cal	2 oz (56 g)	
mizuame (wheat-starch syrup)	722 Cal	about 1½ Tbsps	1 cup weighs about 12⅕ oz (348 g)
mizu-yōkan (recipe, page 463)	421 Cal	2⅖ oz (69 g)	
mochi	560 Cal	1⅖ oz (41 g)	1 piece measuring ⅜ × 1¼ × 2 in (1½ × 3½ × 5 cm) weighs about 1¾ oz (50 g)

FOOD	CALORIES IN $\frac{1}{2}$ lb.	WT. OR VOL. CONTAINING 100 CALORIES	WT. PER CONVENIENT VOL. UNIT
mushrooms			
cloud ear (*kikurage*)	0 Cal		
enokitake	0 Cal		
matsutake	0 Cal		
nameko	0 Cal		
shiitake, fresh and dried	0 Cal		1 fresh medium *shiitake* weighs about $\frac{1}{3}$–1 oz (10–30 g); 1 dried medium *shiitake* weighs about $\frac{1}{6}$ oz (5 g)
noodles, buckwheat (*soba*)			
boiled	263 Cal	3 oz (88 g)	
noodles, *sōmen*			
dried	767 Cal	1 oz (30 g)	
noodles, *udon*			
boiled	261 Cal	3 oz (88 g)	
nori seaweed	0 Cal		1 sheet measures $8 \times 6\frac{7}{8}$ in (20.5×17.5 cm)
octopus (*tako*)			
raw	173 Cal	5 oz (144 g)	
boiled	223 Cal	$3\frac{1}{2}$ oz (101 g)	
oil, vegetable	1989 Cal	about $2\frac{1}{2}$ tsps	1 cup weighs about $7\frac{1}{2}$ oz (216 g)
okara (bean curd "lees")	146 Cal	$5\frac{1}{2}$ oz (156 g)	1 cup weighs about $5\frac{1}{2}$ oz (156 g)
onions, Japanese green (*aonegi*)			
raw	56 Cal	$15\frac{1}{3}$ oz (438 g)	1 stalk weighs about $1\frac{3}{4}$–2 oz (50–60 g)
onions, long (*naganegi*)			
raw	61 Cal	13 oz (375 g)	1 medium stalk weighs about $3\frac{1}{2}$–$5\frac{1}{4}$ oz (100–150 g)
oysters			
raw	176 Cal	$3\frac{3}{4}$ oz (106 g)	
boiled	250 Cal	$3\frac{1}{8}$ oz (90 g)	
pears, Japanese (*nashi*)	90 Cal	$9\frac{1}{5}$ oz (263 g)	1 medium pear weighs about 7 oz (200 g)

FOOD	CALORIES IN ½ lb	WT. OR VOL. CONTAINING 100 CALORIES	WT. PER CONVENIENT VOL. UNIT
peppers, bell (*piman*) raw	47 Cal	13 oz (375 g)	1 medium pepper weighs about 1 oz (30 g)
persimmons, oriental (*kaki*) raw	135 Cal	5⅗ oz (163 g)	1 medium fruit weighs about 7 oz (200 g)
dried	596 Cal	1½ oz (44 g)	
plum liqueur (*umeshu*; recipe page 470)	313 Cal	about 5 Tbsps	1 cup weighs about 9 oz (254 g)
plums, pickled (*umeboshi*)	117 Cal	22 oz (625 g)	
potato starch (*katakuriko*)	747 Cal	1 oz (30 g)	1 cup weighs 3¾–6 oz (108–168 g)
rice, glutinous (*mochi-gome*) dry	790 Cal	1 oz (29 g)	1 cup weighs about 6¾ oz (192 g)
rice, glutinous, (*Dōmyōji-ko* preparation for sweet confections)	812 Cal	1 oz (29 g)	1 cup weighs about 6¾ oz (192 g)
rice, short-grain brown (dry)	758 Cal	1 oz (30 g)	
white dry	790 Cal	1 oz (29 g)	1 cup white rice weighs 6¾ oz (192 g); it increases in weight about 2.2–2.5 times when cooked
cooked	326 Cal	2⅖ oz (69 g)	
saké (rice wine)	about 239 Cal	about 7 Tbsps	1 cup weighs 8⅖ oz (240 g)
salmon raw	371 Cal	2⅝ oz (75 g)	
broiled	405 Cal	2 oz (56 g)	
satsuma-age (deep-fried *kamaboko*)	335 Cal	2⅝ oz (75 g)	1 small piece weighs about 1 oz (30 g)
saury pike (*kamasu*) raw	281 Cal	2⅘ oz (80 g)	1 medium fish weighs 2⅘ oz (80 g)
broiled	358 Cal	2⅕ oz (63 g)	
sea bass (*suzuki*) raw	236 Cal	3 oz (88 g)	1 medium fish weig8s 2¼ lbs (1 kg)

FOOD	CALORIES IN ½ lb	WT. OR VOL. CONTAINING 100 CALORIES	WT. PER CONVENIENT VOL. UNIT
sea bream (*tai*) raw	203 Cal	3½ oz (100 g)	a fish 1 ft (30 cm) long weighs 14–21 oz (400–600 g)
sea trout (*masu*) raw	320 Cal	2⅖ oz (69 g)	
sea urchin (*uni*) raw	333 Cal	2⅖ oz (69 g)	
sesame seeds, white and black	1269 Cal	⅝ oz (18 g)	1 Tbsp weighs ⅓ oz (8.5 g)
*shallots (*rakkyō*) pickled	284 Cal	10 oz (288 g)	
shiso leaves	79 Cal	10⅓ oz (294 g)	1 leaf weighs about .035 oz (1 g)
seed pods	140 Cal	8⅓ oz (238 g)	1 sprig weighs about .035–.11 oz (1–3 g)
shōchū (35 %) (distilled rice, potato, or millet spirits)	452 Cal	about 3½ Tbsps	1 cup weighs 8 oz (230 g)
shrimp (*kuruma ebi*)	243 Cal	4⅛ oz (119 g)	1 medium shrimp weighs 1⅖ oz (40 g)
sillago (*kisu*) raw	216 Cal	3¾ oz (106 g)	1 fish about 5–6 in (13–15 cm) long weighs about 1¾ oz (50 g)
snow peas (*saya-endō*)	101 Cal	8 oz (225 g)	1 cup weighs 3 oz (84 g)
soybeans, dried (*daizu*)	882 Cal	⅞ oz (26 g)	1 cup weighs 5½ oz (156 g)
soybeans, fresh boiled (*edamame*)	299 Cal	2⅞ oz (81 g)	1 cup beans in pods attached to stalks, gross wt about 3⅓ oz (96 g); net wt (beans only) about 2 oz (54 g)
soy sauce (*shōyu*) dark (*koikuchi*)	131 Cal	about 1⅕ cups	1 cup weighs 10 oz (288 g)
light (*usukuchi*)	108 Cal	about 1⅖ cups	

FOOD	CALORIES IN ½ lb.	WT. OR VOL. CONTAINING 100 CALORIES	WT. PER CONVENIENT VOL. UNIT
spinach (*hōrensō*)	63 Cal	13⅛ oz (375 g)	1 bunch weighs about 1 lb (400–450 g)
squash (pumpkin), Japanese (*kabocha*)			
raw or boiled	81 Cal	6⅗ oz (188 g)	1 squash weighs 2¼–3½ lbs (1–1.5 kg)
squid (*ika*)			
raw	171 Cal	4 oz (119 g)	1 medium squid, about 8–10 in (20–25 cm) long, weighs about 9–10½ oz (250–300 g)
boiled	250 Cal	3⅛ oz (90 g)	
broiled	214 Cal	3⅝ oz (105 g)	
sweet potatoes (*Satsuma-imo*)			
raw or steamed	280 Cal	3 oz (88 g)	1 medium potato weighs (7–10½ oz (200–300 g)
tea, Japanese green leaf			
bancha	0 Cal		
sencha	0 Cal		
etc.	0 Cal		
powdered (*matcha*)	0 Cal		1 cup weighs 3 oz (84 g)
tilefish, red (*amadai*)			
raw	230 Cal	3½ oz (100 g)	
boiled	250 Cal	3⅛ oz (90 g)	
broiled	288 Cal	2¾ oz (78 g)	
tōfu (bean curd)			
"cotton" (*momen*)	131 Cal	6⅛ oz (175 g)	1 pc weighs about 8¾–10½ oz (250–300 g)
"silk" (*kinu*)	106 Cal	7⅖ oz (213 g)	
grilled (*yakidōfu*)	185 Cal	4⅓ oz (123 g)	1 pc weighs about 5¼–8¾ oz (150–250 g)
thick deep-fried (*atsuage*)	236 Cal	3⅓ oz (95 g)	1 pc weighs about 4⅕ oz (120 g)
thin deep-fried (*aburage*)	779 Cal	1 oz (29 g)	1 pc weighs about ¾–⅞ oz (20–25 g)
tōfu, freeze-dried (*Kōya-dōfu* or *kōri-dōfu*)	981 Cal	⅘ oz (24 g)	1 pc weighs about ¾ oz (20 g)

FOOD	CALORIES IN ½ lb	WT. OR VOL. CONTAINING 100 CALORIES	WT. PER CONVENIENT VOL. UNIT
trefoil (*mitsuba*)			
raw or boiled	40 Cal	1¼ lb (563 g)	
trout, rainbow (*niji-masu*)			
raw	360 Cal	2⅛ oz (63 g)	
tuna, bluefin (*maguro*)			
lean meat (red), raw	301 Cal	3 oz (88 g)	
fatty meat, raw	706 Cal	1 oz (31 g)	
turnip (*kabu*)			
raw or boiled	44 Cal	15⅓ oz (438 g)	
pickled in rice-bran mash	65 Cal	17½ oz (500 g)	
udo	32 Cal	26¼ oz (750 g)	
vinegar, rice	72 Cal	about 3½ cups	1 cup weighs about 8½ oz (240 g)
wakame seaweed	0 Cal		sold in various weights
wasabi horseradish			
raw root	164 Cal	4⅜ oz (125 g)	1 average root weighs about 2 oz (60 g)
powder	752 Cal	1 oz (30 g)	
wheat gluten (fu)	821 Cal	1 oz (28 g)	sold in various forms
yams, field (*sato imo*)			
ko-imo type, raw	205 Cal	4 oz (113 g)	1 yam about egg size weighs about 2 oz (50–60 g)
yams, mountain (*yama no imo*)			
raw	223 Cal	3 oz (88 g)	
yellowtail (*buri*)			
raw	565 Cal	2⅛ oz (63 g)	
broiled	668 Cal	1⅕ oz (34 g)	
yuba (soy-milk skin)	972 Cal	⅘ oz (24 g)	1 average sheet weighs about .07 oz (2 g)
yuzu (citron) peel	207 Cal	4 oz (113 g)	

Liquid Measures

ounces $\times$ 29.57 = milliliters (mL)
milliliters $\times$ 0.034 = ounces
quarts and liters are almost the same:
quarts $\times$ 0.95 = liters (L)
liters $\times$ 1.057 = quarts

CUPS, PINTS, QUARTS	SPOONS	FLUID OUNCES	MILLILITERS
$\frac{1}{48}$ cup	1 tsp	$\frac{1}{16}$ oz	5 mL
$\frac{1}{16}$ cup	1 Tbsp	$\frac{1}{2}$ oz	15 mL
$\frac{1}{5}$ cup	3 Tbsps+1 tsp	$1\frac{3}{5}$ oz	47 mL (50 mL)
$\frac{1}{4}$ cup	4 Tbsps	2 oz	59 mL
$\frac{1}{3}$ cup	5 Tbsps+1 tsp	$2\frac{2}{3}$ oz	79 mL
$\frac{2}{5}$ cup	6 Tbsps+1 tsp	$3\frac{1}{5}$ oz	94 mL
	7 Tbsps−1 tsp		100 mL
$\frac{1}{2}$ cup	8 Tbsps	4 oz	118 mL (120 mL)
$\frac{3}{5}$ cup	10 Tbsps−1 tsp	$4\frac{4}{5}$ oz	142 mL
$\frac{2}{3}$ cup	11 Tbsps−1 tsp	$5\frac{1}{3}$ oz	157 mL
$\frac{3}{4}$ cup	12 Tbsps	6 oz	177 mL
	13 Tbsps+1 tsp		200 mL
1 cup	16 Tbsps	8 oz	236 mL
$1\frac{1}{4}$ cups		10 oz	296 mL (300 mL)
$1\frac{1}{3}$ cups		$10\frac{2}{3}$ oz	315 mL
$1\frac{1}{2}$ cups		12 oz	355 mL
$1\frac{2}{3}$ cups		$13\frac{1}{3}$ oz	394 mL (400 mL)
$1\frac{3}{4}$ cups		14 oz	414 mL
2 cups (1 pt)		16 oz	473 mL
3 cups		24 oz	710 mL
4 cups (1 qt)		32 oz	946 mL (1 L)

Some general points of information that may prove valuable or of interest:

1 British fluid ounce=25 mL

1 American fluid ounce=30 mL

1 Japanese cup=200 mL

1 British cup=200 mL=8 British fl oz

1 American cup=240 (236) mL=8 American fl oz

1 British pint=500 mL =20 British fl oz=$2\frac{1}{2}$ British cups

1 American pint=480 (472) mL=16 American fl oz=2 American cups

Weights

$$grams \times 0.035 = ounces$$
$$ounces \times 28.35 = grams$$

POUNDS	OUNCES		GRAMS	KILOGRAMS
	.035	oz	1 g	
	⅛ (.14)	oz	4 g	
	⅙ (.175)	oz	5 g	
	⅕ (.21)	oz	6 g	
	⅓ (.35)	oz	10 g	
	⅜ (.385)	oz	11 g	
	½ (.49)	oz	14 g	
	⅗ (.595)	oz	17 g	
	⅝ (.63)	oz	18 g	
	⅔ (.665)	oz	19 g	
	⅘ (.805)	oz	23 g	
	⅞ (.875)	oz	25 g	
	1 (1.05)	oz	30 g	
	1⅖ (1.4)	oz	40 g	
	1¾ (1.75)	oz	50 g	
	2	oz	60 g	
	2½ (2.45)	oz	70 g	
	2⅘ (2.8)	oz	80 g	
	3 (2.975)	oz	85 g	
	3⅙ (3.15)	oz	90 g	
	3½ (3.5)	oz	100 g	
¼ lb	4	oz	115 g	
	4⅕ (4.2)	oz	120 g	
	4½ (4.55)	oz	130 g	
	5 (4.9)	oz	140 g	
	5¼ (5.25)	oz	150 g	
	5⅖ (5.6)	oz	160 g	
	6 (5.95)	oz	170 g	
	6¼ (6.3)	oz	180 g	
	6⅔ (6.65)	oz	190 g	
	7	oz	200 g	
½ lb	8 (7.875)	oz	225 g	
	9 (8.75)	oz	250 g	
	10 (9.975)	oz	285 g	
	10½ (10.5)	oz	300 g	
	11 (11.025)	oz	315 g	
¾ lb	12 (11.9)	oz	340 g	
	13 (12.95)	oz	370 g	
	14	oz	400 g	

POUNDS	OUNCES		GRAMS	KILOGRAMS
1 lb	16	oz	450 g	
	18 (17.5)	oz	500 g	
1¼ lbs	20 (19.95)	oz	570 g	
	21	oz	600 g	
1½ lbs	24 (23.975)	oz	685 g	
	24½ (24.5)	oz	700 g	
	26 (25.9)	oz	740 g	
1¾ lbs	28	oz	800 g	
	30 (30.1)	oz	860 g	
2 lbs	32 (31.5)	oz	900 g	
2¼ lbs	35	oz	1,000 g	1 kg
2½ lbs			1,125 g	1¼ kg
3 lbs			1,350 g	1⅓ kg
3½ lbs			1,500 g	1½ kg
4 lbs			1,800 g	1¾ kg
5 lbs				2¼ kg

Linear Measures

inches × 2.54 = centimeters

centimeters × .39 = inches

INCHES	CENTIMETERS (*nearest equivalent*)	INCHES		CENTIMETERS (*nearest equivalent*)
1/16 in	¼ cm		5 in	13 cm
⅛ in	½ cm		6 in	15 cm
¼ in	¾ cm		7 in	18 cm
⅜ in	1 cm		8 in	20 cm
½ in	1½ cm		9 in	23 cm
⅝ in	1½ cm		10 in	25 cm
¾ in	2 cm	1 ft	12 in	30 cm
1 in	2½ cm		14 in	35 cm
1½ in	4 cm		15 in	38½ cm
2 in	5 cm		16 in	40 cm
2½ in	6½ cm	1½ ft	18 in	45 cm
3 in	8 cm		20 in	50 cm
3½ in	9 cm		21½ in	55 cm
4 in	10 cm	2 ft	24 in	60 cm
4½ in	11½ cm			

Temperatures

$$\text{Fahrenheit} = \frac{\text{Celsius} \times 9}{5} + 32$$

$$\text{Celsius} = \frac{(\text{Fahrenheit} - 32) \times 5}{9}$$

FAHRENHEIT	CELSIUS		FAHRENHEIT	CELSIUS	
75°F	24°C	(23.9°C)	275°F	135°C	(135°C)
80°F	27°C	(26.7°C)	300°F	150°C	(148.9°C)
85°F	29°C	(29.4°C)	320°F	160°C	(160°C)
100°F	38°C	(37.8°C)	325°F	163°C	(162.8°C)
110°F	43°C	(43.3°C)	330°F	165°C	(165.5°C)
115°F	46°C	(46.1°C)	335°F	168°C	(168.3°C)
120°F	49°C	(48.9°C)	340°F	170°C	(171.1°C)
130°F	54°C	(54.4°C)	350°F	175°C	(176.7°C)
140°F	60°C	(60°C)	360°F	180°C	(182.2°C)
150°F	66°C	(65.6°C)	365°F	185°C	(185°C)
160°F	71°C	(71.1°C)	370°F	188°C	(187.7°C)
165°F	74°C	(73.9°C)	375°F	190°C	(190.6°C)
170°F	77°C	(76.7°C)	380°F	193°C	(193.3°C)
180°F	82°C	(82.2°C)	400°F	205°C	(204.4°C)
190°F	88°C	(87.8°C)	425°F	220°C	(218.3°C)
200°F	95°C	(93.3°C)	450°F	230°C	(232.2°C)
205°F	96°C	(96.1°C)	475°F	245°C	(246.1°C)
212°F	100°C	(100°C)	500°F	260°C	(260°C)
225°F	110°C	(107.2°C)	550°F	290°C	(287.8°C)
250°F	120°C	(121.1°C)			

DEEP-FRYING OIL TEMPERATURES
300°F/150°C—330°F/165°C=low
340°F/170°C—350°F/175°C=medium
350°F/175°C—360°F/180°C=high

Index

定価3,800円
In Japan